CAGE KINGS

How an Unlikely Group of Moguls,
Champions & Hustlers Transformed
the UFC into a $10 Billion Industry

MICHAEL THOMSEN

SIMON & SCHUSTER
NEW YORK   LONDON   TORONTO   SYDNEY   NEW DELHI

Simon & Schuster
1230 Avenue of the Americas
New York, NY 10020

First Simon & Schuster hardcover edition June 2023

SIMON & SCHUSTER and colophon are registered trademarks of Simon & Schuster, Inc.

For information about special discounts for bulk purchases, please contact Simon & Schuster Special Sales at 1-866-506-1949 or business@simonandschuster.com.

The Simon & Schuster Speakers Bureau can bring authors to your live event. For more information or to book an event, contact the Simon & Schuster Speakers Bureau at 1-866-248-3049 or visit our website at www.simonspeakers.com.

Interior design by Carly Loman

Manufactured in the United States of America

10   9   8   7   6   5   4   3   2   1

Library of Congress Cataloging-in-Publication Data has been applied for.

ISBN 978-1-5011-9847-2
ISBN 978-1-5011-9853-3 (ebook)

Do not try to change yourself—you are unlikely to succeed.

—Peter M. Drucker, "Managing Oneself," *Harvard Business Review*

CONTENTS

Author's Note

This book is based on more than four years of research and reporting, including interviews with current and former UFC employees, fighters, trainers, managers, media executives, promoters, and journalists. Other information is drawn from court documents, depositions, video interviews, and dozens of books on the history, business, and culture of prize-fighting and mixed martial arts. I have generally referred to people by last name, but in some instances where people with the same family name appear, I have used first names to avoid confusion.

Introduction

THE LAST SPORT ON EARTH

One Saturday morning in early August, I tried to find my way through the backstage tunnels in the Prudential Center arena in Newark, New Jersey. The long white corridors felt like a casino that had been stripped to the girders, placeless and impossible to navigate unless you already knew where you were going. I followed Chris Bellitti, the UFC's vice president of corporate communications, who had helped me arrange a press pass to see *UFC on ESPN: Covington vs. Lawler*, one of the forty-two events the Ultimate Fighting Championship would hold in 2019. Bellitti had made the trip from the front box office to the press room several times that morning, but even he seemed to second-guess himself after we turned a corner and found ourselves looking down another long white corridor nearly identical to the one we'd just come from. It was easy to see how arenas could blur together for people who worked for the UFC. The week before, the UFC had held an event in Edmonton, Canada, and in the coming week it would travel to Montevideo, Uruguay, then on to Anaheim, Shenzhen, Abu Dhabi, Vancouver, Mexico City, Copenhagen, and Melbourne.

The unrelenting pace is part of what has made the UFC one of the most valuable sports franchises in the world, with annual revenue close to $1 billion and an estimated worth as high as $10 billion, according to president Dana White, more than any team in the NFL, NBA, Major League Baseball, or international soccer. The UFC's near weekly events are broadcast in 129 countries, including Saudi Arabia, South Africa, Mexico, China, Argentina, Finland, France, and Kenya. Fifteen of the fifty bestselling pay-per-views of all time are UFC events or co-promotions, including the one in the top position, a boxing match between Conor McGregor and Floyd Mayweather Jr. that generated more than 6.7 million buys and more than $1 billion in global sports betting. In 2016, when the UFC was acquired for $4.2 billion by WME-IMG—now called Endeavor—it ranked as the biggest single transaction in sports history, worth the equivalent of what Disney paid for the rights to Marvel Comics, and nearly three times the estimated value of The Beatles catalog. Measured by revenue, the UFC accounts for around 90 percent of the global mixed martial arts market, and in 2020, the company's biggest star, Conor McGregor, was the highest paid athlete in the world, topping Lionel Messi, Cristiano Ronaldo, Lebron James, Tom Brady, and Roger Federer with a reported $180 million in income, most of which came from the sale of his whiskey brand Proper No. Twelve.

The company describes itself as a "quintessential American success story," as Marc Ratner, the UFC's vice president of government and regulatory affairs, told a congressional committee in 2017. Once banned in thirty-six states, and hovering on the edge of bankruptcy, the UFC created a multibillion-dollar global industry that seemingly emerged out of thin air, bringing wealth and opportunity to those who previously had neither. "Today, collegiate and Olympic wrestlers, judo specialists, and other mixed martial artists have a professional outlet for their athletic endeavors that barely existed fifteen years ago," Ratner told Congress. First conceived as a marketing pitch for a beer importer in the early 1990s, the UFC built an entirely new sport around the idea of testing the real combat effectiveness of different martial arts. Fighters trained in Brazilian jiu-jitsu, judo, muay Thai, taekwondo, sambo, and dozens of other disciplines were locked inside a chain-link cage and made to fight until one was knocked out, choked unconscious, or forced to submit to the pain of a joint lock. Over time, the differences between the disciplines began to blur, and a new sport emerged from the amalgam: mixed martial arts. The UFC has made millionaires out of "dozens upon dozens" of fighters who've become students of this new hybrid discipline. And it's created billions in spillover revenue for hotels, arena concessions, apparel companies, video game publishers, energy drink makers, sports bars, and gym owners. Even the UFC's competitors have benefitted from its success. With a thriving global market, dozens of regional and international promotions have offered the public their own particular variations on cage fighting, including Bellator, Professional Fight League, Cage Warriors, ONE Fighting Championship, and Extreme Fighting Championship.

The UFC's success has also forced many to reconsider the role violence plays in society. What Arizona senator John McCain infamously called "human cockfighting" in 1996, and what the *New York Times* described as part of a "pay-per-view prism" onto the decline of Western civilization, is now spoken of in more admiring terms, as a kind of "human chess" played out in real-time between two bodies. While the objective is still "leaving someone as close to death as you possibly could," as UFC veteran Jorge Masvidal once put it, the spectacle of near-death experiences no longer feels as scandalous as it did when the UFC first debuted in 1993. Head kicks that land with the force of a two-by-four, submission holds that tear ligaments and muscle from the bone, chokes that starve the brain of oxygen—none of it seems as instinctively wrong as it did to many at UFC 1. To the contrary, today, mixed martial arts has become commonplace as a form of personal fitness, as popular and accessible as yoga or Pilates. The UFC has its own gym franchise with more than 150 locations in thirty-seven countries. American Top Team, Gracie Jiu-Jitsu Academies, American Kickboxing Academy, Straight Blast Gym, Tiger Schulmann's Martial Arts, and dozens of other chains also have their own global networks, with locations in Rome, Johannesburg, Moscow, Phuket, Mexico City, and Minot, North Dakota. Celebrities have flocked to mixed martial arts training, including Demi Lovato, Will Smith, Kate Upton, Halle Berry, Wiz Khalifa, Idris Elba, Shaquille O'Neal, Russell Brand, Tool's Maynard James Keenan, and the late Anthony Bourdain. Some have even become decorated black belts, including comedian Kevin James and former *Modern Family* star Ed O'Neill.

Yet, despite the success, many of the UFC's events often feel like throwaways, as if something about the company's public identity can't always match the reality of its business, where fights have to be held regardless of whether they serve any larger point or purpose. As I walked through the streets of downtown Newark on my way to the arena earlier that morning, there were few signs that one of the world's most popular sporting companies was in town for an event. I only saw one other person on the streets who was clearly headed to the same place I was—a man dressed as Chuck Liddell, with satiny blue "Ice Man" shorts, UFC gloves, and a recently shaved mohawk, who was walking next to a woman in a T-shirt and jean shorts. A little more than half the available tickets had been sold, and the staff had kept seats in the upper half of the arena closed off to make it look more crowded around the cage for the television cameras.

When Bellitti and I finally arrived at the press room inside the Prudential Center, which had been set up in a giant storage room filled with hundreds of stacked chairs just off the arena floor, there was only a handful of bloggers and YouTube personalities staring into their laptops next to a buffet of fruit, pastries, and giant metal coffee carafes. At the far end of the room, a few streamers were setting up tripods in front of a black backdrop with the UFC and ESPN logos printed on it, where fighters would be led to answer questions after their bouts. The majority seemed like fans that covered the sport as a side gig instead of a full-time job. The most professional group appeared to be the UFC's own team of backstage reporters, who recorded interviews and short preview pieces that would air on the company's YouTube channel or be excerpted on the ESPN broadcast.

While the UFC once coveted attention from major news outlets like the *New York Times* and the *Washington Post*, the promotion no longer seems particularly interested in having other people tell its story. The company has gradually shut itself off from the traditional media, and many of the sport's longtime beat reporters and investigative journalists have been denied press credentials so often they no longer even bother trying to apply. The most notorious example came in 2016, when well-known reporter Ariel Helwani was ejected from UFC 199 and banned from the UFC for life, as ostensible punishment for publishing a news story—about WWE star Brock Lesnar returning to the UFC after a four-year absence—just a few hours before the promotion had planned to announce it during the pay-per-view broadcast. (Helwani's ban was later rescinded, but company president Dana White has maintained a hostile attitude toward him, variously calling Helwani a "pussy," "douche," and a "crybaby victim.")

Today, it seems like the UFC would prefer to report on itself, using an array of media that often blurs the line between self-promotion, reportage, and genuine matters of public interest. There's a weekly podcast series, *UFC Unfiltered*, hosted by former welterweight champion Matt Serra and comedian Jim Norton, a video series that gives technical breakdowns of upcoming fights, several different long-form interview series with fighters, and the reality series *Dana White: Lookin' for a Fight*, which follows White and two friends around the country as they scout promising regional fighters. The promotion also broadcasts a series that matches top prospects against each other for a chance at a UFC contract at the end of the night, called *Dana White's Contender Series*. Before each of its pay-per-view events, the UFC airs an hour-long mini-documentary profiling the fighters booked in the main and co-main events, and during the week leading up to the event, the promotion releases six or seven short YouTube videos called *UFC Embedded*, which document the final days and hours of the card's main fighters. The company also produces its own historical documentaries, reporting on past milestones and struggles as if it were a neutral observer rather than a promoter.

In the few instances when the UFC has agreed to let a media company tell a part of its history, the promotion has still played a substantial role in shaping the narrative. After the UFC signed a landmark broadcasting agreement with ESPN in 2018, worth a reported $1.5 billion over five years, the network produced an episode of its documentary series *30 for 30* on the rivalry between Tito Ortiz and Chuck Liddell in the early 2000s. In an interview after the episode debuted, director Micah Brown admitted that while ESPN had final cut on the project, the UFC had participated throughout the editing process. "Sometimes I win some battles," Brown said. "Sometimes I don't win some battles, and I think that's just kind of one of those things." According to Ortiz, the documentary was repeatedly recut to accommodate specific feedback from White, who was also one of the main characters in the story.

In 2018, White had a hardbound book made for UFC employees called *Don't Believe Anything You Read*, with stories from *Bloody Elbow*, *Deadspin*, and other news websites accompanied by White's criticisms of each. "Nobody knows anything about this sport," White told TMZ in 2019. "Nobody, not even the so-called experts, because all this stuff is new." White would later describe the journalists who cover the UFC as "the weakest, wimpiest people on earth." In White's mind, he had created something for the media to cover with the UFC, and he expected they would be both grateful and motivated to present the sport in the best possible light. Most of the media who depended on covering UFC events for a living found it easier to limit their coverage to the dramas of matchmaking, new rivalries, and unusual techniques that new stars brought to the sport. Public criticism of the company—about low fighter pay relative to the amount of revenue the UFC generates; drug testing and sponsorship policies that often change dramatically without input from fighters; and the lack of a pension fund or post-career healthcare for former fighters, many of whom suffer with symptoms of chronic traumatic encephalopathy (CTE) from prolonged brain trauma—often seems like it's coming from an alternate universe, delivered by people who fundamentally misunderstand the realities of the universe the UFC operates in.

Before I arrived in Newark, I'd spent five months trying to find a way into the UFC's universe, to better understand how a cage fighting company had become so consistently popular and profitable. As I had exchanged phone calls and emails with Bellitti, a veteran of corporate communcations who had previously worked for Fox Sports and then WWE, I got the impression that he, like many who worked for the UFC, had to squeeze much of his life into the small slivers of time in between Sunday-night red-eyes and Tuesday-morning takeoffs to wherever the company's next event would be. There was little time for anything that wasn't part of the promotional cycle, and our plans were continually being unmade and re-made by circumstance. Eventually, Bellitti suggested the best way to understand the UFC would simply be to see an event in person. That would explain things better than any of the company's executives could.

I had been to UFC events in the past, but always as a fan in the rafters looking down on the cage where the fighters seemed even smaller than action figures. I had never seen a fight cage-side, or wandered through the bowels of an arena, puncturing the fictive veil of the television, to see what was on the other side of the camera lens. At first, the *Covington vs. Lawler* event seemed like a strange choice. Like many of the company's events, it had come together almost by happenstance, announced just six weeks earlier, with no scheduled fights or main event, just a vague plan to go live on ESPN on August 3. The event had initially been planned for Sochi, Russia, as part of a new broadcasting agreement with Media-Telecom, a joint media venture between two of Russia's largest television companies. After it became clear negotiations wouldn't be concluded in time for the event, the UFC tried to relocate to Manchester, England, then Tampa, Florida, before finally settling on Newark, where, because of previous scheduling conflicts, the whole card would start six hours earlier than normal, with early prelims beginning at 12:00 p.m. and the main card going live at 3:00 p.m.

The matchup between Robbie Lawler and Colby Covington seemed as haphazard as the final venue. It was framed as a title eliminator, but Covington had already earned that right a year earlier, when he'd won the interim welterweight championship against Rafael dos Anjos. After the fight, he had undergone surgery to repair a nose injury and asked for a two-month delay in scheduling his title unification fight, against then-champion Tyron Woodley. Instead, the UFC had stripped Covington of his interim title and given his contender spot to another fighter, one who was younger and less accomplished, but who had no problems accepting the UFC's terms and time frame. And though Lawler was a fan favorite and former champion, he had lost three of his last four fights and seemed closer to the end of his career than the peak. More than anything, the fight seemed like a stopgap to fulfill the UFC's broadcasting agreement with ESPN, something that would be easy to forget about almost as soon as it was over and the promotion packed up for its next destination the following week.

Yet I got a small chill as Bellitti led me to the long press table a few feet from the cage, minutes before the event was scheduled to start. In spite of it all, I was still unsure what I was about to see as the arena PA crackled to life while the first fighter stood on the edge of the floor with her coaches huddled behind her, waiting for the show to begin.

For most of my adult life, I had followed mixed martial arts as if it were a full-time job, a kind of shadow career to which I committed an extra thirty or forty hours each week. I refreshed mixed martial arts blogs almost hourly, listened to a dozen fight-related podcasts, and scrolled through YouTube looking for backstage interviews, slow-motion fight breakdowns, body language analysis during face-offs, and professional gamblers sharing their picks. On weekends, I'd skip out on seeing friends and stay home alone watching cage fights until 3:00 a.m. For pay-per-views I'd end up at a bar or a Buffalo Wild Wings, slowly drinking beer and watching one of a half-dozen screens showing the fights. At night, I'd fall asleep replaying submission sequences and punch combinations, faceless bodies with no backstories moving around each other like gangly planets.

I first discovered cage fighting in 1993, a few months after my sixteenth birthday, when the local news in my hometown of Fresno, California, aired a short but shocking segment on UFC 1. The newscasters framed the event as a public crisis, a new form of cultural contagion that threatened the safety of its competitors and the character of those who watched in amusement. Without access to pay-per-view at home and no friends as curious to see firsthand what had provoked so much outcry and agitation, I would have to wait another three years before I could see a UFC event for myself, when a college friend shared a collection of pirated UFC tapes he'd copied from a former high school wrestling teammate. We'd spend weekend afternoons watching the ghostly footage, images degraded through duplication as they had passed from one set of teenage hands to another. The production had the flat and timeless look of pornography, something that could have taken place in 1976 as easily as in 1996. Like many, I was mesmerized by Royce Gracie, a thin Brazilian in a disheveled white gi, the pajama-like uniform of a traditional martial artist, who dominated the UFC's early years. He seemed to be on the verge of losing every fight, overpowered and outmatched, right up until the moment his opponent would frantically tap in submission. His victories were as inexplicable as street magic, an urban legend come to life. While other fighters came and went, it was Royce who proved the only real and lasting point: No one was safe in a fight, no matter the size or record. Everyone could be broken and beaten.

After college, I lost track of the UFC, along with almost everything else in America, when I enrolled in the Peace Corps and spent almost four years living abroad, first in China and then Madagascar. When I returned in 2005, a few months after the first season of *The Ultimate Fighter* had debuted, the UFC was everywhere. The handful of fighters I recognized from my roommate's pirated tapes—Tito Ortiz, Matt Hughes, Chuck Liddell, Randy Couture—were now on magazine covers and late-night television shows, as if they had the same celebrity stature as movie stars and musicians. Newspapers covered UFC events as reliably as *Monday Night Football*, and there was a whole new ecosystem of consumer brands tied to cage fighting: Xyience energy drinks; Affliction jeans; Tapout T-shirts; mixed martial arts video games; and even an official malt liquor, Mickey's, which became a featured UFC sponsor in 2006. It was suddenly possible to watch the UFC on basic cable, and also wear it, drink it, play it, eat it as a supplement, and even get drunk on it at the end of the day. And follow-ing on the UFC's success, a new group of promotions began airing its own versions of cage fighting on Fox Sports Net, NBC's Versus, CBS, Show-time, and MTV2. Everything was growing, and it seemed as if everyone was making money.

At the same time, it had started to feel as if my own life was com-ing together. After years of trying to make a living as a writer, I finally landed a full-time job as an editor at a website that mostly focused on video games. I had been living on credit cards and part-time jobs with no benefits or security. I'd shelved books in a library and been a movie extra. I'd worked as a production assistant and a video game tester; I delivered balloon bouquets to children's birthday parties and pushed a mailroom cart around a corporate office. With a $40,000 salary and my own cubicle, I felt almost decadently rich. At thirty-one, in 2008, I was able to afford living without roommates for the first time in my adult life. I bought gro-ceries with cash instead of credit, invited friends out for drinks and forgot about overdraft fees. A year and a half later, I moved to New York and began writing freelance stories for publications I'd thought would never have someone like me. While work was plentiful—usually there was too much of it—money had begun to grow scarce again. Checks came two weeks too late, and were never quite big enough to cover the bills that had come due. To keep from going broke, I went back to doing side jobs and part-time hustles. I dog-sat, ghostwrote letters of recommendation for visa applications, translated wiretapped phone calls for a government contractor, donated bone marrow, and worked as an apartment and office cleaner. I would periodically sublet my apartment and stay with family or on a friend's couch for a few days. Sometimes, I ended up with nowhere to go for a night and I'd walk around my neighborhood until my legs grew sore, and then wait out the sunrise in the twenty-four-hour diner below my apartment. When I was sure the subletter had left for the day, I'd let myself back in and sleep on the living room couch for a few hours and then leave again in the afternoon.

The harder my life became, the easier it was to drift into fandom, trail-ing the lives of UFC fighters as if they were old friends who'd fallen back in touch through the magic of modern media. The UFC became a sec-ond home I kept in my mind at all times, a place I could retreat to when

I was exhausted from work or afraid of the future. The sport's coldness and complexity were calming. There were so many variables that no one fighter could master them all. You could give your life over to training and still end up beaten by someone a little younger, taller, stronger, or hungrier. The outcomes were usually fair, but fairness rarely felt just. Even undefeated fighters had an air of vulnerability, their winning streaks no less safe or certain than the odds of a coin toss. It reminded me of my own circumstances, and whenever there were new fights to look forward to, I felt less alone.

This affinity wasn't accidental, nor was it quite as personal as it felt. The average UFC fan looked a lot like me, and according to a Scarborough Research survey, there were a lot of us. In America, three-quarters of the UFC's audience were men between eighteen and forty-four, and 53 percent were white. (Women made up just 25 percent of its audience.) More than half made less than $50,000 a year, and one in five earned less than $25,000 a year. The highest concentration of "avid" UFC fans came from working-class suburbs or semirural cities with significantly higher poverty rates than the national average, including Honolulu, Bakersfield, El Paso, Mobile/Pensacola, Memphis, Albany, Colorado Springs, Las Vegas, Jacksonville, and Fresno, where I had grown up. The UFC's rise seemed to track with a long period of generational decline, which had encircled both its fans and fighters. Roughly half of the people in my generation, born in the late 1970s or early 1980s, would be poorer than their parents, and 47 percent of full-time workers would be unable to come up with $400 in cash to cover an emergency expense.

To this generation, the UFC offered a vision of cathartic prosperity, a world where hard work and sacrifice could still be repaid with wealth and recognition instead of burnout and alienation. Even more important, it tied success to a certain kind of sadism, reinforcing the idea that winners required victims. For one person to advance, another had to suffer both the physical and financial burdens of defeat. The UFC's pay structure divided purses into two halves—$10,0000 to fight and $10,000 to win was typical for new fighters—ensuring that winners would leave the cage with double pay, while their opponents would have to live on half pay until their next fight. It was often easy to cheer for one person's pain and failure even more loudly than it was to be thrilled by another's triumph, giving in to what Sam Sheridan, a writer who traveled the world practicing different martial arts, described as a "berserker emotion that doesn't discern friend from foe but simply rejoices in blood."

While the UFC had rehabilitated its once dire reputation and neutralized its loudest critics, it was sometimes hard not to wonder whether people had been too eager to accept cage fighting as popular entertainment. For Antonio McKee, a trainer and fighter who briefly competed in the UFC, there was something ominous about the sport's sudden growth. "It takes a special person to get in a fuckin' cage and beat the shit out of somebody until there's a submission," he said in a 2007 interview. "There's no sport about that. That's sick. That's why society is now embracing it, because our society is becoming sick."

The houselights were still on in the Prudential Center when the opening video montage for *UFC on ESPN: Covington vs. Lawler* played to thousands of empty seats that encircled the few hundred fans on the arena floor who'd come early enough to see two women's flyweights (125 pounds), Hannah Goldy and Miranda Granger, make their UFC debuts. I had the impression I was watching a dress rehearsal as each walked toward the cage from the media table just a few feet away. Most of the reporters and bloggers stayed in the press room, watching the fights on the arena's closed-circuit television as they waited for their first post-fight interviews.

As the fight began, the sound of the PA system gave way to a strange silence, which was broken only by the sporadic shouts of advice from Goldy's and Granger's coaches. I had never seen a UFC event from such close distance, and I was struck by just how much detail was lost on the eight television cameras gathered around the cage. Even seemingly light punches landed with a disturbingly sharp, wet slap. On television, it sounded as if someone was being hit. In person, it was the unmistakable sound of someone being hurt, something that focuses the senses and triggers a small burst of adrenaline. Without commercial breaks or camera edits, the fight moved at a strange pace. It seemed both faster and less clear in terms of what was happening at any moment, and yet more dangerous and damaging. The lack of color commentary to trace a narrative around the two fighters as they clashed and came apart gave the fight a cold sense of purposelessness, like watching two rams batter each other on the mountainside until one relents and wanders away for no apparent reason.

After three rounds, Granger was declared the winner by unanimous decision, having used her seven-inch reach advantage to keep Goldy at bay, and then smothering her in clinches whenever Goldy got close enough to punch. As the decision was announced, there was a brief outcry of joyful voices from the other side of the arena. After a victory speech, Granger was shuttled backstage for a medical examination and media interviews. The next fighters were queued at the side of the arena floor, waiting for their entrance music to start. Over time, the fights began to seem almost like a background activity. What for the fighters was a brief, high-stakes opportunity to double down on their futures, was for dozens of production assistants, security guards, and ushers just another Saturday-morning shift. The fighters were shuttled to the cage for their moment under the lights, like tourists arriving in Vegas for a three-day weekend, expecting a once-in-a-lifetime experience that was reproduced tens of thousands of times a day all around the strip.

And with each new bout, the houselights steadily dimmed while the arena speakers grew louder with thudding dance music. When the main card finally started, the arena had somehow transformed into a coliseum-sized discotheque, with bright neon beams of light pinwheeling across the scattered crowd, while the sound of electronic drums and bass pounded the air.

Halfway through the main card, a conflicted burst of boos and cheers cut through the arena in the middle of a fight between Nasrat Haqparast, the son of Afghan refugees who'd grown up in Hamburg and later moved to Toronto to train full time, and Joaquim Silva, a former contestant on the Brazilian version of the UFC's reality series *The Ultimate Fighter*. The cheers weren't meant for either fighter, but for Eric Trump, Donald Trump Jr., and Kimberly Guilfoyle, who had been escorted into front row seats halfway through the second round. They had been invited as guests of White, a longtime Trump supporter, and Colby Covington, who had created a quasi-fictional persona as a Trump fan who made a point to wear "Make America Great Again" hats and shirts in all his media appearances, and had even visited the White House and met Trump in the Oval Office in 2018.

Covington had become a widely hated figure in the UFC for both his fealty to Trump and for his frequently racist and confrontational attitude. In 2017, he referred to Brazilians as "filthy animals" and called their country a "dump" after a bloody win over UFC veteran Demian Maia in São Paolo, Brazil. He'd described his next opponent, Rafael dos Anjos, as a "filthy animal" too, and nicknamed him "Ralphie dos Nachos." He said those who supported the Black Lives Matter group were "criminals" and "bad people" and called NBA star LeBron James a "spineless coward" for supporting the group.

Many in the crowd in Newark had come to see Covington hurt, expecting that whatever punishment he would endure in the cage would be righteous and well deserved. Some in the media speculated that Covington's persona was a put-on, a deliberate theatricality he used to draw attention to his fights, and make it feel as if there was something at stake in them. Public records showed he hadn't voted at all in 2016, despite his incessant Trump boosterism. Before the Maia fight in Brazil, Covington had been modest and respectful to both his opponents and fans. But, after winning seven of his first eight fights in the UFC, he claimed the promotion told him it wasn't interested in renewing his contract, which had been set to expire after the Maia fight. "That was the time where I was just like, You know what, fuck it," Covington said in an interview with ESPN. To stand out, he decided to make himself into a heel, creating derogatory nicknames for other top contenders, wearing Trump apparel, and insulting audiences wherever he went. The gambit worked, and helped make Covington a main-event draw instead of a space-filler on the prelims. Asked before the Newark event about Covington's behavior, White said it was just another part of the business. "I sell fights for a living," White said. "So if you're different or whatever your deal is, I'll work with it. The thing with Colby is I don't know what's real and what's not. He really did go meet the president, and he really was excited about it."

The houselights went out before Covington made his entrance. The arena sound system began playing "Medal" by Jim Johnston, the walk-out song made famous by WWE star Kurt Angle, while the crowd began chanting "You suck!" in time with the beat. Covington jogged out of the backstage tunnels onto the arena floor, an American flag draped over his shoulders, and pumped his arm at Eric and Donald Jr. as they clapped for him. "Fight hard tonight, Colby. You are a real champ!" Trump Sr. posted on Twitter, along with a picture from the previous summer at the White House.

As Covington climbed into the cage, I scrolled through my phone past Trump's tweet, looking for news about another story. Midway through the main card, in El Paso, Texas, a twenty-one year-old Trump supporter had walked into a Walmart with an assault rifle and killed twenty-three people, while leaving another twenty-two injured. In a manifesto, the shooter, Patrick Crusius, said he had been inspired to take up arms "as a response to the Hispanic invasion of Texas," driven both by legal and illegal immigrants from Mexico and Central and South America, the same kinds of people Covington might have called filthy animals. Months earlier, Trump had threatened to declare a national emergency over immigration at the southern border, claiming there was a caravan of migrant invaders preparing to storm the country. "Criminals and unknown Middle Easterners are mixed in," he wrote in a Twitter post on October 22, 2018. "I have alerted Border Patrol and Military that this is a National Emergency. Must change laws!"

As Covington bounced on the balls of his feet across from Lawler in the cage, smiling to himself in a cascade of boos, the collective anger in the arena suddenly felt ominous and unpredictable, like it could lead a person anywhere, and make them capable of anything. That feeling of fearsome liberation had always been part of the UFC's appeal, a revelation that any of us were still capable, in the right setting, of wild, remorseless cruelty. As the referee prepared Covington and Lawler for the start of the fight, Covington pumped his fist in affirmation at Don Jr. and Eric. The crowd began chanting "Robbie! Robbie! Robbie! Robbie!" in anticipation of the violence that still lay ahead, that would surely rip through the seams of the imaginary fiction that we had all confused for reality.

The fight ended up being a one-sided and anticlimactic win for Covington, who smothered Lawler for five rounds, pinning him against the side of the octagon, then dragging him to the mat with twisting takedowns. Covington won every round on all three judges' scorecards, and as the final result was announced the crowd broke out in a conflicted mix of boos and cheers. In his post-fight interview, Covington launched into a flagrantly personal attack on one of Lawler's closest friends and former training partners, Matt Hughes, who had been hit by a train while driving in his truck two years earlier. The accident had nearly killed Hughes, and he had been placed in a medically induced coma to treat severe bleeding in his brain. Hughes was left with permanent brain damage, and when he finally woke, he spent months learning how to speak and walk again.

"Hey, let's talk about the lesson we learned tonight," Covington said in Newark. "It's a strong lesson Robbie should have learned from his good buddy Matt Hughes. You stay off the tracks when the train's coming through, Junior. It don't matter if it's the Trump train or the Colby train. Get out the way!"

While Covington celebrated backstage with Eric and Donald Jr. and later took a call from Trump himself, I left the arena and wandered back to Newark's Penn Station to catch the train. After nearly seven hours of fights, I felt disoriented and numb, my ears still ringing from the arena sound system, and my muscles still stiff from adrenaline and the frigid arena air. I was surprised to see the sun still out, a bright orange glow on the horizon, half-hidden by the arena. I was used to feeling that way after fights, but not in the daylight, with so much time left before I could crawl into bed and slowly replay strange fragments of violence in my mind again and again until I fell asleep. It felt like all of those new memories were trapped inside me, with nowhere to go, and I carried them with me up the stairs, onto the train platform, and back into the city.

Every generation has its blood sports, popular but disturbing pastimes that exist just outside the bounds of decent society. Gouging spread across the American colonies in the seventeenth and eighteenth centuries, a freeform style of fighting with the objective of tearing out an opponent's eye or ripping the skin around the mouth, nose, or ear. In England, bare-knuckle boxing was a popular but mostly illegal entertainment in the eighteenth and nineteenth centuries that sometimes attracted crowds of more than ten thousand people. Catch wrestlers traveled the world in the early twentieth century competing in violent submission grappling matches that would lay the foundation for both the UFC and WWE. In the 1970s, the Professional Karate Association aired bloody full-contact kickboxing matches on *ABC's Wide World of Sports* and ESPN, drawing scrutiny and criticism from members of the Association of Boxing Commissions who worried about the potential damage from headkicks. During the same period, tough-man contests became popular across the American suburbs, one-night-only tournaments in which mostly blue-collar men brawled with each other for cash prizes.

For White, what distinguished the UFC from everything that had come before it was its timelessness. "Before any guy ever threw a ball through a circle or hit a ball with a stick, someone hit somebody else with a punch and whoever was standing around ran over to watch it," he once told the New York Times. "I believe fighting was the first sport on earth, and it'll be the last sport on earth. It works everywhere, and we're going to take it everywhere."

As I wandered back home in the last smoggy rays of daylight, it was hard not to wonder whether the UFC's version of fighting was closer to being the first sport on earth or the last. I thought back to a conversation with Campbell McLaren, when I'd first started looking into the UFC's history. McLaren had been an executive at Semaphore Entertainment Group, the small pay-per-view company in New York that helped fund the first UFC in 1993. At the time, McLaren had been eager to play up the UFC's apocalyptic qualities. One of his inspirations had been *The Morton Downey Jr. Show*, a contentious interview program that frequently ended with panelists coerced into shouting matches, and sometimes even fistfights.

To increase the likelihood of a confrontation, the producers would slowly change the color of lighting on set. Each segment would begin with a calm blue background, and over the course of the hour-long episodes it would slowly change, until the final few minutes took place against a sweltering red. "He knew how to pump up an audience," said McLaren, "I saw that too and I think that if we had a plan—I'm not sure we ever articulated it, but the idea was to outlive the controversy, but keep the edginess. We never wanted the realness to go away."

Today, reality often feels like a special effect, as if someone in the background has been slowly raising the temperature of the studio lights to prime all of us in the audience for something inevitable and terrible. When I asked what McLaren thought about the UFC's new entanglements with Trump and his political movement, he said simply that the times have changed. "What was counterculture is now culture," he said. "The angry nineties have become the really angry two thousands. The UFC doesn't seem that angry anymore. The whole world has changed. And in some ways the world has caught up with the UFC."

What follows is an attempt to tell the history of the UFC over the last three decades, and to look at what exactly has changed about our world to make it ready to embrace a sport like cage fighting, a sickness, a spectacle, a celebration.

1

GOD FORGIVE ME!

Before the broken noses and bloodied mouths, the hair pulled in tufts from scalps, the shards of human tooth embedded in a man's bare foot, before the 3,997 beer-drunk fans gathered into an arena to cheer for it, before it was anything at all, the Ultimate Fighting Championship was just a thought trying to find a way out of Art Davie's head as he sat in the reading room at the Torrance Public Library. He'd spent months going through histories of prizefighting and martial arts, collecting stories and taking notes for his pitch folder. He was especially interested in matches that had pitted fighters from different martial arts disciplines against each other, not to prove who was the better man but to see who had chosen the more effective form of self-defense. His notes were filled with strange curiosities, including a 1963 exhibition bout between judo black belt Gene LeBell and boxer Milo Savage—LeBell won in the fourth round, using his gi lapels to choke Savage. In 1976, Vince McMahon Sr. booked Shea Stadium in New York for an exhibition fight between wrestler Andre the Giant, née André René Roussimoff, and heavyweight boxer Chuck Wepner. The match was followed by a closed-circuit television broadcast of an event from the Nippon Budokan arena in Tokyo in which Muhammad Ali fought wrestler Antonio Inoki. That match was originally supposed to be fixed—with Inoki coming from behind to beat Ali by a submission hold—but the rules were hastily rewritten at the last minute and Inoki was forbidden from using wrestling takedowns. Instead, he spent the majority of the fifteen-round match lying on his back kicking Ali's knees. Midway through the fight, some in the crowd began throwing garbage into the ring and chanting, "Money back! Money back!" Beginning in 1976, *ABC's Wide World of Sports* would periodically air Professional Karate Association events, which matched fighters from different styles of karate against each other. Around the US, amateur events like *Tough Guys*, a one-night-only tournament held at a Pittsburgh Holiday Inn, had matched workers from different backgrounds against each other—farmer, blacksmith, construction worker. "Anything goes," a local flyer for the event had promised. "Punching, striking, kicking, throwing, and grappling (ground fighting)." While most events were one-off stunts or short-lived spectacles, Davie was convinced he was onto something big.

An excitable ad man who spoke in story-length sentences, Davie always seemed to be on the verge of something new. He saw the secret wink of possibility everywhere he looked. Where others saw bad ideas or wastes of time, he saw the future, opulent but still invisible to the naked eye. He had grown up in a middle-class family in Sheepshead Bay, Brooklyn, and gone to high school at the New York Military Academy. (He was roommates for a semester with a young Donald Trump.) Davie later enlisted in the Marines, and served in Vietnam for eleven months, then found work as a used car salesman after returning to the US. In the mid-1970s, Davie worked for Toyack Motors, a large discount car brokerage in San Diego, where he appeared in a series of outlandish television commercials. In one, he wore a Kevlar vest while someone shot him in the chest with a handgun. In another, he was suspended by a harness below a helicopter as it flew across San Diego. He eventually talked his way into a job working for the Los Angeles ad agency that Toyack worked with, and a few years later he had made another jump, to J&P Marketing, which handled accounts for StarKist Tuna and Original New York Seltzer. In 1989, one of J&P's clients, Wisdom Imports, asked for help developing a new marketing campaign for Tecate beer. As he worked on pitch ideas, Davie started thinking about fighting.

Growing up, his favorite show had been *Greatest Fights of the Century*, a weekly program that showed old boxing matches, sponsored by a new Vaseline hair tonic for men. Davie tried to imagine what a contemporary series sponsored by Tecate might look like. Boxing would likely be too costly, and pro wrestling too juvenile, but he saw potential with martial arts. In Vietnam, he'd heard a story about an underground fight a group of soldiers had seen on an R & R trip to Bangkok. The fight had been an extreme mismatch, between a small muay Thai fighter and a hulking Indian wrestler, which had ended with the smaller man winning. Davie wasn't sure if the story was true, but he thought it had the start of a good idea in it. Were there other kinds of unusual fighters that could be matched against each other? Could a Japanese wrestler beat a heavyweight boxer? Could an American kickboxer fend off a sumo wrestler? Would a Krav Maga fighter be able to protect themselves against a judoka? Davie put together a pitch for a television series that would answer those questions, *The World's Greatest Fighter*, sponsored by Tecate.

When he laid out his vision to Wisdom Imports, in the winter of 1990, it politely passed and asked what other ideas Davie's colleagues had. Rejection was the rule in advertising and Davie didn't take it personally, but the idea of *The World's Greatest Fighter* lingered in his imagination. As part of his research he'd read a profile in *Playboy* of Rorion Gracie, a Brazilian jiu-jitsu black belt who had challenged heavyweight boxing champion Mike Tyson to a street fight and promised to pay $100,000 to any other martial artist willing to come to his gym and beat him. *Playboy* described Rorion as "the toughest man in the United States," and the Gracie version of jiu-jitsu as the "most devastating of all martial arts," a sort of counterintuitive ground fighting that could give even the smallest and weakest fighters a chance to win. A few months after Wisdom had turned down his pitch, Davie wandered into the Gracie Academy in Torrance and left his card for Rorion with an invitation to dinner and discussion about a potential business opportunity. A few days later, they met in person.

Rorion reminded Davie of a bird of prey. He was charming but distant, kind but also ready to fight at any moment, humble but outspoken in his belief that no one on earth could beat him. For the Gracies, jiu-jitsu had been a birthright. Rorion's grandfather, Gastao Gracie, a wealthy businessman in Belém, Brazil, helped produce a local circus and hired the pupil of a traveling Japanese prizefighter and judo expert, Mitsuyo Maeda, to fight in one of his shows. Gastao would later become friends with Maeda and sent his sons to learn self-defense at one of the expert's gyms. They were eager students and later adapted what they had learned into their own unique variant they called Gracie jiu-jitsu, which placed greater emphasis on grappling on the ground, where smaller and weaker fighters could use leverage to better neutralize bigger and stronger opponents. When Rorion arrived in America in 1978, at twenty-six, he saw an opportunity to bring the family's extensive jiu-jitsu business to a new market. Initially, he worked as a house cleaner and as an extra on television shows like *Hart to Hart* and *Fantasy Island*, but he would often invite actors and executives he'd met to visit his small rental home in Torrance, where he'd teach them basic jiu-jitsu on mats spread across the garage. Many of his early clients were celebrities, including John Milius, the cigar-gnashing screenwriter of *Red Dawn*, *Conan the Barbarian*, and *Apocalypse Now*. His reputation helped him land a job as a stunt coordinator for *Lethal Weapon*, and eventually he developed a large enough client list to lease a gym in Torrance and begin teaching full-time.

Rorion wasn't impressed with Davie's pitch. Rorion had already produced his own video series, *Gracie Jiu-Jitsu in Action*, crude camcorder footage of different Gracie family members using jiu-jitsu in old Brazilian prizefights or gym challenges against fighters from other disciplines. In 1982, another producer had asked him to help launch an open rules fighting league, called the World Freestyle Fighting Championship, with a match against champion kickboxer Benny "The Jet" Urquidez. Davie's idea seemed like old hat. Despite his apparent disinterest, Rorion agreed to lend his name to an event if Davie could put it together, assuming it would be another venue to demonstrate the effectiveness of jiu-jitsu. Over the next year, Davie became a gadfly around the gym, taking weekly lessons and befriending other members of the Gracie family who helped run classes. (Davie had previously dabbled with muay Thai lessons as a way to stay fit, after first learning some basics in Vietnam.) Davie helped organize a direct marketing campaign for a five-volume VHS series called *Basics of Gracie Jiu-Jitsu*, sending out a mailer to every student who had ever taken a class with Rorion, and advertising in *Black Belt* magazine. Tape sales were soon bringing in more than $21,000 a month. Rorion had agreed to share the profits with Davie, and he realized his share would be more than enough to support himself while he tried to produce *The World's Greatest Fighter* full-time. It would be a step down from what he was making in advertising, but he decided it was worth the risk.

In the summer of 1992, Davie quit his job and began making regular afternoon trips to the Torrance Public Library, which he would refer to as his "de facto office." Davie gave himself a crash course in state athletic commission regulations and the broadcasting industry, learning as much as he could from trade papers about how to get a television show on the air. He knew the event, which he had decided to rename *The War of the Worlds*, would likely be too violent for traditional broadcast networks, and instead decided to target cable, a sector that had grown dramatically, from 850,000 US subscribers in 1962 to more than 53 million by 1989. Over the same period, the number of available channels had risen to seventy-nine, creating thousands of new broadcast hours each week, which had created openings for new kinds of shows for specialty audiences that would have been unthinkable a few decades earlier. Davie cold-called executives at HBO and Showtime. They both agreed to hear him out, but turned him down. Showtime's Jay Larkin joked that Davie would have had better luck with a show about "marital arts" instead of martial arts. ESPN and Prime Ticket, a local sports channel in Los Angeles, showed some interest but neither responded to follow-up calls after Davie faxed over his business plan.

In early spring of 1993, Davie decided to try reframing the event as a pay-per-view instead of a cable series. It was a smaller market—only 37 percent of US cable subscribers had the capability of ordering pay-per-views through their cable boxes—but it still reached more than twenty million homes and had been more open to what Scott Kurnit, president of Showtime's pay-per-view division, called "niche-casting." While the fine arts attracted a small but profitable pay-per-view audience—the Metropolitan Opera generated thirty-five thousand buys and $1.2 million with a live broadcast of a twenty-fifth anniversary special at Lincoln Center—the more popular programming had come from forbidden arts. One of the biggest early successes was Howard Stern's *Underpants and Negligee Party*, an amateurish variety show performed in front of a small studio audience. Dressed in underwear and lingerie, Stern and his costars acted out short comic sketches and interviewed celebrity guests, including Richard Belzer, Jessica Hahn, and Penn Jillette. "I'm never gonna get credibility like this," Stern exclaimed as he simulated a ménàge a trois with two hired models in negligees, who took turns simulating oral sex on him underneath a sheet.

Stern had been a consistent performer on pay-per-view, reveling in the fact that almost everything he was doing would have been censored on standard broadcast television. He had a modest hit with *U.S. Open Sores*, built around a tennis match between Stern and producer Gary Dell'Abate in front of sixteen thousand fans at Nassau Coliseum in Long Island. He'd followed that with *Butt Bongo Fiesta*, which featured segments like "Lesbian Dial-a-Date" and "Guess the Jew," a skit that pitted Ku Klux Klan member Daniel Carver against Kurt Waldheim Jr., whose father was president of Austria and had been tied to the Nazi Party in Germany. Stern's biggest hit would come later with 1993's *New Year's Rotten Eve*, which featured a woman eating live maggots and another covering herself in ice cream to make a "human sundae." The broadcast generated more than 270,000 pay-per-view buys and grossed more than $12 million, substantially more than less offensive material like a Rolling Stones concert from the *Steel Wheels* tour that generated $4 million, or the 1992 Summer Olympics, a high-profile joint venture between NBC and Cablevision, which reportedly lost more than $100 million. On pay-per-view, having credibility often felt like a liability, while amateurism and irreverence were taken as markers of authenticity, something worth paying a premium for.

As Davie read more about the peculiarities of pay-per-view, one company in New York caught his attention: Semaphore Entertainment Group. A subsidiary of music publishing giant Bertelsmann Music Group, SEG had built a small but steady business broadcasting pay-per-view concerts of BMG's musical acts, including Iron Maiden, Bette Midler, Lynyrd Skynyrd, The Who, and New Kids on the Block. SEG had been looking for ways to expand its business beyond musical performances, ideally with something that could grow into a recurring series and compete in the market segment where Stern had found chart-topping success. In 1992, SEG produced an update to the iconic *Battle of the Sexes* tennis matches that originally took place in 1973, first between Bobby Riggs and Margaret Court, and later with Riggs and Billie Jean King. SEG's update was called *Battle of the Champions*, and featured Jimmy Connors and Martina Navratilova. It attracted some press attention, but much of it was critical—the *New York Times* described the event as "silly" and CBS tennis analyst Mary Carillo compared it to a pie-eating contest. As Davie read more about SEG, he became convinced that *The War of the Worlds* was just what the company was looking for. It was a series, not a one-off, and dramatically less costly than sharing profits with world famous musicians or tennis stars. Most important, the taboo-inflected tone had a better chance of appealing to pay-per-view audiences, promising not just violence but revelation. Just as Howard Stern had broken through the artificial congeniality of broadcast television with nudity and neo-Nazis, Davie was confident *The War of the Worlds* would show viewers the reality of martial arts culture, exposing the frauds and "strip mall gurus" who had filled the American suburbs with karate and kung fu gyms that promised their students an unattainable "aura of invincibility."

In early March, Davie decided to cold-call SEG and was surprised when instead of an assistant or receptionist he reached Campbell McLaren, the recently hired vice president of original programming who liked to make a point of picking up his own phone as often as possible. "It was some great pitch," McLaren says. "It went something like this: Campbell, HBO turned me down, Showtime turned me down, everybody turned me down. You're my last hope. I was like, Who is this? I literally had no idea what he was talking about." Yet, as Davie told his story about a wholesome family of Brazilians who also happened to be trained killers and had been campaigning to fight Mike Tyson, McLaren was immediately interested. Like Davie, he was a theatrical showman with a taste for spectacle and surprise. He had studied documentary filmmaking at MIT before dropping out and moving to New York. He worked in marketing for Young & Rubicam, before landing a job as an assistant at Carolines on Broadway, the legendary comedy club that helped launch the careers of Mitch Hedberg, Richard Belzer, Louis C.K., Bill Hicks, Jerry Seinfeld, and Chris Rock. McLaren worked his way up to being the club's talent director and then left to work as a manager, representing Joy Behar, Larry David, and Lewis Black, among others. He'd joined SEG in 1992 to help the company branch out into comedy and other original programming. McLaren had a bawdy sense of humor and seemed to have internalized the comedian's mantra that the most offensive thing a person could be was boring. He was unsure what kind of event Davie was proposing, but as he listened he had the sense that it was just the kind of thing he'd been hired to find— part sporting event, part stunt show, and part costume drama. Whatever it was, he was sure it wouldn't be boring.

McLaren asked Davie to send him a formal business plan to circulate with his colleagues and promised to set up an in-person meeting in New York in a few weeks' time. In addition to his pitch documents, Davie mailed copies of *Gracie Jiu-Jitsu in Action* videos, which became instant hits with SEG's staff. David Isaacs, SEG's chief operating officer, recalled putting one of the tapes on in his office. Within a few minutes, he was surrounded by other staffers who had stopped to gawk as they'd walked past his open door. "You were like, Oh my gosh, I've never seen anything like this," Isaacs would later say.

In April, Davie met with McLaren and SEG president Bob Meyrowitz for a cigar-fueled meeting at the company's offices on West 57th Street. Meyrowitz struck Davie as a "modern day business buccaneer," with styled hair, a trimmed beard, and a suit that he assumed had cost more than most people pay for their mortgages in a month. He had made a name for himself in the music world in the 1970s, producing the hit syndicated radio series *King Biscuit Flower Hour*, which featured live performances from some of the biggest bands in the world, including Bruce Springsteen, Eric Clapton, and the Grateful Dead. Though he didn't know much about martial arts, Meyrowitz had been a longtime boxing fan and liked the idea of producing a series that involved fighting in some form. Meyrowitz told Davie that he would have SEG's lawyers start negotiating the basic terms of a deal with Davie's lawyers. To celebrate, McLaren and Isaacs took Davie out for a martini-soaked steak dinner at McCormick & Schmick's.

Davie was thrilled, but as he flew back to California, he realized he didn't have any lawyers for SEG to negotiate with. For almost a year, Davie had been doing everything himself. He'd had official company letterhead printed, but he'd never even registered an LLC. With a tentative debut set for Halloween weekend, just six months away, he realized that for all the time and money he had already invested, he was still just getting started.

With the green light from SEG, Davie settled on Denver, Colorado, as the best location for *The War of the Worlds*. It was one of just three states in the country where bare-knuckle boxing was actually legal, thanks in part to a 1977 law that had repealed all regulatory statutes for boxing and wrestling events in the state. The state also lacked a boxing commission that would have been required to provide legal oversight or, potentially, interference with Davie's vision. The only legal requirement as far as Davie could tell, was to ensure every fighter would be over eighteen years old. Davie took a short trip to Denver after returning from New York and set up War of the Worlds Promotions as a Colorado LLC. He also hired a local lawyer, Mark Field, and an accountant in Denver to handle the company's accounts. Back in Torrance, he rented a small office in a building that shared a back alley with the Gracie Academy, and began working with SEG's production department on what exactly the first *War of the Worlds* event would look like. Davie and SEG had settled on an eight-man tournament structure, with each fighter representing a different martial arts discipline. The tournament winner would fight three times in one night, and would earn a $50,000 prize. Davie had wanted to give the tournament winner a crown rather than a championship belt or trophy, something that pointed to the ancient Greek roots of hand-to-hand combat. After sketching out several rough designs, he decided to go with another idea that had come from one of Rorion's students: a simple medal similar to those given to Olympic athletes. Engraved on the back would be the phrase *Per Aspera Ad Astra*. Through adversity to the stars.

There was a protracted debate about what kind of platform the fights should take place on. A boxing ring seemed like it would make grappling exchanges more dangerous with its tangle-prone ropes. Davie suggested a cage with an electric fence, or perhaps one enclosed from above by razor wire. John Milius, who had joined the production as a consultant, suggested building a moat filled with piranhas. They also considered using a Plexiglas cube to provide an unobstructed view of the fighters, but the likelihood of humidity and sweat smearing the surfaces made it unworkable. SEG's art director Jason Cusson finally settled the issue with a design for an octagonal cage, framed with padded posts and chain-link fencing in between. Cameramen would be able to film over the top edge of the fence while standing on small crates, and for long grappling exchanges on the mat, the chain-link would be in the foreground, adding an element of illicitness and taboo. The shape had been inspired by *The Octagon*, a 1980 movie in which Chuck Norris infiltrates a terrorist organization that holds sparring sessions in an octagonal space marked out by eight heavy wooden posts. To lend an aura of credibility, Davie invented the International Fight Council to serve as the event's formal sanctioning body and rules enforcer, with Rorion listed as commissioner.

SEG and Davie continued to negotiate the final points of the deal throughout the summer, but they had reached a general agreement that SEG would cover the marketing and production costs and Davie and Rorion would be responsible for finding the fighters and covering their prize money, which would total $102,500–$50,000 for the winner, $15,000 for the runner-up, $4,000 for the two losing semifinalists, and $1,000 for the four first-round losers, plus $2,500 to be divided between two alternate fighters who would be available as backups in case of injury. (Davie had also agreed to secretly pay two fighters extra guaranteed fees regardless of whether they won or lost, for $17,000 and $6,000 respectively.) Davie raised the money over the summer, by sending out a mass mailer to every current and former student of the Gracie Academy and offering them the chance to be investors in WOW Promotions. SEG would later ask for a name change, fearing it would be exposed to copyright infringement lawsuits if it went forward with *The War of the Worlds* as the event name, which was identical to both the H. G. Wells novel and the 1953 film adaptation, both of which were still protected. Davie began using *World's Best Fighter* as a placeholder, and in August, Michael Abramson, SEG's head of marketing, suggested *Ultimate Fighting Championship*. No one was enthused by the name. Davie thought it was too long and cumbersome, and McLaren thought it sounded too much like Ultimate Frisbee. But no one could think of a better alternative, and with just weeks left, they decided to run with it as the least objectionable option. SEG's design team created a logo for the new brand featuring a bald fighter, standing astride the Earth, arms raised in victory. The image reminded Davie of Mr. Clean more than anything else, but he decided to not make an issue of it with so little time left before the event.

In the final weeks of preparation, a sense of uncertainty hung over everything. They pushed the date back two weeks, to November 12, because of a scheduling conflict. SEG paid just $4,000 to rent the McNichols Sports Arena, home of the NBA's Denver Nuggets, who were playing an away game against the Los Angeles Lakers that night. To help market the event, Davie hired a pair of local Denver promoters, Barry Fey and Zane Bresloff, who spread flyers around the city advertising the UFC as "The End of Civilization As We Know It," an angle they'd settled on after seeing that the fighter contracts included an acknowledgment they might be injured badly enough to die during the event. SEG faxed fliers to gyms and dojos all over the country and asked their owners to post them in locker rooms and lobbies, hoping students would be interested in watching. SEG's fliers didn't mention death or the end of civilization, but instead promoted the fact that that there would be no rules, no judges, and no point system, just pure uncontrolled violence. "THERE ARE NO RULES!" one of it's posters said, using bold block letters with little fissures running through them, as if they had been damaged in an earthquake.

There actually were rules, a full typewritten page of them, but the fighters weren't given them until the night before the event. The only way a fight could be stopped was if there was a knockout, or a fighter tapped three times on the mat in submission, or their corner threw in the towel on their behalf. Fights would be divided into five-minute rounds with a two-minute rest period in between, and there would be as many rounds as necessary to produce a finish. Biting, groin strikes, and eye gouges were forbidden. Fighters who chose to wear wrestling or boxing shoes wouldn't be allowed to throw kicks, but those who chose to go barefoot would be. When Davie handed out the rules to the fighters in a small conference room at the Tower Inn, a hotel he'd booked to be the event headquarters during fight week, there was nearly a mass walkout. Everyone had their own particular issue with the rules, and they all mistrusted Rorion's role in creating them, suspecting they had been designed to tilt the field in favor of Gracie jiu-jitsu. "The fighters and their camps were all loudly arguing, and I could see that the whole event was coming apart before it had even started," Davie recalled. The unrest dissipated after Teila Tuli, a sumo wrestler from Hawaii, grew sick of the bickering, and announced he was signing his release form. "I don't know about you guys, but I came here to party," Tuli said. "If anyone else came here to party, I'll see you tomorrow night at the arena."

When the cameras finally started rolling at 6:00 p.m. the next day, no one seemed ready for what was about to happen. Davie hadn't signed the final contract with SEG until just hours before the first fight. The event had the feel of community theater, the world's most lavish public access show. It opened with an introduction from American kickboxing legend and lead commentator Bill "Superfoot" Wallace, who belched mid-sentence and twice misidentified the event as *The Ultimate Fighting Challenge*. He also introduced sideline reporter Brian Kilmeade as Brian

Kilmoore, and rambled unintelligibly throughout much of the broadcast. At one point, Wallace described the benefits of handwraps to retired NFL star Jim Brown, whom Davie had persuaded to provide color commentary. "Don't you wish you could tape your whole body, Jim?" he said "Pain hurts. Let me tell you, it ruins your whole day."

The first fight, between Dutch kickboxer Gerard Gordeau and Tuli, fell apart within the first thirty seconds. After circling each other for a few seconds, Tuli suddenly rushed forward, waving his arms hoping to catch Gordeau in a blitz. An experienced kickboxer, Gordeau calmly skipped backward on the balls of his feet and delivered a short right hook to Tuli's jaw that sent him stumbling to the mat. It happened so quickly it wasn't clear there had even been a punch. It looked like Tuli might have lost his balance, but then Gordeau took a step forward and kicked Tuli in the face while he was trying to pull himself up. The blow sent one of Tuli's front teeth flying into the audience, while a few shards remained embedded in Gordeau's foot.

The referee, João Alberto Barreto, an experienced fighter from Brazil and friend of Rorion's, was shocked into action. Barreto called a time-out, though there was no rule stating time-outs could be called, by the referee or anyone else. Gordeau, who had been ready to throw more punches, was irate and protested that Barreto was giving Tuli a chance to recover and costing him a chance to win. Tuli's cornermen flooded into the cage to check on their fighter, while Rorion jumped onto the octagon apron, yelling at Barreto in Portuguese that he had to let the fight continue. On commentary, Wallace stumbled through an explanation of what was happening, though it was clear no one knew. After nearly two minutes of confusion, Tuli's team finally determined that he was too hurt to continue and conceded the fight. Gordeau was declared the winner.

A group of executives from Gold's Gym, one of the event's few sponsors, was so repulsed that it walked out and vowed to never again work with the UFC. For the few thousand fans who had bought tickets, however, the moment was just what they had hoped for. As Davie listened to their cheers, he knew he had created a hit. "I can smell the bloodlust of young guys all over the planet," he thought to himself. "This is fucking real, and I fucking love it. And we still have the rest of the tournament to go—the night has just begun. God forgive me!"

In the second fight, Zane Frazier and Kevin Rosier, two aging and out-of-shape kickboxers, had the kind of brawl you might expect two drunken fathers to have in a parking lot after a Little League game. At one point, Frazier grabbed a tangle of hair on the back of Rosier's head and used it as a grip while he threw short uppercuts and knees. "That's something that wasn't talked about in the rules," Kathy Long, the third member of the commentary team and a women's kickboxing world champion, observed while trying to process how quickly the idea of martial arts competition was transforming into something wilder and less familiar. "You see some of the hair falling on the ground there. There's quite a bit coming out." The fight ended with a surprise comeback after Frazier, exhausted from having punched Rosier for so long and to so little effect, lost his balance and fell to the mat. Rosier grabbed the top of the octagon fence and began stomping his heel down onto Frazier's head, which prompted Frazier's cornerman to throw in the towel.

The third fight was the first to feature a Gracie. Rorion had ruled out competing himself because he was a co-promoter and co-owner of WOW LLC. Instead, he chose his younger brother Royce to represent the family. When Royce entered the arena floor, he was part of a human train made up of Gracies, one standing behind another in a long single-file line, jogging in unison, each with their hands resting on the shoulders of the person in front of them. At twenty-six years old and 178 pounds, Royce was both the youngest and smallest of the eight fighters in the tournament. His opponent, Art Jimmerson, a top-ten–International Boxing Federation–ranked cruiserweight boxer, outweighed him by nearly twenty pounds. When they stood across from each other in the octagon, Royce seemed physically outmatched. Thin and loose-limbed, he seemed to disappear inside his crisp white gi. He refused to make eye contact with Jimmerson in the seconds before the fight began and kept his face in a scowl, as if trying to persuade himself of something. Royce had never thought of himself as a fighter, but had practiced fighting as a vocation. He'd arrived in the United States at seventeen, and had lived with Rorion and worked as a babysitter until his English was good enough to help at the academy. Initially, Rorion had wanted his brother Rickson Gracie to represent the family in the tournament. Rickson was older and bigger than Royce, and had competed in Brazil throughout the 1980s and frequently fought in the *Gracie Jiu-Jitsu in Action* tapes. But after Rickson opened his own Gracie jiu-jitsu academy in Los Angeles, Rorion feared the family brand would become diluted, and had instead chosen Royce to compete, rather than giving Rickson a platform to promote his own offshoot.

As the fight began, Royce seemed tense and out of place. He stood up straight and almost stork-like, his elbows flared outward like bent wings. Even the way he made a fist seemed wrong, with his fingers loose and fanned out like an old grandmother holding a steering wheel. Jimmerson circled Royce with short, rhythmic steps, controlling the distance between them and feinting to imply the threat of an intercepting punch should Royce move closer. As the fight wore on, Jimmerson refused to throw any punches, in spite of how confidently he controlled the space between them. As he continually circled away, it started to seem as if Jimmerson was, for some reason, afraid of Royce, and after nearly a minute of caution and hesitation, Royce suddenly ran forward, bent at the waist, and wrapped his arms around Jimmerson's legs as he tried to backpedal. Royce drove Jimmerson backward onto the mat and quickly leapt into mount position, straddling Jimmerson's hips. Jimmerson wrapped his arms around Royce's shoulders in a tight bear hug to keep him from pulling back to throw punches. After forty seconds of struggling to hold his grip, with just one free hand and one hand in a boxing glove, Jimmerson's hands slipped apart and he immediately began tapping the mat in submission. Though there was no observable threat or damage inflicted, Jimmerson had nevertheless seemed helpless and terrified, totally lost in the labyrinth of Royce's body. There was a surreal calm after the fight, and even as Royce graciously went to hug Jimmerson and said "Good job" into his ear, there was something fearsome in his face, a surprising, stoic fury.

Royce's next fight was against Ken Shamrock, who was even bigger than Jimmerson, outweighing Royce by more than forty pounds. Shamrock had flown into Denver from Japan, where he had built a career in professional wrestling. Shamrock had also competed in Pancrase, a Japanese mixed martial arts promotion that had debuted just six weeks earlier, which was loosely based on the ancient Greek martial art of pankration, a free-form mix of boxing and grappling. He had fought three times in the previous two months, earning the title of King of Pancrase, including a win over the famous Japanese heel Masakatsu Funaki. Shamrock came to the cage in a black silk robe with a white towel stuffed into the collar.

When he pulled it off in the cage, he revealed a tight red wrestling Speedo and a thickly muscled torso that made him seem more like a superhero than a sportsman.

As the fight began, it appeared that Royce had finally met a physical limit that he wouldn't be able to overcome with technique or trickery. He immediately took a long skip step toward Shamrock and bent over to tackle him, but Shamrock instead stepped backward, ran his arms under Royce's armpits, and turned the Brazilian over onto his back as if he were repositioning an anvil. For a few seconds, Royce seemed overwhelmed as he tried to keep rolling away from Shamrock and find a way back to his feet, but Shamrock held him tightly around the torso. Royce fell backward onto the mat and pulled Shamrock down on top of him. He seemed doomed for a few seconds, his left leg seemingly trapped against his own body by Shamrock, while Royce tried to use his free right leg to drive down heel strikes into Shamrock's back. Shamrock got back to his feet, scooped Royce's free leg into his arms, and dropped onto his own back, trying to use Royce's trapped foot as a lever to twist his knee out of joint. As Shamrock leaned back, searching for a solid point of leverage, Royce jumped up and fell forward on top of Shamrock, taking away all Shamrock's leverage on his knee. Royce began cuffing Shamrock on the ears with open palm strikes, and when Shamrock tried to sit up and again reached out for Royce's ankle, Royce slid to his side and ran his left arm under Shamrock's throat, cinching a choke and using his hips to press as much of his body weight onto the back of Shamrock's neck as possible. After a second of hesitation, Shamrock realized he was caught and began pounding the mat in submission. Royce released the choke, but the referee appeared to have missed the tap and seemed unsure of what had actually happened. When it seemed as if the fight might be allowed to continue after he had already won, Royce became irate.

"You tapped! You tapped!" Royce shouted angrily at Shamrock, who finally confirmed that he had been beaten, prompting the referee to officially end the fight.

Before the finale, it became a little clearer why Royce was in such an irate state, when a special ceremony was held in the cage to honor his father Hélio Gracie, whom Rorion introduced as the "original ultimate fighter." Royce had quickly put a blue Gracie Academy warm-up jacket over his now rumpled gi and stood in a line with his older brothers as Rorion dedicated the event to their father, "a pioneer warrior" who had fought anyone, regardless of style and for sixty-five years had participated in "the most realistic, bone-breaking bare-knuckle fights that the world has ever seen." It was an odd description for Hélio, who had just turned eighty, and seemed gaunt and frail, the only person in the cage who was lighter and shorter than Royce. The crowd in Denver was restless throughout much of the ceremony, booing intermittently at the interruption and reacting to the absurdity of giving a lifetime achievement award to someone at an event presented as the first of its kind.

After the presentation, the cage was cleared for the finale, between Royce and Gordeau, who had won his semifinal against Rosier, in less than a minute, with a methodical barrage of leg kicks and hard elbows. Gordeau had taped his right foot, which still had fragments of Tuli's tooth in it and had begun to swell, prompting some worries of infection. There was a muted quality to the finale. Both men had spent substantial energy and focus on earlier fights and seemed to move more cautiously. Gordeau opened by pushing Royce back to the octagon fence with a steady series of feints. Trapped, Royce sprinted forward and tried to take Gordeau down, but the Dutchman used the lapels of his gi to pull him up and away from his hips while hopping back to the opposite side of the cage for support. Royce stubbornly held on to his chest and wrapped his leg around Gordeau's left calf hoping to trip him, but Gordeau held on to the octagon fence and kept his feet. After forty seconds of struggle against the fence, Royce instead ran his leg through the inside of Gordeau's and tripped him in one smooth motion, landing in mount position atop Gordeau's hips. Gordeau turned to one side to wriggle free, and Royce again ran his arm across Gordeau's throat for a choke that forced Gordeau to tap the mat in submission. For several seconds, Royce refused to release the choke, perhaps fearing a repeat of the confusion that had taken place after the Shamrock fight. Gordeau began tapping Royce's shoulder, then the mat, and then he stretched out and reached for the referee's shoes as he bent down to finally pry Royce away from Gordeau's neck.

When Royce was announced as the winner, the crowd cheered and an air horn sounded from somewhere in the front rows. His brothers ran into the cage and lifted him on their shoulders as Royce held his arms aloft in victory. There was a sense of unreality to the scene, or perhaps more accurately it seemed as if a new reality had been exposed. People who looked like Royce weren't supposed to be capable of beating people who looked like Shamrock and Jimmerson. And yet he had, consecutively beating three larger men in less than five minutes total. The mechanics he had used to take control of a fight while on his back, legs helplessly waving in the air, seemed almost supernaturally effective.

Davie would later compare the fighters who competed in Denver to Chuck Yeager's test pilots attempting to break the sound barrier. In reality, they often seemed closer to the Wright brothers at Kitty Hawk, sending experimental gliders over the dunes, simply hoping to prove that flight was possible for humans. Even the few moments of ascent were brief and bookended by crash landings, and a lingering sense of confusion about what had worked, and what had gone wrong when everything came crashing down. It was captivating, both revelatory and repulsive, comic and catastrophic. Nothing quite like it had ever before been broadcast on mass media.

"I think I found my sport," Jim Brown said as the broadcast drew to a close. As Royce stood in the cage holding an oversized check for $50,000 while flanked by his family, Brown spoke for many in the audience when he signed off with an attempt to condense everything he had seen over the last eighty-six minutes.

"What we've learned tonight is that fighting is not what we thought it was."

Meyrowitz didn't bother attending the first UFC. He watched it from his house on Long Island with a friend and his friend's thirteen-year-old son. He was uncomfortable with much of what he saw, but his friend's son was transfixed. As Meyrowitz watched the boy over the course of the night, he realized SEG had something special on its hands, though he wasn't sure exactly what it was. The press reaction did little to clarify things for Meyrowitz. The first wave of reviews and reports on the event alternated between horrified and contentious or dismissive. *TV Guide* called it "disgusting, dumb, and depraved." The *Los Angeles Times* critic Howard Rosenberg described the mix of barbarism and amateurism as unexpectedly funny. "Leaning forward on the edge of my chair in front of my TV set shortly before 6 p.m. Friday, I was poised to wince, flinch, shudder, and scream out in terror as never before. To say nothing of laugh," Rosenberg wrote. *Black Belt* magazine suggested the event had been skewed to give jiu-jitsu an advantage and ensure the Gracies won. *Sports Illustrated* decided to cancel a feature on the event altogether, after being disturbed by the violence described in the draft filed by the reporter they'd flown to Denver.

The early sales estimates were much less confusing. Despite the bare-bones marketing campaign, the event would sell eighty-six thousand pay-per-view buys at $14.95 each, surpassing SEG's internal estimates. It generated nearly $1.3 million, and after cable companies took their percentage—the typical split at the time was around 45 percent—SEG was left with a little more than $700,000. SEG had spent around $400,000 on marketing and production costs, but that still left a substantial profit. And there was the potential for even more money with VHS sales and rentals, merchandising, and video game adaptations. SEG had hoped the UFC would become a regular series, and the agreement Davie had finally signed had given SEG the right to produce up to four events if the debut performed well enough. After seeing the sales figures and press response to the first event, Meyrowitz exercised the option for a second event, which was planned for just four months later.

As Davie began looking for a new set of fighters, SEG tried to settle on a branding strategy for the UFC. The arguments were as divided internally as the press response had been. Isaacs, SEG's chief operating officer, had wanted to sell the UFC as "pro wrestling, only real," following on the recent success of the World Wrestling Federation, which had built itself into one of the most successful pay-per-view companies of the era. "When wrestling is big, it's huge," Isaacs said in an interview with *MMA Fighting*. "But when wrestling isn't hot, it's still a good business." McLaren felt the company should continue with the apocalyptic slogans that had helped sell the first event. In radio and newspaper interviews, he tried to play up the violence and implicit risk all the fighters were accepting. On an episode of *Good Morning America*, McLaren emphasized the possibility that someone might be killed during a fight. "You can win by tapout, knockout, or even death," he explained. In an interview with the

New York Times, McLaren claimed that following the success of the first UFC, a Saudi production company had pitched him the idea of airing live executions on pay-per-view. McLaren claimed he had turned them down in part because the UFC already offered viewers the possibility of seeing someone die on camera. "I don't want anyone to die," he said. "It may be good for the buy rate. But I don't want anyone to die." The *New York Times* published the story with a scandal-friendly headline: "Death Is Cheap. Maybe It's Just $14.99."

The strategy made the UFC a media sensation, but it also provoked the ire of politicians, including Denver mayor Wellington Webb. Angered that SEG had organized the event in Denver without giving anyone in the city government advance notice, Webb contacted the management at the McNichols Arena to ensure it wouldn't host the UFC again. SEG adapted to the ban by moving UFC 2 to the Mammoth Gardens, a small concert venue that doubled as a roller skating rink during the day, located just a few miles away from McNichols Arena. As SEG promoted the show, many of the details were still left up to Davie, who functioned like a freelancer, working independently from his small office behind the Gracie Academy in Torrance. Davie had decided to move forward with an expanded tournament, featuring sixteen fighters instead of eight. He claimed to have faxed McLaren about the idea, but no one else at SEG had signed off on it, and they didn't realize what Davie had planned until they arrived in Denver for fight week. The decision added to the logistical issues the crew was facing working in a smaller venue. SEG had to rent out rooms from a small hotel next to the arena to use as dressing rooms for the fighters, leaning the mattresses against the walls so there would be a place to warm up and rest between bouts. The production crew was so short-staffed that no one could leave the venue and escort fighters back and forth from their hotel rooms, so SEG asked Fred Ettish, one of two backup fighters hired to be ready to take the place of anyone too injured to advance, to do the job.

Despite the organizational issues, the second UFC sold even better than the first, generating more than 125,000 buys, a nearly 50 percent increase. It also established Royce as the promotion's unlikely hero, as he beat four other fighters in less than ten minutes total to reclaim his title as the Ultimate Fighter. Eager to build on the momentum, SEG organized another two popular events in 1994. In April 1995, it promoted a super-fight rematch between Royce and Ken Shamrock as the main event of UFC 5. The event generated 286,000 pay-per-view buys at an increased price of $24.95, more than double the previous high, bringing in millions instead of hundreds of thousands. And still more began coming in from VHS rentals and sales, the rights to which SEG had licensed to Vidmark, a subsidiary of Trimark Studios, best known for low-budget genre films, such as *Leprechaun*, *Kickboxer 2*, Peter Jackson's zombie farce *Dead Alive*, and Ken Russell's *Whore*. Vidmark embraced McLaren's branding, placing a black-and-white "Unrated" label on the cover of each tape, along with shock-centric marketing copy: "Unedited! Uncensored! Unleashed!" The company sold tapes for $45 each to national rental chains—Blockbuster Video, Musicland, and Tower. Vidmark also sold tapes and T-shirts for cash at UFC events. Don Gold, the executive in charge of the operation, was responsible for all the merchandising, and would sometimes leave events with bags of cash—as much as $50,000 some nights. "I would walk into my CFO's office at Trimark with my laundry bag and just dump all my cash in there," Gold says. "He was like, What the fuck are you doing? [But] that's how I got paid. They weren't writing checks."

With so much money coming in, SEG consolidated control over the UFC in 1995, buying Davie's and Rorion's 50 percent share of the brand and dissolving WOW LLC. Davie stayed on as contractor for SEG, earning $25,000 as UFC commissioner and its official matchmaker. Rorion decided he didn't want to be associated with the event if he didn't have any control over how it would continue to evolve. Royce left the UFC with Rorion, and soon several of his brothers and cousins instead began appearing in the growing number of competitor promotions that had sprung up. As Davie continued to recruit new fighters, the UFC's roster grew even more bizarre, filled with a collection of characters drawn from the suburban murk of strip mall dojos, where eccentric, and sometimes wholly fictional, forms of martial arts were practiced. At UFC 3, Kimo Leopoldo had introduced the world to Jo Son Do, a discipline his lead trainer, twenty-three-year-old Joe Son, had invented and taught as if it were a real offshoot of taekwondo. Leopoldo was also a devout Christian and walked to the octagon carrying a full-sized wooden cross over his shoulder, while his cornermen held up a banner that showed Jesus bleeding on the cross, with the caption "If I'm OK and your [sic] OK, then explain this!" At UFC 5, John Hess was introduced as a master of his own proprietary martial art called SAFTA, Scientific Aggressive Fighting Technology of America. His opponent, Andy Anderson, was a Texas nightclub owner and member of the Aryan Brotherhood who had been offered a spot in the tournament after helping SEG hire ring card models from one of his venues, the Totally Nude Steakhouse in Gregg County. At UFC 8, a towering Canadian named Gary "Big Daddy" Goodridge debuted, one of the few black fighters to compete in the promotion. Goodridge promoted his skills as a championship arm wrestler, claiming to have beaten a thousand consecutive men in less than two hours at a Japanese arm wrestling tournament. "I don't know what that has to do with martial arts, but he puts that on his résumé," said Jeff Blatnick, the avuncular former Olympic wrestler that SEG hired to replace Bill Wallace.

David Abbott was introduced as a "pit fighter," a discipline Davie had invented, along with Abbott's more familiar nickname, "Tank," to accentuate the intimidating aura of his six-foot-one, 260-pound frame. In reality, Abbott was a hard-drinking construction worker who had developed a minor reputation as a bar brawler around Long Beach. He liked to brag he could drink a bottle of vodka in a single sitting, and seemed to take genuine pleasure in seeing other people hurt. One of Abbott's friends, Dave Thomas, knew Davie and recommended Abbott as a perfect fit for the promotion. In his debut fight, at UFC 6, he brutally knocked out his opponent, John Matua, in eighteen seconds. Matua would remain unconscious on the mat for more than a minute after, legs involuntarily convulsing while his arms were held out stiff at either shoulder in the "fencing response" position, a common symptom of significant brain trauma. As Abbott walked away from Matua, he held out his own arms in the same position and rolled his eyes back in his head in a mocking gesture. In his next fight, Abbott beat Paul Varelans in just under two minutes, taking him down and crushing Varelans's head to the mat with his knee while pulling on the cage fence for extra leverage. As Abbott watched a replay in a post-fight interview with Blatnick cage-side, he said, "I'm starting to get sexually aroused, you better turn that off." On commentary, Jim Brown encapsulated Abbott's appeal as a fighter: "He has no respect. He's from the streets. He's doing a lot of things that are different—it has nothing to do with the martial arts. This guy is a street fighter."

Abbott was an ideal avatar for the UFC's target audience, working-class white men who had started to feel alienated from other sports that were no longer dominated by white athletes. According to Davie, an early survey of the UFC's audience found that 79 percent were white men and more than half were single. "UFC was so successful because it was a sport white guys could win," McLaren says. "This was not for LA, it was not for San Francisco. We did very well in Detroit, Denver, Buffalo, Charlotte. You know, kind of a Walmart strategy in a way, a working-class strategy. Guys that were priced out of boxing, guys that didn't want to see black fighters. That's a reality of it." John Lober, who fought in Pancrase and the UFC, came to the sport after a failed Spanish language test derailed his hopes of becoming a full-time fireman. He blamed "affirmative action." Without the job, Lober felt "lost and that anger was building." For Vare-lans, who competed in four UFC events in 1995 and 1996, mixed martial arts "created a space where people kind of started feeling their liberties again. We've lost so many rights to just live your life and do what the hell you want. . . . You know what, if I want to risk my life, I'm going to fucking do it."

The rebellious attitude and reckless spirit of amateurism drew the attention of Arizona senator John McCain, who, like Wellington Webb, was revolted by the idea that cage fighting was being openly promoted in the United States without any government oversight. McCain had been working on a bill to create a federal sanctioning organization to regulate boxing. He was a lifelong fan of the sport, having trained as a boxer at the US Naval Academy before he became a politician, and had been disturbed by the lack of consistent legal and medical standards to protect fighters from being unnecessarily endangered or exploited. In a September 1994 hearing, McCain pointed to the UFC as an example of the lawless barbarism that would eventually take over any sport without federal standards. "That is what is being done in America today," McCain said as he played several short clips from UFC 2. "Maybe there are comments that can be made about the degeneracy of our society, but the fact is that this kind of thing, I think, continues to occur. The only way it can be stopped is through regulation." In 1995, McCain sent an open letter to all fifty

US governors asking them to support legislature banning the UFC. Ben Nighthorse Campbell, a senator from Colorado who had also competed on the US Olympic judo team in 1964, responded by promising the UFC would never again be allowed in his state. The Illinois state legislature followed suit and passed a bill banning all mixed martial arts events. At an event in Charlotte that year, SEG found itself facing resistance from local law enforcement for the first time, when the city's chief of police arrived at the arena and warned McLaren that he would personally be arrested if the UFC returned to the city. "I don't know what the charge is, I don't know what the law is that you're breaking," McLaren recalls him saying. "But I guarantee you, you'll be in jail until I figure it out." It was an ominous moment for McLaren. "I love the UFC," he said, "but I'm a TV producer. I'm not Amnesty International fighting dictators. I don't want to go to jail. Those kinds of things were very sobering."

Anticipating that serious legal troubles might be closer than anyone at SEG had considered, Meyrowitz decided to lobby the New York State Athletic Commission to formally sanction the UFC. He hired a local lobbying firm and began pitching legislators on the economic benefits of bringing UFC events to the state. The promotion had had one of its biggest hits in Buffalo, drawing a crowd of more than nine thousand to the Memorial Auditorium and generating an estimated 190,000 pay-per-view buys. Meyrowitz promised the UFC could produce a similar burst of economic activity in a number of other working-class cities around the state, and promised to bring UFC events to Albany; Syracuse; Rochester; and Hempstead, Long Island. He also promised he would initially avoid holding events in Manhattan and Brooklyn in order not to attract undue controversy. After months of meetings, the New York state legislature passed a bill allowing mixed martial arts events, with provisions that there would be no eye gouging, throat striking, biting, or kicks to the head from fighters in shoes.

To celebrate the new legal recognition, SEG scheduled two additional events in New York State for 1997: UFC 12 in Niagara Falls, on February 7—the day the bill was scheduled to go into effect—and another at Nassau Coliseum on Long Island, set for later in the year. However, the week of the first event, Meyrowitz learned that Governor George Pataki had put a stay on the bill after increasing public backlash following a series of critical stories in the *New York Times* and threats from New York City mayor Rudy Giuliani to orchestrate a citywide ban on mixed martial arts in defiance of state law. At the last minute, the New York State Athletic Commission had substantially altered its regulatory guidelines in a way that would effectively make it impossible for the UFC to hold its event as planned. Every fighter would be required to wear protective headgear and boxing gloves, and takedowns and trips would be banned to ensure there would be no fighting on the ground. "It basically melded the UFC into amateur boxing," longtime UFC referee John McCarthy, who was also part of the negotiation, wrote in his memoir. The changes were unacceptable to SEG, and the company went to court to request an emergency injunction. The day before the event, the court ruled against SEG, saying there was no evidence that the new restrictions would cause the company "irreparable harm," defined as "injury for which money cannot compensate." Faced with the prospect of putting on an event with no grappling or submission holds, in which everyone wore headgear and boxing gloves, Meyrowitz decided to find a new location. Because SEG had already booked its broadcasting slot with cable pay-per-view providers and spent hundreds of thousands on print marketing, the company decided it couldn't change the time or date. Instead, it quickly came to an agreement with the city of Dothan, Alabama, a small town of sixty thousand near the state border with Florida. SEG chartered a 747 to transport the octagon, production crew, and fighters from Buffalo to Alabama the night before the event. The last-minute move saved the show but wiped out most of the profits. It also left SEG's staff demoralized about the future. "That would have been the end of our business," SEG's Isaacs would later say. "After all the problems, if we couldn't provide a show, the cable companies would have never put us back on."

Things would only become more difficult after UFC 12. In 1997, John McCain was appointed chairman of the Senate Commerce Committee, which was responsible for overseeing the cable industry. He made it a priority to have the UFC taken off the air and began calling the heads of every major cable company in the US to encourage them to drop the promotion. TCI was the first to comply, removing the UFC from its pay-per-view services just a few weeks after UFC 12 in February 1997. Time Warner followed suit, and then Viewers Choice (which would rebrand as In Demand in 2000). By the summer, Cablevision and Request had removed the UFC from their pay-per-view services too. The number of US homes that could buy UFC pay-per-views dropped from 36 million to 7.5 million, most of which were satellite cable subscribers. Seventy percent of the UFC's revenue had come from pay-per-view sales, and the sudden but swift bans devastated SEG's business model. It went from earning between $1 and $2 million in revenue per event to losing $100,000 to $150,000, with some events selling as few as fifteen thousand pay-per-view buys.

SEG responded with aggressive counterattacks against US cable companies. Meyrowitz took out a full-page ad in *Newsday* defending the UFC and encouraging fans to call Cablevision CEO James Dolan directly, listing his home phone number at the bottom. On UFC broadcasts, the company took a similarly plaintive tone. "This may be your last chance to watch the UFC," color commentator Mike Goldberg said during an event in early 1998. "Pick up your phone, call your local cable provider." While SEG waited for an outpouring of fan support, Isaacs and the production crew scrambled to find places that would still allow the UFC to hold events without the threat of legal or political intervention, mostly smaller, rural markets in the South, including Birmingham and Mobile, Alabama; Bay St. Louis, Mississippi; and Augusta, Georgia. The company also began looking for international partners, holding events in São Paolo, Brazil, and Tokyo, Japan, the latter of which was arranged through UFC-J, a subsidiary that was partnered with a local Japanese production company.

The struggles added to the growing tensions between SEG and Davie. In 1997, Meyrowitz fired Davie after he learned he had been talking with outside investors about starting another cage fighting promotion, tentatively titled Thunderdome. McLaren left SEG a few months after Davie, and in 1998 Isaacs left the company too. Many of the UFC's star fighters began to follow the executives' lead and left for more lucrative contracts elsewhere. In 1997, Ken Shamrock joined the WWF, and Don Frye, Dan Severn, Gary Goodridge, Marco Ruas, Oleg Taktarov, and Mark Kerr all left for Pride, a new Japanese promotion backed by one of the country's biggest television networks. The few stars who had stayed with the UFC were asked to take pay cuts to help the promotion avoid bankruptcy, including Tito Ortiz, who had been contracted to make

$25,000 for a title fight against Frank Shamrock, Ken's brother through adoption, but was told SEG could only pay him $10,000. SEG continued to develop other pay-per-view series to bring in new revenue, including a 1998 broadcast called *Street Legal*, which pitted teams of underground car racers from America and Japan against one another. But nothing seemed to work.

Growing more desperate, Meyrowitz flew to TCI's offices in Denver to convince company president Leo Hindery Jr., that the UFC deserved a second chance. Like McCain, Hindery was a proud antagonist of the UFC. When he had run a regional TCI subsidiary in San Francisco, Hindery had refused to carry the franchise, and after he was promoted to president of the whole company he said one of his top priorities was dropping the UFC. "I came here, found out where the bathrooms are, and I canceled it," he said at the time. Meyrowitz argued that mixed martial arts had become a legitimate sport that was already legally sanctioned by several state athletic commissions, including in Mississippi, Louisiana, and Iowa, the latter of which had reversed its ban from a few years earlier, thanks in part to the state's enormous college wrestling fan base. In response, Hindery offered Meyrowitz a bit of hope and promised to reconsider airing the UFC if Meyrowitz could persuade one of the major state athletic commissions—California, Nevada, or New York—to approve mixed martial arts.

Encouraged by the news, Meyrowitz decided to focus on Nevada, often described as the "fight capital of the world" because of its famed history with boxing. Meyrowitz hired Sig Rogich, a former George H. W. Bush adviser turned lobbyist and political strategist, and spent several days in Las Vegas meeting with commissioners, hoping to persuade them to formally sanction mixed martial arts in the state. Two of the five commissioners had been outspoken critics of the UFC, including executive director Marc Ratner, whom Meyrowitz debated in 1995, on an episode of *Larry King Live*. Ratner remained a UFC skeptic, but Meyrowitz believed he had been able to persuade at least three of the five commissioners and was prepared to ask for a vote, until Rogich warned him that they likely wouldn't win.

Meyrowitz had more success with the New Jersey State Athletic Commission, which was run by Larry Hazzard Sr., a jiu-jitsu black belt who had previously worked as a martial arts instructor for more than a decade. After meeting with Meyrowitz, Hazzard agreed to grant the UFC provisional approval to hold three trial events in the state. If there were no major safety or logistical concerns, Hazzard agreed to fully sanction mixed martial arts. It was good news but not quite enough to persuade Hindery. As Meyrowitz scrambled to cover the event's production costs, he started looking for outside investors, and made a tentative deal with Dan Lambert, a real estate developer in south Florida and a jiu-jitsu fanatic who'd bankrolled his own burgeoning fight team. Lambert promised he would pay SEG $200,000 to fund the first New Jersey event, and place another $1 million in an escrow account to fund future events, in exchange for 51 percent ownership of the UFC. It was a lifeline, but as Meyrowitz began preparing for the UFC's first show in New Jersey, scheduled for November 17, 2000, at the Trump Taj Mahal in Atlantic City, the situation began to feel hopeless. Everyone who had sold Meyrowitz on the idea of the UFC had left the promotion, yet he had stayed behind, trapped in someone else's dream. Meyrowitz had dreams of his own, including a new side business he'd helped found, eYada.com, a website that streamed original talk radio programs over the internet. Meyrowitz had gotten a $25 million investment for the company from Time Warner and several banks. As the UFC was wavering on the edge of bankruptcy, he started to wonder why he was still trying to save it.

"I was in court all the time," Meyrowitz would later say. "I was fighting the cable operators who had all been my friends. Your budget keeps shrinking, so you're doing less and less shows rather than bigger and better shows. Why am I doing this?

"At that point, I wanted out. I just really did not want to do this anymore."

EVERYTHING THESE GUYS TOUCH TURNS TO GOLD

Dana White was on the phone with Bob Meyrowitz in the fall of 2000 when he realized the UFC might be for sale. An affable thirty-one-year-old with a tinny voice and faint Boston accent, White was a relative newcomer to the world of cage fighting. He'd made a name for himself in personal fitness, teaching group classes and private lessons to out-of-shape suburbanites and executives in Las Vegas. He'd later branched out into managing a small number of gyms and tried to launch his own apparel line, Bullenbeisser, named after a dog breed he'd had as a child. White had initially thought the UFC was "ridiculous," but he'd quickly changed his mind after a few months of private jiu-jitsu lessons with John Lewis, a former UFC fighter who ran his own fight gym in Las Vegas, Academy J-Sect Jiu Jitsu. A perpetual entrepreneur, White had also talked his way into representing a few fighters from J-Sect, including Tito Ortiz, who'd won the UFC's light heavyweight championship in April.

White was determined to get Ortiz more money before his first title defense, and he laid out two options for Meyrowitz, over speakerphone in the basement office at one of the executive gyms he managed: the UFC could either pay Ortiz what he was owed from his Frank Shamrock fight the previous year, when he'd been contracted to earn $25,000 but had only received $10,000, or it could give him a percentage of the pay-per-view revenue for his next fight. If Meyrowitz wouldn't do either, White was ready to take Ortiz to Pride, or any other promotion that would pay him his full worth. As if to prove how serious he was, White hung up before Meyrowitz had a chance to explain his position. Ortiz, who had been sitting in on the call in White's office, was shocked. "Can you do that?" he remembers saying.

"I don't know. We'll find out," White said.

Over the summer, White had acted on a similar threat, when he'd gotten another client—Chuck Liddell, one of Ortiz's occasional training partners—to reject a three-fight offer from the UFC that started at $1,000 to fight and $1,000 to win. White had instead gotten Liddell a one-fight offer from the IFC, a smaller regional promotion that mostly held events in central and northern California, for $4,500. After Liddell won that fight, and the IFC's light heavyweight championship, by a spectacular headkick knockout, the UFC, fearing it was on the cusp of losing a new young star and knockout artist, offered Liddell a new three-fight deal that would start at $5,000 and $5,000 for his first fight, then rise to $7,500 and $7,500, and $10,000 and $10,000. Liddell happily accepted.

When Meyrowitz later called White back about Ortiz, it became clear that things with the UFC had taken a turn for the worse, and even small concessions were no longer going to be possible. "You know what," White remembers Meyrowitz saying in an exasperated tone, "there is no pay-per-view. There is no money. And pretty soon there's probably not going to be a UFC."

As Meyrowitz attempted to explain his dire situation trying to raise funding to cover the UFC's first event in New Jersey, White heard the sound of opportunity in Meyrowitz's defeated tone. He immediately thought of someone he knew who did have money: Lorenzo Fertitta, president and co-CEO of Station Casinos, a Las Vegas gaming conglomerate he ran with his brother, Frank Fertitta III, six years his senior. While Meyrowitz and the UFC were nearly bankrupt, Station was having its best year ever, on track to generate $990 million in revenue from seven properties in 2000. In January, Station would add two new properties to its portfolio, the Fiesta Rancho and the Fiesta Henderson, consolidating its control of close to half of the Las Vegas locals market, which catered to residents who liked to gamble but didn't want to deal with the tourists and traffic on the Strip.

Whatever sums of money Meyrowitz had been struggling for would have been rounding errors to the Fertittas and Station Casinos. As soon as White hung up with Meyrowitz, he called Lorenzo, who was in Miami on a corporate retreat with other Station executives, making plans for the new year. "Dude," White remembers telling Lorenzo, "I think we might be able to buy this thing, and I think we should."

Lorenzo and Frank III had been with White at the Hard Rock Hotel and Casino when he'd first met Lewis, mulling around the casino floor after a Limp Bizkit concert. And they'd joined White for private jiu-jitsu lessons with Lewis at J-Sect, where they'd become as enthralled with the sport as White was. Learning submission holds and all of the counterintuitive mechanics of grappling opened up a new hidden reality for Lorenzo. "It was like in *The Matrix*—take the pill and it opens your eyes," Lorenzo would later say. "I was obsessed with it. I wanted to train every day." When Frank III learned that Lewis was planning to launch his own mixed martial arts promotion in Las Vegas, what would become the World Fighting Alliance, he offered to fund the project. Lewis initially supported the idea, but he says Frank III later lost interest when Lewis told him he would have to share ownership with another investor. Lorenzo and White had also talked about ways of getting involved with boxing but hadn't found the right idea.

Lorenzo's mind was already filled with ideas about what he would do differently with the UFC. Lorenzo had already met Meyrowitz a year earlier, when Meyrowitz had come to Las Vegas to lobby the Nevada State Athletic Commission. Lorenzo had been appointed to the commission in 1997, and at twenty-eight, he had been its youngest member. Meyrowitz had hoped Lorenzo would help tip the balance away from the older and more conservative members of the NSAC, but Lorenzo had wanted to wait to see if an athletic commission in another large state would approve it first. "I just didn't feel like we had to be the commission that was blazing the trail at the time," Lorenzo later said of his reluctance.

Meyrowitz had invited a small delegation from the NSAC to UFC 21 in Cedar Rapids, Iowa, hoping that seeing an event in person would be more persuasive than his presentations. It had been unusually violent, even by UFC standards, with two fights that were stopped by the presiding ringside physician, and an infamous mismatch between a visiting Japanese fighter, Daiju Takase, and American Jeremy Horn, who outweighed Takase by nearly twenty-five pounds. In the first round, Horn mounted Takase and battered the smaller man with punches and elbows as he wriggled in vain to find an escape route. The event had disturbed Lorenzo and the other commission representatives who'd made the trip. "When you first see it and you're right there in person and a guy's head is bouncing from an elbow or a forearm off the canvas," Lorenzo would later say, "we were like, Wow."

A year-and-a-half later, Lorenzo's reluctance had turned to admiration, and after he hung up with White, he immediately cold-called Meyrowitz at his office in New York. When Meyrowitz heard Lorenzo's voice, he was filled with a sense of rue. Lorenzo, who had resigned from his position on the NSAC in July, told Meyrowitz that he'd heard the UFC was looking for buyers. Meyrowitz admitted he was, and suggested he would consider selling half of the company for $1 million. Lorenzo said he wasn't interested in working with partners and instead offered $2 million for the whole company.

Meyrowitz accepted. Lorenzo would later describe it as the easiest deal he'd ever made. Meyrowitz assured him that running the company would be simple. "He's like, Look, this is super easy," Lorenzo would later say. "You go out, get the production team, sign some fighters and go do your deals with pay-per-view distributors, cut your commercial and go on."

Lorenzo's first act as the UFC's new owner was to appoint White as president. Despite his newfound business in fighter management, White was a peculiar choice for the job. He had no previous executive experience, had nearly flunked out of high school, and had dropped out of college after just a few weeks. To Lorenzo, White's inexperience was an asset. He thought it would be easier for fans to relate to someone who didn't speak like a Harvard MBA, but who was still obsessive about work, driven by a desire to succeed at any cost, the kind of people Lorenzo thought of as "killers."

White and Lorenzo had first met as teenagers, at Bishop Gorman, a private Catholic high school in an upscale suburb on the western edge of Las Vegas ten miles west of the Strip—an enormous checkerboard of gated subdivisions and mile-long plains of undeveloped dirt between them. Lorenzo and White were friendly but not quite friends. It seemed as if their lives were on opposite trajectories. Lorenzo was a starter on the school's football team, well dressed, and a disciplined student. White was trouble waiting to happen, raised by a single mother who'd worked her way through nursing school in Massachussets, then moved to Las Vegas for a job, with White and his older sister, Kelly. He was cheerful but impulsive, cut class as often as he attended, and spent most of his time either partying or fighting with students from rival schools. In the middle of their senior year, White disappeared altogether, after his mother sent him to live with his grandparents in a small town outside Bangor, Maine. After graduation, White moved to Boston and enrolled in classes at the University of Massachusetts, Boston, but stopped going in the middle of the first semester. Over the next several years, he worked as a bar bouncer, bike courier, a bellhop at the Boston Harbor Hotel, and an asphalt layer for EJ Paving, a small company that did road repair work and built curbs around the suburbs north of Boston. ("That was the hardest job I've ever had in my entire life," White would later say of EJ Paving. "That was the job that showed me what real work was, man. If this is real work, I don't ever want to do this.")

Feeling directionless and bored by his life, he decided to launch a career as an amateur boxer, which had been one of his childhood fantasies. He became a regular at the McDonough Boxing Training Center, a run-down gym attached to the Boston Municipal Court in Southie, and persuaded another promising amateur and former Golden Gloves winner, Peter Welch, to help train him. White loved being in the gym. In sparring sessions with more experienced fighters, he impressed Welch with his persistence, even when he was taking a beating. "From the first blow he took on his chin, he proved he had the stuff to stick around the game," Welch would later tell the *Boston Globe*.

To make ends meet, Welch and White started teaching fitness classes at the gym. Too poor to afford a car, White would bicycle to the gym every day, and he sometimes listened to audiobooks on the ride. White became a fan of Tony Robbins, whose motivational books on entrepreneurship and career development were written with an almost mystical sense of optimism and destiny. In one characteristic section, from *Unlimited Power: The New Science of Personal Achievement*, Robbins described how the world had been remade after the Industrial Revolution so that "any kid in blue jeans can create a corporation that can change the world." In pre-industrial times, the world was defined by feudal caste systems that dictated a person's destiny almost before they were born. But because of electronic media and the arrival of the information age, in Robbins's telling, anyone could rise above their rank and make their life "a masterpiece," so long as they have the courage to act, to "live what they teach" and "walk their talk." According to Robbins, these are "the models of excellence the rest of the world marvels about. Join this unique team of people known as the few who do versus the many who wish—result-oriented people who produce their life exactly as they desire it."

White wasn't sure where his own life was heading, but as he listened to Robbins's exhortations, he felt confident he was on the right path. That confidence was shaken one day in late 1995, when Kevin Weeks walked into the McDonough Boxing Training Center. Weeks interrupted White in the middle of one of his adult fitness classes and asked him to step outside. Weeks was well known and widely feared in Southie. He worked for the Winter Hill Gang, a crime syndicate then run by Whitey Bulger (née James Joseph Bulger Jr.), who trafficked guns, sold marijuana and cocaine, and extorted regular payments from local businesses in exchange for being allowed to operate in what Bulger thought of as his territory. Weeks told White he would have to pay $2,500 if he wanted to keep teaching fitness classes at the gym. The sum was unimaginably large to White, and after a few fear-filled months trying to raise the money, followed by a final ominous threat from Weeks, White decided to get out of Boston. He booked a one-way ticket to Las Vegas, the only other place he could imagine going, and twenty-four hours later was on an outbound flight. White moved in with the parents of an ex-girlfriend from Bishop Gorman, Anne Stella, and started looking for work as a fitness instructor. He went to a Kinko's and printed business cards for "Dana White Enterprises" and then drove around Las Vegas introducing himself at every gym he could find to pitch his services as a trainer. Within a year, White had built a steady business teaching both group classes and private lessons for executives like Steve Cavallaro, the Hard Rock Hotel and Casino's chief operating officer. His group classes could attract as many as 140 people for a ninety-minute session that promised the high caloric burn of boxing-derived conditioning exercises.

He'd reconnected with Lorenzo a year after returning to Las Vegas, at the wedding of a mutual friend from Bishop Gorman, Adam Corrigan. Lorenzo was amazed by how much White had changed. All the things that had seemed like negatives in high school—White's impulsiveness, his short attention span, his inability to self-censor—seemed to have become positives in adulthood. By the end of the night, White had sold Lorenzo on private training sessions and over the next several months, they became closer friends than they had ever been in high school. They went to concerts, boxing matches, and nightclubs, often with Frank III in tow, and they hired White to build and manage an executive gym in the basement of Station's corporate offices.

When Lorenzo and Frank III returned to Las Vegas from Miami, they asked their father, Frank Jr., to lunch to tell him about the newest addition to the family business. A kindly man with a monkish rim of gray hair circling a bald spot, Frank Jr. had always encouraged his children's ambitions. In 1993, he'd stepped down from his position as CEO of Station and transferred control of the company to Lorenzo and Frank III. He'd been proud of what they'd accomplished, steering Station through a $294 million IPO, the largest ever for a gaming company at the time, while expanding from one property to nine, and growing to more than ten thousand employees. When he heard the plan to buy into the cage fighting business, however, Frank Jr. was alarmed. "I really don't want you doing this," Lorenzo recalled him saying. "It doesn't make any sense."

It seemed like a flight of fancy, what even Lorenzo would later describe as a "vanity business," that might risk Station's standing in Las Vegas and on Wall Street for a brand that had been publicly attacked by the chief of police in Charlotte, North Carolina, the state attorney general in Michigan, the governor of New York, and one of the most powerful senators in the country who'd just narrowly lost a bid to win the Republican presidential primary. And what would the upside even be, from a company worth a fraction of 1 percent of Station's annual revenue? A few extra million dollars a year? Lorenzo and Frank III practiced all their talking points—the fighters weren't hooligans, most had college degrees and many had competed at the Olympic level, the barbaric appearance in clips was the result of bad regulatory standards and a misunderstanding of the complexities of the sport. None of it sounded convincing to Frank Jr.

Reputation was a sensitive subject for Frank Jr. Much of his career, and Station's success, had been staked on the good standing he'd cultivated in Las Vegas's insular gaming community. He'd moved to Las Vegas from Galveston, Texas, in 1960, newly married and in search of work at just twenty-two years old. His uncle had a job at the Stardust and helped him get hired as a bellhop. Eager to move up in the world, Frank Jr. began taking classes to learn how to become a blackjack dealer. Over the next decade, he worked his way through the ranks up and down the Strip—

including stints as a shift manager, baccarat manager, pit boss, and general manager at the Fremont Hotel and Casino, the glimmering centerpiece of downtown Las Vegas. In 1976, Frank Jr. was able to organize a group of investors to back construction of his own casino on a dusty five-thousand-square-foot plot of land on Sahara Avenue, a mile from the Strip. Simply called The Casino, the property was attached to a Mini-Price Motor Inn and offered four blackjack tables and one hundred slot machines in a space no bigger than a typical chain restaurant, like a Denny's or Bob's Big Boy. In 1978, he renamed the casino the Bingo Palace, and in 1983, he again rebranded it as Palace Station.

Also in 1983, one of Frank Jr.'s partners in Palace Station and a former coworker at the Fremont, Carl Thomas, was sentenced to fifteen years in prison for his role in an elaborate skimming operation at the Fremont, which involved stealing coins collected from slot machines before they were officially tallied in counting rooms off the casino floor. Prosecutors alleged the scheme was organized by members of the Civella family in Kansas City, who had helped fund loans for casino construction and renovation through the Teamsters Union pension funds, sometimes using vendors like Valley Bank, a Las Vegas lending institution that had helped fund the construction of Palace Station, as a go-between. After Thomas was charged, Frank Jr. bought out his share of Palace Station to preserve the good standing of the casino. FBI wiretaps of Thomas from 1979 had captured Frank Jr. making a number of vague but suggestive statements about coins. "So if these coins cost us say $20,000," Frank Jr. said in one recording, "we got $150,000 on, you know we're going to have like $130,000 in excess cash." No criminal charges were brought against Frank Jr., but the Nevada Gaming Control Board opened a multiyear investigation into his past and present business practices, which had cast a pall over Palace Station. While he was being investigated, Frank Jr. developed an interest in charitable donations—in 1988, he donated $300,000 to the University of Nevada, Las Vegas, and contributed another $70,000 to Leslie Randolph, a single mother of three, to help cover the costs of a heart transplant. In 1989, he contributed $1 million toward the construction of a new tennis complex at UNLV. Later that year, the gaming control board would vote two-to-one to take no further disciplinary action against Frank Jr. Despite the vindication, Frank Jr. stepped down from his role at Station, while preparing for the company's vaunted 1993 public offering. Before the IPO launch, he transferred control of Station to his sons, with Frank III becoming president and CEO, while Lorenzo would be a board member and president of the investment-focused subsidiary Fertitta Enterprises.

Lorenzo had been twenty-four at the time, just weeks removed from finishing his MBA at New York University's Stern School of Business. As he'd traveled the country, making the case for Station's IPO to the largest institutional investors in the world, he'd been aware of the fact that he was often the youngest and least experienced person in the room. He'd pushed through by relying on everything he'd learned about the casino business from his father while he was growing up. Even after he left home at eighteen, for an undergrad program at the University of San Diego, Lorenzo would fly back to Las Vegas after his last class on Thursdays and spend his weekends working at Palace Station. He was too young to work in any of the gaming departments and instead learned everything about the food, beverage, and hotel side of the business, which treated human vice analytically, an experience carefully constructed from the ground up, like a Swiss clock, to produce a steady, stable profit. The work could sometimes seem more custodial than entrepreneurial, as if Lorenzo and Frank III were groundskeepers entrusted with the responsibility of keeping their father's estate in full flower. The UFC presented a chance to build something new for themselves. But without their father's blessing, Lorenzo and Frank III weren't sure what to do. Many of the Station executives and lawyers they'd enlisted to work on the deal "hated" the idea of running the UFC, White would later say. Had they tricked themselves after a few private jiu-jitsu lessons into seeing something that wasn't really there? Were they setting themselves up for failure?

If they were, it was too late to do anything about it. Lorenzo and Frank III decided to push ahead with the plan. In December, they flew to Tokyo with White for UFC 29, what would be the final event under SEG ownership. White had already planned to make the trip to help corner Ortiz, who had finally agreed to make his first defense of the light heavyweight championship, and Chuck Liddell, who was scheduled for the first fight of the night. They made the drive from central Tokyo to the Differ Ariake arena in Koto City, an archipelago of industrial buildings and port warehouses on Tokyo Bay. It was a damp and overcast Saturday, and the event had a glum aura that was amplified by the reserved Japanese audience. The event itself wouldn't air live in the United States and wouldn't be available on pay-per-view until a week later. Mike Goldberg and Jeff Blatnick recorded their commentary after the fact, in front of a green screen on a US soundstage while pretending they were in the arena live. Lorenzo and Frank III took advantage of the occasion to see how the show was organized, wandering backstage in between fights and talking to everyone they could.

The fights were again acutely violent, with three first-round knockouts and a main event that ended with Ortiz submitting Pancrase star Yuki Kondo with a choke in just under two minutes. Ortiz celebrated after in the cage by pulling on a hand-printed T-shirt he'd made for the occasion: "RESPECT I don't earn it I just fucken take it." After, Lorenzo and Frank III invited referee John McCarthy to dinner with White and continued asking about how the company had been run. Why had so many fighters left for other promotions? What were Meyrowitz's biggest mistakes? Who were the best fighters outside the UFC? What were the biggest political hurdles for the sport? McCarthy was used to answering questions about the UFC—he had been a frequent public advocate, testifying on its behalf in court, appearing on television talk shows, and making presentations to athletic commissioners, including Lorenzo in 1999—and he didn't think much about the friendly interrogation. The next day, the referee found himself on the same flight back to Las Vegas with Lorenzo and Frank III and saw them going through some paperwork together at the gate. It slowly dawned on him that they might have come to Meyrowitz's rescue.

A few weeks later, in early January, Lorenzo and Frank III made the news public for the first time. They would take over the UFC through a newly formed LLC called Zuffa, the Italian word for a fight. Lorenzo and Frank III invited the few remaining key staff members from SEG, including McCarthy and Jeff Blatnick, to Las Vegas to discuss the transition. Everyone was treated to a free room at Palace Station and a tour of what would be the UFC's new offices. Instead of SEG's suite on 57th Street and Madison Avenue in Manhattan, the new UFC would be run from a small office park on Sahara Avenue, in a modest three-story building on a long Las Vegas city block down from Palace Station where Lorenzo had leased space for some of the family's ancillary businesses, including a small investment firm called Fertitta Enterprises and Gordon Biersch, a beer brewery and restaurant chain they partially owned. In place of Rockefeller Center and the Russian Tea Room, the Zuffa offices were surrounded by a nail salon, mortgage brokers, personal injury lawyers, and an In-N-Out Burger.

At a group dinner later that night, Lorenzo tried to reassure everyone that there would be no major layoffs; in his view, the main problems with the UFC had come from strategy not staffing. With the Fertittas' business experience and access to capital, alongside Lorenzo's connections at the Nevada State Athletic Commission, they were sure a turnaround was imminent. To reinforce the point that the company was in good hands, the Fertittas had invited a number of family friends and business associates to the dinner to vouch for them. "Everything these guys touch turns to gold," McCarthy remembers one Fertitta friend telling him. "They don't fail at anything."

The UFC's problems had seemed simple to White and Lorenzo, a matter of plain arithmetic. Meyrowitz had wasted the company's reputation and resources on unnecessary legal fights, alienated executives at the cable companies he relied on, and watched his best fighters leave for other promotions. Lorenzo was convinced everything could be reversed with a few key adjustments. Get sanctioned in Nevada, return to cable pay-per-view in the US, invest more in marketing, and the UFC would quickly return to profitability. It was similar to Meyrowitz's plan, but after years of burning bridges, he'd ended up without the social capital to make it work. Lorenzo and Frank III were confident that with their reputation and resources, they could succeed where Meyrowitz had failed. Lorenzo estimated the new UFC would be able to generate 150,000 pay-per-view buys for each event, around half of what SEG's most successful cards had sold. Zuffa's share would add up to a little more than $2 million per event—at around 45 percent of the revenue from each $29.95 purchase. It would be more than enough to cover a rough production and marketing budget of around $1.3 million. Even more money would come from live ticket sales Lorenzo and Frank III expected would follow when they moved from two-thousand-person arenas in rural Louisiana to ten thousand-person arenas in Las Vegas, after Lorenzo's old colleagues on the NSAC voted to sanction the sport. Adding in VHS and DVD sales and rentals, plus merchandising rights, it was hard to see how it could fail.

Looking for comparable business models to emulate, Lorenzo had found a ready template in professional wrestling and downloaded as many publicly available files on the World Wrestling Federation's business that he could. While the UFC had been stumbling toward bankruptcy, the WWF had grown its annual revenues to more than $377 million in 2000, an all-time high and more than quadruple what it generated in 1995. Unlike the boxing industry—which was spread across a labyrinthine tangle of promoters, sanctioning bodies, state regulators, and broadcasting partners—the WWF had built a self-contained ecosystem that gave it broad control over its athletes and events. WWF's wrestler contracts were notoriously restrictive, making performers exclusive to the promotion despite treating them as "work for hire," or independent contractors without health benefits or any of the federal protections given to full-time employees. Performers were expected to pay their own wrestling license fee and training costs, provide their own costumes and props, and cover any travel and transportation expenses required to perform at an event.

The WWF also claimed exclusive ownership of all original intellectual property related to a character or costume that a performer used, even if it predated their signing with the WWF. The contracts further required the performer to agree to be available to help promote or produce licensed goods, with no guarantee of extra compensation, and stipulated the performer would be paid nothing if WWF used their likeness in magazines. More important, performers had no influence over their own characters or story lines and no recourse to protest in cases of disagreement with the WWF. With near total control over their wrestlers, the WWF was able to maintain an aggressive schedule with more than one hundred live events a year, relying on lesser-known wrestlers and newcomers for shows in smaller markets like Greenville, South Carolina, and Hershey, Pennsylvania. In larger markets, more recognizable stars would be used, building their story lines toward a climactic match that fans could only see on one of a dozen or so annual pay-per-view broadcasts like *WrestleMania* and *SummerSlam*. It was hard to see how the UFC might one day be able to operate at a similar scale as the WWF, especially after having scheduled just six live events in 2000. But it was a starting point, and Lorenzo asked Lawrence Epstein, a friend and lawyer who'd previously served as outside counsel on some projects for Station, to work on a new set of agreements for the UFC.

In Zuffa's first event—UFC 30 on February 23, 2001, at the Taj Mahal in Atlantic City—White introduced himself on-camera as the UFC's new president, though he looked more like a stand-in than a head executive. Wearing a shapeless navy blue suit, he spoke with sideline reporter James "The Worm" Werme on the broadcast, promising that the UFC was on the verge of a major transformation. "Tonight signifies a new beginning, with new leadership, with great vision," White said, in a thin and tenuous voice. Unused to making eye contact with the camera lens, his gaze kept drifting down to the floor as he spoke, like he was a student called into the principal's office after being caught skipping school. "Tonight we promise you to take what is already the Super Bowl of mixed martial arts to a higher level, and some day everyone will talk about the UFC as the premier sporting event in the world."

White had overseen a dramatic overhaul of the UFC's live event production during his first month as president. Like Lorenzo, he thought that SEG's events felt like "morgues," with little effort put into lighting or music, and no screens in the arena to help fans follow the action from afar. With tickets that ranged from $30 to $300, White wanted the audience to feel as if they were seeing something momentous, as lavish and loud as the Super Bowl halftime show. "It's expensive to go to a live event, so when someone comes to one of our live shows, I want them to walk out of that arena and go, 'Holy shit! That just happened,'" White would later say. UFC 30 was the first chance to put a rough version of White's theory into practice, and the end result felt as unfamiliar as he was. The broadcast opened with a chorus of angry male voices chanting "Crush!"—a remixed version of Megadeth's "Crush 'Em" that replaced SEG's generic synthesizer fanfare—as a series of slow-motion, sepia-tinted replays of violent knockouts and wrestling slams played in montage. The arena was styled like a nightclub, with an elaborate entry ramp built for fighters, wreathed with laser lights and fog machines. And before the main event, Zuffa had arranged for a smoky indoor fireworks display, which according to referee

John McCarthy, added $100,000 to the production budget, including a pre-show trial run for the local fire marshal, and left the arena covered in a wispy mist that hung over the octagon with nowhere to go.

The event would culminate with a showcase fight for Ortiz, who, along with Lidell, White had stopped representing as a manager. (Las Vegas lawyer Jim Gallo initially took over managerial duties for both fighters.) It was a sobering and violently abrupt counterpoint to the event's lavish theatrics, ending in just twenty seconds, after Ortiz knocked out his opponent, a formerly undefeated Texan named Evan Tanner, with a brutal wrestling slam that left Tanner's head trapped against the mat as Ortiz drove his weight down from above. As the crowd cheered, Ortiz ran around the cage shooting imaginary pistols at Tanner's body with his fingers, and then pantomimed digging a fresh grave, dragging a corpse into it, and covering it with invisible dirt. Tanner remained unconscious and on his back for more than three minutes after the fight was called, a stream of blood rolling out of his mouth and his eyes rolling back into his head as he came in and out of consciousness while the cage-side physician tried to revive him. The sight was so disturbing the production crew stopped showing Tanner and focused solely on Ortiz, who capped his celebration by putting on a custom T-shirt that proclaimed: "If You Can Read This I Just Stomped Your Ass!"

Fans in the arena were exultant, and Lorenzo wanted White to ensure every new show would be either "a step up or parallel step" from the last, in terms of spectacle, scale, and hopefully sales. The next major escalation would come just four months later, with a June event planned for the twenty-thousand-seat Continental Airlines Arena in East Rutherford, home to the New Jersey Nets and the New Jersey Devils. It would be the UFC's largest event to date, an occasion to mark the New Jersey State Athletic Commission removing the UFC's provisional status and fully recognizing mixed martial arts as a legitimate sport. To help pull off the newly expansive live events, Zuffa hired several veterans from the boxing industry, including Bernie Dillon, who had previously worked at Ceasars Palace in Atlantic City and helped organize major boxing cards with Sugar Ray Leonard, Mike Tyson, and Oscar De La Hoya. In March, White had also recruited Burt Watson, who had once been Joe Frazier's manager and gone on to a prolific career as an event coordinator, handling everything from hotel scouting and picking up fighters from the airport, to keeping weigh-in scales calibrated and shuttling fighters from their dressing rooms into the arena to make sure broadcasts stayed on time. Watson was working one of the biggest boxing events of the year, a match between Oscar De La Hoya and Arturo Gatti at the MGM Grand in Las Vegas, when White introduced himself backstage and asked if he'd be interested in working on a few UFC events each year. Watson didn't know anything about mixed martial arts at the time but he was impressed by White, who struck him as a "peacock." He was even more impressed by Lorenzo and Frank III, whose reputations he knew from his years working in Las Vegas. He assumed any offer that was connected to the Fertittas must be legitimate. "I knew they were playing with real strong house money," says Watson.

Despite their reputation, he was surprised by how unruly UFC events were compared to boxing. At his first event, the UFC's final provisional show in New Jersey, on May 4, 2001, Watson saw several fighters go straight to the hotel bar, as he manned the fighter check-in desk in the lobby of the Taj Mahal a few days before the event. "In boxing they just never did that," he says. "I very seldom saw a boxer at a bar fight week. I'm kind of like, Okay, is this gonna work?" Watson's misgivings grew when he saw a bill the hotel had sent to the UFC's makeshift production office in a small conference room on the mezzanine floor, for damages to one of the lobby bar's bathrooms. A group of fighters had stayed out late in the lobby bar and ended up in an argument with another guest, who thought cage fighting was as fake as pro wrestling. To defend the honor of their sport, the fighters chased the man into the bathroom, where he locked himself in a stall. "He wouldn't open the door, so they went and tore the door off. They tore the stall off the wall to get to him," Watson says. "I think the bill was like six grand or some crazy number. I was totally shocked."

In June, Zuffa held a press conference in Manhattan to promote its upcoming event in Newark and to celebrate the milestone of being sanctioned by the NJSAC. Though ESPN wouldn't cover the event itself, Zuffa rented out the ESPN Zone restaurant and used the ESPN logo as a prominent part of the backdrop as they spoke about its future plans, which included introducing Carmen Electra as the company's new spokesperson. "I'm sure everyone here is wondering: What the hell does Carmen Electra have to do with the UFC?" the singer and former model said from the podium. "Well, basically, absolutely nothing."

Electra would be the centerpiece of an extravagant marketing campaign to promote the UFC's new ownership, with full-page print ads in *Sports Illustrated*, *GQ*, *FHM*, *Rolling Stone*, and *Maxim*, nationally syndicated radio spots on *Opie and Anthony* and *The Howard Stern Show*, and a billboard at the exit to the Holland Tunnel. White would later claim the UFC spent $2.4 million to market UFC 32. Lorenzo told the small gathering of journalists and reporters that Electra's lack of a specific connection to mixed martial arts was less important than her mass media appeal. (Both *Entertainment Tonight* and *Extra* had sent reporters to cover the press conference, hoping to get interviews with Electra.) "We decided that we wanted to rebrand the UFC, we wanted to roll it out in a whole new package," Lorenzo said. "And in order to do that, we picked one of the most exciting, beautiful, lovely, nice ladies to be the cornerstone of that campaign, and that's Carmen Electra."

While the public reaction to the strategy was still uncertain, it had been enough for executives at In Demand. Dan York, In Demand's vice president of programming, followed Electra at the podium in New York, and announced that the pay-per-view provider had reached an agreement with Zuffa to bring the UFC back to US cable subscribers for the first time since 1997. The terms of the deal were less favorable than SEG's had been, with Zuffa reportedly having to sell at least seventy-five thousand buys just to break even. But the deal would expand the UFC's market reach into more than thirty million pay-per-view-equipped homes, pushing the total number of homes in the US where the UFC pay-per-views would be available for purchase to forty-eight million. Lorenzo was determined to try and reach as many of those households to pitch his and White's new vision for the UFC. In Demand's York praised Zuffa's commitment to improving the sport's public reputation and said that with new ownership, In Demand was ready to "provide a true national platform for this franchise to really take off."

When UFC 32 went live two days later, it was clear that Zuffa expected a nationwide audience to be watching. White had wanted everyone involved with the production to ensure "the UFC looked like a big fucking deal" as soon as the broadcast started. The production crew had hired a helicopter to circle the arena for live overhead shots, and the indoor crew had set up a crane-mounted camera for sweeping shots of the audience around the cage. The show opened with the most elaborate indoor fireworks display yet, and the VIP section around the octagon was filled with an exclusive list of celebrities, including Fred Durst, Dennis Rodman, Kendall Gill of the Charlotte Hornets, and Donald Trump and Melania Knauss, who beamed for the cameras in between fights. The commentators boasted that they had the biggest live audience in UFC history, with more than 12,500 people in attendance, surpassing the previous high of 10,000 at UFC 9 in Detroit in 1996, though most had been given free tickets through promotions and seat-filler companies.

Despite the production's sweep and grandeur, it was filled with moments of bumbling awkwardness. A fog machine was placed next to the fighter entry ramp, but it fired out of sync throughout the event. In the first fight on the broadcast, Vladimir Matyushenko stood at the top of the ramp for several moments after Bruce Buffer announced him to the audience, waiting for the fog machine to fire. He appeared trapped in space for a few moments before turning back to his cornerman to ask if he should start walking. As they prodded him forward, the fog machine finally turned on, giving the strange impression that he was running away from the fog instead of emerging from it. Other fighters covered their mouths with towels as they walked out, fearful that breathing in the fog fumes would hurt their endurance.

The fights themselves were starkly violent, with four of the six matchups on the main card ending by knockout or TKO—a technical knockout, typically ruled when a fighter is no longer able to intelligently defend themselves but aren't completely unconscious. The lone submission, a first-round armbar, in a heavyweight fight between Josh Barnett and six-foot-nine Dutch kickboxer Semmy Schilt, was punctuated by Barnett triumphantly rising from Schilt's defeated body, wiping away a thick layer of blood from his own face, and sticking his bloodied fingers into his mouth as the crowd cheered. For the main event, White had again booked Ortiz, his former client, in a title defense against Elvis Sinosic, an Australian jiu-jitsu specialist with a mixed record of four wins, three losses, and one draw, and only one previous fight in the UFC. Before Ortiz entered the arena, the houselights were turned off, leaving the audience in darkness.

On the overhead screens, animated orange flames offered the first new light, matching the iconic graphics Ortiz wore on his fight shorts. White strobe lights lit up the walkout ramp like muzzle flashes when Ortiz appeared, wearing a black Gordon Biersch Brewing Company shirt and beanie, plumes of artificial fog around his legs as he rhythmically jumped from one foot to the other, part war dance and part warm-up exercise. Orange bursts of fireworks exploded above the audience, like mortar fire launched from a dozen points around the arena, then Ortiz's choice for a walkout song, Limp Bizkit's "Break Stuff," began to play as Ortiz marched to the octagon. *Give me something to break! Just give me something to break! How about your fuckin' face!*

It seemed strange, when the fight began, that it had been preceded by so much pomp. What had seemed like a climactic confrontation between two of the most dangerous humans in the world became a straightforward mismatch under the shadowless arena lights. Ortiz was visibly larger and stronger than Sinosic, and his early punches sent the Australian backpedaling toward the fence, sometimes losing his footing in his haste. After nearly a minute, Ortiz sprinted toward Sinosic, slammed him to the mat and held him down as perfunctorily as an older brother might have done. After ensuring Sinosic was securely trapped under his weight, Ortiz began battering him with punches and elbows, until the referee stopped the fight after just three minutes and thirty-two seconds, declaring Ortiz the winner by TKO. Ortiz sprinted across the cage and celebrated with his customary gravedigger pantomime, then donned another T-shirt he'd had made for the event, printed upon which was "That's American for 'Whoop Ass' Mate."

As the final result was announced, NJSAC commissioner Larry Hazzard wrapped the UFC's championship belt around Ortiz's waist as White celebrated with Liddell, Frank III, and Lorenzo along the edge of the cage.

Three weeks later, Ortiz appeared in Las Vegas, alongside White, Lorenzo, Frank III, Liddell, John Lewis, and several other Zuffa representatives to formally request that mixed martial arts be sanctioned by the Nevada State Athletic Commission, a prerequisite for holding a UFC event in Las Vegas. Despite the commission's former antagonism toward the sport, Lorenzo's involvement had been enough to persuade even the skeptics to give cage fighting the benefit of the doubt. "I'm never going to like this sport, and it's not what I consider a good athletic event. But I am friends with Lorenzo Fertitta. He believes in it, and I will vote for it," John McCarthy recalled Commissioner Glenn Carano telling him before the hearing. Under SEG, the UFC had been a self-regulating organism, hiring its own referees and judges, several of whom were journalists, like longtime wrestling reporters Dave Meltzer and Eddie Goldman. Moving forward, hiring and training judges and referees would be the responsibility of the athletic commission in any US state where the UFC would put on an event.

The fights themselves would be governed by the Mixed Martial Arts Unified Rules of Conduct, the product of an April meeting White and Lorenzo had organized with NJSAC officials and representatives from several other key mixed martial arts promotions, including Pride, IFC, and King of the Cage, all of which had their own rules. The Unified Rules standardized nine weight classes, ranging from flyweight (125.9 pounds) to super heavyweight (anything over 265 pounds), and mandated a fighting area as no smaller than eighteen feet by eighteen feet and no larger than thirty-two feet by thirty-two feet. Any type of ring or cage enclosure would be permissible so long as it would prevent fighters from falling out. Fights would take place over three five-minute rounds with a one-minute rest period between each, and championship fights would be five rounds. Fights would be scored by the Ten-Point Must System, borrowed from boxing, with the round-winning fighter earning ten points and the round-losing fighter earning nine or fewer. A consulting physician from the NJSAC made a brief attempt to ban wrestling slams for fear of serious neck and back injuries, but Zuffa persuaded Hazzard to allow them after showing a video of highlights from the 1996 Summer Olympics in Atlanta, which featured several similarly violent slams. A compromise was agreed to, whereby slams would be allowed, but "spiking" or intentionally slamming a person headfirst onto the mat, would be illegal. Also banned were soccer kicks, head butts, knees to the head of a grounded opponent, the "downward pointing of elbow strikes," which the consulting physician feared could cause blindness or other serious injury if the tip of the elbow struck the eyeball. The UFC's approach to apparel also became the new standard, with fighters being allowed to wear only shorts, groin protection, a mouthguard, and some type of glove.

The Nevada Commission took the Unified Rules as a basic framework but added a few extra wrinkles. Promoters would be required to have at least two video screens at any event to ensure the audience could follow the action clearly, and no event would be allowed with fewer than twenty-five total rounds scheduled, the rough equivalent of eight fights. Fighters would also be required to submit up-to-date MRI and MRA test results as well as the results of a full blood panel test completed within the last twelve months, to ensure they didn't have any serious medical conditions that would make it unsafer than normal for them to compete. Fighters would also be required to undergo a general physical exam no more than seven days before their scheduled event.

With those final few alterations agreed to, the commission unanimously voted to sanction mixed martial arts, a little over two years after Meyrowitz had first tried to sway them with a broadly similar set of rules and regulations. The following week, Zuffa officially announced the UFC's first ever event in Las Vegas, planned for September 28 at the Mandalay Bay, headlined by a fight between Ortiz and Vitor Belfort, a former UFC tournament winner who had become a star with Pride in Japan. After a year of escalations, White and Lorenzo believed the event would be a culmination. Every major obstacle had been cleared away—the government regulations, the broadcaster bans, the lack of marketing, the modest production budgets. In Las Vegas, the public would see, for the first time, what they saw in cage fighting. Lorenzo promised "one of the best cards in the history of the Ultimate Fighting Championships," and the response from the UFC's fan base had been encouraging. Tickets sold out in just two weeks, a rarity in Las Vegas, Lorenzo explained, because of the number of other entertainment options, including Cirque du Soleil, Blue Man Group, Siegfried & Roy, and Penn & Teller.

The sporting press was less excited by Zuffa's advancements, and most outlets ignored the milestone. The *Los Angeles Times* was one of the few major news outlets to cover the event, sending T. J. Simers to a press junket at the House of Blues in Hollywood to interview Electra, Ortiz, and several other fighters booked on the card. The story ran in print with the headline "Keeping a Straight Face Was Real Fight." Simers misidentified White as "Dan" instead of Dana, and described Ortiz not as a world champion but a "big lug with a gold ring around his waist." He dedicated most of the article to learn about Electra's short-lived marriage to NBA star Dennis Rodman, and concluded that "without Carmen, this is a press conference that would lack only one thing: the press."

Shortly after, the card's main event appeared to be in jeopardy when Belfort withdrew due to a freak injury—he had inadvertently punched a window next to the sparring area in his gym, which cut through his right bicep and would leave him unable to compete for months. White began a frantic search for a replacement. He tried to lure Frank Shamrock out of retirement for a rematch against Ortiz—whom he had previously beaten in 1999, in what SEG had awarded its "Match of the Year"—but negotiations fell apart over the weight limit. White also tried to book Ken Shamrock, who hadn't fought in the UFC since 1996. White offered Ken a reported $180,000, more than any fighter had previously been paid. Ken countered with a request for $500,000, a sum that was so unthinkably large that White decided to simply move on. He settled on Matyushenko, a cult favorite among fans but little known outside of mixed martial arts blogs, in what would be his second fight in the promotion, just three months after his debut.

With one unexpected crisis averted, an even bigger one emerged when members of Al Qaeda attacked the World Trade Center in New York and the Pentagon building in Arlington County, Virginia, on September 11. As images and video emerged of the horrific events, the idea of promoting consumer entertainment of any kind seemed ghastly. Lorenzo and White debated canceling the show altogether, but after so much persistence and planning, that felt equally unthinkable. With only a matter of days to make up their minds, they decided to move forward, but to reframe the event as a display of patriotic determination, proof that Americans would carry on with business as usual despite the attacks and the lingering threat of international terrorism. The broadcast opened with a live performance of "The Star Spangled Banner" by A Moment in Time, a women's a cappella group from Las Vegas. Uniformed members of the Las Vegas Fire Department's Color Guard lined the fighter entrance ramp holding American flags as they sang, and during the final verse, a barrage of fireworks were set off over the octagon, leaving a layer of smoke hanging in the air that remained throughout the entire broadcast.

White and Lorenzo had hoped the fights would live up to the pomp and pyrotechnics, but each of the five fights on the main card was halting and hesitant affairs that ended in uneventful decisions. Two of the five would later be identified as the least active fights in UFC history, according to Fight Metric, a mixed martial arts statistics tracking group, with as much as thirty-five seconds passing between punch attempts or other significant actions. Worse still, without any knockouts or submissions, each fight took more than its allotted share of the three-hour broadcast window the UFC had booked with In Demand. By the time Ortiz and Matyushenko entered the cage, the UFC had used up almost all of its time, and just after the fourth round began, the broadcast abruptly cut off. Fans who had ordered the pay-per-view would have no idea who had won the fight, and those without internet access or subscriptions to one of the small number of monthly magazines that covered the UFC, like *Black Belt* or *Full Contact Fighter*, would have to wait for weeks until the event was released on VHS to see what had happened. (Ortiz won by unanimous decision.) Early returns on pay-per-view sales suggested there hadn't actually been many fans watching in the first place, with roughly seventy-five thousand buys, half what Lorenzo had hoped for as a new baseline. White would later describe the event as the "worst show we've ever had." Bruce Buffer, the UFC's longtime announcer, had persuaded one of his business contacts, Jeremy Zimmer, cofounder of United Talent Agency, to attend the event in hopes that he might see some potential in the sport and its roster of fighters, and possibly help open doors with other media companies. But when Buffer caught up with him backstage, Zimmer was unimpressed. "I just don't see it," Buffer remembers him saying.

UFC attorney Lawrence Epstein would later hear a similar sentiment, when he tried to pitch the UFC to one of his own personal connections, Mark Lazarus, a friend from college who had gone on to become the president of Turner Sports. During Lazarus's tenure, Turner had expanded its sports coverage to include NCAA football, NASCAR, WCW, and the Goodwill Games, which featured competitive judo, taekwondo, and wrestling. Epstein had hoped that the UFC could fit with the network's new emphasis on less conventional sporting events, but Lazarus was certain he'd be overruled by Ted Turner, who had become an ardent critic of boxing. "Ted's never gonna go for this thing," Epstein recalled Lazarus saying.

After close to a year of searching for a new audience, it was starting to seem less clear who would go for the UFC. It wasn't just the UFC's audience that seemed to have moved on. The market for original pay-per-view programming that SEG had initially wanted to take advantage of had also largely disappeared. In place of cage fighting and Howard Stern specials, Hollywood studios had overtaken the pay-per-view market with second-run blockbusters like *Shallow Hal, Jurassic Park III, Training Day, Ocean's Eleven,* and *Harry Potter and the Sorcerer's Stone.* With a burgeoning DVD market and dozens of new channels to choose from as part of a basic cable subscription, sports and wrestling pay-per-views found it harder to capture people's attention and declined more than 25 percent between 1999 and 2002, dropping from $486 million to $363 million. Even boxing struggled to sustain its market reach, with the best-selling boxing pay-per-view of 2000, a middleweight championship bout between Felix Trinidad and Bernard Hopkins, selling just 450,000 pay-per-view buys, less than a quarter of the top-selling event from 1997, a controversial rematch between Mike Tyson and Evander Holyfield that had generated nearly two million buys.

There seemed to be a broad communal fatigue with the extreme attitude and aura of transgression the UFC embodied, a once popular trend that appeared suddenly dated and exploitive in the early 2000s. In early 2001, the high-profile collapse of the Xtreme Football League (XFL) signaled that audiences had moved on from taboo and defiance in mass entertainment. A $100 million co-venture between NBC and WWF to create a more violent and less regulated alternative to the NFL, with shorter time limits in between plays, and fewer restrictions on when and how players could tackle one another, the XFL had seen its ratings drop by nearly 80 percent in its first month. Both audiences and critics seemed to have caught on to the fact that extreme aesthetics were often a way for investors to cut costs by hiring less experienced athletes while keeping a greater share of the profits for themselves. *Los Angeles Times* TV critic Howard Rosenberg described the XFL as "just another football league, with fringe and over-the-hill players who are surely serious about what they're doing, but putting on a tedious, inept show while doing it." After a disappointing ten-week season and two-round playoff, NBC canceled the XFL and took a reported $70 million loss.

The UFC was starting to look like the same kind of failed enterprise, played out on a smaller scale. With White and the Fertittas in charge, the UFC had managed to sell just 145,000 pay-per-views total for its five events in 2001, far less than the 150,000 per show that Lorenzo had targeted. While he and White had proved that cage fighting could be a legitimate sport, few people seemed to care. It began to seem like exactly the wrong kind of investment at the wrong time. After nearly a decade, the sight of a strange group of eccentrics fighting one another in a cage seemed desperate and depressing. What kind of person would willingly subject themselves to something so arduous, unpleasant, and seemingly irrelevant?

NO ONE CAN DO WHAT YOU DID

Randy Couture had never been anywhere like the Avalon Hotel in Beverly Hills, when he stepped through the front entrance one bright June morning in 2001. From the outside it could have passed for an apartment complex, elegantly secluded behind a bank of palm trees and tall bamboo stalks, but inside it was like an avant-garde amphitheater. The balconies attached to each room encircled a courtyard pool, where a mix of celebrities, executives, and tourists mingled while the hotel staff stood by like stagehands waiting for their cues. It was a world away from the one Couture had entered when he won the heavyweight tournament at UFC 13 in Augusta, Georgia, in 1997. Fighter check-in had taken place at a folding table in the lobby of a Holiday Inn, after a two-and-a-half-hour drive from the Atlanta airport. Weigh-ins were done with a cheap household scale, and there were no athletic commission officials or doctors present to perform pre-fight medicals. Everything had seemed improvised and uncertain, even the promotion's slogan at the time—"reality combat fighting"—seemed like a non sequitur, three words that lost their meaning when put together. The Avalon staff directed Couture to a private conference room in the back of the hotel, where a photo shoot was being organized with Carmen Electra and some of the UFC's top fighters.

At thirty-eight, Couture was the oldest in the group. Everything about him seemed worn and weathered. His sinewy build and prematurely receding hairline gave him the look of a pair of old running shoes, both beyond repair and indestructible. A small white replica UFC octagon had been constructed on set, and the fighters, stripped to their fight shorts, fanned out around Electra, who wore four-inch heels, a gold bikini bottom, and a white halter top with "UFC" written in sparkling text across the chest. Couture smiled through each new setup, but he was still unsure of where he stood with the UFC's new owners. Beneath the lavish productions and extravagant marketing, he felt as if he had started off at immediate odds with White.

They had first met in November 2000, when White cold-called Couture to offer his services as a manager. "I think we could do something with you," Couture recalls him saying. White pitched himself as a former boxer who understood the realities of the fight world, and Couture agreed to meet with him in person a month later in Japan, where Couture would be traveling to corner a teammate at UFC 29. The meeting had been friendly, but Couture decided to instead sign with Jeremy Lappen and Peter Levin, respectively a former movie producer and entertainment industry lawyer, who he hoped would be able to get him acting jobs in between fights—something he'd become interested in after Doug Crosby, a UFC judge who moonlighted as a stunt coordinator, helped him get a small part on the HBO series *Oz*. When the Zuffa acquisition was announced after he returned from Japan, Couture was surprised to learn the promotion would now be run by the same person who had offered to represent him just a few weeks earlier.

White was eager to sign Couture to a new UFC contract in the spring, but he was unhappy about having to deal with Lappen and Levin. He continued to call Couture directly and referred to Lappen and Levin as "hair fags" who didn't know anything about the fight world, and tried to persuade Couture that it would be easier if they could figure things out themselves, without outside interference. Lappen and Levin were shocked by White's behavior. They told Couture that White had been aggressive and unprofessional and would often resort to "screaming and yelling and cussing."

Lappen and Levin found the deal White was offering just as shocking as his behavior. "They were like you can't sign this contract, this is a horrible contract," Couture would later say. The UFC wanted the right to release Couture following a single loss, regardless of ranking or the number of fights still remaining on his contract. It also demanded Couture's image rights for merchandising and licensing with no additional compensation or end date. Lappen and Levin countered with a provision that Couture could only be cut after two consecutive losses, and they asked that he be granted favored nations status as long as he held the heavyweight championship, guaranteeing that he would always be the highest paid fighter in the UFC. The demands exasperated White, but when Couture had refused his entreaties, White abandoned the negotiations entirely and let match-maker Joe Silva finalize the deal and accede to Couture's demands.

The drama had confused Couture in part because he'd never really considered cage fighting as a career path. He'd stumbled into the sport on a whim when he was working as an assistant wrestling coach at Oregon State University in Corvallis. A student had showed him a tape of UFC 8, and Couture recognized his former college teammate, Don Frye, who went on to win the eight-man tournament. Couture thought it was a "wacky" event, but he was intrigued by how unfamiliar it seemed. The $50,000 prize Frye won was also close to double what the average assistant wrestling coach would make in a year. A few months later, a friend helped Couture make an audition tape composed of clips of his wrestling matches, and he mailed it to the UFC. Initially, they turned him down, but a few months later they asked if he would be willing to fill in for an injured fighter at UFC 13. Couture agreed, and after a five-day crash course in jiu-jitsu, he won the event's heavyweight tournament. The prize payment had been cut down to just $20,000 a year after Frye's win, but even that was close to what Couture would earn for a full year of coaching. By the end of the year Couture had fought at two more UFC events and become the promotion's heavyweight champion, for which he was given a $4,500 monthly retainer and a minimum guarantee of $60,000 per fight.

At the time, Couture had been more focused on making it to the Olympics, and he saw his newfound success in cage fighting as a way to help pay for his wrestling training. Couture had been to the Olympics twice before—as an alternate on the US men's wrestling team in 1992 in Barcelona, and as a fan in 1996 in Atlanta. He was already thirty-six and knew that the 2000 Summer Games in Sydney would likely be his last chance to win a gold medal, something that had been a lifelong obsession. Couture had discovered wrestling as a junior high school student in Lynnwood, a quiet suburb north of Seattle, after a friend talked him into tagging along for a local wrestling tournament and the school's coach invited Couture to join the school team. Couture loved the grueling training sessions and the way the coaches exhausted the team with intense warm-up exercises—rope climbs, push-ups, sprints, a pegboard challenge where they would pull themselves up a large plywood board using two wooden dowels—before turning the boys on one another. There was something equalizing about it, everyone in the room brought to the same lowly state where adolescent egos evaporated in a sweaty haze of deadened limbs and physical depletion.

It was revelatory, in part because Couture had always struggled with feelings of inadequacy. His father had left the family when he was just three—his first memory was of clinging to his father's leg in tears as his father carried his bags to the front door. He'd been raised by a single mother who supported Couture and his two older sisters by working as a bartender and bookkeeper. As a child, Couture had been afflicted with a range of health conditions that made him feel like a "freak." An abnormally enlarged bladder made him a chronic bedwetter until eighth grade, and when he occasionally wanted to spend the night at a friend's, his mother would have to call ahead and warn his friend's parents that there might be an accident. Couture also suffered from severe asthma and had to sleep in a plastic oxygen tent for much of his childhood. On family vacations, Couture would use a bulky vaporizer that his mother packed in with the luggage. When he was wrestling, however, Couture felt a new sense of self. There was little time or space for shame on the wrestling mat, only the urgency of the moment, a struggle for balance and position that overtook every other stray thought or loose anxiety.

The sport also left him with a hope that if he worked hard enough, he might be able to lure his father back, if not to the family than at least to the wrestling meets. "I heard stories my whole life about my father and what a good wrestler he was and what a tough guy he was and so I kind of thought that if I started wrestling I'd get his attention and he'd come around a little more," Couture would later say. Instead, while his father remained aloof, his mother drove him to every practice, and when he came home he'd continue drilling with his sisters. He made long, branching lists of techniques to use in different positions, and at night, he'd fall asleep imagining lateral drops, arm drags, and headlocks, limbs moving against one another in slow motion like planets.

After graduating high school, he earned a spot on the wrestling team at Washington State University in Pullman as a walk-on freshman, and for a few happy months he seemed on his way to a promising career as a collegiate wrestler. Those plans were derailed after his first semester, when he learned his ex-girlfriend from high school, Sharon King, had become pregnant after they'd slept together during a trip home for Thanksgiving break. Couture asked if she would consider an abortion, but Sharon, who had been raised in a conservative Lutheran family, said no. Six weeks later, they were married and Couture dropped out of college, determined to find a way to provide for his newfound family. He found one in the army, which had just launched a recruiting program promising $5,000 bonus payments to people who enrolled in an aviation program, part of the Reagan administration's long-term plan to replace the eleven thousand striking air traffic controllers that had been fired in the summer of 1981.

Shortly after Sharon gave birth to their son Ryan, Couture shipped off to boot camp, and then was stationed at a base in Hanau, West Germany, where he worked in the base's air traffic control tower, and learned how to set up impromptu landing zones in fields and farmyards. He was surprised to learn the base also had a club wrestling team that periodically competed against teams from other bases, and Couture began training with them after his shifts, while Sharon cared for Ryan in the small apartment they were renting behind an old gas station in town. After a little over a year on base, Sharon gave birth to their second child, a daughter they named Aimee Jean, and a year after that Couture was invited to join the All-Army team, which competed at the Olympics every four years as well as major international tournaments throughout the year. Couture moved to Fort Dix in New Jersey for an intensive six-month wrestling program, and was then reassigned to an administrative post managing the sports department at Fort Campbell in Kentucky, which would allow him to spend even more time training for upcoming tournaments and, eventually, Olympic qualifiers. Sharon found a job working as a paralegal and took care of the children while Couture was mostly on base, training in the mornings, then working a full shift, training after his shift, and then going on nightly runs after his second training session to keep his weight down. Couture eventually became the third-ranked wrestler in the US military for his weight class, and in 1988 he was chosen as second alternate for the US Olympic team. Though he wouldn't travel with the team to Seoul, the achievement made him a top prospect with college recruiters, and after his service contract with the army expired, he accepted a wrestling scholarship at Oklahoma State University.

At twenty-five years old and married with two children, Couture was out of step with most students on campus and older than all but a handful of other members of the team. On the mats, he continued to excel. He qualified as an All-American in three of his four years, won first place two times at the Pan American Games, and competed in the NCAA championships in 1991 and 1992, losing both times to another future UFC champion, Mark Kerr. In 1992, Couture was chosen as first alternate for the US Olympic team and traveled to Barcelona to see the Summer Games firsthand. Though he didn't get to compete, he was enthralled by the crowds and the spectacle—the way Iranian fans flooded the arena with horns and rattles, and the boisterous, boozy cheers of Finns who spurred their teams on—and the experience left him even more motivated to cross the threshold from alternate to competitor. "I knew next time it was going to be my turn no matter what," Couture wrote in his memoir. After graduation, he accepted a job offer as an assistant wrestling coach at Oregon State University, which would allow him to continue to train and compete for the next Olympic Games. The salary was less than half what he would have earned from the army, but as he neared thirty, the desire to fulfill his own ambitions had become too powerful to resist.

At the same time, Couture realized he wasn't happy in his marriage. Though he and Sharon rarely fought, he'd felt unsure about their marriage from the start. The relationship felt lifeless to Couture, and he'd allowed himself to cheat repeatedly. He'd had his first brief affair with another woman who worked on the base in Hanau. As he'd traveled around Europe for tournaments with the All-Army team, he would cap off celebratory nights of drinking with his teammates in Sweden or Bulgaria with a string of one-night stands, a habit he continued while traveling to collegiate competitions when he was at Oklahoma State. In his first year at Oregon State, Couture fell into another affair, with a woman named Trish, an assistant coach for the women's volleyball team. Though she was eight years younger than Couture, he felt an unexpected connection with Trish, who, after four years as a college athlete, found it easy to appreciate the importance Couture placed on wrestling. As they spent more time together, around the gym and in weekly coaches' meetings, Couture found the excitement and vitality that had often seemed to be missing from his marriage. Couture thought he could keep his affair with Trish secret by limiting his encounters with her to after-hours meetings at the gym, where they both had offices. Near the end of the first school year, Sharon stopped by Couture's office unannounced and found him and Trish together, half-undressed on top of his desk. After a brief attempt to save their marriage with counseling, Sharon filed for divorce and moved back to Seattle with Ryan and Aimee, while Couture moved into a small apartment off-campus. "I felt a tremendous sense of failure," Couture wrote. "I thought everyone looked at me differently."

Despite his shame, Couture decided there was little reason to stop seeing Trish, and in 1994, at the end of his second year in Corvallis, they moved in together, and two years later they married. In the 1996 Olympic trials, Couture advanced far enough to be a second alternate, a step back from his 1992 performance. Though Couture wouldn't be allowed to travel with the team as a second alternate, he and Trish decided to attend the 1996 Summer Games in Atlanta as fans for their honeymoon trip. Trish was studying to be a nurse practitioner and had just one year left on her program. She was eager to start a family and move beyond the world of gyms and athletics, which had started to seem like a holdover from her college years. Though Couture had just turned thirty-three, the idea of giving up on his Olympic dreams to have children felt like moving back into an older life that he'd already had. They agreed to a compromise: Trish would support Couture through one last run for the 2000 Summer Olympics in Sydney, Australia. And after, no matter what happened, he would retire from competition and they would focus on building a family. Less than a year later Couture won his first UFC tournament, and after realizing that he had made more in his first two fights than he had in a whole year of coaching, he decided to leave his job at the University of Oregon and use the financial windfalls from cage fighting to fund his Olympic training.

Couture felt ambivalent about his early experiences in mixed martial arts. He distrusted Meyrowitz, whom he found stiff and pompous, and he disliked John Perretti, SEG's matchmaker, who was in charge of recruiting new fighters and contract negotiations, especially after he tried to persuade him into taking $25,000 for his first title defense instead of the $80,000 he'd been contracted to earn. Couture had declined and vacated the UFC's title, deciding to focus on training for the Sydney Olympic trials. Despite his dedication, Couture again made it only as far as second alternate, losing the match that would have earned him a place on the team to Garrett Lowney, a twenty-one-year-old from the University of Minnesota. When Lowney went on to win a bronze medal in Sydney a few weeks later, Couture realized the window on his own competitive wrestling career had likely closed for good. "I was now thirty-six years old, watching a young kid come up on the international circuit at the open level—and it hit home," he wrote. "I think it's time to focus on something else."

Before he had time to think seriously about what that something else would be, Couture began training for another mixed martial arts competition that he'd agreed to compete in, for a new Japanese promotion called Rings. The tournament would take place in Tokyo over the course of two events five months apart, with the winner earning $200,000. Couture won his first two fights in October and advanced to the semifinals scheduled for early 2001. When he returned to Oregon, Perretti called him and asked if he would be willing to return to the UFC to fight for the heavyweight title, promising that big changes would soon be taking place in the promotion. Couture was skeptical but told Perretti he'd be willing to fight for $85,000. Perretti eventually agreed, and a little over a month later, Couture beat Kevin Randleman at UFC 28 in Atlantic City to reclaim the UFC's heavyweight championship, in what would be SEG's second-to-last event. While the win lifted Couture's spirits, it left Trish uneasy. She had just entered the final year of her master's program and had been eager to start building a new family with Couture. Instead, Couture was often away from home, training or traveling for an event, and he and Trish began arguing more frequently. Couture responded by withdrawing into training even further. He asked Trish to stop coming by his local gym and found excuses to travel out of town for competitions and training sessions more often.

In his first fight under the new Zuffa banner, Couture was suspicious that White and the Fertittas wanted him to lose. His opponent, Pedro Rizzo, a sweet-natured and boyish twenty-eight-year-old from Brazil who had won five of his first six fights with the promotion by knockout or TKO, was much younger and seemed much easier to market. The two were booked as the main event of UFC 31 at the Trump Taj Mahal in Atlantic City on May 4, 2001, just three months after the Zuffa acquisition was announced. With the contentious contract negotiations still unresolved, Couture suspected that White and the Fertittas had wanted to use him as a stepping stone to build Rizzo's reputation and turn him into the promotion's next star.

In the early moments of the fight, it seemed as if Couture's intuition was right, as Rizzo whipped leg kicks into Couture's quadriceps, leaving the older fighter visibly hobbling around the cage. (The kicks were so forceful they would leave a permanent "dent" in Couture's upper thigh, where a small section of muscle tissue had been killed.) Despite Rizzo's early success, Couture persisted, even with one badly damaged leg, and by the third round Rizzo was visibly fatigued, and had slowed enough for Couture to catch him in an upper body clinch, blanketing the Brazilian along the cage and dragging him to the mat with trips and slow but steady pressure. By the end of the five rounds, Couture had turned what seemed like a certain loss into a unanimous decision win, in a bout that the UFC would later recognize as its Fight of the Year for 2001.

After the fight, Couture thought he had performed well enough to earn a place among the other stars in the UFC, obscure as they may have been at the time. He was shocked, then, to discover he had been airbrushed out of the UFC's new print advertising campaign based on the photo shoot in Beverly Hills earlier that year. "Back with a vengeance!" the ad copy read as Liddell, Pulver, Electra, Rizzo, Newton, and Ortiz fanned out across the white octagon. Couture should have been hovering in the back between Pulver and Electra, but there was just empty air where he had been—his place, position, and prestige erased without warning or explanation. A few weeks later, he learned that Zuffa had asked Crave Entertainment to cut him out of its licensed video game, *UFC: Tapout*. Both decisions had been made during the contract negotiations, and even after he and Zuffa seemingly resolved their differences, an air of resentment and mistrust lingered.

Shortly after, Couture agreed to a rematch against Rizzo at the MGM Grand Garden Arena in November, in what would be the UFC's second event in Las Vegas. Couture remained baffled by the UFC's stance toward him. When he learned that Rizzo had been given a new six-fight contract ahead of the rematch, he again felt that he was being set up to fail, even after having established himself as the promotion's most accomplished fighter. Despite his frustration, a part of Couture had always taken some pleasure in conflict. It simplified things, making it seem as if the most reasonable response was to disconnect and let himself descend into the ardors of training. Even as a new recruit in boot camp, Couture had secretly loved the hostility of drill sergeants as they bullied him around. He'd often found himself incapable of suppressing a smile in the midst of long streams of verbal abuse, which led to even more laps and mandatory push-ups as punishment. "It was almost a luxury, to be told what to do and not have to make my mind up for myself," Couture wrote. With lingering uncertainty of what his life would look like without wrestling, he happily threw himself into training sessions in an unventilated warehouse behind a used-car dealership with one of his former wrestling teammates, Matt Lindland, who had transitioned to mixed martial arts.

When Couture and Rizzo finally met again, at UFC 34, it was a one-sided pummeling. Couture skillfully avoided Rizzo's leg kicks and took him down with relative ease, and slowly battered Rizzo from the top position over the course of two-and-a-half rounds. The fight was finally stopped less than two minutes into the third round, after Rizzo was again taken to the mat and seemed helpless to protect himself from a slow but steady barrage of Couture's punches. As Rizzo sat on a stool after, with the ringside physician inspecting the long crescent-shaped gash that had opened over his left eye, he looked as if he was lost in a bad memory, violently ejected from his own dreams and left stranded in some unwanted future.

As the final result was read out, Rizzo stood up and walked back to the locker room alone while Couture was interviewed in the cage with the championship belt wrapped around his waist. Couture thanked God, his sponsors, and the USA for the victory. After the interview, White walked over to Couture and shook his hand, which turned into a joyous hug. "No one can do what you did," White shouted in Couture's ear over the arena sound system; Rizzo had never been finished in a fight before. A few moments later, Lorenzo joined Couture and White, and they posed for a picture with the UFC's reigning and defending thirty-eight-year-old champion. "Number one!" White yelled, as if trying to preemptively caption the photo before it was published. For Couture it seemed as if another new beginning in a life that had been filled with them. For a few moments, he seemed to have turned into a whole new person, appearing ten years younger behind a toothsome, boyish smile as the UFC's photographer captured the moment for the bosses. Couture was still unsure where exactly this would take him, but as he had always done before, he pushed the concerns out of his mind. His biological father watched from the audience for the first time in his career as either a wrestler or fighter, after he'd reached out unexpectedly to make amends for having abandoned his son decades earlier. In the exhausted afterglow of the fight, Couture felt a new sense of completeness, as if every part of his life that had been separate from the others was woven back together into one celebratory whole, like a photo shoot in which everyone had forgotten they were posing for a camera and just let themselves be captured in the moment, smiling and happy.

THERE IS NO PLAN B

Dana White sat in quiet awe inside the Saitama Super Arena, one humid, overcast night in August 2003. Seated at the ringside commentary table and surrounded by 40,316 fans, it seemed as if he could barely speak for a few moments, overwhelmed by the scene. Even the biggest UFC events seemed like miniatures by comparison—UFC 43 in June had drawn an estimated ninety-eight hundred fans to the Thomas & Mack Center at the University of Nevada, Las Vegas, just enough to fill the arena halfway. To cover up the thousands of empty seats, the production team had staged the octagon on one side of the arena floor and used the fighter entry ramp and background draping to block out a large part of the arena. There was no need for that kind of stagecraft at Pride events. More tickets had been sold for that night's show, Pride Total Elimination 2003, than there were seats in the arena. "It's unbelievable," White said on the Pride broadcast. "When we're in the states and we get thirteen thousand people we're blown away. When I just walked into the arena twenty minutes ago, I just couldn't believe it. It's amazing to see this many people together in one place at one time."

White had traveled to Japan with two of the UFC's best fighters, Ricco Rodriguez and Chuck Liddell, as part of a talent-sharing agreement he'd negotiated with Pride. Rodriguez and Liddell would be allowed to compete in a two-event Grand Prix for the Japanese promotion's heavyweight and light heavyweight championships. In return, Pride had agreed to send two of its stars, Kazuyuki Fujita and Kazushi Sakuraba, to compete in the UFC at a later date. If things went according to plan, Liddell would win his fight that night, against a lanky Dutch kickboxer named Alistair Overeem, and show that UFC fighters could compete with the best fighters in the world; they weren't just a rabble of backroom brawlers who'd mistakenly stumbled onto the world's mainstage for a few confusing years in the 1990s and were still, for some inexplicable reason, trying to command ordinary people's attention.

As Liddell walked through the characteristically silent Japanese crowd, toward the oversized cube of blue light in the center of the darkened arena where the ring was waiting, White's nervousness was palpable on commentary. "Dana, I know you're trembling, I know you're feeling it right now," Pride play-by-play announcer Stephen Quadros said. "I'd be lying if I said I wasn't," White answered. White claimed he had bet $250,000 on Liddell to win not just the fight, but the entire tournament. He had spent much of the preceding three years putting similarly ambitious plans in place, but they had rarely worked as intended. In 2002, White succeeded in getting the UFC on standard cable in the US and elsewhere. He signed a six-month deal with Sky Sports in the United Kingdom to air a one-hour anthology of the UFC's best fights every Thursday at 11:00 p.m. He'd also secured a deal with Wowow, a premium-pay Japanese broadcaster that reached 2.5 million homes, to air tape-delayed UFC events on Sunday evenings. The Brazilian cable and satellite TV giant Globosat had also agreed to air one-hour compilations of past top bouts on its free subsidiary SportTV, as well as to make the UFC's pay-per-views available to all its subscribers. In June 2002, it seemed as if White was on the verge of a major breakthrough when he persuaded producers from Fox Sports Net in the US to air a full fight on *The Best Damn Sports Show Period*, a talk show that sometimes aired UFC highlights and brought fighters into the studio for live interviews as an irreverent novelty. Eager to take advantage of the opportunity, White assembled a live six-fight card in between two previously booked pay-per-view events, called UFC 37.5. Instead of an arena, the event had taken place in a ballroom at the Bellagio Hotel & Casino. The Fox producers picked one fight from the event to air as a special during its hour-long 8 p.m. time slot, a violent brawl between Robbie Lawler and Steve Berger, which ended with a second-round knockout win for Lawler.

The episode had proved unexpectedly popular with the Fox audience, generating one of the highest rated episodes in *The Best Damn Sports Show Period*'s short history, and for a few weeks, it had seemed like the start of a promising new partnership. But some Fox executives had been uncomfortable with the association and when the executive who had championed the sport, Dan Harrison, left for a job at NBC, the show's remaining producers lost interest in the UFC. A few months later, it seemed as if White might have scored another coup when *ESPN The Magazine* agreed to send Bill Simmons to cover a UFC event for his popular "Page Two" column. White and Lorenzo had hoped for an endorsement from one of the most influential sportswriters working in the US at the time, but Simmons had been broadly dismissive of what he'd seen at UFC 39. He described a fight between heavyweights Tim Sylvia and Wesley "Cabbage" Correira as "practically Amateur Night," comparing Sylvia and Correira to rejects from a Tough Man Contest. Simmons had seemed particularly disturbed by another fight between Phil Baroni and Dave Menne, which ended in an alarming eighteen-second knockout. "The camera zoomed in on a discombobulated Menne—face already swelling up, vacant eyes, blood dripping from inside his left eyeball— and everyone hushed," Simmons wrote. "Yikes. *This guy doesn't look good.* They quickly brought a stretcher out for him, as one of the dudes behind us gleefully shouted, There's your ride! Suddenly, I wasn't sure I wanted to be there anymore."

In Japan, Pride was seen very differently from the UFC. The promotion had a lucrative broadcasting deal with Fuji TV, which reached more than 98 percent of Japan's total population. Some Pride events had been watched by more than twenty million Japanese viewers, drawing a bigger audience than some NBA Finals or World Series games. Pride events had an unexpected sense of grandeur and elegance. Instead of the guttural, angst-drenched metal soundtrack the UFC used, Pride's main theme was a dramatic orchestral suite. Broadcasts often opened with a ceremonial introduction of the fighters, who would enter the ring one by one to salute the audience or else line up together on risers along the edge of the arena floor surrounded by glowing orbs of white light. Before the individual championships were introduced in 2001, every winning fighter was presented with a trophy in the ring, as if each fight was its own self-contained triumph, a chance to test oneself in an extraordinary setting against overwhelming odds, instead of an incremental struggle to rise a few rankings.

Pride's star fighters often came out of the country's legendary professional wrestling circuit and had a folkloric aura, as if they weren't athletes but actors in parables that imparted some fleeting lesson about how

life should be lived. Sakuraba had become a cult favorite, an unassum-
ing former wrestler from Japan's Universal Wrestling Federation who
had earned the nickname of "the Gracie Killer," for beating four different
members of the Gracie family over a thirteen-month span, including a
ninety-minute battle against Royce that ended with the Brazilian's cornerman throwing in the towel, the former UFC star's first professional loss.
Pride had siphoned off many of the UFC's best fighters and made it hard
for the UFC to compete for new prospects. In 2001, White had helped
sign Anderson Silva, a promising Brazilian fighter with a seven-and-one
record who had just won the Shooto middleweight championship. A
month before his scheduled debut, Silva backed out of the agreement to
pursue an offer from Pride instead. Both White and Lorenzo had grudgingly understood Pride's appeal to fighters. On weekends when Pride had
an event, White, Lorenzo, and Frank III would sometimes sneak down to
a library-themed meeting room Frank Jr. kept in Station's office to watch
Pride events while drinking Gordon Biersch beer from kegs that had been
installed for guests. Because White understood its appeal, he'd been especially aggressive about trying to undermine Pride's public recognition.
In an interview, Joel Gold, editor-in-chief of *Full Contact Fighter*, recalled
how White would call him whenever he chose to put Pride fighters on
the cover of an issue. "Every time he saw the paper, if there was something he didn't like—Oh boy!—he'd call me up and start yelling," Gold
said. Jeff Sherwood, who created and ran Sherdog.com, one of the most
popular mixed martial arts websites at the time, was also a regular target
for White's Pride rants. "He would call me and say like, Hey, we're going
to take over the world. We're going to be the only MMA show around, I
guarantee you," says Sherwood. "You need to get on board. You don't need
to cover that shit in Japan anymore. Be one of my guys."

White had often tried to be as controlling with the UFC's fighters. In
2002, he'd tried to orchestrate a title fight between his two former clients,
Liddell and Ortiz, who had held the UFC's light heavyweight champion
for three years. Liddell was a clear title contender with six consecutive
wins in the UFC. According to Ortiz, White had wanted him to call out
Liddell in his post-fight interview at UFC 40 on November 22, 2002,
following a win over Ken Shamrock. Instead, with 13,265 fans in MGM
Grand Garden Arena and more than one hundred thousand pay-per-

view buyers watching, Ortiz used the interview to complain about his pay. "I guess we gotta renegotiate things because me and Chuck—I mean our friendship's not worth the money we're getting paid, if you ask me," Ortiz said. "I love Chuck as a friend. If we're going to get in here and do what we just did right now, I'm going to make it worthwhile for myself and hisself."

White would later say that trying to negotiate with Ortiz had made him angrier than he had ever been. Ortiz had reportedly wanted a new deal worth $1.1 million to fight his former training partner. It was an astronomical fee for the time, worth almost as much as the entire production budget for an event. When Ortiz turned down a $160,000 offer, the UFC decided to work around him, booking Liddell into a fight for an interim light heavyweight championship against Randy Couture, who would come down a weight class from heavyweight for the chance at a second title. (Ortiz would later claim he tried to persuade Liddell to join him in holding out for money, but Liddell wasn't interested.)

Couture had seemed like a safe opponent at the time. After his two wins over Rizzo, Couture had lost his next two fights to younger fighters by disturbingly violent TKOs, the last of which had left him with a shattered orbital bone and six months of double vision. He had only one fight remaining on his UFC contract and had promised Trish that he would retire after. Instead, Couture once again upended the odds by beating Liddell in a shocking third-round TKO. "Unbelievable!" newly hired color commentator Joe Rogan said on the broadcast, repeating the word three times, each louder than the last. "What an incredible athlete and what an incredible upset. Randy Couture is an animal!"

Two months later, White had arrived in Tokyo with Liddell. It wasn't how White had planned for things to play out, but as he watched Liddell in the ring, bouncing from foot to foot as he waited for Overeem to make his way through the crowd, he reflexively focused on the positive. "I two hundred percent believe in Chuck Liddell," White told Stephen Quadros.

In the opening seconds of the fight, that belief seemed ill-founded, when Overeem exploded forward with a knee into Liddell's midsection, which landed with the force of a pneumatic piston. As Liddell reeled backward, Overeem hit him again with a sudden, leaping left cross as he backpedaled toward the ropes. Liddell's knees buckled and he instinctively tried to rush forward, grabbing Overeem around the waist to smother any further punches and buy time for his newly confused mind to clear. He seemed outmatched by a younger, faster, and longer fighter. Overeem calmly worked himself free of Liddell's bodylock and returned to the center of the ring, where he landed several more knees and straight lefts, which easily shot through the loose defensive barricade Liddell tried to make with his arms. Another knee glanced off the crown of Liddell's head and opened a cut along the edge of his mohawk, leaving a small trickle of blood running down Liddell's face. Liddell tried to back Overeem away with looping counterpunches as Overeem advanced on him, but the looping punches all seemed to sail wide of Overeem's head while leading Liddell off-balance and open for more counterstrikes.

Feeling his chances narrowing, Liddell ducked under one of Overeem's long straight punches just as he was beginning to hunt for a knock-out, and slammed Overeem to the mat. Liddell tried to create enough leverage to land punches from above, but Overeem used his legs to create a barricade that was just too big for Liddell to punch through. Overeem rolled onto his knees with his head tucked between his arms. Liddell tried to maintain top position by digging his arms under Overeem's shoulders and tried to punish him with knees to the head. Overeem deflected the worst of the blows with his arms and used the brief windows after Liddell had thrown himself off-balance to work his way back to his feet.

For a moment, it seemed as if Liddell had run out of options. All that remained was for the fighters to play out their parts for a few more exchanges before the younger and faster man would inevitably bring things to a cruel end. But then, something changed. As they exchanged punches again, Overeem's youthfulness seemed to have faded. His punches traveled a slightly slower arc than they had been, and his body seemed to sag slightly as he retracted his arm afterward. It seemed defending against Liddell's wrestling had strained Overeem's energy stores. Still alert enough to sense the lull, Liddell suddenly seemed like the younger and stronger fighter. Overeem began to back away from Liddell's punches, searching for breathing room instead of confidently ducking and countering. Liddell prowled after in an excited predatory hunch and threw a long, whipping overhand left, which smashed through Overeem's guard onto the edge of his jaw like a thrown brick. Overeem's eyes went vacant for a moment, even as he continued to look directly at Liddell. As Overeem took a step backward, his legs seemed to have stopped working and he tottered like a foal on wet rocks. Sensing vulnerability, Liddell stormed forward, and began punching with the fury and franticness of a twenty-four-year-old. Overeem tried to shield his head with upheld arms, but Liddell continually found new angles for his punches.

Overeem leaned back into the ropes and turned away to one side, hoping to lessen the number of available targets for Liddell. As he hunched down and kept his arms up to cover his head, he was unable to see the left straight Liddell threw from across the far side of his own body. The punch landed as simply as a finger flicking a light switch and sent Overeem into a sudden free-fall. As his half-conscious body hit the floor a second later, the referee jumped in front of Liddell and called the fight off. Liddell celebrated by circling the perimeter screaming at the audience as the tendons and arteries in his neck bulged through the skin, his arms crossed behind his back as if he were handcuffed. Overcome with joy and relief, White ripped his broadcasting headset off and jumped onto the ring apron. Liddell ran to him in an exultant rage, and White reached across the ropes and held Liddell's face in his hands, leaned over, and kissed him on the top of his head. After the official results were read, Liddell handed White the small trophy he'd earned for the victory. "I'll give you the other half in November," he promised, in reference to the second and final round of the Grand Prix, when Liddell would have to fight and win twice in one night to claim the Pride middleweight championship.

The relief White felt was short-lived. As he returned to Las Vegas to work on the final two events of the year for the UFC, including one to commemorate the ten-year anniversary of the first UFC in 1993, Lorenzo and Frank III had begun to worry. Despite White's and Liddell's triumph in Japan, the UFC was no nearer to turning a profit than it had been under SEG ownership. While revenues had risen, from $4.5 million in 2001 to $8.7 million in 2002, expenses had risen even faster. Production costs for 2002 had been more than $10 million, and fighter pay had added another $3.6 million. Coupled with marketing expenses, legal costs, and everyday overhead, the Fertittas' total losses after three years were nearly $20 million, around ten times what they'd originally paid for the promotion. And the first three events of 2003 had underperformed even the 2002 levels, making it likely the latest round of losses would be the biggest yet. In the press, Lorenzo admitted his vision for mixed martial arts might never match the public's. "The miscalculation was that it's not the same sport that it was before," Lorenzo said in 2002. "Unfortunately, it seems that [the fans] were more interested in tuning in to a spectacle or a car wreck than a true sporting event."

White buried himself in work. He felt as if he'd struck on another viable formula by focusing on the small but loyal group of fans who had followed the sport since the beginning. He'd crisscrossed the country for "meet-and-greets" at local pubs and chain restaurants, trying to build a grassroots promotional campaign for the UFC's fighters in their hometowns, including trips to Mac's Smokehouse in Seattle with Randy Couture and Evan Tanner, the Bw-3 Grill and Pub in Houston with Yves Edwards, and Hooters on 56th Street and 7th Avenue in New York, where White appeared with Tito Ortiz, Phil Baroni, and a local broadcasting crew from K-Rock 92.3 FM. "I don't care if three people show up," White told *Full Contact Fighter*. "If there's three fans, we're here to do it. I'll go anywhere and do anything for the fans."

As White traveled the country, he struck up an unexpected friendship with one ardent fan, Charles Lewis, who had started an apparel company called Tapout. Lewis and the two friends he'd enlisted to help him, Dan Caldwell and Timothy Katz, were always in the audience, both at UFC events and the dozens of smaller regional shows White scouted, selling T-shirts in parking lots and befriending hundreds of fighters, many of whom they gave small sponsorship fees, typically $300, to wear their shirts into the cage. "Mixed martial arts and fighting didn't have any identity," Lewis would later say. "You couldn't put on a uniform and feel the way we felt in the gym. So I, kind of—just as a need to identify what I was feeling on the inside of myself, came up with a T-shirt." From the outside, Tapout appeared more like a traveling cabaret than an apparel company. Lewis, Katz, and Caldwell would try to attract attention by wearing face paint and elaborate costumes with sequined jackets, feather boas, and army surplus camouflage pants. The company was run mostly on cash, and they gave shirts away for free as often as they sold them. To keep the operation solvent, Lewis often found himself sleeping on friends' couches or staying up all night driving home after an event to save on hotel costs. Lewis papered his bedroom with inspirational quotes, like "To quit does not exist." He liked to tell the story of Hernán Cortés arriving in Mexico in 1519 and burning his own ships after he arrived, to prevent his soldiers from fleeing in fear of the Aztecs. The story was apocryphal, but for Lewis it had become a rubric that guided him through life. "There is no Plan B," Caldwell would later say. "We have to win. There is no escape. Burn these ships and we're going to go win this fucking war. That was our mentality. That's how we thought."

White saw a kindred spirit in Lewis and decided to make Tapout a regular part of the UFC brand. At UFC 36, the Tapout logo appeared on the octagon mat, making it seem like the event's biggest sponsor. Lewis hadn't paid anything for the placement, and no one at Tapout knew it would be featured so prominently until the day of the event. "They didn't even tell us," Caldwell would later recall. At the time, Zuffa had been struggling to attract sponsors, something Lorenzo had hoped would become a major source of revenue. The travel website Expedia.com had been the highest profile sponsor to sign on, for UFC 33, but the company had declined to continue the partnership after one event. Unable to attract other mainstream sponsors, Zuffa had resorted to promoting Station subsidiaries like Gordon Biersch and *UFC: Tapout 2*, a video game series produced through a licensing deal SEG had negotiated with Crave Entertainment. The association with Tapout had given the UFC the air of a larger commercial ecosystem, even as the apparel company was run mostly out of a van in parking lots. Lewis, Caldwell, and Katz were frequently shown in the VIP section during pay-per-view broadcasts, and in 2003, the UFC began giving a "Tapout Award of the Night" prize to the night's most exciting fighter. At UFC 43, White had Lewis film a bizarre introductory video for Liddell before he walked out into the arena to fight Couture. Lewis appeared in full face paint covered in blue light, filmed from a bizarre variety of tilted angles punctuated with rack zooms, describing Liddell as if he were a comic book villain instead of a cage fighter. "Who's in the house?" Lewis asked. "The Ice Man's in the house. I'm talking about Chuck Liddell. A professional killer, an assassin." The video would be widely mocked by fans, but it conveyed a bizarrely persuasive sense of reverence for the sport that was often missing in other media. More important, the association with Tapout suggested there was a group of consumers who had remained loyal to the sport, and would continue to buy not just its pay-per-views but a range of peripheral products—shirts, beanies, sweat pants, and more—a kind of self-contained universe of institutions nested within one another that had gone largely ignored by all but the true believers.

White had found another true believer in Joe Rogan, a television personality and stand-up comedian, who would become even more enmeshed in the UFC's public branding than Tapout. Rogan had briefly worked as the UFC's backstage interviewer in 1997, something his talent manager at the time had arranged with Campbell McLaren, whom he had known from his days working at Carolines. Rogan had grown up practicing martial arts. At nineteen, he had won the US Open Taekwondo Championships, and after seeing the first UFC he'd begun training in jiu-jitsu, first at Rickson Gracie's academy in West Los Angeles, and then later at Carlson Gracie's academy in Hollywood, where he had trained alongside UFC fighters Vitor Belfort, Allan Góes, and Wallid Ismail. After the UFC was kicked off US cable, SEG hadn't been able to afford Rogan's $1,500 fee and he stopped appearing on broadcasts. But he had remained a dedicated fan and continued coming to events on his own, which was where he first met White shortly after SEG sold the company. They quickly bonded over their love of fighting and similar upbringings—like White, Rogan had also grown up in Massachusetts, in an exurb fifteen miles outside of Boston. They would often end up at dinner together after fights, and White aggressively pressed Rogan to rejoin the broadcast team. "I was like, I don't want to work, man," Rogan would later say. "I just want to go watch the fights and swear and scream and get drunk like everybody else."

White had been dissatisfied with the UFC's commentary team since the beginning. Jeff Blatnick was let go after UFC 32 because, according to McCarthy, White "didn't like anything about him, from his looks to his commenting skills." Blatnick was an Olympic medalist in Greco-Roman wrestling and had been quick to appreciate the complexity of mixed martial arts, but his enthusiasm could sometimes feel clumsy and inarticulate. He was also in his mid-forties, and his earnest approach to the sport seemed out of step with the push toward celebrity and youthful spectacle that Zuffa had brought in. Blatnick was replaced at UFC 33 by Jeff Osborne, an experienced martial artist who ran his own small promo-

tion based in Indiana, called HOOKnSHOOT. Osborne spoke with more
clarity and comfort about techniques and new fighters, yet he had a slow
Texas drawl, sweetened by a faint smoker's rasp. And though his famil-
iarity with mixed martial arts gave him an air of authority, it sometimes
muted his response to what was happening in the cage. He could be both
comforting and tranquilizing, and he sometimes sounded like he was
struggling to keep pace with the energy of the crowds when they reacted
to big punches or wrestling slams. After a year, Osborne was politely fired.
He was told by executive producer Steve Tornabene that the company
simply wanted to "shake things up a little."

Rogan replaced Osborne as color commentator at UFC 40 in November 2002, a decision he ultimately credited to White. "I only did it because [White] was a friend," Rogan would later say. Initially, he agreed
to work for no salary, and asked only for the UFC to pay for his travel
expenses and a few extra tickets to share with his friends. Rogan was a
strange addition to the broadcast team. He had already attained a level of
celebrity and stardom playing a belligerently self-absorbed sportscaster
on the NBC hit sitcom *NewsRadio*, then gone on to host *Fear Factor*, a
surprise 2001 hit that was often the number one rated show in its time
slot, drawing more than fifteen million viewers by challenging contestants
to eat cooked horse rectum, or crawl through a pit filled with two thousand scorpions. Seeing a famous entertainer and game show host provid-
ing technical analysis gave UFC events a sense of surreal confusion, as if
a casting director had mistakenly sent Rogan the wrong call sheet for his
next gig.

Rogan described himself as a "professional fan," and his commentary
immediately changed the tone and intensity of the UFC's broadcasts. He
revered fighters and described everything in the cage with awed super-
latives. Where others saw Tough Man rejects, Rogan saw "world-class"
athletes and "elite" martial artists, who were among the most developed
and dangerous human beings on the planet. His own experience in jiu-
jitsu and taekwondo allowed him to explain the sometimes counterintuitive drama of grappling, helping audiences to absorb a new vocabulary
of technical terms for different jiu-jitsu positions and submission holds.
He also dramatized the small battles for limb control or hip position that
were constantly taking place, which to the untrained eye might have

looked just like two tired men slouching on each other. More important, he modeled how viewers should react to what they were seeing, with frequent screams of disbelief whenever a fighter appeared hurt or in danger, almost as if he were a human seismograph tuned solely to violence. He seemed to relish the damage fighters would endure, underscoring, and sometimes overselling, the consequences. After Ortiz beat Ken Shamrock at UFC 40, Rogan memorably said Shamrock's bloodied and misshapen face "looks like he got hit with Howitzer." In Rogan's telling, moments of extreme violence lent the sport a kind of grave but essential nobility that made the public caricature of an amateurish freak show feel cynical and ill-informed.

White shared many of Rogan's views on the sport's cruelty, and tried to weave them into a range of licensed goods pitched at the UFC's most committed fans. White had helped create Zuffa Records, which published an official soundtrack for the UFC, filled with guttural metal songs from bands like Damageplan, Hatebreed, Sepultura, and Scars of Life. White had a special affinity for one band in particular, a little-known group from Buffalo called Stemm. A Las Vegas producer who was working with Zuffa Records had given White a demo tape of unpublished songs from the band after seeing them perform at a music festival in 2002, and five days later White had set up a call with Lorenzo and all of the band members to negotiate a licensing deal for some of the band's songs. They also asked for Stemm to write a few new songs specifically for use during weigh-ins, fighter walkouts, and as background music during prepackaged fight previews. White also asked if they would write a new theme song to open pay-per-view broadcasts, something that, in White's words, would be "about the mindset of a fighter, something that lyrically explains what they go through when they step into the ring." The result was "Face the Pain," which debuted at UFC 40, the same event where Rogan would take over as color commentator. The song opens with three thin, muted notes tightening like a garrote, before blasting into an angular syncopated drop-C guitar riff that spirals toward a car crash of a chorus with lead singer Joe Cafarella screaming variations on: "Face the pain, no escape, can you step to this?" White loved the song, especially when he heard it played on the MGM Grand Garden Arena speakers during the walk-through before UFC 40. The deal Zuffa offered Stemm to use "Face the

Pain" as the UFC's main theme for all future events was, Cafarella would later say, "not the greatest," but the band had been together for less than three years, and like many fighters, they were just happy to have someone interested in their work. "At the time, all we cared about was exposure and getting our name out there, and they were a massive vehicle to do that," Cafarella said.

In addition to selling CDs, White had also hoped to boost revenues by selling DVDs through a newly created UFC Video label. VHS sales and rentals had been a significant source of revenue for SEG throughout the 1990s, when video rental chains like Blockbuster and Hollywood Video had helped the UFC preserve a small foothold in the public imagination even after it had been dropped from cable pay-per-view. White had seen Don Gold's name in the credits of an old UFC tape and cold-called Gold in his Los Angeles office in the summer of 2003 to ask if he'd be interested in rejoining the UFC to help with its struggling DVD business. "I was like, No," Gold says of the call. "It's so difficult to take a brand that went up and then crashed when all the carriers stopped showing the fights, and then reignite it."

After the UFC had begun its collapse, Gold had moved on with his life. In 1996, he'd traded cage fighting for children's entertainment, taking a job with Harvey Comics, the company behind *Casper the Friendly Ghost*, *Baby Huey*, and *Richie Rich*. He later joined Itsy Bitsy Entertainment to work on *Teletubbies*, and then started his own production company in 2000, focusing on family friendly television. Moving back into cage fighting seemed like a bad choice. But White steadily broke down Gold's skepticism and convinced him to fly to Las Vegas to meet with Lorenzo and Frank III. White's insistent optimism impressed Gold, and when White and Lorenzo agreed to let him handle not just DVD distribution but the UFC's entire licensing and distribution business he decided to take the job. Gold's connections had an immediate effect, as he persuaded Best Buy to purchase five hundred DVDs to sell at a set number of locations across the country. It was a small number, but White was ecstatic. He made a point of finding out which branches in Las Vegas stocked the DVDs and would periodically stop in to move the UFC titles to the front of the sales rack.

As White prepared to return to Japan with Liddell in November, it seemed as if things were finally beginning to move in the right direction. The last three years had been difficult and filled with disappointments, but he'd built a stable foundation for the promotion that wouldn't require the approval or acknowledgment of people in the mainstream media. Liddell's expected triumph in the second and final event of the Pride Grand Prix would be an inarguable sign that the UFC had returned to the top of sport, something that people wouldn't be able to continue ignoring for long. In Liddell's first fight of the night, he was matched against Quinton "Rampage" Jackson, a powerful twenty-four-year-old who wore a chain-link necklace and howled like a werewolf at the arena lights on his way to the ring. If Liddell won, he would likely have to fight Wanderlei Silva, the favorite to win the tournament, nicknamed "the Ax Murderer" for his aggressive style that sometimes resulted in blood-drenched brawls.

The finale, subtitled Final Conflict 2003, took place on November 9 in the Tokyo Dome, which was filled with 67,450 fans, enough to populate a small city, and six times more than the total population of White's childhood hometown of Ware, Massachusetts. Lorenzo had also made the trip and sat in the ringside VIP section near the commentary desk, where White was again invited to sit during Liddell's fights. Rodriguez had lost his fight at the start of Pride's heavyweight tournament in August, leaving Liddell as the only remaining hope of usurping a title from the UFC's biggest competitor. Though White was optimistic, the tension in his voice was clear when he began speaking on commentary. He was again barely audible when he spoke, as if his diaphragm had clenched shut and wouldn't allow any air into his lungs. Liddell's plan for beating Jackson had seemed straightforward: continually circle away from Jackson's powerful right hand while kicking his calves and thighs to slow his movement. After the first ten-minute round Jackson would tire himself out with missed punches while suffering from new contusions on his legs, and Liddell would be safe to start throwing knockout punches. One would inevitably find its way to Jackson's chin, bringing the fight to a sudden, violent end. As the fight began, that triumphant image slowly disappeared and a confusing new reality set in. Instead of fighting evasively, Liddell seemed to have abandoned the game plan. He seemed to continually be drawn toward Jackson, and when the younger and more powerful fighter threw his heavy right hand, Liddell would plant his feet and try to punch back, as if trying to prove he was the stronger man.

In practice, Liddell's punches were neither powerful nor fast. They seemed to land either too soon or too late, often skidding off Jackson's shoulders or gloves as he protected his head. Halfway through the first round, it became clear that it was Jackson who was leading Liddell into exhaustion. "Very slow pace," White said, as if he were quietly talking to himself. "Chuck isn't implementing the game plan at all." By the end of the round, Liddell seemed depleted. Every inhale left him short of breath, and the dull, distant fog of repeated brain trauma from Jackson's counter-punches had begun to gather at the outer edges of his mind. "Chuck looks exhausted," White said on commentary, as the bell sounded to end the round. "He looks tired. I'm shocked."

In the second round, a glassy-eyed Liddell, conspicuously breathing through his mouth, tried to pull himself out of the fatigue that had hi-jacked his body, but his punches seemed more like pleas than threats, swings filled with the hope of undoing the reality of the moment, all of which missed and left Liddell lurching and off-balance. Two minutes into the round, Jackson grazed Liddell with a quick, flashing uppercut that finally knocked him to the canvas. Liddell struggled back to his feet, but Jackson immediately slammed him back down with a wrestling trip. For seventy seconds, Jackson pounded Liddell's ribs, stomach, and head from above. Too tired to do anything else, Liddell waved his arms above his head to deflect the punches, until the referee finally jumped in to stop the fight while Liddell stayed on his back staring into the noth-ingness of the overhead lights and the mix of familiar and unfamiliar faces that came in and out of view. "What happened?" White asked. It wasn't until the slow-motion replay ran over the monitors at the com-mentary table that he saw the small white towel from Liddell's corner flying through the air.

The disappointment of the loss was followed by another, when White and Lorenzo returned to the United States and closed out the year with *UFC 45: Revolution*, which also coincided with the promotion's ten-year anniversary. It should have been an exultant celebration of how far mixed martial arts had come in its first decade, and how central the UFC remained to the sport. During the broadcast, White and Lorenzo announced the creation of the UFC Hall of Fame and made Royce Gra-cie and Ken Shamrock its first official entrants. They also awarded ten additional "Legends" awards that fans had voted on through the UFC

website, which went to, among others, Don Frye, Dan Severn, Randy
Couture, and Mark Coleman, each of whom was invited into the cage
and given a glass trophy. Despite the gestures, the event was largely a de-
bacle. An anticipated bout featuring former SEG star Tank Abbott ended
after two sloppy minutes of fighting, when a huge gash opened above
Abbott's right eye and the doctor ruled it unsafe for him to continue.
As Abbott's opponent, Wesley "Cabbage" Correira, celebrated by flipping
him off, a shoving match broke out between the two camps, forcing the
cage to be cleared. As the final results were read, Abbott tried to pull the
microphone out of Bruce Buffer's hand to address the crowd, but he was
taken away by security. In the main event, welterweight title challenger
Frank Trigg came to the octagon wearing a shirt promoting VinceVoy-
eur.com, the website of a notorious porn actor. The event would generate
just forty thousand pay-per-view buys, the second lowest of the year, one
in which every event had lost money. Despite all of White's efforts to
build a more organic business around a smaller but loyal fandom, the
UFC's revenues for 2003 would fall to $7.5 million, $1 million less than
it had made in 2002. Total losses for the UFC after three years of Fertitta
ownership topped $30 million.

The size of the losses from the UFC had unsettled Frank III. While running the UFC had been a fun distraction from the complexities of managing an ever-growing network of casinos, the spell had begun to wear
off. In some months, when Zuffa's accounts had been depleted, Lorenzo
would walk across the street from Station to the UFC's offices and deliver
a handwritten check to ensure it wouldn't miss a payroll date or fail to pay
its contractors. The more money they spent, the more Frank III had worried that fandom might have prevented them from seeing the plain truth:
it wasn't a sustainable business. "It's like going to a craps table saying, Am
I just gonna go there and play all night and not have a budget on what I'm
going to lose," Frank III would later say. "And wake up tomorrow and say,
How the hell did I lose this much money?" While the UFC's losses were
a small fraction of the $858 million in revenue Station was on track to
generate in 2003, it seemed like a bad bet to keep spending money to see if
their luck might improve. As White began to plan 2004's events, it became
clear that Pride had no intention of sending Sakuraba or Fujita to compete
in the UFC, and it was hard to see how things could reverse course. With

pressure from Frank III, Lorenzo reluctantly decided to tell White that it was time to cut their losses. "I can't keep spending my family's money," he told White.

The words stung White. Growing up, he'd always felt a twinge of self-consciousness around the students at Bishop Gorman, many of whom came from rich families. They dressed differently, talked differently, drove different kinds of cars, and lived in different kinds of houses. White hadn't taken the differences seriously as a teenager, but one night in his junior year, after he'd totaled his girlfriend's car driving home from an under-twenty-one nightclub near the Strip, his mother had reminded him those differences would likely only grow with time. "Let me tell you the difference between you and all these fucking rich kids you hang around with," he recalled her saying. "They're always going to be rich and you're not. And if you fucking blow it, you'll be pumping gas into their cars one of these days. You're their pal now, but just you wait."

As White hung up with Lorenzo and began going through his contact list looking for people he thought might be willing and able to buy the promotion from the Fertittas, the sadness of the situation slowly sunk in. "It's over," he thought to himself. "We didn't make it."

Lorenzo had begun second-guessing the decision to sell almost as soon as he'd made it. He hated the idea of failure. When White gave him the short list of potential buyers he'd been able to find, the reality of how much money they'd have to write off set in. There had been some interest—including from Dan Lambert, who, after being shut out of his initial agreement with Meyrowitz, had launched the American Top Team gym in Coconut Creek, Florida—but the best offers had come in between $6 and $7 million, less than a quarter what the Fertittas had spent to keep the UFC running. The losses had always seemed temporary as they had accumulated year over year, but selling the company would make those losses permanent, an eight-figure reminder of Lorenzo and Frank III's bad judgment. It was a hard thing to accept. "We hadn't lost at anything," Lorenzo would say of the dilemma. "We weren't losers."

Despite his misgivings, Lorenzo decided it would be at least worth a few more months of time and effort to try to save the UFC. "Fuck it,"

Lorenzo told White, after he'd made up his mind. "Let's keep going." Normally, Lorenzo avoided cursing in business settings, and instead spoke with the practiced innocence of a teenager caught coming home after curfew. He'd start sentences with *Gosh*, and slip into a folksy western drawl that rounded the edges off certain syllables, making him sound more like a ranch hand than an MBA from NYU. *Wasn't* would sometimes come out as *wadn't*; *isn't* became *idn't*. It seemed less like an organic way of speaking than a private vernacular he'd trained himself to fall back on when he needed to make sure he wouldn't say the wrong thing. Only rarely did he lower his guard enough to let the wrong thing slip out. When White heard the phrase—*fuck it*—he knew Lorenzo was serious, and he decided to commit himself to whatever plan Lorenzo wanted to move forward with.

Unsure of what exactly to do next, Lorenzo did what his father had taught him to, and looked for advice from someone who might know better than he would how things were supposed to work. That person was Craig Piligian, a television producer whom Lorenzo had met in early 2003, when he approached Station with a pitch for a reality series about the day-to-day operations of a Las Vegas casino. Piligian had become a magnate in reality television after helping launch *Survivor* in 2000. He'd seized upon the overheated market to convert a wide range of niche interests and industries into raw material for small screen drama, including motorcycle custom shops (*American Chopper*), blue-collar service work (*Dirty Jobs*), and paranormal investigation (*Ghost Hunters*). Lorenzo and Frank III had agreed to let Piligian follow the staff at Green Valley Ranch for *American Casino*, a reality series that would run on Discovery Channel for two seasons. The series wasn't drawing big ratings, but Lorenzo trusted Piligian's instincts. When he mentioned the UFC's struggles, Piligian suggested approaching television broadcasters with something called a barter deal. Barter deals had first become popular in the 1980s, with shows like *Fame*, *Lifestyles of the Rich and Famous*, *Solid Gold*, *Entertainment Tonight*, and *Too Close for Comfort*. Sometimes called first-run syndication, they were a way for projects that had been rejected or canceled by television networks to find a second life with independent financiers, who would cover the production costs and then license the finished product to networks in exchange for a percentage of the advertising revenue. Television executives loved barter deals because they didn't have to risk any of their own money to produce shows, and independent producers like Piligian liked them because they would be able to collect revenue from multiple broadcasters in different markets while also controlling second-run syndication and all other ancillary licensing rights.

If Zuffa approached a basic cable network with a barter deal, offering the chance to air a fully funded cage fighting series, Piligian was sure they'd be able to find a partner. It was a scary idea for Lorenzo. Covering the costs of a full season of a television show would be the biggest expense to date for the UFC, with the only hope of recouping the costs coming from how much advertisers would be willing to pay for a thirty-second spot, something that could end up being no more than a few thousand dollars. It felt like a desperate gamble, the same sort of deluded decision-making that might drive a blackjack player to make up a lost hand by doubling their bet on the next one. But it was the last best option and Lorenzo decided to go with it.

The first idea was for an hour-long show of fights between promising young contenders, loosely modeled after *Tuesday Night Fights*, a short-lived but influential boxing series that had aired on the USA Network in the early 1980s. The initial response from networks was not positive. Executives from ABC, NBC, Fox, MTV, and ESPN had all been willing to meet with White and Lorenzo, but none had been impressed by the idea of airing fights. Even without having to spend money on the production, the risk of controversy and public backlash outweighed any potential ratings upside from the sport's small but fervent audience. When White and Lorenzo walked into Kevin Kay's office one day in early 2004, their expectations were low. Kay had recently been appointed as vice president of programming at Spike TV, a cable channel that debuted in 2003 with the hope of attracting a young male audience. Kay had spent much of his tenure at Spike trying to find new kinds of sports to put on air. He'd thought he'd found one with *Slamball*, a cross between rugby and basketball that was played on a court with trampolines underneath each basket. *Slamball* had aired for two short seasons on Spike, wedged in between syndicated reruns of *Baywatch* and *WWF*. The acrobatic slam dunks and alley-oops had initially amazed viewers, but by the end of the second season, ratings had collapsed as fans caught on to the fact that it was less a sport than a series of stunts that didn't really add up to anything outside of a few weightless, slow-motion highlights.

Kay had spent the end of 2003 looking for something to take *Slamball*'s place. He'd taken meetings with promoters for a roller derby league, traveled to Tokyo to meet with the Japanese kickboxing promotion K-1, and scouted out sumo matches, wondering if American audiences could learn to appreciate the drama of two men colliding like monster trucks in a ringed arena. One of the office assistants, a recent NYU graduate named Gil Ilan, had brought Kay a stack of UFC DVDs and tried to sell him on the idea, but Kay hadn't bothered to watch them. A few months later, Spike's head of talent, Casey Patterson, told Kay people from the UFC had reached out with an idea for a series and said it might be worth a meeting. When Kay finally got around to watching the UFC DVDs, he saw what had so excited Ilan's classmates in the dorms, but was convinced the sport was too violent for a major cable channel. Despite his misgivings, he agreed to meet with White and Lorenzo to hear them out.

"The first meeting was not particularly good," says Kay. "There was a lot of Dana pounding on the desk saying, You don't know what you're missing, this is the greatest fucking thing in the world. I was like, No I've watched it, it's cool, but I don't know how to put it on TV." Kay liked Lorenzo and White, and he liked what he had seen of the UFC, but he couldn't imagine pitching cage fighting to the kinds of corporate sponsors Spike depended on, and even if he could, he wasn't sure audiences would be able to see past the shock factor. "If it's just the fights, people aren't gonna understand it," he recalls telling White and Lorenzo. "They don't understand the rules, they don't understand why it's in a cage, there's blood on the mat. I can't sell it to advertisers. We needed a better idea."

Spike had been formed in large part to appeal to advertisers. It appeared in the aftermath of Viacom's 1999 acquisition of CBS, one of the largest media deals of the 1990s, which consolidated CBS's massive network of local affiliates and cable channels into Viacom's broadcasting portfolio, which included MTV, VH1, Comedy Central, Nickelodeon, and BET. Included in the package was the Nashville Network, a smaller country-themed channel that CBS had acquired in the early 1990s, mostly known for airing NASCAR, *WWF Raw*, and a range of hunting and fishing programs. By 2000, TNN was available in more than seventy-eight million homes and generated an estimated $350 million in advertising revenue. But Viacom already owned a country-themed network of its own, Country Music Television, which offered similar programming, but had a much younger and more lucrative audience than TNN, which had a prime-time audience that was mostly over fifty-five. Instead of keeping both channels running, Tom Freston, president of Viacom's cable operations, decided to rebrand TNN. Freston put out a call for pitches and settled on one that came, improbably, from Albie Hecht, a president of Nickelodeon, who proposed turning TNN into "the first network for men," a channel that would be "contemporary, aggressive, and irreverent," the television equivalent of *Esquire* magazine.

At the time, no demographic was more desirable than young men aged eighteen to thirty-four. Advertisers were willing to pay more than double to reach them—with average rates of $23.54 per one thousand viewers, according to NBC News president Lawrence K. Grossman, compared to $9.57 per one thousand viewers for audiences over thirty-five. "You're dealing with a very small pool, but it's a group advertisers love to target, and they will pay a premium for it," Brad Adgate of market research firm Horizon Media said in 2003, praising Viacom's strategy to rebrand TNN into Spike. Young men had become so desirable, in part, because many had stopped watching television altogether, making it harder for advertisers to find them. Men between eighteen and thirty-four were the least likely demographic to watch TV, according to a Comscore survey, and most seemed to have instead migrated to the internet for their daily media consumption, accounting for more than 40 percent of web traffic on any given day. While younger men had less purchasing power and financial stability, they also had more leisure time and fewer social commitments, which made them more susceptible to impulse buying.

"We found that men were looking for a new identity, a strong identity," says Hecht. In part, that search had been driven by generational economics, which by the early 2000s had left young men fresh out of high school or college with few clear career paths or reliable ways of earning a basic income. The real hourly wage for the average American had remained almost unchanged between 1973 and 2003, rising from $10.49 an hour to $10.53 an hour, according to a report from the Economic Policy Institute. Over the same period, the value of the real minimum wage had fallen from $7.65 an hour in 1973 to $6.66 in 2003, while rents and the cost of living had exploded. After the 9/11 attacks, the US had fallen into a recession that wiped out 2.4 million jobs, while unemployment rates hit 6 percent. The number of high school graduates who worked jobs with employer-provided health insurance had been cut in half between 1989 and 2003, and for college graduates, only 41 percent got jobs with health insurance after graduating in 2003, compared with 61 percent in 1989. With interest rates close to zero and banks rolling back requirements for loan qualifications, consumer debt ballooned as many turned to credit cards and bank loans to support themselves. By 2004, the average US household had more than $7,000 in credit card debt, more than triple what it had been in 1986.

Against that kind of generational decline, there had been a strong incentive for young people, and men in particular, to define themselves through something other than families or careers. Pastimes gradually became personas. People no longer just followed a local sports team but evolved into all-purpose fans who followed every team and league as zealously as voting board members. People didn't just play video games, they became "gamers." Men with an interest in fashion became metrosexuals. Everything people used to fill their free time came with some built-in expectation that it would represent something personal, as if the products had come to endorse the people using them. Hecht had created Spike to speak to this generation of men like a friend they hadn't known they had. He'd chosen the name because it sounded rugged, connoting industrial objects like the spikes found in railway ties or medieval weaponry, and aggressive actions like spiking a volleyball or football after a big play. More important, it was a person's name, suggesting a kind of surrogate friendship that viewers could rely on, even as everything around them seemed to be dissolving into thin air.

The most popular programming on Spike tended to be reality shows that offered a glimpse of vocational wish fulfillment, with young men given the chance to compete for the kinds of dream jobs they'd only be eligible for on a television set. *I Hate My Job* was an early hit, improbably hosted by Reverend Al Sharpton. It followed the lives of eight men who had recently quit their jobs to pursue careers in standup comedy, male modeling, and nightclub promotion. There was also *The Club*, which followed the travails of managers at Ice, a newly opened disco in Las Vegas famous for a dance floor flooded with a special liquid nitrogen fog. *The Joe Schmo Show* was another early hit, which followed a regular guy who was tricked into thinking he was competing against seven other people for a $100,000 prize in an imaginary reality series called "Lap of Luxury." The other contestants were hired actors whom producers asked to coerce the unwitting protagonist into more and more extreme behavior for comic effect.

Kay had helped put together this lineup with Hecht, whom he had first worked with at Nickelodeon, where he helped oversee shows like *SpongeBob SquarePants* and *The Adventures of Pete & Pete*. Viacom had given Spike a programming budget of $75 million a year, and it had largely fallen to Kay to make sure that money could stretch for more than eight thousand broadcasting hours a year. Nearly a third of the budget—an estimated $24 million a year—went to a deal with WWE they'd inherited from TNN, which gave them roughly 260 hours of original content annually, including *Monday Night Raw*. Kay had divided the remaining $50 million among a few adult-oriented animated series, like the Pamela Anderson vehicle *Stripperella* and *Ren & Stimpy: Adult Party Cartoon*, alongside syndicated reruns of *CSI: Crime Scene Investigation*, *American Gladiators*, *Unsolved Mysteries*, and *Blind Date*. There were also shows that repurposed newsreel footage and archival material into magazine-style compilation shows like *World's Wildest Police Videos*, *100 Most Beautiful Women*, and *Takeshi's Castle*, an obscure obstacle course show that had aired in Japan in the 1980s, which Spike paid to re-edit and overdub with sarcastic, and frequently offensive, commentary from American voice actors. While Kay still wasn't sure how the UFC could fit into Spike's lineup, the chance to add more original programming without having to tie up more of Spike's already limited programming budget was appealing, and he continued to meet with Lorenzo and White, trying to find the right idea for a show. If airing live fights wouldn't work, Lorenzo and White suggested a reality series about White's day-to-day life as a mixed martial arts promoter. Kay liked the idea better but still wasn't sure it would work. Would viewers really see running the UFC as a dream job? Was being a fight promoter anyone's fantasy other than White's?

Frustrated by the response, Lorenzo and White decided to invite Kay to see a UFC event in person, hoping the experience might give him some ideas of his own. Kay agreed and flew to Las Vegas for UFC 47, in early April 2004. The night was a turning point for Kay. "It was just magical," he says. Instead of watching old DVDs on his living room television, he found himself among a sellout crowd of 11,437 in the Mandalay Bay Events Center, most of whom were wearing branded mixed martial arts T-shirts and drinking Budweiser from the arena concessions, a brand that had been one of Spike's biggest sponsors. The main event was the long awaited match between White's two former clients, Tito Ortiz and Chuck Liddell, who had finally agreed to fight each other. The crowd was deafening as the men made their entrances—raucous cheers for Liddell and an avalanche of boos for Ortiz. Celebrities filled the cage-side VIP section, including Shaquille O'Neal; George Clooney; Juliette Lewis; Joe Pantoliano; Zab Judah; MTV host Carson Daly, who wore a *Full Contact Fighter* T-shirt; Cindy Crawford and her husband Rande Gerber, the bar and restaurant mogul who was a friend of Lorenzo's.

Ortiz walked into the arena carrying a double-sided flag representing both Mexico and the United States, while boxing star Fernando Vargas walked behind him yelling like a hype man in a music video. When Ortiz entered the cage, he took off his Punishment-branded beanie and threw it into the crowd, but a few seconds later someone threw the beanie back into the cage, prompting an even bigger cheer. When Liddell finally knocked Ortiz out a little over thirty seconds into the second round, it felt as monumental as Kirk Gibson hitting a home run in the bottom of the ninth inning in the 1988 World Series, or Michael Jordan scoring thirty-eight points with a flu in the 1997 NBA Finals. The cheers had the intensity of an earthquake, and the fact that few people outside the arena were even aware such an extraordinary moment in sports history was taking place gave it even more power for the drunken lunatics who had ensured they would be there to see it in person.

For Kay, it was a dealmaking night, and when he met with White and Lorenzo after, he promised they would find a way to get the UFC onto Spike in some form or another. "I was just like, This is amazing," says Kay. "This isn't what I expected at all. We should figure this out."

5

A REVERSE SOCIALIZATION PROCESS

White hated the idea of turning the UFC into a reality show. It had been the one approach he wanted to avoid, but after months lost to the limbo of meeting rooms and conference calls, he accepted that a reality series would be the only way forward with Spike. White convened a meeting with Piligian and Zuffa's small production team to come up with a concept that Kay could sell to the more conservative Viacom executives he and Hecht reported to. "I finally just said we're pulling an all-nighter," White said. "So we went into my office at 10 p.m. and came out at 4 a.m. with the basic concept for the show." Instead of a behind-the-scenes documentary series, they settled on a standard formula used by shows like *Survivor*, *The Bachelor*, and MTV's *The Challenge*. Eighteen fighters would live together in a Las Vegas mansion and compete in a series of weekly stunts. The losing group would have to eliminate a teammate, and at the end of the season, the two finalists would have to fight each other in the octagon. Whoever won the fight would win the tournament and be offered a six-figure contract to compete in the UFC. As soon as Kay heard the concept, tentatively called *The Ultimate Fighter*, he knew he would be able to sell it. "It was perfect as a pitch," says Kay. "It was like, Okay, now the audience can get to know who these guys are. They'll understand the discipline, the training, the rigor, the respect. You start to know them as characters, you figure it out, and it ends in a fight thirteen weeks later. By then, hopefully they'll be prepared."

Freston approved the pitch when Kay and Hecht presented it to him, and Lorenzo asked Piligian to help produce the show, which would consist of twelve episodes. Each would last forty-three minutes, leaving seventeen minutes of advertising time that Spike and Zuffa would split. It would be the biggest bet Frank III and Lorenzo had made on the UFC, and if it failed would likely be the last. Piligian put together a budget and shooting schedule for fifty-two days of filming in Las Vegas, which would cost roughly $10 million, more than an entire year of revenue for the UFC. Ortiz and Ken Shamrock were the first choices to coach the two rival teams of fighters. Both were interested, but negotiations quickly fell apart over money. So White offered the coaching jobs to Couture and Liddell, thinking they could rematch for the light heavyweight championship at the end of the season. Zuffa offered each $800 a week for the eight-week shoot, the equivalent of less than 5 percent of the purse both had earned for their most recent fights. According to Liddell, it was a sum so low that his manager, Jim Gallo, dropped him after he insisted on taking it.

White and Joe Silva spent much of the spring and early summer looking for regional fighters to cast as contestants. Two of Couture's training partners were offered parts on the show, Nate Quarry and Chris Leben, the latter a charismatic but uncontrollable twenty-five-year-old with flame-dyed hair. White found another candidate when he stopped by a local gym in Las Vegas, where he saw an undefeated twenty-six-year-old from Boston named Alex Karalexis holding his own in a sparring session with current UFC middleweight contender Phil Baroni. On a trip to Boston, White recruited Kenny Florian after seeing him compete in a small event called *Combat Zone 7: Gravel Pit*. It was just Florian's third professional fight, and he lost to a five-year veteran with a twenty-two-and-two record, but White had been impressed with Florian's intensity and refusal to concede even in a clear mismatch.

As White was casting, Lorenzo grew anxious about another fight-focused reality series he feared could undercut the UFC's *The Contender*, which was being produced by *Survivor* mogul Mark Burnett for NBC. Burnett had already undercut Lorenzo with another series, called *The Casino*, which debuted on June 14, 2004, less than two weeks after *American Casino*, which followed the inner workings of the Golden Nugget in downtown Las Vegas. NBC had targeted a March 2005 launch for *The Contender* and had committed a reported $30 million to produce fifteen episodes, with Sylvester Stallone and Sugar Ray Leonard as hosts. Though it was built around boxing instead of cage fighting, Lorenzo was worried it would hurt *The Ultimate Fighter*'s chances, and he began pressuring Kay to debut their series as far in advance of *The Contender* as possible. But Spike had already set its schedule for the fall and spring and the only available time slots were in off-hours outside of prime time. The company had also allocated its marketing budget for the rest of the year to other shows, so he knew it wouldn't be able to help Zuffa market the launch. Kay was skeptical that Zuffa would be able to put the production together on such a tight timeline, even with Piligian's help. "He was really pushing me hard," says Kay. "I was like, Can you be ready? Can you deliver a show?"

When Lorenzo insisted on a January debut, two months before *The Contender*, Kay decided the best option would be to slot it after *WWE Monday Night Raw*, in the spot that had previously been taken by Spike's re-edited episodes of *Takeshi's Castle*. Because Vince McMahon had a special agreement that his shows could run more than an hour depending on the storytelling needs of the episode, *The Ultimate Fighter* would have the unusual start time of 11:08 p.m. Despite the late-night positioning, the spot would guarantee a large lead-in audience, and would serve as a good barometer for how appealing the UFC would really be to the WWE's young and mostly male audience. Lorenzo agreed, and everyone at Zuffa rushed to have everything in place for filming to start in September, several months earlier than they had initially expected.

The hasty nature of the production was apparent to all the cast members as soon as they arrived on set for the first day of filming. The number of contestants had been cut to sixteen instead of eighteen to accommodate the fast start, and when they walked into the large tract home that Zuffa had rented for the shoot in a North Las Vegas suburb, many immediately complained about the amenities, especially the kitchen, which had been stocked with Hot Pockets, Snickers ice cream bars, and other processed junk foods. It was as if the production crew, many of whom had little firsthand knowledge of fighting, had been preparing to host a kids' slumber party instead of professional athletes. As cameras captured the first few hours of the fighters in the house, choosing bunk beds and jumping into the backyard pool, White arranged an impromptu grocery store run and personally delivered fresh meats and vegetables to the house later that afternoon. The gym Zuffa had arranged for the training sessions was an even stranger fit. Zuffa had acquired a small warehouse in an industrial office park behind the Palms, beside a long, trash-filled drainage ditch where haphazard homeless encampments would sometimes peek out of the concrete storm tunnel that opened onto the ditch. The production team had filled the warehouse with heavy bags, treadmills, grappling mats, and a small octagon for sparring sessions, but they couldn't run the air-conditioning system during filming because of noise and electrical load, which forced fighters to suffer through long and intense workouts with no ventilation. In the opening episode, Couture and Liddell evaluated the fighters in the sweltering gym as they ran through a gauntlet of training exercises that concluded with a thirty-minute treadmill run, during which the pace automatically increased every five minutes, from five miles an hour to twelve miles an hour. It drove several into serious dehydration and some began vomiting after.

The elimination challenges at the end of each episode seemed as poorly planned as everything else. The first required each team to carry their respective coach on their shoulders while seated in a two-hundred-pound La-Z-Boy recliner. The teams would then have to move the recliners through a race course circuit that had been set up on the rocky shores of Lake Mead, thirty miles outside Las Vegas. Almost immediately, fighters began getting injuries which they worried might prevent them from being able to compete in the finale. One of the fighters, Mike Swick, tripped and fell on the rocks on Lake Mead, opening a huge gash on his shin that he worried could sideline him for the rest of the season. "That's a dumb thing to say you got injured by," says Swick. "How'd you get injured? I was carrying Randy Couture on a La-Z-Boy across Lake Mead. It was so pointless."

After two weeks of filming, the production team began to have many of the same concerns as the fighters. They were making a show about how demanding and technically complex mixed martial arts was, but no one was ever shown fighting. Instead, fighters were supposed to prove their worth in what looked like overcomplicated games from a child's birthday party. It felt as if they had gotten the formula wrong.

After discussing options with the production team, Lorenzo and White decided to restructure the show so that they could build each episode around an actual fight. Though no one from the crew told the cast members about the change in format, many began to suspect something was happening behind the scenes. "As we were walking in [to the gym one morning] we saw the red and blue chairs out front," says Swick.

"They just spray-painted them and they were sitting on cardboard boxes and we were like, Oh shit, that's corner chairs. There's only one reason why they would have corner chairs painted blue, so we were like, Oh man what's going on?" The fighters were initially excited by the change, but when they learned they would also have to weigh in at their officially sanctioned weight class before every bout, potentially having to lose as much as twenty pounds or more on just a few days' notice, eagerness turned into uncertainty. "We were kind of just stuck in the moment. Like, Whoa, whoa, whoa, we're going out there and fighting and not getting paid?" Karalexis would later say. While none of the cast members had been able to make cage fighting their sole source of income, most had received at least a few hundred dollars for being willing to fight, even in the smallest regional promotions. "This is a business," Karalexis said. "We risk our health, a lot of things, every time we get in there. You break a hand, you break an arm, an ankle, and you're not getting paid for it? That's an issue."

Lorenzo had been at the gym with the production crew when the announcement was made—he'd made a habit of stopping by the set on his way to or from the Station offices at the end of the day. As he saw resistance spreading through the cast, he called White, who was working at Zuffa's offices a ten-minute drive away, and asked him if he could talk to the fighters. "I literally walked out of a meeting, jumped in my car and broke every driving law in the state of Nevada," White later said. When he arrived on set, he was so agitated that he forgot to turn his car engine off. It was unthinkable to White that anyone would put money above opportunity. "I'm not happy right now," White told the fighters, as they lined up in their team jerseys along the wall. He could feel himself getting angrier as he spoke, fanned by flickers of fear that the show might be in jeopardy because some ungrateful cast members wanted a few thousand dollars more.

"Does anybody here not want to fight?" White said. "Did anybody come here thinking that they would not fight?"

The only answer came from Bobby Southworth, a thirty-four-year-old veteran who had fought in regional promotions for five years and once in Pride, against former UFC champion Vitor Belfort. "Some of us thought we weren't going to fight until the finals," Southworth said. "None of us have a problem with the fighting, Dana. Nobody here has a problem with that."

Southworth had been singled out for the first fight of the season, against Lodune Sincaid, an undefeated light heavyweight from North Hollywood. Southworth hadn't fought in over a year, and his weight had crept up to 230 pounds during the time off. He had expected to lose some of it during daily training sessions over the eight-week shoot, but because of the format change he would suddenly have to lose twenty-five pounds in two days to make the 205-pound weight limit for light heavyweight.

"I can't explain to you what a unique opportunity this is," White said, enervating himself as he spoke. "You have nothing to fucking worry about every day except coming in and getting better at what supposedly you want to do for a living." As he spoke, he grew into an intimidating figure, completely unlike the cautious and ingratiating man in a suit that had appeared during Zuffa's first broadcast in 2001. "We picked who we believe are the best guys in this country right now," White went on. "We did, and you guys are it. Fuckin' act like it, man. Do you want to be a fighter? That's the question. It's not about cutting weight, it's not about living in a fuckin' house. It's about, Do you want to be a fighter? It's not all signing autographs and bangin' broads when you get out of here. It's not. It's no fuckin' fun man, it's a job just like any other job. So the question is not, Did you think you had to make weight, did you think you had to do this—Do you want to be a fuckin' fighter?" As he spoke, the cast fell into a sheepish silence. White ended with a disorienting combination of threat and affection, which the fighters instinctively responded to with a submissive silence. "Anybody who says they don't [want to be a fighter], I don't fuckin' want you here," White said. "And I'll throw you the fuck out of this gym so fuckin' fast your head'll spin. It's up to you, I don't care. Cool? I love you all, that's why you're here. Have a good night gentlemen."

White knew as soon as he walked out of the gym that he had "flipped out." As his temper subsided, fear followed. Everything he had done and said had been recorded and would be played back on national television. "I don't even remember exactly what I said to them or anything like that," he said. "I was like, Oh, man, this is going to be bad." For the people who worked with White, his tendency to turn arguments into all-or-nothing standoffs was familiar, but in public, he had forced himself to behave like the successful entrepreneur instead of an ex–bar bouncer who'd developed Ménière's disease and had had his hearing permanently damaged after losing a street fight, one of many his mind and mouth had led him into over the years. White had always been kind and cordial to Tommy Rojas, who had previously been Southworth's manager. "When I met Dana, I never saw him act the way he does on TV," says Rojas. Rojas had first gotten to know White in late 2000, just before Zuffa acquired the UFC, when they were both focused on representing fighters, and he had never heard White raise his voice or swear.

For the cast, White's sudden loss of temper persuaded them, grudgingly, to accept the show's new format and fight one another for free. Though it felt exploitive, so too had life outside of the show. On camera, they at least had the chance to get something in return for that exploitation. "I don't have anywhere to go after this," Lodune Sincaid admitted after White's speech. "I have no job, no apartment, no car." Swick had an apartment and car, but had been working three jobs to support himself and pay for his training costs—painting houses, pressure washing driveways, and tending bar at night. "I was fighting just to not have to go back to work," he says. "I was going all or nothing." For Quarry, there was no work to go back to. "I just stood there with my arms crossed and listened because, to me, this was, Yeah, I do want to be a fucking fighter," he later said. "That's why I quit my job with a two-year-old baby at thirty, to try and pursue this dream. So if you tell me I have to fight—I get to fight, to pursue that dream—well, that's what I signed up for."

The addition of regular elimination fights escalated tension that had been building in the house, with many in the cast starting to crack under the pressure of being filmed around the clock. A production trailer was parked next to the house with a feed of what was being filmed, and the camera crew would remain in the house for up to an hour after everyone went to sleep in case there were any late-night incidents. "If they saw us talking or some shit going on, they would just storm in there," Swick says. "The second they would see something, the camera crew would run in, they would be there in seconds." The crew had conditioned the cast to not just expect intrusions but to monitor their own conversations for potentially filmable material. "There was a term they used called 'conserve reality,' so anytime we had good conversation in the van or somewhere else there wasn't cameras, the producers would yell out, Conserve reality, guys, conserve reality," says Swick. "Which meant we basically had to stop that conversation or continue when we got in front of the cameras."

Producer Andrea Richter described the filming as a psychological experiment that would inevitably push people toward atypical and extreme behavior. "That's the thing that outsiders don't necessarily know coming into this situation is that being in this house and not having anyone you can talk to and not having any control over your lives, it affects people in ways that they never understand or have any grasp of," Richter told the *Canadian Press*. "It's a very strange environment for these guys. So a lot of times are they going to do things that they would do at home? No, they're going to act completely different." Forrest Griffin, a former college football player from Georgia who was competing as a light heavyweight, said it took him two weeks to return to his old normal self after the production ended. "It's a reverse socialization process," he would later say. "There are sixteen dudes with that knuckle-dragger in them, and if you put them in that situation, they'll devolve. We all turned into cavemen."

Midway through filming, the producers tried to return a small sense of normalcy to the cast by allowing them a night out in Las Vegas. They were treated to dinner at the Hard Rock Hotel and Casino and given tickets to a Kid Rock concert afterward. Some cast members drank excessively, including Leben, who had earned a reputation after drinking himself to a near blackout state on the first night of filming and then urinating on fellow contestant Jason Thacker's pillow. Following the Kid Rock concert, the heavily intoxicated cast returned to the house. Leben continued to drink from the stocked bar the producers kept in the house throughout filming, as did Southworth and Josh Koscheck, a former All-American wrestler who had turned to mixed martial arts after graduating in 2002. The trio eventually began arguing, and Southworth called Leben a "fatherless bastard." Just as a punch might send someone into unconsciousness, the phrase sent Leben back in time. Overwhelmed by too many conflicting emotions—rage, pain, embarrassment, confusion—the only response was a full shutdown.

As hard a drinker as his son, Leben's father had abandoned his family when Leben was two years old. Though no one on the show knew at the time, Leben had met his father again for the first time just before filming began. Over drinks in a casino bar, his father, still no closer to stability or sobriety, asked Leben for money to help him survive until his next pay-check, as if Leben, simply by virtue of being on television, might have some hidden surplus of cash to share. The experience had unsettled Leben, like catching a glimpse of yourself in a mirror in the dark. It had been both a comfort and a terror, reminding him he was no less alone with his father in the flesh than he had been as a child growing up without him. Drunk and hurting after the Kid Rock concert, Leben decided he would sleep on the lawn in the backyard rather than go back into the house, fearing that he might lose control of his temper. Waking in a wet puddle on the grass to see Southworth and Koscheck laughing at him was the last memory Leben would have of the night. After, he snapped into a dissociative rage and chased Koscheck and Southworth back into the house. He punched through the glass window in the front door and sheered the skin off the knuckle of his left index finger to the bone. Inside, he punched his way through Koscheck's bedroom door before Griffin eventually subdued him and the producers separated him from the rest of the cast and took him to the emergency room just as the first rays of light broke over the horizon. The event opened just the kind of social schism that reality television had been designed to both encourage and decry. Some felt Leben should be kicked off for safety concerns, and others wanted Southworth and Kos-check removed for baiting Leben to his breaking point.

For White, the simplest solution was to let Koscheck and Leben fight each other in the following week's elimination bout. The crew seized on the rupture and framed it as the season's centerpiece, a prismatic conflict spread across two episodes that would culminate in a fight to restore the group's moral symmetry by giving Leben the chance to punish Koscheck. Instead, the match showed that fighting rarely gives moral clarity to con-flict; it simply proved who would win in a fight between the two, and that was, in the cold logic of combat, Koscheck, a lifelong athlete and colle-giate standout who used his wrestling to smother Leben for two rounds before winning a clear but anticlimactic decision. It was a cruel and cold moment, underscoring the fact that fairness was fleeting in mixed martial arts. It was just as often a sport where bullies triumphed over their vic-tims, who could fall still further than was thinkable, in spite of their hard work and self-sacrifice.

After Leben was eliminated, the second half of the season seemed to deflate, as if the plot had resolved itself and the remaining players were trying to figure out why they were still on stage. Stephan Bonnar, a jiu-jitsu specialist from Chicago who trained with Carlson Gracie, grew irritated with Diego Sanchez's inconsiderate habit of taking the heads off asparagus for his "health shakes." Near the end of filming, a house-wide conspiracy spread alleging that Sam Hoger was hoarding free Tapout apparel from the gym. In early November, the crew officially wrapped filming on the last episode, and the cast was sent back home while the editors rushed to finalize the cut on the first few episodes of the season, which were scheduled to debut on January 17, 2005.

While Spike didn't have marketing funds available because of the quick turnaround, the company promoted the launch on *Monday Night Raw* for several weeks beforehand. Kay was less interested in the ratings than in measuring how big the dropoff would be in the handover from *Raw*, which typically peaked at between five and six million viewers. Kay figured the break-even point for *The Ultimate Fighter* would be somewhere between 700,000 and 800,000 viewers. The first episode more than doubled that number, with 1.667 million viewers. And the ratings held steady through the first four episodes, bringing in an average 1.4 share for the time slot. When the episodes featuring Leben's meltdown hit the air in February, ratings jumped to more than two million viewers, and the sixth episode, which showed Leben's elimination fight with Koscheck, brought in the highest ratings of the season, with an audience share of 1.8. Despite the higher-than-expected ratings, Spike remained noncommittal about the future. Ahead of the season finale, White had flown to New York to meet with Viacom executives in the hopes of signing a deal for a second season but had left empty-handed. According to White, Spike had also agreed to a full-page advertisement in *USA Today* to promote the finale, but the ad never ran. As the finale began, White was "freaking out" about the possibility that Spike might not renew the agreement.

The season finale was a full night of fights that aired live on April 9, 2005, with all of the cast mates who'd lost matches against one another on the prelims. The main card had just three fights: a main event between Ken Shamrock and a rising contender, Rich Franklin, who'd fought in the UFC since 2003, and the two *Ultimate Fighter* finalist bouts, in the middleweight and light heavyweight divisions. As the first fight, between middleweight finalists Sanchez and Florian, began, there was still no deal in place for a second season. After Sanchez easily overwhelmed a smaller and hopelessly mismatched Florian in just two minutes and forty-nine seconds, winning the first of two UFC contracts planned to be given during the event, White felt even less sure about the prospects for another season. Before the light heavyweight finale, White went into the locker rooms to wish both Bonnar and Griffin luck. "I think I cracked a joke that you would think he was the one going in there and fighting," Bonnar said, recalling how nervous White looked.

There had been little drama or buildup around the Bonnar-Griffin matchup. The two had become close friends over the course of filming and had mostly avoided the house dramas. Griffin was mischievous but kind and spoke with a gentle Southern drawl. His left ear stuck out from his head a little more than his right ear, giving his face a friendly, hound-like aura. Bonnar seemed just as likeable. Though he had adopted "American Psycho" as his nickname, he had been as conflict averse as Griffin, and often served as a mediator in the house with other cast members, de-escalating conflicts with his gentle Midwestern accent. "You had Nobody Special Average Joe One versus Nobody Special Average Joe Two," Bonnar would later say. "Not only athletically weren't we like totally gifted athletes, ego-wise we weren't projecting these huge egos and identities, which like made everyone be able to project themselves into us that night."

As the fight began, they circled each other in a slow, cautious orbit, testing each other with jabs and calf kicks. Soon these were followed by long clubbing overhands that seemed more like formal obligations than heartfelt attacks meant to do lasting harm. Then Griffin discovered he could land a short inside uppercut serious enough to snap Bonnar's head back as Bonnar marched forward. Bonnar ignored the punches and took them as signs to swing back even harder. After each exchange, they'd both stagger backward, off-balance and in a slight daze, then drift back toward each other as if they'd been magnetized. Neither seemed interested in fighting from a safer distance. Instead, as the first round wore on, they stood their ground in front of each other, feet rooted to the mat, and traded head-snapping, hair-whipping punches, until one of them had to circle away to regain his balance. "These are two walls colliding with each other and looking for a weakness," Rogan said on the broadcast.

As the blows continued, Griffin's kindly face was covered in blood, which leaked out of a new cut on the bridge of his nose. The small crowd of two thousand people inside UNLV's Thomas & Mack Center rose to their feet, applauding and howling in ecstatic disbelief. For a miraculous few minutes, it seemed as if the laws of nature had been suspended to allow the brain to absorb more direct trauma than should have been possible. At the end of the second round, the miracle began to abate, as both Griffin and Bonnar seemed to have exhausted themselves to a point where they could no longer punch with enough force to hurt the other. But they continued into the third round. There was still an extraordinary intensity in the heaving lurches, as if they would sooner be maimed for life than disengage.

When the fight ended, White jumped out of his seat and clapped as if his hands were on fire. "That's the craziest fight I've ever seen," Rogan exclaimed on the broadcast. Bonnar slumped in exhaustion against the octagon fence, propping his arms over the edge. Griffin turned him by the shoulder and they hugged for a moment, hands cradling each other's necks. As the judges' scores were collected, Lorenzo and White huddled with Piligian along the octagon fence and decided they should give both fighters UFC contracts regardless of who the judges would score the fight for.

Before *The Ultimate Fighter* had begun filming, Griffin had been on the verge of giving up mixed martial arts altogether. He hadn't competed in over a year, after suffering a broken arm in a fight he'd taken in a small coastal city in Brazil. He had managed to win that fight, despite the pain of the broken bone, but when he returned to the US he had been unable to afford treatment and had let the arm mend on its own instead, which left a large knot on his forearm. As a teenager, Griffin had dreamed of becoming a star football player and made it as far as the practice squad at the University of Georgia as a freshman. Despite having excelled in high school, he had often felt outmatched and overpowered by his college teammates. He had tried to add muscle to his lanky frame by switching to a six-thousand-calories-a-day diet and working out two to three hours a day. He lifted weights, ran wind sprints, went on long-distance runs, and tried everything he could think of to make himself into more of an athlete.

By the end of the year, he had made peace with a new idea: that he wasn't as talented as the other players on the team, and he wouldn't be able to make up the difference just by trying. His life wasn't going to play out like a movie montage, and four years wouldn't be long enough to create the happy ending he'd dreamed of as a teenager. Griffin had quit the team and taken a job as a campus police officer, where he began training in self-defense. He found the intense sessions both familiar and cathartic, and after graduating he continued training at the Hardcore Gym in Athens, Georgia. His coaches encouraged him to start fighting professionally, and soon he was driving across Florida and Georgia to compete in small regional promotions. Over two years, he recorded nine wins and two losses and beat two fighters who had previously been in the UFC, Travis Fulton and Jeff Monson. During the same period, he'd gotten a new job at the Richmond County Sheriff's Department in Augusta, and after more than a year off following his arm break he had begun to think it was time to "grow up," that cage fighting, like college football, had been a boyhood fantasy that wasn't worth derailing his life over.

In September 2004, just seventeen days before shooting was supposed to begin, he'd gotten the offer to appear on *The Ultimate Fighter* after another contestant had withdrawn. He'd accepted, but as he was walking through the Atlanta airport for his flight to Las Vegas, Griffin felt a surge of self-doubt. He had been given leave at the one decent job he'd had since finishing school and packed all of his earthly possessions into an eight-by-ten self-storage unit just for a chance to be on a reality show. "What have I done?" he thought as he walked through the airport. "Why have I done this? I didn't want to come out to Vegas, quit my job, get my ass beat, and end up with nothing." He called one of the producers from the airport and said he didn't think he could go through with it. Shortly after, White called him back while he was still in the terminal. "Convince me to do this," Griffin had said. White did just that, winding him up in the same way he had Kay, Gold, and all of the partners he'd so far been able to persuade about the UFC's bright future. If Griffin tried and failed, White counseled, it might hurt, but if he gave up before he even tried, he would have to carry the regret with him for the rest of his life. Every time he looked in the mirror, there would always be a question hanging over his life, of what he could have become, if he had had a little more faith in himself. He was already living life as the version of himself who couldn't make it as a professional fighter. But what kind of life was waiting for him if he succeeded?

As Griffin stood in the octagon after he was announced the winner by unanimous decision he beamed with glee as White presented him with prizes from the new life he was about to begin, including a glass trophy that anointed him as "the Ultimate Fighter," keys to a Scion xA, a Thump-star dirt bike, an Audemars Piguet wristwatch, and a "six-figure" con-tract with the UFC—which was in reality an eight-fight agreement that started at $8,000 to fight and $8,000 to win, and rose in $4,000 increments with consecutive wins. After collecting his prizes and allowing Bonnar to speak, Griffin rushed back to the center of the octagon realizing he had forgotten something. He grabbed the microphone and thanked the Fertit-tas for keeping the UFC alive and then he stretched his arm out to point at White who was leaning against the edge of the octagon grinning. "Hey, Dana," Griffin said, "thanks for the opportunity, brother."

As Griffin and Bonnar celebrated with their families and teammates in the arena, Lorenzo and Frank III huddled with Kay and some other ex-ecutives from Spike in a loading dock behind the arena. After seeing how the crowd had responded, Kay was determined to keep the UFC on Spike. "We were just standing there talking about it, how great a night it was, and I said, Guys, how do you want to go forward?" says Kay. "I think we have to make a deal now." As the production crew began disassembling the cage and moving lights into box trucks around them, Kay and the Fertittas laid out the terms for a new deal between Spike and Zuffa, which would include a new season of *The Ultimate Fighter*, four cards a year of free fights featuring former *Ultimate Fighter* cast members, in what would become the *Ultimate Fight Night* series. Zuffa would continue to pay for the production of *The Ultimate Fighter*, and Spike would pay a $1 million licensing fee per episode, and around $1.5 million for each of the four *Ultimate Fight Night* cards. Spike would handle all of the advertis-ing and Zuffa would own all of the rights to the shows and would be free to negotiate its own sponsorship deals for in-episode product placements and logos on the octagon mat. As they shook hands, the UFC's annual revenue more than doubled what it had been one year earlier before even a single pay-per-view had been sold, all but guaranteeing the company would turn a profit for the first time since the Fertittas had acquired it.

When the ratings for the *Ultimate Fighter* finale came out a few days later, it had outperformed every other episode of the season, drawing an average of 2.6 million viewers, and peaking at more than ten million during the Bonnar-Griffin fight. The Tapout website crashed shortly after the episode ended, as online orders jumped from around ten an hour to more than three thousand an hour. A week later, when Couture and Liddell fought at UFC 52, pay-per-view buys jumped to a reported 280,000, making it the bestselling UFC event in close to a decade, spurred by Zuffa continuously running commercials for it with the company's share of ad inventory on *The Ultimate Fighter*. Another $2.5 million came in from ticket sales at the MGM Grand Garden Arena. All together, the event grossed almost as much as the UFC had earned in all of 2003, and in the months that followed money continued to flow in frictionless streams, while White and the Fertittas rushed to expand Zuffa's production capacity. The second season for *The Ultimate Fighter* was fast-tracked for production in the summer of 2005, and Zuffa used the newfound celebrity of the cast from the first season to fill out its *Fight Night* cards on Spike, the first of which featured Leben, Bonnar, Koscheck, Florian, Swick, and several other runners-up. Zuffa also increased pay-per-view prices from $29.95 to $34.95, while White began negotiating for a better share of revenue from cable providers, which had previously been stuck at less than 50 percent. By the end of the year, the UFC's annual revenues had more than tripled, to $48.3 million, and brought in more than $6 million in profit. As White found himself fielding media requests instead of chasing them, he was exultant, and praised the transformative effect that Spike and reality television had had on the UFC. "We got people watching mixed martial arts without even realizing it," he told the *Baltimore Sun*. "And by the time they did, they were hooked."

White also ended up fielding calls from a number of media executives who'd watched the UFC's sudden and unexpected success and begun trying to find a place for themselves in it. Ari Emanuel had first read about

The Ultimate Fighter's breakout ratings in *Variety* and the *Hollywood Reporter* in the spring of 2005, and he began calling Zuffa's offices to pitch his services. Emanuel was president of Endeavor, one of the major talent agencies in Hollywood, which he'd cofounded in 1995, and which represented star actors like Adam Sandler, Matt Damon, Ben Affleck, Hugh Jackman, Mark Wahlberg, and dozens of other major celebrities, writers, and directors. Emanuel had become a notorious figure in the entertainment world, and was disliked by many of his peers. Joy Harris, a literary agent who worked with Emanuel early in his career, described him as "cocky, ambitious, and arrogant. Oh my God, this kid, you wanted to pinch him on one cheek and slap him on the other." The HBO series *Entourage* famously caricatured Emanuel as Ari Gold, a robotic and amoral agent who tried to steer his star client's career to frequently ridiculous ends. In real life, Emanuel spoke in a galloping monotone and seemed to have conditioned his face to remain expressionless, which gave him the look of a computer model that hadn't yet been animated.

He'd started his career in the mailroom at International Creative Management (ICM), and quickly worked his way up to agent, representing television show runners and writers. Unsatisfied with how ICM was being run, Emanuel had planned to break away and start his own agency, what would become Endeavor, with three of his colleagues. Before they could finalize their plans, ICM president Jeff Berg found out and fired everyone involved. Despite its contentious start, Endeavor had grown quickly, often poaching agents and filling its own roster with some of its rivals' biggest clients. Yet, there often seemed to be no special purpose or reasoning to Emanuel's drive. Asked about his career goals in an early profile, he said, "Besides getting money and power, I haven't figured it out yet."

White hated Emanuel when they first met, after his initial barrage of calls. To Emanuel, it didn't make sense to tie up all of the UFC's programming with one broadcaster. He was sure the promotion would be able to grow even faster by partnering with a range of different networks, each of whom would have to compete against the others for the right to air a portion of the company's content, just as the NBA, the NFL, and MLB all had contracts with multiple networks. The message was appealing, but the messenger wasn't. Emanuel reminded White of everyone who had told him "No" throughout his career, someone in a suit who thought he knew better because he had a Rolodex filled with all the right names. As a test to see whether Emanuel could deliver anything close to what he was promising, White asked if Emanuel could get the UFC a deal with HBO, one of the prestige networks in boxing that White had always coveted.

HBO Sports executives had mostly turned their noses up at the UFC in the past. Seth Abraham, who had signed Mike Tyson to an exclusive ten-fight contract in 1986, and who helped build HBO Boxing throughout the 1990s, thought the UFC was ridiculous and would ruin the network's reputation if it ever agreed to air the sport. "When HBO attaches itself to boxing, it attaches itself to Joe Louis, Sugar Ray Robinson, and Muhammad Ali. It attaches itself to history, achievement, and glory," he said in an interview with the boxing site *Seconds Out*. "UFC has none of those things, and it will tarnish HBO's boxing franchise. Will UFC get good ratings? Probably. But so would naked boxing." Ross Greenburg had replaced Abraham as president of HBO Sports in 2000, but he proved to be equally skeptical about the UFC, as were most of HBO Sports' production team. "What I see with the UFC are bar fights," HBO's Jim Lampley said in 2006. "They may be very good bar fights, but they're still bar fights."

Instead of trying to change Greenburg's or Lampley's minds, Emanuel simply went around them and pitched the UFC to HBO CEO Chris Albrecht. Albrecht had built his career on gambling with what could be made to seem like good taste, championing unconventional hits like *Sex and the City*, *Da Ali G Show*, *The Sopranos*, *The Wire*, and *Deadwood*. *Sopranos* creator David Chase described him as "an impetuous guy who believes in his own convictions and is not afraid to say them, but they do not come from a place of fear and worry. They come from a place of excitement, from a little bit of a warlike stance." One of Albrecht's worries was HBO's audience aging out of its programming. "We need to make sure we're not your father's HBO," he said in an interview with *Variety*. Unlike Greenburg, Albrecht was less concerned with the UFC's lack of a dignified past. He was convinced that the sport would have a long future and he wanted Greenburg to make sure HBO Sports would be a part of it.

Negotiations began grudgingly, in the spring of 2006, with the idea that the UFC would produce an additional four to five events a year exclusively for HBO. The events would occupy a middle tier between Spike's

Fight Night cards and pay-per-view events, where championship fights were expected to almost always be the main event. HBO would handle the production of each UFC event it aired through its own in-house team, something the company had considered a standard requirement. That was a problem for the UFC, which had always managed its own productions through ConCom Inc., an external production company in Connecticut founded by early ESPN executive Scotty Connal and his son Bruce. SEG had originally contracted with ConCom to handle its pay-per-view productions in the 1990s, and the Fertittas had continued the relationship. To Lampley, a longtime sports commentator who had also covered the Olympics, the NFL, and Wimbledon, there was something suspicious about the UFC handling its own productions. "We're talking about an organization where the promoter has hired the commentators," he would later say. "Now that's an entirely different kind of broadcast than what we do or what anybody in boxing does. That's really a lot more like pro wrestling. Because then they tell the story that they want to tell."

After having invested so much time and money to modernize the UFC's event production, White was especially reluctant to give up control, but they agreed to consider letting HBO handle the production on the condition that the UFC approve all of the changes it would make to the presentation. In 2006, a team from HBO Sports drew up a list of everything they would do differently, which they presented to Zuffa. The scope of the list shocked White and Lorenzo. The HBO team wanted to change almost everything, including making their own pre-fight introduction videos, lowering the volume of fighters' walkout music, and having fights take place in a roped-off ring like Pride rather than the UFC's iconic octagonal cage. "I think that's when Dana was like, Wait a second," says Epstein, who had transitioned from external counsel to Zuffa's full-time general counsel. "We've controlled our own destiny, we've controlled our own brand, our look and feel is unique and special, and then we're gonna essentially allow HBO to slap their production standards and all that [on our event]?" According to Epstein, White and Lorenzo were also concerned that letting HBO Sports handle the live event production could keep Zuffa from signing deals with broadcasters in territories outside North America that wouldn't be covered by HBO Sports. "If you got Jim Lampley with the HBO mic sleeve talking about the event, you can't use

any of that on any other platforms around the world," says Epstein. With
Zuffa controlling the production, it could theoretically send one master
live feed to broadcasting partners all over the world, and allow each to
overlay its own graphics and logos on top.

Though international broadcasting deals were a fraction of the UFC's
total revenue in 2006—just $1.8 million compared to the more than
$27 million that *The Ultimate Fighter* brought in from Spike, and far less
than the $87 million that residential pay-per-views would bring in for
the year—Lorenzo had made expansion outside the US a priority. In October 2006, Zuffa hired Marshall Zelaznik to oversee that expansion, a
job that required him to relocate from New York to London. While his
role sounded grandiose, Zelaznik spent most of his days alone with a laptop working in a Caffè Nero, a chain of sterile espresso shops that offered
cheap caffeine, free Wi-Fi, and long-term seating. Zelaznik had initially
been skeptical of the UFC. He'd previously worked at In Demand, where
he specialized in sports broadcasting, negotiating deals with the English
Premier League, the International Olympic Committee, HBO Boxing,
and Showtime Boxing. Zelaznik had first met White in 2003, at a conference about the broadcasting industry in New York. White had been trying unsuccessfully to get a meeting with Zelaznik to talk about improving
Zuffa's pay-per-view deal with the cable giant, and instead decided to
speak with Zelaznik in person after the panel. "I didn't quite understand
mixed martial arts and I didn't quite understand UFC," he would later say.
That changed after White persuaded him to come see UFC 47 in person,
the same event that had persuaded Kay to put the UFC on air. "That was
the fight that really changed it all for me," Zelaznik said. "It was in Vegas
and it was the most compelling thing I'd ever seen."

In London, Zelaznik spent months calling and emailing every broadcasting contact that he could find, and he quickly learned to mirror
White's work ethic and intensity. "We're a brand that will be your best
friend and your worst nightmare," Zelaznik said, echoing a phrase White
often used himself. "We'll give you a tape and then we're on the phone
with you every week saying, How did it do? What else do you need?
Are you running a tune-in spot? Oh, you don't have anyone to create a
tune-in spot? We'll create it. Send us your graphics, we'll produce it." One
of the first breakthroughs in Europe came with plans to host an event in

Manchester, England, UFC 70, which was also tentatively targeted to be the first event aired by HBO in North America. Zelaznik helped finalize a deal with the Irish broadcaster Setanta Sports, which also broadcast across the UK and in parts of Africa, to air the event as a pay-per-view in Europe. Yet, with just weeks to go before the event, Zuffa and HBO still hadn't come to terms on how to handle production. With commitments already made to Setanta, the UFC suddenly found itself with the possibility of not being able to broadcast in North America. With the deadlines already passed to book time from North American pay-per-view broadcasters, White persuaded Spike to air the event as a free broadcast instead of a pay-per-view.

Executives at Spike were eager to get as much UFC programming as possible. In 2005, just as *The Ultimate Fighter* was peaking, Spike's agreement with WWE had come to an end and Spike had decided not to renew it, in part because of the flat ratings and a diminishing interest in pro wrestling from advertisers. That had freed up more than $25 million of Spike's programming budget and opened up dozens of hours that needed to be filled each week. Zuffa had accommodated them by creating even more shoulder programming for the network, including an anthology series that repackaged old fights, called *UFC Unleashed*, and a biography series called *All Access* hosted by Rachelle Leah, one of the UFC's regular "Octagon Girls," who walked the perimeter of the cage in bikinis in between rounds. There was also a newsmagazine series hosted by Rogan called *Inside the UFC*, and *Countdown to the UFC*, a pseudo-documentary series that promoted the main event fighters for upcoming pay-per-views.

While Zuffa had only four people working full-time in its production department, the company relied heavily on external contractors to keep up with the huge volume of programming it was expected to deliver every month. One of the biggest was Echo Entertainment Inc., a video production house in Calabasas that specialized in producing video packages for *The World Series of Poker*, the NFL, and the US Olympics Committee. Paul Cambria was a post-production supervisor at Echo and oversaw *All Access* and *Countdown* for Spike. He also helped create "barkers" and "features," respectively thirty-second- and two-minute-long video montages that would introduce fights during events. "At the time the UFC just had no infrastructure to do anything in-house," says Cambria. "We cut a piece and I remember talking with Dana, it was like one of the one and only times where Dana got on the phone, and he was just like, I want to see more blood. I want to see more blood. I'm like, What is wrong with this guy? What the fuck? He wanted the barker to be like as violent as it possibly could be." Echo kept an editor on call for the Friday and Saturday before each event, in part to be available if there was a last-minute injury or incident, but more often because White would frequently ask for last-minute changes, which could be anything from cutting in a new sound bite during a fighter interview to completely restructuring a story arc. White reacted instinctively to things he didn't like, and it was often hard to know what would or wouldn't work. "If he liked something, he'd just be like, It's fine," Cambria said. "But if he hated something it was very black and white. It was either Fine, good, or I hate this, you gotta fix it, recut the whole thing. He wouldn't really give specific notes, he'd just leave it to us to glean what he wanted. It was a total nightmare."

While it could be nightmarish, the approach had continued to deliver huge windfalls for both Spike and Zuffa. In 2006, the UFC's annual revenue swelled to $180 million, nearly triple what it had generated in 2005 and more than twelve times what the company had earned in 2004. The finale of the third season of *The Ultimate Fighter* drew 5.7 million viewers. It was the most watched event in Spike TV history, and outperformed the first game of the 2006 American League Championship Series between the Detroit Tigers and the Oakland Athletics, which had aired at the same time. The UFC also overtook both the WWE and HBO Sports as the market leader in pay-per-view, with $222 million in gross revenue, of which Zuffa took roughly $91 million, leaving the remainder to their various cable provider partners. And the company again increased the price of its pay-per-views, to $39.95, bringing in still more money. As Lorenzo and White continued to close the HBO deal with Emanuel and Greenburg, it suddenly began to feel as if maybe they no longer needed to chase after the vaunted legacy broadcasters. Lorenzo would later say he had a "gut feel" that giving HBO control of the UFC's broadcasts would kill promotion's appeal. "Our brand is about irreverence," he'd say, "it's about changing things up, the music is pumping the announcers are yelling at the top of their lungs because the music's pumping and they have to break through. And that energy that we create translates to our generation—I shouldn't say my generation, the younger generation. We figured out what that formula was and we weren't willing to let go of that."

In May 2007, the UFC lost its biggest advocate at HBO when Albrecht announced he was taking a leave of absence after he had been arrested in Las Vegas for assaulting his girlfriend in the parking lot at the MGM Grand after a boxing match between Floyd Mayweather Jr. and Oscar De La Hoya. In an email sent to staff explaining the leave of absence, Albrecht pointed to alcoholism. "I had been a sober member of Alcoholics Anonymous for thirteen years," he wrote. "Two years ago, I decided that I could handle drinking again. Clearly, I was wrong." Albrecht entered a no-contest plea and was issued a $1,000 fine and suspended sentence for the incident. In the weeks that followed, rumors circulated that other women who had worked for Albrecht had had behavioral complaints, and according to a report in the *Los Angeles Times*, HBO had paid a six-figure settlement to one dating as far back as 1991. In September, Albrecht officially cut ties with HBO and moved to IMG, a sports-focused talent agency with a client list that included Tiger Woods, Roger Federer, Rafael Nadal, Peyton Manning, Cam Newton, Daniel Boulud, Tyra Banks, and Justin Timberlake. In public, White continued to hint that negotiations were ongoing with HBO, but in October Greenburg told *ESPN* the deal was off. "After lots of discussion it became apparent that the business model doesn't make sense for either one of us," Greenburg said. "So, we agreed to go our separate ways." Despite the failure, White and Lorenzo had grown to trust Emanuel during the negotiations and decided to let him continue to represent Zuffa moving forward.

For John McCarthy, all of the changes and new faces had been disorienting. McCarthy had been with the promotion as a referee since UFC 2. He had testified in court with Meyrowitz and McLaren, and traveled to meet with the Association of Boxing Commissions to advocate for the UFC. He'd helped write the unified rules with Larry Hazard and the New Jersey State Athletic Commission in 2000. But as he'd watched newcomers like Emanuel begin to steer the sport, he struggled to see where exactly he stood with the promotion. After UFC 70, he began to think he might not have a place at all. The six-foot-four and 275-pound McCarthy had asked if the UFC would be willing to buy him a first-class ticket to London for the eleven-hour flight from Los Angeles, after hearing the promotion had booked Rogan and ring announcer Bruce Buffer in first class. The request had made its way to White, who was indignant. "What the fuck is up with you?" he'd texted McCarthy. When McCarthy apologized and said he'd be willing to fly coach if there was no other alternative, White told him not to bother making the trip. The UFC would find another referee to replace him in England.

After the event, White summoned McCarthy to Zuffa's offices and told him about how unhappy he'd been with the referees in England. "We can't have this happen again," he'd told McCarthy, as if the mistakes were somehow his. White asked if there was a way McCarthy could do more work to train other referees as the UFC continued to hold events in new locations. McCarthy had held on to his full-time job as a trainer at the Los Angeles Police Department and had already felt like he had been operating past his capacity by refereeing the UFC's events once a month. The meeting ended without any real conclusion or reconciliation. White said he would take his issues to the athletic commission instead, and ushered McCarthy out of Zuffa's offices. "I'd looked around at the army of employees bustling about preparing for a handful of upcoming events, and I hadn't recognized any of them," McCarthy wrote in his memoir. "I think it was in that moment I knew I wasn't really part of the UFC anymore."

PROBLEM CHILD

On February 24, 2007, Nick Diaz stepped out onto the arena floor in front of 12,911 fans at UNLV's Thomas & Mack Center for Pride 33: *The Second Coming*. Though he'd spent most of his still-young career in the UFC, he'd always dreamed of fighting in Pride. In the days leading up to the event, he'd imagined how the fight, against the Japanese promotion's lightweight champion Takanori Gomi, would play out so many times that it felt as if he were slipping into a memory as he made his way toward the ring in the darkened arena. The audience was filled with celebrities and other familiar faces. Harrison Ford and Chuck Norris were seated in the front row, and so was Nicolas Cage, who wore a black suit with gleaming, slicked-back hair. Lorenzo Fertitta and Joe Silva were seated three rows from the ring, watching one of their former stars make his debut for one of their biggest competitors.

Three months removed from his last fight in the UFC, Nick had been surprised by how respectfully he'd been treated by Pride. Backstage, the event staff addressed the twenty-three-year-old as "Mr. Nick Diaz," and left a platter of cold-cut sandwiches for him in his locker room before the fight. Though Nick wasn't able to eat any of the sandwiches because he kept a mostly vegetarian diet during training, the gestures made him feel appreciated in a way that he hadn't with the UFC, where ten of his twenty professional fights had taken place. Despite the reception, a part of Nick's mind remained unsure that he deserved it. "I look at my career, and past things, accomplishments that I've done," he'd later say, "it's a small little stack of stuff, is what it looks like to me. I haven't done much of anything, is what it looks like to me."

Nick had become a star as much for his disarming honesty as for his aggressive fighting style. He had a handsome sulk that made him seem older than his age, and spoke in halting floods, as if he was both

overflowing with thoughts and irritated by the work of having to make
them scrutable to others. He often ended sentences with quick question marks instead of periods—*Okay? You know?*—as if there was a part
of his own mind that he was still uncertain of. His eyes were in constant motion when he spoke, but they didn't look at things or people
so much as they scanned the distance for potential threats. He had the
detachment of someone who had been dragged into adulthood before
his time, and he often avoided direct eye contact when he spoke, as if
he were self-conscious about what he was, or had to become. "I was
meant to fight," he would later say. "I wasn't meant to do shit else, that's
for sure."

He'd created one of the UFC's most iconic moments when he
knocked out Robbie Lawler at UFC 47 with a sharp right hook that sent
him falling face-first onto the canvas. "I literally have chills," Mike Goldberg said on commentary as the crowd cheered. The moment would be
repurposed in highlight reels and cut into the opening credits sequence
for the UFC's pay-per-view broadcasts. White had hoped Nick would
help promote the UFC to a wider audience, and offered him a chance to
appear in an episode of *Blind Date*, a syndicated television series that set
up strangers on first dates that were later annotated with comic thought
balloons and superimposed animations. One of the show's field producers had been an avid UFC fan and together with White had negotiated
a full week of shows that would feature fighters awkwardly stumbling
their way through first dates. To Nick, it sounded like a terrible idea, a
chance to be humiliated by TV producers who would take every opportunity to make fun of him and his profession. White was indignant that
Nick wasn't willing to go along with anything that would help expand
the UFC's reach at a time when it was still losing money each year. According to Steve Heath, one of Nick's teammates who was in the room
at the time, the conversation quickly escalated into a shouting match.
"Nick was like, Fuck you and your stupid show," says Heath. "And Dana
was yelling back at him."

After the confrontation, Nick seemed to have suddenly fallen out of
favor with the UFC's matchmakers. His next three fights were booked
for the prelims, which weren't part of the live pay-per-view broadcast
and would only be seen by the few hundred people who'd bothered

to make it to the arena three or four hours early, or those who would later buy a DVD of the event. When Nick was finally booked for a live broadcast close to two years later, he suspected he was being used to build up the reputation of an even younger and more agreeable fighter, Diego Sanchez, the middleweight division winner from the first season of *The Ultimate Fighter*. Though it would be Nick's sixth fight in the UFC, and just Sanchez's second, Sanchez would earn more for the fight—with a disclosed payout of $12,000 to fight and $12,000 to win, compared to $10,000 and $10,000 for Nick. "He gets on a TV show and then he wins one fight and now they put him on a main event?" Nick said in the pre-fight interview. "I don't think he should be where he's at right now."

Nick lost the fight in a competitive decision, and then lost two more decisions over the next five months, mostly by being controlled by larger wrestlers who held him down as he searched in vain for submission openings. In fights, Nick seemed to seek out worst case scenarios, marching forward and throwing himself into harm's way, forcing himself into scenarios where he would have the fewest advantages, only to show that even then he was capable of surviving without breaking. It was that attitude more than his wins and losses that had made Nick a fan favorite. Even when he lost, he seemed to emerge as the better man, who'd been willing to take more risks and face more danger, while his opponents had been forced to take Pyrrhic victories, holding him down when he was just as happy to fight from his back.

The UFC was less impressed with the approach than the fans were, and initially released him in early 2006, after his third loss. A month later it offered him a chance to return as a contestant on the fourth season of *The Ultimate Fighter*, which was themed around former UFC fighters getting a second chance to fight their way back into the promotion. Nick turned the offer down, but a few months later, he replaced an injured fighter at UFC 62 on four days' notice, facing another hopeful prospect, Josh Neer. Nick unexpectedly won by a third-round kimura, a submission hold that involves rotating the opponent's arm backward at a ninety-degree angle to the point where the shoulder socket begins to tear apart. He was awarded Submission of the Night— part of a bonus program the UFC had first implemented in 2003 to reward fighters for exciting performances—and in his next fight he again won, by a second-round TKO. The performances drew attention from Pride's matchmakers, and Nick decided to sign a two-fight deal with the promotion, gambling that he would be better treated than he had been in the UFC.

The version of Pride that Nick had signed with was very different from the one that had been the global market leader in mixed martial arts for most of the past ten years. In the summer of 2006, Pride had abruptly lost its agreement with its Japanese broadcasting partner, Fuji TV, after an investigative series of stories was published in *Shūkan Gendai*, a weekly newsmagazine, documenting the promotion's extensive financial connections with the Japanese mafia. The series, published over the course of several months, made a number of damning allegations, including that the yakuza had illegally skimmed event revenues and coerced matchmakers into booking fights with favorable betting odds for yakuza-backed fighters, many of whom were also managed by people closely connected to the crime syndicate. Fuji TV management decided the scandal was too significant to ignore and terminated its contract with Pride early, effectively cutting off the promotion's single biggest source of revenue. Pride executives scrambled to replace the lost revenue by expanding its US pay-per-view operations. The company had a disappointing debut event in the US in October 2006, with weak ticket sales and several weeks of controversy after, when two fighters tested positive for steroids and a third was accused of using a fake urine sample to clear a post-fight drug test. Pride 33 would be the promotion's second event in the US, and the company had hoped it would build the reputation of some of its star fighters, who were revered by mixed martial arts fans but lacked the recent mainstream celebrity of Couture, Liddell, or Ortiz. Gomi had been one of Pride's most active and violent new stars, amassing a thirteen-and-one record since joining the promotion in 2003, most often by knockout or submission.

When the fight started, it seemed as if Gomi might be fast on his way to his fourteenth win after an early scramble left Nick on his back, trying to defend himself from a long flurry of punches. For a moment, it seemed as if the fight might play out just as every other loss Nick had had, caught beneath an opponent searching for submissions that never quite materialized while the clock ticked away at the timekeeper's table. "Gomi like a blanket, all over him!" Mauro Ranallo exclaimed on commentary. After nearly a minute and a half of smothering punches from above, Nick found enough space to lever his legs up to Gomi's shoulders and tried to spin on his back for an armbar. Gomi defended for a few seconds, then decided to stand back up instead of risking a submission. The two began trading punches, but Nick's lanky six-foot frame seemed to work against him with the shorter Gomi. Nick's long straight punches seemed too loose and free of force as they thudded off Gomi's forearms and shoulders, while the champion darted in and out of range with blinking flurries of right and left hooks, one of which crashed into Nick's temple and sent him falling backward just ten seconds after he'd gotten up. Gomi seemed surprised the punch had landed and had to jolt himself out of a planned retreat to jump back on top of Nick, again trying to land long ground punches through the slippery tangle of Nick's outstretched legs. The crowd blared with excitement, sensing an imminent ending.

Moving on instinct, Nick rolled to his knees and hunched forward in a turtle position as Gomi sent a dozen punches whipping into the side of his head and forearms. After half a minute, Nick snatched one of Gomi's wrists as he punched and tried to roll back with the arm to set up a shoulder lock, but Gomi again pulled away and stood up. The referee cued Nick to get back up and continue the fight on his feet. Again Nick inched forward throwing long half-speed punches, while Gomi countered with leaping hooks and crosses thrown from his hips. His punches continued to land, but Gomi's torso began to slouch noticeably in between exchanges. There was a labored desperation in his movements, as if each punch might be the last he would be able to throw, and so he tried to put every last bit of force into it. Nick seemed to notice too and steadily corralled Gomi back to the ropes with his own steady flood of punches. "What a slobberknocker!" Ranallo exclaimed.

With Gomi trapped, Nick held his arms straight up as if they were antlers, then spread them out to the side trying to make himself inescapable. Gomi struggled to catch his breath, his heart apparently galloping in oxygen deficit as his muscles went slack with fatigue. Nick steadily pummeled Gomi with punches to the body and the head, half-speed blows that seemed intended to disorient more than damage. "What's he doing here!? Gomi's exhausted," color analyst Frank Trigg said in disbelief as the champion staggered along the edge of the ropes trying to escape Nick's onslaught. At the end of the first round, Gomi stumbled back to his corner, barely keeping his balance. For a moment, Nick stopped in the center of the ring and raised his arms like a conductor in a symphony hall, a small braid of blood falling down his cheek from a long cut above his left eyebrow. The crowd cheered more loudly than they had all night.

As the second round began, a huge contusion had begun to form under Nick's right eye, with a horizontal gash running across it. As Nick and Gomi traded punches, blood spread across Nick's face, making it seem as if he were wearing an eye mask. Sensing a chance for a technical stoppage, Gomi began pointing at the eye and yelling to the referee that Nick couldn't see. The referee obliged and called a short time-out to have the ringside physician see if Nick's vision was too impaired. The doctor spent between two and three seconds examining the swelling and cuts, then asked Nick if he wanted to continue. Nick nodded affirmatively. As the referee restarted the fight, Nick plodded forward punching impatiently, seemingly aware he might also be racing against the time he had left, before his eye would be completely closed by the swelling. Gomi tried to counterpunch in short bursts as Nick moved forward, but his punches seemed to have lost most of the force they'd had in the first round. Hoping for time to regain some stamina, Gomi abandoned punching and ducked onto Nick's hips and took him down. Nick fell back as if he were getting into a recliner, but as he hit the mat, Nick pulled his left leg around Gomi's right arm into a gogoplata, hooking the shoulder joint in the crook of his knee and running the length of his shin bone across Gomi's throat. Nick pulled Gomi's head down into his shin, crushing his windpipe, while at the same time wrenching Gomi's shoulder to a breaking point. Gomi froze for a few seconds searching for the smallest sliver of open space to turn into to alleviate the pressure. But there was none, and he tapped in submission.

Nick stood up with his arms raised in triumph as the referee tended to Gomi, who slumped on the mat. The fans rose to their feet and howled and cheered Nick as he walked around the ring, his face covered in blood and bruises and his right eye now nearly swollen shut. As his training partners and coaches rushed into the ring to celebrate, Nick looked out into the audience, keeping a scowl on his face, as if winning had somehow made him even angrier than he had been when the fight started. Nick saw an arena full of faces who hadn't believed in him, who had paid to see him lose, in a system that had been designed to ensure he would have no other option. And he had won. Nick had beaten the lightweight champion in what most still viewed as the best promotion in the world, less than a year after the UFC had branded him a failed prospect and released him. Though the match had been booked as a non-title fight, meant to introduce Gomi to American audiences, the implication was clear. Nick was the best in the world, regardless of whether one company or another was willing to put a gold belt around his waist.

The glory was short-lived, as the Nevada State Athletic Commission flagged one of Nick's drug test samples for containing marijuana metabolites. Though not considered a performance-enhancing drug, marijuana was still illegal in Nevada and the commission treated it as a banned substance, fining Nick 15 percent of his purse from the Gomi fight, which had been just $15,000. The commission also overturned Nick's win, changing the official result to a "No Contest," and suspended him for six months. A month later it became clear that by the time Nick would be eligible to fight again, Pride would no longer be operational. The shocking announcement came at a press conference in March 2007, where White and Lorenzo announced that Zuffa would be acquiring the struggling Japanese promotion. The deal was estimated to be worth between $65 and $70 million, which included a $10 million non-compete agreement with Pride president Nobuyuki Sakakibara, who wouldn't make the transition and would be prevented from working with any other competitors for seven years. "This is really going to change the face of [mixed martial arts]," Lorenzo said from the podium in Tokyo. "Literally creating a sport that could be as big around the world as soccer. I liken it somewhat to when the NFC and AFC came together to create the NFL."

While Lorenzo and White initially said they hoped they would be able to keep Pride running in Japan, internal memos from Zuffa's lawyers suggested otherwise. An email from Zuffa's outside counsel Thomas Paschall, of Milbank, Tweed, Hadley & McCloy LLP, a New York–based law firm specializing in global finance, summarized Zuffa's position in negotiations with Pride as having been "strategic/preemptive . . . (i.e. to stop others from buying it)," and further suggested Zuffa had "seriously contemplated acquiring [Pride] only to shut their business down and use their fighters in the UFC." In a deposition, Deutsche Bank's Drew Goldman, an analyst covering Zuffa at the time, drew the conclusion, based on conversations with Zuffa personnel, that the acquisition had "unique offensive and defensive purposes" that would result "in Zuffa's roster of elite fighters expanding significantly." A month later, the UFC began booking Pride's biggest stars in UFC events, including former heavyweight champion Mirko "Cro Cop" Filipovic, who was booked for the main event at UFC 70 in April, and Quinton Jackson, who was booked in a rematch against Liddell for the light heavyweight championship at UFC 71 in May. By September, Zuffa had announced it would be permanently closing Pride and would cease to hold a regular schedule of events in Japan, whether under the Pride or UFC branding. "It makes me very angry that the US management would do this in a way that betrays the people who have supported us," Keiichi Sasahara, a former Pride public relations executive, said at the time. "We believed in Lorenzo's message of restarting Pride." White had claimed Pride's brand had been so badly damaged by its former scandals that he hadn't been able to find any Japanese broadcasting partners to work with in the first few months after the acquisition. "I've pulled everything out of the trick box that I can and I can't get a TV deal over there with Pride," he said in the weeks leading up to the announcement. "I don't think they want us there."

With the possibility of another fight in Pride gone, Nick found himself once again on the outside of his own career trying to find a way back in. After six years of self-sacrifice and an almost monastic commitment to training, it seemed as if he was back where he had been when he started, which was nowhere.

Nick had grown up in Stockton, California, an interlocking maze of suburbs surrounded on all sides by the flat and hopeless geometry of industrial farming—long, straight lines of tomatoes, strawberries, cherry and peach trees, and grapevines, grown atop dusty voids of land, all tended by migrant workers paid well below the federal minimum wage. It was both the most profitable 250-square-mile stretch of farmland in the world, and one of the poorest regions in the US. One in five lived below the poverty line in Stockton, and per capita personal income was among the lowest in California, ranked 304th out of 361 cities in the state, according to a report from the Congressional Research Service.

Nick's parents met at a diner in Stockton, where his father worked as a line cook and his mother was a server. They flirted and fell in love, and later had three children together, two sons and a daughter. Nick was the oldest, and when his father left the family, he was forced to become a stand-in parent. After school, he would come home to the thin-walled motel rooms they often stayed in while searching for more permanent housing, to look after his younger brother and sister, Nathan and Nina, while his mom went to work the night shift. His siblings were still young enough that they could lose themselves in cartoons, but Nick couldn't lose himself in anything. He was too aware in his own body, too alert in his own mind, and even at seven years old, he knew that the smell of old cigarette smoke, the footsteps of strangers in the hallways, and the unpredictable shouting matches rising up from the sidewalks were not what many of his other classmates went home to at night.

By second grade, Nick had begun to show disruptive behaviors in school. For his second-grade class photo, while all the other students smiled at the camera, Nick had turned sideways in a fighting stance and raised a fist in front of his face. In class one day, he'd gotten up from his desk and pulled the fire alarm, forcing everyone in the school to evacuate to the playground. "It's just the way he was," Gail Tutt, his second-grade teacher, would say of the alarm-pulling incident. "Nick was Nick, and Nick was going to do what he was going to do." He was later medicated for attention deficit hyperactivity disorder, and assigned to special education classes. His classmates often teased him, and occasionally even his teachers would join in. Nick was quick to defend himself and developed a reputation as a fighter, something that he came to see as an inescapable part of the environment he was growing up in. "You'd get in fights—everybody would. Out here, you get in fights when you're a kid, unless you go to a private school—and I didn't go to a private school," he'd later say.

When Nick started high school, his mother moved everyone to Lodi, an even smaller suburb ten miles north of Stockton, where she supported the family by working at a Lyon's Restaurant, a diner chain in central and northern California. She enrolled Nick in classes at Tokay High School, on a tree-lined campus with its own small football stadium, nestled in a quiet suburb of low-slung ranch houses with streets named after wine grape varietals—Pinot Noir Drive, Chenin Blanc Drive, Colombard Circle, Chianti Drive, Tawny Port Drive. Nick felt even more out of place at Tokay and would ask to be dropped off down the street from campus so his classmates wouldn't see the kind of car his mom drove. To fit in, he signed up for the swimming and wrestling teams, but he was often bored by his classes and started skipping or sleeping late. In his sophomore year he dropped out and was assigned to a continuation program, intended to help students with special needs continue their coursework and earn a diploma. Free of a conventional school schedule, Nick began smoking cigarettes and marijuana, and spent his days skateboarding and listening to metal music—the Deftones, Ill Niño, Biohazard, Nirvana, and Metallica. He also became even more interested in fighting and built a makeshift gym for himself in his mother's backyard, with a weight bench and a small sparring area, where he practiced moves he stitched together from Jean-Claude Van Damme movies he'd rent from the local Blockbuster Video.

On one trip to the Blockbuster, he found an old UFC tape among the kickboxing and wrestling videos in the special interest section. He was enthralled by what he saw and began practicing many of the strange jiu-jitsu moves he got from the tape. When a friend mentioned there was a fight gym in Lodi, called Animal House Mixed Martial Arts, in a large shopping center less than a mile from Tokay High, Nick decided to stop by. Soon he was a regular, affectionately nicknamed "the Problem Child," for his brooding and standoffish demeanor. "He'd come in, wouldn't talk much, but you could be kind of rough on him," says Steve Heath, an Animal House regular who also competed in regional promotions across California. The gym had become home to a small group of fighters that had left Ken Shamrock's gym, the Lion's Den, in Lockeford—another tiny farming town outside of Lodi—and Nick soon found himself training side by side with a number of professional fighters. Future UFC champion Jens Pulver spent a few months training at Animal House and was impressed with Nick's intensity and work ethic. "He was in there every day when I walked into the gym, already sweating, working the bag. Then, when I was leaving, he was still there, working. I remember thinking, Who is this kid?" Pulver would later say.

Nick became obsessed with training. He would spend his afternoons and evenings at Animal House, and he often kept training on his own after he left, doing wind sprints or going on long runs across Lodi at two in the morning. The harder he worked the more his dysfunctions came to seem like assets. "I would tell Nick's mom what a fast learner he was," says Heath. "She said, What? They were telling me at the school he had a learning disability. I was like, No, he's not a slow learner, he's just not interested." While still a teenager, Nick would often spar with adults, and was amazed to find he could hold his own, even against the doctors and dentists from the nicer parts of Stockton who'd sometimes come in for jiu-jitsu lessons. "I'd come home and tell my friends, like, Yo, dude, I just tapped out this guy, he's buff. I'd be like, Dude, I could choke your dad, you don't understand," Nick would later say. "I'm fourteen, I could whoop your dad's ass. I was fanatical about it then." Heath recognized a darkness in Nick's approach to training, a stubbornness that wouldn't allow him to give up, no matter how overmatched he might be. "I would watch him train for two hours, because that's what he'd do, he'd train for two hours, and if it took him two hours to get you, he'd take two hours," says Heath. "You stick Nick in a dark alley, I don't care who it was, you put two people in a dark alley and say only one guy comes out—that's what Nick was. That was his mentality."

After a few months, Heath introduced Nick to Cesar Gracie, who taught jiu-jitsu to many of Animal House's professional fighters. Gracie had his own gym in the idyllic suburb of Concord outside Oakland but would periodically make the hour-and-a-half drive into Lodi for seminars and to help fighters prepare for upcoming fights. Though less famous than other members of the enormous Gracie family, Cesar had grown up learning jiu-jitsu as if it were a second language. Rorion and Rickson Gracie were his uncles, and he had helped both establish their gyms in Southern California in the early 1990s, before moving to the Bay Area to be closer to his mother. He had opened a gym in San Jose with Ralph Gracie, whom he had also managed during his early career as both a mixed martial artist and jiu-jitsu competitor, but they had a falling out and Cesar had relocated to Concord to open his own facility. Like Nick,

Cesar had a combative streak. Heath had first met him at a "smoker" that Cesar was refereeing in a small gym in Stockton. After one fight ended, according to Heath, Cesar calmly walked across the cage and punched one of the losing fighter's coaches, a man who had briefly trained with Cesar and disparaged his training methods and gym. Cesar had a pragmatic approach to martial arts and was less doctrinaire about the purity of jiu-jitsu. He understood that he was ultimately training his students for fights, violence that had the potential to spin out of control of even the most well-thought-through techniques and theories. "His attitude was like, Do whatever it takes," says Heath.

Cesar had just started his own fight team, Gracie Fighter, with a handful of his best students, including Heath, Dave Terrell, and Gil Castillo, and helped them book fights with small events held on tribal lands around the San Joaquin Valley. Nick had become one of Heath's main training partners as he prepared for his fight against Liddell in 1999, and he suggested that Nick should join the Gracie Fighter team. Cesar was impressed with Nick and agreed to help him book a professional fight when he became legally eligible at eighteen. "I could tell Nick was a thinker," says Cesar. "He was really smart when it comes to jiu-jitsu, he was like a natural . . . very natural movement, flexible, thought about his stuff." Nick had never really thought about a career in anything, but getting paid to fight made sense to him. "I never knew what I wanted to do with my life or anything, but when I was doing better than some of these guys in training, I decided, Hey, maybe I should get paid too," he would later say.

Nick's first professional fight took place at the Gold Country Casino Resort in Oroville, California, on August 31, 2001, four weeks after his eighteenth birthday. He was scheduled as the third fight of thirteen at Warriors Challenge 15, hosted by the International Fighting Championship, one of dozens of small mixed martial arts promotions that hosted events at tribal casinos in California. Though mixed martial arts was still illegal in California—the state athletic commission had formally voted to allow it, but the governor's office refused to release the additional funding needed to oversee a new sport—tribal lands were exempt from following state law and would offer promoters event fees ranging from $50,000 to $125,000 with the hopes that some percentage of the audience would end up staying around to gamble after the fights. The Gold Country Casino was an unlikely setting for a night of cage fights. Set back in the rolling foothills of the San Joaquin Valley, the gleaming white edifice looked like a cruise ship that someone had cut into pieces and abandoned halfway between an RV park and a discount smoke shop. Inside, locals whittled down cigarettes and complimentary cups of weak coffee in between pulls at the slot machine, and just outside the rear entrance, a semi-permanent tent structure had been built in the open-air parking lot to serve as the casino's events center.

Nick didn't know anything about his opponent other than his name and the gym he trained at—Mike Wick from Team X in Sacramento, founded by UFC veteran Cal Worsham. Before the fight, one of Wick's teammates asked if Nick would agree for both sides to go easy on each other since it would also be Wick's first fight. They were both beginners, and neither would be well served by ending up with a serious injury they couldn't afford to treat. Nick thought that was the plan when he stepped toward the center of the pentagonal cage, where on some other night, people might have been dancing at a wedding reception or watching a Los Lobos concert. Instead, Wick charged him and caught Nick on the nose with the hardest punch he could throw. It was like a setup, confirmation of Nick's suspicion that the odds had been against him from the start. No matter how dutifully he had prepared, something would slip out of his control that would leave him no chance to win. The feeling enraged him, and he fought against it until three minutes and forty-three seconds later, Nick caught Wick in a triangle choke, locking his long, gangly legs in a figure-four to cut off blood flow through the carotid artery in Wick's neck. As his consciousness started to slip away into a faint white snowfall in the back of his mind, as if time itself had been turned on its side, Wick tapped in submission.

Backstage after the fight, Nick was paid $700, more than he'd ever been given for anything. Nick celebrated by allowing himself the small luxury of a used Honda ATC250R, a three-wheel off-road bike that cost him $400. But after a few celebratory weeks riding beside the irrigation ditches that broke up the fruit fields outside Lodi into mile-long squares, the thrill waned. Nick began to feel guilty about having wasted more than half his fight earnings on an overgrown toy, and he put the three-wheeler up for sale and decided to dedicate himself to training full-time. For the next several years Nick adopted a quasi-nomadic lifestyle, having his mother drive him to Concord to train jiu-jitsu with Cesar, and sometimes hitching rides with other Animal House fighters to cross to Mountain View, the small town south of San Francisco where Ralph Gracie ran his own gym and helped train UFC fighters like BJ Penn, then a highly touted prospect in the 155-pound division. Nick would tag along to Pleasanton, where one of Ralph's students, Dave Camarillo, had opened his own gym. Cesar also began driving Nick into Oakland to train at King's Boxing Gym, a renowned facility where Nick sparred with young amateur and pro boxers, including then eighteen-year-old Andre Ward, a future two-weight world champion who was then training to qualify for the US Olympic team in boxing. While Nick was frequently overmatched by the most experienced boxers at King's, he quickly earned a reputation for his indefatigability. "King's trainers quickly learned they could rotate in fresh boxers every three or four rounds to match Nick's pace," says Cesar. "Their pros would do good [against him], but after a while they would get tired. And Nick's got a head full of rocks, you can't really hurt him. You hit him as hard as you can, he just looks at you like, And? Nobody there had ever seen anything like it in their entire lives."

Cesar also began acting as Nick's manager, and helped him book fights in several regional promotions. "I realized it's not rocket science," Cesar says. "At the time managers were charging like 20 percent, it was insane. So you'd pay your manager 20 percent and you'd pay your trainer 15 percent, whatever it was. It was a ridiculous amount of money you were giving up. I said, Look, I'll do both for 15 percent. I'll represent you, and you're training at my gym anyway. So I pretty much managed the whole team at the time."

Over the next two years, Cesar booked Nick in fights as often as he could, including three times in one night in a cramped tent at the Mono Wind Casino on the pine-studded slopes of the Sierra Nevada foothills. Later, Nick traveled to Honolulu and fought on a card Heath headlined. He won a championship in the IFC, and then a second championship in a new promotion called World Extreme Cagefighting, where he'd stepped in as a late replacement for another teammate, Jake Shields, who'd developed a staph infection and couldn't be cleared

to fight. Despite his accomplishments, Nick's payouts never amounted
to more than a few thousand dollars. He was always out of money,
and among his teammates had developed a reputation for dining and
dashing at local restaurants. "I would always hear about it," says Heath,
who worked as a bar bouncer and as a sanitation manager for an industrial baker that mass-produced hamburger buns for local McDonald's franchises. "I'd always be like, Do you have money? Do I have to
pay for it?"

When Nick was finally offered a spot in the UFC, just two years after
he'd made his professional debut, it was mostly by accident. He was
booked against Jeremy Jackson, an exciting young prospect with spiky
blond hair and a tattoo of a scorpion on his chest, who'd finished four of
his last five fights by knockout. Jackson had already signed with the UFC
for a fight in the fall of 2003 but had decided to take one more booking beforehand. Nick seemed like a safe opponent. He had already beaten
him once a year earlier, in what had been Nick's first loss, a brutal first-
round knockout. In the rematch, Nick unexpectedly dominated Jackson,
smothering his punches with standing clinches, before taking him down
and finishing him with thirty seconds of uninterrupted punches from the
mount position. When the UFC learned its newest signee would be entering the promotion on a loss, it decided to offer Nick a contract and
booked him in a trilogy fight against Jackson as part of the prelims at
UFC 44, on September 26, 2003.

It should have been a vindication, but the lead-up to the fight was beset
with more unexpected complications and compromise. Nick's pay would
be close to the scant amounts he was making in regional promotions—
the UFC's standard entry-level contract at the time was just $2,000 to
fight and $2,000 to win. According to Heath, legal complications related
to an arrest after a violent street altercation added further distraction to
Nick's already truncated training camp and left him in nowhere near the
kind of shape he had hoped to be in. When Nick finally entered the octagon, in front of a mostly empty arena at the Mandalay Bay in Las Vegas,
in the second of nine fights scheduled for the night, he seemed angry but
not excited, as if he were being forced to do something he wasn't ready
for and didn't want to do. The fight had an unexpected sluggishness compared to the two earlier meetings. Nick moved at an almost reptilian pace,

attempting to repeat his earlier winning strategy of smothering Jackson in clinches and baiting him into throwing punches that Nick could duck under for takedowns. But Nick seemed a half step slower than he had been in their earlier fight, and when he got Jackson down in the first minute of the first round, Jackson worked his way back to his feet with only passing resistance from Nick, who seemed to be steadily growing more tired.

In the second round, it seemed clear that Nick was becoming fatigued, and halfway through the round Jackson was able to reverse one of Nick's takedown attempts and spent the remainder of the round above Nick trying to punch through his guard. In the third round, Nick tried to lock an anaconda choke around Jackson's neck after a sluggish takedown, but his arms were too tired to maintain the position for more than a few seconds, and Jackson was able to escape and eventually wound his way back on top. It seemed as if the fight might be on the cusp of slipping away from Nick when he suddenly trapped one of Jackson's arms as he was trying to punch. Nick swiveled his hips while keeping his hands clamped on Jackson's wrist, putting enough pressure on the back of Jackson's elbow to provoke a tap in submission.

As Nick stood in the center of the octagon after the fight, waiting for the official results to be read, he seemed dejected, as though he knew that despite winning the fight there would be nothing to show for it. Nick stared at himself in one of the four huge LCD screens that hung from the arena rafters. The bridge of his nose had been cut open, his left eye had begun to swell, and his right eye was surrounded by the dark bruising of a new black eye. He shook his head in disappointment. "Fucked up," he said to himself, as if he were all alone in the center of the arena, with almost every camera around the cage trained on him.

After Nick's marijuana suspension was up in September 2007, the options for continuing his career seemed limited. Zuffa had tried to hold on to its position at the center of mixed martial arts by acquiring as many of its competitors as possible. In December 2006, the UFC announced its first major acquisition, three months before the Pride announcement, of the World Fighting Alliance, another Las Vegas promotion that had backing from Jeremy Lappen, Couture's former manager, and which had spent lavishly to build a large roster of former Pride and UFC stars. After the acquisition was finalized, White announced that Zuffa would close the WFA, and all of the fighters still under contract would be absorbed into the UFC. That same month, Zuffa also acquired World Extreme Cagefighting. Instead of closing it, the UFC would treat the WEC as a kind of minor league to develop new talent and sign fighters who competed in weight classes below the 155-pound limit.

The companies that the UFC didn't acquire, it instead went to war with, using frequently aggressive tactics to limit their business. The biggest target was the International Fight League, a new promotion started by Gareb Shamus, the publisher of a large network of fan-centric magazines, including *Wizard: The Comics Magazine* and *Anime Insider*, and Kurt Otto, a real estate developer from New Jersey who'd grown up training in martial arts and had lately become a student at Renzo Gracie's jiu-jitsu academy in New York. Shamus and Otto had decided they could develop a promotion that was "cleaner and more professional" than the UFC, giving mixed martial arts a chance to appeal to an even more mainstream audience. "We don't want to create an underground comic book. We want to be Spiderman," Shamus told the *New York Times*.

The IFL was organized around four teams of fighters, each representing a prominent mixed martial arts gym from a different city—Los Angeles, New York, Seattle, and the "Quad Cities" region of Iowa. The teams would compete against one another during a regular season, and the one with the most victories would advance to a playoff round where their head coaches, former UFC stars like Pat Miletich, Bas Rutten, and Maurice Smith, would compete. Otto and Shamus claimed they had reached basic terms on a broadcasting deal with Fox Sports Net, and recruited several of the UFC's top executives to help launch their first season, including Zuffa's vice president of production Steve Tornabene; operations executive Keith Evans; event logistics manager Lisa Faircloth, who had previously helped White manage gyms around Las Vegas; and Shannon Knapp, who had worked as a backstage interviewer on pay-per-view broadcasts.

White was furious when he learned about the IFL. "It's a war," he would later say of his approach to competing promotions. "And in a war there's gonna be some casualties. Whether you're a fighter or an employee, you need to pick sides." According to Miletich, White called him before the start of the first season and said that any fighters or trainers who went to work with the IFL would be blacklisted by the UFC. White promised Miletich that the UFC "was going to fucking crush these guys," and he was no less harsh with Zuffa employees. "It was not a real good situation," says Burt Watson, recalling White's reaction to Faircloth and others leaving. Though most felt they were well within their rights to change employers and further their careers, White considered the departures a betrayal, and many dreaded having to explain the decision to him. "Everybody was so afraid, and very intimidated," says Knapp of her last days at the Zuffa office. White's reputation for having a temper only added to the dread many felt about leaving.

Zuffa would later file a lawsuit against the IFL before its first event had aired, accusing Tornabene of inviting Otto and Shamus to UFC 55 on October 7, 2005, and illegally giving them access to trade secrets related to Zuffa's live event production. Zuffa also alleged that Evans had illegally copied the contents of his work computer, including fighter contracts, bout agreements, and marketing materials, and that Tornabene had violated a non-compete clause in his contract with Zuffa when he took his new position with IFL. According to Otto and Shamus, the suit, and Zuffa's further threats to sue Fox if it went ahead with their plans to air the IFL, caused the network to put its broadcasting deal on indefinite "hold." As the lawsuit, and a countersuit from the IFL against Zuffa, worked its way through the courts, Otto and Shamus struggled to secure a new broadcasting deal. They eventually reached an agreement with My-NetworkTV, an obscure collection of former CW affiliates that would pay just $50,000 per event, far below what the IFL needed to recoup its production costs, which were reportedly more than $1 million.

Zuffa had also tried to use the courts against Elite Xtreme Combat (EliteXC), a promotion run by former boxing promoter Gary Shaw; Kelly Perdrew, a software engineer who had won the second season of *The Apprentice*, a reality television series hosted by Donald Trump; and others. EliteXC had signed a broadcasting agreement with Showtime, which had been eager to gain an edge on HBO Sports, by chasing a younger and potentially more lucrative demographic than its older and more con-

servative rival drew with boxing. Zuffa's lawsuit against Showtime and
EliteXC alleged the network had illegally used old footage from past UFC
events in the opening montage of its broadcasts. (A confidential memo
prepared by Zuffa in 2007 and later shared with investors would describe
how the UFC's "complete control and ownership" of all content it created
would discourage "competing organizations from soliciting UFC fighters
by restricting ability to market prior fights for promotional purposes.")
Despite the efforts, EliteXC had grown quickly, through acquisitions
of its own—including a 2007 deal to purchase King of the Cage—and
partnerships with Dream, a Japanese promotion started by former Pride
executives, and Strikeforce, a California promotion that was focused on
live events at San Jose's HP Pavillion. EliteXC also captured headlines by
introducing a women's division, featuring Gina Carano, the daughter of
former Nevada State athletic commissioner Glenn Carano, who became
a sudden star for her aggressive fighting style and historic role as one
of the first women's cage fighting stars to break out of the regional circuit. In mid-2007, EliteXC attracted still more attention when it hosted
the mixed martial arts debut of WWE superstar Brock Lesnar, alongside
the anticipated rematch between Royce Gracie and Sakuraba, in a co-
promotion with Dream and K-1.

Nick had signed a nonexclusive contract with EliteXC in early 2007,
which would pay him a reported $60,000 per fight, more than he had ever
made. As his suspension ended that fall, EliteXC was eager to promote
him as one of its new generation of stars, part of a roster that was quickly
growing even more colorful and accomplished than the UFC's. After a
warm-up bout in September, Nick was booked to fight for EliteXC's inau-
gural lightweight championship, against K. J. Noons, a little-known Ha-
waiian who'd previously had a brief career as a professional boxer. The
card would be one of the promotion's biggest to date, and would also feature the debut of Kevin Ferguson, better known as Kimbo Slice, a street
fighter from south Florida who had become an internet sensation for his
prolific backyard fight videos.

As Nick trained for the fight, it seemed as if things in his life might
finally be coming back into place after being derailed by the NSAC.
While he'd continuing his nomadic training routine, he had also begun
competing in triathlons and going on long mountain bike rides in the

Sierra Nevadas. His younger brother, Nathan, had come into his own as a fighter, after first tagging along with Nick to his evening training sessions at Animal House, starting when he was just fourteen. Nathan had quietly built up his own reputation in regional promotions, amassing a five-and-two record and earning an invitation to compete on the fifth season of *The Ultimate Fighter*. Nathan hadn't initially wanted to accept the offer, but Nick had persuaded him to agree if only because the UFC would pay to update all of his costly medical exams and clearances, which he would be able to use for a year or more in other promotions, without having to pay out of pocket for MRIs or blood work. In July 2007, just as Nick's suspension was ending, Nathan had won the season finale and signed an eight-fight contract with the UFC, taking over where his older brother had left off, while Nick continued to break new ground for them both.

As Nick waited in the wings to step out onto the arena floor at the American Bank Center in Corpus Christi, Texas, it was as if he were finally going to be allowed back into the life he should have been living all along. As ring announcer Jimmy Lennon Jr. bellowed his name over the arena's PA system, Nick stepped through a plume of artificial smoke and ran down the Plexiglas runway that led to the cage, fans pressed up against either side hoping to steal a touch of his calf or ankle for luck. A strange sense of history hung over everything. In a pre-fight video montage, Nick and Noons had faced off against each other on the deck of the USS *Lexington*, a decommissioned aircraft carrier dating to World War II that had been converted into a public museum at a naval air station in town. On the broadcast, play-by-play announcer Mauro Ranallo laid out the stakes in dramatic terms. "John L. Sullivan was the first heavyweight boxing champion of the world; the Green Bay Packers, the first Super Bowl champs; the first Major League Baseball World Series champion was Boston," he said. "Tonight, November 7, 2007, another world first takes place as EliteXC crowns its first 160-pound champion. Who's it going to be? Nick Diaz or K. J. Noons?"

As Nick stood across the circular cage from Noons, bouncing from foot to foot, he believed that no matter what happened, he would find a way to survive and eventually win. As the bell rang, Nick began inching toward Noons with short, cautious steps. He held his arms out and threw several probing, noncommittal punches, while Noons planted his feet and counterpunched, throwing his entire body weight into almost every blow. Beginning to sense a manipulable pattern in Noons's reactions, Nick tried to bait out another series of counterpunches and then ducked down onto Noons's hips and tried to pull one of his legs up and use it as a lever to throw him off-balance. Noons seemed to expect the move and dug his arms under Nick's armpits, lifting him up while he angled his own hips backward to preserve his center of gravity. After a few seconds he was able to twist away and return to the center of the cage, while Nick trailed after. The sequence repeated itself for the first few minutes of the fight, with Noons learning to anticipate the moment when Nick would duck under his counterpunches, gaining slightly more leverage to reverse his momentum each time.

Halfway through the round, Nick had walked Noons back to the edge of the cage and again tried to duck into his hips, but Noons anticipated the move. He stepped forward and rammed his right knee into Nick's head just as he was ducking down. The collision left Nick on his back with a long cut across the bony ridge between his eyelid and eyebrow. Seeing the blood stream directly into Nick's eyes, the referee called an immediate time-out and waved in the ringside doctor to examine Nick. After Nick assured the doctor he could still see, the referee restarted the fight. And almost immediately after, Nick was hit by a hard counter right hand that Noons landed against Nick's eye socket, which sent him tumbling backward onto the mat. Noons hovered over Nick and hurled punches as Nick tried to cover his head with his arms. After half a minute, Noons pulled away, fearing Nick might catch one of his legs from below and pull him off-balance, and Nick cautiously got back to his feet, now with a second cut, above his other eye, leaving his face covered in a splotchy skein of blood. For the remainder of the round, Noons continuously circled away from Nick, trying to lead him into more counterpunches, but neither was able to land anything conclusive. In the final seconds of the round, Nick finally trapped Noons against the cage and clasped his arms underneath Noons's hips, hoisted him upward, and dragged him to the mat for the first time, just as the horn sounded.

As Nick returned to his stool, the ringside physician hovered over his cornermen's shoulders staring into the long cuts over Nick's eyes, each of which had begun to widen into something more like an open gash. Nick's left eye had also begun to swell significantly, and it seemed likely to be fully closed in a few minutes. The doctor turned away, walked to the referee, and quietly whispered in his ear that Nick's vision was compromised and he could no longer safely fight. The referee immediately waved his arms over his head, indicating the fight was over. Noons jumped up from his stool and began celebrating, while his teammates tried to hoist him onto their shoulders. As Nick realized what had happened, he walked to the middle of the cage in protest and flipped Noons off.

Disgusted, Nick turned around and stormed out of the cage before the final results were announced. Jared Shaw, Gary Shaw's son who also worked as an executive at EliteXC, trailed after Nick pleading with him to return to the cage. Nick ignored him, and when he reached the top of the entry ramp, he turned around and again raised both middle fingers into the air, cursing everyone in the cage and seemingly everyone in the arena watching. A cameraman trailed after Nick backstage as he marched to his dressing room loudly cursing the unfairness of the entire event. As the cameraman tried to jog in front of Nick to capture his anguished face, Nick swung at the lens and shoved the cameraman away from him.

When Nick had first started training on the mats of Animal House, it had felt "like freedom," he would say. "I was happy that I could do what I want. I could fight my way out of anything. Like, I failed at this. Okay, I'll go fight my way out. I failed at that, I'm gonna go fight my way out." After nearly seven years and twenty-two professional bouts, Nick had fought his way out of failure enough times to seem as if he might be on the verge of beginning a new life, finally proving he was a different and better person than the one his classmates and teachers had seen him as. Instead, his body had betrayed him. The accumulated scar tissue he had taken on, from the fight to make it as far as he had, had finally given way and left him broken open at the seams. In the days and weeks that followed, fans seemed to turn on him and his embarrassing meltdown, seeing it as a display of bad sportsmanship and self-pity, just what you would expect from an undisciplined kid from the streets. It was as if he were slipping backward into a caricature of the kind of person everyone had always expected him to be: classless, uneducated, out of control, and bound to fail, no matter what he did.

THIS IS NOT *FANTASY ISLAND*

By 2008, White was far removed from the timorous young man who'd first appeared on camera at UFC 30. Success seemed to have freed him of the need to pretend to be something he wasn't, and he'd reverted to a version of himself that he might have fantasized about becoming as a high school student, both boyish and joyfully hostile to other people's judgments. He had traded boxy suits and neckties for loose-fitting jeans, canvas sneakers, and colorful graphic T-shirts. After he'd started showing signs of balding in 2004, White had begun shaving his head—and he'd even started shaving his forearms, "'cause I'm a fuckin' gorilla," he explained to a journalist from *Esquire* who later inquired about the choice. He'd also grown visibly bulkier as a result of a semi-regular weight-lifting routine, which he liked to admit was largely to offset his frequent binges on candy and junk foods.

He'd also grown more comfortable with his notoriously unpredictable temper. "I'm mad a lot," White would later admit. "I guess that's what I do. I yell a lot, I scream." While White could still be cheery and charming, an avatar of Tony Robbins–inspired positive thinking, he had little problem using intimidation when it became clear persuasion wouldn't work. "The one thing was that Dana was always in control, from the beginning," says Watson. "Total control. And he needed you to know that. And he needed you to know that without him telling you that."

His controlling attitude and aggressive public image continued to pay off for the UFC. Annual revenue reached an all-time high of $226 million in 2007, $46 million more than the previous all-time high in 2006. The UFC also continued to break records for Spike, consistently delivering the network's highest rated programming. In 2007, Spike drew its biggest audience in network history with a free broadcast of UFC 75, headlined by two former Pride fighters, Dan Henderson and Quinton

Jackson, who had again beaten Liddell to win the UFC's light heavy-weight championship when he moved over after the Pride acquisition. The three-hour broadcast drew an average of 4.7 million viewers, and a peak of 5.6 million during the main event. Spike's semi-monthly *Fight Night* broadcasts also remained popular, and periodically outperformed Major League Baseball or NBA games that aired at the same time. And ratings had remained highest with the lucrative eighteen-to-thirty-four-year-old male demographic, with an average audience share of 2.9 over the first three years of the Spike deal, meaning 2.9 percent of the total number of people watching television in the US at the time were tuned in to the UFC. The young audience allowed the network to boost its rates with advertisers eager to pitch their energy drinks, video games, body sprays, and beer brands. Spike had also helped the UFC counterprogram against EliteXC and other competing promotions' events by broadcasting free pay-per-view reruns or short-notice *Fight Night* cards that hadn't been part of their original agreement, often requiring previously planned programming to be pre-empted.

To take advantage of the growing demand, the UFC nearly doubled the number of fight cards each year—from ten in 2005 to nineteen in 2007—and began traveling outside Las Vegas for major pay-per-views and *Fight Night* cards, including Los Angeles, Houston, Hollywood, Florida, and Columbus, Ohio. Marc Ratner, the former executive director of the Nevada State Athletic Commission, joined Zuffa as senior vice president of government and regulatory affairs in mid-2006 to help drive the expansion into new markets, by lobbying legislators and other athletic commissions in the thirty-one US states where mixed martial arts still wasn't legally recognized. Though Ratner had long been a UFC skeptic—he had debated Meyrowitz on CNN in 1995 and had opposed voting to sanction the sport after Meyrowitz's lobbying efforts in 1999—he had an even longer relationship with both Lorenzo and Frank III. Ratner had worked as an advertising executive in Las Vegas throughout the 1980s—for R&R Partners, the firm that famously created the "What Happens in Vegas Stays in Vegas" campaign—but he'd also volunteered as a high school sports referee, and had worked several Bishop Gorman football games that Lorenzo and Frank III had played in as teenagers.

After they had worked together on the NSAC through the late 1990s,

Ratner had grown to trust Lorenzo, and after several months of meetings, decided to accept the offer to join the UFC. Much of Ratner's work involved overseeing the distribution of money, meeting with politicians, making campaign contributions, or hiring lobbyist groups to pitch state legislators. "We had a big map of the US in my office, and the goal was to get it all green," says Ratner. "Every time we would get a state approved, we had it in red and then we'd have another map made, saying Nebraska's in now." He'd often travel with Mike Mersch, formerly an attorney for the Nevada State Attorney General's Office, who also joined Zuffa, as assistant general counsel, in early 2007. They found the most persuasive arguments tended to focus on the economic benefits a UFC event could generate for a city or state, with potentially thousands of fans traveling across the country for the chance to see a UFC event firsthand. "One of the things I always talked about was the room nights we would bring into a city," says Ratner. "It was probably five or six hundred room nights with the UFC staff and all the corners. We'd be there for four nights, so if we have 150 rooms, that's a lot of business. Then you got bars and people coming in and renting cars and going out for food. It was great for the cities. That was one of my selling points."

To keep up with the aggressive new production schedule, Zuffa signed more than eighty new fighters in 2008, pushing the total roster count to more than three hundred. White kept a long list of fighter names written in temporary marker on the double-height window in his office, which he used to help track rankings for each division and plan future fights. White had to make sure each event would have enough fights to fill the allotted broadcast windows the UFC had agreed to with Spike and the growing list of international networks that licensed its programming, typically between nine and twelve fights per event. White worked closely with matchmaker Joe Silva to guide most contract negotiations, and many fighters and managers had learned to dread Silva's blunt and ultimatum-prone style of negotiations.

White relished Silva's role as an enforcer, not just in negotiating new contracts but in coercing fighters to take fights, even when the timing or particular matchup wouldn't be in their best interest. "I can tell you this man, if you fucking call Joe Silva and turn down a fight, you might as well say, Fucking rip up my contract," White would later say. While Silva lacked White's zest for conflict and sometimes felt guilty about how the UFC treated fighters, he had accepted that doing his job well would necessitate some cruelty. "I read an interview recently with a fighter talking about the depression that comes on after being cut. It's impossible to read that and not feel responsible," he would later say, "but the job dictates it. It's not like we decided, this would be fun. It's that this is the only way it can work." Despite his mixed feelings, Silva was clinical and dispassionate in his approach to negotiations, often fighting over even $1,000 pay increases for ten-year veterans of the sport.

Chris Leben would describe Silva as "a little Napoleon," who operated in close concert with White to push fighters into taking unfavorable matchups for little or no extra compensation. "First, Joe makes negotiating as difficult as possible," Leben wrote, in his memoir. "Then, when the deal seems close to falling apart, Dana steps in with some smooth talk." After building a five-fight win streak in the UFC after the first season of *The Ultimate Fighter*, Leben had hoped to fight middleweight champion Rich Franklin. Instead, Silva offered Leben a fight against Anderson Silva, the highly skilled Brazillian kickboxer, who had finally agreed to sign with the UFC. Leben's head coach, Matt Hume, adamantly opposed the matchup, especially on the relatively short timeline of less than two months that the UFC was offering. It was a difficult stylistic matchup for Leben, and because most fans weren't familiar with Silva's career outside the UFC, a win would do little for Leben's standing. Leben agreed and asked Joe Silva for other options, but there were none. "Chris, you are taking this fight. Plain and simple," Joe Silva told him.

After a heated argument between Leben and Joe Silva, White called Leben and coaxed him with flattery instead of intimidation. He described the fight as the "opportunity of a lifetime," and assured Leben he could beat the Brazilian. A fighter of Leben's quality, he recalled White saying, shouldn't be afraid of fighting anyone. Without an agent or manager to mediate, Leben found it hard to not be persuaded by White's encouragement. When Leben learned he had earned a spot on *The Ultimate Fighter*, he would describe it as the first time in his life he "actually had value in the world." Growing up, Leben had periodically collected old aluminum cans out of the trash to pay for bus fare to get to school, and he hadn't learned to read until his late teens. He'd gone AWOL after attempting a career in the army and struggled to find steady work in his twenties. His still-young career with the UFC was as much a personal conviction as it was a business commitment, and after White promised that the UFC would repay Leben for his loyalty in his next fight, Leben decided to accept the bout over his coach's objections. "That's why you're my guy," White told Leben, promising a small pay increase—$5,000 more than Joe Silva had offered according to Leben. (Anderson Silva would go on to knock Leben out in less than a minute—one of the most lopsided losses of his career—and claim Leben's place as title contender against Franklin in his next fight. Leben would never again come close to fighting for a championship.)

Even for fighters who had agents or managers, negotiations were often one-sided and frustrating. In December 2006, White had been eager to sign a new contract with Brandon Vera, an exciting young heavyweight who'd won his first four fights in the UFC, including a TKO over former champion Frank Mir. Vera sent his manager, Mark Dion, to Las Vegas to negotiate with White at Zuffa's offices. After some discussion, White wrote down an offer on a blue Post-it Note with two options written on either side. One side offered a three-fight deal that would pay Vera $90,000 to fight and $90,000 to win, then $100,000 and $100,000, and $115,000 and $115,000. If he was booked to fight against the UFC's current heavyweight champion in any of those fights, his pay would be guaranteed to increase another $50,000. On the other side of the Post-it Note was an option for a four-year contract that would pay a total of $7 million while remaining exclusive to the UFC. Both options, White said, would come with a $100,000 signing bonus.

Dion took the Post-it Note and returned home to discuss the options with Vera and a business lawyer, and after a few weeks he emailed White with two counteroffers of his own: a one-year, three-fight deal that would pay Vera $150,000 and $150,000, $175,000 and $175,000, and $200,000 and $200,000; or a three-year deal that would pay Vera $9 million total for ten fights. Dion proposed a $1.5 million signing bonus for either offer. Dion had expected White to counter his counter and that they would eventually work their way to some middleground, but he later claimed White responded by simply cutting him off and telling Joe Silva to take over the negotiations. Silva threw out White's previous opening terms and came in with a deal that was roughly half the size: three fights for

$50,000 and $50,000, $60,000 and $60,000, and $70,000 and $70,000, with a $100,000 signing bonus. As Vera saw what was unfolding, he worried Dion was damaging his relationship with the UFC, and according to Dion, Vera contacted Zuffa and told them to work out a deal with him directly. Vera severed ties with Dion and signed a new deal with the UFC starting at $100,000 and $100,000. Dion would later file for arbitration with the California State Athletic Commission, claiming Vera owed Dion a percentage of the pay from his new contract in exchange for his services. In court, Dion claimed that Zuffa's approach to negotiations had contributed to his dispute with Vera. "This is all I got from Dana White," Dion testified, in reference to the Post-it Note. "This is all I could show to Mr. Vera. There was no e-mails. Dana White likes to keep—keep himself covered on all aspects." The CSAC arbitrator would eventually rule in Dion's favor and required Vera to pay him a percentage of his future earnings, and called out the UFC's habit of negotiating without a clear paper trail, relying mainly on undocumented conversations and vague Post-it scrawls.

The UFC's frequent use of secret locker room bonuses also added tension to the relationship between many fighters and their managers. White and the Fertittas had developed the tradition, typically delivering envelopes with handwritten bonus checks to fighters backstage during events if they felt like a fighter's performance had merited it. In an interview with *ESPN,* Lorenzo described the process: "Essentially if me and Dana and my brother sit down and say, Okay, did that fighter perform? Did he exceed his performance? Did he really go out and lay it on the line?" Sometimes the envelope would contain a check for a few thousand dollars, and other times it could contain as much as $500,000, the sum White and Lorenzo handed Couture in 2006, after his third fight with Liddell. According to Monte Cox, a manager who represented Matt Hughes, Tim Sylvia, Jens Pulver, and dozens of other fighters, the envelopes often came with a precondition that the money not be mentioned to the fighters' agents or managers. That was what Cox claimed White had told former middleweight champion Rich Franklin when he handed him an envelope with an extra $100,000. "When you tell someone like that, Here's money, and they need money, and you're not to give it to your manager, it's hell to get them to give it to their manager.

It broke up a lot of people," Cox would later say. "And I think they did it intentionally."

The UFC also regularly used side-letter agreements to pay fighters extra sums of money that wouldn't have to be publicly reported to athletic commissions, which made it harder for fighters to learn what their peers were making and to more accurately evaluate their own relative market value. The UFC's side-letter agreements also provided more incentive for violence, such was the case for light heavyweight Lyoto Machida, who was secretly contracted to earn an additional $100,000 for every fight he won by knockout or submission. The UFC also organized a separate public bonus system for each event, awarding fighters between $25,000 to $75,000 for "Knockout of the Night," "Submission of the Night," and "Fight of the Night." Entry-level contracts at the time started at $3,000 to fight and $3,000 to win, meaning that a fighter could earn more than ten times their base pay based on luck or the UFC's largesse.

The UFC's tight control over fighter pay left little financial incentive for more established sports agents and managers to expand into mixed martial arts, and many UFC fighters conceded that their lives would be easier if they didn't push back on the promotion's demands. Mixed martial arts came to seem less like a career than a kind of violent lottery. Just as casinos bathed gamblers in the glimmering possibility of jackpots going off in every direction, the UFC fighters lived on a kind of hopefulness that they might one day be transformed into millionaires or moguls, even as they competed for wages that, in the worst cases, averaged out to less than the federal minimum wage over the course of a year. And while most didn't make it any further than the average gambler who found an open seat at a casino table, there was something affirming about being in the same room where people's lives truly were transformed with the roll of the dice. The chance to walk out into the hysteria of a full arena, to a sound system that turned a favorite song into a pulsing quake in the air, while ten thousand faces hung in the neon twirl of the houselights, made it seem for a few sweet moments as if life had become a scene in a television show someone else was watching. And then the eerie clarity of the octagon, so brightly lit even one's shadow disappeared inside, leaving only a body poised to collide against another like human dice tumbling along the octagon fence.

Instead of leveraging the UFC for better pay, many managers found it easier to make money for their fighters through sponsorship deals, selling off small pieces of advertising space on their fight shorts, or custom-printed T-shirts and baseball hats that would ensure a company's logo would be visible on-camera as the fighter walked out to the octagon. By 2008, fighters often earned several times more than their standard fight purse from the UFC by covering themselves in a bizarre mix of corporate logos and branding, like: Dynamic Fastener Services, a power tools and construction wholesaler; the Gun Store, a firearms and ammunition shop in Las Vegas; Condom Depot, an online retailer specializing in sex toys, lubrication, and condoms; and PittbullMortgageSchool.com, a short-lived website that claimed to teach people about flipping homes. "What on earth is that?" Rogan asked, after seeing the latter on Chris Leben's shorts during an event in 2007. No one on the commentary team or in the UFC production truck knew.

Many gyms had their own in-house sponsorship groups to help supplement their incomes, which could be anything from a local car dealership to international software giants like Microsoft and Salesforce. "We all rode the wave together. It just literally went from something that was kind of like helping a buddy out to a business, like literally overnight," says Bob Cook, one of the head coaches of American Kickboxing Academy and co-owner of Zinkin Entertainment, which helped the gym's fighters find sponsors. Mike Swick, a contestant from the first season of *The Ultimate Fighter,* who went on to become a UFC mainstay for nearly ten years after, says he would earn between $60,000 and $70,000 from sponsors for each fight, at a time when his reported purses were as low as $7,000 and $7,000. "I had like ten to fifteen patches on my shorts—I looked like NASCAR," Swick says. "Some of those patches were $5,000 and $10,000."

For a time, it seemed as if everyone was making money together, but soon the UFC found itself in direct competition with its fighters as both sides tried to find new ways to monetize the sport. In 2007, Zuffa announced a deal to produce a new UFC video game series with THQ, a publisher that also created licensed games for WWE, Pixar, and Nickelodeon. It was the first major video game deal Zuffa had negotiated, and most fighter contracts at the time didn't have clear language covering the rights to use a fighter's likeness specifically in a video game. Instead of negotiating with the fighters on the roster that THQ wanted to use, Zuffa attached a rider to new fighter bout agreements, which required fighters to grant Zuffa full rights to use their likeness in a game with no extra compensation. In 2008, Jon Fitch, a fighter who trained at AKA, caught the changed language in a bout agreement. He told the UFC he wanted to negotiate terms before signing away his likeness in perpetuity. He asked for a set limit on the number of years the likeness could be used and a clause that would ensure family members could continue receiving royalties in the case of his death. The move infuriated White, and he responded by announcing Fitch would be cut from the UFC, as would any other fighters who refused to sign the new rider. "We're looking for guys who want to work with us and not against us," White told *Yahoo! Sports* after the news of Fitch's release became public, "and frankly, I'm so fuckin' sick of this shit, it's not even funny. . . . These guys aren't partners with us. Fuck them. All of them. Every last fuckin' one of them."

White's response was extreme, even by his standards. It made it seem as if the UFC's business interests had become entangled with White's sense of self, and anything that threatened one was an implicit danger to the other. White liked to think of himself as someone who helped others. He was a loyal person and took pride in the fact that many of his closest friendships had been formed years before his newfound wealth and celebrity. "I like having people around me who I can trust, the friends who were your friends when you were broke," White would later say. In 2008, White had let an old friend from Boston, Bobbie Moore, move into a house he owned but no longer used in the Southern Highlands, a special subdivision of luxury homes on the Las Vegas outskirts. Moore had been struggling financially, and White helped him start a new business as a personal trainer and invited him to use the basement gym at the UFC offices to meet with clients while he got back on his feet. White felt like he had provided a similar kind of custodial care for the UFC's fighters. While not every fighter would personally benefit from every new development in the UFC, the promotion's continued growth would multiply the opportunities they'd have to make money, whether through sponsorships, side businesses, or increased visibility for their own gyms. Without White and the UFC, they'd still be hobbyists forced to work as accountants or construction workers while they squeezed all of their life's dreams into a few practice sessions on the weekends. As the subprime mortgage market collapse of 2008 had suddenly sent the US economy into free-fall, with some of the biggest banks in the country on the verge of insolvency, White felt that if anything, fighters should be grateful they still had an opportunity to earn six-figure incomes from the UFC.

Fitch's attitude had represented a unique kind of betrayal, because he seemed to not just be ciritcizing the terms of the deal but calling White's approach to dealmaking itself into question. "It was not a very good agreement. There was not really a reason for us to sign it," Fitch said. Fitch's objections made it seem like there was something haphazard and improvisatory in the way the UFC was run, chasing after half-cooked partnerships seemingly without forethought or basic planning, while fighters were left to ratify whatever new riders or arrangements the UFC concocted. "The way they bring the contracts and stuff to us, I don't know," Fitch said, "it's just not how business is done."

Faced with the possibility that his UFC career was finished, and that his training partners and others connected to his gym might also be permanently blacklisted, Fitch would eventually relent and sign the new merchandising agreement. But it was just one of a growing number of messy public disputes the UFC had found itself in with its own fighters, including its own heavyweight champion.

On January 14, 2008, Randy Couture became the first UFC fighter sued by the promotion. Zuffa filed the suit in the Clark County District Court alleging that Couture had "combined, conspired, confederated and agreed" together with up to one hundred individuals and/or LLCs, who "induced Couture to violate his contractual obligations by enticing him to disclose confidential information and to promote MMA events in direct competition with Zuffa." Zuffa claimed Couture's actions had caused damages "in excess of $10,000," which it requested he repay along with an unspecified sum for punitive damages. Zuffa also demanded an immediate injunction to prevent Couture from fighting outside the UFC, claiming, in essence, that his future as a fighter was UFC property.

That Couture was still trying to fight in 2008, at forty-four, was almost as surprising as the fact that he was being sued by the company he had

helped go mainstream. He had retired in 2006 following his second loss
to Liddell, at UFC 57, laying his gloves down in the center of the octagon
as a celebrity-filled audience of eleven thousand plus watched, including
Paris Hilton, Charles Barkley, Cindy Crawford, and Lee Majors. After
having broken every rule of age and anatomy, Couture accepted that it
was time for him to leave the future of the sport in other hands. After the
announcement, White and Lorenzo had showered Couture with praise
and gratitude. In the locker room immediately following the fight, they
handed him an envelope with a handwritten check for $500,000, the first
bonus he had ever received from the UFC. Lorenzo and White promised
that they would do whatever Couture wanted to ensure he would remain
a part of the UFC in his retirement years. A few months later, White had
offered Couture the chance to work on a series of branded gyms the UFC
was planning to open around the country, or even become president of
the UFC's expanding European division. Couture wasn't interested in either option, but accepted a role as the third member of the UFC's commentary team alongside Goldberg and Rogan, for which he was paid
$56,000 a year.

Despite his beloved standing among fans, Couture still felt uneasy
with his own life. Success had done little to protect him from the recurring thought that he was defective in some way, as if some part of his
mind hadn't believed he deserved his achievements and had set about trying to undo everything. Couture's marriage to Trish had begun to fracture
during the filming of the first season of *The Ultimate Fighter*. She had
come to Las Vegas with their one-year-old son, Caden, and stayed with
Couture in an apartment Zuffa had rented for the eight-week shoot, but
they had fought often. Three years after he had first promised to retire,
Trish was frustrated by how often Couture still seemed to prioritize his
fighting career. He had won the tournaments, been a heavyweight champion, fought in Japan, and come back from a three-fight losing streak to
win the UFC's light heavyweight championship. At forty-one, what was
left to prove? During filming in Las Vegas, Trish grew even more frustrated when she found herself taking care of Caden at home while Couture made VIP media appearances with White, Lorenzo, and Liddell at a
star-studded boxing match between Oscar De La Hoya and Bernard Hopkins. Later, when Couture told Trish he had agreed to teach a seminar at a

friend's gym in Australia after filming wrapped, she became even angrier with him. Why was it so much easier to focus on his training partners and opponents than his family?

While Couture was resented at home, he was revered on set of *The Ultimate Fighter*. The young cast members treated him like a trailblazer and guru, and he relished the feeling of being helpful. Halfway through filming, Trish decided to fly back to Oregon with Caden, and soon after, Couture let himself fall into an affair with Kim Borrego, an executive at the Bellagio, whom he met at a club one night after the day's filming had wrapped. Couture found Kim accepting and easy to talk to. When he was with her, he felt strangely settled, and he looked back on all of the stress and self-doubt he'd felt when he was with Trish. After filming ended a few weeks later and Couture returned to Portland, he and Trish entered marriage counseling. He also stayed in contact with Kim and would call her in secret to vent about the mounting tension in his marriage. As the first episodes of *The Ultimate Fighter* were beginning to air, Trish said she wanted a divorce, and Couture agreed. Shortly after, he decided to relocate to Las Vegas to pursue a new relationship with Kim. He also found himself fielding more offers to act, and accepted small roles on *The King of Queens*, *The Unit*, and in the Rob Schneider comedy *Big Stan*.

Many of his closest friends found it hard to understand Couture's choices and expressed concern about his relationship with Kim, including his former teammates at Team Quest, a small fight gym he had helped found in an unusued warehouse on a friend's used-car dealership lot in Oregon. Many had been especially offended by Couture's decision to bring Kim to his retirement fight against Liddell, just weeks after agreeing on a divorce. Couture found it hard to understand the negative impressions and wrote it off to envy. It wasn't Kim that his closest friends disliked, he believed, but the newfound celebrity and wealth that was transforming Couture's life.

As the tensions mounted in his personal life, Couture began to have second thoughts about retirement, just six months after he'd announced it. He had sized up the UFC's current heavyweight champion, Tim Sylvia, from the commentary table, and began to think he might have walked away from the sport too early. Couture knew that Sylvia was unpopular with fans for his plodding style—the entire arena had booed Sylvia's most recent title defense, a one-sided but uneventful decision win against Jeff Monson. White had sided with the fans, telling the *Baltimore Sun* that Sylvia should rethink his approach if he wanted to be more popular. "I think Tim's had a couple of fights that people weren't crazy about and now it's up to Tim to work on his game and get in there and finish people," White said. In November 2006, Couture mentioned to some friends over dinner that he thought he could beat Sylvia and become heavyweight champion again. They goaded him to send a text message to White with the same proposition. "Are you serious, bro?" White texted back.

A few weeks later, Couture had signed a new four-fight agreement with Zuffa and was booked against Sylvia in the main event of a pay-per-view in March. Sylvia was hurt when he found out Couture had asked for the fight. The six-foot-eight former trucker had thought they were friends. Sylvia had traveled to Oregon in 2003 to train with Couture at Team Quest and had helped Couture renovate an aging farmhouse he'd bought with Trish outside Portland. Before accepting the fight, Sylvia had called Couture and asked why he had singled him out. As with many mixed martial arts gyms, there was an unspoken rule that teammates not fight one another at the hard-nosed Miletich Fighting Systems in Iowa, where Sylvia had settled. Training partners were supposed to build one another up, not take win bonuses out of each other's pockets and push one another down the rankings, closer toward being cut. Couture tried to explain that it was just business. He still thought of Sylvia as a friend, but they had already fought each other in training for free, Couture reasoned, so they might as well both get paid for another few rounds on television.

When they finally fought, at UFC 68, on March 3, 2007, Couture knocked Sylvia down with the first punch of the fight and proceeded to outwrestle him for a dominant five-round decision. For the sixth time in his ten-year career, Couture became a UFC champion, four months before his forty-fourth birthday. *Sports Illustrated* asked Couture to appear on the cover of an upcoming issue and be interviewed as part of a larger feature on the resurgence of cage fighting. Couture was also invited to the White House to meet President George W. Bush, and to lead an informal hand-to-hand combat session with the Secret Service's Counter Assault Team. ESPN introduced a "Best Fighter" category for its year-end Espy Award ceremony, and nominated both Couture and Quinton "Rampage"

Jackson alongside boxing superstars Floyd Mayweather Jr., Miguel Cotto, and Manny Pacquiao. (Floyd Mayweather Jr. would ultimately win.)

Rejuvenated by the accolades, Couture began to think about the remaining fights on his contract and how he might use them to finalize his legacy. After an August title defense against a young Brazilian contender, Gabriel Gonzaga, he decided the only escalation left would be to challenge Fedor Emelianenko, Pride's long-reigning heavyweight champion who had been widely recognized by journalists as the consensus best heavyweight for the last three years running. A devout Russian Orthodox Christian who blessed his hotel rooms and airport buses with rosaries, Emelianenko had cultivated an almost mythic persona among mixed martial arts fans. He looked like everyone should have been able to beat him, with a belly as round as his balding head. He avoided direct eye contact with his opponents before fights, as if he were already remorseful for what he would have to do next. And after finishing his opponents, he often walked back to his corner as if he had done nothing more interesting than check the mail. He had won twenty-four consecutive fights since 2001, against a long list of top-ranked opponents that made Couture's record of mixed wins and losses seem less triumphant.

White and Lorenzo had tried to sign Emelianenko to the UFC after the Pride purchase, but they had failed to come to terms, in part because of the UFC's unwillingness to co-promote with M-1, a Russian company that Emelianenko had a preexisting agreement with. Emelianenko had instead signed with Adrenaline MMA, a newly formed company run by Monte Cox, the former Iowa sports journalist who had become a prodigious manager and promoter. Adrenaline agreed to co-promote all of Emelianenko's fights with M-1, and promised to make Emelianenko a centerpiece of its new business specifically focused on international events, with fight cards promised in Macau, Tokyo, Amsterdam, St. Petersburg, and Seoul. Unlike the UFC, which prohibited its fighters from competing in other organizations without permission, M-1 and Adrenaline said they would be willing to partner with any and all promotions interested in hosting Emelianenko.

After Couture had re-signed with the UFC, he had been offered $3 million to fight Emelianenko in BodogFight, a short-lived promotion funded by online gambling tycoon Calvin Ayre, but he had been unable to because of the exclusivity clause in all of the UFC's fighter contracts. But in the fall of 2007, after negotiations between Emelianenko and Zuffa had fallen apart, Couture decided to pursue a fight with Emelianenko outside the UFC, believing it would be the closest thing to winning an Olympic medal that he could still achieve. Though he still had two fights remaining on his current contract with Zuffa, Couture and his representatives believed they had found a loophole in a stipulation that all four of the fights would have to take place over an eighteen-month period. Couture believed that if he announced he was retiring and waited until the spring of 2008, when the eighteen-month window expired, he would be free to negotiate with other promoters. On October 11, 2007, Couture faxed a letter to Zuffa's offices announcing his retirement. A spokesperson for Couture told reporters immediately after that he had made the decision after learning Emelianenko had turned down the UFC's latest offer. "That was the fight Randy wanted. Without that fight, he felt what did he have to prove," Sean O'Heir said on behalf of Couture. "Everyone always says Fedor is the best. Randy wanted to show he could beat him. Fedor was Randy's last big challenge."

Couture wasn't available for interviews because almost immediately after sending his retirement notice he had flown to South Africa, where he would begin two weeks of filming on *The Scorpion King 2: Rise of a Warrior*, a straight-to-DVD spinoff from the 1999's *The Mummy* remake. In a costarring role, Couture played Sargon, an ancient sorcerer who manipulates the film's hero, played by former *Power Rangers* star Michael Copon, before a climactic confrontation in which Couture morphs into a building-sized scorpion. There was no internet in the hotel the production company had booked for Couture and Kim, and they were effectively cut off from news in the US. On days when Couture didn't have to be on set, he and Kim went to wine tastings, dove with sharks, and took a safari.

When Couture returned, he discovered that his resignation had triggered an outpouring of media requests and controversy, including several long voicemails from White that alternated between threatening and ingratiating. In the press, White had been characteristically blunt and aggressive about Couture's attempts to leave. "He definitely belongs to me," White told a reporter. He described Couture's management as "maggots" and "parasites," the kinds of people who cling to anyone they think they can make a profit from. "There's no way I was going to let anybody come in from another organization and make more money and have better deals than my guys who have been with me for a long time and helped me build this business."

Couture decided to address the subject in an impromptu press conference at Xtreme Couture, a new hybrid gym and apparel company that he'd opened in Las Vegas with Kim. Speaking from a podium in the sparring ring, Couture explained that he felt the UFC had never fully valued him as a star fighter. "For eleven years of my life I've tried to represent this sport with integrity, represent this sport in a particular way, for the owners before and the owners now. And I've never felt like that was appreciated," he said. Couture held up the bout agreements for his Sylvia and Gonzaga fights as evidence of the UFC's mistreatment, pointing out that the promotion had reportedly offered Emelianenko more as a signing bonus—reportedly $1.5 million—than Couture had ever been paid for a full fight purse, which had typically been a $250,000 base purse with another roughly $500,000 in pay-per-view royalties. "I'm tired of swimming upstream at this stage with the management of the UFC. It only makes sense at this point in my career to fight Fedor Emelianenko," he said. "And since he's now signed with another organization, I feel like it's time to resign and focus on my other endeavors."

The UFC claimed Couture had grossly misrepresented the details of his contract in an attempt to damage the promotion's reputation. "The facts are the facts," Lorenzo said days later. "We have the facts." Though the promotion had jealously guarded details about fighter pay, Lorenzo approved the release of payment details from Couture's most recent comeback. The UFC claimed it had given Couture a signing bonus worth $500,000, which had been paid out in two halves, one on signing his contract and the other several months later, after he had completed his first fight against Sylvia. The UFC also revealed that Couture had made $936,000 from pay-per-view participation for the Sylvia fight, not the $500,000 he'd claimed. In public, White was indignant, comparing fighters like Couture to customers in a beauty salon, "sitting around talking about what they're not getting." He reframed the entire question as one of ingratitude for the work he and Lorenzo had done to build the UFC to the point where someone like Couture could be a millionaire. "We know what we've done for Randy, we know who we are," he told the *LA Times*. "We're running a business here. This is not *Fantasy Island*."

While Couture waited for the end of his eighteen-month contract, Emelianenko and M-1 signed a deal with Affliction, another new promotion launched by an apparel company that had become one of the biggest fight sponsors in the UFC, with additional backing by Mark Cuban and Donald Trump, who was especially enamored with Emelianenko. "His thing is inflicting death on people," Trump said of Emelianenko in an interview with Howard Stern. While Zuffa's suit worked its way through the court system, Affliction announced that Emelianenko would appear in its debut event, not against Couture but Tim Sylvia, whom the UFC had released less than a year after his loss to Couture. The pay-per-view event was scheduled for July 17, 2008, at the Honda Center in Anaheim, California.

White responded by banning any UFC fighter from wearing Affliction-branded clothing, and he pushed Spike to counterprogram the event, assembling an unscheduled *Fight Night* card on four weeks' notice, which would air for free at the same time as Affliction's event. The card's highlight was middleweight champion Anderson Silva going up a weight class to fight light heavyweight contender James Irvin in a non-title fight. Affliction would end up generating a reported one hundred thousand pay-per-view buys and more than $2 million in ticket sales for its debut, which ended with Emelianenko beating Sylvia by rear naked choke in just thirty-six seconds. The UFC's *Fight Night* card drew a peak audience of more than 3.8 million. It was one of the highest rated shows of the year for Spike, which outperformed both Affliction and a Major League Baseball game on Fox that had aired on the same day.

Though Affliction had lost money on its debut, the promotion was confident a super-fight with Emelianenko and Couture would be a hit and began preparing commercials to advertise the bout between the two, which was initially targeted for its second pay-per-view event, scheduled to take place on the UFC's home turf, UNLV's Thomas & Mack Center in Las Vegas, on October 11, 2008. But Zuffa's lawsuit with Couture was an unworkable obstacle. Zuffa argued it was entitled to a twelve-month extension on Couture's original contract because he had turned down a fight offer in the fall of 2007, against another former Pride champion,

Antônio Rodrigo Nogueira. Couture had hoped for a quick resolution to the dispute, but a scheduling conflict with the courts delayed an arbitration hearing by six months, meaning Couture wouldn't be legally cleared to compete in October. Nearly a year removed from his resignation and seemingly no closer to making the fight with Emelianenko a reality, Couture began to lose heart. As his legal fees mounted—nearing $500,000, he'd later estimate—and each passing day pushed him further away from his athletic prime, Couture began to fear he had made a mistake in trying to challenge the UFC. Instead of ending his career in a moment of glory, he worried it would end in a courtroom. Whatever the outcome, he would be left with millions in legal fees for his troubles, and no guarantee of success.

In August, Affliction announced that its next event would be delayed until January. Shortly after, Couture decided to swallow his pride and sent another text to White, asking if there were any opponents other than Emelianenko that the UFC could book him against to fight out his contract. "I couldn't afford to spend another year spending money on lawyers to see what may or may not happen," Couture would later say of the decision. "I got a fairly short window of competition left here and I had to do what I had to do to take care of myself and my career." White replied with two words: "Brock Lesnar."

During Couture's interregnum, the former WWE star had swept through the UFC like a hallucination. A belligerent heel with a bull-like appearance, Lesnar had been fast-tracked to UFC championship contention after just one fight as a professional mixed martial artist. At six-foot-three and 286 pounds, he seemed more like an inflated arena mascot than an athlete. His pectoral muscles were the size of barbell plates, split by the tattoo of a saber that ran the length of his torso from his navel to the base of his throat. Lesnar had started training in mixed martial arts with one of the wrestling coaches from the University of Minnesota, where he had been an All-American and national champion. After graduating, Lesnar had found an unexpected career in professional wrestling, where his size and naturally rebellious personality had made him stand out. He'd been offered a contract with the WWE, and quickly became one of the company's biggest stars, but he'd still dreamed of becoming a professional athlete. In 2004, he'd tried to earn a spot in the NFL, and played with the Minnesota Vikings' pre-season practice squad, but was cut before the start of the regular season.

Like Couture, Lesnar decided to turn to cage fighting to fulfill his athletic dreams. After an impressive debut in 2007, White had signed him to the UFC. Lesnar had lost his UFC debut, to former heavyweight champion Frank Mir, but he'd dominated former Pride veteran Heath Herring in his second fight over the summer of 2008, at UFC 87, just as Couture was preparing for a potential fight with Emelianenko. White was eager to build up Lesnar as an even bigger star and more fearsome fighter than Emelianenko, and he offered Couture the chance to return to the UFC and defend his title against Lesnar in November. Couture accepted. While far less accomplished than Emelianenko, Lesnar was a global superstar and Couture decided the fight could be an even bigger cultural event than the Emelianenko fight, even if it lacked its pure sporting significance. The bout was scheduled as the main event for UFC 91, at the MGM Grand Garden Arena on November 15, 2008—a year and a month after Couture had faxed his resignation to Zuffa.

When the fight began, Couture looked dramatically smaller than the pro wrestler, who outweighed him by almost fifty pounds. Much of the round was fought along the fence, where Couture would turn and hold Lesnar after the younger fighter had tried and failed to take him down. After the air horn sounded the end of the first round, it seemed as if Couture had defused much of Lesnar's power and arguably come out ahead on the scorecards. Halfway through the second round, however, Lesnar hit Couture on the ear with a short right hook. It was a slow, glancing punch that seemed like it had barely made contact, but it caused Couture's body to go limp, as if all the musculature that held him upright had collectively turned off. Couture dropped to one knee and then tumbled backward to the mat. Lesnar jumped on top of him and began to pound the side of his head with short, almost childlike hammer fists. Couture tried to roll over on his side and bury his head behind Lesnar's thigh to block the punches, but Lesnar kept rolling him back, and after a few more seconds the referee pulled Lesnar off Couture and waved the fight off.

Lesnar rose from Couture's slumped body and jumped up onto the top of the cage wall. He put his hand above his brow and looked across the audience like a mariner scanning an angry, roaring sea. "Can you see me now!?" he roared back, claiming his place as the best fighter in the UFC's most competitive division. Couture tried to get back up to his feet but fell down to the mat in an exhausted confusion. He remained on his back for nearly a minute and a half, before he was finally able to stand on his own.

The event generated $4.8 million in ticket sales and more than a million pay-per-views, making it the most successful UFC event to date. The UFC's annual revenue for the year would climb to $275 million, a $50 million increase from 2007, and another all-time high.

STATION TO STATION

Lesnar quickly became the biggest star in cage fighting, bringing in a new crossover audience of professional wrestling fans who helped drive the UFC's estimated value to more than $1.1 billion in 2009, while *Forbes* included Lorenzo and Frank III on its list of the nine hundred richest people in the world. Ratner had succeeded in getting mixed martial arts legally sanctioned in forty-four states across the US, and the UFC had aggressively pushed into new markets, holding events in Minneapolis, Atlanta, Omaha, Nashville, and Philadelphia, as well as new international markets like Montreal, Dublin, and Cologne, where throngs of young men were as captivated as Americans had been by the spectacle of two people fighting in a cage for a bigger paycheck and a better life.

At the same time, Affliction had struggled to organize new events. Without the possibility of a superfight between Couture and Emelianenko, the promotion had instead matched the Russian against Andrei Arlovski, another former UFC champion, for an event in January 2009. Despite a triumphant first-round TKO win for Emelianenko, the event had lost money for Affliction, with $500,000 less in ticket sales than their first event. A costly new co-promotion agreement with Oscar De La Hoya's Golden Boy Promotions further cut into the company's share of pay-per-view revenue, and a disclosed fighter payroll of $3.3 million— substantially higher than the UFC typically paid and nearly triple the disclosed fighter pay for UFC 91—left the promotion even deeper in debt. White had added more pressure to Affliction by pushing Spike to air a free replay of UFC 91, featuring Lesnar's victory over Couture, at the same time as their second event went live. The Spike broadcast would draw a peak audience of 3.3 million and had the highest rating among eighteen-to-thirty-four year-old male viewers on both cable and standard broadcast television.

Lesnar's next fight, a rematch against Frank Mir, was booked as the main event at UFC 100 on July 11, 2009. It broke almost all of the UFC's previous records, generating 1.3 million pay-per-view buys, the most ever for a UFC event, passing Lesnar's own previous high at UFC 91. Ticket sales brought in another $5.1 million, the second-highest in UFC history. Two weeks later, Affliction would be forced to cancel its third event when Emelianenko's opponent, Josh Barnett, tested positive for anabolic steroid metabolites. (The UFC had had its issues with fighters testing positive for steroids and other performance enhancing drugs, but most happened in the days and weeks after events, most often with samples collected on the night of the fights.) Unable to find a short-notice replacement for Barnett, the company found itself with millions more in lost marketing and preproduction expenses. As the promotion's executive board considered the prospect of spending even more to move the event to the fall, they instead decided to abandon fight promotion altogether. White would later celebrate by posing in his office with a faux tombstone printed with the logos of all the competitors the UFC had driven out of business, including Affliction, IFL, and EliteXC, which had been acquired by Strikeforce after two years of operating at a loss.

While the UFC was surging, Station Casinos was hanging by a thread. And that thread snapped on July 28, 2009, just two weeks after UFC 100. Though Station's revenues had grown steadily since 2000, peaking at $1.3 billion in 2008, the company's long-term debt had grown even faster—rising from $1.2 billion in 2001 to more than $6.4 billion in 2008, more than double the size of the entire Las Vegas locals market. Most of the debt had been used to finance the Fertittas' aggressive expansion plans, which relied on larger and larger loans to fund new property acquisitions or lavish construction projects to consolidate their place as Las Vegas's biggest off-strip gaming company. The pattern had started almost as soon as Frank Jr. had stepped down and given his sons full control of the company, which at the time still just had a single property. In 1994, Frank III oversaw the $103 million construction of a second property, on the eastern edge of Las Vegas, Boulder Station, a railroad-themed casino built on twenty-seven acres of land, which featured twenty-two hundred slot machines, along with an eight-thousand-square-foot electric sign in front, with what Station described as the world's largest color screen.

While some gaming analysts worried it was far too big an expense for the growing but still very niche locals market, Frank Jr. eagerly supported his sons' decision. "People said we overspent, that it was too nice and too fancy. But that's been a common theme at Station," Frank Jr. would later say of the property. "We try to exceed people's expectations. We want to get the oohs and aahs and wows." In 1997, Station spent more than $200 million to open Sunset Station, a 130,000-square-foot property in Henderson, Nevada, a sprawling suburb south of Las Vegas, modeled after a Spanish piazza, with faux terra-cotta villas and tiled roofs. It would be the largest off-strip casino in Las Vegas, with a larger casino floor than either the Luxor or the Mirage Hotel & Casino. In 2001, Station acquired a 50 percent stake in Green Valley Ranch in Henderson, in a deal that included a $165 million loan from a varied group of bankers. The deal would entitle Station to 2 percent of the property's annual revenue plus an annual management fee of more than $4 million. "The late nineties really was a discovery period that defined the capacity of the locals market. And every time [the Fertittas] built a new property, it got a little nicer," Dr. Tony Lucas, a gaming professor at the University of Nevada, Las Vegas, and a former Station employee, said in an interview with the *Las Vegas Sun*.

By 2006, Lorenzo and Frank III had used similar financial structures to expand Station's list of properties to sixteen, with another seven hundred acres of land that the company would describe as "the best portfolio of un-developed, gaming entitled real property in the Las Vegas Valley." In 2007, Station took on another $3.4 billion in debt to buy back all of the company's stock and go private, in a deal brokered by Tom Barrack's Colony Capi-tal, which Station claimed would allow it more flexibility to develop new properties and expand into other markets. When the subprime mortgage crisis sent the US real estate market into free-fall in 2008, Station's debt load began to seem like a death sentence, as revenues plummeted across the gaming and hospitality sector. Monthly slot machine revenues dropped from $3.8 billion in July 2007 to $2.9 billion in July 2009, according to Apertor Hospitality, an asset management and advisory company. Unem-ployment rates in Las Vegas would rise as high as 14 percent, and Nevada would become the number one state in the country for home foreclosures. An estimated 65 percent of home mortgages in the state were underwater.

Station's annual revenue would decline by $300 million in 2009, with gaming revenue down 17 percent across all its properties, and hotel book-ings dropped another 22 percent. The total worth of the company's assets fell more than $1.5 billion—from $5.8 billion to $4.3 billion—between 2008 and 2009, while its debt had grown to more than $6.6 billion. The situation was worsened by the November 2008 opening of Aliante Station, a lavish $662 million casino and resort in North Las Vegas, with twenty-five hundred slot machines and video poker machines, that Station had built in partnership with the Greenspun Corporation, a Las Vegas–based media conglomerate.

The Fertittas had tried to negotiate a lower interest rate for their out-standing debt with Station's note holders. One proposed offer would have repaid senior note holders $540 for every $1,000 of bonds they had bought. Subordinated note holders would be paid just $200 per $1000 bond. The offer was rejected by a margin of nearly two-to-one after Sta-tion's bond holders voted on it. Boyd Gaming, one of Station's only major competitors in the locals market, which owned Sam's Town, the Orleans, and a number of historic casinos on Fremont Street, floated a potential offer to buy all of Station's properties for a reported $2.4 billion, but the Fertittas decided instead to enter bankruptcy, leaving the company's fu-ture to the courts. In the best case, the court would determine a fair rate for Station's various note holders and allow the company to continue op-erating. In the worst case, all of its properties and other assets would be sold off piecemeal, leaving Lorenzo and Frank III with nothing.

In many ways, the UFC's success had been as precariously constructed as Station's. The Fertittas had often relied on new loans and lines of credit to bankroll the promotion's growth, cover acquisition costs, and issue lav-ish dividend payments to themselves and White. After reaching terms to acquire Pride in 2007, Zuffa took out a loan worth $275 million to help cover the costs, but reportedly allocated the majority of the funds—$199 million—to dividend distributions for the Fertittas and White. The re-ported dividend was nearly four times as much as the $55 million the UFC had paid to its two-hundred-plus fighter roster in 2007. The annual fees required for the loan were $23.9 million, high enough to prompt Standard & Poor's to downgrade Zuffa's credit rating from BB to BB- in 2007, even as the promotion was continuing to grow at record-breaking levels. Among other concerns, S&P cited the fact that Zuffa had doubled its operating expenses in just one year, and 75 percent of the company's total revenue came from live events, a single source that left its long-term profitability susceptible to a similar kind of market volatility that would later push Station into bankruptcy.

A few months later, as Station was racing toward insolvency, Lorenzo announced he would focus on the UFC full-time, with the goal of expanding the company's revenue sources beyond pay-per-views and its deal with Spike. While Frank III tried to save the family business, Lorenzo struck a deliberately optimistic tone in describing the UFC's still untapped growth potential. Within five years, he told the *Sports Business Journal*, he believed the UFC could surpass the global reach and popularity of the NFL, which would generate $7 billion in revenue in 2008. "As huge as the NFL is [in North America], they don't give a shit about the NFL in Europe," Lorenzo said in an interview announcing his new role. "But fighting transcends continents. Everybody on every continent understands a fight." Lorenzo promised to pursue broadcasting agreements in dozens of new markets around the world, including China, India, and Russia. He was also eager to add more money from corporate sponsorships and licensed merchandising to take advantage of the UFC's popularity with advertisers, something that both Spike and the UFC's fighters seemed to be profiting from more effectively than Zuffa.

Before *The Ultimate Fighter*, sponsorship revenue had been a negligible part of the UFC's business, generating just $200,000 in 2004, from mostly obscure or down-market brands like Pit Bull Energy Drinks, 42 Below vodka, and Superior Bindery Inc., an industrial printing company outside Boston. By 2006, sponsorship revenue had risen to $16 million, but the mix of brands remained dubious. It included Mickey's, which had become the official malt liquor of the UFC, and Amp'd, a prepaid mobile provider that would declare bankruptcy in 2007 after accruing more than $100 million in losses over just two years of operation. The UFC's biggest sponsor in 2006 had been Xyience, a brand of science-adjacent energy drinks and health supplements that had become enmeshed in every part of the UFC's programming. Its logos were printed on the octagon mat at almost every event, and the company had hired Chuck Liddell to be its official sponsor, reportedly paying him $75,000 a month and $1 million for two cross-promotional appearances for the Warner Bros. movie *300*. Xyience products were given to contestants throughout the second season of *The*

Ultimate Fighter, and the winner was promised a personal $100,000 sponsorship deal with the brand. In 2007, Xyience signed a new three-year deal with Zuffa worth a reported $32 million over three years, consolidating its position as the UFC's biggest and most recognizable sponsor.

Yet, like many of the UFC's sponsors, Xyience was a deeply unstable business that ran up enormous losses despite its relative popularity. In 2006, the company had generated $22 million but had spent more than $77 million on operating costs, including more than $42 million on marketing. In 2007, a Zuffa-connected subsidiary, "Zyen," which was owned by Fertitta Enterprises and operated out of the same Sahara Avenue offices as the UFC, issued more than $12 million in loans to Xyience, $5.5 million of which would be repaid to Zuffa in the form of sponsorship and other fees. Court documents would later show another Zuffa-connected subsidiary, Bevanda Magica (UFC), which in Italian means "magic drink," had acquired more than five million shares of Xyience, representing roughly 10 percent of the total voting shares. Lorenzo and Frank III were listed as managers, and John Mulkey, the UFC's chief financial officer, was also listed as a shareholder. From the outside, it appeared as if Zuffa had been propping up Xyience to create the illusion of a thriving sponsorship market, while supplying the company with enough capital to cover its operating costs and avoid a bankruptcy or buyout. In January 2008, three months after announcing the groundbreaking Xyience deal, Zuffa closed an even bigger sponsorship agreement with Harley-Davidson, the first "blue chip" advertising brand to associate itself with the UFC. In February, Zuffa reached a long-coveted agreement with Anheuser-Busch to make Bud Light the official beer of the UFC for three years. "Every year, we've taken this thing to another level, but the one thing that wasn't there was the big, blue chip sponsor," White said. "I think it's just the beginning."

As the UFC's sponsorship revenue grew, the promotion began placing new restrictions on the kinds of deals its fighters could sign. While sponsorship approvals had once been a relatively permissive process—at UFC 69, welterweight Mike Swick brought a six-foot banner filled with logos of his sponsors into the octagon without showing it to anyone at the UFC—the list of banned brands steadily expanded to some of the most popular fighter sponsors, including CondomDepot.com, the Gun Store, and AmmoToGo.com. In 2009, Zuffa further restricted its fighter sponsor policy by requiring that all apparel brands first pay Zuffa a $50,000 "brand affiliation" fee before making individual deals with any of the UFC's fighters. "The standard procedure is to have the prospective sponsors contact me directly and I will handle working out an agreement with them so they can sponsor you and other fighters in the UFC," Zuffa's Mike Mersch wrote in an email to a fighter, explaining the new policy. The new policy would also require any sponsors who promoted individual fighters to be exclusive to Zuffa and not sponsor fighters in any other promotion. The changes were deeply unpopular with fighters and led to an immediate loss of supplemental income for many. Even Lesnar seemed unhappy with the UFC's approach to sponsors. In his post-fight interview after UFC 100, standing in a cascade of boos, Lesnar said, "I'm gonna go home tonight, I'm gonna drink a Coors Light—that's a Coors Light because Bud Light won't pay me nothing." The comment infuriated White, and he went straight to Lesnar's locker room after, for what Lesnar would describe as a "whip-the-dog session," followed by a public apology. "I acted very unprofessionally after the fight," Lesnar said. "I screwed up and I apologize. I apologize to Bud Light."

As other fighters and managers began to criticize the UFC's sponsorship policies, both for the bans and for not cutting fighters in on the profits from the deals with Bud Light and other blue chip sponsors, White naturally fell into the role of a public enforcer. He used his newfound celebrity as a bully pulpit to shout down critics, making public "whip-the-dog" sessions its own kind of spectacle. In 2009, White targeted Loretta Hunt, a reporter from the website *Sherdog*, who had written a short news story reporting that the UFC had begun revoking backstage passes for some managers. "They're telling fighters they can go directly to them," one anonymous manager who'd had their credentials taken away told Hunt. "They're telling fighters they'll be doing sponsorships themselves in the near future that will put the managers and agents out of business. They're trying to minimize the managers' and agents' role in the fighter's life so they can better control salaries." Hunt's story sent White into a characteristic rage, and the day after it was published, he recorded a video response in his office that was later posted on the UFC's YouTube channel. He called Hunt's anonymous source a "pussy and a fuckin' faggot and a fuckin' liar and everything else."

He then addressed Hunt directly: "Hey Loretta, if you're gonna write a story, you fuckin' moron, make sure it's fuckin' true and get some facts. And if you're gonna put some quotes in there, get quotes from people who have the balls to put their fuckin' name on it." White ended the video by flipping off the camera and saying, "You fuckin' dumb bitch. Fuck you, Loretta Hunt." The video almost immediately generated dozens of news stories and opinion pieces, and within a few hours the UFC removed it from its YouTube channel. The following day, White offered an apology. "I never intended to hurt anybody in the gay community, or be malicious, or look like a hateful guy," he said in an interview with *ESPN*. However, he refused to take anything back that he had said about Hunt. "I absolutely, positively meant to attack the reporter, Loretta Hunt from *Sherdog*," he said. "Absolutely."

Later that year, White used the UFC's YouTube channel to attack another *Sherdog* columnist, Jake Rossen, who had written a short piece criticizing the UFC's decision to ban CondomDepot. White had a friend film him as he called an unnamed editor at *Sherdog* to complain, then posted the video to a YouTube channel the UFC had recently started. White called Rossen a "fuckin' assbag" and "typical fuckin' douchebag reporter," and asked why he had a job. "What the fuck has this guy ever done to move the sport of MMA forward, okay?" White said. After hanging up, White spoke directly to fans through the camera, explaining that Rossen was effectively a parasite whose main interest was writing "bullshit stories smashing MMA" in order to trick readers into giving him attention. "Jake Rossen, go fuck yourself," White said directly into the camera as the video ended. The behavior might have been disqualifying for the president of another company, but for many fans, White's aggression and authoritarian aura had become part of the UFC's appeal. "The thing that sucks is that video rant, the feedback I got was not negative," White would later say of his Hunt tirade. "It was overwhelmingly positive from our fans. It was, Yeah, you go, Dana. You're the man." For many fans, White simplified ethical and economic complications into a satisfying question of us against them, and everyone who joined him and his vision for the UFC was included in a comforting collective.

White had a similarly charismatic effect on people in the UFC's offices, where despite his public apologies for the term, the word "fag" had become commonplace. One former employee recalled being surprised by how freely the term was used when they started with the company, a default pejorative for any person or thing that wasn't cooperating with the UFC's plans. After a few months, they found it had seeped into their everyday vocabulary, and had simply become the easiest way to understand and be understood. White's penchant for pranks and hazing rituals had also become a regular occurrence. One new hire had their office rigged with a speaker that would play loud farting noises when they were on business calls. Another worker had takeout food snuck into their car's air-conditioning vents, where it quickly spoiled after a day in the desert heat. When Zuffa's chief financial officer, John Mulkey, a former Station executive Lorenzo had persuaded to work on the UFC in 2006, took a few days' vacation to attend a car race, White had his office furniture replaced with children's decorations, including a tiny desk modeled after a race car.

White had also become a decadent and generous figure around Las Vegas. He was a frequent guest at the N9NE Steakhouse in the Palms, where, according to a report in the *Las Vegas Review-Journal*, he had run up dinner bills of $15,000, and left tips as large as $10,000. White was a prodigious gambler, and was rumored to have tipped blackjack dealers as much as $100,000. "He's changed people's lives," one anonymous source told the *Review-Journal*. White also tried to be as open and generous with fans, making a point to say hello or pose for pictures, sometimes for an hour or longer. "If you're excited to meet me, I'm excited to meet you," he told a CNBC documentary crew as they trailed him through the streets of Cologne, Germany. White tried to cultivate the communal spirit with impromptu giveaways and meetups on social media. On a whim one night in New York, White sent out a post on Twitter inviting fans to a Pinkberry frozen yogurt shop in Midtown, which he had a private agreement with to stay open late when he was in town, catering to his notorious sweet tooth. He promised free frozen yogurt and a ticket giveaway for an upcoming UFC event. The shop flooded with people and was surrounded by a group of NYPD officers who'd been called out for crowd control. "I get out of the car and everybody starts cheering and going crazy," White said. "I look at the police and I'm like, Are you guys mad? And they're like, We didn't believe you were coming. I get out, I sign autographs, take pictures. We hand out like a zillion tickets. We're there for two hours. And this is the craziest fucking thing about this whole story: not only is it Monday night, raining, in Midtown Manhattan on a Jewish holiday, I'm giving away tickets to a fight in fucking *Los Angeles.*" Among strangers, it often seemed as if White had found a new home.

For Lorenzo, White's outsized public profile was a boon. His aggressive attitude helped normalize even more aggressive policies meant to consolidate and defend the UFC's position as market leader. In addition to banning certain sponsors, Zuffa had begun using exclusivity clauses with venues, requiring them to not host any other mixed martial arts promotion for a set period of time, typically between thirty days and ninety days, in order to host a UFC event. The company had also used exclusivity clauses with some of their international television partners, which ensured that any network that wanted to air UFC events would agree to not broadcast any other mixed martial arts promotions.

With a bankruptcy court in Las Vegas working through Station's ledgers to determine whether the company should be auctioned off piece by piece to pay off its debtors, business dictated that Lorenzo do as much as possible to keep the UFC growing as quickly as possible. And as the UFC's Spike agreement was set to expire at the end of 2011, Lorenzo wanted its next broadcasting deal to be the promotion's largest to date. Even if that meant leaving Spike.

There was no particular date when Kevin Kay realized Spike was going to lose the UFC. For years, the two brands had been inseparable. "It overtook the whole schedule—we became the UFC channel," says Kay. In October 2007, Spike and Zuffa signed an expansive four-year deal that paid Zuffa $75 million a year for the rights to broadcast UFC content, a fivefold increase on the previous agreement. Each year, Spike would get two seasons of *The Ultimate Fighter*; up to five *Fight Night* events; thirty-nine episodes of *UFC Unleashed,* an hour-long micro-anthology of old fights; *UFC Countdown,* a documentary series that followed fighters through their final weeks of training before an event; the news show *UFC All Access*; and periodic compilation shows like *The 25 Tuffest Moments of All Time,* which featured memorable moments from past seasons of *TUF* (*The Ultimate Fighter*). Within a year, the UFC was outperforming every other major sport except the NFL in ratings for eighteen-to-thirty-four-year-old males, while Spike would add more than twenty million new homes to the seventy-eight million it had inherited from TNN in 2003.

Along with the success came a slow-motion barrage of calls from Emanuel, who began arguing that Spike was underpaying for the UFC's rights less than a year after it had finalized the deal. Brock Lesnar's debut in early 2008 had added new value, Kay recalls Emanuel telling him, and Spike should pay more for the benefit. His calls came with a kind of metronomic persistence once a week, each time adding a new rationale or angle. It was maddeningly repetitive, as if he were reaching out from an alternate dimension where time had come to a full stop until he got his way. "He just kept calling me and calling me and that's when I walked it upstairs and people were like, No, that's not how this works," says Kay. "And that's when people started to realize, Okay, we don't own anything here. . . . That really was the moment where I think they sort of woke up and started questioning the value. What are we paying? What are we getting? We don't own it. There's so many hours of it."

While the UFC's global audience had continued to grow at a staggering pace, most of the growth had come from outside North America, in markets where Zuffa collected licensing fees for repackaged versions of the same events and shows that were airing on Spike. In 2009, Zuffa had announced a deal with Televisa in Mexico for a newly launched sports network that would initially reach six million homes. The UFC also secured broadcasting deals covering Germany, France, Portugal, Congo, Nigeria, and it signed its first major broadcasting deal in China through NMTV, a terrestrial broadcaster that reached more than eighty million homes in Inner Mongolia, a province in Northern China. By the end of 2009, the UFC was available in more than four hundred million homes around the world, and the promotion's November pay-per-view, UFC 105, was broadcast live in more than fifty countries. In 2010, Zuffa opened a full-time office in China, run by Mark Fischer, who had previously worked for the NBA in Taipei, Hong Kong, and Beijing. One of Fischer's main priorities would be reaching some of China's more than 250 million men between eighteen and twenty-four years old, with the goal of making the UFC available in more than a billion homes worldwide by 2012. Also in 2010, Zuffa announced it had sold a 10 percent ownership stake to Flash Entertainment, a sports and entertainment subsidiary of the Arab Emirates government in Abu Dhabi, with the expectation that Flash would help broker new deals in the Middle East and Asia.

For Lorenzo, the value in the company's international business wasn't in the up-front revenue—collectively, international licensing accounted for around 10 percent of the UFC's yearly revenue, roughly $45 million. Instead, each new deal substantially increased the UFC's global audience reach, which Lorenzo believed would prime each new market for all of the other parts of the UFC's business model, including its licensed merchandise and apparel, new franchise gym locations, local sponsorship deals, and, eventually, converting international viewers into pay-per-view customers. "We'd rather go out and get a license fee and expose the product to as many people as we can and, over time as big fights come up, move to a pay-per-view platform," Lorenzo said in a 2009 interview.

The strategy had produced a string of broken records for ratings and audience size, which affirmed White and Lorenzo's view that the drama of two people in a cage fighting could translate to any culture or country, drawing the same kind of fascinated awe in Macau or Manilla as it did in Las Vegas. In 2011, the UFC held an event in Brazil, UFC 134, for the first time since UFC 17.5 in 1998, as part of a deal with RedeTV!, a brash new network that had launched in 1999. Tickets sold out in seventy-four minutes, and the live broadcast captured a peak audience of thirty-five million viewers, helping Rede pass the country's biggest television broadcaster, Globo, for fourteen minutes. Another *Fight Night* event featuring heavyweight champion Junior dos Santos drew fifty-two million viewers, and another event that aired between 1:00 a.m. and 3:00 a.m. local time drew an audience of sixteen million, or 70 percent of everyone in the country watching television at the time. *The Ultimate Fighter* would regularly draw ten million viewers, several times more than the English-language version of the show was drawing for Spike in the US. That same year, Zelaznik helped close a new broadcasting deal in the UK with ESPN, promising to bring another four to six live events to the territory. By the end of 2010, the UFC had added another one hundred million homes to its global broadcasting reach, and the company had begun targeting a future broadcasting deal with India, with help from Flash Entertainment's connections in the region.

The international expansion had little effect on the UFC's ratings in the United States, which had been mostly flat since the debut of *The Ulti-mate Fighter* in 2005. Four of the first five seasons of *The Ultimate Fighter* saw rating declines, and the sixth produced an all-time low, with an average audience share of 1.1 for each of its twelve episodes, compared to an average of 1.6 from the first season. The first ten UFC *Fight Night* events had drawn an average 1.7 share, with audience size ranging from between one and two million viewers. There had been periodic highs—such as when Zuffa allowed UFC 92 or UFC 100 to be replayed on Spike a few weeks after they originally aired, or when Kimbo Slice was cast as a contestant in the tenth season of *The Ultimate Fighter*—but most events had begun to feel perfunctory and almost interchangeable, with mostly unfamiliar fighters competing for stakes that seemed to dissolve after each broadcast's end credits.

Spike had played on the UFC's facelessness, promoting its generic aura of hypermasculinity as an antidote to a generation that had lost its sense of self in a bewildering fog of consumerism and dead-end day jobs. One typical ad featured a man in hunting clothes sharpening a knife in the woods. "The other day I was shopping for a lavender duvet cover to match my canopy bed and I thought, How do I know what a duvet cover is?" an off-screen voice said as the camera slowly zoomed in on the man. "And why do I own a canopy bed? And why the hell am I wearing capri pants? I've become a real Nancy. Then I switched to UFC on Spike TV. One dropkick to the face and I was back to my old self. You know, reading nudie magazines and scratching my junk. Thanks, Spike TV." In some ways, the facelessness was what gave UFC events their power, framing the rare moments of triumph in a fight as life-changing jackpots, something that could lift bouncers and baristas living in crowded house shares or their parents' spare bedrooms into a new reality, where everyone watching saw indisputable proof that they were what they had always said they were, world-class mixed martial artists and elite athletes.

The 2008 financial collapse had only made the appeal more powerful for young men in the US, who could see their own circumstances in many of the fighters' backstories, and dutifully tuned in each week as both a distraction from their worsening financial prospects and a reminder that there were still ways out for those willing to make the right sacrifices. By 2009, the average net worth of people under thirty-five had dropped to

$3,662, a nearly 70 percent decline from 1984, and one in five Americans under thirty-five were living below the poverty line. A quarter of Americans between eighteen and thirty-four had moved back in with their parents, in part because they'd been unable to find steady income. Of those living with their parents, one in four was idle, meaning they were no longer actively seeking work or had plans to return to school. Many were struggling with student loan debt—thirty-seven million Americans owing more than $760 billion, and more than four million overdue on at least one payment. Others were buried in credit card debt, which in the US had grown to more than $704 billion, the equivalent of about one-fifth the size of all government spending for the year.

When Lorenzo spoke about the UFC, he liked to describe it as an "eat what you kill" sport, in which the athletes were competing for basic survival, not just medals or rankings. The company didn't guarantee its fighters a living, it promised them the opportunity to make one for themselves, as if a steady paycheck with benefits were a kind of prey animal waiting to be stalked and killed for meat. That gave the UFC the awe and drama of a nature documentary. And Lorenzo began to think of the promotion less as a variation of the WWE business model, with weekly television shows leading to monthly pay-per-views. Instead, he began to compare it to Discovery Communications, the expansive reality and documentary programming conglomerate that operated the Discovery Channel, Animal Planet, the Food Network, TLC, HGTV, and the Travel Channel. "It sounds kind of crazy on the face of it," he would later say. "But you think about what helped their company go from producing this dangerous type of content to being a global media player and owning all these networks around the world, there's something generic. . . . People will watch baby seals in Alaska. Anyone. It's interesting, whether you're from Alaska or you're from Africa, or you're from the Caribbean, it's interesting programming." In the same way that Discovery had turned the stark images of animals fighting for a place around a dwindling seasonal watering hole into a consumerist fiefdom, with plushy toys, T-shirts, television shows, chain restaurants, branded cruises, and slippers shaped like hippos and stingrays, Lorenzo wanted to transform the UFC into a global media company that used fighting as a foothold to break into dozens of new industries—gyms, nutritional supplements, documentaries, music and movie co-ventures, apparel co-ventures, toys and video game deals, and more, all of which would feed back into a central but nebulous brand.

It was hard to see where Spike would be useful in that vision. As negotiations about a new deal to keep the UFC on Spike beyond 2011 began, Zuffa was eager for even more broadcast hours and made plans for more than thirty events in 2012. The company also wanted to start producing stand-alone seasons of *The Ultimate Fighter* designed specifically for the UFC's new list of international markets, including Brazil, Mexico, and potentially India. It felt counterintuitive to Kay and others at Viacom, who had begun to fear the UFC was becoming overexposed and that the huge amount of programming it put out each week often diluted what was special about the sport. Kay had wanted Zuffa to book bigger stars in its *Fight Night* cards rather than reserving them for pay-per-views, making it easier for the network to build up each new event. He had also wanted to pull *The Ultimate Fighter* back to one season a year instead of two, but for Lorenzo and White, rollbacks were out of the question. With pay-per-view sales accounting for around 55 percent of the UFC's annual revenue, there was little incentive to divert stars to *Fight Night* cards, where Zuffa would receive a set licensing fee regardless of ratings.

Throughout 2010, Zuffa had met with other networks to see what options were available, including NBC, which was already broadcasting World Extreme Cagefighting, the regional promotion in California that Zuffa had acquired as a feeder league in 2005 and that aired on NBC's sports-themed cable network Versus. White also met with Fox, which was planning to consolidate its vast array of regional sports affiliates into a national network to rival ESPN. The most unusual option came from meetings with NBC's parent company, Comcast, which was looking to sell G4TV, a cable network that competed against Spike for the eighteen-to-thirty-four year-old male audience with programming that was mostly focused on video games, science fiction, and consumer technology. While the network was available in more than sixty million homes in the US, it had seen its ratings steadily decline as the number of cable networks available in the US had grown. By 2011, the average American household had access to 168 television channels, but regularly watched just seventeen. Zuffa had discussed buying 60 percent of G4TV, which was valued at roughly $600 million, and remaking it into a platform for cage fighting, and a convenient outlet for the company's growing library of fights, both its own and those from defunct competitors like Pride, which had been absorbed into the UFC brand.

Spike's options should the UFC leave were more limited. Viacom had begun airing events from Bellator, a small tournament-based promotion launched in 2008, on MTV2, but the ratings had been a fraction of what even the least-watched UFC events on Spike drew, with audiences that typically ranged between two hundred thousand and three hundred thousand. The only other major promotion at the time was Strikeforce, a California promotion that had broadcasting agreements with both CBS and Showtime. Originally founded as a small kickboxing promotion in 1985 by Scott Coker, a former stunt coordinator and martial artist, Strikeforce had rebranded as a cage fighting company in 2006. Initially, the company had focused on promoting local fighters from Northern California, which had been home to a number of top-tier fight teams, including American Kickboxing Academy and Cesar Gracie's Gracie Fighter. The company's debut featured a fight between Frank Shamrock and Cesar Gracie, and drew a record-breaking live audience of 18,265 at the HP Pavillion in San Jose, the largest ever for a mixed martial arts event in the United States at the time. In 2008, Silicon Valley Sports & Entertainment, the company that operated the HP Pavillion, acquired 50 percent ownership of Strikeforce and made it a key part of a plan to turn the arena into an events hub. In 2009, the company acquired EliteXC and took over the promotion's broadcast slots with both CBS and Showtime, steadily amassing its own roster of unique stars like Kimbo Slice, Nick Diaz, and Cristiane "Cyborg" Venâncio, who beat Gina Carano and became the reigning women's featherweight champion. In 2009, Strikeforce scored its biggest coup to date by signing Fedor Emelianenko after the collapse of Affliction, giving it an argument that it had an even better heavyweight division than the UFC, despite the fact that the company's annual revenue, around $30 million, was less than one-tenth the UFC's.

In November 2010, Zuffa had made an attempt to acquire Strikeforce, when Lorenzo and a small delegation of Zuffa lawyers flew to New York to meet with Strikeforce's management. According to Coker, Lorenzo had argued that it would be in the best interest of the sport if there was only one major global brand instead of two, not unlike the NFL and NBA. It

had been a tempting offer. Just two years after buying into the mixed martial arts business, executives at Silicon Valley had begun to question the
decision. While the promotion's revenue had grown more than 700 percent since 2006, close to two-thirds of the company's total revenue went
to paying fighters, including its costly agreement with Emelianenko, who
had unexpectedly lost two of his first three fights, including a horrific
doctor's stoppage TKO to Antônio Silva, which left his right eye swollen
shut and his face purpled with bruising and fresh blood. In early 2010,
Strikeforce lost another important revenue source when CBS canceled its
contract after a post-fight brawl broke out in the cage during an event in
Nashville, driven by Nick Diaz, who had been cornering a teammate from
Gracie Fighter, Jake Shields. Coker had hoped to make up the shortfall
with new revenue through DVD sales and launching an online streaming
platform to show old fights from both the Strikeforce and EliteXC catalog,
but the promise of a buyout from Zuffa seemed like a surer bet for Silicon
Valley, and they agreed to enter negotiations with Zuffa.

Coker had tried to argue against the sale, asking for another year to
bolster revenues and find a new domestic television partner to replace
CBS. Silicon Valley's executives weren't persuaded by Coker, and decided to accept an offer from Zuffa reported to be roughly $40 million. In
March 2011, White announced the deal in a YouTube interview with Ariel
Helwani, a reporter from *MMA Fighting*. The news came a week before
Coker had planned to announce the sale to Strikeforce's staff and fighters,
and the off-the-cuff statement from White sent the promotion into confusion for days after, with people scrambling to figure out whether they
would have jobs in a month's time. The announcement had also come as
a surprise to many at Spike, who realized the once promising market for
alternatives to the UFC—Pride, Affliction, IFL, WEC, EliteXC—had been
wiped out. Knowing Viacom wouldn't approve a new deal that was substantially bigger than the last, Kay did his best to sell Lorenzo and White
on staying with the network. "The only argument I could make was: I
want you to stay here. You should take less money to stay here because
you're the most important thing at Spike and you're promoted all over the
network, all day, every day," says Kay. "You're gonna go [to Fox] and then
you're gonna see one spot on the NFL and you're not gonna get treated
like that [anymore]."

It was a losing strategy, and in August 2011, Zuffa announced that it would be leaving Spike at the end of the year for an agreement with Fox Sports, which would pay more than $700 million over the course of seven years, with annual licensing fees rising from $90 million in the first year of the deal to $115 million in the last year of the deal. In addition to paying more than Spike, Fox had also agreed to Zuffa's plans for even more programming, with thirty-six events spread across several Fox channels, including FX, Fuel, Fox Sports 1, Fox Sports 2, and main Fox. The UFC would account for 15 percent of Fox Sports's weekly programming, and even more on its subsidiaries, including 646 hours a year on Fuel, with a mix of *Fight Night* events, rebroadcasts of old events, news shows, fighter documentaries, archival compilations, and two seasons a year of *The Ultimate Fighter*.

Zuffa announced the deal in Los Angeles, at Studio 2A on the Fox Network Center soundstages, where a weekly UFC news show *UFC Tonight* would be filmed. "We're not second class anymore," lightweight champion Frankie Edgar said at the event, flanked by Chuck Liddell, Rashad Evans, and Georges St-Pierre. "We're right up there with MLB, the NFL—you know, we're mainstream. And I still think this is just the tip of the iceberg. The opportunities this is going to lead to are endless."

Asked about the split from Spike, Lorenzo claimed it had come down to broadcast hours. "We need more fights, we need more programming, we've got more weight classes, we've got fights that we need to do from an international standpoint, so when you have one channel that you broadcast on, one channel can only take so much programming, right?" he said. While Lorenzo was pragmatic, White was triumphant. "I always talk about monumental moments we've had over the last years," White said. "If you add them all up and put them together, they don't equal this."

For many of Strikeforce's former executives, news of the UFC's split with Spike was shocking. Strikeforce's legal counsel Ken Ellner looked back on the timing of Zuffa's offer to buy the promotion just months before announcing it would vacate all of its time slots on Spike with suspicion. "If they were going to leave Spike that would have left it open for us," Ellner would later say. That possibility could have changed the decision-making process that led to the decision to sell to Zuffa. "I never imagined that the UFC would leave Spike," Coker would say. "If I'd known that, I would have told them to wait and we could have had Viacom as a partner and we would have been on both Showtime and Spike."

Instead, Strikeforce ran as a kind of zombie promotion for another year, fulfilling its remaining obligations to Showtime, while Zuffa brought most of its star fighters into the UFC, including Nick Diaz, who was booked for a welterweight championship fight against Georges St-Pierre in October 2011; Dan Henderson, who was booked as a pay-per-view main event against former Pride star Mauricio "Shogun" Rua that November; and heavyweight contender Alistair Overeem, who was booked against Lesnar in a pay-per-view main event in December. Emelianenko, however, didn't make the transition. After three shocking losses in Strikeforce, he opted to return to Russia to compete for M-1, before finally announcing his retirement in 2012. White had claimed the UFC didn't want Emelianenko after his losses and had cut him. Emelianenko's manager refuted White, saying that Emelianenko had only ever had an agreement with Showtime, through M-1 promotions, and the UFC wouldn't have been able to transfer him into the UFC in the same way it had other fighters.

Ronda Rousey would be one of the last Strikeforce fighters to make the transition. Though she'd had only two professional fights on her record when she made her Strikeforce debut, just a month after Emelianenko's final fight in the promotion, she would become one of its biggest stars. When Zuffa finally announced it would close Strikeforce after the Showtime deal expired, Rousey had nowhere left to go but the UFC.

I WILL MAKE YOU LOOK LIKE A GENIUS

Ronda Rousey worked the day shifts at Gladstones, a beachside bar and grill overlooking the Pacific Ocean at the end of Sunset Boulevard. She spent her afternoons behind the bar, buoyed by ocean air, Vicodin, and stolen sips of a sugary drink she'd invented in honor of that year's Democratic presidential candidate, called "Party Like a Barack Star," a mix of vodka, espresso, Kahlúa, Baileys, cocoa powder, and sweetened half-and-half. At twenty-one, Rousey felt like she had already done enough work for one lifetime. She had spent most of the previous eleven years obsessively chasing an Olympic medal in judo, but after fighting her way back out of the losers' bracket to win a bronze medal at the 2008 Summer Games in Beijing, she'd begun to wonder if the sacrifices had been worth it. When she returned to LA afterward, she'd slept on the couch in her mother's Santa Monica apartment and used her $10,000 winnings to buy a secondhand Honda Accord—painted Olympic gold in honor of the goal she had fallen just short of.

Rousey paid her bills by bartending. She split her weeks up with shifts at three different bars: the Redwood, a pirate-themed bar in downtown Los Angeles; the Cork, a classic neon-lit lounge in West Adams; and Gladstones, where she poured beers and mixed margaritas for tourist families and the locals who'd come down from their bluffside mansions to socialize. (Among Rousey's favorite regulars were a pair of record producers who tipped in both cash and marijuana.) *SportsCenter* on ESPN ran throughout the day on the television above the bar, and UFC highlights were presented in between touchdowns, home runs, and power play goals. The short clips fascinated Rousey, pulling her now dormant athletic senses back into focus. To her eyes, many of the fights looked amateurish, a series of missed opportunities, like watching through night-vision goggles as someone tries to reach for a doorknob in the darkness. "I could totally do that," she thought to herself.

At the time, the idea of women fighting in cages still seemed bizarre. Though women had been part of mixed martial arts from the start, they had rarely gotten credit for their contributions. During the first UFC in 1993, Davie had hired world kickboxing champion Kathy Long to provide color commentary and technical analysis, and she had been the most competent voice on the broadcast. A number of early UFC champions, including Don Frye and Dan Severn, trained with Becky Levi, a judo black belt and physical education specialist. In 1997, Levi became one of the first women in the US to compete in mixed martial arts at IFC 4 in Hogansburg, New York. After the event, the IFC continued to periodically book women's matches, and soon other regional promotions followed suit, including King of the Cage, SuperBrawl, and Cage Rage. In the early 2000s, Jennifer Howe emerged as a regional star in the Midwest, and in 2002, former UFC commentator Jeff Osborne promoted the first card to feature all women fighters, *Hook N Shoot: Revolution* in Evansville, Indiana. It was the first of several women-only events he would promote. In 2007, Gina Carano became an unexpected star in EliteXC, appearing in the first mixed martial arts card to air on network television, *EliteXC Primetime* on CBS. After suffering her first professional loss in 2009, to Cristiane "Cyborg" Venâncio, Carano left cage fighting for a career in acting, including a starring role in Steven Soderbergh's *Haywire*. Despite Carano's breakout success—her fight on CBS drew an average of 4.7 million viewers—White had been uninterested in having women fight in the UFC. In 2011, he famously told a *TMZ* reporter it would never happen. White worried there weren't enough women fighters sufficiently talented to fill out a full weight division. He also thought there was something that was fundamentally unsettling about seeing a woman battered in a cage. He conceded it was a sexist attitude, but the few times he had scouted women fighters at regional promotions had disturbed him in ways that fights between men rarely had.

When Rousey mentioned the idea of competing in cage fighting to some of her teammates at the judo club where she still periodically trained, Gene LeBell's legendary Hayastan MMA Academy in North Hollywood, everyone was supportive. A few had already made the transition to the UFC themselves, including Manny Gamburyan, who was a finalist on the fifth season of *The Ultimate Fighter*, and Karo Parisyan, who had been a top contender in the UFC's welterweight division when

Rousey was a teenager. Like many gyms at the time, Hayastan had its own in-house manager to help book fights and arrange sponsorships for the gym's fighters, Darrin Harvey. Rousey drew up an elaborate fourteen-day training cycle of boxing, weightlifting, surfing, and sand dune sprints that would help her get back into shape for competition while keeping up with her bartending schedule.

"This is the stupidest fucking idea I've heard in my life," Rousey's mother, AnnMaria De Mars, told her when she first heard the plan. De Mars understood why her daughter was drawn to mixed martial arts. She herself had been a lifelong judoka and, in 1984, had become the first American to win a gold medal at the World Judo Championship in Vienna, Austria. De Mars had encouraged her daughter to take up judo at eleven, and had pushed her to be an aggressive competitor who trained not to have fun but to be the best, or empty herself in trying. When Rousey was twelve, she was worried she had broken a toe in practice and was in too much pain to continue. Instead of taking her to the emergency room, De Mars insisted she run laps around the mat until the practice ended. "If you want to win the way you say you do," De Mars had said after, "you need to be able to compete, even when you're in pain. You need to be able to push through. Now you know you can."

De Mars was eager for Rousey to explore the world outside the dojo after more than a decade of competitive judo and two trips to the Olympics, and hopefully realize there was more to life than competition. As she listened to Rousey, she feared the competitive hunger of her teenage years might steer her into a state of stunted adolescence, chasing dreams that would turn out to be both unattainable and unworthwhile. "I am not going to be one of these parents who has a thirty-year-old living in their house and eating their food because you have a dream," De Mars said.

The reaction stung Rousey, and for the next two weeks she refused to speak to De Mars. It was a familiar feeling for Rousey, who had been unable to speak until she was six—the result of a traumatic birth during which the umbilical cord had twisted around her neck and prevented her from breathing for several minutes, leaving parts of her brain associated with language development skills damaged. She had communicated with her parents and two older sisters through gestures and simple syllabic sounds. In public, she had relied on them to translate for her, but she was always aware that there was a wide gulf between what she was trying to communicate in her mind and what came out when she tried to speak. "It wasn't just about words, it was about everything," Rousey wrote in a memoir. "What I felt. What I wanted. What I meant. It was always a struggle."

After she had finally begun to speak, Rousey's family relocated from Santa Monica to Minot, North Dakota, where her mother had gotten a job teaching educational psychology at Minot State University. During their first winter in North Dakota, Rousey's father, Ron, broke his back during a family sledding trip, and spent five months in the hospital recuperating, a process that was further complicated by the fact that he suffered from Bernard-Soulier syndrome, which inhibits the blood clotting process. Before the injury, Ron had been a stay-at-home father, but after he was finally released from the hospital, the family found themselves buried in medical bills and Ron decided to look for work to help keep them out of financial trouble. He ended up moving to the small town of Devil's Lake, a two-hour drive from Minot, and the family decided to temporarily live apart while Rousey's mother looked for another teaching job closer to Ron. While her sisters stayed behind in Minot with her mother, Rousey moved in with her father, and the two lived in joyful bachelor's squalor, eating fast food every day and watching R-rated action movies together at night. Though Ron still struggled with pain from his injury, he took care to make sure it never showed when he was with Rousey.

The family was eventually reunited when Rousey's mother found another teaching job at a school closer to Devil's Lake. Ron decided to stop working and stayed at home with his daughters again, but the pain from his injury had continued to worsen, and he began to slip into depression. One afternoon, he called Rousey's mother at her office and told her to come home, then got into his Ford Bronco and drove to a nearby creek where he'd sometimes taken Rousey to skip stones. He parked, got out and ran a hose from the exhaust pipe through the driver's side window, and started the motor again. A few hours later he was found dead.

De Mars would later decide to move the family back to Santa Monica, and eventually remarried. But Rousey seemed stuck in a lingering depression and began struggling in school. De Mars thought judo classes might help her daughter better deal with her grief. "I thought, well, with judo at least you have to have a partner. She would have to go out and meet some other kids," De Mars would later say. "Maybe that would help her?" Rousey was soon obsessed with judo. The continuous movement of the opponent and all the minute threats that had to be attended to during a match—where you gripped the opponents gi, the angle of your hips, the direction of your feet, the numberless small adjustments and misdirections that happened every second—distracted her from her grief. "One hundred percent of my focus had to be in the present moment," Rousey wrote in her memoir. "There was no time for introspection."

After two weeks of nothing but introspection and silence, De Mars agreed to meet Rousey and Darin Harvey for dinner to hear their plan. While De Mars was still skeptical, she agreed to give Rousey one year to start a career. If it didn't seem like she would be able to support herself after that time, Rousey promised to drop fighting altogether and either apply for college or begin a vocational training program with the US Coast Guard.

A few weeks into her new training routine at Hayastan, one of Rousey's training partners invited her to join him for an afternoon at the Glendale Fighting Club, a small kickboxing gym run by Edmond Tarverdyan. Rousey made the drive across the San Fernando Valley to train with Tarverdyan, but was surprised to learn that he wasn't especially interested in working with her. "I was like, A girl fighting?" he would later say. "Why? Like, go teach judo or something." Rather than guiding her through drills, he told her instead to just watch him hold mitts for other fighters and to emulate the footwork and punching techniques on her own. It was completely unlike the treatment she had gotten at Hayastan, where her teammates had affectionately called her "Ron" and gone out of their way to include her in their hardest workouts. "When Ronda was a kid we used to yell at her and tell her to suck her lip back in and start doing the techniques," Parisyan would later say. "She trained with animals like us and that's why she went and became a world champion in judo."

Though a part of her was offended by Tarverdyan's standoffishness, another part was determined to win his approval, and she spent months returning to the Glendale Fighting Club, doing just what he'd said: watch-

ing him work with other fighters and then patiently trying to replicate the
drills on her own in a corner of the gym. When she wasn't at the Glendale Fighting Club, she would drive to a gym in Sherman Oaks to lift
weights and do cardio conditioning. Some days she would drive into Van
Nuys and work out with SK Golden Boys Wrestling Club, a team of local
wrestlers. A few nights a week, she'd drive to a YMCA in West Los Angeles, where she taught beginner judo classes, and then stayed after to
take jiu-jitsu lessons from a local instructor. On weekends, she'd work the
graveyard shift at 24 Hour Fitness in Hollywood to help cover her training expenses, and on Mondays she'd start the cycle all over again.

Harvey booked Rousey in her first amateur fight after just a few
months of training. She took on another debuting fighter, Hayden
Munoz, at a small smoker event in Oxnard, an hour's drive up the coast
from Santa Monica. The event was held at a jiu-jitsu academy in an industrial park, in between a Costco and a FedEx Ship Center. The lights
were turned down low to give the space a theatrical gloom. As she stood
in the cage for the first time, in an improvised outfit of board shorts and
a rash guard, Rousey felt the world narrow around her until she couldn't
hear or see anything other than Munoz, who stood across the cage pacing
in a small circle. After the opening bell, Rousey and Munoz circled each
other for a few seconds. Then Munoz threw a thigh kick, which Rousey
caught and held while she swept Munoz's other leg out from under her.
Rousey landed on top of Munoz and immediately grabbed onto her wrist
and used it as a lever for an armbar. Munoz tried to get away by standing up, but Rousey's grip was too strong and she dragged her back to the
mat, where the pressure on Munoz's elbow joint became overwhelming.
Munoz had been so nervous about facing a former Olympian that she forgot to tap and simply grimaced in pain, prompting the referee to stop the
fight just twenty-three seconds after the bell had rung. As Rousey took a
short victory lap around the cage, she heard scattered cheers from the few
dozen people who'd come to watch. "Winning feels like falling in love,
except it's like falling in love with everybody in the room all at once," she
would write.

She found herself wanting to re-experience that feeling as often as
possible, and Harvey would book her in another four fights over the next
ten months. Rousey would win each by first-round armbar. Though she

was still a novice, all of her opponents were unprepared to defend themselves against an Olympic-caliber athlete who had been one of the best
competitive judokas in her age group. Her longest fight would last just
fifty-seven seconds. It seemed unreal, too fast and yet indisputable, and
after each win, the scowl she wore into the cage dissolved into a smile that
beamed across the small ballrooms like a searchlight.

Her career developed with the singular haste of a love affair, and with
every win a new door seemed to open. First Tarverdyan agreed to begin
individually training her in kickboxing, and in 2011, a year after she'd
made her amateur debut, Rousey signed with Strikeforce, and fought
on an otherwise forgettable card at Palms Casino Resort in Las Vegas.
Rousey's opponent, Sarah D'Alelio, had originally been signed for a one-
fight deal to face Gina Carano, who had tried to make a return to cage
fighting after a two-year absence. That fight had fallen apart after Carano was deemed medically unfit to compete, and D'Alelio was rebooked
against Rousey shortly after.

Rousey treated it as the most important fight of her career and quit
her job at 24 Hour Fitness so she could focus on training full-time. As
with her earlier amateur fights, Rousey overwhelmed D'Alelio and caught
her in a flying armbar just twenty-five seconds into the first round. After
the fight ended, D'Alelio protested the stoppage, saying that she hadn't
tapped in submission, even though Rousey had her arm torqued to the
brink of hyperextension, prompting her to scream in pain. As Rousey returned to the locker room after the victory, she felt the moment had been
spoiled by D'Alelio's protests, and she decided that from then on, when
she caught an opponent in a submission hold she wouldn't hold anything
back. "From this day on," she told Tarverdyan, "I'm just going to fucking
break everybody's arm."

Rousey soon developed a reputation among fans, not just for the speed
of her victories but for the frequently stomach-turning damage she caused
with her submission holds. In her next fight with Strikeforce, against Julia
Budd, Rousey won in just thirty-nine seconds, by wrenching Budd's arm
backward well past the 180-degree point. "That's a flamingo knee!" color
commentator Pat Miletich cried out in disgust. After she tapped, Budd
seemed overwhelmed by the pain and left her arm lying off to the side, at
a shockingly unnatural angle.

Four months later, Rousey was booked against Miesha Tate, Strike-force's women's bantamweight champion, a comparative veteran of the sport who had competed professionally since 2007. Rousey and Tate would fight in the main event of a card that would air live on Showtime, from the twenty-thousand-person capacity Nationwide Arena in Colum-bus, Ohio. Rousey had developed a peculiar but intense animosity toward Tate, a former high school wrestler who was nicknamed "Cupcake" and preferred to fight in hot-pink spandex skirts that she wore over her fight shorts. Everything about Tate irritated Rousey. In the lead-up to the fight, she described Tate as "just a chick who decided in high school it'd be cool to wrestle, and a few years later decided it'd be cool to do MMA. . . . This is just a fad to her." It was an offensive attitude for Rousey, who had sacri-ficed most of her life preparing to compete at the highest levels possible. More offensive still was Tate's claim that Rousey didn't deserve to be a title contender after just four professional fights spread out over the course of a year. The night before the fight, tensions escalated even further when Tate's boyfriend, who'd competed on the fourteenth season of *The Ulti-mate Fighter*, posted on Twitter that if Rousey ever wanted to fight a man, he would "knock her teeth dwn her throat the break her arm.[*sic*]"

As Rousey and Tate finally faced off in the cage, the mutual disdain was overwhelming. Rousey refused to touch Tate's glove as a customary sign of respect before the start of the fight. Within a minute of the open-ing bell, Rousey had taken Tate down and trapped her in an armbar just as she had with all her other opponents. As Rousey pressed her hips up into Tate's elbow, she wrenched the arm backward at the wrist. Tate's arm began to bend in a similarly gruesome angle to Budd's. As the commen-tary team again groaned in disgust, Tate refused to tap. In a burst of numb adrenaline, she slid out of Rousey's grip and, after a quick scramble, found herself behind Rousey, clamped onto her torso like a backpack, trying to find enough space under Rousey's chin for a choke.

After another minute of struggle, Rousey shook Tate off and got back to her feet. A few seconds later, Rousey again tripped Tate back to the mat, then slipped into the mount position and battered Tate's head with punches. As Tate held out her arms to deflect the blows, Rousey quickly grabbed Tate's wrist and rolled back into an armbar that was even tighter than the first. Rousey pulled back on the arm until the joint buckled, knobs of bone and strained tendon showing through the stretched skin in places where they shouldn't have been visible. Trapped in a sudden flood of pain, Tate tapped in submission a little more than thirty seconds before the end of the first round. An excruciating slow-motion replay showed Tate's arm completely dislocated at the elbow and bent backward at a ninety-degree angle. After the fight, Rousey refused to shake Tate's hand when she offered it, and in her post-fight interview Rousey said she wasn't bothered by the horrific injury she had inflicted on Tate. "I don't feel that bad about it," she said, as waves of boos broke out across the stunned crowd.

Though it was just her fifth professional fight, for which she had been paid a disclosed purse of $32,000, Rousey found herself an overnight celebrity, who had recaptured a large part of the audience that had first become fascinated with Carano four years earlier. There was something virtuosic in the way she pruned back the familiar elements of mixed martial arts, until the only things that remained were exactly the kinds of standing grappling exchanges she had spent her life perfecting. Her body seemed to move faster than her opponents could think, and by the time their minds had caught up with her movements, they were inevitably caught in the vise of Rousey's armbars, isolated and strangely helpless.

In the summer of 2012, the editors of *ESPN* magazine photographed her for their Body Issue. She appeared nude with full body paint, in front of a pastel plume of artificial fog, with pink handwraps clumped over her knuckles. When the editors saw the photos, they decided to put Rousey on the cover. When she saw the issue, she found it hard to recognize herself. She had never seen herself as beautiful. As a teenager, her classmates had teased her over the added muscle mass she'd gained from judo training, calling her Miss Man. "There were days I would look at myself in the mirror and just cry," she'd later say.

Rousey had known a career in mixed martial arts would involve not just fighting but being seen by an audience. She had hoped to build on what Carano had accomplished, proving not just that women fighters could attract attention, but that they could be as technical, athletic, and violently dangerous as men. "I think what we really need right now is a face to the sport that people actually want to look at, so I'm going to try my best to be that person," she said in a 2011 interview. As she found herself suddenly transforming into a public figure, fielding interview requests and beginning to make television appearances, Rousey tried to resist the self-infatuation of celebrity. Before her next fight, against Sarah Kaufman, Showtime made her the subject of a two-part *All Access* documentary, and Rousey proudly shared the disordered squalor of her life as both a world champion cage fighter and cover model. The cameras followed her through the cluttered rental house in Santa Monica that she shared with a roommate. Dirty dishes were piled in the sink, small mounds of unwashed laundry filled the corners of her bedroom, and a wiggly dogo argentino named Mochi perched on ratty thrift store furniture. The only trace of personal indulgence was a forty-two-inch flat-screen television Rousey had bought, but never actually plugged in, after beating Tate. She had also splurged on high-speed internet for *World of Warcraft*, which she played on an old laptop in between training sessions.

Tellingly, the *All Access* episode opened with an endorsement, not from her mother or Tarverdyan, but from Dana White. He described Rousey in admiring terms, someone who had changed his mind about women fighting in cages. "Everything you need in a fighter, she has—yet she's a woman and she's beautiful," he said. "The Ronda Rousey package is different than any package we've ever seen."

When White watched Rousey's fights in Strikeforce, he saw something he rarely saw in men's fights: unapologetic aggression coupled with a near instinctive ability to cause serious damage within a matter of seconds. Like Royce Gracie, Rousey accomplished things that seemed like they shouldn't have been possible, creating moments you had to see to believe. Lesnar's departure from the UFC a year earlier, after two consecutive losses and worsening symptoms of diverticulitis, a chronic intestinal disease, had left a void in the promotion's pay-per-view numbers and its roster bereft of new stars that were as reliably marketable as Lesnar had been. Though Rousey had only been a professional for a little over a year, the potential for bringing in a whole new audience of women fans, along with a new class of blue chip advertisers eager to sell to them, suddenly seemed too lucrative to not at least try.

As Strikeforce entered its final months of operation in the summer of 2012, Rousey was still unsure if she would be able to make the jump to the UFC with many of the promotion's other male stars. After her first

Strikeforce title defense, a fifty-four-second armbar submission against Kaufman in August, White invited Rousey to meet him in Hollywood for the premiere of the fifth season of *Sons of Anarchy*, a show about a biker gang that aired on FX. After, he took her to dinner at Mr Chow in Beverly Hills. It was the same restaurant where, a year-and-a-half earlier, he had told a TMZ reporter that women would never fight in the UFC. As White retold the story of that night to Rousey, he admitted he had been wrong, and told her that she was going to be the first woman to fight in the UFC. She felt a smile break across her face so forcefully it almost hurt. Though neither Harvey nor any of her coaches were there to help her think through the offer, Rousey couldn't see how there was anything to think about. "In my mind, there was confetti, a full marching band, and a choir from heaven singing," she'd recall. White cautioned there were no guarantees—her first fight would be an experiment, and her opponent was still being finalized. If it didn't work, there might not be another one.

"I promise," she said, "I will make you look like a genius."

BROTHER, I LOST EVERYTHING

By 2014, the UFC offices had grown to nearly twenty thousand square feet spread across the business park on Sahara Avenue across from Palace Station, mostly cobbled together from smaller satellite offices that Zuffa had leased as they had become available. White no longer recognized many of the faces as he walked back and forth across the sprawl between meetings, and there were large sections of new office space he had never even been in. He had once taken pride in having a personal relationship with every employee and every fighter who worked with the UFC, but with more than four hundred full-time employees, he often found himself surrounded by strangers. "When we started this thing, guys were at my house for holidays and shit like that," he would later say. "I walk around the UFC offices now and I don't know half the people who work there. I couldn't tell you half their names and I don't have a personal relationship with the majority of the fighters like I used to." White was rarely in the office for more than a few days a month, and instead spent most of his time traveling around the world aboard the Fertittas' private jet, which they had committed to UFC business travel. During one representative three-month stretch, White claimed to have flown more than forty thousand miles, more than an NBA or Major League Baseball team would travel in a full season. "I've done an entire season of *The Ultimate Fighter* in Brazil," White said in an interview. "I'm on episode three of *The Ultimate Fighter* here in the United States. Plus, I've been to Omaha, Nebraska; Atlanta for a press conference; Chicago, Japan, Australia, and a million other places in between that I can't even remember."

The pace had been no less hectic for many of the UFC's employees. Jen Wenk, Zuffa's PR director, described the UFC as operating in a state of "controlled chaos" during most of her six-year tenure. "It got to the point where we didn't clock time by dates or months," she said in a 2012 interview. "We clocked time by events, by what UFC event number it was. For example, my birthday was UFC 152 or Christmas could be 154, or someone's baby is due around 151." The deal with Fox had only added to the intensity. With five channels to provide programming for—Fox, Fox Sports, Fox Sports 2, FX, and Fuel TV—and Fight Pass, a new subscription streaming service launched in late 2013 to provide access to both old and new events, Zuffa's yearly event schedule grew to forty-six in 2014, almost one a week. "There were plenty of times when people in our offices wouldn't know where the fight was being broadcast that weekend," says Don Gold. "Is it a pay-per-view fight? Is it a Fox Sports fight? Is it a big Fox main event? Is it on Fight Pass?" Adding to the confusion, just seven of the UFC's forty-six events for 2014 took place in Las Vegas, and nearly half took place outside the US, with cards in Macau, Mexico City, Stockholm, Singapore, Abu Dhabi, Auckland, Vancouver, and Tokyo. And the international expansion continued, with new deals covering South Africa, Central Asia, and the Middle East, along with renewed agreements with TSN in Canada, Televisa and Globo in Brazil, and BT Sport in the UK and Ireland, to which the UFC promised four hundred hours of programming over a three year term.

The continued international expansion helped make up for a major decline in the UFC's pay-per-view business, which had fallen from an all-time high in 2010 of 7.7 million to just 2.8 million in 2014. The UFC partially offset the decline by raising its pay-per-view prices, from $49.99 in 2009 to $59.99 in 2014, but even more of the difference was made up from media licensing deals, which often included predetermined annual increases that allowed the UFC's bottom line to rise even as its paying audience dwindled. By 2014, nearly three-quarters of the UFC's revenue came from sources other than pay-per-view buys, a stark reversal from a decade earlier. Lorenzo's efforts to transform the UFC into a transmedia lifestyle brand had also contributed. In 2013, Zuffa acquired LA Boxing, a national chain of fitness centers, and converted eighty-one properties into UFC Gyms, part of a franchising operation the company had first started in 2009 as a co-venture with 24 Hour Fitness cofounder Mark Mastrov. The company also released *UFC Fit*, a twelve-DVD crossfit series hosted by former *Ultimate Fighter* contestant Mike Dolce, promising to help people lose weight and get in shape with exercises based on real fighter training drills. "This is the key to changing your life," White said in a prepared statement about the program at its launch. "This is the chance you've always hoped for." In 2014, the first video game in a multiyear agreement with EA, *EA Sports UFC*, was released, and Zuffa announced a new agreement with Future US to produce and distribute the UFC's official print magazine, *UFC 360*. And in December 2014, Zuffa announced a six-year agreement with Reebok to become the exclusive apparel provider for the UFC, worth an estimated $70 million. Under the terms of the deal, Reebok would provide customized "fight kits" for each fighter in the UFC, containing shorts, T-shirts, hoodies, hats, and shoes to wear into the octagon. There would also be a range of commercial apparel for fans, with special designs for star fighters, like Ronda Rousey and light heavyweight champion Jon Jones. For Lorenzo, the deal was a milestone, replacing what had been a disordered and sometimes bizarre mix of outfits—silk boxing trunks, a camouflage combat kilt, or even a minuscule Speedo, which Dennis Hallman famously wore at UFC 133 in 2011—with the consistent look of a team sport. Reebok had also agreed to pay every fighter on a card an individual sponsorship fee in exchange for wearing its apparel, which in the first year would range from $2,500 for new fighters to $40,000 for defending champions. "All [the fighters] have to worry about is performing that night, not running around trying to figure out if they're going to get 1-800-Radiators on their shorts and whether they're going to get paid at the end of the day," Lorenzo would later say.

This transformation had also made the UFC even less dependent on individual stars like Liddell, Ortiz, Couture, and Lesnar, who had helped define the sport, at a time when Zuffa was forced to commit as much as 41 percent of its annual revenue to fighter compensation. By 2014, just 16 percent of the UFC's revenue went to fighter pay, and the company wielded an unusual amount of leverage over its roster, allowing it to fill out the ever-expanding number of events it held each year. In 2009, the UFC spent $67 million on fighter pay for 215 fights spread over twenty events. In 2014, the company spent $72 million on fighter pay for 503 fights spread across forty-six events, nearly half as much on average per fight as it had five years earlier, when the company had made more than $100 million less in total revenue.

Zev Eigen, a labor law professor from Northwestern University, would describe the UFC's contracts as the worst sports or entertainment agreement he had ever seen. In a 2013 interview, Eigen criticized a range of clauses in a UFC contract that had leaked online, including Zuffa's claim to all rights to a fighter's likeness in secondary markets, and automatic extension clauses that allowed the UFC to add six months to any fighter's contract due to injury. If a fighter won a championship, the UFC could automatically extend their contract at its current pay rate for either a full year or an additional three fights, whichever of the two took the longest amount of time. Eigen compared the clause to involuntary servitude and suggested it could be a violation of the Thirteenth Amendment to the United States Constitution. The contract's termination clause summed up the overwhelming imbalance in power between the UFC and its fighters, which Eigen described as "completely one-sided, completely unfair." It authorized Zuffa to cut a fighter following any loss, due to logistical problems obtaining work visas or proper licensing, or after misdemeanor convictions, while fighters had no reciprocal way to end a contract early. "This is an unconscionable term," Eigen said. "The term unilaterally benefits the employer with no reciprocal benefit to the fighter."

The small number of star fighters who could credibly push back on the UFC—Lesnar, Liddell, Rousey, Anderson Silva—typically did so through private side-letter agreements that promised additional pay that wouldn't be reported to athletic commissions, or personalized perks, like the Dodge Challenger SRT Hellcat Zuffa promised to buy for Quinton Jackson as part of a new agreement he negotiated in 2014. Zuffa bought Ronda Rousey a BMW X6 M (with suggested starting price at the time of $92,900), after her first-round armbar submission win against Liz Carmouche in her UFC debut. "I can't have one of my champions driving around in a busted-ass Honda," she recalled White telling her. For most of the roster, these benefits were inaccessible. Without any major competitors to sign with and no fighters' association to collectively bargain for better baselines—as athletes in the NFL, NBA, MLB, and most other major sports had—it often seemed like the most sensible thing was to accept whatever the UFC offered. "I was so driven, if they said to me, Don't eat for a month, I would have done it," says former lightweight Phillipe Nover. "Anything they would have said, I would have done." A finalist on

the eighth season of *The Ultimate Fighter* in 2008, Nover had been undefeated in his six-fight regional career. He would go on to win all three of
his bouts during the filming of *The Ultimate Fighter*, prompting White
to compare him to a young Georges St-Pierre, the UFC's welterweight
champion at the time.

Though Nover went on to lose in the season finale, by unanimous
decision to Efrain Escudero, the UFC offered him a three-fight contract
paying $8,000 and $8,000, $10,000 and $10,000, and $12,000 and $12,000.
It was a substantial pay cut from what the twenty-five-year-old had been
earning as a nurse in New York City, but Nover was convinced he could
become a UFC champion and decided to quit his job and move back in
with his mother to train full-time. "I knew in my head that I was gonna
win," he says. "In my mind, there was never losing. Losing wasn't an option." Despite his self-belief, Nover would lose his next two UFC fights,
the first by TKO and the second by a unanimous decision to Rob Emerson, a former contestant from the fifth season of *The Ultimate Fighter*.
Though he still had one fight left on his contract, Zuffa decided to release
him. In a little over a year, Nover had earned $16,000 in purse money for
his two fights, and was left with a herniated disc in his neck that would require total replacement surgery. He had to cover the cost himself, through
a health insurance plan he had luckily maintained from his former nursing job. "That was a really low point," says Nover. "I pretty much quit my
job, lost all my fights, and I had a broken neck. I was in bad shape."

Experiences like Nover's more often seemed like the rule than the ex-
ception, as the UFC's roster grew along with its event schedule. With 230
new fighters making their debut in 2014, the UFC had begun to seem
less like a star factory than a staffing agency. Each year, excited new faces
arrived, performed well for a few fights, experienced some unexpected
difficulties, and vanished a short time later, replaced by another crop of
new faces. The UFC had introduced a formal rankings system in February 2013 to add some competitive structure and stakes to the hundreds
of prelim and non-title fights that made up the bulk of its events. The initial seventy-three-person panel, chosen by the UFC, was made up mostly
of radio hosts, television personalities, and sports journalists, many of
whom had questionable expertise in martial arts. But with the average
fighter's career lasting just forty-one months, or five bouts, it was rare that
anyone survived long enough to rise dramatically in the rankings.

For US audiences, watching mostly unfamiliar faces batter one an-. other in pursuit of a better life had begun to lose its appeal. During the Fox Sports era, the UFC's domestic television ratings had been as unreliable as they were on Spike. After a strong debut on November 12, 2011—which drew an average audience of 5.7 million and a peak of 8.8 million for a heavyweight title fight between Junior dos Santos and Cain Velasquez, who had won the championship from Lesnar a year earlier—ratings on Fox Sports and its constellation of subsidiaries had steadily declined. *UFC on FOX 2* would draw 4.7 million, and both *UFC on FOX 3* and *UFC on FOX 4* drew an average audience of just 2.4 million. The average audience for the first season of *The Ultimate Fighter* on Fox Sports was 1.16 million, a significant decline from the final season that had aired on Spike, which drew an average of 1.84 million viewers. The semiweekly *Fight Night* events saw similar declines on Fox Sports, drawing an average of 1.35 million viewers, where they had drawn an average of 1.73 million viewers in the final year of the Spike deal. The audience for *UFC Primetime*, a documentary series that followed the lives of two fighters as they prepared for an upcoming pay-per-view, nearly halved, dropping from an average of 933,000 viewers on Spike to 540,000 for the first three installments on FX. The UFC's global television audience showed similar signs of flagging, dropping from 44.7 million in 2012 to 34.9 million in 2014, even as Zuffa continued to expand the number of territories its programming was available in. Despite everything, the UFC would generate $450 million in revenue in 2014, the second-best year in company history.

As cage fighting seemed to be losing some of its spectacle value, many in the media had begun to focus on how the UFC treated fighters outside the cage. In 2012, ESPN produced a segment on UFC fighter pay for its documentary series *Outside the Lines*, alongside a written article on the ESPN website. The pieces presented a largely negative portrait of the UFC, depicting it not as an agent of prosperity and personal transformation, but a corporate robber baron that exploited its athletes to enrich its owners. "We're basically fighting for crumbs," an anonymous fighter told *ESPN*, one of nearly a dozen quoted in the article. "The top five percent [of fighters] are definitely making good money, but you've got to look at the guys at the bottom of the card. They can't fight anywhere else." Rob Maysey, an Arizona attorney who had helped launch the Mixed Martial Arts Fighters Association, a fledgling attempt to organize fighters across promotions, said many lived in fear of being blacklisted by the UFC for speaking out about pay. "The vast majority of people I meet with want to [organize], but 75 percent of that majority fear repercussion, so they won't," he told *ESPN*.

Lorenzo had agreed to be interviewed for the story and disputed many of its claims. "Maybe it's just part of our culture," Lorenzo said. "We came from a corporate background, we pay for performance." He insisted that it was unfair to compare the promotion to other sports leagues because it was newer and paid for all of its own production costs, while boxing promoters and the NFL relied on their broadcasting partners to cover production costs. Yet when asked what percentage of the UFC's annual revenue went to fighter pay, Lorenzo claimed it was "in the neighborhood" of the roughly 50 percent athletes in the NFL, NBA, and MLB earned. Though not public at the time, the actual percentage of the UFC's revenues given to fighters in 2012 was just 16 percent. Nearly half of the $71 million spent on fighters that year would go to just twenty of the promotion's top stars. Only 8 percent of UFC bouts in a year involve fighters earning guaranteed purses of $55,000 or more, according to a later report on fighter pay. Eighty-three percent were contracted to earn guaranteed purses of $30,000 or less per fight.

In 2014, the UFC provoked more public ire when White signed WWE star Phil Brooks, more commonly known as CM Punk, gambling on his potential to become another crossover draw like Lesnar. Despite the fact that Punk had only recently started training and had never fought professionally, Zuffa agreed to pay him a guaranteed purse of $500,000 per fight, more than the publicly disclosed pay of several current UFC champions. One fighter described the signing as a "circus" and another called it a "freakshow," something that underscored how little comparative value the UFC placed on its own fighters.

For some, the UFC's response to public criticism could be swift and severe. Longtime cutman Jacob "Stitch" Duran admitted Zuffa's deal with Reebok had prevented him, like most fighters, from signing his own sponsorship agreements to wear logos on his vest whenever he worked UFC events, something he had relied on for years to supplement his pay as an independent contractor. "Brother, I lost everything regarding sponsors, from pay to a nice vest!" he wrote to a fan on Twitter, who had asked him about Reebok. "Now I have no fees and a generic vest." A day later, Zuffa told Duran it would no longer be using his services to treat fighters' cuts and injuries in between rounds. Duran was shocked by the news, and especially hurt that White hadn't come to him directly to talk about any problem he might have had with what Duran had said. "Dana has definitely changed," Duran would later say. "Now it's all about the economics. It used to be a fighter friendly environment." When asked about Duran's firing shortly after, White said he didn't have anything to do with the UFC's cutmen but confirmed Duran wouldn't work with the UFC again. "We weren't friends," White said. "We're not friends, and no, he shouldn't have been expecting a call from me. And if he's my friend, why didn't he reach out to me?"

In early 2015, Burt Watson found himself in a similarly unexpected conflict with the UFC after the weigh-ins for UFC 184 in Los Angeles. One of the fighters who had been booked to compete on the prelims, Mark Munoz, initially missed weight, and needed the extra sixty-minute grace period allowed by the California State Athletic Commission to shed the last fraction of a pound. The weigh-ins had taken place a short distance from the fighter hotel, in a tent outside of the Staples Center, where the fights would take place the day after. Munoz's weight miss had forced the production crew and event staff to stay behind for an extra hour. Watson told Munoz he wouldn't make the fighter shuttle-bus drivers wait for him too, and he should instead walk back to the hotel on his own. Shortly after, Mike Mersch, the UFC's vice president of legal affairs, called Watson and confronted him about the choice, implying Watson had been negligent in leaving Munoz behind. Watson was shocked and offended by what felt to him like an effort to interfere with a process he had managed since 2001. "I went off on him," says Watson. "I said, You know what, you haven't even been around long enough to wipe your [own ass]. If you got nothing better to do, then you go downstairs and get my ticket so I can go home and you can go kiss my ass."

The next morning, Watson was on a flight back to his home in Philadelphia. He would never again be asked back to work an event with the UFC. As with Duran, he never heard anything from White. "I was disappointed because of the fact I had been there fifteen years without one complaint," says Watson. "Without one." Still, he wasn't surprised. "I didn't expect Dana or Lorenzo to call me. Especially Dana. I know the person that Dana is, and I'm never surprised at what I see or what I hear."

Station Casinos had come out of Chapter 11 bankruptcy protection in an unexpectedly strong position. After two years of negotiations with the company's debtors and Nevada's bankruptcy court, Station had reached a deal to write off $4 billion of debt owed to the company's investors, in what the lead debtor's counsel described as "the biggest-ever in-court restructuring of a gaming company." As part of the deal, the Fertittas were allowed to reacquire eleven of Station's properties that had been on auction, for a total $772 million, paid for by a mix of Station's own money and $455 million in new loans from Deutsche Bank, Colony Capital, and others. It was a fraction of what bondholders had paid three years earlier when the Fertittas had taken the company private. Because Station held such a dominant position in the locals market, even in bankruptcy, most of its competitors had been unable to afford a bid on any of its properties. The one company that could, Boyd Gaming, Station's main rival in the locals market, had decided to withdraw from the process citing concerns about the auction rules and other factors it claimed would give Station an unfair advantage. In one example, it pointed to a stipulation for the Texas Station casino that would require the winning bidder to pay both the full purchase price and an additional $75 million leasing fee to the owner of the land the casino had been built on, which happened to be Victoria Fertitta, Lorenzo's and Frank III's mother. While six other bids for individual properties were registered from smaller investors, after Boyd withdrew from the process, Station was the only remaining party able to submit an offer for all eleven properties, leaving them as the de facto winner of a one-party bidding war. The unsecured bondholders, who had collectively invested $2.8 billion into Station's original plan to go private, were effectively wiped out and offered only the option of buying a 15 percent stake in the new post-bankruptcy Station for $100 million, in the hopes that future profits might offset some of their losses. Frank III and Lorenzo's losses were estimated at close to $700 million, though they would be allowed to retain some $300 million from Station stock sales in 2007, and they would retain majority control of the company post-bankruptcy.

At the same time that Station was fighting with its investors in the courts, the company had found itself fighting its employees, many of whom had been trying to join the Culinary Union Local 226, a near mythic group in Las Vegas that represented more than sixty thousand housekeepers, cooks, bartenders, bellhops, and hotel workers. The Culinary Union had successfully organized almost every major casino on the Las Vegas Strip, including Caesars Palace, the Bellagio, the MGM Grand, the Mandalay Bay, the Luxor, Treasure Island, Circus Circus, Paris Las Vegas, and the Tropicana, often through aggressive workers' strikes. (It held the record for the longest strike in American history, at the Frontier Casino, where the union maintained an active picket line for twenty-four hours a day for nearly seven years, from 1991 to 1998.) Despite its success in organizing on the Strip, the Culinary Union represented workers at just four properties in the locals market, and it had been eager to add Station's thirteen thousand employees to its ranks.

Throughout the 2000s, the Culinary Union had tried to persuade 30 percent or more of Station's workers to sign union authorization cards that would trigger a formal company-wide vote on whether to unionize. In 2010, several hundred Station employees formed an organizing committee to work with the Culinary Union. The members cited concerns about the company's shifting business model, which had relied on outside contractors and leasing floor space to companies like Denny's and Krispy Kreme. As Station had made waves of layoffs across its properties, as part of cost-savings measures during bankruptcy, many had begun to fear they would lose their jobs to outside contractors or employees who worked for external food service franchises that Station was working with more frequently. "Every day we come in in fear," Wayne Brasher, a bartender at Boulder Station, said in a 2010 interview. "What happened to the kitchen worker? What happened to the uniform attendant? Are we next? Everybody feels like they're next."

Fearing that Station would make additional cuts to benefits and pay for its full-time employees, the Culinary Union successfully petitioned to have a group of Station employees sit in on bankruptcy meetings about staffing costs. Also in 2010, the Culinary Union filed a complaint with the National Labor Relations Board, accusing Station of more than four hundred different instances of unfair labor practices, which it argued had undermined its efforts to organize the company's employees. In 2012, a three-member panel from the NLRB ruled that eighty of those instances were in fact violations of federal labor law, including threatening workers with reduced hours as retaliation for organizing activities, directing employees to not wear union buttons while at work, forbidding employees from using Station parking lots to distribute union pamphlets or hold demonstrations, and surveilling an employee who had chosen to wear a union button throughout her shift.

The Culinary Union had also seized on the Fertittas' link to the UFC and began a public relations campaign to argue that Zuffa used unfair business practices to exploit its fighters in the same way that Station exploited its hotel and casino workers. In 2011, after Zuffa announced its plan to acquire Strikeforce, the Culinary Union wrote a letter to Federal Trade Commission claiming the deal would violate US antitrust law by eliminating the industry's last major competitor, leaving the UFC with near total control over both the marketplace and its fighters. "The anticompetitive restrictions it imposes on athlete mobility serve no legitimate business justification beyond stifling competition and increasing Zuffa's already dominant position in the market," the letter argued.

In 2012, the FTC closed its formal investigation into the deal and determined that no further action was warranted, though in a letter announcing the decision, the FTC also said the finding should not "be construed as a determination that a violation may not have occurred, just as the pendency of an investigation should not be construed as a determination that a violation has occurred." A former FTC commissioner familiar with the UFC's business, Dr. Joshua Wright, would later explain that the commission's main concern in merger investigations was the likelihood of imminent harm to consumers, most often in the form of higher prices. With no immediate increases in the UFC's pay-per-view prices or new price barriers for accessing its content, and the UFC's initial public claims that it would keep Strikeforce running, the case for imminent material harm to consumers would have been difficult to make. But the Culinary Union persisted, launching a series of websites—fitforchildren .org and zuffainvestoralerts.org—posting unflattering facts and potentially damning speculation about the Fertittas, the UFC, and Station. The websites ran stories questioning the UFC's partnership with the United

Arab Emirates' Flash Entertainment, while the government enforced bans on homosexuality and limited women's legal rights; highlighting the violent criminal records of some fighters; and speculating about whether the UFC took out life insurance policies on certain fighters as a hedge against the possibility of someone dying in the cage. The union also worked with its national parent organization, UNITE HERE, to successfully lobby legislators in New York to block the UFC's efforts to legalize mixed martial arts in the state, the last in the US where they were still banned. According to Ratner, there was overwhelming support among legislators to legalize mixed martial arts, but the speaker of the state assembly Sheldon Silver ensured a vote never took place. "We'd get through every committee and we would pass the senate twenty-four to ten or something like that," says Ratner. "Then they would go to the assembly and they wouldn't even bring it up, usually. This went for eight years, and I knew—we knew, that this wasn't kosher." Ratner attributed Silver's obstinacy to his close ties to both the Culinary Union and UNITE HERE, which had also successfully organized a large percentage of New York City's hospitality industry. (Silver would later step down from his role in the state assembly after being indicted for money laundering, extortion, and other crimes in 2015, involving more than $5 million in payments in exchange for official acts. He was convicted on all counts and sentenced to seven years in prison in 2018.)

In 2014, a small group of fighters went a step further than the Culinary Union, and filed a class action lawsuit against the UFC, organized in part by lawyer Rob Maysey, who had been a frequent critic of the promotion. The suit argued that Zuffa had used a wide variety of anticompetitive practices to consolidate its status as a monopsony, or the only major buyer of goods or services in the American mixed martial arts market, then used that power to trap fighters in restrictive long-term contracts and suppress fighter pay. As with most antitrust suits, the case would drag on for years, but a ruling against Zuffa could result in a maximum penalty of $4.8 billion. (As of 2023, it remains unresolved.) As the case went through the early stages of litigation to determine the appropriate jurisdiction and timeframe over which to examine the fighters' allegations, the Federal Trade Commission quietly reopened its 2011 investigation into the UFC, interviewing fighters, managers, and promoters at a Seattle branch office, though a spokesperson declined to comment on the nature of the investigation or what had prompted it.

Despite the growing political and legal uncertainty that hung over the promotion, the UFC continued generating record-breaking amounts of money. In 2015, the UFC was set to earn an estimated $128 million from its domestic television deal with Fox Sports, and another $83 million from international broadcasters. Ticket sales would add $67 million, $52 million would come from sponsorships, and licensing and merchandising would add another $19 million. The company could cover all its operating expenses—roughly $335 million—before it sold even a single pay-per-view, something that would have been hard to imagine a decade earlier. The company's remaining profit—$119 million—could be accounted for almost entirely by the difference between the $237 million those pay-per-views would bring in and the $113 million that would go to fighter pay. Just as casinos ran on the gulf between the odds of winning and the odds paid out at the cashier's cage—in video poker, a royal flush typically pays 250 to 1, but the odds of getting one are around 649,740 to 1—the UFC had transformed fighting into a kind of elaborate differential equation played out by humans. As automated as a slot machine, its events spun into motion at semiweekly intervals, and periodically exploded with flashing lights and the bell clatter of a jackpot, while its fighters and fans fed the company their free time like coins from a plastic tub sitting next to a bottomless gin and tonic and a half-filled ashtray.

The business had become almost self-regulating; similar to Lorenzo's casinos, the UFC ran on a string of probabilities played out over hours, days, weeks, and months, across dozens of different games. The main thing was to let the machine do its job and slowly reap its harvest. The UFC had become a platform where hundreds of athletes came to try their luck at hitting a jackpot, stringing together five or six knockout wins and transforming themselves into superstars, even as the underlying math of fighting and the size of the roster ensured that few of them would ever break through.

With more than five hundred fighters on its roster, and just ten weight divisions to win championships in, the odds were stacked against everyone. And even those who won championships often saw only modest pay increases, which didn't accurately reflect the steep odds against them. In

2014, top fifteen UFC welterweight Robbie Lawler fought on a contract that paid him a disclosed purse of $105,000 to fight and $105,000 to win. After winning the UFC's welterweight championship, Lawler's per-fight pay rose to just $150,000 to fight and $150,000 to win, plus a small percentage of pay-per-view royalties. "The reality is the UFC is the ultimate place of capitalism and you earn if you're successful," Lorenzo said in a 2014 interview. "If you're a fighter and you become champion and you become successful, and you're the guy or girl that's bringing people to come watch the show and are buying the pay-per-views—the last conversation we're going to have is about money."

Where some saw antitrust violations and exploitation, Lorenzo saw a kind of artfulness in the way the numbers balanced out. Over the years, he had become a prolific art collector, building a collection that included works from Andy Warhol, Takashi Murakami, KAWS, Dustin Yellin, and Jean-Michel Basquiat. He'd commissioned Damien Hirst to create an original work—the UFC's octagonal logo made from pastel colored butterflies—which he proudly hung in the office lobby. When the UFC prepared a report assessing its financials and future, it was named "Project Basquiat," as if the portrait it painted had the outlines of a modern masterwork, as unconventional as Basquiat's paintings, simple but captivating, both exuberant and ominous. When describing the appeal of cage fighting to others, Lorenzo had often used art as a point of reference. If American football was akin to Mark Rothko's paintings, disorienting blobs of color that sometimes seemed arbitrary and required a degree of concentration to unpack, cage fighting was closer to Andy Warhol's celebrity portraits. The appeal was immediate, but beneath it was a disquieting void of surfaces and automatic replication with no larger purpose. Just as Warhol had traced the outlines of America's transition to mass consumerism in the 1960s and 1970s, the UFC had captured the underlying spirit of precarity and economic desperation in early twenty-first-century, where the cruelty of the profit-making enterprises driving the global economy had become more plainly visible. In Lorenzo's office, on the wall directly behind his desk, he had hung a triptych of Damien Hirst paintings, each of which showed a single word printed on a pharmaceutical label—"Anarchy," "Violence," and "Killer"—as if each were a proprietary chemical compound administered in recommended doses listed in fine print against a numbing white background. Taken from Hirst's *Eat the Rich* series, they reflected a kind of clinical detachment toward barbarism, as if it were a necessary evil that helped propel human history forward, best dispensed in controlled quantities, by impartial administrators who were able to use it for its most productive ends.

As with any great artwork, the UFC had attracted a growing list of enterprising people interested in adding it to their own collections of profit-generating wonders. CBS had reportedly offered $1 billion for the UFC after its agreement with EliteXC fell apart. In 2014, investment firm Blackstone had expressed interest in acquiring the UFC, and in 2015 Fox made a short-lived bid for a reported $2 billion. The terms and timing had never felt quite right to Lorenzo, but as 2015 wore on, he started to think that perhaps his work with the UFC was close to finished, and there might be an even bigger future for him and Frank III elsewhere.

Lorenzo had been a lifelong football fan, and he had long harbored the fantasy of one day owning an NFL team. That dream became even more personal after his youngest son Nicco emerged as a star defensive player for the Bishop Gorman football team. Lorenzo had paid to build a two-story 41,324-square-foot training facility for the team, with a ninety-seat theater for film study, a hydrotherapy pool, and an ice bath—at a rumored cost of $20 million. During Nicco's senior year, Bishop Gorman had gone undefeated and ranked as the top high school football program in the country, according to *USA Today*. In the fall of 2015, Nicco accepted a full scholarship to play for Notre Dame. At the same time, Oakland Raiders owner Mark Davis had been shopping for a new city to move the team to, and had several meetings with Napoleon McCallum, a former Raiders running back who had taken an executive position at the Las Vegas Sands, about the possibility of moving to the city. Though there were competing offers from San Antonio, Texas, and Carson, California, the possibility of investing in the NFL, potentially as part of a group of investors that would finance construction of a new stadium, intrigued Lorenzo. With annual revenue of $10.5 billion in 2013, from just a six-month season, the NFL offered a substantially larger canvas to work with than the UFC, which was on pace to generate $609 million in 2015, an all-time high that was still around 5 percent of what the NFL brought in.

While nothing was certain, Lorenzo and Frank III had begun planning to take Station public again, under the new name of Red Rock Resorts Inc., named after a luxury resort the company had opened near the Red Rock Canyon National Park on the western edge of Las Vegas. The IPO was targeted for the first half of 2016, and they hoped it would raise between $500 and $600 million to use for future investments in gaming and beyond. In November, the FTC announced it was closing the investigation into the UFC following a series of private meetings with Zuffa's vice president and chief legal officer Kirk Hendrick and several other executives. The commission again noted that the announcement should not be construed as proof that a violation had or had not occurred, but rather that the commission had determined no further action was required to benefit the public interest. Around the same time, Lorenzo got a call from what he would later describe as one of the biggest private equity firms in the world, to discuss the possibility of acquiring the UFC. After years of having said no to similar offers, Lorenzo found himself interested to hear more, and he agreed to a meeting at Station's offices.

Ari Emanuel hadn't initially been included in the meeting, but he found out about it shortly after and immediately called Lorenzo to find out what he was thinking. Emanuel was determined to involve himself in some way, and he made Lorenzo promise that he wouldn't move forward with the offer or consider any other options until Emanuel had the chance to organize a potential deal of his own. Like Lorenzo, Emanuel had spent the last several years trying to make his own corporate masterpiece, that would transform his talent agency into its own kind of global media conglomerate. While he hadn't considered acquiring a company from one of his biggest clients, the option filled him with excitement, and he decided, as simply but insistently as he did with everything, that he would make it happen. As he started placing calls to see how much money he could raise for a potential acquisition, he found interest higher than ever. A new fighter from Ireland had emerged from the crowded ranks of the UFC's featherweight division and was on the cusp of becoming the sport's biggest star ever.

MAYBE I CAN

O n the morning before his first fight in the UFC, Conor McGregor straddled the octagon fence inside the Ericsson Globe arena in Stockholm and flexed his biceps for 14,500 empty red seats, listening to the silent roar of the crowd as he practiced the same victory pose he'd seen hundreds of fighters strike on television. Over his spandex shorts, he wore a white T-shirt with "The Notorious" written in Gothic lettering above a screen print of his own picture, shirtless and wreathed in the Irish flag. In his mind, he was already a star, not an unemployed twenty-three-year-old who lived with his parents and paid his gym fees with a weekly social welfare check of €188.

The UFC's standard entry-level contract at the time would pay just $8,000 and $8,000. It was the lowest amount a UFC fighter could make, but to McGregor even that was an unreal sum, enough to imagine a future where a new pair of shoes or a copy of the next *Call of Duty* game would no longer seem like budget-breaking extravagances. And as far as he was concerned, one win would lead to the next; one check would lead to another, like a funhouse corridor in which every door opened onto an even bigger door, until he would arrive at some palatial endpoint where there'd be nothing left to do but turn around and marvel at the strange journey.

There was something less visionary about the week leading up to the fight. The UFC staff treated fighters like new recruits drafted into a war that no one knew was happening. They were addressed not individually but in groups of thirty and forty (counting their coaches and training partners), filling one of the fighter hotel's cavernous conference rooms for orientation sessions that walked them through all the different things that would be expected of them during the week. They were given sheets with their locker room assignments and windows of time when they would be allowed to use a neighboring conference room that had been lined with mats for light training sessions. They had a gear check and were fitted with gloves, and then had to show their sponsorship banners and apparel to another executive to make sure there was nothing the UFC would find objectionable. Then they were sent into an even smaller, windowless conference room where they were measured, for height and arm reach, then filmed shadowboxing in front of a green screen, and finally interviewed about their opponent by a disinterested producer behind the camera, who fed them lines when they stammered or weren't sure what to say. Then there were medical exams, and drug tests, and weight that would be measured the day before the fight, and lists of what they would be allowed to eat and drink after.

The card was a forgettable one, scheduled on an off-weekend between two major pay-per-views. There were twenty-six fighters on the card, and they all seemed to be passing through. One came from the Democratic Republic of the Congo, others from Chechnya, Iran, Australia, and Syria. The main event, between former Strikeforce light heavyweight champion Gegard Mousasi and Alexander Gustafsson, had been canceled after Gustafsson failed his medical clearance. One of his teammates who'd never fought in the UFC before was signed and brought in as a last-minute replacement. Because of the time difference, the card would air in the US on Fuel TV at 2:00 p.m. on a Saturday, rather than the customary prime-time slot. McGregor's fight on the prelims wouldn't make the broadcast, but instead would be streamed on the UFC's Facebook page, an experiment in using social media that the promotion had been testing.

McGregor played along with the anonymity of the event. He amplified the smallness of it when he spoke to the groups of European press that the UFC's PR department had booked him with. "It's just another contest," he said into a loaner cell phone in a small, windowless office in the fighter hotel as two PR reps listened from a folding table. "It could be UFC, PFC, OFC, it makes no difference. It's just another contest at the end of the day and that's the way I see it." Later the same day, at a small roundtable interview in the hotel lobby restaurant, he described his opponent as equally irrelevant. "It's always you versus you," he said. "If you're competing against other people, you become bitter. You'll eventually become bitter. But when you compete against yourself, you become better, you know what I mean?"

The words he left to linger in people's minds were both familiar and hard to place. Had it come from a poster in the gym locker room or a self-help book? Was it something another fighter had said? Or a line from a movie? Everything had the ring of a testimonial, as if he wasn't sharing a thought of his own but endorsing something he'd heard and decided was true.

He'd grown up in the gray and glamorless suburb of Crumlin, on the periphery of downtown Dublin, in a two-bedroom row house with his parents and two older sisters. He was enamored with WWE and Batman movies, soccer, Jay-Z, and Notorious B.I.G. He played video games compulsively, and went with his neighborhood friends to beginners' classes at a local boxing gym. His father worked as a taxi driver, and McGregor spent most of his time with his sisters and mother, who described him as a "mummy's boy." When he was fifteen, the family moved to a bigger house in Lucan, another suburb on the western edge of Dublin, where the grassy hills outside the city loomed between long rows of red brick houses.

At his new school, McGregor befriended Tom Egan, who immediately picked up on McGregor's sullenness. "He was just a lazy prick," he said of their first meeting. "And I don't mean that in an insulting way. He was just at a loss of identity and didn't have anything to hold on to." Egan's mother was a black belt in Shotokan karate, and she had encouraged Egan to take up martial arts. He and McGregor used each other as training partners, turning slumber parties into sparring sessions, practicing moves they'd watched on tape-delayed UFC events, reverse-engineering armbars and chokes and trying to incorporate them into the bits of knowledge they'd learned from karate or boxing class. Sometimes McGregor would spend an entire weekend at Egan's house practicing new techniques, at the end of which the two would fight full-bore in a shed in Egan's backyard to see who would win.

Fighting captured McGregor's imagination in a way that school had never been able to. The endless drilling and repetition of training had an obvious purpose that homework and history lessons lacked. Instead of absorbing dead bits of information that had no immediate application to anything he had known in life, fighting felt like an incremental ascent up a high dive, preparing for a climactic leap of faith into the unplanned chaos of conflict between two bodies, each of which had a mind of its own, a second layer of consciousness embedded in the musculature and nervous system response that could only be impeded by trying to control it with thinking. McGregor and Egan found a local MMA gym, run by John Kavanagh, who, like them, had taught himself the basics of cage fighting with a small group of friends after having discovered an old UFC tape in a Dublin video store in the late 1990s. After finishing a degree in mechanical engineering, Kavanagh had decided to pursue a career in mixed martial arts instead of hunting for an office job. He moved back in with his parents and worked as a bouncer while he ran a small gym in a chilly cement space nicknamed the Shed. McGregor arrived at the Shed as an overstimulated seventeen-year-old, and training quickly became a compulsion, overshadowing everything else in his life. "I couldn't shut it off, so I just rolled with it, kept showing up everyday," McGregor said in a 2015 interview.

His family was less excited about McGregor's desire to become a fighter, and after he announced he didn't want to continue with school, his mother found him a plumber's apprenticeship with a crew that worked in Kilternan, a small village in the foothills south of Dublin famous for a small manmade ski slope. It was an eighteen-mile drive from the McGregor home in Lucan, and his mother would gently wake him up every morning at 5:00 a.m. so he could walk out to the N4 and wait for one of his coworkers to pick him up in the company van. If they had bad luck with traffic, the commute could stretch to two hours. As a first-year apprentice McGregor became the crew's errand boy on the job site, carrying the heavy gear from the van and getting other people's lunch orders. With shifts that could stretch to fourteen hours, it seemed as if he were feeding his life day by day into a furnace, where it burned away to nothing. "I'm looking around on the site, looking at the fully qualified people, bad backs, bad posture, not making—you know what I mean?—not a good life to live," he'd later say. "I just realized I didn't want to go down that route. I thought I could do something with my life."

McGregor decided to quit and instead launch a career in cage fighting. His parents were set against the choice. "The first thing they said was, 'Who else has done it? What other Irish man has made a career of this?'" McGregor would later say. The decision was especially alien to his father, who had married at twenty-one and taken a job at a factory to support his young family. He'd had his own vague dreams of being a poet or rock-and-roll singer, but accepted that being a life partner and a parent would take the place of his vanishing teenage fantasies. McGregor had no answers for his parents, but he promised things would be different for him; he swore that if they trusted him he would be a millionaire by the age of twenty-five. His father didn't believe him, but McGregor didn't care. He applied for social welfare benefits to cover basic living costs and committed himself to training full-time with Kavanagh.

For a short while it seemed as if everything was going McGregor's way. He trained obsessively at Straight Blast Gym, and worked his way into the ranks of the gym's professional fighters, most of whom fought in a series of small events Kavanagh promoted in Dublin called Cage of Truth. The events usually took place at a small venue called the Ringside Club, where crowds of around three hundred people paid €15 or €20 to watch their friends and neighbors and former classmates fight one another for the prize of a few hundred Euros and a small engraved plate. McGregor fought his first two professional fights in two months, winning both by one-sided TKO. He booked his third fight just two weeks before his twentieth birthday, and had sold twenty-five tickets to the event, which Kavanagh had given him in advance. It was supposed to have been a celebration, but instead it was an incomprehensible defeat, with McGregor losing by kneebar to a visiting Lithuanian fighter a little over a minute into the first round. McGregor was humiliated, and it left his once unshakable sense of self-belief broken, compounded by the shame of knowing that the €500 he owed Kavanagh for the tickets was gone. He'd spent it in the weeks leading up to the fight on small indulgences, assuming he'd be able to replace it with his win bonus from the fight. Instead of returning to training, McGregor hid from Kavanagh and his teammates and distracted his wounded ego by staying out late into the night with friends and sleeping into the afternoons.

After two months, Kavanagh assumed he would never see McGregor again. It was a common enough occurrence at fight gyms, overeager newcomers would appear and disappear regularly, and Kavanagh had mistrusted McGregor's attitude from the outset. He had labeled him as a "street kid," and he'd expected there would be a moment when McGregor returned to the streets, once it became clear just how much time and humility were really necessary to become a martial artist. Most people were satisfied with just learning a few unique tricks. But two months after the loss McGregor's mother called Kavanagh and asked if he'd be willing to come to the family house and speak with her son. She was worried about him, she told Kavanagh, and thought maybe he could reach McGregor in a way that she and his father hadn't been able to. Kavanagh almost turned her down, but then decided he couldn't say no to a mother asking for help, and so he arrived at the McGregor home in Lucan late one Friday afternoon. "I was used to this bubbly, charismatic athlete but he looked very down and just didn't look healthy to me," Kavanagh recalled. "So we had a conversation that I've had with a couple of guys since: 'You don't want to be the guy in your forties saying 'coulda, shoulda, woulda' with a pint in your hand at the bar. You've got potential. Use it. Do it. Don't worry about the ticket money—scratch it off, I don't care.'" It was an unexpectedly emotional exchange, one that left them both in tears. McGregor promised he would return to the gym first thing on Monday morning.

Over the next four years, McGregor would grow into one of the most dominant fighters in Ireland, winning ten of his next eleven fights, all but one win coming by TKO and eight of ten coming in the first round. He had developed a free-flowing style that allowed him to attack from a much wider variety of angles and positions than most of his opponents expected. His unusually long arms allowed him to leap in with corkscrewing uppercuts from a distance that many fighters would have assumed was too far away, and he developed a series of spinning kicks that added unpredictability and even more range to his attacks, which forced opponents to either stay as far away as possible or rush in to close the distance, creating an opening for his quick and devastatingly accurate counterpunches. It was a smothering, high-confidence style that worked in tandem with his excitable, boyish energy, something that had been catalyzed by a gift from his sister Erin. Seven years McGregor's elder, Erin had become a fitness model and personal trainer, a line of work that had led her to Rhonda Byrne's self-help sensation *The Secret*.

The project began, by Byrne's account, when her daughter gave her a copy of the 1910 bestseller *The Science of Getting Rich* by Wallace D. Wattles, one of the most prominent self-help authors of the early twentieth century. Byrne was enthralled by Wattles's writing, and immersed herself in his work and ideas, becoming convinced she had stumbled on a blueprint for universal human prosperity, lying dormant in every person's unconscious. She assembled her own selection of insights taken from Wattles and other writers she'd been researching and created a framework for her own updated version of the law of attraction, built around the idea that the shape one's life takes is a mirror of the thoughts one cultivates. Unhappiness, in Byrne's update, relayed in both a book and companion DVD, is a result of thinking too much about the things a person doesn't want or hopes to avoid in life. By creating new habits of thinking that focus on positive outcomes, a person can make their life a kind of magnet for their own dreams, turning fantasy into fait accompli.

Erin had given the book version of *The Secret* to McGregor, but he'd left it unread for nearly a year, until he found out there was a ninety-minute DVD version that would spare him having to read two hundred pages. At first, McGregor thought it was "bullshit." He let himself try it as a joke, attempting to manifest good parking spots for himself and his new girlfriend, Dee Devlin, as they drove around Dublin in her Peugeot 206 hatchback. Strangely, it did seem like they got better parking spots, and McGregor let himself imagine more specific images, seeing himself as the millionaire he'd promised his father he would be, not as something he would become when he turned twenty-five, but as something he already was. For his fights, he stopped thinking about his opponents and started imagining only the pure motion of his own punches and kicks, flying through empty space like the limbs of an animal suddenly possessed by the music of the spheres. Every punch landed, every forward step produced the appropriate counterstep that left his opponent in the perfect position to be hit; it was almost conspiratorial the way things fit together, like a set of puzzle pieces reassembling themselves through some unseen magnetism that would end with McGregor in the same timeless position of victory, arms lifted overhead in triumph, body filled with a warm wave of endorphins, and the crowd erupting in adoration. None of it was to come; it was all one continuous present tense that only McGregor could see.

Nearing his twenty-fifth birthday, McGregor had become one of the most highly ranked prospects in European mixed martial arts and had won the featherweight and lightweight championships in Cage Warriors, a regional promotion based in London. Yet, for all his accomplishments, his life still seemed as unsettled as it had when he was seventeen. For winning his second title in Cage Warriors, he'd earned just €2,500. He was still collecting public assistance and supplementing those weekly payments by teaching beginners' boxing classes at Straight Blast Gym. In early 2013, Kavanagh noticed that McGregor had begun avoiding his calls again, and he feared McGregor was on the verge of another depressive collapse. It seemed as if he had run out of goals to accomplish, and barring an invitation to sign with the UFC, there was nowhere left to escalate. Then in February 2013, one of the UFC's matchmakers, Sean Shelby, who had been hired to help build the promotion's lighter weight classes after the UFC had closed WEC, called and offered McGregor the chance to fight on the UFC's Stockholm card, a throwaway event for the promotion that for McGregor would validate his entire adult life's work.

When he walked into the cage, in the fourth of seven prelim fights, it felt as if he was in his own main event, and he fought even more dominantly than he had in Cage Warriors, battering his opponent, Marcus Brimage, with counterpunches and shifting uppercuts before earning a TKO win in just a minute and seven seconds. After the referee called the fight, McGregor stalked the octagon in a dazed fury, and forgot to jump onto the cage as he'd rehearsed earlier in the day. Instead he carried the Irish flag spread across his back like a sail and stared at himself on the big screen above the cage. After the fight, in the locker room McGregor had shared with a dozen other fighters, White made an unexpected visit to say how impressed he'd been by McGregor's performance. "So there's been a lot of hype," White said, in reference to the fervent Irish following McGregor had built up. "I guess the hype is real." He promised McGregor he could fight again on a card in Boston in a few months, and he said they were planning another event in Ireland that they would want McGregor to fight in as well. McGregor was also awarded a $60,000 bonus for Knockout of the Night that sent him home with $76,000 after starting the week with €188. To celebrate, he put on a shirt and bow tie and snuck back into the arena with Devlin to watch the rest of the card.

From the outset, fighters in the UFC had disliked McGregor's approach and the riotous energy he inspired in his fans. Before the fight in Sweden, McGregor fans had swarmed Brimage's Facebook account with threatening messages and comments. "I'm like, Hey, can't we be just a little bit more respectful?" Brimage had said in a fight week interview. In McGregor's second fight in the UFC, on the prelims of a *Fight Night* card in Boston, McGregor was given a full champion's walkout, with the arena blanketed in darkness before luminous sheets of green and orange lights swept across the audience. The special fanfare was almost always reserved for title fights or main events. No one on the prelims had ever been given a special walkout like that before. The spectacle even forced a note of surprise from Joe Rogan. "Wow," he said, as the arena went dark more than three hours before the night's main event. In his third UFC fight, McGregor was booked as the main event of his own *Fight Night* in Dublin, against Diego Brandão, a Brazilian who stepped in on six weeks' notice to replace Cole Miller, McGregor's original opponent, who had dropped out with an injury. For many veterans it was a scandal to see a newcomer like McGregor being treated with such deference by the UFC. For Lorenzo, McGregor's success was the best-case outcome for the promotion's international expansion, which could be used to draw in experienced fighters with their own local fanbases to create an immediate sense of excitement and stakes. When McGregor fought Brandão, Lorenzo noted, he drew a sixty share in Irish TV ratings, meaning 60 percent of the people watching TV at the time had tuned in to the UFC. For McGregor's fourth fight, against Dustin Poirier, just two months after headlining in Dublin, one-out-of-every-ten tickets went to a fan from Ireland who'd traveled to Las Vegas to watch McGregor. The event, topped by a flyweight championship fight between Demetrious Johnson and Chris Cariaso, brought in close to double the amount of pay-per-view buys that Johnson's previous title defense had, according to estimates at the time. McGregor had signed a new contract with the UFC and was the second highest paid fighter on the card, with a disclosed purse of $75,000 to fight, $75,00 to win. He would also earn another $50,000 bonus for Performance of the Night. For a month prior to the event, McGregor had stayed in a $7,500-a-night suite at the Red Rock Casino Resort with two full-time butlers, a personal chauffeur available for him twenty-four hours a day, and a second suite for Kavanagh and the rest of his training partners who had come from Ireland. The week before the fight, McGregor, Kavanagh, and Devlin had gathered for a catered dinner with White in a VIP suite and watched a *Fight Night* event broadcast from the Saitama Super Arena in Japan.

A month after he knocked out Poirier, one minute and forty-six seconds into the first round, Zuffa paid to fly McGregor to Brazil as a guest fighter in the audience for UFC 179, where José Aldo, the reigning featherweight champion, was scheduled to defend his belt against Chad Mendes. McGregor taunted both fighters throughout the week, playing up his presence in the audience as even more important than the fight. In a media appearance with Mendes, McGregor played up his position of privilege with the UFC and how, even as a contender lower ranked than either Mendes or Aldo, he was being treated better than both of them. "I'm not even in the fighter hotel, I'm in the Fertitta hotel, in the suite, on the Copacabana," McGregor taunted. "So you enjoy your time in the fighter hotel." Mendes, an All-American and former Pac-10 wrestler of the year, tried to pick on McGregor's comparative inexperience as a grappler. "Do you even know what wrestling is?" he said, trying to bait McGregor. "I could rest my balls on your forehead," McGregor replied.

The taunts were juvenile, but their dismissiveness rang true against a backdrop of declining ratings and pay-per-view buys. The fight between Aldo and Mendes was a historic milestone for fans—a violent five-round struggle in which each fighter knocked the other down, and both were pushed to near breaking points. Aldo would win a unanimous decision, his ninth consecutive title defense in a reign that spanned both the WEC and UFC, and his eighteenth consecutive win. He had gone nearly a decade since his last (and only) loss. Despite the historic feat, ratings for the prelims, which aired on Fox Sports 1, were the second lowest since the network began airing UFC events, drawing just 536,000 viewers. The event generated an estimated 180,000 buys, making it the third worst of the year. The promotion itself seemed to have lost its ability to persuade the public that something important was happening in most of its fights. In contrast, McGregor seemed important even when he was simply sitting in the audience. His self-assurance added a touch of destiny to everything he involved himself with. And the surer McGregor seemed to be in his persona, the more doubt he created in his opponents. In a sport where fighters spent their whole careers trying to prove themselves to others—to friends, family members, coaches, training partners, matchmakers, sponsors—McGregor expected the world should have to prove itself to him.

In the spring, McGregor was finally scheduled to fight Aldo, and the UFC arranged a world tour with press appearances in Rio de Janeiro, Las Vegas, Los Angeles, Boston, New York, Toronto, Dublin, and London. Many of the events left Aldo seeming eerily helpless as he relied on an interpreter to translate everything McGregor said into Portuguese, ensuring he would always be the last one in the room to understand McGregor's insults. In Rio, Aldo and McGregor sat on a dais separated by White, who was at a podium. McGregor, in a beige suit and dark sunglasses, leaned back and put his feet up on the dais as if he were in his own living room. When asked about a previous comment in which Aldo had said he was the true King of Rio and McGregor was only a joker, McGregor answered, "I own this town. I own Rio de Janeiro. So for him to say he is the king and I am the joker—if this was a different time, I would invade his *favela* on horseback and kill anyone not fit to work. But we are in a new time, so I'll whoop his ass in July." The crowd booed McGregor as Aldo sat with a fading grin, waiting for the translator. White burst into laughter like a teenager watching two classmates argue in a parking lot.

In Ireland a week later, Aldo tried to mimic McGregor's colonial bravado by telling the crowd that he was the real King of Dublin. McGregor leapt up and reached across White at the podium and grabbed Aldo's championship belt, which had been propped up like a museum piece on the Brazilian's side of the dais. McGregor lifted the belt above his head with one arm as the crowd erupted in an orgiastic cacophony, while Aldo tried and failed to grab the belt back, as aggrieved and ineffectual as a younger brother held back by a parent. For Aldo, one could sense the blot of resentment forming, as if he disbelieved that McGregor would treat him so callously, and worse, that the UFC would allow it. For McGregor, these provocations had little to do with personal animosity. They were simple exercises that reminded him he was free and unrestrainable, there were no limits that he could not simply cross if he so chose. He seemed as carefree and playful as someone making faces at himself in the bathroom mirror, while Aldo writhed behind White's outstretched arm, reduced to a background prop, an extra in a scene that called for some commotion to better frame the star. Before the Poirier fight, McGregor had elaborated on his approach to his opponents. "I'm not here to show these people remorse," he said, "I'm here to get in there and be ruthless and eliminate everybody. It's all fun and games to me. I have no emotions toward him good or bad. I don't like him, and I don't dislike him. For me he does not exist."

In Dublin, McGregor made it possible for everyone watching to see in Aldo what McGregor had seen in him, a collective vision that turned one of the top ranked fighters in the world and the most accomplished featherweight in UFC history into harmless set dressing. It left many in the audience feeling the same dizzy, conspiratorial sense of liberation that McGregor felt. Respects need not be paid. It was the thrill of mass sadism, pleasure in domination that seemed for a few clamorous moments that everyone present wanted to take part in. Would Aldo be able to reassert his own sense of self by beating McGregor?

The question would be delayed when, two weeks before the fight, Aldo pulled out citing a rib injury sustained in sparring, which a doctor in Brazil had told him would be unsafe to fight through. Lorenzo and White both drove to the two-story stucco-and-marble mansion in Las Vegas that McGregor had rented for his fight camp. They arrived in the early afternoon, and McGregor, who had grown accustomed to training in the middle of the night and sleeping until two or three o'clock in the afternoon, was just waking up. As he came down the stairs from the master suite and saw White and Lorenzo standing in the kitchen looking sullen, he knew the fight was off. "This is what you call a rude awakening," White said as McGregor searched their faces for some clue about what was wrong. "He broke his fucking rib." White said they could rebook the fight for another pay-per-view the company had scheduled seven weeks away, on September 5. McGregor brushed the date aside, appearing more interested in the question of whether he could still take another fight before Aldo was fully healed. Lorenzo let out a thin, wavering laugh. "I didn't know that was an option," he said, almost under his breath. A day later the UFC announced McGregor would fight Chad Mendes instead of Aldo, and it would be for the interim featherweight championship. The winner would fight Aldo later in the year after he had recovered. In his first interview about the change, McGregor maintained his sense of complete indifference to opponents. "It means nothing to me, the result will be the same," he said in one of the UFC's corner office meeting rooms, with White and Lorenzo seated around him like handlers. "It doesn't matter who is in front of me, I am the pound-for-pound number one, so whoever is standing across from me will get it."

When McGregor and Mendes stood in front of each other in the cage two weeks later, it seemed as if McGregor might be the one who would get it from Mendes. The event had drawn a sold-out audience of 16,019 at the MGM Grand Garden Arena, breaking the record for the highest live gate in mixed martial arts history, with $7.2 million in ticket sales. It had the air of a pagan hybrid, half-funeral and half-wedding, with each fighter given a live musical accompaniment for his walkout. Mendes stepped onto the arena floor as country singer Aaron Lewis performed "Country Boy," and McGregor emerged to Sinead O'Connor singing the Irish war ballad "Foggy Dew." Within the first five seconds of the fight, Mendes had grabbed McGregor's leg, which was left outstretched after a missed knee attempt, and wrestled him to the mat, which was stained with drying blood from the previous fight, between Rory McDonald and Robbie Lawler. McGregor worked his way back to his feet quickly, but he seemed like a less steady version of himself.

When McGregor planted to kick or punch, he seemed to wobble slightly, the result of a training camp injury that partially tore his ACL, the ligament that connects the interior parts of the knee joint behind the patella, which left his knee loose and unsteady whenever it was forced to bear any weight. Mendes saw many of McGregor's attacks coming and was able to roll and slip out of the way just at the end of McGregor's long, reaching punches. Mendes seemed more able than any of McGregor's past opponents to catch him out of position with sudden forward sprints, punctuated by a clean overhand right to the jaw. McGregor showed no effects from any of the punches and would often raise his arms and shake his head to taunt Mendes for being unable to hurt him. When they reset, McGregor pecked at Mendes with his feet, kicking into the shorter fighter's solar plexus with stabbing flicks, as if he meant to puncture a piece of hanging meat. Mendes began to take deeper and deeper breaths, but he continued to wrestle McGregor back to the mat, and spent the last minute of the round pinning McGregor as blood streamed down from a cut under McGregor's right eye that Mendes opened with an elbow strike that had thudded into McGregor's face and slammed the back of his head into the mat.

At the start of the second round, McGregor rose from his stool, his hair sweaty and mussed, making it seem as if he'd just gotten out of bed. McGregor beamed an enormous smile up at his own image as it played on the giant screens hung from the arena rafters, and then looked across the cage to Mendes and extended his hand toward him, gestured for Mendes to come hither as if he were the neighbor's overeager dog. After a minute of traded punches, Mendes ducked onto McGregor's hips and once again dragged him to the mat, holding him down for almost four minutes. McGregor clattered Mendes's ears with open palm strikes while pinned to his back, and later he tried a barrage of elbow strikes to the top of Mendes's head, which hung over McGregor's chest like an inert pendulum. McGregor later turned to the referee and began complaining that Mendes was stalling.

With forty seconds left in the round, Mendes began edging up McGregor's torso and with an explosive swimming motion brought one of his arms around the back of McGregor's neck, and as McGregor rolled onto his knees to use the brief opening to get back to his feet, Mendes brought his free hand under McGregor's chin and clamped his palms together in an attempted guillotine choke, using his forearm as a lever to crush McGregor's windpipe. For half a second it seemed as if a trap had been sprung and McGregor would be defeated, but then McGregor rolled back to his opposite shoulder, creating a small opening that relieved the pressure on his throat and gave him just enough leverage to break Mendes's grip. McGregor pushed back up to his feet and began marching toward Mendes, throwing an exhausted but incessant barrage of punches, as if the real fight had been paused for most of the round and it was rushing through the buffered footage to catch up. Mendes seemed somehow even more tired than McGregor, and he reached for air with an open, uptilted mouth, as if he were trapped in a flooding cave.

McGregor continued to paw and punch and stab at him with kicks, loose and drained of much of their force but coming ceaselessly and in a confusing order that Mendes retreated from, his back against the fence as he tried to find space to escape. Mendes traced the long arc of the cage as McGregor followed him with greedy sidesteps, and with fifteen seconds left in the round, Mendes seemed to have completely retreated inside himself, exhausted and overwhelmed. He held up his forearms to protect his head, and McGregor hurled his own labored punches at them as if he were bailing water. Mendes's arms began to droop slightly, from soreness or fatigue, and he tried once more to walk away from McGregor, almost as if he were trying to call a time-out. Seeing Mendes's head unguarded, McGregor leapt after him with a predatory instinct and sent one last long, pneumatic left hand into Mendes's jaw. Mendes reeled backward, and then slid down the fence onto his knees and tried to bury his head into the mat as McGregor jumped on him. Mendes remained on his knees, inert, his right arm wrapped around his head trying to blunt McGregor's follow-up punches. After a few more seconds of follow-up punches, it became clear Mendes wasn't able to fight back or protect himself and the referee stepped between them and called the fight off.

McGregor jumped up onto the cage to celebrate with Kavanagh and his team, who reached up to him over the edge. McGregor then jumped back into the cage and dropped to his knees and buried his face in the Irish flag. When he pulled the flag away, he was in tears. An almost agonized look creased his face, as if the flood of happiness had been so intense it had turned to pain. The ringside physician, a pale blond woman in a bright yellow dress, cradled his bearded face and asked if he had any injuries. McGregor shook his head no and knocked her hands away. Mendes walked over to McGregor and bent down to hug him. "Thank you so much," McGregor said, an almost shocking gesture of kindness from a fighter who had committed so much of himself to cruelty and detachment. They stood up together, still wrapped in an embrace, and McGregor lifted Mendes's arm up as if it were he who had won the fight instead of McGregor.

In the locker room after the fight, McGregor collected his check from White, a $500,000 guaranteed purse and a $2.11 million discretionary bonus that would remain undisclosed to both the athletic commission and the other fighters on the card. It was ten times what he had earned for his last pay-per-view appearance, which had been more than ten times what his contracted purse was for his first fight in the UFC, which itself had been six times what his last purse had been in Cage Warriors. In just over two years he had traveled through the whirling magic of exponential growth, where money had magically come from money, the way chips seem to replicate almost on their own on a streak at a craps table, passersby brought to a standstill by the infectious glow of good fortune.

When McGregor was rebooked to fight Aldo at the end of the year, it seemed almost like an afterthought, and the startling glimpses of vulnerability and kindness that he had shown in the cage after the Mendes fight had disappeared again behind the black plastic lenses of his sunglasses and the tight fit of his tailored suits. After the world tour at the start of the year and the aborted buildup over the summer, the fight week had a muted sense of déjà vu, like looking up the answers to a question after you've already had to turn the test in. When the fight finally took place, it lasted just thirteen seconds. Watching live, it seemed almost like a misunderstanding, a false start that could be quickly reset and begun again. McGregor ran to the center of the octagon in a low sideways stance, his arms stretched out, open-palmed, in front of him, as if he expected to be thrown a beach ball. Aldo pumped his lead hand in tense, exaggerated feints. McGregor threw a long left hand, and Aldo slipped under while trying to throw an aborted left hook over the top of McGregor's arm, in an arcing motion he interrupted as he saw McGregor pull back out of range. Sensing Aldo had come prepared to counter, McGregor retreated to just outside the distance where Aldo's arms could reach. He threw a sidekick that angled down into the thigh of Aldo's lead leg, emphasizing the distance between them and the fact that McGregor could still reach across it when Aldo couldn't. For another two seconds they stood in front of each other feinting. Then Aldo took a short step back, as if he expected McGregor to come forward again, but McGregor stayed where he was. Then Aldo stepped forward and sprinted at McGregor, his chest leaning out over his feet.

Strangely, he seemed to stop midstep, and simply fell forward. It looked as if he had tripped over his own feet and found himself suddenly falling face-first to the mat. McGregor, taking advantage of Aldo's bad fortune, jumped on top of him as he rolled to his back in glassy-eyed confusion and was met with long, whipping hammer fists. The referee sprinted in and threw his body over Aldo's and the fight was over. It took the slow-motion footage played on the arena screen above the roaring crowd of Irish fans to see what had actually happened, something so focused and instinctive that it had been imperceptible in real time. As Aldo had lunged forward, McGregor had calmly slid back just a few inches, planted the balls of his feet, and transferred all his weight into a short left hand that landed on Aldo's chin as if it had been pulled there by magnets. The blow twisted Aldo's head sharply to the side and crumpled the flesh around his face, snapping whatever connection had kept his brain and body synchronized. As Aldo fell, already unconscious on his feet, the left hook he'd committed to a split second before bounced off the side of McGregor's brow hard enough to open a fresh cut, leaving a small thread of blood running down his face.

There was something ritualistic about the moment, when played in frame-by-frame detail, like a sacrifice, an act of cruelty so calm and detached it was hard not to think it had some kind of higher purpose. Without the UFC's camera and production booth, it would have been unseeable, but in the glacial movements of the replay, everything seemed to unify—the setting, the people in it, the tools they'd been given to capture the event, the crowds preloaded with cold beer and Irish flags—into one miraculous fabric of time. It was both awe-inducing and anticlimactic: one man had beaten another. Almost immediately, footage of the fight began to circulate online, short enough to fit into an Instagram video or Twitter post, or even an animated GIF.

In 2008, Lorenzo had famously said the UFC's core business wasn't putting on fights but creating moments, what he specifically termed "Holy Shit" moments. "At least one or two times in every UFC show, whether you say it out loud or you say it to yourself, you go, 'Holy shit did that just happen?'" he said. "I mean, you might see somebody do a flip, get kicked in the head, get knocked out with a punch. At some point, you're going 'Whoah, did that just happen? Did I really just see that?' That's the nucleus of what our product is." McGregor's entire career in the UFC had been a series of such moments, knockouts so eerily effective and precise they seemed supernatural, moments that briefly transcended the confines of sport and made cage fighting seem as if it had a public interest. There was a feeling not just of joy in the arena, but jubilation, a burden lifted, a debt dissolved. As McGregor mounted the side of the cage in celebration, he started peeling off imaginary dollar bills from his palm into the crowd as if there had been a bank run and he was the first one who'd made it into the vault.

After the fight, Aldo returned to his locker room with his shirt over his face to mask the tears. He walked to the far wall and squatted on the floor, then fell backward into the arms of one of his cornermen. He threw his shirt aside and sobbed into a towel as his team huddled around him for comfort. For much of his life, Aldo had felt like he was no one, and before he had found a career in cage fighting, he had been. He had grown up in the slums of Manaus, an industrial city in the middle of the Amazon. At seventeen, he had left his family and moved alone to Rio, some seventeen hundred miles away, to train at Nova União, one of the city's most famous mixed martial arts gyms, hoping to make a name for himself as a professional fighter. He'd found a father figure in André Pederneiras, the man who'd given John Lewis his black belt in jiu-jitsu four years before training White and the Fertittas. Having nowhere else to go, Aldo slept at the gym and helped out by cleaning the mats and teaching beginners' classes while Pederneiras mentored him, bringing him up through the harsh regional Brazilian promotions before he finally got a chance to come to America to compete in the WEC in 2008. He had fought nineteen fights over seven years before he'd earned the chance to fight in the UFC, in a weight division the promotion had never before had, and which he helped maintain for another four years, quietly building history with each title defense. When McGregor had come along, it was as if none of that history had been real, like a stack of chips that had been swept back onto the dealer's side of the table after an unlucky hand. Aldo had been certain he would beat McGregor, but with his face pressed into another gym mat in a strange city thousands of miles from his family, tears streaming down his face, he began to doubt himself. Had he ever really been a champion? Had it all been a decade-long misunderstanding? He left the arena without speaking to the press.

Meanwhile, McGregor basked in attention at the post-fight press conference. He broke the long-standing tradition that had all the card's main fighters share the dais and take turns answering questions from the press while White watched from the podium. McGregor instead waited until all the other winning fighters finished taking questions before he made his entrance. And instead of taking questions from the dais, he took White's position at the center podium as if he had just won the UFC presidency and not the featherweight championship. He spoke with the calm detachment of someone addressing shareholders on an earnings call. "How do I look up here, by the way?" he asked, preening in a hand-tailored maroon suit and an $85,000 rose-gold and diamond-set Audemars Piguet wristwatch. "I think it suits me. I think I look good up here."

Something seemed different about him at the press conference. He was kind instead of cocky, considerate more than confrontational, yet he was insistent on his position not just as the UFC's biggest star, but its main source of revenue, after having broken his own record for tickets sales with a $10 million live gate. "I said to Dana and Lorenzo, I'm bringing these big numbers, I'm bringing these half billion dollar revenue numbers," he said, referring to a statement Lorenzo had made to CNN that the UFC would generate more than $600 million in 2015, $150 million more than the company had made the year before. To McGregor, all that growth and all the renewed excitement around the brand had come from him, and he expected only more from the company in the future. He announced his plans to immediately move up a division to fight for the lightweight championship next, and when asked if there was any chance he could bring the UFC back to Ireland, potentially for an event at Croke Park, a soccer stadium in Dublin with more than eighty-two thousand seats, McGregor said he would jump at the chance if White and Lorenzo brought it to him.

"Could you demand it?" the reporter, Kevin Iole from *Yahoo! Sports*, asked.

McGregor tilted his head to one side and smiled, as if he'd never actually had the thought, or hadn't ever allowed himself to say it aloud. "Maybe I can, these days," he said, as if he was about to break out laughing.

"Maybe I can."

FAIR IS DEFINED AS WHERE WE END UP

In early 2016, Ari Emanuel was scrambling to find investors to back his UFC bid. Though new stars like Rousey and McGregor had helped revive the UFC's flagging pay-per-view business and had generated waves of free publicity for the promotion, with cover stories in the *New York Times*, *Sports Illustrated*, and the *New Yorker*, many investors were still unsure of just how long the UFC's winning streak would last. Lorenzo had settled on a minimum price of roughly $4 billion and that figure had posed a problem for Emanuel. It was nearly twenty-two times Zuffa's non-adjusted earnings before interest, taxes, depreciation, and amortization (EBITDA)—a common financial metric used to evaluate a company's overall worth based on its year-to-year profits—which had been $189 million in 2015. It was an unusually high multiple, something that many investors could see as a red flag. And while the UFC's high profit margins were enticing, many investors had been concerned about the sport's volatility and how quickly its earnings could potentially be upended by having to pay even higher purses to hold on to star fighters like McGregor and Rousey. (An internal UFC document prepared for the sale would later acknowledge that the most commonly asked question from investors had been about fighter compensation.) While Zuffa had forecast that it would be able to limit fighter pay to 20 percent or less of total revenues each year, the ongoing antitrust lawsuit added uncertainty of Zuffa's projections, as did efforts from another small group of fighters that had been lobbying Congress to include mixed martial arts fighters in the Muhammad Ali Boxing Reform Act, which had first been enacted in 2000 to protect boxers from predatory or exploitive promoters.

Emanuel had first discussed the idea of a UFC acquisition with Silver Lake Partners, a $10 billion private equity firm that frequently invested in the tech market. Emanuel had befriended one of Silver Lake's managing partners and co-CEO, Egon Durban, in 2011, just after Emanuel pulled off a high-profile acquisition of rival talent agency William Morris. The newly combined entity, renamed WME (William Morris Endeavor), became the biggest talent agency in the entertainment industry, putting more than three hundred agents under Emanuel's leadership and increasing annual revenue from $100 million to $365 million. Durban was impressed with Emanuel's intensity and ambitions, and he agreed to invest $200 million in WME in 2012 to help fund Emanuel's plans for even bigger acquisitions, in exchange for a 31 percent stake in the agency.

Emanuel had long suspected the talent representation business was inherently limited, dependent on an entertainment industry that had started to stagnate. Though the number of original television series being produced had risen throughout the 2000s—from 182 in 2002 to 288 in 2012—advertising revenue had remained flat, with $41.2 billion raised in the US in 2002, and $40.1 billion generated in 2012. The film industry had also seen its revenues flatten. In 2002, nearly 1.6 billion movie tickets were sold in the US, generating close to $9.2 billion. In 2012, fewer than 1.4 billion tickets were sold for a total of $11 billion. Studios had adapted by raising ticket prices and experimenting with 3D and IMAX, while also cutting their yearly releases to consolidate revenue in a small number of blockbusters—Warner Bros. went from distributing twenty-seven theatrical films in 2002, to seventeen in 2012; Paramount tapered from nineteen to fifteen; and 20th Century Fox remained flat, with fifteen in 2002 and fifteen in 2012.

For a company that ran mostly on commission, it was hard to see how WME could continue to grow as a traditional talent agency. Instead, Emanuel had wanted to transform the agency into a new kind of business. Inspired by George Gilder's short but influential book, *Life After Television: The Coming Transformation of Media and American Life*, Emanuel had predicted that the once monolithic entertainment industry would be broken down into thousands of smaller self-contained ecosystems, which no longer depended on the one-way distribution systems that had made the broadcast television, terrestrial radio, and theatrical film industries possible. "The world of ten thousand networks," Emanuel would call it. Gilder had been a favorite of libertarians and techno-futurists like Elon

Musk and Arthur Laffer, who had described Gilder's work as the "bible of the Reagan Revolution." In *Life After Television*, Gilder had predicted people would turn to "teleputers," which they would use to connect with, and perform for, one another directly.

Emanuel imagined a company that would thrive in that future landscape, a kind of Cisco Systems for celebrity, that would collect fees from as many different subcultures as possible, while helping to keep each primed with new forms of content. After William Morris, Emanuel's first major target had been IMG, a sports marketing and events company that had created lucrative ad campaigns for a client list that included Tiger Woods, Pete Sampras, supermodel Kate Moss, violinist Itzhak Perlman, Derek Jeter, and even Pope John Paul II, for whom the company had organized a speaking tour in 1981. IMG also represented more than ninety university athletic programs, on whose behalf it would sell sponsorships and media rights licenses. Like the UFC, IMG was a free-form company that treated its client list as self-contained brands that could be translated into any medium or industry for a fee. Originally founded in 1960 by a corporate lawyer from Cleveland, Mark McCormack, who wanted to help his friend, PGA Tour newcomer Arnold Palmer, supplement his still modest income with some product endorsements, IMG had grown into a corporate conglomerate with seventy offices around the world and more than thirty-five hundred full-time employees.

Though IMG had rejected several previous acquisition attempts, including a hostile takeover engineered by Creative Artists Agency founder Michael Ovitz, Emanuel was able to break through in 2013, with a bid of $2.4 billion, which Durban and Silver Lake had helped put together. The size of the offer shocked everyone involved. It was over $600 million more than the next closest bid, from the the Chernin Group and CVC Capital, and was flagged as "speculative" by Moody's, implying creditors were at a greater risk of losing money through default on loan repayment. Moody's cited WME's suspiciously unrealistic revenue projections and the significant amount of debt required to complete the deal—more than $1.9 billion—as reasons for concern.

Despite the risks, IMG had accepted the offer. Emanuel became CEO of a new corporate amalgam, WME-IMG, while Silver Lake took a 51 percent ownership stake. Over the next several years, Emanuel and

Silver Lake continued their debt-leveraged acquisition spree, hoping to expand WME-IMG's business into even newer and stranger markets. They purchased PWR Events Ltd., a company that built an amusement park in London's Hyde Park every winter; Brand Events, which organized food festivals in Australia; and ELeague, an e-sports company that organized competitive video game tournaments. The global arts company Frieze was also added to WME-IMG's roster, along with Professional Bull Riders, a competitive bull riding promotion, and MADE Fashion Week, the company behind the influential New York Fashion Week.

It was a bizarre mix of businesses, and it was hard to see what one had in common with the other. Even Emanuel could sound muddled when he tried to describe how all of WME-IMG's pieces would fit together. "So the book department is now publishing books from the hot, new chefs out of the UK, the hottest area in chefs," he said in a 2016 interview. "So the people in LA or New York in the reality area, can go sign [the chefs] and create shows. And if we have twenty-eight food festivals, depending on what we're gonna do with food, you can create shows, either sell them or create licensing product off of them. You're constantly being able to learn what's happening in the world through the platform and through the intel inside of the system."

Emanuel's acquisition spree had largely been paid for with new debt that had grown far more quickly than WME-IMG's revenues. And while he was convinced that the UFC would complement his sprawling conglomerate of media properties, the promotion's steady flow of profits would be even more useful to help service WME-IMG's previous debts. The UFC's Fox deal was set to expire in 2018, and the promotion had projected a new deal could bring in as much $450 million a year, more than two-and-a-half times what Fox was paying, something the company believed it could accomplish despite its often flat or declining ratings, because of heightened competition in online streaming between companies like Amazon and Disney.

It was less clear what benefits the UFC would get from tying itself to Emanuel's strange gambit with WME-IMG, but Emanuel was confident that he could assemble a big enough group of investors to hit Lorenzo's target price. And at that point, the money would speak for itself. Over the winter, Zuffa had begun preparing bid books—containing a detailed summary of the UFC's current business and future prospects, with help from merchant bank the Raine Group, which Emanuel had helped launch in 2009—that would be sent to a long list of potential bidders at the end of March. Both Fox and ESPN had expressed interest, as had Time Warner and Dalian Wanda, the Chinese real estate giant that had reportedly expanded into entertainment with the acquisition of AMC Theaters in 2012. Also curious were China Media Capital, a film financier that had purchased percentages of Manchester United F.C. and the racing championship Formula E; Blackstone, an American private equity giant; and leveraged buyout specialist Providence Equity. Silver Lake began its own financial analysis, "deep under the cover of night," Durban would later say, of what it would take for WME-IMG to pull off the acquisition. After nearly a decade of representing the UFC as a client, Emanuel was convinced the next logical step would be to own it outright.

Nick Diaz watched his younger brother, Nathan, fighting on the small monitor mounted to the wall of a locker room in the Amway Center in Orlando, Florida. It was the UFC's last event of 2015, *UFC on Fox: dos Anjos v. Cowboy 2*, and Nathan had been booked against the sixth-ranked lightweight, Michael Johnson, who had started the first round with a series of quick left crosses that seemed twice as fast as Nathan's punches. As Nathan tried to settle into a rhythm, Johnson continually interrupted him with short calf kicks that made Nathan momentarily stumble to the side, as if he had stepped on a trapdoor in the mat. Nick wanted to shout advice at the screen, but there was no point in the empty locker room. He had always hated watching his little brother fight. Seeing Nathan hit, he would later say, hurt him more than any of the punches he'd taken in his own fights.

Nick's own career as a cage fighter had come to an abrupt halt earlier that year, when the Nevada State Athletic Commission suspended him from competition for five years and fined him $165,000, after he tested positive for marijuana metabolites following a fight against Anderson Silva at UFC 183. As part of his punishment, Nick had been barred from being in Nathan's corner, the first time since 2007 that he wouldn't be cage-side for one of his younger brother's fights.

The decision had frustrated Nick, and left him with a renewed sense of responsibility for Nathan. "It's my bad he even got into this sport," Nick had said after his suspension was announced. "And he gets his face kicked in and they don't even pay him. I got us in this, and if I don't make any money, I don't have any way to get us out."

The brothers' lives had been closely entangled throughout their careers as fighters. They'd lived together for a time, in a new tract house Nick had saved up to buy on the outskirts of Lodi. They spent nights training in a small gym they had opened together, and afterward they'd go on long, late-night runs, often with a pack of teammates trailing behind. They competed in triathlons in the pine-flocked mountains surrounding Lake Tahoe and would train with long mountain bike rides in the foothills outside Stockton. They'd come home again in the evening and while away the hours with many of the same friends they'd had since high school.

In the cage, Nick had been one of Strikeforce's biggest stars, winning the promotion's welterweight championship and amassing a ten-fight win streak that included a five-round decision win against K.J. Noons in a much-hyped rematch. In June 2011, Nick had been one of the first fighters brought to the UFC following the Strikeforce acquisition, a move that forced him to abandon plans for a boxing match against Jeff Lacy, who had held the IBF and IBO super middleweight championships. Nick had continued to clash with the UFC management after returning. He missed press conferences, and was pulled from fights, or had last-minute opponent switches. The conflict fueled Nick's sense of paranoia that he was being set up to fail. "They do everything they can in their power to create these problems for me," he said of the UFC in a 2013 radio interview. Nick admitted he was suspicious that people in UFC management hoped he would lose. "I would imagine they do [want me to lose]," he said. "I think the US wants me to lose, especially after what they've been marketed. And you know it's not their fault. It's not their fault. They are educated, okay? But they're educated on what's been marketed to them."

In 2013, when he finally fought Georges St-Pierre—the UFC's long-reigning welterweight champion, the opponent he had originally been promised when he first agreed to abandon the Lacy fight and return to the UFC—a sense of doom hung over the matchup. Nick would lose a slow and largely uneventful five-round decision to St-Pierre, who relied on his wrestling strength to neutralize Nick's high-volume boxing and submission attempts. As Nick waited for the decision to be announced in the cage, he had looked up at himself on the big LCD screens in the corner, as he had done after his first UFC fight ten years earlier, his face still covered in the same gray and purple bruises. He looked away from the sight and stared down at the mat.

In his post-fight interview with Rogan, Nick seemed strangely buoyant, as if something in him had been freed. "You know, I think I'm gonna have to—I'm gonna have to figure out if I want to keep doing this," he said, pausing for a moment to quietly laugh as a new thought formed.

"To be honest, I don't think I got it anymore."

At the same time, Nathan began to think the UFC had "conned" him into signing a restrictive contract that had left him earning little more for his eighteenth fight with the promotion ($15,000 and $15,000) than he had made for his first ($8,000 and $8,000). "I'm over here getting chump change," he'd said in 2014. "At this point, they're paying all my partners and other people I train with are getting real money, and it's too embarrassing for me to even fight again for the money they're paying me." Despite his complaints, Nathan had remained popular with fans, and had produced a steady stream of violent highlights and finishes. He had earned eleven bonuses for Submission of the Night or Fight of the Night in the UFC, with payments that ranged from $50,000 to $125,000. In 2012, his one and only title fight, against lightweight champion Benson Henderson, had drawn an average of 4.4 million viewers and peaked with 5.8 million during the main event, making it the second-most watched UFC event on Fox at the time.

White dismissed Nathan's complaints, and would later describe him as "difficult," someone who, like his older brother, Nick, couldn't be trusted to "play the game." White claimed Nathan had missed a chance to make "Justin Bieber money" by losing to Henderson, and said that if he wanted better pay he would have to prove he was worth it by winning fights. "Guess how much money he makes sitting at home?" White said. "Zero. Get back to work, Nate." When Nathan refused to accept another fight unless the UFC offered him a new contract with better pay, the promotion instead removed him from its rankings.

After holding out for nearly a year, Nathan began to fear he was losing the best part of his career, in a contract dispute he ultimately had
no way of winning. "Fighting drives me crazy," he would later say, "but
not fighting, that shit drives me crazier." A few months after Nathan's
thirtieth birthday, he decided his best option was to return to the cage
and finish the remaining number of fights on his contract, and either negotiate a new deal with the UFC, or find another promotion that would
pay him what he was worth. His first fight back was against Johnson, in
Orlando.

Even without Nick's corner advice, Nathan had gradually found a way
back into the fight after Johnson's fast start. He began timing Johnson's
power punches, leaning just out of the way and countering with a slow
but effective right hook. Nathan had recruited the audience to his side
by pointing at Johnson every time after he landed a counterpunch, as if
disappointed his opponent wasn't adapting as quickly as he was. By the
end of the fight, Nathan had earned a unanimous decision win, his first in
more than two years, along with another $50,000 bonus for Fight of the
Night.

When Joe Rogan approached him in the cage afterward for an interview, Nathan brushed off his question and instead grabbed the microphone and went on an expletive-filled diatribe against Conor McGregor.

"Conor McGregor, you're taking everything I worked for, mother-
fucker. I'm gonna fight your fuckin' ass," Nathan said. Nick had left the
locker room after the fight and watched the short speech from the edge of
the arena floor. The callout had seemed strange at the time, in large part
because almost all of it was censored by the broadcast team on Fox, but
also because Nathan had lost three of his last five fights and seemed an
unlikely choice to match against the surging McGregor.

As if to underscore the strange irrelevance of Nathan's callout, the UFC
announced, just three weeks later, that McGregor's next fight would be
against Rafael dos Anjos, the current lightweight champion on March 5,
2016. For McGregor, it would mark a historic attempt to become a champion in two weight classes simultaneously, something that had never been
done before in the UFC. And for the UFC, another McGregor pay-per-
view would help present a bullish picture of the promotion's business to
potential investors, who would receive bid books just weeks later.

That plan was upended a little over a month later when dos Anjos was forced to withdraw from the fight after breaking his foot in the final sparring session of his training camp. It was the second consecutive pay-per-view main event that had fallen apart at the last minute. The preceding pay-per-view, built around a heavyweight championship fight between Fabricio Werdum and Cain Velasquez, had been canceled altogether after Velasquez withdrew due to an injury. The remaining fights were repackaged as a standard *Fight Night* card that aired on Fox Sports, losing millions in the process. As White scrambled to keep UFC 196 together, he turned to the long list of fighters written in black marker on the floor-to-ceiling windows in his office in Las Vegas, looking for replacements. Nathan wasn't high on the list of options, but after several phone calls, he unexpectedly emerged as the leading contender if only because he wasn't injured and hadn't just been knocked out.

When he got the offer, he was on a short vacation in Cabo San Lucas, Mexico, with a small group of his training partners. According to Urijah Faber, a UFC bantamweight who had also been considered as a potential opponent for McGregor, the promotion had offered Nathan the fight along with a new contract that would pay him $50,000 to fight and $50,000 to win. Nathan rejected the offer and reportedly hung up on the UFC after it was made. When White laid out the remaining options for McGregor, he insisted on Nathan, in part because of his aggressive fighting style and hard-earned reputation among fans. The UFC went back to Nathan with a new multiyear deal that would give him a disclosed purse of $500,000 for the McGregor fight, along with a side-letter agreement that would bring his total pay into the millions.

Nathan accepted the offer, and two days later, he found himself on a dais at the UFC Gym in Torrance, California, a short drive from the beachfront mansion that McGregor had rented for the final weeks of his training camp. McGregor sat on the opposite end of the dais, compulsively flexing and flinching like a horse ready to bolt from its handlers. He seemed energized by the unruly crowd that cheered and heckled, ready to come to life at any slight precursor of real violence. Asked about the change in opponents, McGregor admitted it stung to lose his chance at winning a second title. "Really, I should create my own belt," he said. "Because I am in myself, my own belt. It doesn't matter weight, if it was a featherweight, a welterweight, a lightweight—it's the McGregor belt."

The crowd reacted with shouts and howls when McGregor spoke, as if his mind were a roller coaster they were collectively riding. Energized by the attention, McGregor taunted Nathan. "He's like a little cholo gangster from the hood, but at the same time he coaches kids jiu-jitsu on a Sunday morning and goes on bike rides with the elderly," McGregor said. "He makes gun signs with the right hand and balloon animals with the left hand."

Dressed in a plain black T-shirt and loose-fitting jeans, Nathan spoke in short, single-line sentences, uninterested in matching McGregor's giddy, cackling energy. "I been in these big-ass shows for hella years," he said in an agitated monotone. "Before this guy even existed. So it ain't no thing. I don't give a fuck."

"I don't give a fuck either!" McGregor said, slapping the table with a theatrical cackle.

Later, he belittled Nathan over his pay, claiming the fight would be an act of undeserved charity that McGregor had gifted him. "How does it feel to be a millionaire now?" McGregor said. "It's nice, right? It's nice, right? . . . You're a 'milly' for one night only."

As the fight drew closer, media interest in the two men exploded, with newspaper profiles, billboards, radio spots, television interviews, on everything from Conan O'Brien to CNBC. McGregor closed as nearly a four-to-one favorite. He seemed almost invincible, a rumor of a human being with a supernatural ability to engineer knockouts, who had helped spread the gospel of cage fighting to the kinds of audiences that almost never gave the UFC a second thought. Nathan closed a three-to-one underdog. He felt like a fighter from another era, a great fighter in a sport where greatness rarely led to good long-term outcomes.

When Nathan and McGregor finally stood across from each other in the cage at the MGM Grand Garden Arena, the VIP seats were filled with an incongruous list of celebrities, whose faces hovered in the darkness outside the cage. Tyga, Josh Brolin, Gordon Ramsay, Leonardo DiCaprio, Reggie Bush, Paris Hilton, Bruno Mars, and Gerard Butler, all watched as the referee issued his final instructions while a small phalanx of athletic commission inspectors stood between Nathan and McGregor, as if they were opposing generals in a war tribunal.

As the opening bell rang, it seemed as if the fight might already be close to the end. McGregor bullied Nathan and inched him backward with feints and stomp kicks aimed at Nathan's knee. Twenty seconds into the fight, Nathan found himself trapped against the octagon fence, while McGregor threw a confusing array of spinning heel kicks, feints, and straight punches. Nathan leaned just out of range, and then ducked under McGregor's punches and grabbed him in a clinch. He rotated McGregor onto the fence and used his own torso as a human lean-to, momentarily pinning McGregor against the cage. Nathan's size, three inches taller and ten pounds heavier, had seemed like the one thing that could give him an advantage over the younger and faster McGregor, but McGregor calmly clamped his arm over Nathan's right arm and used it as a fulcrum to rotate himself back off the cage. In a matter of seconds it seemed as if Nathan's only advantage had evaporated.

Nathan tried to push McGregor back with his long jab, but McGregor countered each punch with one or two of his own. Nathan's punches always seemed to come out a half second too late, while McGregor's landed with heavy thuds against Nathan's head. As the round wore on, McGregor's speed advantage became overbearing, and nothing Nathan tried seemed to have any effect at all. With a minute-and-a-half left in the round, McGregor had opened a long cut on Nathan's right eyebrow, and a steady trickle of blood began running down his face, and into his eyes. Near the end of the round, Nathan bent down and grabbed McGregor's ankle after a kick and used it to pull him down to the mat, hoping to use his comparatively advanced jiu-jitsu to gain an advantage. But McGregor refused to be held in place and instead grabbed one of Nathan's own ankles and used it to sweep him onto his back. The round ended with Nathan trapped on his back as McGregor hovered over him, punching down through his outstretched arms and legs.

In the final press conference two days before the fight, McGregor had described Nathan not as an opponent but as prey. "You're like a gazelle, all bunched up together [with your teammates], hoping that you get spared," McGregor had said. "I'm a lion in there and I'm going to eat you alive." As the second round began, it seemed as if something predatory was happening. McGregor continued to slide and roll out of the way of Nathan's long jabs, and countered with quick, piercing punches that snapped Nathan's head backward and sideways, leaving him shocked for a split second, as if he had just hit his head on an unexpectedly low ceiling, before resetting his stance. After a minute-and-a-half, Nathan's face was covered in his own blood. As McGregor's punches steadily widened the cut over his eye, the fight seemed like it might be nearing its terrible conclusion.

But then, something changed.

At first, it seemed like a simple miscalculation by McGregor. After an inconclusive exchange of punches, Nathan circled away from him along the edge of the octagon fence. Instead of skipping laterally to keep Nathan trapped, McGregor walked after him in a leisurely line. Recognizing the opportunity, Nathan quickly stepped around McGregor in a circular motion and trapped him against the fence for a few seconds. McGregor leapt forward with another combination of punches, but they now seemed to come at half speed and no longer had the head-snapping effect. A few seconds later, Nathan landed a long open-hand slap against McGregor's left ear. McGregor smiled at having been caught, and almost immediately Nathan hit him again, with a quick jab that landed on the chin and drove McGregor off-balance, as if he had stepped on a loose floorboard. McGregor tried to regain the initiative with more feints, but Nathan had recognized that McGregor's punches were coming with less speed and force, and he no longer backed away from them. Suddenly, it was McGregor who was taking backward steps, searching for space as Nathan began marching forward. McGregor seemed strangely drained, as if maintaining the upper hand for seven minutes had required energy equivalent to finishing a marathon.

With two-and-a-half minutes left in the round, Nathan stepped forward with a jab and a left cross that hit McGregor on the end of the chin and twisted his head to the side like a bottle cap being twisted off. McGregor sluggishly nodded to acknowledge the hit, as he staggered backward. Sensing weakness, Nathan stepped forward with a slow flood of loose-limbed punches, some of which bounced off McGregor's forearms and shoulders and others of which thudded into the side of his face. As McGregor tried to sag away from more damage, Nathan stepped forward, grabbed him around the back of the neck in a clinch, and used his head to pin McGregor to the fence. "Nate's hurting him! Nate's hurting him!" Joe Rogan shouted on commentary, as if shocked by the sound of his own words.

McGregor gathered his remaining energy and released another short flurry of labored punches to no effect. Nathan hit McGregor with another hard jab-cross that snapped McGregor's head back, and again sent him retreating to the cage, exhaustion mixing with the slow confusion of new brain trauma. As Nathan planted to throw another combination, McGregor ducked under the punches and drove forward for a wrestling takedown. Nathan ran his arm under McGregor's neck and used his forearm to push into McGregor's throat while pushing down on the back of McGregor's head with his own torso. McGregor tried to swivel his feet to the side as they fell, hoping to alleviate the pressure of the choke, but Nathan instead used McGregor's trapped head as a lever to roll him onto his back. Nathan slid his knee across McGregor's stomach and began punching down on McGregor's face, his beard and hair suddenly rust-colored with blood.

McGregor rolled onto his stomach to shield his face from more punches, and Nathan drove his arm back through the crevice between McGregor's shoulder and neck. "That's it!" Rogan screamed like a hysterical father watching a live birth. "He's got the choke! He's got it!" McGregor grimaced in pain as he tried to push up off the mat to alleviate the pressure wrenching his esophagus into the back of his neck. But it was too late. There was no space left to escape to, and McGregor tapped three times in submission. Nathan rose from McGregor's drained body and flexed his biceps, his face creased with anger and defiance as he walked toward the octagon fence and thrust his face into one of the cameras.

For a moment, it felt like a miracle, a violation of the natural order, a gazelle loping across the savanna with the carcass of a lion in its mouth, reality drowning itself in an ecstatic hallucination. Interviewed in the cage after the official result was read, Rogan told Nathan he had just shocked the world. "I'm not surprised, motherfucker," he said, looking away into the crowd, as if he expected Nick to have snuck out of the locker room and onto the arena floor, where his face would have blended in with the dozens of stunned celebrities.

At the post-fight press conference in the MGM Grand Garden Arena,

White said the early returns from pay-per-view sales and social media impressions indicated the event was "breaking every record we've ever had. It's pretty much the biggest fight ever." By most metrics, it should have been a disaster; the UFC's biggest star losing a short-notice fight to an opponent who had gone two-and-three over the preceding three years, puncturing the aura of invincibility that had surrounded a once-in-a-generation talent who turned out to have more limitations than advertised. But the UFC always had the most appeal when it seemed as if things were running off the rails, capturing moments that shouldn't have been possible or weren't supposed to happen. Even the typically reserved VIP section had been shocked to life by the sight of Nathan choking McGregor. "You know you have something exciting when people who have done it all, seen it all, been everywhere and done everything are standing around going, Holy shit what just happened?" White said immediately after the fight. To White, the magic of the moment was simple. "It was a fight, man," White said. "Listen, this thing was what it was—these are two guys that wanted to fight, and everybody saw a fight tonight."

UFC 196 would go on to generate roughly 1.5 million pay-per-view buys, making it the bestselling event in company history, passing the Brock Lesnar–Frank Mir grudge match at UFC 100. It generated $8.1 million in ticket sales, the second highest, behind only McGregor's previous fight, at UFC 194. It was the number one trending topic in Twitter's sports category for a week, and the free prelim fights that aired on Fox Sports 1 were the most watched program across all broadcast and cable for their time slot, drawing more than 1.8 million viewers.

The morning after the fight, Lorenzo and White had driven to the two-story beige mansion McGregor had rented, in a wealthy subdivision on the edge of Las Vegas, and found him still obsessing over the loss. He had kept replaying the fight in his head, trying to find his way back to the slippery moment where everything had spun out of control. He begged for a rematch, but White thought it was a bad idea. He'd sat with hundreds of other fighters after bad losses and heard the same plea for a second chance, someone searching for a way out of their failure. Like a gambler doubling their bets to make up for a lost hand, the wished for immediate rematch seemed like it would only compound the damage. It was a risk for McGregor, but it was also a risk for the UFC. Two consecutive losses wouldn't erase his drawing power, but it would lessen it, and steal from a future timeline where he might otherwise continue breaking records.

White and Lorenzo tried to persuade McGregor to forget about the loss and return to the featherweight division. There were no real stakes in a rematch, other than pride. It was reckless, good for his ego but bad for everything else. To McGregor, ego and business had become interchangeable. Losing to Nathan couldn't be a part of who he was. It had to have been an anomaly; it was incompatible with the story he had told the world, and the story he had wanted to believe about himself. To accept his loss, it had started to feel as if he would have to also accept becoming another person, to abandon some part of himself he had believed in and left behind in that moment on the mat, flattened out on his stomach, drifting toward unconsciousness as Nathan's arms tightened around his neck.

White and Lorenzo weren't convinced McGregor was making the right choice for his career, but a rematch would add at least one more guaranteed blockbuster to the UFC's pay-per-view schedule, to keep investors energized about the company's future earnings potential. And so three weeks later, with the UFC's bid books just beginning to circulate, the UFC officially announced that a second fight between Nathan and McGregor would take place at UFC 200 on July 9 in Las Vegas. Assuming the event would match or potentially surpass UFC 196's performance, it would leave a charmed aura around the UFC as the Fertittas prepared to pass it on to its next owners.

As Lorenzo and Frank III began to think more carefully about who those next owners might be, they kept coming back to White. While they expected White's 9 percent ownership stake in the UFC to be included in any sale agreement they signed, they had also expected him to stay on. Lorenzo wanted the new owners to be people White would feel as comfortable with as he had been with Lorenzo and Frank III. He kept thinking of Emanuel. Though White had disliked Emanuel when they first met, he had developed an uncanny admiration for him. "He's got huge balls," White would later say, "and he's really smart."

Like White, Emanuel had an intense temper. His shouting fits at WME-IMG had become infamous. "I saw him scream at someone on the phone, dropping F-bombs and the like and then he winked at me while still on the phone," a former WME colleague said in 2013. Another employee had reportedly seen Emanuel smashing a laptop to pieces in the WME-IMG parking lot one morning, for reasons that they couldn't quite understand. And just as White had gravitated to Tony Robbins's gospel of self-belief and prosperity, Emanuel was taken in by Preetha Ji's meditation practices at the One World Academy, which offers online courses and in-person seminars that "transform disconnection to connection, division to oneness, suffering to a beautiful state." According to Emanuel, Ji's approach to meditation had helped him to embrace his inner rage instead of trying to fight against it. "It says it's OK to be mad!" Emanuel would say of the course.

At Zuffa's offices, White was infamous for his inability to sit through long meetings. His attention span waned quickly and he fed on continually changing his schedule. Emanuel was likewise so perpetually restless he had treadmill desks installed in every one of his offices. He always wanted to feel as if he was going somewhere, though it was rarely clear what he was supposed to be getting done in any one place. "Most of Hollywood stays in Hollywood," Emanuel said. "No one's getting on a plane and going to Argentina for three meetings. . . . And then getting on a plane and flying to London. Or going to China for a lunch and a dinner and coming back. I don't give a shit. I did it last weekend." Less a visionary than a control freak with a deep competitive streak, Emanuel seemed to value acquisitiveness above all else and he maintained an almost arbitrary sense of ethics. Asked in 1994 to condense his personal philosophy into one sentence, he replied: "Fair is defined as where we end up."

Emanuel still wasn't sure where he'd end up in the bidding process for the UFC. With WME-IMG's substantial debt and limited supply of cash to include in any bid offer, Emanuel tried to find a way to assemble the complex puzzle of different bonds and loan offers from a range of investment banks, private equity companies, and commercial banks. "It was very difficult to come up with the number [the UFC] wanted," he would later say. In March, WME-IMG raised $250 million by selling a 5 percent stake in its operations to the Japanese finance giant SoftBank Group, a sum that Emanuel's co-CEO, Patrick Whitesell, said would be useful for acquisitions. Yet, as more funding became available, Emanuel's ambitions grew in proportion. In the spring, WME-IMG began exploring another and potentially even larger deal to partially acquire F1, the European auto-racing league that was worth an estimated $8.5 billion. Coupled with the UFC, the F1 deal would have expanded WME-IMG's sports portfolio by an order of magnitude, and almost instantly turned WME-IMG into a global sports institution instead of a collection of curiosities.

Yet, at the end of April, Emanuel's efforts grew more complicated when White decided to pull McGregor from UFC 200 just one month after announcing that his rematch with Nathan would serve as the main event. White claimed that McGregor had refused to leave his training camp in Iceland to appear at a press conference in Las Vegas and spend an extra day filming an advertisement for the event. "Joanna Jedrzejczyk came in from Poland. Claudia Gadelha came in from Brazil," White said of the decision. "This is what we do. This is how it works. I didn't prevent [McGregor] from fighting at UFC 200. He knew what the deal was. I told him what the deal was. He opted to do that."

Without a McGregor fight on the card, public interest immediately dropped. The first public press conference livestream for UFC 200 had drawn roughly 33,000 viewers, compared to the more than 360,000 simultaneous viewers for the UFC 196 press conference. Emanuel pushed ahead and by early May had assembled the rough elements of an offer, using a mix of cash, bonds, and loans involving Silver Lake, the private equity firm Kohlberg Kravis Roberts & Co., and Michael Dell's investment firm MSD Capital. Additional financing was provided by Barclays, Credit Suisse, Goldman Sachs, and Deutsche Bank.

As more formal offers began coming in, news stories quickly spread online. A report from ESPN's Darren Rovell said negotiations had reached an "advanced" stage with four different bidders, including Blackstone, the Chinese conglomerate Dalian Wanda, and China Media Capital, a Chinese venture capital firm. Providence Equity reportedly submitted a bid for $2.8 billion, and Fox entered a bid of its own worth a reported $3.6 billion. And an undisclosed Chinese firm outbid the field with a $5 billion offer.

As the stories about the sale circulated in the media, White and Lorenzo denied anything unusual was happening. "Yeah, we're not up for sale," White said, in an appearance on the *Dan Patrick Show* in May. "We're always working on deals and our expansion globally. I've been saying since this thing came out: No, we're not for sale. But let me tell you what: if somebody shows up with $4 billion, we can talk. We can definitely talk." When Patrick asked if the UFC might instead be selling just a portion of the company, White prevaricated. "Obviously, if I'm in the middle of a deal right now, there's a lot of confidentiality involved. But we're working on expanding. We're working on growing the company." White insisted the UFC had received acquisition offers continuously since 2010, and just as continuously turned people down. "I'll tell you this," he said, "the day we decide to sell, I probably don't want to do this anymore." As UFC 200 drew closer, Lorenzo insisted all of the stories were based on a simple misunderstanding. "Look, if we bring on an investor or something happens, we'll let everyone know," he told the *Los Angeles Times*. "I've never been more bullish on the business. I still have massive love for the sport. I never said I was walking away. What's happening—this is standard, any company, this size and magnitude, you don't talk about things you're working on in strategical terms. So there's nothing to report."

Behind the scenes, Lorenzo and Frank III had reportedly narrowed their options down to two bidders: China Media Capital and Emanuel's bid on behalf of WME-IMG, backed by Silver Lake and what had become a sprawling list of other financiers. While WME-IMG's involved substantially more investors and complications, it had come in with a substantially higher total offer than China Media Capital's, and after a late June dinner meeting in Hollywood with Emanual and several other exeutives, Lorenzo decided to accept WME-IMG's offer. As Lorenzo flew with Frank III to a $28 million beachfront mansion in Laguna Beach, California, for the Fourth of July weekend, Emanuel tried to finalize all the excruciating deal terms.

"It was nine days of hell," Emanuel would later say of the process. In early July, three days before UFC 200, another unexpected problem arose when the main event that had replaced McGregor's rematch with Nathan, a light heavyweight championship fight between Jon Jones and Daniel Cormier, fell apart after Jones tested positive for two banned substances, clomiphene and letrozole. As White scrambled to find yet another replacement on just three days' notice, Lorenzo suddenly feared someone in Emanuel's group might use the cancelation to justify lowering the acquisition price at the final minute. Just two days before they were hoping to close, Lorenzo warned Emanuel that if he or anyone else tried to lower the price, Lorenzo would stop negotiations and walk away from the sale entirely.

Meanwhile White persuaded Anderson Silva to replace Jones in a non-title fight against Cormier, flying him up from Brazil for the event on two days' notice. White moved another fight to the main event slot, a women's bantamweight championship fight between number one contender Amanda Nunes and Miesha Tate, who had won the title in March from Holly Holm, who had shockingly beaten Ronda Rousey in late 2015.

In the buildup, UFC 200 had offered a complete microcosm of all the potentially disastrous volatility that was built into almost every UFC event. Lucrative rematches could be scuttled over a press conference. Failed drug tests could wipe out replacement fights. Millions of dollars could be spent promoting fights that would never take place. And the final offering could come together like a patchwork of random pieces, smashed into spaces where they didn't belong. Despite everything, the event managed to be a hit, bringing in $10.7 million in ticket sales and just over a million pay-per-view buys, driven largely by the surprise return of Brock Lesnar, who had been secretly negotiating with White throughout the spring to fight at UFC 200, in what would be his first fight in more than four years.

On Sunday evening, less than twenty-four hours after UFC 200 ended, Lorenzo and Frank III finalized the deal with Emanuel to sell the UFC to WME-IMG, for $4.025 billion. It was the single biggest windfall the Fertittas had ever had, worth $1.6 billion more than Red Rock Resorts' April IPO. After repeatedly courting failure, Lorenzo's and Frank III's decision to go against their father's wishes fifteen years earlier had been a winner. A little after midnight on Sunday, White posted a single smiley face on his Twitter account.

BE HAPPY FOR ME

White had been in denial about the UFC sale through most of the spring and early summer. As the negotiations progressed, he shut it out of his mind, assuming it would come to nothing. "I didn't believe it was gonna happen, at all," White said in an interview after the sale. "We'd been through this before. People had made offers; we'd gone out and talked to people." He had thought of the sale as a part of the company's operations that Lorenzo was overseeing, a technical formality that was necessary for the company's international expansion. The weekend before UFC 200, as Lorenzo and Frank III were in the final throes of negotiation with Emanuel, White had taken a long Fourth of July weekend with his family at his vacation home in Levant, Maine. After UFC 200 came to an end, he had started to realize what was really happening and he felt suddenly overwhelmed. The UFC wasn't expanding. To the contrary, a large part of the company was departing. For fifteen years, Lorenzo and Frank III had treated him like a third brother, and his brothers had decided to walk away. As the reality hit, White would later say, it "fucked me up big time."

In *Unlimited Power*, Tony Robbins describes his search for a mysterious man he had heard rumors about but never actually met, someone who was "young, wealthy, healthy, happy, and successful. I had to see [him] for myself." Just a few years earlier, this young man had been alone in a four-hundred-square-foot studio apartment where he did the dishes in his bathtub. But he had grown into a world traveler who had met with presidents, trained executives, and lived with his wife in a castle overlooking the Pacific Ocean. "How was it that this twenty-five-year-old kid, with only a high school education could have accomplished so much in such a short period of time?" Robbins asked.

He was, of course, describing himself, or the version of himself he envisioned becoming while he was struggling through the early stages of building his self-help business. As a twenty-two-year-old biking around Boston listening to Robbins's thick, marbly voice on his Walkman, White had been excited by the idea of transformation. He knew he was on a path to becoming something. He could make the UFC's future, and his own, sound as promising as a Christmas present when he spoke about them. He hadn't counted on feeling alone again, looking back on two decades of brazen risk, new friends, and new enemies, fights that came to nothing, and fighters who became permanent parts of popular culture, the complaints, the unexpected problems, the canceled shows, the people who seemed to lose confidence in him, those who had stayed loyal—it had all been tolerable because he had had someone who believed in him as much as he had believed in himself. He'd trusted Lorenzo and Frank III as much as anyone in his own family, and he felt an overwhelming sense of lonesomeness as he thought about what running the UFC would be like without them. Instead of celebrating, White went into a state of mourning. He rented a suite at Palace Station, pulled the blinds, and went numb in the placelessness of the beige casino tower. He skipped meals, didn't sleep, and watched cable news reports of the sale, seeing what had become of his life's work transformed into a news item that could be explained in a few minutes of television before moving on. "I never thought I would react that way and I would feel that way," White said. "You don't know until it happens to you."

White stayed in the suite for two days, avoiding calls until Lorenzo finally came to coax him out. As he had done so many times before, Lorenzo simplified things for White, and gave him an explanation he knew White would understand, a comforting thought his mind would be able to take shelter in, like a mantra that you could accept as truth without having to think about it. "Dude, I'm done. Be happy for me," Lorenzo told White. "Be happy for me." Fighting had been everything for White, but for Lorenzo it had been one thing among many, a canvas he'd worked at for years and was ready to frame, hang on the wall, and move on from, to the next empty canvas.

Most people who worked at the UFC learned about the sale by reading the news. Like fans, they'd followed the rumors in *ESPN*, the *Wall Street Journal*, *MMA Junkie*, *FloCombat*, and *Bloody Elbow*. "Nobody had any idea of what really was happening," says Paul Cambria, who had joined Zuffa full-time as director of production in 2008. "They didn't communicate things. Only a handful of people knew what was going on and it was impossible to get any information." On a June episode of the UFC's in-house podcast, *UFC Unfiltered*, White tried to publicly reassure employees, saying the rumors of a sale were false. "It's the last thing anybody who works here needs to worry about," White said. "It's just crazy. It's just the world we live in today. With absolutely no proof or evidence whatsoever, people can just go out and say whatever they want. It's fuckin' nuts."

When the sale was officially announced three weeks later, few people inside the company were surprised. Many employees had grown accustomed to not taking the company at its word, to being promised one thing and receiving another. Some jokingly called it the "Zuffa two-step," according to Cambria. To cover for someone who'd left the company, an employee might be asked to relocate or take on some added responsibilities in exchange for a raise or promotion that would never come. It had been frustrating because of how much the company often demanded of its employees, operating in a continual state of crisis, its future endlessly imploding.

It was hard to hold on to a vision of their lives outside of the company. The urgency of going from an event in Brazil one week to another in Poland the week after, and a third in Idaho or Nova Scotia, the week after that always seemed to take priority. For the employees who had put themselves out to help keep the company on its aggressive schedule, the time for balancing the books and living up to Zuffa's side of old bargains never seemed to arrive. There was always another main event that had fallen apart, a complication with a fighter's visa that needed fixing, a hotel that didn't have the appropriate facilities for fighters to cut weight, an arena that wasn't properly equipped. There was nothing but problems to be solved. Tim O'Toole, vice president of Zuffa's event production department, admitted that working for the UFC had made him dread being asked about his hobbies because a large part of his personal life had been absorbed by his job. "That's the question I hate: What do you do for fun?" he said in a 2016 interview. "Because there isn't a lot. This job consumes a lot of time."

After years of sacrifice, some viewed the sale with pride, a kind of external validation of their efforts that UFC management had never quite managed to provide. It was described as a historic milestone—the biggest single transaction ever in professional sports, *ESPN* would proclaim; worth as much as Disney had paid for *Star Wars*, *Men's Journal* wrote. The UFC was worth more than every team in the NFL save the Dallas Cowboys, and was more than three times as valuable as The Beatles catalog. Emanuel had offered a group of WME-IMG's celebrity clients the chance to buy a small ownership stake of the UFC for a minimum investment of $250,000. At least twenty-three accepted, including Tom Brady, Jimmy Kimmel, Guy Fieri, Sylvester Stallone, Ben Affleck, Conan O'Brien, Tyler Perry, Serena Williams, and Adam Levine. The future had never been brighter, and for some it had grown so bright it was hard to see clearly.

When Marshall Zelaznik, the UFC's European division president, learned the company had been sold, he told his team to be prepared for layoffs, not new job titles or promotions. After relocating from London to Los Angeles in 2011, Zelaznik had spent nearly five years commuting to Las Vegas every week, leaving his wife and son on Monday mornings to catch an early flight and not coming back until Friday night. Though he'd been one of the company's longest running employees and helped assemble its media licensing business, he saw the headlines as a sign his job would likely be absorbed by WME-IMG's own media sales team. The idea of layoffs after having achieved so much success was hard to process, and the lack of communication from management slowly amplified the sense of unease about the future, which might not actually have room for everyone.

That unease was amplified when, in October, the Federal Reserve Bank, after reviewing the details of the sale, warned Goldman Sachs that the debt it had issued to help facilitate WME-IMG's acquisition had a heightened risk of default. Typically, the Federal Reserve considered acquisitions unsafe if the amount of debt rose above six times a company's annual earnings. The debt ratio for the UFC was closer to ten, with $1.825 billion borrowed against the UFC's $189 million in EBITDA for 2015. The risk seemed even greater considering 2015 had been an all-time best year for the UFC and any amount of downward volatility in its business could quickly make the debt even less tenable. Shortly after, WME-IMG sent a document to investors outlining plans to cut $71 million from Zuffa's yearly operating expenses, with savings coming from a proposed budget cut for *The Ultimate Fighter* from a reported $27.6 million to $10 million, and the elimination of the $5.3 million expense the Fertittas had charged to the UFC for using their private jet. The biggest savings would come from layoffs. In mid-October, around sixty full-time Zuffa employees were let go, close to 15 percent of Zuffa's roughly 350 full-time employees at the time. The move would shrink the company's payroll from $55.4 million to $27 million.

From the outside, it was hard to understand why a company coming off the most successful year in its history would need to cut its payroll. But for Emanuel and the UFC's new owners, it was part of a necessary strategy to push earnings even higher to qualify for additional bonus payments. If they could drive the UFC's EBITDA to $275 million in 2017, Emanuel and company would collect an additional $175 million bonus from their lenders and investors. And if EBITDA for 2018 reached $350 million, WME-IMG would get another bonus of $75 million. If the promotion failed to hit either target, WME-IMG would still collect a yearly management fee of $25 million from the UFC.

While regulators were alarmed by the terms of the deal, Goldman Sachs received four times as many offers from investors as they had shares to sell. Risky, debt-leveraged acquisitions had become standard operating procedure for private equity firms like Silver Lake and KKR. In the preceeding decade, private equity fundraising had grown from $93 billion in 2003 to $527 billion in 2015. Those funds had been used as partial down payment on a wide range of acquisitions, including Hilton Hotels, H. J. Heinz Company, Toys "R" Us, Petco, and J.Crew, among many others. The ideal targets tended to be mature companies with steady cash flows, from which new profits could be extracted not through growth but cost-cutting, layoffs, and imposing new limits on customer service. Even if overall revenue remained flat, the private equity firms could point to near-term increases in profitability as evidence of their own success, and either resell the companies to another consortium of investors or take them public and collect hundreds of millions in bonuses, management fees, and earn-outs. The US tax code also provided a series of loopholes that allowed private equity firms to treat loan payments as write-offs that lowered their overall tax burdens. If instead the companies failed, the deals were most often structured so that the companies themselves were responsible for repaying the loans, not the private equity firms, something that only added incentive for risk taking. By 2015, the average private equity acquisition was made for more than ten times the acquisition targets' EBITDA, well above what federal regulators advised.

The UFC had been an intriguing candidate for acquisition in part because WME-IMG's licensing and production staff made it easy to see where cost-saving layoffs could be made at Zuffa without damaging the UFC's core business. Zelaznik would be let go, along with Jamie Pollack, who had helped build the UFC's broadcasting business in Latin America. Tom Wright, who had overseen the promotion's Canadian and Australian events, was cut along with around 80 percent of the UFC's Toronto office. Garry Cook, who'd come to the UFC in 2012 from the Manchester City Football Club to oversee the company's international expansion, was asked to leave. Even Chuck Liddell and former welterweight champion Matt Hughes saw their honorary positions—which paid each a reported $300,000 yearly salary as a kind of hall of fame pension for helping see the promotion through its years of near failure—eliminated.

"It was an awful day for the company," Zelaznik recalled. "It was terrible. You didn't really get a chance to say goodbye to anybody. You kind of got walked out of the building. That was a little funky to me." The layoffs had been expected, and a number of other key executives had left on their own over the summer and fall—Joe Silva had announced he was retiring in August, and Dave Sholler, who had been one of the company's key PR executives and often stood in for White during post-fight press conferences, announced he was leaving for a position with the Philadelphia 76ers in September—but there was still a harsh suddenness to the layoffs.

After the acquisition, legislators showed renewed interest in trying to regulate mixed martial arts. Markwayne Mullin, a Republican member of the House of Representatives from Oklahoma, had been working on a House Resolution to expand the Muhammad Ali Boxing Reform Act to cover mixed martial arts. The Ali Act, which had been signed into law in 1999 and went into effect in 2000, was the culmination of John McCain's years-long effort to regulate boxing at the federal level. Though he ultimately failed in his attempt to create a federal boxing commission, the Ali

Act instead created a legal framework to protect boxers in an open market of competing promoters and sanctioning organizations by standardizing the criteria for how boxers would be ranked, which every sanctioning body would be required to use in creating its own public rankings. In theory, this would protect fighters from capricious or corrupt matchmaking and ensure there was at least some universally recognized standard for working toward a championship. The act also forbid promoters from serving as managers for individual boxers, and forbid managers from having any kind of direct or indirect financial relationship with promoters other than advocating for their client's best interest. Most important, the act required promoters to give state athletic commissions a full accounting of all of the revenue earned from the event, and document the payment given to the top boxers on the card.

The act had rarely been invoked in the years since it was passed, and its effectiveness had been widely questioned. Members of the Association of Professional Boxing Commissions, a collective body that represents all the state boxing commissions in the US, would later claim the US Attorney's Office responsible for prosecuting Ali Act violations had ignored almost all of the cases forwarded to them for further investigation. Promoters likewise often ignored financial transparency requirements for boxers on their cards, and many ringside physicians complained that state athletic commissions often violated a provision requiring them to respect medical suspensions given to a fighter from another state commission after a knockout, concussion, or other traumatic injury, allowing them to compete before it was medically safe.

Despite the criticism, Mullin believed the Ali Act would be the most effective available tool for immediately improving the lives of cage fighters, who he said were treated by the UFC "not as an asset, but as a commodity." Mullin had firsthand experience in the industry. He was unbeaten in regional events around Oklahoma, and negotiated a potential appearance as a contestant on a season of *The Ultimate Fighter* in 2007, which he turned down after seeing the terms of the contract. "I couldn't believe what they were wanting me to do," Mullin said in an interview with *Bloody Elbow*. "Luckily it wasn't my livelihood, it was just a hobby of mine, so I could walk away." Mullin was still concerned with the well-being of those fighters who felt like they couldn't walk away.

"The only way the sport is sustainable is the fighters being treated on an even playing field," he told *Variety*. Without some form of federal protection, he feared the UFC would continue to "spit up athletes and throw them out. That's what happens right now. Athletes are here today and gone tomorrow."

On December 8, 2016, Mullin scheduled an informational hearing on expanding the Ali Act to mixed martial arts, with Lydia Robertson from the Association of Boxing Commissions; neuropathologist and brain trauma expert Dr. Ann McKee from Boston University's Alzheimer's Disease Center; Jeff Novitzky from the UFC, a former federal agent from the Food and Drug Administration whom the promotion had hired to oversee a strict new drug-testing program it had paid to implement through a partnership with the United States Anti-Doping Agency (USADA); and Randy Couture, who would speak on behalf of fighters. According to Mullin, the UFC threatened to pull out of the hearings when it found out Couture would be testifying, but later backed off the threat when Mullin refused to replace him with another fighter. While the speaker list wasn't released until forty-eight hours before the hearing, Mullin said the UFC had found out that Couture had been chosen to appear and began "trying to dictate who we could and couldn't have on the panel." (An unnamed UFC spokesperson disputed the claim at the time.) Mullin went forward with Couture, who despite having headlined eighteen UFC events, more than any other fighter, had once again been blackballed by the company, largely because of White.

Following his loss to Lesnar in 2009, Couture had been treated as a kind of elder statesman and was matched up in a series of age-appropriate legacy matches—first against former Pride heavyweight champion Antônio Rodrigo Nogueira, and then against UFC 10 winner and fellow hall of fame inductee Mark Coleman. Couture also fought former boxing heavyweight champion James Toney, who had hopes of a late-career resurgence in mixed martial arts. Couture won in a dominant TKO after a little more than three minutes. Two months before his forty-eighth birthday, Couture had agreed to one last fight, against the younger and faster Lyoto Machida, who knocked him out in the second round with a jumping front kick so unexpected and impactful it broke one of Couture's front teeth in half. Couture had announced his retirement in the cage after the fight in characteristically modest fashion. "You're not gonna see me again—this was it," he said before making time to praise Machida as a "tremendous fighter" and waving one last time to the crowd.

In retirement, Couture had turned again to show business, acting in *The Expendables 2*, the sequel to a 2010 hit about a group of aging mercenaries played by former 1980s action stars. He also resumed his former role as an occasional guest commentator for UFC events, and continued to train younger fighters at Xtreme Couture, including his son Ryan, who had begun a promising career as a fighter with a six-and-one record in Strikeforce. A few months before Ryan would make his UFC debut, Couture had accepted an offer from Spike to appear on two new reality series that would be used to launch the network's new broadcasting deal with Bellator MMA, the smaller promotion based out of Los Angeles that the network had signed to replace the UFC. One series, called *Gym Rescue*, would see Couture travel the country to rehabilitate failing gym businesses. The other series, called *Fight Master: Bellator MMA*, modeled after *The Ultimate Fighter*, would see Couture as one of four celebrity coaches guiding thirty-two young fighters through a tournament. White was furious when he heard the news, and indignant that Couture would commit to a competitor when he still was under contract as a commentator for one more UFC event. He called Couture's lawyer and went on a tirade—"I went 'me' on the lawyer, is the best way I can explain it," White would later say of the call. He also barred Couture from any future events and refused to let him corner Ryan when he made his UFC debut (on the same card in Sweden where Conor McGregor debuted). "The only time that Randy Couture is ever a man is when he steps foot in that cage," White would say. "As soon as his big toe steps out of that cage, he's the furthest thing from it." White reassured Ryan that he wouldn't let his issues with Couture affect Ryan's standing with the UFC, but he promised that he and Couture were "never going to be good, ever, ever again, as long as I walk this fucking planet." Couture responded as he often did, by detaching from the conflict. "The issues are his, not mine, so it's up to him," he said of the conflict.

Despite the magnitude of the fight, Couture's move to Bellator ended quickly and left him without much to show for his troubles. *Gym Rescue* was canceled after airing just three episodes, while *Fight Master* drew weak ratings and ended up being moved to a late-night time slot for its final three episodes, and plans for a second season were abandoned. Couture carried on with his acting career, taking parts in a long run of mostly low- and mid-budget movies intended for release on Blu-ray and DVD, including the FBI thriller *Ambushed*, a comedy called *3 Geezers!* about the residents of a convalescent home featuring Tim Allen, and an action caper movie called *Stretch* about a limo driver pushed into extreme circumstances to repay a debt to a bookie. In 2013, he began dating Mindy Robinson, seventeen years his junior, whom he would later work with on the set of *Range 15*, a crowdfunded movie about a group of soldiers who wake up from a night of hard drinking to discover a zombie outbreak has wiped out civilization. Robinson was also active in conservative politics and would later host a YouTube series called *Red, White and F U*, which she described as "a show for patriots, by patriots." Couture became more political in his own right, and began working with the Mixed Martial Arts Fighters Association, the group that had originally been founded in 2009 by attorney Rob Maysey to advocate for better working conditions for fighters, with the main focus of expanding the Ali Act. (Maysey was also involved with the antitrust lawsuit filed against the UFC in 2014.)

After years of fighting his own battles against the UFC, it was a relief to find a more organized group effort with a clearly identifiable goal. Couture had opposed the idea of a fighters union, fearing it would force them to become UFC employees rather than independent contractors who could freely negotiate their worth in an open marketplace. Instead, he thought of the Ali Act as a tool that fighters could use to negotiate better terms for themselves individually. In his testimony, Couture criticized the "take-it-or-leave-it attitude" he'd experienced in negotiating with the UFC, something he attributed to the fact that it functioned as both a promoter and a sanctioning body that issued its own rankings and titles. "That conflict of interest gives the promoters a ton of power to manipulate the fighters, manipulate the rankings," he said. "You know, for them it's just business, they're trying to get the most pay-per-views sold and people to buy tickets and they'll do whatever they need to do to manipulate that ranking structure and those titles to do that." He also criticized the fact that the UFC closely guarded information about fighter pay. "Fighters are hamstrung in their ability to negotiate fight purses as promotions, unlike in boxing, are not required to disclose to fighters the revenues earned from such bouts," Couture said.

Rather than negotiate in good faith, Couture said the promotion had built a structure that it used to "coerce, bully, and ensure that its brand remains paramount." With an independent sanctioning body that issued its own rankings and titles, he imagined the UFC and other promoters would have to bid on the services of top fighters and work with their competitors to match contenders who might be contracted to other promotions. Instead of a free market, the UFC had created a kind of hostage situation where anyone hoping to have a career in cage fighting effectively had just one choice. Speaking for the UFC, Novitzky said that giving control of rankings and titles to an outside organization would only add confusion and potentially expose fighters to greater health risks. "If a UFC fighter who is under the most stringent, comprehensive, robust anti-doping program in professional sports in the world is forced to fight a fighter from another promotion that may not have any out of competition anti-doping program, that's clearly a health and safety risk to our fighter," he said.

The hearing lasted a little more than an hour and ended on an inconclusive note. Though it was billed as informational, there were few specifics and no exhibits or other evidence presented, in part a product of how closely the UFC guarded information about its fighter contracts and business operations, leaving little room to do anything but argue in generalities. (The committee did not try to subpoena more specific documents or testimony.) Speaking for the Association of Boxing Commissions, commissioner Lydia Robertson concluded with an air of defeatism, admitting it had little sway over mixed martial arts. "We just don't have any teeth to do any other kind of enforcement," she said. "In boxing . . . the ABC actually recognizes the sanctioning bodies, they have to make applications. That has to be published. The fighters know what the standards are. And we don't have those kind of teeth in the MMA industry."

While Mullin's bill had attracted fifty sponsors in the House of Representatives, there was little momentum to move it out of the Energy and Commerce Committee for a floor vote, and even less hope that it would clear the Senate if it passed in the House. Zuffa and the Fertittas had developed an expansive network of political influence through campaign contributions and targeted lobbying efforts. In 2016, the Fertittas gave a combined $1.5 million to the GOP's Senate Leadership Fund through Zuffa, Station Casinos, and individual donations. The company had also paid $420,000 to several high-profile lobbyist firms to advocate against Mullin's bill, including Brownstein Hyatt Farber Schreck and Farragut Partners. The company had also earmarked more than $210,000 to continue lobbying against the Ali Act in early 2017.

In addition to lobbying, Zuffa had been aggressive in using its fans to create pressure around political issues. In New York, Zuffa had paid a company called Global Strategy Group to educate fans and encourage them to reach out to state legislators' offices to pressure them to legalize mixed martial arts. Zuffa had also shown a tendency to purposefully blur the distinction of whether mixed martial arts was a sport or an entertainment product. In 2001, the company had argued to state athletic commissions that mixed martial arts was merely a composite of different Olympic sports—boxing, karate, wrestling, judo—but in 2011, Zuffa sued the state of New York over its ban, arguing that, "live professional MMA is clearly intended and understood as public entertainment and, as such, is expressive activity protected by the First Amendment." The suit argued that concern about mixed martial arts wasn't a public safety issue but a matter of freedom of speech and that New York's ban suppressed fighters' rights to express themselves through competitive violence.

While the suit had eventually been dismissed, Mullin said that in a private meeting prior to the December hearing, the UFC's Lawrence Epstein had argued that the promotion's championships shouldn't be viewed as formal titles, even as they came with ten-pound gold belts. "Lawrence said to me it's not a championship belt," Mullin said in a 2016 interview. "They are bestowing an award on the best fighter for the night. That's what they think about the ranking system and as a professional athlete, that's insulting. But that was their mentality back then and that is their mentality going forward." It was an echo of how former UFC fighter Jon Fitch had described the promotion, in a statement submitted to the court as part of the ongoing antitrust suit against Zuffa, as not a sport but "a reality show premised around athletic endeavors." That interpretation might have been anathema to UFC executives in the early 2000s, but as WME-IMG began to share it's plans for the promotion, it more often used the language of celebrity and entertainment than sports and rankings.

In an interview with *Fast Company*, Emanuel said WME-IMG had composed a list of "twenty-five male stars and about fifteen female stars" whom it said it would help make money in everything but fighting. "We're in conversations with Hasbro to do dolls," he said. "We're in conversations with some of the magazines to do profiles on the women. We're just now beginning the process of building the brand and building their name recognition. We're then gonna, we got Conor McGregor—he's just not available—an offer to do *Game of Thrones*. . . . [Welterweight champion Tyron] Woodley has done two movies, he met with the agency. So we're now just gonna start building profiles. We'll put teams on 'em and start building profiles with endorsements, etc." WME-IMG's copresident Mark Shapiro distilled Emanuel's vision, and the future of the sport, to one of pure escapism. "We're in the emotion transportation business," Shapiro said. "Our job is to move people."

No one had moved more people in the UFC than Ronda Rousey. In three years with the promotion, her pay-per-views had reportedly generated more than four million buys. She had been profiled in the *New Yorker* and the *New York Times*, and featured on the cover of *Self*, *Sports Illustrated*, *Men's Fitness*, *The Ring*, *Black Belt*, and dozens of other magazines. She had appeared alongside Couture in *The Expendables 3*, played herself on the HBO series *Entourage*, taken a small role in *Furious 7*, and been cast in the Mark Wahlberg action movie *Mile 22*. She'd also agreed to star in *Roadhouse*, a remake of the 1989 Patrick Swayze vehicle about a bar bouncer who helps save a small town from a corrupt businessman, which MGM was developing for her. Paramount had bought the film rights to her autobiography, and she'd agreed to star in *The Athena Project*, a planned Warner Bros. movie in development about a team of women commandos trying to stop an international arms dealer. In 2015, she won ESPN's Fighter of the Year at the ESPY Awards, beating out Floyd Mayweather Jr. and Manny Pacquiao. And in January 2016, she would become the first UFC fighter to host an episode of *Saturday Night Live*.

Rogan described her as "the best female combat sports athlete in the world," and "a mythical human." "When you watch Ronda Rousey fight, especially now, it doesn't just seem like a fight," he said. "It seems like some sort of historical event that you have the privilege of watching live." According to White, Rousey was "the biggest star we've ever had." She had proved her worth, not just by expanding the UFC's core audience beyond the eighteen-to-thirty-four-year-old male demographic, but through her willingness to work on the UFC's terms in instances where other fighters wouldn't. "She'll do the work of twenty male fighters," White said in a 2015 interview. "She'll bury anyone. When guys turn stuff down, she's like, 'You pussy, give it to me.' When you talk about a franchise player—anything we need, she's there for us."

As 2016 drew to a close, it had been more than a year since anyone had experienced that privilege. After six dominant wins, five of which had taken a minute or less, Rousey was dismantled by former Olympic boxer Holly Holm in front of 56,214 fans in Melbourne, Australia, the largest crowd in UFC history, and finally knocked unconscious with a sudden left high kick fifty-nine seconds into the second round. The fight felt monumental, not just because it was Rousey's first loss but because it hadn't been close. Holm had patiently circled around the cage in short, L-shaped steps, moving both back and to the side, always just out of reach as Rousey lunged forward for a judo clinch. There was something almost childlike in the way Rousey followed Holm with outstretched arms, and something cruel in the way Holm consistently repelled her with one or two quick counterpunches, which hit Rousey like unseen doors repeatedly closing in her face. By the end of the first round Rousey seemed concussed and confused, her mouth flooded with blood, making it even harder to breathe in the sudden fatigue brought on by the diaphragmatic shock of being hit in the head again and again. "Champ, beautiful work," her cornerman, Edmond Tarverdyan, had said between rounds, trying to reach through the gathering fog in her mind.

In the second round, Holm met Rousey with still another straight left as Rousey pressed forward. Holm used the same extended arm to push herself away from Rousey and avoid any return punches. Rousey was so battered and disoriented, the shove knocked her off-balance and sent her tumbling to the mat. In a stupor, she turned on all fours and began to get up with her back to Holm, who was waiting with a left high kick that thudded into the side of Rousey's neck, just under her jawline. Rousey's head seemed to fold over Holm's shin, and then she fell, eyes open but va-

cant, staring at the final few hammer fists Holm threw at her without seeing any of them. The fight had the cruelty of a fairy tale, in which Rousey
gradually faded into a ghost of herself. And after she simply vanished. She
was helped out of the octagon without a post-fight interview, and rushed
to the hospital instead of the post-fight press conference.

Two days later, when she landed back in Los Angeles, she pulled her
hoodie over her head and covered her face with a pillow to avoid being
photographed by the paparazzi waiting outside baggage claim. In March,
five months after the loss, she made her first public appearance, on *Ellen*,
during which she admitted to having been knocked out on her feet after
the first punch. "I really don't remember most of it," she said. As the fight
played out, she said, she'd lost her ability to gauge distance, which had left
her feeling as if she couldn't see. In spite of the severity of the damage, she
had refused to give away how compromised she was. "You have to make
it appear as if you're not hurt," she said. "Because if someone can tell,
they're going to swarm in on you, so I was trying my best to make it—to
kind of hide the fact that I wasn't even there anymore." In the hospital,
after the fight, the feeling that she wasn't there anymore lingered. "I was
in the medical room, and I was like down in the corner," she said, tears
filling her eyes and her voice softening, "I was sitting in the corner and
I was like, What am I anymore if I'm not this? And I was literally sitting
there and thinking about killing myself in that exact second. I'm like, I'm
nothing. I'm like, What do I do anymore? And no one gives a shit about
me without this."

For Rousey, becoming a mass media icon had been as bewildering
as Holm's punches, and she seemed to have kept herself steady by retreating into a persona. She had adopted the nickname "Rowdy," taken
to calling other fighters in her division "do-nothing-bitches," or "DNBs,"
and made "Bad Reputation" by Joan Jett her walkout song. At a rematch
against Miesha Tate in her second UFC fight, which she won by armbar
in the third round, Rousey was greeted with a persistent wave of boos
after the fight, when she refused to shake Tate's hand. A part of Rousey
enjoyed the effect her persona had an audiences. "If you're cheering and
the person next to you is booing, you're going to cheer louder," she said in
2014. "I love that. I love creating conflict within the audience."

Her zest for cruelty became most acute when she was asked about Cris

Cyborg, Strikeforce's former women's featherweight champion who'd been stripped of her title and suspended for a year after testing positive for androgen and the anabolic steroid stanozolol two months before Rousey won Strikeforce's bantamweight championship. Rousey had initially been scheduled to fight Cyborg in her UFC debut, which would also have been Cyborg's first fight after completing her suspension. The negotiations eventually fell apart over a dispute about weight class, and Cyborg instead went to fight for Invicta, a small women's promotion based in Kansas City and founded by Shannon Knapp, who'd gone from the IFL to working as one of Strikeforce's matchmakers, before striking out on her own. Cyborg had been undefeated since 2005, winning in wild, cyclonic dervishes that ended in first- and second-round knockouts. She had claimed her title by beating Gina Carano and had defended it convincingly three times before being stripped, yet even in exile there was the sense that she was the lineal champion.

Despite her accomplishments, Cyborg's name seemed to inspire re-vulsion in Rousey, who would sometimes call her "Miss Man" or simply "it," in reference to Cyborg's muscular physique. "In a perfect world, she wouldn't have been taking all those steroids and hormones for so many years that she ceased to be a woman anymore," Rousey said in 2014. "In a perfect world, she would be a girl and not an *it*." After Rousey's comments were criticized as transphobic, White defended Rousey by adding his own transphobic assessment of Cyborg's appearance, saying she looked like "Wanderlei Silva in a dress and heels." He pointed out that Cyborg had also called Rousey a "chicken" and insinuated she was afraid of accepting a fight with her at the featherweight limit. "I think that this is the fight business," he said in a media scrum, trying to create equivalence between the two. "People say mean things about each other."

When Rousey was later matched with Holm, a note of strain appeared to have entered her persona. She seemed overcommitted to a story line that Holm—a soft-spoken and self-deprecating fighter whose father was a preacher in the Churches of Christ—was a "fake respect, fake humil-ity bitch." The loud provocations had started to feel like tells, as if some part of Rousey's subconscious still refused to believe in the image she had projected to the world, even as fans described her as unbeatable and the oddsmakers made her a twenty-to-one favorite.

Like many other fighters, Rousey had tried to hold on to her tenuous
self-confidence by keeping it stoked with a regular supply of motivational
slogans and aphorisms. *Champions do more. Everything is as easy as a decision. Refuse to accept any other reality. Winning is a habit. The only power
people have over you is the power you give them.* Rousey collected them
like carnival prizes and would write new ones down on a whiteboard on
the wall beside the sparring ring at Glendale Fighting Club. One morning in early 2015, she discovered another one while scrolling through her
phone after a training session: *By believing passionately in something that
still does not exist, we create it. The nonexistent is what we have not sufficiently desired.* She read it aloud for the UFC cameras that were in the
gym filming her as part of a promotional mini-documentary. "Oooooh, I
like it!" she said, staring into her phone as if it were an oracle. "Fuck yeah,
I like it. That might be wall-worthy." Sometimes misattributed to Franz
Kafka, the quote comes from Nikos Kazantzakis's lyrical autobiography
Report to Greco. Near the end of the book, the speaker prepares to return home to Crete after a life of study and work across Europe and the
Middle East. Before the last leg of his journey, he marvels, for a moment,
at how far his faith has carried him, how many improbable things it has
made him capable of. Instead of triumph, the thought comes on a wave
of exhaustion. "With everything finally ended, I suddenly felt how tired
I was," Kazantzakis writes. "I could not stand on my feet, could not eat,
sleep, or read; I was exhausted. I had mobilized all my forces up to that
time, as long as the great need lasted; the soul had buttressed the body
and kept it from falling. But immediately the battle ended, this inner mo-
bilization dissolved, the body remained undefended, and fell."

When Rousey finally returned to the octagon after more than a year
away—at UFC 207 against Amanda Nunes, who had won the women's
bantamweight championship from Miesha Tate in July—her self-belief
had become a cloister. She had asked that she not be required to do any
interviews or media appearances leading up to the fight, and White had
waived the boilerplate language in the UFC's contract that requires all
fighters to promote their fights. "Listen, Ronda has given more than anybody," he said of the decision. He admitted her request wasn't "ideal,"
but said she deserved the benefit of the doubt. "She's done a lot for this
company," White said. "She's done a lot for the sport. She's done a lot for

women in this sport, and this is what she asked for. She's never asked for
much. She asked for this and we said yes."

The fight itself would last just forty-eight seconds. Rousey was overwhelmed by Nunes, who battered her in an even more comprehensive
manner than Holm had. Nunes rammed punch after punch into the side
of her head and face, each landing in a broken staccato—the first less a
punch than a slow probe to measure the distance between them, and the
second a hard right hand that traveled the long arc of a javelin toss—
then a breath and a step closer, and then two more punches in a loose
counter-rhythm. Some glanced off Rousey's arms as she tried to protect
her head, and others landed directly on the cheek and nose and mouth,
mushing the skin into a crumped divot for a millisecond before retracting
and leaving the faint discoloration of a new bruise, and a speckled smear
of blood that had somehow traveled up onto her cheeks from her freshly
bleeding nose.

Yet Rousey refused to fall, even as it was clear she had lost control of
her faculties. She stared into some horrific middle distance with glassy,
confused eyes. The part of her mind that governed self-belief refused to
be broken, yet the part of her brain that was a necessary component of locomotion seemed lost, as if someone were explaining to her that the mat
was made of sky and she was walking on it. It felt less like a fight than an
assault, something you might have tried to intervene in had you seen it in
an alley or on a sidewalk.

In the final moments, after all of her training and game-planning had
departed into the fog of new brain trauma, Rousey seemed to have nothing left but her defiance, the drive to not falter, which made it appear as
if she were fighting herself as much as Nunes, refusing to cooperate with
her own body as it tried to shut off for a half second after each punch.
Finally, it was the referee who jumped in to save Rousey, after one final
punch landed and made her knees bend so deeply it appeared, for a second, as if she were trying to sit in a chair that wasn't there. As the referee
waved one arm over his head to signal the end of the fight, Rousey tried
to pull herself back into a standing position, but instead went careening
off to the left in a series of stumbling steps. Nunes stalked around the perimeter of the cage in victory, holding her index finger up to her mouth to
shush the already stunned crowd deeper into silence.

In her memoir, Rousey described a routine she'd developed the night before each of her UFC fights. After the loud weigh-ins, she'd return to her hotel room with Tarverdyan and her sister and mother. One by one everyone would leave again, until it was just her and her mother. "We lie on my bed," Rousey wrote, "and my mom tells me all the reasons why I'm going to destroy the other girl in less than twenty-four hours. It is a ritual we have had since I was a little kid. She lists every reason why I'm the best in the world like it's a bedtime story." As she listened to the affirmations, growing drowsier and drowsier, she would stay up for as long as possible, reliving each step of her training camp, each part of the plan, every moment of sacrifice and struggle, to ensure that no one in this world or any other would be capable of beating her, which would be the last thought in her head before drifting to sleep.

In Rousey's final moments in the UFC octagon, under the hard white of the arena lights, she kept her eyes down on the mat, trying to not see what was happening around her. As Bruce Buffer announced the official result and Nunes leapt up and down, screaming in joy while White tried to wrap the championship belt around her waist, Rousey turned away and walked out of the cage. Nunes ran after to pay her respects, but Rousey had already climbed down the cage stairs and was walking past the media tables where beat reporters filmed her on their phones. Rousey didn't appear at the post-fight press conference, and didn't speak to anyone in the media in the days that followed. As she had done a year earlier, she simply disappeared.

It would be the fifth event of 2016 to sell more than a million pay-per-view buys, pushing the UFC's annual revenue to $690 million, the highest figure in company history.

THE MONEY BELT

The day after Donald Trump was elected president, Conor McGregor rode through the streets of Manhattan in a matte-black Rolls-Royce Ghost, a picture of his screaming face painted on the side panel above the word "NOTORIOUS." He was ebullient, splitting his days between shopping at Gucci and hitting pads in a small Midtown boxing gym, preparing for the culmination of his plan to win a championship in two different weight divisions, in the main event at UFC 205. It would be the UFC's first-ever event at Madison Square Garden and its first card in New York since UFC 7 in 1995, after the New York state legislature finally voted to legalize mixed martial arts, once Assembly speaker Sheldon Silver resigned in 2015 over corruption charges. The event would mark the first time in UFC history that cage fighting would be legal in all fifty states. Despite the celebratory milestone, the presidential election had cast a pall over the day, as impromptu protests had swept across the country, oblivious to the history McGregor was on the verge of making. In Los Angeles, people had marched onto the 101 Freeway and stopped traffic; in Portland, protestors blocked light rail train stations and shut down the I-5; in Chicago, people flooded Lakeshore Drive with chants and anti-Trump signs; and in New York, protestors marched through Columbus Circle and gathered in front of the Trump International Hotel & Tower, just a block from where McGregor had been staying, in a suite overlooking Central Park at the JW Marriott Essex House hotel.

The sound of chants would have echoed through the hotel windows, and played on news footage in the lobby bar television, and popped up in short, angry clips on Twitter. McGregor was perplexed by the sudden political outpouring. He had spent so much of his life focused on developing himself, the idea of a collective in which no one person stood out marching through the streets—it all seemed wrongheaded, ran against everything he'd proved to himself over his still-young career. "It's the wrong mindset," he'd later say, misdirected energy, time wasted blaming others instead of focusing on self-improvement. "Rather than putting your energy into pointing the finger at somebody else, figure out what it is you need to do and do it, and do it right, and get it done, and get your situation right," he said.

In the UFC, Trump had been an uncontroversial figure. Lorenzo and Frank III had each donated $1 million to America First Action, one of the super PACs funding Trump's campaign. White had pledged his support to Trump and spoken at the Republican National Convention in Cleveland, Ohio. (It was held in the same arena where six weeks later the UFC would host a pay-per-view.) In a radio interview, White described Trump admiringly, as "the kind of crook that does it by the rules." Emanuel had represented Trump as an agent until 2016, and helped negotiate the deal with NBC for *The Apprentice*, the reality show that Trump hosted from 2004 to 2015 and which helped salvage his public image after a series of bankruptcies and financial controversies. "I call him a lot, and we talk," Trump said of Emanuel in a 2016 interview. "He's very political. Even though he's not political, he's political. He gets it." In 2015, WME-IMG purchased the Miss Universe Organization from Trump, and kept the archive of old tapes and B-roll from past events private as reports of Trump's backstage abuses and alleged sexual misconduct made headlines. Emanuel was also briefly vetted for a potential position with the Trump administration, but because of his past as a lifelong Democratic fundraiser he was passed over.

Though McGregor was not especially political, he had seen Trump as yet another example of how far self-belief can carry a person, and he struggled to understand what protestors would gain from militating against Trump—who he would later describe as "phenomenal" and possibly the "[greatest of all time]." In a way, seeing anti-Trump protests was as strange as seeing people boo the hero in a theater at the end of a movie. McGregor felt closer than ever to fulfilling his own vision, which he'd first laid out to his skeptical parents in the small kitchen of their home in Lucan, of holding not one championship belt in the UFC but two. It had seemed laughable at the time, but now that he appeared to be on the verge of making his dream a reality, a whole new set of once unimaginable possibilities had opened up before him. He could do anything he wanted, it

had begun to seem. After he'd seen the UFC sold, he'd gone from thinking about championships to ownership. As much money as the UFC was
paying him for his fights—in Rousey's absence, he had become the promotion's highest paid fighter—he knew the UFC was making even more
from him than he was making from them. To McGregor, beating Alvarez
for the lightweight championship started to seem like not just an accolade
or life goal, but more leverage toward getting what he felt he deserved. "I
want to put my analytics forward, man-to-man, and be like, This is what
I'm owed now. Pay me," he'd later say.

After the UFC pulled him from UFC 200, it seemed as if he might have
overestimated his own bargaining power. But he was quickly rebooked
against Nathan Diaz at UFC 202 in August, where he made up for the loss
with a close five-round decision win. "Surprise, surprise, motherfuckers,"
he'd said in the cage after the fight, "the king is back!" It felt like an evic-
tion notice, reclaiming Nathan's post-fight line after their first fight—*I'm
not surprised, motherfuckers*—like a landlord repossessing an apartment.
A little over a month later—after McGregor had cryptically posted "Beg
me" on Twitter—his fight against Eddie Alvarez had been confirmed as the
main event of UFC 205. McGregor treated the fight as an uninteresting formality that was keeping him from his future. When his Rolls-Royce Ghost
finally pulled into the underground parking lot at Madison Square Garden,
and McGregor made his way to the small media room where White had
been hosting the pre-fight press conference for around fifteen minutes, he
seemed more interested in celebrating his wealth than in promoting the
fight. "I run New York City!" McGregor shouted, wearing a white mink
coat he'd bought for $55,000 at Gucci on Fifth Avenue. "I'm a fucking pimp!
Rockin' Gucci mink! And without me, this whole fuckin' ship sinks!"

When the fight finally arrived, playing out in a cold, blue-tinted
bloom of light at the center of the darkened arena, McGregor patiently
dissected Alvarez. At times McGregor was completely inert, almost reptilian as he planted himself in a side stance and dared Alvarez, whose
arms are five inches shorter than his own, to cross the distance between
them. When Alvarez obliged, McGregor calmly slid back and stung
him with straight, precise counterpunches. It seemed as if Alvarez was
trapped wherever he stood, with no good options to move anywhere
but backward. At one point, McGregor held his hands behind his back

and hung his chin out in front of his own feet as a kind of pity offering to Alvarez. The fight was finally stopped in the second round, after Alvarez was knocked down for a fourth time in eight minutes. McGregor circled the cage in victory and checked an imaginary wristwatch, as if he had somewhere better to be. "I just want to say, from the bottom of me heart," he said in the post-fight interview, "I'd like to take the chance to apologize to absolutely nobody! The double champ does what the fuck he wants!" As the crowd cheered his defiance, White draped the second championship belt over his shoulder, which McGregor grasped and then stared up at his own image on the big screen, adjusting the angle as if he were taking a selfie. "This is what I dreamed into reality," he said. "Ooooh, that looks good!"

Later that night, McGregor announced that at the height of his popularity, he was stepping away from cage fighting as his long-term partner, Dee Devlin, was pregnant with their first child. Like the fans, and Zuffa's employees, McGregor had read news of the UFC's historic sale and list of new celebrity shareholders who'd seemingly had no previous connection to fighting, and wondered why he hadn't been cut in on the action. "If you want to come at me, if you want me to stick around and help service that debt and continue to push the company, bring me on board, for real," McGregor said. "I need to be set for life for this. If you want me to be truly on board, then I need to be all-in on this proper, as an owner, and have an equity stake in the company. That's what I'm looking for." Mysteriously, three weeks later, the California State Athletic Commission announced that it had approved McGregor's application for a boxing license.

The first time a fight between McGregor and Floyd Mayweather Jr. was mentioned in public it was a joke on a late-night talk show. Conan O'Brien had asked McGregor about the matchup on an episode of *Conan* in the summer of 2015. "What if you were in the ring with Floyd Mayweather," O'Brien asked, looking up from a cue card, "what do you think would happen?"

"If you're asking would I like to fight Floyd," McGregor answered, "I mean who would not like to dance around the ring for $180 million. . . . I certainly know he would not want to step into my world, the world of pure unarmed combat where there are no limitations. But I would certainly step into his world."

The idea seemed absurd, but like the Trump candidacy, it lingered and quietly spread, until it was in everybody's head as if they had thought of it on their own. Meanwhile, both Mayweather and McGregor continued to poke each other through the media, as if two butterflies on opposite ends of the Earth were competing to see whose wing flaps could cause the most commotion. Mayweather's uncle and trainer, Jeff Mayweather, told reporters that his nephew could beat McGregor with one arm tied behind his back. Later that year, Mayweather said the sudden popularity of cage fighting had been driven, in part, by racist double standards typified by the media's treatment of stars like Rousey and McGregor. "They say he talk a lot of trash and people praise him for it, but when I did it, they say I'm cocky and arrogant," Mayweather said. "After Ronda Rousey fought I think nine, ten, eleven fights, it didn't even take that long, she got all types of endorsements, movies, and everything. Laila Ali did the same thing in better fashion. Ronda Rousey, she's a good-looking woman when she put it on. Laila Ali is a drop-dead gorgeous woman; I mean a naturally beautiful woman and can kick ass, but you never heard them saying when she had I think somewhere around ten, eleven, twelve fights that she was the baddest woman to ever fight on the planet."

McGregor was quick to respond, with an Instagram post: "Floyd Mayweather, don't ever bring race into my success again," McGregor wrote. He said the Irish had been oppressed for their "entire existence," and that "there was a time where just having the name 'McGregor' was punishable by death. Do not ever put me in a bracket like this again." McGregor suggested they could settle their differences in a fight, offering to split the revenues eighty-twenty with Mayweather, as an act of charity since Mayweather's last fight had "bombed at every area of revenue." Later, Mayweather claimed he had contacted McGregor directly with an offer for a fight—promising McGregor $15 million while paying himself $100 million—a provocation designed to highlight the fact that McGregor couldn't actually take him up on the offer, as he was bound by his contract with the UFC and needed its permission to compete in any other combat sport. It was also a veiled insult, as McGregor had never made $15 million in any fight with the UFC, and yet that would still be a fraction of what Mayweather commanded as a minimum starting point. The following day, in January 2017, two months after McGregor's fight against Alvarez, White appeared on Fox Sports' *The Herd with Colin Cowherd* and reasserted himself as the person who would determine whether the fight was made. "You're talking to somebody about the fight, you're talking to me. I'm the promoter. Conor is under contract to me," White said. White made a provocation of his own to Floyd. "I'll tell you what, Floyd: Here's a real offer, and I'm the guy that can actually make the offer, and I'm actually making a real offer," he said. "We pay you $25 million, we'll pay Conor $25 million, and then we'll talk about pay-per-view at a certain number. There's a real offer."

Mayweather ignored the offer, which was almost one-tenth of what he had reportedly earned for fighting Manny Pacquiao in 2015, and instead continued to bait McGregor over the UFC's exclusivity clause. In March, at the Savoy Hotel in London, Mayweather was asked about the possibility of the fight during a press scrum. "If Conor McGregor really wants the fight to happen, stop blowing smoke up everybody's ass," Mayweather said. "Sign the paper," Mayweather went on. "Sign the paper. You said you're a boss. Just sign the paper and let's make it happen."

Mayweather was a strange target for McGregor. He was retired and had just turned forty, after having spent most of his career fighting at weight classes that were between ten and twenty pounds lighter than what McGregor had most recently fought at in the UFC. McGregor was twelve years younger and visibly larger—taller, longer armed, and more thickly muscled—yet the idea of a UFC fighter competing against the best boxer of his generation seemed unthinkable. Mayweather had won every professional fight he'd been in, amassing a forty-nine-and-zero record, with championships in five different weight classes between 130 and 154 pounds. Despite his achievements, Mayweather had become a hateable figure. He approached boxing as a sportsman and won by rule rather than physical domination. Mayweather frustrated his opponents by refusing to engage in the most dangerous parts of a fight and claimed his victories based on how ineffective his opponent had been rather than how badly he was able to hurt them.

In a sport where fans prefer to measure victories by broken bodies instead of accumulated points, Mayweather's career felt almost like a hustle.

He had a way of making even the most hyped fight seem small and flatly workmanlike once it started, like watching a great woodworker methodically turn a log into a small bedside table with a few simple hand tools. What fans had hoped for was the thundering sounds of tall trees crashing down across the forest, breaking everything in their path, and the mythic figure of a lone man with an axe, lathered in sweat, standing at the splintery stump. Mayweather had realized early in his career that the frustration could be lucrative. Being hateable made him a draw, some people would pay in the hopes of seeing him punished. "Let 'em boo, it's no problem," he said in the ring after a smothering win over Hector Arroyo in 1998. "That's a part of boxing—some love you, some hate you. But I love myself."

For Mayweather fighting had been a family craft, a vocation passed down from one generation to another. "It's my job," he said. "I go to the gym, I train, I go home; I do what I have to do." Born in Grand Rapids, Michigan, Mayweather was named after his father, Floyd Joy, one of three brothers who were all accomplished boxers at a time when that conferred little social standing or financial security. When Mayweather was just six months old, his father had begun preparing him for a career in boxing, moving his arms in small punching motions each day in the hopes the movement would sink into muscle memory, as automatic as language. Mayweather's childhood had been one of erratic shifts—with his father there was always money around, and indulgences, but a sense of looming uncertainty over it all, like being at a lavish picnic as heavy storm clouds gather at the horizon. To help keep the family afloat, Mayweather Sr. sold cocaine and crack, to a client list that included his wife, who eventually left the family and moved to New Jersey. As a child, Mayweather sometimes lived with his father, other times with his grandmother, and sometimes traveled to New Jersey to stay with his mother, in a small house shared by eight people, which lost electricity intermittently when the bills piled up.

As a teenager, Mayweather had thought about finding a job, but his grandmother had encouraged him to stay in boxing, which while unpleasant seemed like the surest path to a steady life. Mayweather emerged as a star amateur boxer and qualified for the US Olympic team at the 1996 summer games in Atlanta, where he won a bronze medal. When Mayweather made his professional debut a few months later—at one of the Fertittas' properties, the Texas Station in Las Vegas—his father was still in prison on drug-trafficking charges. Mayweather's uncle Roger took over head training duties and helped him cultivate his elusive style.

As his career progressed, Mayweather famously avoided alcohol and drugs, but wealth itself seemed to become a surrogate vice. Mayweather settled in Las Vegas and founded his own brand—part apparel company, part fighter management group—called the Money Team. He kept a growing collection of luxury cars—a Lamborghini Murciélago, a Ferrari Enzo, an Aston Martin One-77, and even a Bentley golf cart. He also owned two mansions in Las Vegas, a 16,789-square-foot estate worth a reported $8.7 million that he nicknamed "Big Boy," and a smaller $3 million residence in a gated community on the western edge of the city. He owned a $2 million 3,100-square-foot penthouse on the fifty-fifth floor of the Palms casino, and penthouses in Miami and Los Angeles. "He prides himself off [money] more than the belts," Josie Harris, Mayweather's former partner with whom he had three children, said in a 2013 interview. "He loves that he can hop on a private jet or buy any watch or buy any ring." Mayweather fed his acquisitiveness with a string of lucrative broadcasting deals, culminating in a six-fight agreement with Showtime in 2013 that, a press release claimed, would make him the "richest individual athlete in all of sports," reportedly worth $250 million. The deal helped Mayweather transform into his own enterprise, where he no longer worked for promoters, but instead would pay for his own events through an entity called Mayweather Promotions and take the majority of revenue from the live gate, merchandising, and concessions, while paying Showtime a fee to manage marketing and broadcasting logistics. In effect, he had become his own one-man UFC.

At the end of 2016, Mayweather announced another new business, a luxury strip club in Las Vegas called Girl Collection. Mayweather often described women in the same terms as his car collections. In a promotional documentary about his lifestyle produced for Showtime, Mayweather said that even though a person can only drive one car at a time, some have ten cars in their garages. "I feel that, as far as when it comes to females, that same thing should apply," he said. "If you're able to take care of twenty, then you should have twenty." Mayweather had a long and violent history with women, including an incident in 2001, when during an argument he swung open a car door that hit Melissa Brim, the mother of his oldest child. Mayweather pushed her into the open door and repeatedly punched her. He was arrested and eventually pled guilty to two misdemeanor charges of battery, resulting in a $3,000 fine, community service, and forty-eight hours of house arrest. In 2003, Mayweather attacked two women in a nightclub at the Luxor Hotel & Casino, friends of Harris's with whom he had had a previous argument. Mayweather was given a suspended sentence, assigned to impulse control counseling, and a hundred hours of community service. "You may be a terrific and famous fighter, but that doesn't make you a god," Nevada Justice of the Peace Deborah Lippis told him. Perhaps the most disturbing event took place in 2010, when Mayweather confronted Harris at a home he had paid for her and the three children they'd had together. An argument broke out between Harris and Mayweather and he left after she called the police. He returned a few hours later, at around 4:00 a.m., and knocked on the patio door until his son Kouran, then ten years old, woke up and let him in. Mayweather found Harris asleep on the couch and after going through her phone and finding text messages from C. J. Watson, an NBA player with whom she had been having an affair, began punching and kicking her. Kouran heard his mother's screams and ran outside to call for help. The beating left Harris with a concussion and Mayweather with four felony charges that he later pled down to misdemeanors. He was sentenced to ninety days in jail and was released after sixty. Six months later, he signed with Showtime and became the richest athlete in the world.

While fame hadn't yet driven McGregor into the courthouse or prison system, it had given him a sense of hedonic weightlessness. "I've just climbed to another level of this, that I can just reach out and get whatever I desire, at any moment," he'd said, just before the birth of his first son. Throughout McGregor's fighting career he'd vacillated between periods of ascetic training and bacchanalian excess. Kavanagh had first caught a glimpse of this tendency in 2011, when they'd traveled together to Amman, Jordan, for a Cage Warriors event. The promotion had paid for a hotel room for McGregor in addition to his €1,000 purse, and after winning his fight, McGregor had returned to the hotel and spent the night ordering alcohol and room service with teammate Cathal Pendred, not realizing the additional expenses weren't covered by the promoter. When presented with the bill in the morning, which was, according to Kavanagh, almost as much as his fight purse, McGregor had snuck out of the hotel without paying. When he told Kavanagh what had happened, in a taxi on the way to the airport, his coach had made the car turn around so McGregor could settle the bill and apologize.

As his career progressed, McGregor had built in affordances for indulgences. He often slept late into the afternoon, sometimes not waking until 3:00 or 4:00, and he preferred to train late into the night. By early 2016, Kavanagh said McGregor's training habits had become so nocturnal outside of training camps that Kavanagh saw him only in passing as McGregor was just arriving for a late-night session and Kavanagh was on his way home. McGregor's training routines had grown more esoteric, and he began working with Ido Portal, an Israeli martial artist who'd nicknamed himself "the Missionary" and taught a form of movement training that involved mimicking animal locomotion, including crawling across the ground like an alligator or walking in the heavy squatting posture of a gorilla. There were also signs that McGregor's appreciation for lengthy drinking episodes had intensified. Cell phone footage appeared of him poolside in a Las Vegas mansion appearing to be heavily intoxicated in the bright morning sun, slurring his words and speaking at half speed to a woman off-camera. A few months later, he spent three intoxicated days in Liverpool, which one unnamed source described as "carnage" and "just full-on partying." He was filmed walking into the Aintree Racecourse for a horse race with a fully unbuttoned shirt and a half-filled highball glass. A report in the *Sun* also described heavy damage done to a room rented out to McGregor's group at the Hilton Liverpool City Centre Hotel: "There were [nitrous oxide] canisters all over the floor, smashed glass and food lying about. They damaged sofas and left [cigarette] butts and his Irish flag. He got people in there to clean because of the level of damage. It's just been carnage."

In March, he was filmed at a boxing event at Madison Square Garden delivering a strangely confrontational diatribe to reporters. "Watch me take over boxing, trust me on that," he yelled, singling out ESPN's Dan Rafael, coming almost nose to nose with him for a few moments. "No one in this boxing game knows what's coming. Trust me on that. . . . I'm going to step in there and shock the whole god damned world. Trust me on that. Look me in the eyes, twenty-eight years of age, confident as a mother-fucker, long, rangy, dangerous with every hand. Trust me, I'm going to stop Floyd, and you're all going to eat your words. The whole world is going to eat their words." As he walked away in an agitated cloud of handlers, he shouted over his shoulder, to no one in particular, "I am boxing!"

After months of rumor, the fight between Mayweather and McGregor was finally announced on June 14, 2017, first in a Twitter post from McGregor. "THE FIGHT IS ON," he posted, above two side-by-side photos of himself and Mayweather Sr., in a dig at Mayweather Jr.'s age. Twelve minutes later, Mayweather followed up with his own Twitter post of a bland fight poster showing the two men superimposed over a boxing ring. "IT'S OFFICIAL!!!" It seemed unreal for a time, another round of hollow provocations from two showmen who'd never been able to walk away from the spotlight, even when they had little to share or show. Two hours later, Showtime issued its own confirmation with an official fight poster and a date: August 26, 2017.

With the fight confirmed, it seemed even stranger than when it had been a fantasy. There were no particular stakes—no titles, no rankings to rise up through, and McGregor's exclusivity with the UFC made it unlikely more boxing matches would follow. It seemed instead like a clash of vanities, two men with egos large enough to have their own gravitational fields participating in a narcissistic supernova that promised to reveal one as the true star and the other as a pretender who'd tricked the public into seeing something that wasn't really there. Instead of a formal title, the World Boxing Council announced that the winner would be awarded "the Money Belt," a decorative replica of a real championship belt made with alligator skin, 3,360 diamonds, 600 sapphires, 300 emeralds, and 1.5 kilograms of 24-karat gold.

The fight seemed to violate most of the principles White and the Fertittas had built the UFC around—fighter exclusivity, control over live production, and a refusal to work with, or even acknowledge, other promotions. For Mayweather-McGregor, Showtime would pay for the live production, commentary team, marketing, and serve as the exclusive cable pay-per-view distrubtor. Zuffa would distribute the fight for on-line pay-per-views through its Fight Pass website and would produce a week of episodes for its behind-the-scenes YouTube documentary series, *Embedded*. But otherwise, the UFC was effectively a passenger, along for the ride to wherever McGregor, Mayweather, and Showtime would take them, for which it would take a substantial percentage of McGregor's pay, rumored to have been as much as 50 percent. It also seemed to under-score the fact that cage fighting was still largely a niche interest, as it al-ways had been, one that needed to step outside itself to make the kind of money that Mayweather made as a matter of course.

To emphasize the magnitude of the fight, Showtime arranged a world tour for Mayweather and McGregor, with arena-sized press conferences in Los Angeles, Toronto, Brooklyn, and London, which were staged more as rock concerts than question-and-answer sessions. At the first stop, in front of more than eleven thousand fans at the Staples Center in Los Angeles, Mayweather pulled a small check out of his backpack, purport-edly his up-front fee from Showtime. "This is what a $100 million fighter looks like," he said. He again pointed to McGregor's comparatively limited earning power in the UFC, despite his enormous celebrity, as a weakness, almost a character flaw. "He look good for a seven-figure fighter," May-weather said. "I look good for a nine-figure fighter."

Two days later, at the Barclays Center in Brooklyn, Mayweather char-acterized McGregor not as a fighter but a stripper. Mayweather walked a circle around McGregor and showered him in dollar bills pulled from a small bag. "I run this show, this is my ho, and I threw $1 bills on this bitch," Mayweather said. McGregor went shirtless with a new Gucci fur coat that had a coiled turquoise dragon stitched on the back. He seemed in a tense kind of ecstasy, veering between boredom, rage, and joy at his position on stage in front of a reported crowd of 13,165 people. In a mo-ment of confused grandeur, McGregor attempted to refute claims he had displayed racist instincts by referring to Mayweather as a "boy" in their Los Angeles appearance. "A lot of people have me saying I'm against black people," McGregor said, slowly pacing the stage while Mayweather trailed behind him recording video of the speech on his smartphone. "That's ab-solutely fucking ridiculous. Do they not know I'm half-black? Yeeeeah-hhh! I'm half-black, from the belly button down!"

The tour reached its acidic conclusion in London, when Mayweather skipped over McGregor, who'd switched from fur to a tailored suit, and addressed White, who was seated beside him in a bright white boxing ring they'd used as a stage in the Wembley Arena. He reminded White that they had known each other for twenty-one years, since when White was one of Mayweather's early sponsors, through his defunct Bullenbeiser apparel line. Mayweather said the historic event was a testament to his and White's genius, and had nothing to do with McGregor. "We're the smart ones, when it's all said and done," Mayweather explained. "We're going to take these foreign fighters and we're going to use them. We some smart Americans. And you out here running with a quitter, but I forgot—you a pimp, and this your ho."

Despite the garish cruelty, many fans rallied around McGregor after the press conferences, drawn in by the unthinkable idea that he could beat Mayweather. According to the betting odds, McGregor was an underdog for the first time in his career, +325 (depending on the bookie and the day). Despite that fact, the overwhelming majority of bets placed were for McGregor—140 of the first 144 taken at Caesars Palace, and 92 percent of those made with the Westgate Superbook. Kavanagh ensured McGregor was surrounded with an aura of destiny. He had a boxing ring and some gym equipment installed in an empty warehouse near Straight Blast Gym in Dublin and had commissioned a painting of McGregor landing a flush left cross on Mayweather's chin, the immaculate knockout punch that loomed over every round of sparring and every solitary session at the heavy bag.

On social media, McGregor posted cryptic images of sparring, his face changed from the joyful, boyish disobedience of his early career into a stoic, blank stare that almost seemed to convey a distant regret, a pair of sad eyes staring into the lens, whether it was in a concrete-walled gym or coming out of a Day Glo–green Lamborghini, a man just on the verge of feeling regret for the terrible things he was capable of. A little more than three weeks before the fight, McGregor moved his training camp to Las Vegas. His sense of frantic self-belief trilled into a new register when two photos posted on Twitter of McGregor sparring with Paulie Malignaggi, a former world champion boxer who'd agreed to help with the UFC star's training camp. The first photo showed McGregor leaping at Malignaggi, apparently at the start of a round, and the second showed Malignaggi flat on the canvas with McGregor flexed and upright staring angrily at his fallen opponent. A matter of hours after the photos were posted, Malignaggi left the camp and accused McGregor's team of misrepresenting their spars to help build an unrealistic impression of McGregor's abilities. He called for the full video of the twelve-round sparring session to be released so fans could come to their own conclusions.

The McGregor camp refused, but shortly after, White posted two short video clips of the spar, together a little more than thirty seconds, which culminated with Malignaggi stumbling to the mat after an exchange of punches. Malignaggi appeared flushed and exhausted in the footage, missing with punches as McGregor countered with long, powerful crosses that snapped Malignaggi's head back in a bloom of sweat droplets from his drenched headgear. Yet the video only caused more debate, as it was still unclear if Malignaggi had fallen as the result of a punch or whether he had lost his balance and McGregor had simply pushed him. The debate only fed the fanatical optimism of those persuaded that McGregor wouldn't just be competitive with Mayweather but would overwhelm him and knock him out in the second round, as McGregor had predicted.

At the same time, Mayweather spent much of the buildup to the fight in a state of casual repose, making a show of how little effort he was putting into his preparations. He posted videos of evening scooter rides through Miami, where he had flown with his family on a whim. He ate McDonald's and drank Coca-Cola, rode horses through Red Rock Canyon National Conservation Area, spent afternoons hitting golf balls at a driving range, and less than a week before the fight went roller skating at a local rink in Las Vegas. When asked by some fans what he was doing out on the town before such a big fight, Mayweather feigned indignation. "Fuck you all mean, What I'm doing?" he said, in a preacherly cadence. "I'm having fun! I can't be beat. Y'all know I can't be beat. It's impossible for me to lose. Impossible. I could be down eleven rounds to zero and still win!" Mayweather's attitude only added to the surreality around the fight, making it easy to believe that hubris might unmake him, that he had confused his past achievements for current ability, and it had made him greedy and arrogant. It could only be through violence, the instinctive equalizer of the American imagination, that Mayweather would be brought back to his station, the glory of his younger years merely held on loan while the next great fighter was sweating away at a heavy bag, unwatched by cameras or crowds. If one person can rise to the top of the world by virtue of their own actions, then another person can pull them back down again.

The night of the fight, both Mayweather and McGregor were driven to the T-Mobile Arena in a small convoy of Nevada Highway Patrol cars, sirens blazing, as if they were transporting nuclear warheads and not human beings. Despite the enormity of interest in the event, the arena itself was eerily undersold. The final ticket sales were 13,094, and with complimentary tickets the total attendance was 14,623 in an arena that had a capacity of 20,000. Most fans were priced out by tickets that ranged from $500 to $10,000, and secondhand sellers had driven the cost of floor seats as high as $169,000. There was an overwhelming sense of wealth to the fight—everyone who had come could afford it. The first few rows around the ring appeared like a Renaissance painting, filled with celebrities including LeBron James, Chris Hemsworth, Jamie Foxx, Charlize Theron, Jennifer Lopez, Vanessa Hudgens, Karlie Kloss, Don Cheadle, Steve Harvey, Cardi B, and Sean Combs. Despite an arena that was nearly one-third empty, the combined wealth of the audience produced ticket sales of $55.4 million, the second-highest gate in boxing history after Mayweather's 2015 fight with Manny Pacquiao, and more than three times the UFC's biggest ever live gate.

Compared to UFC events, the arena was strangely silent and bright, with none of the thudding DJ music and light shows that swallowed the arena whole. Yet the magnitude of people looking into the event from outside was unmissable, as the number of pay-per-view orders overwhelmed both Showtime and UFC's Fight Pass, leading to both declined transactions and broken streams that forced the production crew to delay the start of the main event by more than forty-five minutes while the audience in the arena was left in an overlit limbo. "Guys," Showtime's Mauro Ranallo said on the broadcast, trying to fill time, "I never thought I'd see an MMA champion against one of the best to ever put on boxing gloves. And yet, the improbable is now imminent." The moment of imminence arrived just after 9:00 p.m. in Las Vegas, as McGregor walked to the ring draped in the Irish flag, eyes dead and cold. He was trailed by Kavanagh and his teammates, who were dressed like role players in old-fashioned suit vests and armbands, as if they were walking into the world's fair. They held up McGregor's two UFC championship belts like a buy-in at a poker table. After, Mayweather walked to the ring in a black ski mask and baseball cap, with a hood pulled over his head, part cat burglar and part medieval executioner.

When the fight began, McGregor came out in a strange, almost prehistoric stance, his lead hand lifted high in the air above him like a prehensile horn, his left hand lower and off to the side, like a tail that he quickly whipped at Mayweather's body. Mayweather grinned to himself and hid behind his raised gloves, less an executioner than a child playing peekaboo in a fort. As he backed away, he ended up pinned against the ropes and McGregor tried to overwhelm him with punches. Mayweather absorbed them the way a sea anemone absorbs the tide, moving with the momentum as they skidded off his gloves or bounced off his elbows and forearms, which formed a barricade around his torso. For almost a minute, Mayweather didn't throw a punch, but simply deflected McGregor's, learning where his reach ended, feeling how much power there was in each punch at different points along the arc, and timing how fast McGregor could throw them. Unable to deliver any damage along the ropes, McGregor began moving backwards, trying to lure Mayweather into counterpunches, especially a rear hand uppercut he wanted to use to split Mayweather's defense. Mayweather obliged and began to inch forward, feinting and pawing with his lead hand, but little else. After a jab from Mayweather fell several inches short of his chest, McGregor paused and looked down at the open space as if almost embarrassed for Mayweather, and then put his gloves behind his back for a split second, daring Mayweather to hit him, just as he'd done with Alvarez.

Mayweather ignored the taunt and kept pushing forward, in short rhythmic steps. For brief periods they both stood rooted in front of each other, stubbornly unwilling to move backward, lead gloves patting the air in front of each other to draw out an attack. In the final minute of the round, Mayweather lunged toward McGregor, and McGregor sprung up with a left uppercut that hit Mayweather squarely on the jaw and lifted his head backward as if he had been attached to a bungee cord in the rafters. It was just the kind of clean power punch McGregor had said Mayweather would be too old and too frail to absorb, the kind of perfectly conceived and timed punch that had sent UFC fighters tumbling to the mat in a jumble of stars and spotlights. In boxing gloves, however, something seemed lost; the punch landed at the right time and place, but lacked the element of force, which boxers spend years learning to deliver, planting the feet, rotating the hips and shoulder in one precise but fluid motion, like a piston. When Mayweather almost instantly regained his stance and continued moving forward again, it seemed clear McGregor had overestimated his ability to generate power in a boxing ring. "All it takes is one," he'd said in press interviews leading up to the fight. He'd gotten that one, highlight-perfect in the first round, and it seemed that he might need another twenty or thirty of the same perfectly timed, perfectly placed punches to begin to have an effect on Mayweather.

In the second and third round, Mayweather continued cautiously moving, rarely attacking, while punches poured from McGregor in a small flood that started to seem both strangely tense and ineffectual. McGregor threw forty-two punches but connected on just eight in the second round. Mayweather threw just ten and connected on five. The fight was filled with activity, but it never felt competitive, and by the scoring criteria of boxing, which counts missed punches alongside connected punches, McGregor's ineffectiveness was slowly filling Mayweather's ledger with points in the same way as had happened in so many fights before. McGregor would periodically pull Mayweather into a clinch and club the side or back of his head with illegal punches the referee repeatedly warned him about. By the end of the third round, McGregor's face was begining to redden from exertion, and he took in furtive breaths through his open mouth. In the fourth round, Mayweather grew more active, and began attacking McGregor with long spearing punches to the stomach, which he sometimes followed with leaping right hands to the head as McGregor lowered his guard. In the fifth, McGregor began backing away from Mayweather faster than in earlier rounds. When Mayweather punched, McGregor would lean his torso back as far as it would go, and then stumble backward as his feet tried to catch up. McGregor's punches seemed labored, placeholders for thoughts he wasn't quite able to complete. Mayweather moved forward more and more aggressively, while it seemed as if McGregor were fighting on a half-second delay, continually trying to catch up to where the fight had been a split second earlier. After the round ended, Mayweather shoved McGregor out of his face, almost in disgust. "When you gonna use your power?" he said.

As the rounds wore on, Mayweather became a constant presence, cautious but persistent, always peering from behind his gloves, taking small steps forward, retreating when McGregor would threaten, and then attacking with long, sharp punches, visibly faster and more forceful than McGregor's. The fight began to seem like a miscommunication more than a mismatch. It had the labored incongruity of a tourist trying to ask for directions in a country whose language he didn't speak. McGregor seemed to be drowning in his own labor, constantly moving backward, flinching and leaning, guessing at what Mayweather would do next. What Mayweather did was slowly increase the pace, throwing twenty-six punches in the fifth round, thirty-seven punches in the sixth, fifty-three punches in the seventh, forty-eight punches in the eighth, and sixty-eight punches in the ninth. "You need to let me know if he's had enough," one of the Nevada State Athletic Commission officials said to McGregor's striking coach, Owen Roddy, midway through the ninth round.

Battered and operating on dulled reflexes, McGregor dipped under a punch and fell forward into the familiar posture of a double-leg takedown, head outside Mayweather's hips, hands behind his knees, a safe escape hatch in mixed martial arts and an illegal move in boxing, which prompted the referee to separate the two. McGregor seemed almost drugged by fatigue as Mayweather hurled punches at him as if throwing baseballs in a carnival game. "Just need to tie him up this round," Roddy told McGregor in the corner before the tenth. "Pop a shot, tie, land. Recover this round. . . . We need to take this round off, okay?"

In the tenth round, McGregor spent the first forty seconds lunging toward Mayweather and grasped him in four consecutive bear hugs, before the referee separated them. After the fourth attempt, McGregor found himself turned against the ropes, unable to move backward or lunge away from Mayweather's punches, which came again like measured hammer strikes, the smaller man bullying the larger one, sending him stumbling with each clean punch, before winding back to chamber the next one. McGregor tried to edge away down the length of the ropes, searching for space. Mayweather hit him with a leaping right hand that buckled McGregor's legs and sent him stumbling backward into the ropes. Mayweather hit McGregor with a left hook and then another, which crashed into McGregor's temple and torqued him sideways as his body momentarily drooped against the ropes. As McGregor tried to straighten himself back up, his arms held low and his eyes glassy, the referee ran in to separate the two men, waving his arm overhead to indicate the fight was over. At one minute and six seconds into the tenth round, Mayweather was declared the winner by technical knockout, and he sprinted across the ring and jumped up onto the opposite turnbuckle and stared out into the crowd, mouth open wide in a primeval snarl.

McGregor watched Mayweather celebrate as the referee held him against the ropes and the ringside physician loomed over his shoulder, looking for the small tells of a concussion or facial fractures. "That was early," McGregor said, elbows supporting his weight against the top ropes, lamenting the damage he hadn't been allowed to take. "That was early, referee. That was early." The ring flooded with people, like a subway at rush hour, and after a minute McGregor pushed through the crowd and embraced Mayweather, conceding defeat. As he milled around the ring, energy flooded back into McGregor's body and he seemed unexpectedly buoyant, grinning in happiness at the scene itself. Already replaying the events of the fight in his mind, he reduced it to its simplest terms. "He's composed, that's it," McGregor said to his cornerman, as they tended to him along the ropes. "That's it. He's composed, that's it. He's not fast, he's not powerful. He's composed and precise." Above him, the replays showed McGregor's head snapping to the side and stumbling backward with every landed punch.

Interviewed in the ring after the official result was read, Mayweather complimented McGregor in the same way he had complimented all of his previous opponents in defeat, calling him a "hell of a champion" and UFC "a hell of a sport." When McGregor spoke, the ringisde reporter asked him why he seemed so happy. "I don't know," McGregor said. "I've been here before. I've been strangled on live TV and came back, so I don't—I'd have liked it if he just let it go. But fuck it. It was some buzz." He blamed the loss on his lapse in stamina, not the damage Mayweather had given him. The fatigue in particular seemed to mystify McGregor—it was a new phenomenon, a sudden but near total collapse that hadn't been present in his earlier fights. Perhaps it was a symptom of his mind and body beginning to pull in two different directions, the super-athlete and the unrestrained hedonist who went on three-day benders that left his heart worse for the wear, which couldn't be completely erased with even a six- or eight-week training camp.

In the dressing room after the fight, White and Lorenzo visited McGregor as he slouched in the corner scrolling through his phone. Frustration and disappointment began to cut through his happiness, the buzz slowly giving way to regret as he saw openings he'd failed to take advantage of, adjustments he'd missed making. When McGregor saw White, he apologized. "Dude, I'm ecstatic," White said. "Very, very badass. You're incredible, I'm telling you, you're unbelievable." McGregor rose and everyone in the room toasted with a shot of whiskey, from McGregor's own forthcoming brand, then called Notorious Irish Whiskey. (It would later be renamed Proper No. Twelve Irish Whiskey.)

The event would go on to break the all-time pay-per-view buys record, according to White, who later told the *Wall Street Journal* it had sold 6.7 million pay-per-views around the world, more than the UFC would generate in an entire year of events. (In the US, the buy rate had been 4.3 million, just behind the 4.6 million pay-per-view buys Mayweather's fight against Pacquiao had generated in 2015.) White also claimed the fight was the most pirated event in history, seen by an estimated one hundred million people around the world using thousands of illegal online streams. The MGM claimed that more than $1 billion in bets had been placed on the fight globally, making it the most heavily bet fight in history. Mayweather made $100 million in disclosed pay, and with pay-per-view participation and other revenue, he would reportedly earn a total of $275 million, making him the highest paid athlete of 2017, worth more than the three next closest candidates combined. McGregor reportedly earned $85 million, including $30 million in guaranteed purse money. The UFC was paid an undisclosed fee as co-promoter, which helped push the company's revenue for the year to a new high of "well over $700 million" according to a Moody's report, making up for a major decline in pay-per-view buys for the company's own events, thanks to the absence of McGregor and Rousey. The event placed McGregor at number four on the *Forbes* list of 2018's highest paid athletes, behind Mayweather, Lionel Messi, and Cristiano Ronaldo, and significantly ahead of LeBron James, Stephen Curry, Tom Brady, Tiger Woods, Clayton Kershaw, and Matthew Stafford. Even in losing he had somehow surpassed every benchmark he'd set for himself as an unhappy plumber's apprentice. He made more from his loss than any of his previous wins, and the UFC had made more from the fight than any of its own events. In hindsight, everything about the fight seemed unreal, both too good to be true, and an overwhelming anticlimax that wouldn't have registered as interesting on its merits were it not for the sums of money involved. "It was almost like the world got a magic trick pulled on them," Rogan would later say of the fight.

After the locker room toast, McGregor had lingered at the post-fight press conference wanting to prolong the last moments of magic as it still hung in the arena air. He was the last to speak, at a podium set up in the half-disassembled ring, wearing a blue paisley suit and large rose-tinted glasses in front of the few dozen journalists and videographers left in the otherwise empty arena. He had brought his bottle of whiskey and a clear plastic cup, from which he took sips as long and slow as breaths, willing the buzz he had felt to remain just a little longer. Asked what his next vision was, McGregor stumbled, at a loss for words for the first time in his career. The future seemed suddenly unseeable. Instead, he looked backward. "To come in and face this man—so many doubters, so many thinking it's never gonna—like, even thinking it's never going to happen, remember that time? This fight is never gonna happen. And I always thought, we can get this fight to happen. Then it was, I'm not gonna lay a glove [on him]. There were so many things to overcome and I've just enjoyed the whole experience, so I'm just relishing in it for now." He spoke from behind the tranquil veneer of chemicals, happy but remote. He was reflective the way a sentimental drunk at a bar on a weekday afternoon might come across as unexpectedly warm and reflective, yet unreachable and alone. After Mayweather rose to leave, taking the Money Belt as his prize, he and McGregor embraced one last time. As Mayweather pulled away, McGregor held on to his arm awkwardly, perhaps wanting some recognition that the fight had been closer than people had thought, that Mayweather had found challenge in it. "You all right," Mayweather said, patting him on the shoulder as he turned away and walked off the stage. "You all right."

McGregor continued taking questions for a few minutes, then a Showtime executive stepped to the podium and announced replay dates for the fight and cued the crew to begin breaking down the rest of the ring, as if the biggest event in modern prizefighting was something that came apart as easily as a piece of IKEA furniture, a collection of mass-produced pieces that would be loaded onto trucks waiting in the delivery bay. Reporters put away their notebooks and laptops, photographers began checking their cameras, videographers started breaking down their tripods. At the edge of the ring, McGregor stopped and walked back toward the podium, and for a moment, the crew stopped and the journalists paused in the middle of zipping up their bags.

Without a word, he started dancing, bottle of whiskey held out in one hand and his cup in the other. It seemed as if McGregor had forgotten about everyone else in the room, as if the stage was the last place in the world he could be by himself. The few remaining people in the arena watched as if there might be some last spark of genius he'd forgotten to share. But there was none. Just someone dancing with himself, feeling the buzz of his own body as it moved through time, the center of his own universe, expanding ceaselessly in every direction. McGregor slowly swiveled around in a half circle and then caught sight of his manager waiting at the bottom of the stage. He stopped mid-step, as if he'd just woken from hypnosis, walked down the stairs, and disappeared into the tunnels beneath the arena.

Epilogue

A MAN MUST EXCEED HIS LIMITS

The UFC's main offices today are far removed from the Torrance Public Library, where Art Davie began organizing the first event. In 2017, the promotion relocated to a 180,000-square-foot campus on the southern edge of Las Vegas, surrounded by shipping warehouses, a plastics factory, and enormous plots of undeveloped desert. Approaching it feels like entering a military outpost more than an office, as if the company's day-to-day operations are so sensitive they need to take place in a walled-in green zone with security checkpoints and a metal fence running around the quarter-mile of desert it sits on. The western half is dedicated to the UFC's corporate offices, and the eastern half is occupied by the UFC Performance Institute, a three-story cube of concrete and tinted glass where any fighter under contract can train with an array of advanced fitness and recovery equipment free of charge. In addition to weight machines, heavy bags, treadmills, and grappling mats, there's also a room-sized hyperbaric chamber, which re-creates the effects of being at altitude, something which causes your body to produce more red blood cells to improve oxygen absorption. There's also a red-light therapy area, which supposedly encourages cellular regrowth in damaged muscle tissue; a cryotherapy room, where fighters spend two to three minutes in a metal cylinder surrounded by air that drops to −100 degrees Celsius. On the top floor, there's a boxing ring and octagon, equipped with multiple cameras to capture footage of sparring and pad work, which can be reviewed in slow motion on one of several wall-mounted televisions. The screens also connect to a server containing the full library of past UFC events, so fighters can break down footage of future opponents in between drills. There are physical therapists and massage therapists on call, along with a small team of dietitians and kitchen staff who prepare free custom meals for any fighter. The UFC hired Forrest Griffin to help oversee the Performance

Institute, which has become a mainstay of fight camps for the few UFC fighters who live in Las Vegas. For the rest of the roster, it remains a utopian glimpse of everything that's missing from their lives as independent contractors used to fill out the prelims on cards pre-sold to the UFC's global network of broadcasting partners.

In 2019, the UFC opened another massive compound on an adjoining piece of land, called UFC Apex, a 90,000-square-foot production facility with a small arena that can accommodate up to fifteen hundred people. The Apex also has a control room with the capacity to remotely operate cameras, and edit live footage from other parts of the world, bringing the UFC a step closer to having the capacity to one day be fully self-sufficient. It's regularly used to film *Dana White's Contender Series*, and during the COVID-19 pandemic, after every major arena in the country shut down, the UFC hosted the majority of its pay-per-view events and *UFC on ESPN* cards in the Apex. In 2020, White announced the promotion was also planning to build its own full-service hotel exclusively for fighters and their trainers, something that would push the UFC one step closer toward being its own self-contained universe, a kind of corporate doomsday prepper ready and able to keep generating profit through a global pandemic or any other conceivable crisis. If every one of its broadcasting partners went bankrupt, if every arena in the country went out of business, if every mixed martial arts gym disappeared, the UFC would still be able to host its own events and stream them over Fight Pass to anyone interested enough to pay the $10 monthly fee. If the world ended, it's not hard to imagine that the UFC would provide the last major sport broadcasting shows to whatever remained of the human population.

Ironically, the UFC had its best year yet during the COVID-19 pandemic. As the new disease spread around the world and killed more than 1.8 million and left more than 114 million newly unemployed in 2020, UFC revenues hit an all-time high of roughly $890 million, 48 percent of which was booked as EBITDA, which helped provide Endeavor a ready cash flow to keep servicing its high debt. According to White, the UFC's total audience grew by 47 percent during the pandemic, and ratings on ESPN grew 16 percent year-over-year. UFC events regularly topped the list of trending topics on Twitter, and the promotion's Instagram account passed twenty-five million followers, five million more than the NFL and second only to the NBA, while its YouTube channel passed ten million subscribers. It was hard not to think that there was some truth in the *New York Times*' first assessment of the UFC, in 1994, as a "pay-per-view prism" onto the decline of Western civilization. As the world steadily lost its sense of normalcy, the sight of two people locked in a cage, fighting for a few months of wages, had never made more sense.

There's always been an apocalyptic aura around the UFC. The promotion has consistently found a way to profit from industries in decline, carving out small pockets of growth in markets that had otherwise failed to live up to their potential. It debuted just as the market for original pay-per-view programming was drying up in the mid-1990s, and it became a born-again hit during the slow decline of cable television subscriptions in the late-2000s, when cable networks tried to keep their numbers up by chasing niche audiences with low-cost, specialty programming. The UFC also offered the same hope to Endeavor, which had largely failed to generate any sort of profit from its strange collection of entertainment subsidiaries, and relied on the UFC for as much as 90 percent of its total revenue. The UFC became the main selling point Emanuel could offer investors as he tried to launch an IPO for Endeavor—first in a 2019 attempt that was abandoned at the last minute, followed by a successful 2021 launch that raised $511 million.

Meanwhile, Lorenzo and Frank III have moved on to new ways of making money. In 2017, Lorenzo started Fertitta Capital, a tech-focused private investment fund with $500 million of seed money from the family. The company's website is filled with the same kinds of inspirational but impenetrable quotes that fighters fill their heads with, from Colin Powell, Lao Tzu, Helen Keller, Aristotle, Peter Drucker, and Winston Churchill. One statement fades into the next, as if they were all part of some hidden master plan: *To see things in the seed, that is genius. Alone we can do so little, together we can do so much. Have a vision. Be demanding. The best way to predict the future is to create it.* The Fertittas' family business, Red Rock Resorts, has continued to thrive after emerging from bankruptcy, generating $1.86 billion from twenty-one properties in 2019, up from the $1.3 billion the company had earned in 2008. Lorenzo and Frank III each have an estimated net worth of $2.5 billion, making them two of the 614 billionaires in the US.

In 2017, Frank III bought a $70 million, 9,138-square-foot town home on Park Avenue, two blocks off Central Park in Manhattan. He's also continued to build his private art collection and took part in what became the most expensive auction for an American artwork ever in 2017, losing a bidding battle for an untitled Jean-Michel Basquiat painting that sold for $110.5 million to Japanese businessman Yusaku Maezawa. In 2018, Frank III spent a reported $25 million to host his daughter Kelly's wedding at the Red Rock, hiring John Mayer, Seal, and Bruno Mars to perform at the reception. In 2019, Lorenzo bought a 285-foot super-yacht reported to be worth $125 million, more than the UFC paid its entire roster of fighters during his last year of ownership. Called the *Lonian*, the yacht has a crew of twenty-seven and comes with annual upkeep fees of $12.5 million. Both Lorenzo and Frank III have also become prodigious political donors, almost exclusively in support of Republican campaigns and super PACs, including the Senate Leadership Fund, Trump Victory, America First Action, the Republican National Committee, and the National Republican Congressional Committee. Both men were heavy Trump supporters in 2016, and donated more than $5.7 million to that year's conservative campaigns. They continued to donate aggressively in 2018 and 2020.

Though still not a billionaire, White has absorbed many of the Fertittas' interests and habits. In 2017, he bought three adjacent mansions in a Las Vegas subdivision—spanning nearly eighteen thousand square feet and collectively worth $6.2 million. White then had them all demolished and built a new mansion on the combined lots, with an indoor basketball court, arcade room, and full-sized gym. He spent a reported $1 million to throw his youngest son a sixteenth birthday party at Drai's Nightclub in the Cromwell Hotel & Casino, and hired Migos, Everlast, and A$AP Rocky to perform. White has also become a committed art collector. One of his most prominent pieces is Nobuyoshi Araki's *Yakuza*, a photograph of a nude Japanese mafia member with an extravagant back tattoo kneeling on a concrete floor having sex with a woman who lies back with her eyes closed, head turned away as the man clasps her ankles for balance. "Isn't that badass?" he said in a 2019 video tour of the office. Another favorite piece is conceptual artist Mel Bochner's *Head Honcho*, a ten-foot-tall oil painting of overlapping crayon-colored words: Head Honcho, Top

Dog, King of the Hill, Master of the Universe, Lay Down the Law, Call the Shots, Crack the Whip, Rule with an Iron Hand, Gotcha By the Balls. White also owns a full set of samurai armor from the fifteenth century, a real sabertooth tiger skull purchased from a museum in Dallas, and an AK-47 made from one-dollar bills, loaded with see-through bullet casings containing cocaine, heroin, oil and blood—"Those are all things we kill for," White likes to explain—made by former Army Special Reserves soldier turned artist Bran Symondson. In 2019, White also donated $1 million to the Trump-tied super PAC America First Action, and in 2020 he again spoke at the Republican National Convention, in support of Donald Trump's re-election campaign.

The connection to conservative politics appeared to have benefitted the UFC when, in 2018, a group of fighters began amassing signatures to create an organization to collectively bargain for improved pay and treatment, under the name Project Spearhead. The group's organizers—Leslie Smith, Kajan Johnson, and Al Iaquinta—tried to persuade fellow UFC fighters to sign authorization cards claiming they wished to be recognized as full-time employees instead of independent contractors. If at least 30 percent of the fighters on the UFC's roster at the time, around 150, signed authorization cards, the group would be eligible to file a claim with the National Labor Relations Board to request a legal ruling on their status. If the NLRB held that because of the UFC's uniform requirements and restrictive contracts fighters were indeed full-time employees and had been improperly classified as independent contractors, they would be eligible to form a union and demand the right to collectively bargain, petition for lost wages, and more.

Within a year of its forming, the UFC had declined to re-sign two of the three fighters organizing the campaign. One, women's bantamweight Leslie Smith, filed a claim of wrongful termination, and the NLRB's Region 4 office determined the claim had merit and would justify a formal investigation. Shortly after the merit finding, a partner at the law firm representing the UFC, Morgan, Lewis & Bockius, who hadn't been involved in the case but had previously served on the NLRB, requested that Region 4's decision be reviewed by the main office in Washington, D.C. According to Lucas Middlebrook, a labor attorney who worked with Project Spearhead, it was a move he had never seen in all his years of practicing law. "The fix was in politically," says Middlebrook. Unable to win the case on the merits, the UFC, Middlebrook was convinced, had instead resorted to the "pulling of political strings" to prevent the investigation from moving forward. Three days after Middlebrook traveled to the main NLRB office in Washington to argue on behalf of Smith, White visited Donald Trump in the White House for a photo shoot with interim welterweight champion and MAGA booster Colby Covington, followed by a lengthy private dinner, which Middlebrook found suspicious. A little over a month later, the NLRB overturned the Region 4 finding, effectively ending Smith's case. According to Middlebrook, the UFC's treatment of Smith had a chilling effect on the signature drive, as many feared they would find themselves at risk of losing their place in the promotion. Left without any current UFC fighters willing to take over the leadership position, Project Spearhead effectively stalled out.

For many fighters, returning to life outside the UFC has been a struggle. Renato Sobral, who fought in the UFC from 2000 to 2007, has said the effects of chronic traumatic encephalopathy (CTE), a degenerative brain condition associated with concussive blows to the head, have caused him to go blind in his left eye. "People only talk about the good things today, what they have accomplished, what happened," he said in a 2019 interview. "But what about what you've lost? What happened to you?" Since retiring in 2010, former UFC and Pride veteran Gary Goodridge has struggled with severe CTE. He's lost his short-term memory and sense of smell, can no longer balance on one leg, and has developed impulse control issues that cause him to periodically snap at people for reasons he doesn't understand. "I've gone on trips with him and we'll be in the hotel at night and he'll ask me, What did we do today?" friend and coauthor of Goodridge's memoir Mark Dorsey said in an interview with *MMA Fighting*. "I won't give it to him right away and he'll sit there and try to rack his brain and remember."

One of Goodridge's former opponents, multiple UFC tournament winner and Pride star Don Frye, had to have two titanium rods screwed into his vertebrae to treat years of chronic back injuries. The rods later broke, and Frye developed a bacterial infection and chronic fever, and suffered a brain hemorrhage during one of the surgeries to repair the rods. He was eventually placed in a medically induced coma for two months to give his body a chance to heal. Former UFC heavyweight champion Kevin Randleman struggled with a number of chronic health issues during his career, including an undiagnosed lung infection that he lived with for close to two years, and severe kidney dysfunction. In 2007, he suffered a life-threatening staph infection that entered his bloodstream and opened two gaping holes on the side of his torso. The infection caused his liver, kidneys, and lungs to fail. In 2016, he died unexpectedly from heart failure after checking in to the hospital to treat a pneumonia infection. He was just forty-four.

Even winning efforts could often prove devastating in the UFC. Cal Worsham, who fought just three times in the UFC in 1995 and 1996, suffered one of the most serious injuries in the sport to date at UFC 9, when Zane Frazier kneed him in the sternum, causing his left lung to collapse. Worsham had shown no signs of pain in the cage and went on to win the fight by first-round TKO, but in the dressing room the pain became overwhelming and he was rushed to the emergency room. "I beat Zane," he would later say of the night, "but it almost cost me my life."

After retiring, lightweight Spencer Fisher, whom White once called his favorite fighter in the UFC, was diagnosed with brain lesions and suffered steadily worsening neurological symptoms consistent with CTE. He experiences regular bouts of vertigo, short-term memory loss, and often finds speaking unexpectedly difficult. White had arranged for Fisher to remain on a $5,000-a-month retainer after he retired in 2013, one of several such agreements that Zuffa had made with fighters that White and Lorenzo wanted to reward for their services to the company. But after the sale to Endeavor in 2017, the UFC informed him the promotion wouldn't renew the agreement. In 2020, former heavyweight champion Tim Sylvia found himself hoping the UFC would help him with medical expenses after unexpected complications from a broken arm he'd suffered in a 2004 loss to Frank Mir. Sylvia's right forearm had snapped in an armbar, and the bone was later mended with screws and a metal plate. Sixteen years later, the screws had begun to push back out of the bone, breaking through the skin on Sylvia's arm and posing an infection risk. Syvlia's doctor had asked the UFC to cover the costs of surgery to repair the arm, but according to Sylvia, it declined. When asked about Sylvia's request, White said he hadn't heard about it but implied that it would be unfair for the UFC to be held accountable for Sylvia's healthcare since he had fought for so many other promotions after leaving the UFC in 2008. (Sylvia later raised more than $15,000 from fans through a crowdfunding website to pay for the treatment.)

While the UFC has been reluctant to pay healthcare costs for retired fighters, it has made a nominal effort to fund research into the long-term effects of brain trauma. In 2014, the promotion announced it would join Bellator, Top Rank Boxing, Glory Kickboxing, and several other promotions in donating to the Cleveland Clinic's Lou Ruvo Center for Brain Health's work studying professional fighters. The center has published several studies suggesting that fighters—in cage fighting, kickboxing, or boxing—have elevated risk for a number of degenerative brain conditions. A 2017 study of 291 active fighters and 44 retired fighters over a five-year period found elevated levels of blood markers associated with permanent traumatic brain injury compared to a control group of non-fighters. Another study, published in 2019, tracked 173 boxers and mixed martial arts fighters and found they lost at least one hundred cubic millimeters of brain volume each year, a condition that's associated with both CTE and Alzheimer's disease. A control group of thirty-one people with no fight experience had brains that grew instead of shrank over the same period.

Many former UFC fighters have publicly struggled with other symptoms frequently linked to CTE. In 2018, *Ultimate Fighter* season one finalist Stephan Bonnar was arrested for driving under the influence after several motorists saw him swerving recklessly at 90 mph on I-15 outside Las Vegas. They surrounded him with their cars as he drove and forced him to slow down and pull over onto the shoulder, where he passed out at the wheel. When police arrived, they found an empty vodka bottle in the passenger seat, an AR-15 in the trunk, and a bottle of celecoxib, an anti-inflammatory pain reliever sometimes given to people suffering from chronic arthritis or experiencing chronic joint or back pain. In late 2022, Bonnar would pass away at the age of forty-five. Initial reports attributed the death to "presumed heart complications."

Nick Diaz also seemed to have "gotten a little out of control" in the years following his 2015 suspension, according to friend and training partner Jake Shields. Nick began spending more time in Las Vegas and often posted photos and short videos to Twitter and Instagram of him drinking or taking shots in clubs. Sometimes he appeared drunk to the point of incoherence. Heath found it hard to recognize the person he'd trained with for so many years in the videos and photos, and many people who had previously been close with Nick were quietly worried about his behavior. "Nick didn't have the childhood, the carefree life. He had to put it together, to live this monk lifestyle, train, eat, do the triathlon," said Heath. "I think he just woke up one day and said, Hey to hell with this stuff."

In May 2018, Nick was arrested in Las Vegas after a woman he had been dating accused him of throwing her to the ground, choking her close to unconsciousness, and then pushing her into a pool. A grand jury would later decline to indict Nick over the charges, based in part on inconsistencies in the woman's testimony. In 2019, Nick appeared in a bizarre and frequently incoherent forty-eight-minute interview with Ariel Helwani that left many fans disturbed. Nick's thoughts seemed to dissolve in his mind before he was able to get them out. He frequently fidgeted and pulled at his clothes, and at one point revealed a mysterious bite mark on his arm without any clear explanation. When asked if he was happy at that moment in his life, Nick answered, "No." Helwani later said the interview had lasted even longer but there were other, lengthy exchanges that were cut because they felt inappropriate.

"It's not a good thing at the end of this tunnel," says Cesar Gracie. "I'd tell him that, but when you're in that lifestyle you're not going to want to [hear it]." Nick finally returned to the UFC in 2021, after a seven-year absence, and lost to Robbie Lawler in a rematch twenty years removed from their first. The fight ended in a bizarre TKO by retirement in the third round, when Lawler hit Nick with a hard right-hook counter that sent him tumbling to the mat. Lawler waved for Nick to stand back up and continue the fight, but Nick shook his head no and the referee immediately waved off the fight. In the cage after, Lawler seemed genuinely concerned about Nick's condition. Instead of celebrating, he circled back to his former rival. He knelt down, clasped Nick's hand, and leaned his forehead onto Nick's. When they rose a few moments later, Lawler asked: "Are you good in life? . . . Let me fuckin' know if I can help."

Even McGregor seemed to fracture under the weight of his own success, growing manic and megalomaniacal after his loss to Mayweather. In April 2018, he was arrested and charged with felony criminal mischief and three counts of misdemeanor assault in Brooklyn after attacking a bus transporting fighters from media day appearances at the Barclays Center for UFC 223. McGregor wasn't booked on the card but had a long-running feud with Khabib Nurmagomedov, who would be fighting for the lightweight championship McGregor had vacated to take on Mayweather. McGregor smashed one of the bus windows with a hand truck in the parking lot underneath the arena and challenged Nurmagomedov to come out and fight him on the spot, leaving two other fighters—Michael Chiesa and Ray Borg—injured and unable to fight after sustaining lacerations from the shattered glass. (He would later plead guilty to one count of disorderly conduct and be sentenced to five days of community service and required to enroll in an anger management program.)

The UFC seized on the scandal to promote a fight between Nurmagomedov and McGregor at UFC 229 on October 6, 2018. At a press conference in New York a little over a week before the fight, McGregor drank his own brand of whiskey, Proper Twelve, on stage and tried to force a glass on to Nurmagomedov, a practicing Muslim who doesn't drink. McGregor described himself as "psycho bred" and said that if Nurmagomedov had gotten off the bus in April he "would be dead right now. This man would be in a box and I would be in a cell." McGregor seemed unusually dour at the press conference, lacking the puckish joy he had had when he first entered the UFC. Even White was disturbed by McGregor's demeanor. "It was dark, man. It was the darkest press conference I've ever been a part of," White would later say. According to Kavanagh, he hardly saw McGregor during the training camp for the Nurmagomedov fight. Instead, McGregor would show up late at night with an entourage, spar against a handpicked selection of partners in sessions that resembled raw, unstructured fights more than training sessions. After knocking his training partners out, McGregor would disappear again for days at a time on long drinking sessions.

When the fight finally took place, McGregor lost by a fourth-round choke, and a huge brawl erupted immediately after, when Nurmagomedov jumped out of the cage and attacked one of McGregor's training partners, Dillon Danis. Several of Nurmagomedov's training partners jumped into the octagon and attacked McGregor. White had the octagon cleared without any post-fight interviews or presentation of the championship belt, and three of Nurmagomedov's teammates were later arrested backstage. It felt as if McGregor's dark energy had turned the entire event into a public safety hazard.

It would go on to generate a reported 2.4 million buys, making it the bestselling UFC event of all time, surpassing McGregor's previous record by more than seven hundred thousand buys.

In the years that followed, McGregor continued to spiral out of control, seeming to test the limits of his own celebrity. In January 2019, a story in the *Irish Times* claimed a "sportsman," later identified by the *New York Times* as McGregor, had been accused of rape by a woman who claimed to have gone with him and several others to a penthouse suite at Dublin's Beacon Hotel at the end of a long night out. After an investigation, no charges were filed against McGregor. In 2021, the alleged victim filed a civil suit against McGregor, seeking between €1.4 million and €1.7 million, claiming she had not been able to work since the 2019 attack because of the psychological trauma. A spokesperson for McGregor told the *New York Times* that he "categorically rejected" all charges. In March 2019, McGregor was arrested in Miami on felony robbery charges after he knocked a cell phone out of a fan's hand and then stomped on it while leaving a dance club early one morning. Charges were later dropped after the victim's attorney claimed he had been "made whole" by McGregor.

The following month, McGregor sucker punched a fifty-year-old man in a Dublin pub after the man refused McGregor's offer of a whiskey shot. "He is a bit of a bully," the man told the *Irish Post*. "A bully with money." McGregor would later plead guilty to charges over the incident, and was fined €1,000. In October, the *New York Times* reported that McGregor had been accused of sexual assault for a second time, in a parked car outside a Dublin pub. No charges have resulted from the investigation. A publicist representing McGregor at the time said he "emphatically denies any report accusing him of sexual assault." In a radio interview, the UFC's chief operating officer Lawrence Epstein would joke about the difficulties of negotiating with McGregor: "I tell Dana, You did too good of a job. You made this guy too much money."

For long-term followers of the sport, it can be difficult to rationalize its effects on those who make it possible. Over time, it can sometimes seem as if you're watching people come apart in slow motion, like a windowpane shattering in footage that takes ten or fifteen years to play out. Ivan Trembow, an influential blogger who began covering the sport in 2002 and contributed some important reporting on fighter pay, television ratings, and steroid abuse, eventually decided he could no longer cover cage fighting with a good conscience. In a blog post announcing his decision, Trembow cited the lack of pension plans, collective bargaining rights, and long-term healthcare for fighters. He was also disturbed by an apparent pattern of substance abuse among current and former fighters, and "the avalanche of emerging science about concussions, CTE, Alzheimer's-like syndromes, and even ALS-like syndromes, it adds up to a recipe for disaster in the years to come," he wrote, "and I just can't watch it anymore."

Beneath the promotional bravura, many fighters seem as conflicted about their profession. "A lot of these guys in the MMA and all other fighters out there will say they love to fight," Nick Diaz said in a 2015 interview. "I'm going to tell you all that I'm a nonviolent person—I'm *not* somebody who loves to fight. I fight because I have to." In a way, part of the UFC's magic is that it distorts reality, making it appear as if people really do have to fight each other, as if the sight of two people locked in a cage with no way out were as normal and natural as deer grazing in a forest glade. Within that artificial reality, conjured by the lights and cameras and blaring music, it can still sometimes appear as if the fighters are themselves reluctant to give in completely to their basest instincts for cruelty, as if they are fighting against their own natures when they turn on one another. Even Royce Gracie, the sport's most iconic figure, would later concede he hadn't been born a fighter, but had become one through circumstance. "In a perfect world," he said in 2015, looking back on his career, "I wouldn't be a fighter."

After more than two decades as president, White has outlasted almost everyone in the UFC. He remains the most important person in cage fighting and has made more from the UFC than any of its fighters, hundreds of millions more. Part of his longevity has come from an ability to disassociate his sense of self from the requirements of his job. "Some people think I'm a classless moron," White said in an interview with *Rolling Stone*. "Other people think I'm this monster that screws my fighters over. And other people like me. You can't make everybody happy. But you gotta understand too, in this business, I'm the promoter. My role is I'm always gonna be the fucking bad guy."

The UFC benefitted from having White be the villain, a mean-spirited authoritarian who punished those he didn't like and made life easy for the few he did. It added an extra sense of drama to the fights themselves, and it gave critics a specific target to blame for all of the UFC's flaws. Colby Covington would describe White as a "piece of shit person" who has "no morals or values," after negotiations for his title fight fell apart. "He got all that money, and he let it get to his head," Covington said. White's own mother publicly renounced him in a short, rambling biography, *Dana White, King of MMA*, published in 2011. She described White as "egotistical, self-centered, arrogant, and cruel." During his tenure as UFC president, she writes, White went "from being a true friend, a good son, and a truly nice person to being a vindictive tyrant who lacks any feelings for how he treats others." When asked about the book, White declined to comment. "I got no thoughts on that," he said. White's older sister, Kelly, with whom he has maintained a close relationship, would later say she was mystified by their mother's turn against White. "Dana never did anything to her. It makes no sense to me," she said in an interview.

Not everyone has bad things to say about White. Former welterweight Mike Swick describes him as a kind of mentor. "Every time I run into problems or I have some situation, he's the first guy that I text," says Swick. "I don't know why, but he's always made time for me, always answers my texts. I can't really explain why because there's no real interest for him to be nice to me and to include me, but he just always has." White was especially supportive in helping Swick open his own gym in Thailand, a sister location of the American Kickboxing Academy. When Swick lost his entire life savings trying to launch the gym without fully understanding Thai building permits and business regulations, White offered him a chance to come out of retirement and rebuild his savings. After another two fights, Swick had enough to return to Thailand in 2014 and finally open the gym.

In 2018, White also gave $1 million to a support fund for the families of those killed during a mass shooting at an outdoor concert in Las Vegas. He decided to leave a permanent memorial to the event in the UFC octagon, writing "#VegasStrong" on the upper edge of the octagon door. (Previously, the space had read, "Charles 'Mask' Lewis Jr." in honor of the Tapout founder, who died in a car accident in 2009.)

White once fixated on his critics, but today he seems to have made peace with the fact that he doesn't have any final sway over how people think about him. In place of his former combativeness, he's cultivated a new sense of detachment, as if he's lost faith in some portion of humanity. The rest of the world—criticism from fighters, the press, even his own mother—has become a kind of white noise he's learned to ignore, like the dull rumble of an airplane engine on a transatlantic flight. "At the end of the day, they really don't matter," White said of his critics in the media in 2020. Instead, White has focused on making the UFC even more profitable. At the end of 2018, the promotion hosted an event in Russia for the first time, and in early 2019 announced a three-year agreement with Media-Telecom, a joint broadcasting operation between two of Russia's largest television companies. (The company also continued broadcasting in Russia in 2022, after the country's invasion of Ukraine, through a new agreement with a media subsidiary of Gazprom-Media Holding, the government-owned energy giant.) Also in 2019, the UFC opened a second Performance Institute in Shanghai, in a bid to make the sport more appealing to viewers in China. In 2020, Zhang Weili became the UFC's first Chinese champion when she won the women's strawweight title in a Shenzhen event, and helped to drive the UFC's fan base in the country to more than 173 million. The following year, the UFC signed a new deal in China with broadcaster Migu, a subsidiary of the state-owned media giant China Mobile.

The UFC also announced a multiyear agreement with SuperSport, the largest sports broadcaster in sub-Saharan Africa, as part of a strategy to promote the growing number of fighters with roots in West Africa, including middleweight champion Israel Adesanya, welterweight champion Kamaru Usman, heavyweight champion Francis Ngannou, and *Dana White's Contender Series* recruit Sodiq Yusuff. The promotion also signed a new five-year agreement with the Department of Tourism and Culture of Abu Dhabi to host fight cards in the city in exchange for an undisclosed site fee, and during the COVID-19 pandemic, the UFC relied on the United Arab Emirates to host multiple events inside a quarantine zone on Yas Island, which White temporarily branded as "Fight Island."

White relished all these accomplishments and offers them as proof that his haters were always wrong, quibbling at the margins of what is or isn't fair, while White and his colleagues were building the future. "If you didn't believe me fifteen years ago," White proudly said in a 2020 interview with *Sportsnet*, "you have to believe me now." The UFC's continued success hasn't served to repudiate claims it also treats fighters unfairly, pays them too little, has illegally misclassified them as independent contractors, purposefully hid star compensation in non-public side-letter agreements, and cut fighters off from taking full advantage of independent sponsorship revenue. Instead, the promotion's success simply overwhelmed its critics with new developments, which has made pointing out its flaws and failings seem futile, a distant echo of what an unnamed George W. Bush aide once told journalist Ron Suskind as the administration plowed forward with its plans for an Iraq invasion: "When we act, we create our own reality. And while you're studying that reality—judiciously, as you will—we'll act again, creating other new realities, which you can study too, and that's how things will sort out."

The UFC's approach is in many ways a reversal of what Jigoro Kano—the old Japanese master, whose pupil, Mitsuyo Maeda, traveled to Brazil and first trained the Gracie family in the early twentieth century—believed the purpose of martial arts should be. In a lecture given to the Parnassos Literary Society in Athens in 1934, just a few years before his death, Kano argued that the fundamental principle of martial arts wasn't to overpower one's adversaries or outmaneuver one's critics, but to produce "mutual aid and concession, leading to mutual welfare and benefit." The combined physical and mental rigors of training were meant to humble people, showing them how much their own advancement depended on the generosity and support of others. According to Kano, "so long as a man lives in society he himself is benefited by its progress, while on the other hand, if society deteriorates he loses what he might otherwise get. . . . To maintain social life every individual member of it must know how to refrain from egoistic conduct and must concede to help others whenever that is necessary to that end."

Kano isn't on White's short list of heroes. Before he starts work each day, he spends an hour exercising in the private gym he had installed as part of his office suite at the new UFC campus. The walls are covered with inspirational quotes taken from White's personal heroes. "Don't be surprised if I behave like a savage. I am a savage," from Mike Tyson. Another, from Bruce Lee: "Seriously, if you always put limits on what you can do, physical or anything else, it'll spread over into the rest of your life. It'll spread into your work, into your morality, into your entire being. There are no limits. There are plateaus, but you must not stay there, you must go beyond them. If it kills you, it kills you. A man must exceed his limits."

White's most prized possession isn't in his gym, but in his office, a small trophy with two clear glass playing cards—an ace and a jack— fanned out above a pedestal that he keeps on a long credenza opposite his desk. He won it along with a $250,000 prize during a fifty-two-person blackjack tournament at the Rio Casino in 2010. It was White's first competitive tournament, and he managed to make it to the finals. Before the last session began, one of the four other finalists approached him and explained that he and the others had all agreed to split the prize money equally no matter who won the final round.

"I'm like, Yeah, fuck that shit," White would later say of the offer. Instead, White went on to beat the other finalists and claim the prize money and the glass trophy for himself. "When I tell you these people hated me, they fuckin' *hated* me," White said. As he got ready to leave the Rio, one of the tournament organizers tried to direct him to the cashier to collect his winnings, but White told them to hold the money for him, assuming he would just come back and use it to gamble again some other day. Today, the money is long gone, but he's kept the trophy in his office ever since. "I told my wife and everybody else, when I die, I literally want this to be buried with me in my hands like this," he said in an interview, leaning back pharaoh-like, with the trophy over his stomach.

In the past, White had sometimes wondered why he's so attracted to gambling. Thinking about the question hadn't made it any easier to answer. For him, the impulse is its own explanation. "Do I need to play cards?" he said. "I'm not gambling to win money. It's just such a weird mental psyche thing.

"I like to fucking win."

ACKNOWLEDGMENTS

A huge number of people helped shape this book over the years. Steven Salpeter, my friend and, later, my agent, has been there from the start. He convinced me, one night in 2016, that I could write something meaningful about fighting and encouraged me to sketch out the first rough outline. The initial idea was for a historical anthology about prizefighting, with each chapter telling the story of a different bout from the early 1600s to the present day, which later morphed into anthology about the history of mixed martial arts told through twelve historic fights.

A few months later, Megan Hogan, my editor at Simon & Schuster, and Priscilla Painton, executive editor at Simon & Schuster, gave this overcomplicated idea a very generous first hearing and suggested I might write something even more revealing and wide-ranging if I just told a more straightforward history of the UFC. Without their creative instincts and belief in my potential as a writer, I couldn't have written this book.

I'm deeply grateful to everyone who agreed to talk with me, both on and off the record. Their insights and experiences helped me see the sport through new eyes. I'm even more indebted to the many journalists who've covered the sport over the last thirty years, and whose work created a public record of the UFC's struggles and extraordinary growth, including Loretta Hunt, Josh Gross, Joel Gold, Ivan Trembow, Erick Krauss, Clyde Gentry III, Jeff Sherwood, Jonathan Snowden, Steven Marrocco, Jack Encarnacao, TJ De Santis, and John S. Nash, among many others.

I also owe special thanks to Kristina Rebelo, an extraordinary reporter in her own right, who helped fact-check the manuscript and ensured everything was both accurate and fair; and to Joanna Oliveros and Carlos Fernandez, who provided invaluable assistance navigating California's court records system.

Jonathan Evans provided exceptional copyediting that helped make this a much more elegant and readable book than I could have. Alison Forner designed a beautiful cover that perfectly encapsulates the book's spirit and sense of history; and Sarah Perillo was a tireless advocate who helped find a readership for this book outside the US. I'm also grateful to Chris Perry, who performed the magical feat of getting me to look normal on camera for a few seconds, and to Patrick Harrison, who delivered a heroic and absorbing performance of the text for the audiobook. There was also an incredible group of people at Simon & Schuster who helped bring the book to life, including: Carly Loman, Allison Har-zvi, Amanda Mulholland, Lauren Gomez, Zoe Kaplan, Omesha Edwards, Elizabeth Venere, Elizabeth Herman, Stephen Bedford, Julia Prosser, Irene Kheredi, and Jonathan Karp.

A huge number of friends also helped keep me on track as I tried to navigate the abyssal murk of building a coherent story out of my years of notes, interview transcripts, court documents, and press clippings. Elizabeth Greenwood's wisdom, sympathy, and humor about the drafting and publishing process was a continual comfort. Chris Byrd was an inexhaustible source of optimism and reassurance. Ashley James helped me keep the lights on as I crawled across the finish line, and Anthony, Amber, Julia, Stephanie, Lionel, and Wes kept me company as I tried to put the last pieces of the puzzle into place.

I'm grateful to those friends who agreed to read early drafts of the book—including River Niles, Ben Bush, Rachel Rosenfelt, Malcolm Harris, Vicky Osterweil, Rob Horning, and Evan Calder Williams, and for those who helped indulge my interest in the sport over the years— including Mark Loo, who first shared his collection of pirated UFC tapes with me in 1996; and Peter Giannascoli, who took me to see my first Tim Sylvia fight at a long-gone sports bar on Sunset Boulevard; Jonathan Zungre, who took me to my first live event; and Pete Fishman, Mike Zweig, and Brian Justman, who indulged my fandom and reluctance to do anything other than watch fights on Saturday nights.

I'm even more grateful for Siobhan Burke, who gave me space and patience over the nearly five years it took to get this book right, which often entailed retreating into the spare room of our apartment until four or five in the morning. She was an unwavering lifeline who helped me find my way back into the world outside when it seemed like I was most in danger of getting lost inside the one I was trying to reconstruct inside my own head.

Finally, I'm indebted to my dad, a gangly and good-humored accounting professor from Denmark who I saw beaten by four other men on the front driveway of our house in Fresno when I was fourteen. My older brother had picked a fight with another eighteen-year-old, and then driven home when he realized the young man had three other friends with him. The young men followed him, and when my dad came out to de-escalate the situation, they turned on him instead.

Lacking the instinct to fight back, he could only hold his arms out to try and protect his head as they took turns battering him. After a minute, one last punch sent him stumbling down to a knee with his hands spread out on the ground in front of him, while the men ran back to their cars in a cloud of celebratory laughter. The beating left my dad with a broken eye socket and a cloud of bright red blood around his iris, which slowly faded to purple-brown over the following few weeks. Surgeons would later have to drill a small metal plate into his skull to help the bone mend.

Despite the injuries, he refused to see his attackers as enemies. He declined to press charges with the police and over the next several weeks, he tracked down each of the four men at their day jobs, determined to continue the conversation he had tried to start before the attack. He wanted each to see the afterlife of their actions on his face and asked for a promise: to try and find some way to resolve their conflicts other than violence.

I don't know if any of them kept their word. But my dad's stubborn belief that you should always fight to see people as more than the monsters that one moment in time might make them seem, has changed how I see the world, and all us in it.

This book is for him.

SELECTED READING

Buffer, Bruce. *It's Time: My 360° View of the UFC.* Crown Archetype, 2013.

Couture, Randy, with Loretta Hunt. *Becoming the Natural: My Life In and Out of the Cage.* Simon Spotlight Entertainment, 2008.

Cruz, Jason J. *Mixed Martial Arts and the Law: Disputes, Suits, and Legal Issues.* McFarland, 2019.

Daly, Lee. *Before a Fall: A History of Pride Fighting Championships.* 2018.

Davie, Art, with Sean Wheelock. *Is This Legal: The Inside Story of the First UFC From the Man Who Created It.* Ascend Books, 2014.

Davies, Richard O. *Sports in American Life: A History.* John Wiley, 2012.

Gentry, Clyde III. *No Holds Barred: The Complete History of Mixed Martial Arts in America.* Triumph Books, 2011.

Gerbasi, Thomas. *UFC Encyclopedia.* DK, 2011.

———. *UFC: A Visual History.* DK, 2015.

Gorm, Elliott J. *The Manly Art: Bare-Knuckle Prize Fighting in America.* Cornell University Press, 1986.

Jhaly, Sut. *The Spectacle of Accumulation: Essays in Culture, Media, and Politics.* Peter Lang, 2006.

Kano, Jigoro. *Mind Over Muscle: Writings From the Founder of Judo.* Kodansha USA, 2013.

Kavanagh, John. *Win or Learn: MMA, Conor McGregor and Me: A Trainer's Journey.* Penguin, 2016.

Kosman, Josh. *The Buyout of America: How Private Equity Is Destroying Jobs and Killing the American Economy.* Portfolio, 2009.

Krauss, Erich, and Bret Aita. *Brawl: A Behind the Scenes Look at Mixed Martial Arts Competition.* ECW Press, 2002.

Kuhn, Reed, with Kelly Crigger. *Fightnomics: The Hidden Numbers and Science in Mixed Martial Arts . . . and Why There's No Such Thing as a Fair Fight.* Graybeard Publishing, 2013.

Liddell, Chuck, with Chad Millman. *Iceman: My Fighting Life.* New York: Dutton, 2008.

Lober, John. *Memoirs of a Machine: Inside the Mind of a Cagefighter.* CreateSpace, 2014.

Mayeda, David T., and David E. Ching. *Fighting for Acceptance: Mixed Martial Artists and Violence in American Society.* iUniverse, 2008.

McCarthy, John, with Loretta Hunt. *Let's Get It On!: The Making of MMA and Its Ultimate Referee.* Medallion Books, 2011.

Mee, Bob. *Bare Knuckle: The History of Bare-Knuckle Prize-Fighting.* Overlook Press, 2001.

Merlino, Doug. *Beast: Blood, Struggle and Dreams at the Heart of Mixed Martial Arts.* Bloomsbury, 2015.

Mills, Keith. *Declaration of Independents: MMA Outside the UFC, Vol. 1 (1996?2005)*. Keith Mills Photography, 2020.

Pedreira, Robert. *Choque: The Untold Story of Jiu-Jitsu in Brazil 1856?1949, Volume 1*. GTR Publications, 2015.

Ortiz, Tito, with Marc Shapiro. *This is Gonna Hurt: The Life of a Mixed Martial Arts Champion*. Simon Spotlight Entertainment, 2008.

Peligro, Kid. *The Gracie Way: An Illustrated History of the World's Greatest Martial Arts Family*. Invisible Cities Press, 2003.

Porter, Michael E. *Competitive Advantage: Creating and Sustaining Superior Performance*. New York: Free Press, 1985

Pulver, Jens, with Erich Krauss. *Little Evil: One Ultimate Fighter's Rise to the Top*. ECW Press, 2003.

Ribeiro, Saulo, with Kevin Howell. *Jiu-Jitsu University*. Victory Belt Publishing, 2008.

Robbins, Anthony. *Unlimited Power: The New Science of Personal Achievement*. New York: Free Press, 1986.

Rodriguez, Robert G. *The Regulation of Boxing: A History and Comparative Analysis of Policies Among States*. McFarland, 2008.

Roman, James. *Love, Light, and a Dream: Television's Past, Present, and Future*. Praeger, 1996.

Rousey, Rhonda, with Maria Burns Ortiz. *My Fight/Your Fight*. New York: Regan Arts, 2015.

Shamrock, Frank, and Charles Fleming. *Uncaged: My Life as a Champion MMA Fighter*. Chicago Review Press, 2012.

Sheridan, Sam. *A Fighter's Heart: One Man's Journey Through the World of Fighting*. Grove Press, 2007.

Slack, Jack. *Notorious: The Life and Fights of Conor McGregor*. John Black Publishing, 2017.

Snowden, Jonathan. *Total MMA: Inside Ultimate Fighting*. ECW Press, 2008.

———. *Shamrock: The World's Most Dangerous Man*. Hybrid Shoot, 2020.

Snowden, Jonathan, and Kendall Shields. *The MMA Encyclopedia*. ECW Press, 2010.

Srnicek, Nick. *Platform Capitalism*. Cambridge, UK: Polity, 2017.

Stevens, John. *The Way of Judo: A Portrait of Jigoro Kano & His Students*. Shambhala Publications, 2013.

St-Pierre, Georges, with Justin Kingsley. *The Way of the Fight*. New York: William Morrow, 2013.

Thrasher, Christopher David. *Fight Sports and American Masculinity: Salvation in Violence from 1607 to the Present*. McFarland, 2015.

Wenner, Lawrence A., ed. *Media, Sports, and Society*. Newbury Park, CA: Sage Publications, 1989.

Wertheim, L. Jon. *Blood in the Cage: Mixed Martial Arts, Pat Miletich, and the Furious Rise of the UFC*. Mariner Books, 2010.

White, June. *Dana White: King of MMA*. Enterprises Unlimited, 2011.

NOTES

Websites

Bleacher Report
Bloody Elbow
CagePotato
Fightland
Full Contact Fighter
Ivan's Blog
MMA Fighting
MMA Junkie
MMA Payout
MMA Weekly
Sherdog
Wrestling Observer Newsletter

Interviews

Anonymous 1
Anonymous 2
Anonymous 3
Paul Cambria
Bob Cook
Lawrence Epstein
Don Gold
Cesar Gracie
Steve Heath
Albie Hecht
Kevin Kay
Shannon Knapp
John Lewis
Campbell McLaren
Lucas Middlebrook
John S. Nash
Phillipe Nover
Richard Perez
Howard Petschler
Marc Ratner

Tommy Rojas
Frank Shamrock
Jeff Sherwood
Leslie Smith
Mike Swick
DinThomas
Burt Watson

Introduction: The Last Sport on Earth

xi *The unrelenting pace is part of what has made the UFC* John S. Nash, "Documents Now Show UFC Makes Over $1 Billion a Year; Minimal Costs and More Growth Expected," *Bloody Elbow*, June 10, 2022, https://www.bloodyelbow.com/2022/6/10/23155850/doc uments-show-ufc-now-makes-over-1-billion-a-year-minimal-costs-and-more-growth -expected.

xi *The UFC's near weekly events are broadcast in 129 countries* Zuffa LLC Board Summary, submitted to Clark County Development Authority, September 20, 2018, https://www .diversifynevada.com/wp-content/uploads/2018/10/6-H.-Zuffa-LLC-dba-Ultimate -Fighting-Championship-UFC-Board-Packet.pdf.

xi *including the one in the top position, a boxing match* Steven Marrocco, "Dana White Now Claims Mayweather-McGregor Did 6.7 Million PPV Buys; Showtime Still Mum," *MMA Junkie*, October 25, 2017, https://mmajunkie.usatoday.com/2017/10/dana-white -mayweather-mcgregor-pay-per-view-buys-6-7-million-buys-showtime; David Purdum, "The Betting Event of the 2010s: Mayweather vs. McGregor" *ESPN*, December 27, 2019, https://www.espn.com/chalk/story/_/id/28366850/the-betting-event-2010s-mayweather -vs-mcgregor.

xi *In 2016, when the UFC was acquired for $4.2 billion by WME-IMG* Jonathan Snowden, "For Dana White and Fertittas, UFC Sale Leaves Behind Complex Legacy," *Bleacher Report*, July 11, 2016; Walt Disney Company Form 10-K, Fiscal Year 2009, https://www .sec.gov/Archives/edgar/data/1001039/000119312509245848/d10k.htm.

xii *Measured by revenue, the UFC accounts for around 90 percent* Hal J. Singer, *Redacted Expert Report of Hal J. Singer* (Case No. 2:15-cv-01045-RFB-BNW; July 12, 2019) pp. 18–19; Brett Knight, "The World's 10 Highest Paid Athletes" *Forbes*, May 12, 2021, https://www.forbes.com/sites/brettknight/2021/05/12/the-worlds-10-highest-paid-ath letes-conor-mcgregor-leads-a-group-of-sports-stars-unfazed-by-the-pandemic/.

xii *"quintessential American success story"* Marc Ratner, "Statement Before the Committee on Energy and Commerce Subcommittee on Digital Commerce and Consumer Protection U.S. House of Representatives for a Hearing on 'Perspectives on Mixed Martial Arts,' " November 9, 2017, available at https://docs.house.gov/meetings/IF/IF17/20171109/10 6604/HHRG-115-IF17-Wstate-RatnerM-20171109.pdf.

xiii *What Arizona senator John McCain infamously called "human cockfighting"* Richard Sandomir, "TV SPORTS; Death Is Cheap: Maybe It's Just $14.95," *New York Times*, March 8, 1994, https://www.nytimes.com/1994/03/08/sports/tv-sports-death-is-cheap -maybe-it-s-just-14.95.html.

xiii *While the objective is still "leaving someone as close to death"* Jorge Masvidal, interview on *Ariel Helwani's MMA Show*, ESPN, April 7, 2021, https://www.youtube.com/watch?v =0vE5HlDdhKk.

xiii *The UFC has its own gym franchise* UFC Gym website, accessed May 17, 2021, https://www.ufcgym.com/.

xiii *A little over half the available tickets had been sold* "UFC Newark: Attendance, Gate, Bonuses," *Fight Sports*, https://www.fightsports.tv/ufc-newark-attendance-gate-bonuses/.

xiv *While the UFC once coveted attention* Anonymous, author interview.

xiv *in 2016, when well-known reporter Ariel Helwani was ejected* Justin Tasch, "Dana White Confirms Journalist Ariel Helwani Is Banned from Covering UFC Events," *New York Daily News*, June 6, 2016, https://www.nydailynews.com/sports/more-sports/dana-white-confirms-ariel-helwani-banned-covering-ufc-article-1.2663639.

xv *After the UFC signed a landmark broadcasting agreement with ESPN* Phil Rosenthal, "ESPN Pays $1.5 Billion for Rights to UFC," *Chicago Tribune*, May 23, 2018, https://wwwchicagotribune.com/sports/breaking/ct-spt-espn-ufc-rights-20180523-story.html.

xv *In an interview after the episode debuted* Alexander K. Lee, " 'Chuck & Tito' Director Micah Brown Talks Origins of Documentary, Adding to Lore, Tito Ortiz's Response," *MMA Fighting*, October 15, 2019, https://www.mmafighting.com/2019/10/15/20914165/chuck-tito-director-micah-brown-talks-origins-of-documentary-adding-to-lore-tito-ortizs-response.

xv *According to Ortiz, the documentary was repeatedly recut* Gustav Garcia, "UFC Tito Ortiz Slams Dana White for 'Assassinating' His Character in Documentary," *International Business Times*, November 11, 2019, https://www.ibtimes.com/ufc-tito-ortiz-slams-dana-white-assassinating-his-character-documentary-2863694.

xv *In 2018, White had a hardbound book made* Jeremy Botter, "Dana White Wrote a Book for UFC Employee and We Have It," *Whizzered*, July 7, 2019, https://www.whizzered.com/p/dana-white-wrote-a-book-for-ufc-employees.

xv *"Nobody knows anything about this sport," White told TMZ* Harvey Levin and Charles Latibeaudiere, Dana White interview with TMZ, March 26, 2019, https://www.youtube.com/watch?v=Mjf0bsR0Dyk.

xv *White would later describe the journalists who cover the UFC* Damon Martin, "Dana White Blasts Media Criticizing UFC During Coronavirus Outbreak: 'Weakest, Wimpiest People on Earth," *MMA Fighting*, March 20, 2020, https://www.mmafighting.com/2020/3/20/21188290/dana-white-blasts-media-criticizing-ufc-during-coronavirus-outbreak-weakest-wimpiest-people-on-earth.

xvi *a veteran of corporate communications who had previously worked for Fox Sports* Sean Czarnecki, "UFC Recruits WWE Veteran Chris Bellitti," *PR Week*, March 23, 2018, https://allwrestling.com/2018/03/23/116015-former-wwe-executive-joins-ufc/.

xvi *The event had initially been planned for Sochi, Russia* Raphael Marinho, "*Invicto no UFC, Claudio Hanibal busca quinta Victoria sequida no UFC Sochi contra Ramazan Emeev*" *Combate*, May 29, 2019, https://sportv.globo.com/site/combate/noticia/invicto-no-ufc-claudio-hannibal-busca-quinta-vitoria-seguida-no-ufc-sochi-contra-ramazan-emeev.ghtml.

xvii *Instead, the UFC had stripped Covington of his interim title* Ariel Helwani, "Tyron Woodley to Defend Welterweight Title Against Darren Till at UFC 228 on Sept. 8," *ESPN*, July 24, 2018, https://www.espn.com/mma/story/_/id/24185799/tyron-woodley-defend-welterweight-title-darren-ufc-228.

xx *he average UFC fan looked a lot like me* Scarborough Research, "Tracking Fan Avidity for the Fight Game," *Sports Business Journal*, April 22, 2013, https://www.sportsbusinessjournal.com/Journal/Issues/2013/04/22/In-Depth/Fight-fan-avidity.aspx.

xx *Roughly half of the people in my generation* Neal Gabler, "The Secret Shame of Middle-
Class Americans," *Atlantic*, May 2016, https://www.theatlantic.com/magazine/archive
/2016/05/my-secret-shame/476415/.

xx *It was often easy to cheer for one person's pain* Sam Sheridan, *A Fighter's Heart: One Man's
Journey Through the World of Fighting* (New York: Grove Press, 2007), p. 7.

xxi *"It takes a special person to get in a fuckin' cage"* David T. Mayeda and David E. Ching,
Fighting for Acceptance: Mixed Martial Arts and Violence in American Society (Lincoln,
NE: iUniverse, 2008), p. 199.

xxii *The cheers weren't meant for either fighter* Ryan Young, "Ahead of UFC Newark, Colby
Covington Draws Support from Trump Family amid Latest Mass Shooting," *Yahoo!
Sports*, August 3, 2019, https://sports.yahoo.com/colby-covington-support-donald
-trump-sons-donald-jr-eric-ufc-newark-mass-shooting-el-paso-215217566.html?guc
counter=1.

xxiii *Public records showed he hadn't voted* Jeremy Botter, "Colby Covington Didn't Vote for
Donald Trump," *Whizzered*, August 6, 2019, https://www.whizzered.com/p/colby
-covington-didnt-vote-for-donald.

xxiii *But, after winning seven of his first eight fights* Mike Rothstein, "How Colby Covington
Became the UFC's Biggest Villain," *ESPN*, August 2, 2019, https://www.espn.com/mma
/story/_/id/27295062/how-colby-covington-became-ufc-biggest-villain.

xxiii *"So if you're different or whatever your deal is"* Ibid.

xxiv *In a manifesto, the shooter* John Eligon, "The El Paso Screed, and the Racist Doctrine
Behind It," *New York Times*, August 7, 2019, https://www.nytimes.com/2019/08/07/us
/el-paso-shooting-racism.html.

xxv *"Hey, let's talk about the lesson we learned tonight"* Colby Covington Post-Fight Octagon
Interview at UFC Newark: Covington vs. Lawler, August 3, 2019, https://www.youtube
.com/watch?v=n0e4mMm7orM.

xxv *Gouging spread across the American colonies in the seventeenth and eighteenth centuries*
Christopher David Thrasher, *Fight Sports and American Masculinity: Salvation in
Violence from 1607 to the Present* (Jefferson, NC: MacFarland, 2015), pp. 38–39.

xxv *In England, bare-knuckle boxing was a popular* Bob Mee, *Bare Fists: The History of Bare-
Knuckle Prize-Fighting* (Woodstock and New York: Overlook Press, 2001).

xxv *Catch wrestlers traveled the world in the early twentieth century* Jonathan Snowden, *The
MMA Encyclopedia* (Toronto, Ontario: ECW Press, 2010), p. 58.

xxv *In the 1970s, the Professional Karate Association aired bloody* Clyde Gentry III, *No Holds
Barred: The Complete History of Mixed Martial Arts in America* (Chicago: Triumph
Books, 2011), pp. 10–12.

xxvi *During the same period, tough man contests became popular* Oliver Lee Bateman, "Two
Pittsburgh Tough Guys Made MMA Safe for Everyone but Themselves," *Mel Magazine*,
May 2019, https://melmagazine.com/en-us/story/two-pittsburgh-tough-guys-made
-mma-safe-for-everyone-but-themselves.

xxvi *"Before any guy ever threw a ball through a circle"* Barry Bearak, "Ultimate Fighting Dips
a Toe in the Mainstream," *New York Times*, November 11, 2011, https://www.nytimes
.com/2011/11/12/sports/ultimate-fighting-championship-comes-of-age-financially.html.

Chapter 1: God Forgive Me!

1   *Before the broken noses* Art Davie, *Is This Legal?: The Inside Story of the First UFC from the Man Who Created It* (Olathe, KS: Ascend Books, 2014), p. 72.

1   *His notes were filled with strange curiosities* " 'Judo' Gene LeBell vs. Boxer Milo Savage: America's First MMA Fight," *Black Belt Magazine*, April 4, 2014, https://blackbeltmag .com/judo-gene-lebell-vs-boxer-milo-savage-americas-first-mma-fight.

1   *In 1976, a young Vince McMahon Sr. booked Shea Stadium* Bill Gallo, "Andre the Giant's Fight with Boxer Chuck Wepner at Shea Stadium in 1976," *New York Daily News*, March 1993, https://www.nydailynews.com/sports/andre-giant-fight-boxer-chuck-wepner -1976-article-1.2487638.

1   *The match was originally supposed to be fixed* Josh Gross, *Ali vs. Inoki: The Forgotten Fight That Launched Mixed Martial Arts and Launched Sports Entertainment* (Dallas: BenBella Books, 2016), p. 4.

1   *Beginning in 1976, ABC's Wide World of Sports would* Gentry III, *No Holds Barred*, pp. 10–12.

1   *Around the US, amateur events like* Tough Guys Bateman, "Two Pittsburgh Tough Guys Made MMA Safe for Everyone But Themselves."

2   *He had grown up in a middle-class family* Davie, *Is This Legal?*, pp. 25–31.

2   *In 1989, one of J&P's clients* Ibid., pp. 31–37.

2   *Growing up, his favorite show had been* "Greatest Fights of the Century," *Internet Movie Database*, https://www.imdb.com/title/tt0390714/. (Sample episode, via the Museum of Classic Chicago Television: https://www.youtube.com/watch?v=vVRs8xACLsY.)

3   *Davie put together a pitch for a television series* Davie, *Is This Legal?*, pp. 39–40.

3   Playboy *described Rorion as "the toughest man in the United States"* Pat Jordan, "Bad," *Playboy*, September 1989.

3   *Rorion reminded Davie of a bird of prey* Davie, *Is This Legal?*, p. 47.

3   *Rorion's grandfather, Gastao Gracie* David Samuels, "One Hundred Years of Arm Bars," *Grantland*, August 26, 2015.

3   *When Rorion arrived in America in 1978* Kid Peligro, *The Gracie Way: An Illustrated History of the World's Greatest Martial Arts Family* (Montpelier, VT: Invisible Cities Press, 2003), pp. 73–76.

4   *Many of his early clients were celebrities* Davie, *Is This Legal?*, pp. 49–51.

4   *His reputation helped him* Peligro, *The Gracie Way*, p. 76.

4   *In 1982, another producer had asked him* Davie, *Is This Legal?*, p. 89.

4   *Tape sales were bringing in more than $21,000* Ibid., p. 68.

4   *In the summer of 1992, Davie quit* Ibid., p. 72.

5   *He knew the event, which he had decided to rename* California Cable & Telecommunications Association, "History of Cable," https://calcable.org/learn/history-of-cable/.

5   *Davie cold-called executives at HBO* Davie, *Is This Legal?*, p. 93.

5   *It was a smaller market* Bill Carter, "Pay-Per-View Scales Back Ambitions for 'Event' Shows," *New York Times*, May 24, 1993, https://www.nytimes.com/1993/05/24/business /the-media-business-television-pay-per-view-scales-back-ambitions-for-event-shows. html. "21 million homes," which is 37 percent of the 57.1 million total subscribers in the US at the time, per FCC report. https://transition.fcc.gov/Bureaus/Cable/Reports /fcc97423.pdf.

5   *what Scott Kurnit, president of Showtime's pay-per-view division, called "niche-casting"*

Andrew L. Yarrow, "Pay-Per-View Television Is Ready for Takeoff," *New York Times*, November 14, 1988, https://www.nytimes.com/1988/11/14/business/the-media-business-pay-per-view-television-is-ready-for-takeoff.html.

5 *One of the biggest early successes was Howard Stern's* Underpants and Negligee Party Kay Gardella, "A Party for Animals," *New York Daily News*, March 14, 1988, https://www.newspapers.com/image/?clipping_id=56626943&fcf.

5 *"I'm never gonna get credibility like this," Stern exclaimed* Shea Garage, "Howard Stern's 1st Pay-Per-View NSFW," *Shea Magazine*, https://sheamagazine.com/howard-sterns-1st-pay-per-view-nsfw/.

6 *The broadcast generated more than 270,000 pay-per-view buys* John Lippmann, "Stern's Gross Special Tops Pay-TV Grosses," *Los Angeles Times*, January 4, 1994, https://www.newspapers.com/image/?clipping_id=56747086&fcf; Thomas Mulligan, "Facts About the Olympic Triplecast," *Los Angeles Times*, May 20, 1992, https://www.latimes.com/archives/la-xpm-1992-05-20-fi-306-story.html; James Roman, *Love, Light, and a Dream: Television's Past, Present, and Future* (Westport, CT: Praeger, 1996), pp. 76–79.

6 *SEG had been looking for ways to expand its business* Campbell McLaren, author interview.

6 *SEG's update was called* Battle of the Champions Richard Sandomir, "More Adventures in Pay-Per-View," *New York Times*, August 28, 1992, https://www.nytimes.com/1992/08/28/sports/tennis-tv-sports-more-adventures-in-pay-per-view.html.

7 *Just as Howard Stern had broken through* Davie, *Is This Legal?*, p. 149.

7 *"It was some great pitch," McLaren says* Campbell McLaren, author interview.

7 *McLaren asked Davie to send him a formal business plan* Davie, *Is This Legal?*, pp. 94–95.

8 *David Isaacs, SEG's chief operating officer, recalled* Dave Meltzer, "The Pitfalls That Faced UFC Before Its Television Success," *MMA Fighting*, November 16, 2013, https://www.mmafighting.com/2013/11/16/5105738/the-pitfalls-that-faced-ufc-before-its-television-success.

8 *In April, Davie met with McLaren and SEG president* Davie, *Is This Legal?*, pp. 95–99.

8 *He had made a name for himself in the music world* Robert Levine, "Who Owns the Live Music of Days Gone By?" *New York Times*, March 12, 2007, https://www.nytimes.com/2007/03/12/technology/12video.html.

8 *He'd had official company letterhead printed* Davie, *Is This Legal?*, pp. 99–100.

8 *With the green light from SEG* Gentry III, *No Holds Barred*, pp. 34–35.

8 *The state also lacked a boxing commission* Paul Dalrymple, "Boxing Commission for Colorado?," *Denver Rocky Mountain News*, January 29, 2000, http://sporttoday.org/13_dedd3dbf75bea5e5_1.htm.

9 *Davie took a short trip to Denver* Davie, *Is This Legal?*, pp. 99–100.

9 *After sketching out several rough designs* Ibid., p. 186.

9 *Davie suggested a cage with an electric fence* Ibid., p. 161.

9 *John Milius, who had joined the production* Jake Rossen, "Changing the Shape of Fighting," *ESPN*, May 22, 2013, https://www.espn.com/mma/story/_/id/8515933/changing-shape-fighting.

9 *SEG's art director Jason Cusson finally settled the issue* Ibid.; also Campbell McLaren, author interview.

9 *To lend an aura of credibility* Davie, *Is This Legal?*, pp. 177–78.

9 *SEG and Davie continued to negotiate* Ibid., p. 260.

10 *Davie raised the money over the summer* Gentry III, *No Holds Barred*, p. 37.

10 *Davie thought it was too long* Davie, *Is This Legal?*, p. 168; also Campbell McLaren, author interview.

10 *The image reminded Davie of Mr. Clean* Davie, *Is This Legal?*, p. 169.

10 *To help market the event, Davie hired a pair* Ibid., pp. 196–97.

10 *SEG faxed fliers to gyms and dojos* Campbell McLaren, author interview.

11 *There actually were rules, a full typewritten page* Davie, *Is This Legal?*, p. 208.

11 *When Davie handed out the rules to the fighters* Ibid., pp. 206–10.

11 *Everyone had their own particular issue with the rules* The True Story of UFC 1, https:// ufcfightpass.com/video/63342/the-beginning-the-true-story-of-ufc-1 (https://www .youtube.com/watch?v=lo6n2hcvUwc&t=2295s).

11 *Davie hadn't signed the final contract with SEG* Davie, *Is This Legal?*, p. 213.

11 *It opened with an introduction from American kickboxing legend* UFC 1 (video), UFC Fight Pass, https://ufcfightpass.com/video/30323/ufc-1-the-beginning?playlistId=2524.

12 *A group of executives from Gold's Gym* Davie, *Is This Legal?*, p. 24.

13 *"That's something that wasn't talked about in the rules"* UFC 1 (video), UFC Fight Pass.

13 *He'd arrived in the United States at seventeen* Samuels, "One Hundred Years of Arm Bars."

16 *Rorion dedicated the event to their father, "a pioneer warrior"* UFC 1 (video), UFC Fight Pass.

17 *"I think I found my sport," Jim Brown said* Ibid.

17 *He watched it from his house on Long Island* Luke Thomas, "Bob Meyrowitz Recalls the Remarkable Genesis of the First Ultimate Fighting Championship Event," *MMA Fighting*, November 12, 2013, https://www.mmafighting.com/2013/11/12/5096720/bob-meyrow itz-recalls-the-remarkable-genesis-of-the-first-ultimate; Art Davie interview, *Lytes Out Podcast*, May 20, 2021 (1:03:30), https://www.youtube.com/watch?v=z34lWDXu5L4

17 *TV Guide called it "disgusting"* Gentry III, *No Holds Barred*, p. 73.

17 *The Los Angeles Times critic Howard Rosenberg* Howard Rosenberg, " 'Ultimate Fight' Lives Up to Name: Pay-Per-View Battle, Instead of Being Merely Gory and Funny, Gets Interesting After the First Two Bouts," *Los Angeles Times*, November 15, 1993, https:// www.latimes.com/archives/la-xpm-1993-11-15-ca-57200-story.html.

18 Sports Illustrated *decided to cancel a feature* L. Jon Wertheim, *Blood in the Cage: Mixed Martial Arts, Pat Miletich, and the Furious Rise of the UFC* (New York: Mariner Books, 2009), pp. 60–61.

18 *Despite the barebones marketing campaign* Davie, *Is This Legal?*, p. 260.

18 *the typical split at the time was around 45 percent* Campbell McLaren, author interview.

18 *Isaacs, SEG's chief operating officer, had wanted to sell the UFC* Meltzer, "The Pitfalls That Faced UFC."

18 *On an episode of* Good Morning America John McCarthy, with Loretta Hunt, *Let's Get It On!: The Making of MMA and Its Ultimate Referee* (Medallion Press, 2011), p. 173.

18 *In an interview with the* New York Times, *McLaren claimed* Sandomir, "TV SPORTS; Death Is Cheap: Maybe It's Just $14.95."

19 *Angered that SEG had organized the event in Denver* Gentry III, *No Holds Barred*, p. 73.

19 *He claimed to have faxed McLaren about the idea* Ibid., p. 68.

19 *SEG had to rent out rooms from a small hotel* McCarthy with Hunt, *Let's Get It On!*, p. 154.

19 *Despite the organizational issues, the second UFC sold even better* Gentry III, *No Holds Barred*, p. 73.

20 *In April of 1995, it promoted a super-fight rematch* Ibid., p. 103.

20   *The company sold tapes for $45 each* Don Gold, author interview.

20   *With so much money coming in, SEG consolidated* Gentry III, *No Holds Barred*, p. 108.

20   *Royce left the UFC with Rorion* Peligro, *The Gracie Way*, pp. 107–223.

20   *At UFC 3, Kimo Leopoldo had introduced the world to Jo Son Do* Jen Yamato, "The Strange Saga of Joe Son: Bond Villain Parody, Gang Rapist, and Possible Murderer," *Daily Beast*, November 6, 2015, https://www.thedailybeast.com/the-strange-saga-of-joe-son -bond-villain-parody-gang-rapist-and-possible-murderer?ref=scroll.

21   *His opponent, Andy Anderson* "Andy Anderson," *MMA Fighting*, https://www.mmafight ing.com/fighter/2409/andy-anderson.

21   *a discipline Davie had invented, along with Abbot's more familiar nickname* Gentry III, *No Holds Barred*, pp. 113–14.

21   *Matua would remain unconscious on the mat* Scott Frothingham, "What Is Fencing Response and Why Does it Happen?," *Healthline*, August 24, 2018, https://www .healthline.com/health/fencing-response.

22   *According to Davie, an early survey of the UFC's audience* Gentry III, *No Holds Barred*, p. 187.

22   *"UFC was so successful because it was a sport white guys could win"* Campbell McLaren, author interview.

22   *John Lober, who fought in Pancrase and the UFC* John Lober with Tam Marquitz, *Memoirs of a Machine: Inside the Mind of a Cage Fighter* (CreateSpace Independent Publishing Platform, 2014), Loc. 337/4567 in Kindle.

22   *For Varelans, who competed in four UFC events* Paul Varelans interview, *Between Rounds Radio Podcast*, January 9, 2019, https://soundcloud.com/betweenroundsradio/varelans.

22   *He was a lifelong fan of the sport* Kevin Iole, "Sen. John McCain Was a Passionate Boxing Fan and His Criticisms Helped Shape Modern MMA," *Yahoo! Sports*, August 25, 2018, https://sports.yahoo.com/sen-john-mccain-passionate-boxing-fan-criticisms-helped -shape-modern-mma-032407860.html?guccounter=1.

22   *In a September 1994 hearing, McCain pointed to the UFC* John McCain, "Health and Safety of Professional Boxing: Hearings Before the Committee on Commerce, Science, and Transportation, United States Senate" September 22, 1994, https://archive.org /details/healthsafetyofpr00unit.

22   *In 1995, McCain sent an open letter* McCarthy with Hunt, *Let's Get It On!*, p. 197.

23   *The Illinois state legislature followed suit* Wertheim, *Blood in the Cage*, p. 101.

23   *At an event in Charlotte that year* Mark La Monica, "How Four Words from Campbell McLaren Shaped the Early Days of the UFC," *Long Island Newsday*, November 13, 2013, https://www.newsday.com/sports/mixed-martial-arts/how-four-words-from-campbell -mclaren-shaped-the-early-days-of-the-ufc-c98313.

23   *Anticipating that serious legal troubles* Gentry III, *No Holds Barred*, pp. 155–58.

23   *To celebrate the new legal recognition* Dave Meltzer, "A Look Back at the 1990s Hysteria Which Got MMA Banned in New York," *MMA Fighting*, April 3, 2016, https://www .mmafighting.com/2016/4/3/11312322/new-york-was-both-the-first-and-last-state-to -pass-a-law-legalizing.

24   *Every fighter would be required to wear protective headgear* McCarthy with Hunt, *Let's Get It On!*, p. 218.

24   *Instead, they quickly came to an agreement with the city of Dothan, Alabama* Jonathan Snowden, *Total MMA* (Toronto, Ontario: ECW Press, 2008), pp. 92–93.

24   *The last-minute move saved the show* Meltzer, "The Pitfalls that Faced the UFC."

24 *In 1997, John McCain was appointed* McCarthy with Hunt, *Let's Get It On!*, pp. 223–24.

24 *TCI was the first to comply* Snowden, *Total MMA*, p. 94.

25 *The number of US homes that could buy UFC* David Plotz, "Fight Clubbed," *Slate*, November 17, 1999, https://slate.com/news-and-politics/1999/11/fight-clubbed.html.

25 *They went from earning between $1 and $2 million* "Blackout: The Story of the Political Crusade to Keep the UFC Off TV," UFC Fight Pass, https://www.ufc.com/video/black out-story-political-crusade-keep-ufc-tv.

25 *Meyrowitz took out a full-page ad* Gentry III, *No Holds Barred*, p. 127.

25 *In 1997, Meyrowitz fired Davie* McCarthy with Hunt, *Let's Get It On!*, pp. 247–48.

25 *The few stars who had stayed* Tito Ortiz, *This Is Gonna Hurt: The Life of a Mixed Martial Arts Champion* (New York: Simon Spotlight Entertainment, 2008), p. 91.

26 *Growing more desperate, Meyrowitz flew* McCarthy with Hunt, *Let's Get It On!*, pp. 226–27, 265.

26 *"I came here, found out where the bathrooms are"* Gentry III, *No Holds Barred*, p. 213.

26 *Meyrowitz hired Sig Rogich* McCarthy with Hunt, *Let's Get It On!*, pp. 276–77.

26 *Meyrowitz had more success with the New Jersey State Athletic Commission* Ibid., p. 274.

27 *Lambert promised he would pay SEG $200,000 to fund* "Dan Lambert Screwed by Bob Meyrowitz on Contract to Buy UFC—Episode 20," *Punchin' In*, December 2, 2021, https://www.youtube.com/watch?v=967cUTg_arQ; Steven Marrocco, "How American Top Team's Owner and an Ex-Matchmaker Almost Bought the UFC," *MMA Junkie*, July 23, 2016, https://mmajunkie.usatoday.com/2016/07/how-american-top-team -owner-and-ex-matchmaker-almost-bought-the-ufc; "Dan Lambert," *Fighter Interviews*, February 3, 2019, http://web.archive.org/web/20200928212344/https://www.fighterinter views.com/en/interviews/2019/02/dan-lambert.

27 *Meyrowitz had dreams of his own* Jose Alvear, "eYada No More," *Streaming Media*, July 10, 2001, https://www.streamingmedia.com/Articles/ReadArticle.aspx?Article ID=64264.

27 *"I was in court all the time," Meyrowitz would later say* Bob Meyrowitz interview, *Lytes Out Podcast*, December 24, 2021 (1:29:00), https://www.youtube.com/watch?v=ywe SHTxWqJA.

Chapter 2: Everything These Guys Touch Turns to Gold

28 *Dana White was on the phone with Bob Meyrowitz* "Dana White Talks About the Early Days of the UFC," January 30, 2017, https://www.youtube.com/watch?v=Mh4dH4b4jSM; UFC Holdings, "Three Guys and Three Letters: The Story of the Fertitta Brothers and Dana White," May 30, 2019, https://www.ufc.com/news/ufc-25-years-short-docuseries -premieres-youtube.

28 *He'd made a name for himself in personal fitness* Tim Willert, "Box Aerobics Class Packs Serious Punch," *Las Vegas Review-Journal*, April 16, 1997, https://reviewjournal.newsbank .com/doc/news/0FD38E4C6B2C80F7; June White, *Dana White: King of MMA* (J. M. White, 2011), p. 96; "Floyd Mayweather's Early Fight Outfits Sponsored by UFC's Dana White," *Yahoo! Sports*, April 30, 2015, https://sports.yahoo.com/blogs/boxing/floyd-may weather-s-early-fight-outfights-sponered-by-ufc-s-dana-white-233757891.html.

28 *White had initially thought the UFC was "ridiculous"* Marcus Kowal, "UFC's History and In Depth Interview with Dana White," *MMAnytt*, March 30, 2012, https://www.youtube .com/watch?v=HqPtGbdtKg0&t=6s.

28 *A perpetual entrepreneur, White had also talked his way* John Lewis, author interview; "Dana White Talks About the Early Days of the UFC," YouTube, available at https://www .youtube.com/watch?v=Mh4dH4b4jSM.

28 *White was determined to get Ortiz more money* "Dana White Talks About the Early Days of the UFC."

28 *As if to prove how serious he was, White hung up* Joe Rogan, "#247—Tito Ortiz," *The Joe Rogan Experience,* July 31, 2012, https://open.spotify.com/episode/2QAu0gOr068 ACXOb7hE2Br.

28 *Over the summer, White had acted on a similar threat* Chuck Liddell with Chad Millman, *Iceman: My Fighting Life* (New York: New American Library, 2008), pp. 119–21.

29 *After Liddell won that fight, and the IFC's* Ibid.

29 *"You know what?" White remembers Meyrowitz saying* "Dana White Talks About the Early Days of the UFC."

29 *White heard the sound of opportunity in Meyrowitz's defeated tone* Ibid.

29 *While Meyrowitz and the UFC were nearly bankrupt* Station Casinos 2002 Annual Report, p. 12.

29 *In January, Station would add two new properties* Ibid, p. 3.

29 *As soon as White hung up with Meyrowitz,* UFC Holdings, "Three Guys and Three Letters."

29 *Lorenzo and Frank had been with White at the Hard Rock* Ibid.; John Lewis, author interview; Mike Straka, "Fighting Words: Interview with Lorenzo Fertitta," March 6, 2011, https://www.youtube.com/watch?v=zLQ7Bkp8UZw.

30 *"It was like in* The Matrix—*take the pill"* Graham Bensinger, "Lorenzo Fertitta: Repairing the UFC's Wreckage," *In Depth with Graham Bensinger,* https://www.youtube.com /watch?v=RhiH3Mj7i6A&list=PLW5qT4HIAd1Yxu7xA-xuHND97K-XIGhRc.

30 *When Frank learned that Lewis was planning to launch* John Lewis, author interview.

30 *Lorenzo and White had also talked about ways of getting* "Dana White Talks About the Early Days of the UFC."

30 *Lorenzo's mind was already filled with ideas* David Samuels, "Lorenzo Fertitta Interview," *Atlantic,* November 2008, https://www.theatlantic.com/magazine/archive/2008/11/loren zo-fertitta/307183/.

30 *Meyrowitz had hoped Lorenzo would help tip the balance* Scott Wapner, *Ultimate Fighting: Making Money Hand Over Fist,* CNBC, October 12, 2008, https://www.cnbc.com/ulti mate-fighting/; "Zuffa Seeks Retraction of Statements by Former UFC Owner," *MMA Fighting,* January 17, 2008, https://www.mmafighting.com/2008/01/17/zuffa-seeks-re traction-of-statements-by-former-ufc-owner.

30 *"I just didn't feel like we had to be the commission that was blazing"* UFC Holdings, "Three Guys and Three Letters."

30 *Meyrowitz had later invited a small delegation from the NSAC* McCarthy with Hunt, *Let's Get It On!,* pp. 276–77; Marc Ratner, author interview; UFC Holdings, "Three Guys and Three Letters."

30 *It had been unusually violent, even by UFC standards* UFC Holdings, "UFC 21: Return of the Champions," *UFC Fight Pass,* July 16, 1999, https://ufcfightpass.com/video/31763 /ufc-21-return-of-the-champions?playlistId=3477.

30 *"When you first see it and you're right there in person"* UFC Holdings, "Three Guys and Three Letters."

31 *A year-an-a-half later, Lorenzo's reluctance had turned to admiration* Bensinger, "Lorenzo Fertitta: Repairing the UFC's Wreckage."

31 *When Meyrowitz heard Lorenzo's voice* Bob Meyrowitz interview, *Lytes Out Podcast*;
    Wapner, *Ultimate Fighting*.

31 *Lorenzo, who had resigned from his position* Gentry III, *No Holds Barred*, p. 276;
    Bensinger, "Lorenzo Fertitta: Repairing the UFC's Wreckage."

31 *"He's like, Look, this is super easy," Lorenzo would later say* Gareth A. Davies, "Lorenzo
    Fertitta Podcast," *Gareth A. Davies Podcast*, October 24, 2018, https://www.garethadavies
    .com/2018/10/24/lorenzo-fertitta-podcast/.

31 *He thought it would be easier for fans to relate* Lee Hawkins, "WSJ Live: UFC's Lorenzo
    Fertitta and Dana White: UFC Bigger Than NFL," *Wall Street Journal*, May 7, 2012, video
    available at https://www.youtube.com/watch?v=E5EYyZ5ABrQ.

31 *White and Lorenzo had first met as teenagers* Graham Bensinger, "Dana White: My
    Alcoholic Dad and Getting Expelled," *In Depth with Graham Bensinger*, 2011, https://
    www.youtube.com/watch?v=aGNkNt9DT-U&list=PLW5qT4HIAd1aK9vr0bzZpb
    2CZiGT-WwrL&index=3; Mike Straka, "UFC CEO Lorenzo Fertitta Interview," *Mike
    Straka*, March 26, 2011, https://www.youtube.com/watch?v=zLQ7Bkp8UZw.

31 *In the middle of their senior year, White disappeared altogether* Kevin Paul Dupont,
    "UFC President Dana White Has Deep Bond with Boston," *Boston Globe*, January
    16, 2016, https://www.bostonglobe.com/sports/2016/01/16/ufc-president-dana
    -white-has-deep-connection-with-boston/77kJjod5RPgnTy3HaJD7iJ/story.html.

32 *Over the next several years, he worked as a bar bouncer* Ibid.; UFC Holdings, "Dana
    White UFC 111 Video Blog—3/25/10," *UFC—Ultimate Fighting Championship*,
    March 26, 2010, https://www.youtube.com/watch?v=_AZZ5WukhqA.

32 *"That was the hardest job I've ever had"* Bensinger, "Dana White: My Alcoholic Dad and
    Getting Expelled."

32 *He became a regular at the McDonough Boxing Training Center* Billy Baker, "Dana White's
    Billion-Dollar Baby," *Boston Globe*, August 1, 2010, http://archive.boston.com/boston
    globe/magazine/articles/2010/08/01/dana_whites_billion_dollar_baby/?page=full.

32 *"From the first blow he took on his chin"* Ibid.

32 *Too poor to afford a car, White would bicycle* Tony Robbins, "Tony Robbins Business
    Mastery—Dana White (UFC President) interview (2018 Aug)," *Master Your Life with
    Tony Robbins*, August 20, 2018, https://www.youtube.com/watch?v=hQ8smKskDT8.

32 *In one characteristic section, from* Unlimited Power Anthony Robbins, *Unlimited Power:
    The New Science of Personal Achievement* (New York: Free Pres, 1986), p. 6.

32 *But because of electronic media and the arrival of the information age* Ibid., p. 413.

33 *That confidence was shaken one day in late 1995* Dupont, "UFC President Dana White
    Has Deep Bond with Boston."

33 *Weeks told White he would have to pay $2,500* Ibid.

33 *White moved in with the parents of an ex-girlfriend* "UFC Boss Fights the Clock," *Las
    Vegas Review-Journal*, July 7, 2009, https://www.reviewjournal.com/sports/mma-ufc/ufc
    -boss-fights-clock/; White, *Dana White: King of MMA*, p. 95.

33 *Within a year, White had built a steady business teaching* Willert, "Box Aerobics Class
    Packs Serious Punch"; Royce Feour, "For Convenient and Effective Workout, Trainer
    Says Skip It," *Las Vegas Review-Journal*, January 11, 1997, https://reviewjournal
    .newsbank.com/doc/news/0FD38E10392F2902?search_terms=q%20the%20sports%20
    club&text=q%20the%20sports%20club&content_added=&date_from=&date_to=&
    pub%5B0%5D=LVRB&sort=old&pdate=1997-01-11.

33 *He'd reconnected with Lorenzo a year after returning* "UFC Boss Fights the Clock."

33 *All the things that had seemed like negatives in high school* Bill King, "Deep Ties for UFC

Execs, Celebrated HS Program," *Sports Business Journal*, November 10, 2014, https://
www.sportsbusinessjournal.com/Journal/Issues/2014/11/10/People-and-Pop-Culture
/UFC-high-school-football.aspx.

34 *When Lorenzo and Frank returned to Las Vegas from Miami* Bensinger, "Lorenzo Fertitta:
Repairing the UFC's Wreckage."

34 *A kindly man with a monkish rim of gray hair* Howard Stutz, "Station Casinos Company
Chief Frank Fertitta Jr. Dies at 70," *Las Vegas Review-Journal*, August 22, 2009, https://
www.reviewjournal.com/news/station-casinos-company-chief-frank-fertitta-jr-dies-at
-70/.

34 *In 1993, he'd stepped down from his position as CEO* Mary Manning, "Frank Fertitta Jr.,
Patriarch of Station Casinos, Dies," *Las Vegas Sun*, August 21, 2009, https://lasvegassun
.com/news/2009/aug/21/frank-fertitta-jr-patriarch-station-casinos-dies/; Matthew
G. Miller, "Fertittas Made Billionaires by Head Blows with Chokeholds," *Bloomberg*,
August 1, 2012, https://www.bloomberg.com/news/articles/2012-08-01/fertittas-made
-billionaires-by-head-blows-with-chokeholds.

34 *"I really don't want you doing this," Lorenzo recalled* Bensinger, "Lorenzo Fertitta:
Repairing the UFC's Wreckage."

34 *what even Lorenzo would later describe as a "vanity business"* Samuels, "Lorenzo Fertitta
Interview."

34 *He'd moved to Las Vegas from Galveston, Texas, in 1960* Alan Balboni, *Beyond the Mafia:
Italian Americans and the Development of Las Vegas* (Reno: University of Nevada Press,
1996), pp. 32–33; Kyle B. Hansen, "Fertitta Remembered for 'Kindness, Generosity,
Integrity' at Funeral," *Las Vegas Sun*, August 29, 2009, https://lasvegassun.com/news
/2009/aug/29/fertitta-remembered-kindness-generosity-integrity-/; "The Fertitta Family,"
Southern Nevada Sports Hall of Fame, 2010, https://snshf.com/hall-of-famers/the
-fertitta-family/.

34 *Over the next decade, he worked his way through the ranks* Balboni, *Beyond the Mafia*,
pp. 32–33; "Frank Fertitta Jr. 1938–2009," *Las Vegas Sun*, August 23, 2009, https://
lasvegassun.com/news/2009/aug/23/frank-fertitta-jr-1938-2009/.

35 *In 1976, Frank Jr. was able to organize a group of investors* Balboni, *Beyond the Mafia*, pp.
32–33.

35 *Simply called The Casino, the property was attached* Ashley Powers, "From Bellman to
Pioneer of Neighborhood Vegas Casinos," *Los Angeles Times*, August 23, 2009, https://
www.latimes.com/archives/la-xpm-2009-aug-23-me-frank-fertitta23-story.html;
Joel Stein, "Ultimate Fighting Machines," *Business 2.0 Magazine*, November 8, 2006,
https://money.cnn.com/2006/11/07/magazines/business2/stationcasinos.biz2/; "Brand
Creator—Lorenzo Fertitta," *STERNBUSINESS Magazine*, Fall 2018, https://www.stern
.nyu.edu/sternbusiness-magazine/brand-creator-lorenzo-fertitta-mba-93.

35 *Also in 1983, one of Frank Jr.'s partners in Palace Station* Al Delugach, "5 Mob Figures
Guilty in Las Vegas Skimming Case," *Los Angeles Times*, January 22, 1986, https://www
.latimes.com/archives/la-xpm-1986-01-22-mn-31381-story.html; "Carl Thomas Sr.
Banned from Nevada Casinos," Associated Press, November 11, 1993, https://www
.latimes.com/archives/la-xpm-1993-11-11-mn-55577-story.html.

35 *Prosecutors alleged the scheme was by organized members* "Businessman Testifies That
Mob Figure Threatened Him, Cut Off Teamster Loans," *Los Angeles Times*, November 8,
1985, https://www.latimes.com/archives/la-xpm-1985-11-08-mn-2778-story.html; Tim
Curran, "Reputed Mob Leaders Convicted in Casino Skimming Case," Associated Press,

January 21, 1986, https://apnews.com/article/e09494d905eb719718e5d28f8d8e066b; Balboni, *Beyond the Mafia*, pp. 32–33; Ronal Koziol, "Skimmer to Testify in Fraud Trial," *Chicago Tribune*, December 2, 1985, https://www.chicagotribune.com/news/ct-xpm -1985-12-02-8503230240-story.html.

35 *"So if these coins cost us say $20,000"* Rich Burgeron, "From Bellboy to Gambling Tycoon: How Frank Junior Built the Fertitta Empire in Las Vegas," *Writingfortruth.com*, July 11, 2010, https://writingfortruth.blogspot.com/2010/07/from-bellboy-to-gambling-tycoon -how.html.

35 *While he was being investigated, Frank Jr. developed an interest* Balboni, *Beyond the Mafia*, p. 102; Caryn Shetterly, "Vegas Heart Transplant Recepient Doing Well," *Las Vegas Review-Journal*, November 26, 1988, https://reviewjournal.newsbank.com/doc/image /v2:1508AFD0E83DBED6@NGPA-NVLVRJ-16EDBA05B0C3D50A@2447492-16EDB 823257AB26F@16-16EDB823257AB26F@?search_terms.

36 *Before the IPO launch, he transferred control of Station* Joel Gold, "The Time Has Come— The New Face of the UFC," *Full Contact Fighter*, February 2001, https://www.fcfighter .com/news0103.htm.

36 *Lorenzo had been twenty-four at the time* Graham Bensinger, "Lorenzo Fertitta: On Running a Casino at 24," *In Depth with Graham Bensinger*, https://www.youtube.com /watch?v=9A69xZfZVxM.

36 *Even after he left home at eighteen, for an undergrad program* Ibid.

36 *In December, they flew to Tokyo with White for UFC 29* McCarthy with Hunt, *Let's Get It On!*, p. 278.

36 *White had already planned to make the trip* Randy Couture, with Loretta Hunt, *Becoming the Natural: My Life In and Out of the Cage* (New York: Simon Spotlight Entertainment, 2008), p. 142.

37 *The event itself wouldn't air live in the United States* "UFC XXIX: Defense of the Belts," *Full Contact Fighter*, December 11, 2000, https://fcfighter.com/ufc-xxix-defense-of-the -belts/.

37 *Mike Goldberg and Jeff Blatnick recorded their commentary* UFC Holdings, "UFC 29: Defense of the Belts," *UFC Fight Pass*, December 16, 2000, https://ufcfightpass.com /video/33218/ufc-29-defense-of-the-belts?playlistId=1866.

37 *Lorenzo and Frank took advantage of the occasion to see* McCarthy with Hunt, *Let's Get It On!*, p. 279.

37 *After, Lorenzo and Frank III invited referee John McCarthy* Ibid., p. 279.

37 *The next day, the referee found himself on the same flight* Ibid., pp. 279–80.

37 *They would take over the UFC through a newly formed LLC* Gold, "The Time Has Come."

37 *Lorenzo and Frank III invited the few remaining key staff members* McCarthy with Hunt, *Let's Get It On!*, p. 287.

38 *"Everything these guys touch turns to gold," McCarthy remembers* Ibid., p. 287.

38 *The UFC's problems had seemed simple* Tommy Rojas, "Dana White UFC President Interview," *Primetime Fighters*, January 2001, http://www.primetimefighters.net /interview2.htm.

38 *Lorenzo estimated the new UFC* Peter Kafka, "Brothers in Arms," *Forbes*, November 11, 2002, https://www.forbes.com/forbes/2002/1111/154.html?sh=b8a6d303e44a ; Campbell McLaren, author interview.

38 *It would be more than enough to cover a rough* Kafka, "Brothers in Arms."

39 *Looking for comparable business models to emulate* Jon Show, "Tapped Out or Still Ready

to Scrap?" *Sports Business Journal*, November 3, 2008, https://www.sportsbusinessjour
nal.com/Journal/Issues/2008/11/03/SBJ-In-Depth/Tapped-Out-Or-Still-Ready-To-Scrap
.aspx?hl=ufc&sc=0; Gareth A. Davies, "UFC Owner Lorenzo Fertitta Fighting for a
Generation of Mixed Martial Artists," *Telegraph*, October 9, 2013, https://www.telegraph
.co.uk/sport/othersports/ufc/10368329/UFC-owner-Lorenzo-Fertitta-fighting-for-a-gen
eration-of-mixed-martial-artists.html.

39 *While the UFC had been stumbling toward bankruptcy* Chris Harrington, "Pure
WWF/WWE Financials 1994–2013," *Indeed Wrestling*, February 20, 2014, https://
indeedwrestling.blogspot.com/2014/02/pure-wwfwwe-financials-1994-2013.html;
Grahame Herbert, "13 Most Profitable Years in WWE History," *What Culture*,
June 24, 2016, https://whatculture.com/wwe/13-most-profitable-years-in-wwe-his
tory?page=13.

39 *WWF's wrestler contracts were notoriously restrictive* World Wide Wrestling Federation
Entertainment Inc. Booking Contract (Exhibit 10.3, circa 2000), available at https://www
.sec.gov/Archives/edgar/data/1091907/000095013000004115/0000950130-00-004115
-0002.txt.

39 *The WWF also claimed exclusive ownership* Ibid.

39 *With near total control over their wrestlers* "WWE Live Events—2000 Results," *Online
World of Wrestling*, https://www.onlineworldofwrestling.com/results/wwelive/_2000/.

39 *In larger markets, more recognizable stars* Patrick Riley, "WWF Pay-Per-Views for 2000,"
available at http://www.patrickriley.com/WWF2000.html.

40 *In Zuffa's first event—UFC 30 on February 23, 2001* UFC Holdings, "UFC 30: Battle on
the Boardwalk," February 23, 2001, https://ufcfightpass.com/video/30905/ufc-30-battle
-on-the-boardwalk?playlistId=1865.

40 *Like Lorenzo, he thought that SEG's events felt like "morgues"* Duane Finley, "The Fighting
Life: The Fire of Dana White," *Bleacher Report*, February 4, 2015, https://bleacherreport
.com/articles/1949634-the-fighting-life-the-fire-of-dana-white.

40 *With tickets that ranged from $30 to $300* Ken White, "Restoring Its Image," *Las Vegas
Review-Journal*, September 28, 2001, https://reviewjournal.newsbank.com/doc/news
/0FD3947B0F5C5FAD?search_terms.

40 *"It's expensive to go to a live event, so when someone comes to one"* Finley, "The Fighting
Life."

40 *The broadcast opened with a chorus of angry male voices* UFC Holdings, "UFC 30: Battle
on the Boardwalk."

40 *And before the main event, Zuffa had arranged for a smoky* McCarthy with Hunt, *Let's Get
It On!*, p. 328.

41 *Las Vegas lawyer Jim Gallo initially took over managerial* Tommy Rojas, "Dana White
UFC President Interview."

41 *The next major escalation would come just four months later* Aaron Crecy, "First New
Jersey, Then the World: Zuffa's Plans for the UFC Biggest Story at Pre-Fight Press
Conference," *Full Contact Fighter*, May 3, 2001, https://www.fcfighter.com/news0105
.htm.

41 *Bernie Dillon, who had previously worked* McCarthy with Hunt, *Let's Get It On!*, p. 298;
Abe Rakov, "UFC: A New Spin on Martial Arts," *Sun-Sentinel*, October 9, 2006, https://
www.sun-sentinel.com/news/fl-xpm-2006-10-09-0610080192-story.html.

41 *In March, White had also recruited Burt Watson* Burt Watson, author interview.

42 *"I knew they were playing with real strong"* Ibid.

42 *In June, Zuffa held a press conference in Manhattan* Aaron Crecy, "Big News from the Big Apple," *Full Contact Fighter*, June 27, 2001, https://fcfighter.com/big-news-from-the-big -apple/; Josh Gross, " 'New' Jersey 'Rules,' " *Full Contact Fighter*, April 4, 2001, https:// fcfighter.com/new-jersey-rules/.

42 *"I'm sure everyone here is wondering: What the hell"* Ibid.

43 *Electra would be the centerpiece of an extravagant new* Ibid.

43 *White would later claim the UFC spent $2.4 million* Steve Cooper, "Meet UFC President Dana White," *Entrepreneur,* June 21, 2007, https://www.entrepreneur.com/starting-a -business/meet-ufc-president-dana-white-entrepreneurcom/180692.

43 *Both* Entertainment Tonight *and* Extra *had sent reporters* Erich Krauss and Bret Aita, *Brawl: A Behind the Scenes Look at Mixed Martial Arts Competition* (Toronto, Ontario: ECW Press, 2002), p. 225.

43 *Dan York, In Demand's vice president of programming* Crecy, "Big News from the Big Apple."

43 *The terms of the deal were less favorable than SEG's* Gentry III, *No Holds Barred*, p. 277.

43 *But the deal would expand the UFC's market reach* Crecy, "Big News from the Big Apple."

43 *White had wanted everyone involved with the production* Cooper, "Meet UFC President Dana White."

43 *The production crew had hired a helicopter to circle the arena* UFC Holdings, "UFC 32: Showdown in the Meadowlands," *UFC Fight Pass*, June 29, 2001, https://ufcfightpass .com/video/32144/ufc-32-showdown-in-the-meadowlands?playlistId=1865.

44 *The commentators boasted that they had the biggest* McCarthy with Hunt, *Let's Get It On!*, p. 298.

45 *Three weeks later, Ortiz appeared in Las Vegas, alongside White* Aaron Crecy, "It's a TKO—Mixed Martial Arts Sanctioned in Nevada!" *Full Contact Fighter*, July 23, 2001, https://www.fcfighter.com/news0107.htm.

45 *"I'm never going to like this sport"* McCarthy with Hunt, *Let's Get It On!*, p. 299.

46 *The fights themselves would be governed by the Mixed Martial* New Jersey State Athletic Control Board, "Mixed Martial Arts Unified Rules of Conduct—Additional Mixed Martial Arts Rules," https://www.state.nj.us/lps/sacb/docs/martial.html.

47 *The Nevada Commission took the Unified Rules as a basic* Nevada Athletic Comission, Chapter 467—Unarmed Combat, https://www.leg.state.nv.us/NAC/NAC-467.html #NAC467Sec204.

47 *The following week, Zuffa officially announced the UFC's* Aaron Crecy, "UFC 33 Victory in Vegas Press Conference," *Full Contact Fighter*, September 25, 2001, https://fcfighter.com /ufc-33-victory-in-vegaspress-conference/.

47 *Lorenzo promised "one of the best cards in the history"* Ibid.

47 *The* Los Angeles Times *was one of the only major news outlets* T. J. Simers, "Keeping a Straight Face Was Real Fight," *Los Angeles Times*, August 8, 2001, https://www.latimes .com/archives/la-xpm-2001-aug-08-sp-31814-story.html.

48 *Shortly after, the card's main event appeared to* Aaron Crecy, "Freak Injury Forces Belfort Out of UFC 33—UFC 'Devastated' by Untimely News," *Full Contact Fighter*, September 19, 2001, https://www.fcfighter.com/news0109.htm.

48 *He tried to lure Frank Shamrock out of retirement for a rematch* Aaron Crecy, "Randleman to Replace Belfort at UFC 33," *Full Contact Fighter*, September 20, 2001, https://www .fcfighter.com/news0109.htm.

48 *He settled on Matyushenko, a cult favorite among fans* "UFC Light Heavyweight

Champion Tito Ortiz to Defend His Title Against Vladimir Matyushenko at UFC 33," *Full Contact Fighter*, September 21, 2001, https://www.fcfighter.com/news0109.htm.

48   *The broadcast opened with a live performance of "The Star Spangled Banner"* UFC Holdings, "UFC 33: Victory in Vegas," *UFC Fight Pass*, September 28, 2001, https://ufc fightpass.com/video/32071/ufc-33-victory-in-vegas.

49   *Two of the five would later be identified as the least* FightMetric, "Worst Title Fight Ever? Check the Numbers," *Bloody Elbow*, April 19, 2009, https://www.bloodyelbow .com/2009/4/19/845024/worst-title-fight-ever-check-the.

49   *Worse still, without any knockouts or submissions* Aaron Crecy, "The Fray at the Mandalay Bay," *Full Contact Fighter*, September 27, 2001, https://fcfighter.com/the-fray-at-manda lay-bay/.

49   *Early returns on pay-per-view sales suggested* "The Blue Book—Pay-Per-Views," *MMA Payout*, http://web.archive.org/web/20170121034505/http://mmapayout.com/blue-book /pay-per-view/.

49   *Bruce Buffer, the UFC's longtime announcer, had persuaded* Bruce Buffer, *It's Time! My 360° View of the UFC* (New York: Crown Archetype, 2013), p. 98.

49   *UFC attorney Lawrence Epstein would later hear* Lawrence Epstein, author interview.

50   *"Ted's never gonna go for this thing," Epstein recalled* Ibid.

50   *In place of cage fighting and Howard Stern specials* R. Thomas Umstead, "'02 Was Kind to PPV, VOD," *Multichannel News*, February 16, 2003, https://www.nexttv.com/news/02 -was-kind-ppv-vod-145944.

50   *With a burgeoning DVD market and dozens of new channels* John Dempsey, Meredith Amdur, "A Pay-per Tiger?" *Variety*, February 10, 2003, https://variety.com/2003/film /news/a-pay-per-tiger-1117880380/.

50   *Even boxing struggled to sustain its market reach* "HBO Will Replay Fight on Saturday," Associated Press, October 4, 2001, http://a.espncdn.com/boxing/news/2001/1004 /1259539.html; Larry Stewart and Lance Pugmire, "A Real Heavyweight in Pay-Per-View Stats," *Los Angeles Times*, May 10, 2007, https://www.latimes.com/archives/la-xpm-2007 -may-10-sp-boxing10-story.html.

50   *A $100 million co-venture between NBC and WWF* "NBC and WWE Entertainment Form Strategic Partnership for XFL," WWE.com, March 29, 2000, https://corporate.wwe .com/news/company-news/2000/03-29-2000; Larry Stewart, "XFL, NBC Working Out the Kinks," *Los Angeles Times*, February 7, 2001, https://www.latimes.com/archives/la -xpm-2001-feb-07-sp-22325-story.html.

50   *the XFL had seen its ratings drop* "PRO FOOTBALL; 54 Million Watched XFL," *New York Times*, February 7, 2001, https://www.nytimes.com/2001/02/07/sports /pro-football-54-million-watched-xfl.html; "XFL Ratings Plummet for Fourth Straight Week," Associated Press, February 25, 2001, https://www.espn.com/otherfb/news /2001/0225/1109574.html.

50   Los Angeles Times *TV critic Howard Rosenberg described* Howard Rosenberg, "XFL Kickoff Puts a Yawn in 'Smash Mouth' Football," *Los Angeles Times*, February 5, 2001, https://www.latimes.com/archives/la-xpm-2001-feb-05-ca-21219-story.html.

50   *After a disappointing ten-week season and two-round* "XFL: Xtreme Financial Loss," Reuters, May 11, 2001, https://www.wired.com/2001/05/xfl-xtreme-financial-loss/.

51   *With White and the Fertittas in charge, the UFC had managed to sell* Matthew Miller, "Ultimate Cash Machine," *Forbes*, May 5, 2008, available at http://mcqfineart.com /wp-content/uploads/2020/02/Forbes-4.5.08-UFC-F-L.pdf.

Chapter 3: No One Can Do What You Did

52 *Fighter check-in had taken place at a folding table* Couture with Hunt, *Becoming the Natural*, pp. 102–3.

52 *A small white replica UFC octagon* 207 Postcards, "Print Ad 2001 UFC Carmen Electra Chuck Liddell Tito Ortiz Back with a Vengeance," Ebay, https://www.ebay.com/itm /403394427885?hash=item5dec2e7bed:g:4ZMAAOSwKJ5h1aip.

52 *Beneath the lavish new productions and extravagant marketing* Kelsey McCarson, "Randy Couture Opens Up About Beef with Dana White," *Heavy*, May 8, 2021, https://heavy .com/sports/ufc/dana-white-beef/.

53 *They had first met in November of 2000* Couture with Hunt, *Becoming the Natural*, p. 142.

53 *The meeting had been friendly, but Couture decided* Ibid., pp. 144–46.

53 *White was eager to sign Couture to a new UFC contract* Ibid., pp. 152–53.

53 *"They were like you can't sign this contract"* Kenny Rice, "One on One with Randy Couture," AXS TV, April 2, 2016, https://www.youtube.com/watch?v=DtsCsM7GxQw.

54 *He'd stumbled into the sport on a whim* Brent Brookhouse, "Randy Couture Tells the Story of Choosing to Stay with UFC Instead of Signing with Pride," *MMA Junkie*, May 25, 2015, https://mmajunkie.usatoday.com/2015/05/randy-couture-tells-story-of-choosing -to-stay-with-ufc-instead-of-signing-with-pride.

54 *A student had showed him a tape of UFC 8* Couture with Hunt, *Becoming the Natural*, pp. 96–99.

54 *The $50,000 prize Frye won* Fernanda Prates, "With Horse Gone and Wife Leaving, Don Frye Says UFC Hall of Fame Came at the Right Time," *MMA Junkie*, June 26, 2016, https://mmajunkie.usatoday.com/2016/06/with-horse-gone-and-wife-leaving-don-frye -says-ufc-hall-of-fame-came-at-the-right-time.

54 *a friend helped Couture make an audition tape* Ibid., pp. 96–99.

54 *The prize payment had been cut down* Ibid., p. 109.

54 *By the end of the year Couture had fought* Ibid., p. 124.

54 *Couture had discovered wrestling as a junior high school* Randy Couture interview, National Wrestling Hall of Fame, Randy Couture Induction Profile, July 8, 2019, https:// nwhof.org/hall_of_fame/bio/4404.

54 *Couture loved the grueling training sessions* Couture with Hunt, *Becoming the Natural*, pp. 33–34.

55 *His father had left the family when he was just three* Ibid., p. 6.

55 *An abnormally enlarged bladder made him a chronic bedwetter* Ibid., p. 27.

55 *Couture also suffered from severe asthma* Ibid., p. 12.

55 *"I heard stories my whole life about my father"* Randy Couture Interview, National Wrestling Hall of Fame Induction Profile.

55 *After graduating high school, he earned a spot on the wrestling team* Couture with Hunt, *Becoming the Natural*, pp. 42–44.

56 *He found one in the army* Ibid., p. 46; Joseph B. Treaster, "13,000 Air Controllers Defy Reagan Dismissal Deadline, 72% of Flights in Operation," *New York Times*, August 5, 1981, https://www.nytimes.com/1981/08/05/nyregion/13000-air-controllers-defy-reagan -dismissal-deadline-72-of-flights-in.html.

56 *Shortly after Sharon gave birth to their son* Couture with Hunt, *Becoming the Natural*, pp. 51–54.

56 *He was surprised to learn the base* Randy Couture Interview, National Wrestling Hall of Fame Induction Profile.

56 *After a little over a year on base* Couture with Hunt, *Becoming the Natural*, pp. 55–62.

56 *Couture moved to Fort Dix in New Jersey* Ibid., pp. 59–66.

56 *Though he wouldn't travel with the team to Seoul* Ibid., pp. 67–73.

57 *He qualified as an all-American in three of his four years* Randy Couture Alumni Biography, Oklahoma State University website, https://cas.okstate.edu/honors/alumni/distinguished-alumni/randy-couture.html.

57 *In 1992, Couture was chosen as first alternate* Couture with Hunt, *Becoming the Natural*, p. 81.

57 *The salary was less than half what he would* Ibid., p. 70 ("At home, Sharon and I never discussed me going back to school. She seemed happy with whatever I wanted to do and she never gave me a hard time about it," ibid., p. 76).

57 *Though he and Sharon rarely fought* Ibid., p. 76.

57 *In his first year at Oregon State* Ibid., p. 84.

58 *After a brief attempt to save their marriage* Ibid., pp. 86–87.

58 *Less than a year later Couture won his first UFC tournament* Mayeda and Ching, *Fighting for Acceptance*, p. 84.

58 *Couture felt ambivalent about his early experiences* Couture with Hunt, *Becoming the Natural*, pp. 124–26.

59 *When Lowney went on to win a bronze medal* Garrett Lowney Profile, Wisconsin Wrestling Hall of Fame, https://wiwrestlinghofhonorees.org/alpha/l/lowney-garrett/.

59 *"I was now thirty-six years old, watching a young kid"* Couture with Hunt, *Becoming the Natural*, p. 133.

59 *The tournament would take place in Tokyo* Ibid., pp. 127–31.

59 *Perretti eventually agreed, and a little over* Ibid., pp. 135–36.

59 *She had just entered the final year of her master's program* Ibid., pp. 163–66.

59 *In his first fight under the new Zuffa banner* Ibid., pp. 154–55.

60 *The kicks were so forceful they would leave* Ibid., p. 151.

60 *He was shocked, then, to discover* Ibid., pp. 153–54.

60 *"Back with a vengeance!" the ad copy read* Ebay listing reference, https://www.ebay.com/itm/403521739265?hash=item5df3c51a01:g:52IAAOSwkEFeO~3D.

60 *A few weeks later, he learned* Couture with Hunt, *Becoming the Natural*, p. 153.

61 *Even as a new recruit in boot camp* Ibid., p. 49.

61 *With lingering uncertainty of what his life would look like* Ibid., p. 135.

Chapter 4: There Is No Plan B

63 *Seated at the ringside commentary table* Levi Nile, "MMA in 2003: A Retroactive Look at the Sport a Decade Later," *Bleacher Report*, December 17, 2013, https://bleacherreport.com/articles/1892894-mma-in-2003-a-retrospective-look-at-the-sport-a-decade-later.

63 *To cover up the thousands of empty seats* Joe Rogan, "Episode 327 – Dana White," *The Joe Rogan Experience*, February 20, 2013, https://open.spotify.com/episode/7FLIl7U9bjuPvz9vxdeoZH.

63 *White had traveled to Japan with two of the UFC's best fighters* Zuffa LLC, *UFC 25 Years: A Matter of Pride*, documentary video series, UFC Fight Pass, June 3, 2019.

64 *As Liddell walked through the characteristically silent Japanese crowd* Dana White (audio commentary track), *Pride Total Elimination 2003*, August 10, 2003, https://ufcfightpass.com/video/34257/chuck-liddell-vs-alistair-overeem-pride-total-elimination-2003.

64 *In 2002, White succeeded in getting the UFC on standard cable* Josh Hedges/Zuffa LLC,

"Ultimate Fighting Championship to Air Weekly Show on Sky Sports in UK, Ireland, Starting on Feb. 7," *Full Contact Fighter*, February 5, 2002, https://www.fcfighter.com/news0202.htm.

64 *He'd also secured a deal with Wowow* Josh Hedges/Zuffa LLC, "UFC to Broadcast Fights on Wowow-TV in Japan, Globosat in Brazil Starting in March, April," *Full Contact Fighter*, March 2, 2002, https://www.fcfighter.com/news0203.htm.

64 *The Brazilian cable and satellite TV giant Globosat* Ibid.

64 *In June of 2002, it seemed like White was on the verge* Jonathan Snowden, "The First Time: This Isn't the UFC's First Foray on Fox," *SB Nation*, August 19, 2011, https://mma.sbnation.com/2011/8/19/2372250/UFC-on-Fox-MMA-news-Joe-Rogan-first-foray-on-fox.

64 *Eager to take advantage of the opportunity* Josh Hedges/Zuffa LLC, "UFC to Debut on Network Television June 25 on FSN's Best Damn Sports Show Period 'All-Star Summer' Celebration," *Full Contact Fighter*, June 17, 2002, https://www.fcfighter.com/news0206.htm.

64 *The episode had proved unexpectedly popular* Loretta Hunt, "For MMA Fans, August 4th's UFC Special Will Be 'As Real As It Gets,'" *Full Contact Fighter*, August 3, 2002, https://www.fcfighter.com/news0208.htm; Dana White, "UFC on Fox Sports' Sunday Night Fights!!," Open Letter, *Full Contact Fighter*, July 29, 2002, https://www.fcfighter.com/news0207.htm.

65 *A few months later, it seemed as if White* Bill Simmons, "Sodom, Gomorrah, and the UFC," *ESPN The Magazine*, November 2002, https://www.espn.com/espn/page2/story?page=simmons/021001.

65 *The promotion had a lucrative broadcasting deal with Fuji TV* N/A, "Ten highest rated Japanese MMA matches," *Yahoo! Sports*, December 21, 2007, https://news.yahoo.com/news/ten-highest-rated-japanese-mma-182200552—spt.html?guccounter=2 ; N/A, "NBA Conference Finals Ratings History (2000-Present)," *Sports Media Watch*, https://www.sportsmediawatch.com/nba-conference-finals-ratings-eastern-western/; Richard Sandomir, "TV Sports; World Series Ratings Are the Lowest Ever," *New York Times*, October 30, 2002, https://www.nytimes.com/2002/10/30/sports/tv-sports-world-series-ratings-are-the-lowest-ever.html.

65 *Before the individual championships were introduced in 2001* List of Pride Champions, Wikipedia, https://en.wikipedia.org/wiki/List_of_Pride_Fighting_Championships_champions.

66 *Sakuraba had become a cult favorite* Lee Daly, *Before a Fall: A History of Pride Fighting Championships*, 2018, pp. 97–112.

66 *In 2001, White had helped sign Anderson Silva* Eduardo Alonso, "Anderson Silva vs. Carlos Newton OFF!" *Full Contact Fighter*, October 4, 2001, https://www.fcfighter.com/news0110.htm.

66 *A month before his scheduled debut* FCF Staff, "The Other Side . . . ," *Full Contact Fighter*, October 4, 2001, https://fcfighter.com/fcf-caption-contest-8/.

66 *On weekends when Pride had an event* Joe Rogan, "Episode 327 – Dana White," *The Joe Rogan Experience*, February 20, 2013, https://open.spotify.com/episode/7FLIl7U9bjuPvz9vxdeoZH.

66 *In an interview, Joel Gold* Gentry III, *No Holds Barred*, p. 284.

66 *Jeff Sherwood, who created and ran Sherdog.com* Jeff Sherwood, author interview.

66 *In 2002, he'd tried to orchestrate a title fight* Micah Brown, "30 for 30: Chuck & Tito," ESPN, October 15, 2019, https://www.espn.com/watch/player/_/id/3610954.

67   *"I guess we gotta renegotiate things"* UFC Holdings, "UFC 40: Vendetta," November 22, 2002, https://ufcfightpass.com/video/30404/ufc-40-vendetta?playlistId=3422.

67   *White would later say that trying to negotiate* Robbie Fox, "Dana White Talks Conor McGregor's Return, Jorge Masvidal vs Nate Diaz and More with Barstool Sports," Barstool Sports YouTube Channel, September 19, 2019, https://www.youtube.com /watch?v=WeO0K2PdT7Q.

67   *Ortiz had reportedly wanted a new deal worth $1.1 million* Ivan Trembow, "Full Story on Mir Being Stripped of Title," *MMA Weekly,* August 13, 2005, https://www.mmaweekly .com/full-story-on-mir-being-stripped-of-title.

67   *When Ortiz turned down a $160,000 offer* Ortiz, *This Is Gonna Hurt,* p. 131.

67   *the last of which had left him with a shattered orbital bone* Couture with Hunt, *Becoming the Natural,* p. 170.

67   *He had only one fight remaining on his UFC contract* Ibid.

67   *"Unbelievable!" Rogan said on the broadcast commentary* UFC Holdings, "UFC 43: Meltdown," *UFC Fight Pass,* June 6, 2003, https://ufcfightpass.com/video/31226/ufc-43 -meltdown?playlistId=3531.

69   *While revenues had risen* John S. Nash, "What We Now Know About the UFC's Finances," *Bloody Elbow,* September 9, 2019, https://www.bloodyelbow.com/2019/9/9 /20851990/what-we-now-know-about-the-ufc-finances.

69   *Production costs for 2002 had been more than $10 million* Peter Kafka, "Brothers in Arms," *Forbes,* November 11, 2002, https://www.forbes.com/forbes/2002/1111/154.html ?sh=60abc6923e44.

70   *"The miscalculation was that it's not the same sport that it was before"* FCF Staff, "Lorenzo Fertitta Interview," *Full Contact Fighter,* October 2002, https://fcfighter.com/pick-up-the -october-2002-issue-of-fcf-today/.

70   *He'd crisscrossed the country for "meet-and-greets" at local pubs* Josh Hedges/Zuffa LLC, "UFC Meet and Greet Schedule," *Full Contact Fighter,* September 18, 2001, https://www .fcfighter.com/news0109.htm.

70   *"I don't care if three people show up"* Loretta Hunt, "UFC Meet-n-Greet Charms New York," *Full Contact Fighter,* January 8, 2002, https://www.fcfighter.com/news0201.htm.

70   *Lewis and his two friends he'd enlisted* Michael Lev-Ram, "A $200 Million Headlock on Mixed Martial Arts," *CNN Money,* August 18, 2010, https://money.cnn.com/2010/08/18 /smallbusiness/tapout/index.htm.

70   *"Mixed martial arts and fighting didn't have any identity"* Andrew Galvin, "Tapout Founder 'Mask' to Be Memorialized at Service Today," *Orange County Register,* April 12, 2009, https://www.ocregister.com/2009/04/12/tapout-founder-mask-to-be-memorial ized-at-service-today/.

70   *The company was run mostly on cash* Bobby Razak, *Mask: The Life and Times of Charles Mask Lewis* (Razak Sport Films, 2018).

71   *"There is no Plan B," Caldwell would later say* Jonathan Snowden, "The TapouT Crew Remembers Charles 'Mask' Lewis," *Bloody Elbow,* March 11, 2011, https://www. bloodyelbow.com/2011/3/11/2037545/tapout-mask-death-interview-skyskrape-punk ass-charles-lewis.

71   *Lewis hadn't paid anything for the placement* Andrew Warner, "How Dan Caldwell Grew TapouT from Nothing to $100,000 in Revenue," *Mixergy,* August 31, 2015, https:// mixergy.com/interviews/dan-caldwell-tapout/.

72   *Rogan had briefly worked as the UFC's backstage interviewer* Campbell McLaren, author interview.

72 *At nineteen, he had won the US Open Taekwondo Championships Black Belt* Staff, "Joe Rogan Owes His Success to Taekwondo, Thai Boxing and Brazilian Jiu-Jitsu," *Black Belt*, January 21, 2019, https://blackbeltmag.com/joe-rogan-martial-arts.

72 *They would often end up at dinner together after fights* Joe Rogan video interview with Sherdog/Greg Savage, YouTube, February 8, 2007, https://www.youtube.com/watch?v=KgK1Hilokqk.

72 *Jeff Blatnick was let go after UFC 32* McCarthy with Hunt, *Let's Get It On!*, pp. 290–91.

73 *He was told by executive producer Steve Tornabene* Jeff Osborne, *MMA Underground*, https://www.mixedmartialarts.com/forums/UnderGround/Why-Did-Jeff-Osbourne-Get-Fired:1066918.

73 *He had already attained a level of celebrity* "Fear Factor Tops Nielsen Ratings," Associated Press, August 8, 2001, https://www.mediapost.com/publications/article/12636/fear-factor-tops-nielsen-ratings.html.

73 *Rogan described himself as a "professional fan"* Joe Rogan interview, YouTube, https://www.youtube.com/watch?v=vPPMW8bsP48.

74 *White had helped create Zuffa Records* Profile Page, "UFC Ultimate Beat Downs, Vol. 1," *All Music*, August 24, 2004, https://www.allmusic.com/album/release/ufc-ultimate-beat-downs-vol-1-mr0001227409.

74 *A Las Vegas producer who was working with Zuffa Records* Tim Bissell, "How 'Face the Pain' Became the Sound of the UFC," *Bloody Elbow*, February 26, 2017, https://www.bloodyelbow.com/2016/11/7/13260198/how-face-the-pain-became-sound-of-ufc-stemm-mma-interview-history-music-zuffa-dana-ortiz-shamrock.

75 *In addition to selling CDs, White had also hoped* J. Michael Plott, "Xtreme Fighting: The State of the UFC," *Black Belt*, April 2003.

75 *White had seen Don Gold's name in the credits* Don Gold, author interview.

78 *Despite all of White's efforts to build a more organic business* Nash, "What We Now Know About the UFC's Finances."

78 *In some months, when Zuffa's accounts had been depleted* Don Gold, author interview.

78 *The size of the losses from the UFC had unsettled Frank III* UFC Holdings, "Three Guys and Three Letters."

78 *While the UFC's losses were a small fraction* Station Casinos Investor Report 2003, http://media.corporate-ir.net/media_files/irol/10/103083/2003ar.pdf.

79 *White hadn't taken the differences seriously as a teenager* "UFC Boss Fights the Clock."

79 *"Let me tell you the difference between you and all these fucking rich kids"* Erik Hedegaard, "What Is UFC President Dana White Fighting For?" *Rolling Stone*, June 12, 2008, https://www.rollingstone.com/culture/culture-features/ufc-dana-white-mma-940798/.

79 *Lorenzo had begun second-guessing the decision* Straka, "Fighting Words: Interview with Lorenzo Fertitta."

79 *When White gave him the short list of potential buyers* Steve Cooper, "Meet UFC President Dana White," *Entrepreneur*, June 21, 2007, https://www.entrepreneur.com/article/180692.

79 *There had been some interest—including from Dan Lambert* Marc Raimondi, "American Top Team Owner Admits UFC Wouldn't Have Been As Big As It Is Now If He Had Bought It," *MMA Fighting*, July 7, 2015, https://www.mmafighting.com/2015/7/7/8904565/merican-top-team-owner-admits-ufc-wouldn't-have-been-as-big-as-it-is.

79 *"We hadn't lost at anything," Lorenzo would say of the dilemma* Mike Straka, "Fighting Words: Interview with Lorenzo Fertitta," March 6, 2011, https://www.youtube.com/watch?v=zLQ7Bkp8UZw.

79 *"Fuck it," Lorenzo told White, after he'd made up his mind* UFC Holdings, *Three Guys and Three Letters.*

80 *Barter deals had first become popular in the 1980s* Richard W. Stevenson, "Bartering for TV Ad Time," *New York Times*, August 3, 1985, https://www.nytimes.com/1985/08/03/business/bartering-for-tv-ad-time.html.

81 *The first idea was for an hour-long show of fights* Kevin Kay, author interview.

81 *Executives from ABC, NBC, Fox, MTV, and ESPN* Luke O'Brien, "UFC Tries to Prove It's Capable of a Knockout," *Fast Company*, November 18, 2012, https://www.fastcompany.com/3002947/ufc-tries-prove-its-capable-knockout.

81 *When White and Lorenzo walked into Kevin Kay's office* Kevin Kay, author interview.

81 *He'd thought he'd found one with* Slamball Lily Oei, " 'Slamball' Hits Pay Dirt," *Variety*, August 7, 2003, https://variety.com/2003/tv/news/slamball-hits-pay-dirt-1117890556/.

82 *He'd taken meetings with promoters for a roller derby league* Kevin Kay, author interview.

82 *"The first meeting was not particularly good"* Ibid.

82 *By 2000, TNN was available in more than seventy-eight million* Sally Beatty, "New TNN Embraces Populist Culture, Hopes to Dethrone Cable Ratings Kings," *Wall Street Journal*, October 5, 2000, https://www.wsj.com/articles/SB970703012437628882.

83 *Instead of keeping both channels running* Albie Hecht, author interview; Allison Romano, "TNN Hopes Mainly Men Will Watch 'Spike TV,' " *Broadcasting & Cable*, April 21, 2003, http://broadcastingcable.com/article/CA293348.html.

83 *At the time, no demographic was more desirable than* Ibid.

83 *Men between eighteen and thirty-four were the least likely demographic* "Marketers Take Note: The Elusive 18-34 Year-Old Is Habitually Online," *Comscore*, March 29, 2004, https://www.comscore.com/Insights/Press-Releases/2004/03/18-34-Year-Olds-Are-Habitually-Online.

83 *"We found that men were looking for a new identity"* Albie Hecht, author interview.

83 *The real hourly wage for the average American had remained almost unchanged* Lawrence Mishel, Elise Gould, and Josh Bivens, "Wage Stagnation in Nine Charts," Economic Policy Institute, January 6, 2015, https://www.epi.org/publication/charting-wage-stagnation/.

84 *By 2004, the average US household had more than $7,000 in credit card debt* Alex Morrell, "Americans Haven't Had This Much Credit Card Debt Since the Eve of the Financial Crisis," *Business Insider*, December 16, 2016, https://www.businessinsider.com/american-credit-card-debt-nearing-all-time-highs-2016-12.

84 *Hecht had created Spike to speak to this generation of men* Albie Hecht, author interview.

84 *The most popular programming on Spike* "Spike TV Highlights—November 2004," press release, Spike TV, October 12, 2004, http://www.thefutoncritic.com/news/2004/10/12/spike-tv-highlights-november-2004—17069/20041012spiketv01/.

84 *There was also* The Club: Jack Colton, "Nightclub Obituaries," *Las Vegas Weekly*, October 2, 2008, https://lasvegasweekly.com/nightlife/2008/oct/02/nightclub-obituaries/.

85 *Viacom had given Spike a programming budget of $75 million* Albie Hecht, author interview; Kevin Kay, author interview.

85 *Nearly a third of the budget—an estimated $24 million* Denise Martin, "Spike TV Smacks Down WWE," *Variety*, March 10, 2005, https://variety.com/2005/scene/markets-festivals/spike-tv-smacks-down-wwe-1117919243/.

85 *Frustrated by the response, Lorenzo and White decided to invite Kay* Kevin Kay, author interview.

86 *For Kay, it was a dealmaking night* Ibid.

Chapter 5: A Reverse Socialization Process

87 *White convened a meeting with Piligian and Zuffa's small production team* Childs Walker, "Fighting to Be the Ring Leader," *Baltimore Sun,* July 30, 2006, https://www.baltimore sun.com/news/bs-xpm-2006-07-30-0607290332-story.html.

87 *Instead of a behind-the-scenes documentary series* Kevin Kay, author interview.

87 *Piligian put together a budget and shooting schedule* Dana White, Speech at Stanford Graduate School of Business, April 18, 2013, https://www.youtube.com/watch?v=94w2l wU-To0.

88 *Ortiz and Ken Shamrock* were the first chosen Loretta Hunt, "The Ultimate Fighter Origins, Part 1," *Sports Illustrated,* December 1, 2011, https://www.si.com/mma/2011/12 /01/tuf-origin.

88 *Zuffa offered each $800 a week* Chuck Liddell, with Chad Millman, *Iceman: My Fighting Life* (New York: Dutton, 2008), p. 224.

88 *White and Joe Silva spent much of the spring and early summer* Bob Cook, Mike Swick, Kevin Kay, author interviews.

88 *Two of Couture's training partners were offered parts* Couture with Hunt, *Becoming the Natural,* p. 198.

88 *White found another candidate when he stopped by a local gym* Michael Rothstein, "The Inside Story of How 'The Ultimate Fighter' Saved the UFC 15 Years Ago," *ESPN,* April 9, 2020, https://www.espn.com/mma/story/_/id/29014001/the-story-how-ultimate-fighter -saved-ufc-15-years-ago.

88 *On a trip to Boston, White recruited Kenny Florian* Eddie Matta, "How Dana White Discovered UFC Fighter Kenny Florian," *Where Are They Now in Sports with Eddie Matta,* October 4, 2014, https://www.youtube.com/watch?v=MWW5m1jeWSM.

88 *As White was casting, Lorenzo grew anxious* Maria Elena Fernandez and Scott Collins, "No Contender, He's the Champ," *Los Angeles Times,* May 17, 2004, https://www .latimes.com/archives/la-xpm-2004-may-17-et-burnett17-story.html; Kevin Kay, author interview.

88 *But Spike had already set its schedule for the fall and spring* Kevin Kay, author interview.

89 *Because Vince McMahon had a special agreement* Ibid.

89 *The number of contestants had been cut* Rothstein, "The Inside Story."

90 *The production team had filled the warehouse* Dana White interview, "Dana White UFC Apex Opening Media Scrum," *MMA Fighting,* June 18, 2019, https://www.youtube.com /watch?v=i9NUHBuiigk.

90 *"That's a dumb thing to say you got injured by"* Mike Swick, author interview.

90 *Though no one from the crew told the cast members* Ibid.

91 *"We were kind of just stuck in the moment"* Rothstein, "The Inside Story."

91 *"This is a business," Karalexis said* Ibid.

91 *"I literally walked out of a meeting, jumped in my car"* Ibid.

91 *"I'm not happy right now," White told the fighters* UFC Holdings, *The Ultimate Fighter,* Season 1, Episode Three, https://ufcfightpass.com/video/29715/tuf-1-ep3-making -weight?playlistId=1705.

92 *White knew as soon as he walked out of the gym* Rothstein, "The Inside Story."

93 *White had always been kind and cordial* Tommy Rojas, author interview.

93 *Swick had an apartment and car, but had been working three jobs* Mike Swick, author interview.

93 *For Quarry, there was no work to go back to* Rothstein, "The Inside Story."

93 *A production trailer was parked next to the house* Hunt, "The Ultimate Fighter Origins, Part 1."

93 *"There was a term they used called 'conserve reality'"* Mike Swick, author interview.

94 *Producer Andrea Richter described the filming as a psychological experiment* Neil Davidson, "A Look Behind the Scenes on the Set of 'The Ultimate Fighter,'" *Canadian Press*, March 31, 2009, https://www.cp24.com/a-look-behind-the-scenes-on-the-set-of -the-ultimate-fighter-1.384764.

94 *"That's the thing that outsiders don't necessarily know"* Ibid.

94 *Forrest Griffin, a former college football player from Georgia* Rothstein, "The Inside Story."

94 *They were treated to dinner at the Hard Rock Hotel and Casino* UFC Holdings, *The Ultimate Fighter*, Season 1, Episode Five.

94 *As hard a drinker as his son, Leben's father had abandoned* Chris Leben, with Daniel J. Patinkin, *The Crippler: Cage Fighting and My Life on the Edge* (New York: Skyhorse, 2017), pp. 13–14.

96 *While Spike didn't have marketing funds available* Kevin Kay, author interview.

96 *The first episode more than doubled that number* Hunt, "The Ultimate Fighter Origins, Part 2."

96 *According to White, Spike had also agreed to a full-page advertisement* Rothstein, "The Inside Story."

97 *Before the light heavyweight finale, White went into the locker rooms* Ibid.

97 *"You had Nobody Special Average Joe One versus"* UFC Holdings, *Fight Lore: Accidental Saviors—Griffin vs Bonnar*, video documentary, https://ufcfightpass.com/video /146028?playlistId=3798.

98 *As a teenager, Griffin had dreamed of becoming a star football player* UFC Holdings, *Finding Forrest: The Story of Forrest Griffin*, June 7, 2019, https://www.youtube.com /watch?v=n2fnUiAZL9Q.

98 *He had tried to add muscle* Frank Curreri, "Lunch with Forrest Griffin," UFC.com, April 19, 2012, https://www.ufc.com/news/lunch-forrest-griffin.

99 *Griffin had quit the team and taken a job as a campus police officer* Dan Arritt, "Keeping a Low Profile," *Los Angeles Times*, July 4, 2008, https://www.latimes.com/archives/la-xpm -2008-jul-04-sp-mma4-story.html.

99 *"What have I done?" he thought* UFC Holdings, *Finding Forrest*.

99 *He called one of the producers from the airport* Bob Emanuel Jr., "Forrest Griffin Entering UFC Hall of Fame," *Newsday*, June 27, 2013, https://www.newsday.com/sports/mixed -martial-arts/forrest-griffin-entering-ufc-hall-of-fame-a25544.

100 *As Griffin and Bonnar celebrated with their families* Kevin Kay, author interview.

100 *As the production crew began disassembling the cage* Ibid.

101 *When the ratings for the* Ultimate Fighter *finale came out* Hunt, "The Ultimate Fighter Origins, Part 2."

101 *The Tapout website crashed shortly after the episode ended* Warner, "How Dan Caldwell Grew TapouT."

101 *A week later, when Couture and Liddell fought* "UFC Pay-Per-View Buys Explode in 2006," *MMA Weekly*, July 13, 2006, https://www.mmaweekly.com/ufc-pay-per-view -buys-explode-in-2006.

101 *All together, the event generated almost as much* Nash, "What We Now Know About the UFC's Finances."

101 *"We got people watching mixed martial arts"* Childs Walker, "Fighting to Be the Ring Leader," *Baltimore Sun*, July 30, 2006, https://www.baltimoresun.com/news/bs-xpm -2006-07-30-0607290332-story.html.

101 *Ari Emanuel had first read about* The Ultimate Fighter's *breakout ratings* UFC Holdings, "Agents of Change: The Story of the Biggest Deal in Sports History."

102 *Joy Harris, a literary agent who worked with Emanuel* William D. Cohan, "The Inside Story of Ari Emanuel's Big, Risky WME-IMG Merger," *Vanity Fair*, March 2015, https:// www.vanityfair.com/news/2015/02/wme-img-merger-ari-emanuel.

102 *Before they could finalize their plans, ICM president Jeff Berg* Claudia Eller and James Bates, "ICM Fires 4 Top Agents Who Planned to Form Rival Agency" *Los Angeles Times*, March 30, 1995, https://www.latimes.com/archives/la-xpm-1995-03-30-fi-48968-story .html.

102 *Asked about his career goals in an early profile* Borys Kit, "Backlot: 80 Years of The Hollywood Reporter," *Hollywood Reporter*, November 17, 2010, https://www.holly woodreporter.com/business/business-news/backlot-80-years-hollywood-reporter -45138/.

102 *White hated Emanuel when they first met* UFC Holdings, "Agents of Change."

103 *As a test to see whether Emanuel could deliver* Ibid.

103 *Seth Abraham, who had signed Mike Tyson* Thomas Hauser, "HBO Boxing: The Challenge," *Seconds Out*, https://www.secondsout.com/features/main-features/hbo-box ing-the-challenge.

103 *"What I see with the UFC are bar fights"* Walker, "Fighting to Be the Ring Leader."

103 *Albrecht had built his career on gambling* Amy Wallace, "Violence, Nudity, Adult Content: The Story of Chris Albrecht," *GQ*, November 2010, https://www.gq.com/story/chris -albrecht-profile-2010.

103 Sopranos *creator David Chase described him* Ibid.

103 *One of Albrecht's worries was HBO's audience aging out* Steven Zeitchik, "HBO: Just the Same, but Different," *Variety*, June 22, 2007, https://web.archive.org /web/20080303230020/http://www.variety.com/article/VR1117967504.html?category Id=2526&cs=1.

103 *Negotiations began grudgingly, in the spring of 2006: MMA Weekly* Staff, "UFC Reaches Deal with HBO," *MMA Weekly*, April 17, 2007, https://www.mmaweekly.com/ufc-reach es-deal-with-hbo-2.

104 *HBO would handle the production of each UFC event it aired* Lawrence Epstein, author interview.

104 *That was a problem for the UFC, which had always managed* John Morgan, "Bruce Connal, Who Spent 20 Years Producing UFC Broadcasts, Remembered by MMA, Sports World," *MMA Junkie*, March 5, 2018, https://mmajunkie.usatoday.com/2018/03/bruce -connal-ufc-producer-remembered-by-mma-sports-world.

104 *To Lampley, a longtime sports commentator* Salvatore Difalco, "Talking to Jim Lampley," *Toro Magazine*, January 27, 2009, http://web.archive.org/web/20090202141946/http:// toromagazine.com/?q=node/1224.

104 *After having invested so much time and money to modernize* Lawrence Epstein, author interview.

104 *The HBO team wanted to change almost everything* Ibid.

105 *Though international broadcasting deals were a fraction* Nash, "What We Now Know About the UFC's Finances."

105 *In October of 2006, Zuffa hired Marshall Zelaznik* MCN Staff, "In Demand's Zelaznik Jumps to UFC," *Multichannel News*, August 11, 2006, https://www.nexttv.com/news/demands-zelaznik-jumps-ufc-332288.

105 *"I didn't quite understand mixed martial arts and I didn't quite understand UFC"* "UFC: Fighting Its Way to the Mainstream," *Sports Pro Media*, February 3, 2010, http://web.archive.org/web/20180825194246/http://www.sportspromedia.com/analysis/ufc_fighting_its_way_to_the_mainstream.

105 *One of the first breakthroughs in Europe* Ivan Trembow, "UFC 70 Will Air on Spike TV with Tape Delay," *MMA Weekly*, March 13, 2007, https://www.mmaweekly.com/ufc-70-will-air-on-spike-tv-with-tape-delay-2.

106 *With the deadlines already passed to book time* Ibid.

106 *In 2005, just as* The Ultimate Fighter *was peaking* Denise Martin, "Spike TV Smacks Down WWE," *Variety*, March 10, 2005, https://variety.com/2005/scene/markets-festivals/spike-tv-smacks-down-wwe-1117919243/.

106 *While Zuffa had only four people working full-time* Max Miceli, "Minding My Business with UFC VP/Event Production Tim O'Toole," *Sports Business Journal*, August 31, 2016, https://www.sportsbusinessjournal.com/Daily/Issues/2016/08/31/People-and-Pop-Culture/MMB.aspx.

106 *Paul Cambria was a post-production supervisor at Echo* Paul Cambria, author interview.

107 *In 2006, the UFC's annual revenue swelled* Nash, "What We Now Know About the UFC's Finances."

107 *The finale of the third season of* The Ultimate Fighter Ivan Trembow, "Ortiz-Shamrock Shatters UFC Ratings Records," *MMA Weekly*, October 12, 2006, https://www.mmaweekly.com/ortiz-shamrock-shatters-ufc-ratings-records-2.

107 *The UFC also overtook both the WWE and HBO Sports* "UFC Wrestles a Share of Paying Viewers," Associated Press, March 1, 2007, https://www.dailynews.com/2007/03/01/ufc-wrestles-a-share-of-paying-viewers/.

107 *Lorenzo would later say he had a "gut feel"* C. J. Tuttle, "Lorenzo Fertitta on Learning from WWE, TUF United Kingdom, UFC Fighter Pay, and Selling Adrenaline" *MMA Mania*, March 9, 2014, https://www.mmamania.com/2014/3/9/5480468/ufc-video-lorenzo-fertitta-learning-from-wwe-tuf-united-kingdom-fighter-pay-mma.

108 *In May of 2007, the UFC lost its biggest advocate* Jacques Steinberg, "HBO's Chief, Chris Albrecht, Resigns Over Assaulting Girlfriend," *New York Times*, May 10, 2007, https://www.nytimes.com/2007/05/10/technology/10iht-hbo.1.5646579.html.

108 *In the weeks that followed, rumors circulated* Ibid.; also Nikki Finke, "What Happens in HBO, Stays in HBO . . . But Should It?" *Deadline*, May 9, 2007, https://deadline.com/2007/05/what-happens-in-hbo-stays-in-hbo-2157/

108 *In September, Albrecht officially cut ties with HBO* Reuters Staff, "Former HBO Chief Joins Talent Agency IMG," Reuters, September 17, 2007, https://www.reuters.com/article/img-albrecht-idUKN1729132320070917.

108 *In public, White continued to hint that negotiations* Dan Rafael, "HBO Says Talks to Broadcast UFC Cards Fall Apart," *ESPN*, October 6, 2007, https://www.espn.com/extra/mma/news/story?id=3051318.

108 *Despite the failure, White and Lorenzo had grown to trust Emanuel* UFC Holdings, "Agents of Change."

108 *For John McCarthy, all of the changes and new faces* McCarthy with Hunt, *Let's Get It On!*, pp. 375–77.

Chapter 6: Problem Child

110 *In the days leading up to the event* Nick Diaz, post-fight interview with Sherdog/Josh Gross, February 24, 2007 ("Actually I felt like I was having deja vu in there or something weird like that when I was fighting, because I had already fucking done all that shit, you know, replayed it or thought about it in my head again again"), https://www.youtube.com/watch?v=2CS5NWKrROw.

110 *The audience was filled with celebrities* UFC Holdings, "Pride 33: The Second Coming," February 24, 2007, https://ufcfightpass.com/video/32588/pride-33-the-second-coming.

110 *Backstage, the event staff addressed the twenty-three-year-old* Nick Diaz interview, "Nick Diaz Talks Ring vs. Cage, Pride vs. UFC, and Much More," *NickDiaz.TV*, February 25, 2007, https://www.youtube.com/watch?v=5O95Q42UoeY.

110 *"I look at my career, and past things"* Ibid.

111 *"I was meant to fight," he would later say* Josh Gross, "Born to Brawl," Sherdog, November 8, 2007, http://www.sherdog.com/news/articles.asp?n_id=9858.

111 *White had hoped Nick would help promote* Geno Mrosko, "Nick Diaz Problems with UFC Stem from Refusal to Go on 'Blind Date' Reality Show," *MMA Mania*, May 11, 2011, https://www.mmamania.com/2011/5/11/2165176/nick-diaz-problems-with-ufc-stem-from-refusal-to-go-on-blind-date.

111 *One of the show's field producers had been an avid UFC fan* Loretta Hunt, "UFC Fighters Get 'Blind Dates,' " *Full Contact Fighter*, July 23, 2004, https://www.fcfighter.com/ufc-blinddate-040723.htm.

111 *To Nick, it sounded like a terrible idea* Steve Heath, author interview.

111 *White was indignant that Nick wasn't willing* Ibid.

111 *"Nick was like, Fuck you and your stupid show"* Ibid.

112 *When Nick was finally booked for a live broadcast* Thomas Gerbasi, "Nick Diaz—100% Fighter," UFC.com, November 2005, https://www.ufc.com/news/flashback-nick-diaz-meets-diego-sanchez.

112 *"He gets on a TV show and then he wins one fight"* UFC Holdings, *The Ultimate Fighter*, Season 2 Finale, November 5, 2005, https://ufcfightpass.com/video/28963/diego-sanchez-vs-nick-diaz-tuf-2-finale.

112 *Nick turned the offer down* "UFC 62: Diaz to Replace Alves," Sherdog, August 22, 2006, http://web.archive.org/web/20061019234136/http://www.sherdog.com/news/news.asp?n_id=5362.

113 *The performances drew attention from Pride's matchmakers* Ivan Trembow, "Nick Diaz Signs with Pride," *MMA Weekly*, January 20, 2007, https://www.mmaweekly.com/nick-diaz-signs-with-pride-2.

113 *In the summer of 2006, Pride had abruptly lost* Zach Arnold, "Fuji TV Cancels Pride for Good," *Fight Opinion*, June 5, 2005, http://web.archive.org/web/20060615172310/http://www.fightopinion.com/2006/06/05/fuji-tv-cancels-pride-for-good/.

113 *The series, published over the course of several months* Lee Daly, *Before a Fall: A History of Pride Fighting Championships* (Middletown, DE: CreateSpace, 2018), pp. 195–208; also Jonathan Snowden, "Sex, Drugs, Gangsters, and MMA: Remembering Pride, UFC's Wild Predecessor," *Bleacher Report*, July 6, 2017, https://bleacherreport.com/articles/2718986-sex-drugs-gangsters-and-mma-remembering-pride-ufcs-wild-predecessor.

113 *The company had a disappointing debut event* Ivan Trembow, "Kevin Randleman Charged with Faking Urine Test After Pride USA Event," *MMA Weekly*, November 7, 2006, https://www.mmaweekly.com/randleman-charged-with-faking-urine-test-2.

116 *The glory was short-lived* Ken Pishna, "Suspensions Handed Down for Diaz, Cope, Pearson," *MMA Weekly*, April 10, 2007, https://www.mmaweekly.com/suspensions -handed-down-for-diaz-cope-pearson-2.

116 *The shocking announcement came at a press conference* "Source: UFC Buys Pride for Less than $70 million," *Associated Press*, March 27, 2007, https://www.espn.com/sports/news /story?id=2814235.

116 *The deal was estimated to be worth* Shakiel Mahjouri, "Zuffa Paid Pride CEO Nobuyuki Sakakibara $10 million for a 7-year Non-compete Clause," *Bloody Elbow*, September 1, 2019, https://www.bloodyelbow.com/2019/9/1/20842916/zuffa-paid-pride-ceo-nobuy uki-sakakibara-10-million-non-compete-clause-ufc-news.

116 *"This is really going to change the face"* "Source: UFC Buys Pride for Less than $70 million."

116 *An email from Zuffa's outside counsel* Singer, *Redacted Expert Report of Hal J. Singer*," p. 30.

117 *In a deposition, Deutsche Bank's Drew Goldman, an analyst covering* Ibid.

117 *By September, Zuffa had announced it would be* Taro Kotani, "Pride Worldwide Japan Office Officially Closed," *MMA Weekly*, October 5, 2007, http://web.archive.org /web/20071012180841/https://www.mmaweekly.com/absolutenm/templates/dailynews .asp?articleid=4838.

117 *"It makes me very angry that the U.S. management"* Ibid.

117 *"I've pulled everything out of the trick box"* Loretta Hunt, "What's Happening in the World of Mixed Martial Arts Now . . ." *Fight Network*, August 26, 2007, http://web.archive.org /web/20071103024447/http://www.thefightnetwork.com/news_detail.php?nid=4671.

117 *It was both the most profitable 250-square-mile* Tadlock Cowan, "California's San Joaquin Valley: A Region in Transition," Congressional Research Service Report for Congress, December 12, 2005, https://www.cdfa.ca.gov/agvision/files/California/California _CRSReportforCongressSanJoaquinValley-ARegioninTransition.pdf.

118 *One in five lived below the poverty line in Stockton* Congressional Research Service, *California's San Joaquin Valley: A Region in Transition*, December 12, 2005, https://www .everycrsreport.com/files/20051212_RL33184_37b57a2e671c0d0d0d653ab619576d 45f940a81b.pdf.

118 *Nick's parents met at a diner in Stockton* John Branch, "UFC Needs an Antihero: Nate Diaz Returns Just in Time," *New York Times*, August 15, 2019, https://www.nytimes .com/2019/08/15/sports/nate-diaz-fight-pettis.html.

118 *After school, he would come home to the thin-walled motel rooms* Ben Fowlkes, "A Tale of Two Diaz Brothers," *MMA Fighting*, May 4, 2012, https://www.mmafighting .com/2012/5/4/2998733/a-tale-of-two-diaz-brothers.

118 *For his second-grade class photo* UFC Holdings, "UFC Primetime: Condit vs. Diaz: Episode 1," January 28, 2012, https://www.youtube.com/watch?v=tHPTZ2n5O0s.

118 *"It's just the way he was"* Ibid.

118 *He was later medicated for attention deficit hyperactivity disorder* Dan Skye, "High Times Interview: Nick Diaz," *High Times*, February 17, 2016, https://hightimes.com/sports /high-times-interview-nick-diaz/; Ryan Hockensmith, "MMA Submission: Nick Diaz's Life Choices," *ESPN*, April 10, 2009, https://www.espn.com/espnmag/story?id=4059271.

118 *His classmates often teased him* Ariel Helwani, "Nick Diaz Opens Old Wounds on a Dark Day in His Career," *MMA Fighting*, September 14, 2015, https://www.mmafighting .com/2015/9/14/9327767/nick-diaz-opens-old-wounds-on-a-dark-day-in-his-career.

118 *You'd get in fights—everybody would* Skye, "High Times Interview: Nick Diaz."

118 *When Nick started high school* Steve Heath, author interview.

119 *Nick felt even more out of place at Tokay* "Nick Diaz Full Interview," *The Opie Show*, November 23, 2016, https://www.youtube.com/watch?v=XqsGp2WxJPA

119 *To try and fit in, he signed up for swimming* Ibid.

119 *In his sophomore year he dropped out* Ibid.

119 *On one trip to the Blockbuster* Skye, "High Times Interview: Nick Diaz."

119 *When a friend mentioned there was a fight gym in Lodi* "Q&A W/ Nick Diaz: The Hunger for More Pt. 1," *The Formula*, http://web.archive.org/web/20180324112656/http://dformula.bizland.com/thaformula_sports_nick_diaz_the_hunger_for_more.html.

119 *Soon he was a regular, affectionately nicknamed* Steve Heath, author interview.

119 *Future UFC champion Jens Pulver spent a few months* Jens Pulver, with Erich Krauss, *Little Evil: One Ultimate Fighter's Rise to the Top* (Toronto, Ontario: ECW Press, 2003), pp. 142–45.

119 *"He was in there every day when I walked"* Elias Cepeda, "Finding the Diaz Brothers," *Fansided*, August 19, 2016, https://fansided.com/2016/08/19/finding-diaz-brothers/.

120 *He would spend his afternoons and evenings at Animal House* Nick Diaz interview, "Fight Week," Sherdog, January 20, 2011, https://www.youtube.com/watch?v=IX6nHMGAXFI.

120 *"I would tell Nick's mom what a fast learner"* Steve Heath, author interview.

120 *While still a teenager, Nick would often spar* "Nick Diaz Full Interview," *The Opie Show*.

120 *"I would watch him train for two hours"* Steve Heath, author interview.

120 *After a few months, Heath introduced Nick to Cesar Gracie* Ibid.

120 *Rorion and Rickson Gracie were his uncles* Cesar Gracie, author interview.

121 *Heath had first met him at a "smoker"* Steve Heath, author interview.

121 *After one fight ended, according to Heath* Cesar Gracie interview, "Episode 21," *Inside BJJ Podcast*, May 16, 2012, https://insidebjj.libsyn.com/-21-cesar-gracie-and-braulio-estima; see also https://forums.mixedmartialarts.com/t/alex-silva-ruas-plagiarizing/2053265; Steve Heath, author interview.

121 *He understood that he was ultimately training* Cesar Gracie, author interview.

121 *"His attitude was like, Do whatever it takes"* Steve Heath, author interview.

121 *Cesar had just started his own fight team, Gracie Fighter* Cesar Gracie, author interview.

121 *Nick had become one of Heath's main training partners* Steve Heath, author interview.

121 *"I could tell Nick was a thinker"* Cesar Gracie, author interview.

121 *Nick had never really thought about a career* Joe Ferraro, "Nick Diaz interview," *UFC Central* (SportsNet cable television), February 16, 2012, https://www.youtube.com/watch?v=oImkV6oaZV0.

121 *"I never knew what I wanted to do"* Ibid.

121 *Though mixed martial arts was still illegal in California* "Mixed Martial Arts Suffers a Terrible Blow," *Full Contact Fighter*, January 8, 2001, https://fcfighter.com/mixed-martial-arts-suffers-a-terrible-blow/.

121 *tribal lands were exempt from following state law* Howard Petschler, author interview.

122 *Nick didn't know anything about his opponent* Steve Heath, author interview.

122 *dancing at a wedding reception or watching a Los Lobos concert* "2001 Los Lobos Tour Dates," *Setlist*, http://loslobos.setlist.com/2001.html.

122 *It was like a setup, confirmation of Nick's suspicion* "Q&A W/ Nick Diaz: The Hunger for More Pt. 1."

122 *Backstage after the fight, Nick was paid $700* Josh Gross, "Born to Brawl."

122 *Nick celebrated by allowing himself the small luxury* Nick Diaz, video interview, https://www.youtube.com/watch?v=qrhn1-atuoI.

123 *Cesar also began driving Nick into Oakland* Cesar Gracie, author interview.

123 *"King's trainers quickly learned they could rotate"* Ibid.

123 *Cesar also began acting as Nick's manager* Ibid.

123 *Over the next two years, Cesar booked Nick* "Nick Diaz—Fight History," Sherdog, https://www.sherdog.com/fighter/Nick-Diaz-2831#!.

124 *He was always out of money, and among his teammates* Steve Heath, author interview.

124 *"I would always hear about it"* Ibid.

124 *Jackson had already signed with the UFC* Keith Mills, "IFC Results," *Full Contact Fighter*, July 19, 2003, https://fcfighter.com/reality-fighting-4score-one-for-the-little-guy/.

124 *Nick's pay would be close to the scant amounts* Ivan Trembow, "UFC 44 Fighter Salaries," *Ivan's Blog/MMA Weekly*, October 6, 2003, http://www.ivansblog.com/2003/10/mixed-martial-arts-ufc-44-fighter.html.

124 *Halfway into his already truncated training camp* Steve Heath, author interview.

125 *In December 2006, the UFC announced its first major acquisition* Carlos Arias, "Zuffa LLC, Subsidiary Purchases WFA," *Orange County Register*, December 11, 2006, https://www.ocregister.com/2006/12/11/zuffa-llc-subsidiary-purchases-wfa/; "Spiked Punch," *Los Angeles Business Journal*, October 15, 2006, https://labusinessjournal.com/news/spiked-punch/.

126 *That same month, Zuffa also acquired World Extreme Cagefighting* Ken Pishna and Ivan Trembow, "UFC Buying World Extreme Cagefighting," *MMA Weekly*, December 6, 2006, https://www.mmaweekly.com/ufc-buying-world-extreme-cagefighting-2.

126 *Shamus and Otto had decided they could develop a promotion* Michael Weinreb, "A Sport Out on the Edge Takes Aim at the Mainstream," *New York Times*, February 6, 2007, https://www.nytimes.com/2007/02/06/sports/othersports/06fight.html.

126 *The IFL was organized around four teams of fighters* Ibid.

126 *Otto and Shamus claimed they had reached basic terms* Jeffrey Thaler, "Breaking Down the Matchup: UFC vs. IFL," Sherdog, March 2, 2006, https://www.sherdog.com/news/articles/Breaking-Down-the-MatchUp-UFC-vs-IFL-4051; Burt Watson, author interview; Shannon Knapp, author interview.

126 *"It's a war," he would later say* Wertheim, *Blood in the Cage*, p. 230.

126 *According to Miletich, White called him* Pat Miletich, "Pat Miletich's Statement in UFC-IFL Case," *MMA Weekly*, June 17, 2006, https://www.mmaweekly.com/pat-miletichs-statement-in-ufc-ifl-case.

127 *"It was not a real good situation"* Burt Watson, author interview.

127 *"Everybody was so afraid, and very intimidated"* Shannon Knapp, author interview.

127 *Zuffa would later file a lawsuit against the IFL* Thaler, "Breaking Down the Matchup: UFC vs. IFL."

127 *They eventually reached an agreement with MyNetworkTV* Jonathan Snowden, "Disastrous Debut Costs IFL Millions: The History of MMA on Television, Part 2," *Bleacher Report*, December 12, 2012, https://bleacherreport.com/articles/1442316-disastrous-debut-costs-ifl-millions-the-history-of-mma-on-television-part-2.

127 *Zuffa had also tried to use the courts* "Elite Xtreme Combat Overview," EliteXC Homepage, December 7, 2006, http://web.archive.org/web/20070103224444/http://www.elitexc.com/?page=about.

127 *EliteXC had signed a broadcasting agreement* Ivan Trembow, "Analyzing Elite XC's Public

Unveiling," *MMA Weekly*, December 18, 2006, https://www.mmaweekly.com/analyzing
-elite-xcs-public-unveiling-2.

128 *Zuffa's lawsuit against Showtime and EliteXC* "Zuffa LLC v. Showtime Networks, Inc.,"
Casetext, April 30, 2007, https://casetext.com/case/zuffa-llc-v-showtime-networks.

128 *A confidential memo prepared by Zuffa* Singer, *Redacted Expert Report of Hal J. Singer*,
pp. 46–47.

128 *Despite the efforts, EliteXC had grown quickly* "Press Release: ProElite Acquires King of
the Cage," *MMA News*, September 13, 2007, https://www.mmanews.com/2007/09/pro
-elite-acquires-king-of-the-cage/.

128 *and partnerships with Dream, a Japanese promotion* "Press Release: Gracie-Sakuraba
Rematch Among Key Bouts on Star-Studded Dynamite!! USA Fight Card," *PR Newswire*,
May 8, 2007, http://web.archive.org/web/20070929135605/http://www.prnewswire.com
/cgi-bin/stories.pl?ACCT=104&STORY=/www/story/05-08-2007/0004583688&E
DATE=.

128 *EliteXC also captured headlines by introducing* Damon Martin, "Shamrock DQ'd; Ladies
Steal the Show," *MMA Weekly*, February 11, 2007, https://www.mmaweekly.com/sham
rock-dqd-ladies-steal-the-show-2.

128 *In mid-2007, Elite XC attracted still more attention* "Press Release: Gracie-Sakuraba
Rematch Among Key Bouts on Star-Studded Dynamite!!"

128 *Nick had signed a nonexclusive contract with EliteXC* Ken Pishna, "Nick Diaz Signs with
EliteXC," *MMA Weekly*, January 18, 2007, https://www.mmaweekly.com/nick-diaz-signs
-with-elite-xc-2; Tim Ngo, "EliteXC 'Unfinished Business' Fighters' Salaries," *5th Round*,
July 30, 2008, http://www.5thround.com/1346/elitexc-unfinished-business-salaries/.

128 *As Nick trained for the fight, it seemed as if things* Josh Gross and TJ DeSantis, "Nick Diaz
Interview," *Beatdown Podcast/Sherdog Radio Network*, https://www.youtube.com
/watch?v=aXryeoI50Q8.

129 *His younger brother, Nathan, had come into his own* Brett Okamoto, "How Nate Diaz
Fought His Way from Stockton to UFC Royalty," *ESPN*, August 16, 2016, https://www
.espn.com/mma/story/_/id/17322102/to-understand-nate-diaz-first-understand-where
-comes-from.

129 *As ring announcer Jimmy Lennon Jr. bellowed his name* UFC Holdings, "EliteXC:
Renegade," *UFC Fight Pass*, November 10, 2007, https://ufcfightpass.com/video/33000
/elitexc-renegade.

131 *When Nick had first started training on the mats* Gross and DeSantis, "Nick Diaz
Interview."

Chapter 7: This Is Not *Fantasy Island*

132 *After he'd started showing signs of balding in 2004* Mike Sager, "Meet Dana White, the
King of Mixed Martial Arts," *Esquire*, January 7, 2010, https://www.esquire.com
/news-politics/a6863/dana-white-ufc-0210/.

132 *"I'm mad a lot," White would later admit:* "*Dana White en toute intimité dans L'nticham-
bre*" (video), *RDS*, March 15, 2013, http://web.archive.org/web/20130319013627/https://
www.rds.ca/vidéos/dana-white-en-toute-intimité-dans-l-antichambre-1.596839.

132 *"The one thing was that Dana was always"* Burt Watson, author interview.

132 *Annual revenue reached an all-time high* Nash, "What We Now Know About the UFC's
Finances."

132   *In 2007, Spike drew its biggest audience in network history* MMA Junkie Staff, "UFC
      75 Broadcast Breaks Spike TV and North American Ratings Records," *MMA Junkie*,
      September 11, 2007, https://mmajunkie.usatoday.com/2007/09/ufc-75-broadcast-breaks
      -spike-tv-and-north-american-ratings-records.

133   *Spike's semi-monthly* Fight Night *broadcasts* Ivan Trembow, "UFC Ratings Report: TUF &
      UFC Fight Night," *MMA Weekly*, September 22, 2007, https://www.mmaweekly.com
      /ufc-ratings-report-tuf-ufc-fight-night.

133   *Spike had also helped the UFC counterprogram* MMA Fighting Staff, "UFC to Counter
      CBS-EliteXC with Replay of UFC 84," *MMA Fighting*, July 9, 2008, https://www
      .mmafighting.com/2008/07/09/ufc-to-counter-cbselitexc-with-replay-of-ufc-84; Singer,
      Redacted Expert Report of Hal J. Singer, pp. 35–40.

133   *Marc Ratner, the former executive director* "UFC Hires Wall Street Gaming Analyst,"
      MMA Weekly, March 30, 2006, https://www.mmaweekly.com/ufc-hires-wall-street-gam
      ing-analyst.

133   *Ratner had worked as an advertising executive* Marc Ratner, author interview.

134   *He'd often travel with Mike Mersch* Ibid.

134   *To keep up with the aggressive new production schedule* "Debut UFC Fighters—UFC in
      2008," Wikipedia, https://en.wikipedia.org/wiki/2008_in_UFC.

134   *White kept a long list of fighter names written in temporary marker* Tom Zenner, "Dana
      White Interview HD," *Jetset Magazine*, September 9, 2014, https://www.youtube.com
      /watch?v=O0t-ar6GMPI&t=445s.

134   *"I can tell you this man, if you fucking call"* "Dana White Post-fight Media Scrum at UFC
      on Fuel TV 7," *Fighters Only*, February 16, 2013, cited in Singer, *Redacted Expert Report
      of Hal J. Singer*; https://www.youtube.com/watch?v=y0NTilTqn2w&t=729s.

135   *Despite his mixed feelings, Silva was clinical* Jason Cruz, "More Documents from UFC
      Antitrust Hearing Reveals Joe Silva's Negotiations," *MMA Payout*, October 10, 2019,
      https://mmapayout.com/2019/10/10/more-documents-from-ufc-antitrust-hearing
      -reveal-joe-silvas-negotiations/.

135   *Chris Leben would describe Silva as "a little Napoleon"* Chris Leben, with Daniel J.
      Patinkin, *The Crippler: Cage Fighting and My Life on the Edge* (New York: Skyhorse
      Publishing, 2016), p. 120.

135   *When Leben learned he had earned a spot* Ibid., p. 12.

136   *In December of 2006, White had been eager to sign a new contract* "Arbitration Hearing
      Lifts Curtain on Backstage World of the UFC," *Canadian Press*, March 20, 2008, https://
      web.archive.org/web/20080324231213/http://canadianpress.google.com/article/ALe
      qM5gJurqcC7Mrxwe1XoGHEAt1EPnmyg.

136   *After some discussion, White wrote down* Ibid.

136   *Dion took the Post-it note and returned home to discuss* Ibid.

137   *As Vera saw what was unfolding, he worried Dion* Ibid.

137   *In court, Dion claimed that Zuffa's approach* Ibid.

137   *In an interview with ESPN, Lorenzo described the process* "Lorenzo Fertitta Interview—
      Uncut—filmed for ESPN's Outside the Lines," UFC YouTube Channel, January 16, 2012,
      http://web.archive.org/web/20120117002233/https://www.youtube.com/watch?v=ck$Lb
      8pDmVg.

137   *Sometimes the envelopes would contain a check* Josh Gross, "Money Matters," Sherdog,
      October 27, 2007, https://www.sherdog.com/news/articles/Money-Matters-9684.

137   *According to Monte Cox, a manager who represented* "MMA Stories Podcast: What It's

Like to Negotiate with Dana White," Sherdog Radio Network, April 2, 2020, https://www
.sherdog.com/radio/MMA-Stories-What-Its-Like-to-Negotiate-with-Dana-White-5552
(starting at 47:00).

138   *The UFC also regularly used side-letter agreements* Erik Magraken, "Did Regulators
Deceive the Public About Brock Lesnar's UFC Pay?" Combat Sports Law, August 9,
2019, https://combatsportslaw.com/2019/08/09/did-regulators-deceive-the-public-about
-brock-lesnars-ufc-pay/; Singer, *Redacted Expert Report of Hal J. Singer*, pp. 23–23.

138   *The UFC's side-letter agreements also* Singer, *Redacted Expert Report of Hal J. Singer*,
pp. 23–23.

138   *Entry-level contracts at the time started at $3,000* "UFC Fight Night 15 Fighter Paydays
and Salaries for 'Diaz vs Neer,' " *MMA Mania*, September 22, 2008, https://www
.mmamania.com/2008/09/22/ufc-fight-night-15-fighter-paydays-and-salaries-for-diaz
-vs-neer/.

139   *"What on earth is that?"* UFC Holdings, "Chris Leben vs. Terry Martin," *UFC Fight
Night: Thomas vs. Florian*, September 19, 2007, https://ufcfightpass.com/video/33210
/ufc-fight-night-thomas-vs-florian?playlistId=3696.

139   *"We all rode the wave together"* Bob Cook, author interview.

139   *Mike Swick, a contestant from the first season* Mike Swick, author interview.

139   *In 2007, Zuffa announced a deal to produce* Ben Fritz, "UFC Signs New Videogame Deal
with THQ," *Variety*, January 14, 2007, https://variety.com/2007/digital/features/ufc
-signs-new-vidgame-deal-with-thq-1117957393/.

139   *most fighter contracts at the time didn't have clear language* Singer, *Redacted Expert Report
of Hal J. Singer*, p. 27.

140   *In 2008, Jon Fitch, a fighter who trained at AKA* Kevin Iole, "UFC Drops Fitch, AKA
Fighters," *Yahoo! Sports*, November 20, 2008, https://sports.yahoo.com/ki-ufcakaf
eud111908.html?guccounter=1.

140   *The move infuriated White, and he responded* Ibid.

140   *He was a loyal person and took pride in the fact* "UFC Boss Fights the Clock."

140   *"I like having people around me who I can trust"* Ibid.

141   *As the subprime mortgage market collapse of 2008* Iole, "UFC Drops Fitch, AKA Fighters."

141   *"It was not a very good agreement"* Ibid.

141   *Faced with the possibility that his UFC career* Chad Dundas, "Fitch Back in UFC,"
MMA Rated, November 20, 2008, http://web.archive.org/web/20081220011319/http://
mmarated.com/blogs/blog/20081120/rated_exclusive__fitch_back_in_ufc-1081.html.

141   *Zuffa filed the suit in the Clark County District Court* Case No. A555208, filed January 14,
2008, https://web.archive.org/web/20160926013725/https://www.aolcdn.com/tmz
_documents/0116_couture_wm.pdf.

142   *In the locker room immediately following the fight* Couture with Hunt, *Becoming the
Natural*, p. 255.

142   *Lorenzo and White promised that they would do whatever* Ibid., p. 255.

142   *A few months later, White had offered Couture* Ibid., p. 262.

142   *Couture wasn't interested in either option* Ken Pishna and Jeff Cain, "UFC Disputes
Couture's Claims About His Pay," *MMA Weekly*, October 30, 2007, https://www
.mmaweekly.com/ufc-disputes-coutures-claims-about-his-pay-2.

142   *Success had done little to protect him from the recurring* Couture with Hunt, *Becoming the
Natural*, p. 223.

142   *She had come to Las Vegas with their one-year-old son* Ibid., pp. 196–97.

142 *Three years after he had first promised* Ibid., p. 200.

142 *During filming in Las Vegas, Trish grew even more frustrated* Ibid., p. 201.

143 *The young cast members treated him like a trailblazer* Ibid., pp. 198–99.

143 *Halfway through filming, Trish decided to fly back* "Kim Couture Bio," http://www
.kimcouture.com/bio.html.

143 *After filming ended a few weeks later* Couture with Hunt, *Becoming the Natural*,
pp. 208–9.

143 *Shortly after, he decided to relocate to Las Vegas* Ibid., p. 240.

143 *He also found himself fielding more offers to act* "Randy Couture," Internet Movie
Database, https://www.imdb.com/name/nm1330276/.

143 *Many of his closest friends found it hard to understand* Couture with Hunt, *Becoming the
Natural*, pp. 217–21.

143 *Couture found it hard to understand the negative impressions* Ibid., p. 222.

143 *He had sized up the UFC's current heavyweight champion* Ibid., pp. 262–63.

144 *White had sided with the fans* Pramit Mohapatra, "One on One with UFC President
Dana White," *Baltimore Sun*, January 22, 2007, https://www.baltimoresun.com/sports/bal
-whiteqa122-story.html.

144 *A few weeks later, Couture had signed* Couture with Hunt, *Becoming the Natural*, p. 263.

144 *Sylvia had traveled to Oregon in 2003 to train* Ibid., p. 183.

144 *He still thought of Sylvia as a friend* Ibid., p. 263.

144 Sports Illustrated *asked Couture to appear* Michael David Smith, "Randy Couture
Heading for Sports Illustrated Cover?" *MMA Fighting*, May 9, 2007, https://www
.mmafighting.com/2007/05/09/randy-couture-heading-for-sports-illustrated-cover.

144 *Couture was also invited to the White House* Couture with Hunt, *Becoming the Natural*,
p. 258.

144 *ESPN introduced a "Best Fighter" category* Michael Shalik, "Rampage and Couture
Nominated for 'Best Fighter' ESPY Award," *MMA News*, June 25, 2007, https://www
.mmanews.com/2007/06/rampage-best-fighter-espy-award/.

145 *Fedor Emelianenko, Pride's long-reigning heavyweight champion* "Fedor Tops Sherdog.com
Pound-for-Pound," Sherdog, August 20, 2007, https://www.sherdog.com/news/articles
/Fedor-Tops-Sherdogcom-PoundForPound-8670.

145 *A devout Russian Orthodox Christian who blessed* Shannon Knapp, author interview.

145 *White and Lorenzo had tried to sign Emelianenko* Evgeni Kogan, "Finkelstein Discusses
UFC, Fedor Emelianenko," Sherdog, July 27, 2007, https://www.sherdog.com/news
/interviews/Finkelstein-Discusses-UFC-Fedor-Emelianenko-8422.

145 *Emelianenko had instead signed with Adrenaline* Ken Pishna, "In Depth: Details About
Fedor and M1-Global," *MMA Weekly*, October 23, 2007, https://www.mmaweekly.com
/in-depth-details-about-fedor-m-1-global-2.

145 *After Couture had re-signed with the UFC* Couture with Hunt, *Becoming the Natural*,
p. 274.

146 *But in the fall of 2007, after negotiations between Emelianenko and Zuffa* Ibid.

146 *On October 11, 2007, Couture faxed a letter* Lance Pugmire, "Couture Retires from
MMA," *Los Angeles Times*, October 12, 2007, https://www.latimes.com/archives/la-xpm
-2007-oct-12-sp-ufc12-story.html.

146 *Couture wasn't available for interviews* Jack Bratcher, "Randy Couture as King Sargon,"
Pro MMA Now, July 12, 2008, https://prommanow.com/2008/07/12/randy-couture-as
-king-sargon/.

146 *There was no internet in the hotel the production company* Couture with Hunt, *Becoming the Natural*, pp. 272–73.

146 *"He definitely belongs to me," White told a reporter* Alex Marvez, "UFC's White: Couture's Still Mine," Fox Sports, October 18, 2007, https://web.archive.org/web/20071020051545 /http://msn.foxsports.com/boxing/story/7349878.

147 *Couture decided to address the subject* "Randy Couture Press Conference Scheduled for Thursday," *MMA Junkie*, October 23, 2017, https://mmajunkie.usatoday.com/2007/10 /randy-couture-press-conference-scheduled-for-thursday.

147 *Speaking from a podium in the sparring ring* "Randy Couture Press Conference October 2007," originally aired on *Inside MMA* (HDNet), October 25, 2007, available at Scott's Wrestling Collection, https://www.youtube.com/watch?v=ZH1CMfDvF9c.

147 *"The facts are the facts," Lorenzo said* Ken Pishna and Jeff Cain, "UFC Disputes Couture's Claims About His Pay," *MMA Weekly*, October 30, 2007, https://www.mmaweekly.com /ufc-disputes-coutures-claims-about-his-pay-2.

147 *In public, White was indignant, comparing fighters* Lance Pugmire, "It's a Battle for Money at the Top of the UFC," *Los Angeles Times*, December 27, 2007, https://www.latimes.com /archives/la-xpm-2007-dec-27-sp-ufc27-story.html.

148 *Emelianenko and M-1 signed another deal with Affliction* "Trump's Affliction-M1 Entertainment Opens Up the MMA," press release, *MMA Mania*, January 9, 2009, https:// www.mmamania.com/2009/01/09/trumps-affliction-m1-entertainement-opens-up-the -mma.

148 *"His thing is inflicting death on people" Trump said* "Donald Trump: Fedor Emelianenko's 'thing is inflicting death on people' (audio)," *MMA Mania*, July 17, 2008, https://www .mmamania.com/2008/07/17/donald-trump-fedor-emelianenkos-thing-is-inflicting -death-on-people-audio.

148 *While Zuffa's suit worked its way through the court system* "Fedor: Fight with Sylvia Now Official," *MMA Junkie*, April 19, 2008, https://mmajunkie.usatoday.com/2008/04/fedor -fight-with-sylvia-now-official.

148 *White responded by banning any UFC fighter* Tim Ngo, "Report: Affliction Banned from Sponsoring UFC Fighters," *5th Round*, January 25, 2008, http://www.5thround.com/356 /report-affliction-banned-from-sponsoring-fighters-in-the-ufc/#more-356.

148 *The card's highlight was middleweight champion Anderson Silva* Singer, *Redacted Expert Report of Hal J. Singer*, pp. 35–36.

148 *Affliction would end up generating a reported one hundred thousand* "Mailbag: The UFC's Affliction," *Yahoo! Sports*, July 22, 2008, https://sports.yahoo.com/ki-mmamail bag072208.html.

148 *The UFC's Fight Night card drew a peak audience* "UFC Ratings for 'Silva vs. Irvin' on Spike TV Were Impressive," *MMA Mania*, July 22, 2008, https://www.mmamania .com/2008/07/22/ufc-ratings-for-silva-vs-irvin-on-spike-tv-were-impressive.

148 *Though Affliction had lost money on its debut* Ryan Harness, "Tom Atencio Opens Up About Affliction, MMA, Donald Trump, and UFC 'Spies,' " *MMA Mania*, September 6, 2020, https://www.mmamania.com/2020/9/6/21425255/tom-atencio-opens-up-about -affliction-mma-donald-trump-and-ufc-spies; "Couture: Could Fight Fedor in October '08," Sherdog, December 15, 2007, https://www.sherdog.com/news/news /Couture-Could-Fight-Fedor-in-October-08-10406; Fedor Emelianenko and Randy Couture filming Affliction commercial circa early 2008, available at https://www .youtube.com/watch?v=wifIDszDLKI.

148　*Zuffa argued it was entitled to a twelve-month extension* Tom Hamlin, "Randy Couture Turns Down Title Defense," *MMA Weekly*, December 3, 2007, https://www.mmaweekly.com/randy-couture-turns-down-title-defense-2.

149　*As his legal fees mounted—nearing $500,000* Steven Marrocco, "Randy Couture Spent $500,000 Fighting UFC in Court, Expects Tough Road for Goerges St-Pierre," *MMA Junkie*, October 21, 2016, https://mmajunkie.usatoday.com/2016/10/randy-couture-spent-500k-fighting-ufc-in-court-expects-tough-road-for-georges-st-pierre.

149　*In August, Affliction announced* "Sources: Couture vs Emelianenko Targeted for Early 2009," *MMA Junkie*, August 30, 2008, https://mmajunkie.usatoday.com/2008/08/sources-couture-versus-emelianenko-targeted-for-super-bowl-weekend.

149　*Shortly after, Couture decided to swallow his pride* Mark Chalifoux, "Q&A with Randy Couture," *Baltimore Sun*, November 4, 2008, https://www.baltimoresun.com/bs-mtblog-140976-qa_with_randy_couture-story.html.

149　*In 2004, he'd tried to earn a spot in the NFL* "Lesnar Shows Vikings Some Raw Ability, But Will They Give Him a Shot?," Associated Press, June 14, 2004, http://www.espn.com/espn/wire/_/section/nfl/id/1821029.

151　*The event generated $4.8 million in ticket sales* "Report: UFC 91 PPV Buys Top 1 Million—Second Biggest Haul Ever for Promotion," *MMA Mania*, December 11, 2008, https://www.mmamania.com/2008/12/11/report-ufc-91-ppv-buys-top-1-million-biggest-haul-ever-for-promotion.

151　*The UFC's annual revenue for the year would climb* Nash, "What We Now Know About the UFC's Finances."

Chapter 8: Station to Station

152　*Lesnar quickly became the biggest star* Lance Pugmire, "The Driving Forces Behind the UFC," *Los Angeles Times*, July 11, 2009, https://www.latimes.com/archives/la-xpm-2009-jul-11-sp-ufc-fertitta11-story.html.

152　*Ratner had succeeded in getting mixed martial arts legally sanctioned* Jon Show, "UFC Feeling Scrappy as Footprint Expands," *Sports Business Journal*, October 12, 2009, https://www.sportsbusinessjournal.com/Journal/Issues/2009/10/12/SBJ-In-Depth/UFC-Feeling-Scrappy-As-Footprint-Expands.aspx?hl=ufc&sc=0.

152　*Despite a triumphant first-round TKO win for Emelianenko* "Arlovski's $1.5 Million Payday Tops Affliction's $3.3 Million Payroll," *MMA Junkie*, February 4, 2009, https://mmajunkie.usatoday.com/2009/02/andrei-arlovskis-1-5-million-payday-tops-afflictions-3-1-million-payroll; Mike Sloan, "Affliction, Golden Boy Join Forces," Sherdog, September 13, 2008, https://www.sherdog.com/news/news/Affliction-Golden-Boy-Join-Forces-14384.

152　*White had added more pressure to Affliction by pushing Spike* Singer, *Redacted Expert Report of Hal J. Singer*, p. 36.

152　*The Spike broadcast would draw a peak audience of 3.3 million* "UFC 91 Replay on Spike TV Peaks with Record 3.3 Million Viewers," *MMA Junkie*, January 28, 2009, https://mmajunkie.usatoday.com/2009/01/ufc-91-replay-on-spike-tv-peaks-with-a-record-3-3-million-viewers.

153　*Lesnar's next fight, a rematch against Frank Mir* John S. Nash, "Pay the Man: Making the Case for Giving Conor McGregor Equity in the UFC," *Bloody Elbow*, March 22, 2017, https://www.bloodyelbow.com/2017/3/22/14850590/pay-the-man-making-the-case-for-giving-conor-mcgregor-equity-ufc.

153 *Ticket sales brought in another $5.1 million* "Nevada's Top 35 MMA Gates," State of Nevada Athletic Commission, retrieved on March 22, 2022, http://web.archive.org /web/20220324004203/https://boxing.nv.gov/results/Top_MMA_Gates/.

153 *Two weeks later, Affliction would be forced to cancel* "CSAC: Affliction's Josh Barnett Tested Positive for Anabolic Steroid, License Denied," *MMA Junkie*, July 22, 2009, https://mmajunkie.usatoday.com/2009/07/csac-afflictions-josh-barnett-tested-positive -for-anabolic-steroid-fined-and-suspended.

153 *The UFC had had its issues with fighters testing positive* Josh Gross, "An Open Letter to Dana White," Sherdog, July 20, 2007, https://www.sherdog.com/news/articles/An-Open -Letter-to-Dana-White-8345.

153 *As the promotion's executive board considered the prospect* Craig Jolicoeur, "Affliction Closes Doors; Now in Bed with UFC," *Bleacher Report*, July 24, 2009, https://bleacherre port.com/articles/223888-affliction-closes-doors-now-in-bed-with-ufc.

153 *White would later celebrate by posing* Jonathan Snowden, "Dana White Adds Another Name to the Tombstone," *Bloody Elbow*, December 21, 2010, https://www.bloodyelbow .com/2010/12/21/1887977/dana-white-adds-another-name-to-the-tombstone; "Tapping Out: ProElite, EliteXC Shut Doors, Declare Bankruptcy," *Sports Business Journal*, October 21, 2008, https://www.sportsbusinessjournal.com/Daily/Issues/2008/10/21 /Leagues-Governing-Bodies/Tapping-Out-Proelite-Elitexc-Shut-Doors-Declare-Bank ruptcy.aspx.

153 *And that thread snapped on July 28, 2009* Station Casinos Form 10-K, filed with the United States Securities and Exchange Commission, March 31, 2011, available at https:// www.sec.gov/Archives/edgar/data/1503579/000104746911003010/a2203162z10-k.htm.

153 *Though Station's revenues had grown steadily since 2000* Ibid.; Tamara Audi, "Hurt by Debt, Casino Firm Station Files for Chapter 11," *Wall Street Journal*, July 29, 2009, https://www.wsj.com/articles/SB124881967460688103.

154 *"People said we overspent, that it was too nice"* Liz Benston, "Neighborhood Draw," *Las Vegas Sun*, December 23, 2005, https://lasvegassun.com/news/2005/dec/23/neighbor hood-draw/.

154 *In 1997, Station spent more than $200 million to open Sunset Station* Ibid.

154 *In 2001, Station acquired a 50 percent stake in Green Valley Ranch* Jeff Simpson, "Regulators Recommend License for Green Valley Ranch," *Las Vegas Review-Journal*, November 8, 2001, https://web.archive.org/web/20020220175847/http://www.lvrj.com /lvrj_home/2001/Nov-08-Thu-2001/business/17403410.html.

154 *The deal would entitle Station to 2 percent of the property's annual revenue* Station Casinos 2002 Annual Report, p. 28.

154 *By 2006, Lorenzo and Frank III had used similar* Ibid., p. 1.

154 *In 2007, Station took on another $3.4 billion* "Station Casinos Accepts Offer from Founder and Buyout Firm," *New York Times*, February 27, 2007, https://www.nytimes .com/2007/02/27/business/27casino.html.

154 *Unemployment rates in Las Vegas would rise as high as 14 percent* Cy Ryan, "Clark County Jobless Rate Hits 14 Percent," *Las Vegas Sun*, August 19, 2011, https://lasvegassun.com /news/2011/aug/19/unemployment-again/; Apertor Hospitality, *The Outlook for the Las Vegas Locals Casino Market*, July 1, 2010, available at https://www.slideshare.net/Gregg Carlson/apertor-las-vegas-locals-casino-market-1a-8228469.

154 *Nevada would become the number one state* Michael Snyder, "The Stunning Crash and Burn of Las Vegas," *Business Insider*, June 11, 2010, https://www.businessinsider.com /the-stunning-crash-and-burn-of-las-vegas-2010-6.

154 *Station's annual revenue would decline $300 million* Steve Green, "Station Casinos Reports
     Revenue Drop in Fourth Quarter," *Las Vegas Sun*, March 31, 2010, https://lasvegassun
     .com/news/2010/mar/31/station-casinos-reports-decline-revenue-quarter/.

155 *The total worth of the company's assets fell* Ibid.

155 *The situation was worsened by the the November 2008 opening* Amanda Finnegan,
     "Alianta Station Opens Its Doors," *Las Vegas Sun*, November 11, 2008, https://
     lasvegassun.com/news/2008/nov/11/aliante-station-set-open-tonight/.

155 *One proposed offer would have repaid senior note holders* "Holders Deem Station Casinos
     Bond Offer 'Deficient,' " Reuters, December 3, 2008, https://www.reuters.com
     /article/stationcasinos-bonds/holders-deem-station-casinos-bond-offer-deficient
     -idUSN0334751620081203.

155 *Boyd Gaming, one of Station's only major competitors* Lauren Silva Laughlin and Una
     Galani, "Bankruptcy Fight, Las Vegas Style," *New York Times*, December 1, 2009, https://
     www.nytimes.com/2009/12/02/business/02views.html.

155 *After reaching terms to acquire Pride in 2007* John S. Nash, "What Investors Are Being
     Told About UFC Debt," *Bloody Elbow*, November 3, 2015, https://www.bloodyelbow
     .com/2015/11/3/9561981/ufc-finances-zuffa-debt-deutsche-bank-moodys-standard-and
     -poor-investors-bonds#_edn2.

155 *The reported dividend was nearly four times* Nash, "What We Now Know About the
     UFC's Finances."

155 *The annual fees required for the loan were $23.9 million* Adam Swift, "S&P Cuts Zuffa's
     Credit Rating, Issues Negative Outlook," Sherdog, November 28, 2007, https://www
     .sherdog.com/news/articles/SP-Cuts-Zuffa146s-Credit-Rating-Issues-Negative-Out
     look-10140.

155 *Among other concerns, S&P cited the fact* Adam Swift, "Behind the Curtain: Zuffa's
     Finances Come into Focus," Sherdog, October 17, 2007, https://www.sherdog.com/news
     /articles/Behind-the-Curtain-Zuffas-Finances-Come-Into-Focus-9528.

156 *A few months later, as Station was racing* "Lorenzo Fertitta to Work Full-Time as UFC
     Chair and CEO," *Sports Business Journal*, June 19, 2008, https://www.sportsbusiness
     journal.com/Daily/Issues/2008/06/19/Leagues-Governing-Bodies/Lorenzo-Fertitta-To
     -Work-Full-Time-As-UFC-Chair-CEO.aspx.

156 *Within five years, he told the* Sports Business Journal "NFL Average Team Value Tops
     $1 Billion: Forbes," Reuters, September 10, 2008, https://www.reuters.com/article/us
     -nfl-valuations/nfl-average-team-value-tops-1-billion-forbes-idUSN1020214220080911.

156 *By 2006, sponsorship revenue had risen to $16 million* Nash, "What We Now Know About
     the UFC's Finances"; James S. Granelli, "Amp'd Mobile Looks to Enter Chapter 11," *Los
     Angeles Times*, June 4, 2007, https://www.latimes.com/archives/la-xpm-2007-jun-04-fi
     -ampd4-story.html.

156 *Its logos were printed on the octagon mat at almost every event* "More Money Than Meets
     the Eye in the UFC," *Yahoo! Sports*, April 30, 2008, https://www.yahoo.com/news/more
     -money-meets-eye-ufc-050500030—mma.html?guccounter=1; Liddell, *Iceman: My
     Fighting Life*, p. 253.

157 *In 2007, Xyience signed a new three-year deal* Adam Swift, "Details on Xyience's UFC
     Sponsorship," *MMA Payout*, December 17, 2007, https://web.archive.org/web/201810
     23002213/http://mmapayout.com/2007/12/details-on-xyiences-ufc-sponsorship/.

157 *In 2006, the company had generated $22 million* Ibid.

157 *In 2007, a Zuffa-connected subsidiary, "Zyen"* Daniel Fisher, "Fertitta Treasurer Accused

of Lying in Energy Drink Case," *Forbes*, September 13, 2011, https://www.forbes.com
/sites/danielfisher/2011/09/13/fertitta-treasurer-accused-of-lying-in-energy-drink
-case/?sh=13de5a5e8790.

157 *Court documents would later show another Zuffa-connected subsidiary* Adam Swift,
" 'Bevanda Magica': Xyience Bankruptcy Filings Reveal Deep Ties to Zuffa," Sherdog,
January 30, 2008, https://www.sherdog.com/news/articles/145Bevanda-Magica146
-Xyience-Bankruptcy-Filings-Reveal-Deep-Ties-to-Zuffa-11061.

157 *From the outside, it appeared as if Zuffa had been propping up Xyience* Adam Swift, "UFC
Owners Defendents in Xyience Lawsuit," Sherdog, March 21, 2008, https://www.sherdog
.com/news/articles/UFC-Owners-Defendants-in-Xyience-Lawsuit-11914.

157 *In January of 2008, three months after announcing* "A-B Signs Deal for Bud Light to Be
Official Beer Sponsor of UFC," *Sports Business Journal*, February 29, 2008, https://www
.sportsbusinessjournal.com/Daily/Issues/2008/02/29/Sponsorships-Advertising-Market
ing/A-B-Signs-Deal-For-Bud-Light-To-Be-Official-Beer-Sponsor-Of-UFC.aspx.

157 *In February, Zuffa reached a long-coveted agreement* Ibid.

157 *In 2009, Zuffa further restricted its fighter sponsor policy* Singer, *Redacted Expert Report of
Hal J. Singer*, pp. 128–29.

157 *In 2009, Zuffa further restricted its fighter sponsor policy* Singer, *Redacted Expert Report of
Hal J. Singer*, pp. 128–29.

158 *"The standard procedure is to have the prospective sponsors"* Ibid.

158 *The new policy would also require any sponsors* Ibid., p. 47.

158 *In his post-fight interview in the octagon after UFC 100* "The Lesnar Show," *Yahoo! Sports*,
July 12, 2009, https://sports.yahoo.com/dw-lesnar071209.html?guccounter=1.

158 *The comment infuriated White, and he went straight to Lesnar's* Ibid.

158 *"The standard procedure is to have the prospective sponsors"* Ibid.

158 *The new policy would also require any sponsors* Ibid., p. 47.

158 *In his post-fight interview after UFC 100* "The Lesnar Show," *Yahoo! Sports*, July 12, 2009,
https://sports.yahoo.com/dw-lesnar071209.html?guccounter=1.

158 *The comment infuriated White, and he went straight to Lesnar's* Ibid.

158 *In 2009, White targeted Loretta Hunt, a reporter* Anthony Stalter, "UFC's Dana White
Unleashes Profanity-Laced Tirade at Reporter," *Scores Report*, April 2, 2009, https://www
.scoresreport.com/2009/04/02/ufc's-dana-white-unleashes-profanity-laced-tirade-at
-reporter/; video available at https://www.youtube.com/watch?v=xzliovVCxR8.

158 *"They're telling fighters they can go directly to them"* Loretta Hunt, "Some Managers,
Agents Lose Backstage Pass," *MMA Fighting*, April 1, 2009, https://www.sherdog.com
/news/articles/1/Some-Managers-Agents-Lose-Backstage-Pass-16813.

158 *Hunt's story sent White into a characteristic rage* Stalter, "UFC's Dana White Unleashes
Profanity-Laced Tirade at Reporter."

159 *The video almost immediately generated dozens* Michael David Smith, "UFC Pulls Video
of Dana White Trashing Loretta Hunt," *MMA Fighting*, April 2, 2009, https://www
.mmafighting.com/2009/04/02/ufc-pulls-video-of-dana-white-trashing-loretta-hunt/.

159 *The following day, White offered an apology* Mary Buckheit, "Questions and Answers
from UFC President Dana White," *ESPN*, April 3, 2009, https://www.espn.com/espn
/page2/story?page=buckheit/090403.

159 *Jake Rossen, who had written a short piece criticizing* Jake Rossen, "The Condom Depot
Ban and Hypocrisy," Sherdog (syndicated on *ESPN*), December 29, 2009, https://www
.espn.com/blog/mma/post/_/id/425/the-condom-depot-ban-and-hypocrisy.

159   *White had a friend film him as he called an unnamed editor* Mike Fagan, "Breaking Down Dana White's Jake Rossen Rant," *Bloody Elbow*, December 30, 2009, https:// www.bloodyelbow.com/2009/12/30/1225266/breaking-down-dana-whites-jake; video available at https://www.youtube.com/watch?v=DHn96ZOWE1w.

159   *"The thing that sucks is that video rant"* ESPN.com staff, "White Sorry for Anti-Gay Slur," ESPN, April 3, 2009, https://www.espn.com/extra/mma/news/story?id=40 38944.

159   *One former employee recalled being surprised by how freely* Anonymous, author interview.

160   *One new hire had their office rigged with a speaker* Ibid.

160   *Another worker had takeout food snuck* Ibid.

160   *When Zuffa's chief financial officer, John Mulkey* UFC Holdings, *Dana White's Video Blog, UFC 129, Day 1*, April 26, 2011, video available at https://www.youtube.com/watch?v=s 5bO0Gqmsu0.

160   *He was a frequent guest at the N9NE Steakhouse in the Palms* Norm Clarke, "UFC's White Cuts Ties to The Palms," *Las Vegas Review-Journal*, October 29, 2012, http://www.lvrj .com/news/ufc-s-white-cuts-ties-to-the-palms-176221331.html.

160   *White was a prodigious gambler* Ibid.

160   *"If you're excited to meet me, I'm excited to meet you"* Wapner, *Ultimate Fighting*.

160   *On a whim one night in New York, White sent out a post* Mike Sager, "Meet Dana White, the King of Mixed Martial Arts"; video also available at https://www.youtube.com /watch?v=IMUAKwfdzOM.

160   *"I get out of the car and everybody starts cheering"* Ibid.

160   *For Lorenzo, White's outsized public profile was a boon.* Lee Hawkins, "WSJ Live: UFC's Lorenzo Fertitta and Dana White: UFC Bigger Than NFL," *Wall Street Journal*, May 7, 2012, video available at https://www.youtube.com/watch?v=E5EYyZ5ABrQ.

161   *In addition to banning certain sponsors, Zuffa had begun* Singer, *Redacted Expert Report of Hal J. Singer*, pp. 128–29.

161   *The company had also used exclusivity clauses with some of their international* Ibid., p. 82.

161   *"It overtook the whole schedule—we became"* Kevin Kay, author interview.

161   *In October of 2007, Spike and Zuffa signed an expansive* "UFC and Spike TV Officially Announce Contract Renewal Through 2011," *MMA Junkie*, October 25, 2011, https:// mmajunkie.usatoday.com/2007/10/ufc-and-spike-tv-officially-announce-four-year-con tract-renewal.

161   *Within a year, the UFC was outperforming every other* Miguel Lopez, "UFC Is Off and Running for 2009," *Los Angeles Daily News*, December 25, 2008, https://www.dailynews .com/2008/12/25/ufc-is-off-and-running-for-2009/; Mike Chiappetta, "UFC Looking to Buy G4 Cable Channel, Spike Execs Prepared to Move On," *MMA Fighting*, June 8, 2011, https://www.mmafighting.com/2011/06/08/ufc-looking-to-buy-g4-cable-channel-spike -execs-prepare-to-move/; Sally Beatty, "New TNN Embraces Populist Culture, Hopes to Dethrone Cable Ratings King," *Wall Street Journal*, October 5, 2000, https://www.wsj .com/articles/SB970703012437628882.

162   *Along with the success came a slow-motion barrage* Kevin Kay, author interview.

162   *Brock Lesnar's debut in early 2008* Ibid.

162   *"He just kept calling me and calling me"* Ibid.

162   *In 2009, Zuffa had announced a deal with Televisa* Jennifer Wenk, "UFC Signs Television

Deal with Grupo Televisa," UFC.com, July 8, 2009, https://www.ufc.com/news/ufc-signs
-television-deal-grupo-televisa.

162 *The UFC also secured broadcasting deals covering* "UFC Continues European-Market
Expansion with Portuguese Broadcast Deal," *MMA Junkie*, May 30, 2009, https://
mmajunkie.usatoday.com/2009/05/ufc-continues-european-market-expansion-with-por
tuguese-broadcast-deal; "UFC Announces TV Deal to Broadcast in France," *MMA Junkie*,
February 18, 2009, https://mmajunkie.usatoday.com/2009/02/ufc-announces-deal-to
-broadcast-in-france; "UFC Signs Agreement with DSF," UFC.com, February 19, 2009;
Jennifer Wenk, "UFC Enters Home of Martial Arts with NMTV Deal," UFC.com, June 28,
2009, https://www.ufc.com/news/ufcr-enters-home-martial-arts-nmtv-deal.

162 *By the end of 2009, the UFC was available in more* Ken Pishna, "UK MMA Arrives, UFC
105 in 400 Million Homes," *MMA Weekly*, November 12, 2009, https://www.mmaweekly
.com/u-k-mma-arrives-ufc-105-in-400-million-homes-2.

162 *In 2010, Zuffa opened a full-time office in China* "UFC Officials Announce Asian
Operations, NBA Exec Mark Fischer Named Head," *MMA Junkie*, August 29, 2010,
https://mmajunkie.usatoday.com/2010/08/ufc-officials-announce-asian-operations-nba
-exec-mark-fischer-named-head.

162 *One of Fischer's main goals would be reaching* Jonathan Landreth, "UFC Expands
Presence in China, Asia," *Hollywood Reporter*, August 29, 2010, https://www.holly
woodreporter.com/news/general-news/ufc-expands-presence-china-asia-27203/.

162 *Also in 2010, Zuffa announced it had sold a 10 percent ownership stake* Jennifer Wenk,
"Flash Entertainment Purchases Minority Interest in UFC," UFC.com, January 12, 2010,
https://www.ufc.com/news/flash-entertainment-purchases-minority-interest-ufc.

163 *For Lorenzo, the value in the company's international business* Bill King, "UFC's Global
Ambitions," *Sports Business Journal*, June 11, 2012, https://www.sportsbusinessjournal
.com/Journal/Issues/2012/06/11/In-Depth/UFC-global.aspx?hl=US&sc=0.

163 *"We'd rather go out and get a license fee and expose"* Jon Show, "UFC Expands TV Reach
to China and Mexico," *Sports Business Journal*, June 29, 2009, https://www.sportsbusi
nessjournal.com/Journal/Issues/2009/06/29/This-Weeks-News/UFC-Expands-TV
-Reach-To-China-And-Mexico.aspx?hl=ufc&sc=0.

163 *Tickets sold out in seventy-four minutes* King, "UFC's Global Ambitions"; "Globo
Dreams of UFC Like in Days of Tyson; Rede TV! Prepares Defense," *Gracie Magazine*,
August 30, 2011, http://web.archive.org/web/20210512202607/https://www.graciemag
.com/en/2011/08/30/globo-dreams-of-ufc-like-in-days-of-tyson-rede-tv-prepares
-defense/.

163 *Another* Fight Night *event featuring heavyweight champion* King, "UFC's Global
Ambitions."

163 *That same year, Zelaznik helped close a new* "TUF 13 to Air on ESPN in UK," *ESPN UK*,
April 6, 2011, http://en.espn.co.uk/ufc/sport/story/83854.html?CMP=OTC-RSS.

163 *By the end of 2010, the UFC had added another* King, "UFC's Global Ambitions."

163 *The international expansion had little effect on the UFC's ratings* Kelsey Philpott,
"The State of the UFC Address," *MMA Payout*, October 4, 2010, https://mmapayout
.com/2010/10/04/the-state-of-the-ufc-address/; Marcus Vanderberg, "UFC Prelims See
an Increase in Ratings," *AdWeek*, September 29, 2010, https://www.adweek.com
/tvnewser/ufc-prelims-see-an-increase-in-ratings/87327/; "Payout Perspective: UFC-Fox
TV Deal Q2 2012 Performance Review," *MMA Payout*, July 27, 2012, https://mmapayout
.com/2012/07/27/payout-perspective-ufc-fox-tv-deal-q22012-performance-review/.

164 *Four of the first five seasons of* The Ultimate Fighter Ivan Trembow, "Ultimate Fighter 5 Finishes as Lowest-Rated Season To-Date," *MMA Weekly/Ivan's Blog*, December 9, 2007, http://www.ivansblog.com/2007/12/.

164 *The first ten UFC Fight Night events had drawn an average* Ivan Trembow, "UFC Fight Night 10 Draws 1.2 Rating," *MMA Weekly*, June 22, 2007, https://www.mmaweekly.com /ufc-fight-night-10-draws-1-2-rating-2.

164 *There had been periodic highs—such as when Zuffa* "The Ultimate Fighter 10 Finale Draws 3.7 Million Viewers, Peaks with 5.2 Million for Kimbo," *MMA Junkie*, December 8, 2009, https://mmajunkie.usatoday.com/2009/12/the-ultimate-fighter-10 -finale-draws-3-7-million-viewers-peaks-with-5-2-million-for-kimbo.

164 *One typical ad featured a man in hunting clothes* Viacom, "UFC on Spike TV" commercial, circa 2011, available at https://www.youtube.com/watch?v=7ITE785Kq80.

164 *By 2009, the average net worth of people under thirty-five* Richard Fry et al., "The Rising Age Gap in Economic Well-Being," *Pew Research Center*, November 7, 2011, https://www .pewresearch.org/social-trends/2011/11/07/the-rising-age-gap-in-economic-well-being/.

165 *A quarter of Americans between eighteen and thirty-four* Paul Taylor et al., "Young, Underemployed, and Optimistic: Coming of Age, Slowly, in a Tough Economy," *Pew Research Center*, February 9, 2012, https://www.pewresearch.org/social-trends /2012/02/09/chapter-1-overview-2/.

165 *Of those living with their parents, one in four was idle* Joshua Vespa, "The Changing Economics and Demographics of Young Adulthood: 1975–2016," United States Census Bureau, April 2017, https://www.census.gov/content/dam/Census/library/publica tions/2017/demo/p20-579.pdf.

165 *Many were struggling with student loan debt* Eric Pianin, "Student Loans Seen as Potential 'Next Debt Bomb' for U.S. Economy," *Washington Post*, March 10, 2012, https://www .washingtonpost.com/business/student-loans-seen-as-potential-next-debt-bomb-for-us -economy/2012/03/05/gIQAM0iF4R_story.html.

165 *Others were buried in credit card debt* Ibid.

165 *it was an "eat what you kill" sport* Samuels, "Lorenzo Fertitta Interview."

165 *Instead, he began to compare it to Discovery Communications* Gareth A. Davies, "UFC Owner Lorenzo Fertitta Fighting for a Generation of Mixed Martial Artists," *Telegraph*, October 9, 2013, https://www.telegraph.co.uk/sport/othersports/ufc/10368329 /UFC-owner-Lorenzo-Fertitta-fighting-for-a-generation-of-mixed-martial-artists.html.

165 *"It sounds kind of crazy on the face of it"* Ibid.

165 *Lorenzo wanted to transform the UFC into a global media company* Ibid.

166 *The company also wanted to start producing standalone seasons* King, "UFC's Global Ambitions."

166 *It felt counterintuitive to Kay and others at Viacom* Kevin Kay, author interview.

166 *With pay-per-view sales accounting for around 55 percent* Nash, "What We Now Know About the UFC's Finances."

166 *Throughout 2010, Zuffa had met with other networks* Ben Grossman, "UFC Chief Says Broadcast Deal Coming in 2011," *Broadcasting & Cable*, October 25, 2010, http://www .broadcastingcable.com/article/458947-UFC_Chief_Says_Broadcast_Deal_Coming_ in_2011.php; Franklin McNeil, "Reports: UFC, NBCUniversal discuss G4," *ESPN*, June 9, 2011, https://www.espn.com/extra/mma/news/story?id=6645058.

166 *White also met with Fox, which was planning* Grossman, "UFC Chief Says Broadcast Deal Coming in 2011."

166 *The most unusual option came from meetings with NBC's* Brian Stelter, "UFC Looking to Buy Part of G4 Channel," *New York Times*, June 8, 2011, https://archive.nytimes.com /mediadecoder.blogs.nytimes.com/2011/06/08/ufc-looking-to-buy-part-of-g4-channel/.

166 *By 2011, the average American household had access to 168* Megan Geuss, "On Average, Americans Get 189 Cable TV Channels and Only Watch 17," *Ars Technica*, May 6, 2014, https://arstechnica.com/information-technology/2014/05/on-average-americans-get -189-cable-tv-channels-and-only-watch-17/.

166 *Zuffa had discussed buying 60 percent of G4TV* Andy Fixmer and Alex Sherman, "NBC Universal G4 Channel May Get $600 Million in Sale to UFC," *Bloomberg*, June 9, 2011, https://www.bloomberg.com/news/articles/2011-06-09/nbc-universal-s-video-game -channel-may-bring-600-million-in-sale-to-ufc.

167 *Viacom had begun airing events from Bellator* "Bellator Season 5 Debut on MTV2 Garnered 386,000 Viewers," *Fighting Insider*, September 14, 2011, http://m.fighting insider.com/2011/09/14/bellator-season-5-debut-on-mtv2-garnered-386000-viewers/; "Bellator Ends Season 4 Strong with Strong Record TV Ratings for MTV2," *MMA Weekly*, May 24, 2011, https://www.mmaweekly.com/bellator-ends-season-4-strong -with-record-tv-ratings-for-mtv2#!.

167 *Originally founded as a small kickboxing promotion in 1985* Jonathan Snowden, "The Rise and Fall of the Pepsi to UFC's Coke: A Strikeforce Oral History," *Bleacher Report*, January 11, 2013, https://bleacherreport.com/articles/1479906-the-rise-and-fall-of-the -pepsi-to-ufcs-coke-a-strikeforce-oral-history.

167 *The company's debut featured a fight between Frank Shamrock* Dave Meltzer, "After Grand MMA Opening, Strikeforce Will Turn Out the Lights Saturday Night," *MMA Fighting*, January 10, 2013, https://www.mmafighting.com/2013/1/10/3859420/after-grand-open ing-strikeforce-will-turn-out-the-lights-saturday.

167 *In 2008, Silicon Valley Sports & Entertainment* Snowden, "The Rise and Fall of the Pepsi to UFC's Coke."

167 *In 2009, the company acquired EliteXC* Josh Nason, "Strikeforce Acquires EliteXC Contracts, Inks TV Deals with CBS, Showtime," *Bleacher Report*, February 5, 2009, https://bleacherreport.com/articles/120226-strikeforce-acquires-elitexc-contracts-inks -tv-deals-with-cbs-showtime.

167 *In 2009, Strikeforce scored its biggest coup* Ken Pishna, "Sweepstakes Over; Fedor Signs with Strikeforce," *MMA Weekly*, August 3, 2009, https://www.mmaweekly.com/sweep stakes-over-fedor-signs-with-strikeforce-2; Eli Segall, "Strikeforce Makes Millions on Mixed Martial Arts," *Silicon Valley Business Journal*, January 28, 2011, https://www .bizjournals.com/sanjose/print-edition/2011/01/28/strikeforce-makes-millions-on -MMA.html.

167 *In November of 2010, Zuffa had made an attempt* Singer, *Redacted Expert Report of Hal J. Singer*, pp. 33–34.

168 *While the promotion's revenue had grown more than 700 percent* John S. Nash, "Fighter Pay Details Revealed During Monday's UFC Antitrust Hearing," *Bloody Elbow*, August 27, 2019, https://www.bloodyelbow.com/2019/8/27/20835161/fighter-pay-de tails-revealed-during-mondays-ufc-antitrust-hearing-mma-news.

168 *In early 2010, Strikeforce lost another important revenue source* Dave Meltzer, "The Demise of Strikeforce," *MMA Fighting*, January 11, 2013, https://www.mmafighting. com/2013/1/11/3859604/the-demise-of-strikeforce.

168 *Coker had tried to argue against the sale* John S. Nash, "The Secret History of

Strikeforce—Part 5: Business as Usual," *Bloody Elbow*, May 1, 2014, https://www
.bloodyelbow.com/2014/5/1/5665136/the-secret-history-of-strikeforce-part-5-business
-as-usual.

168   *an offer from Zuffa reported to be roughly $40 million* Geno Mrosko, "How Much Did
the UFC Pay for Strikeforce?," *MMA Mania*, March 13, 2011, https://www.mmamania
.com/2011/3/13/2049233/how-much-did-the-ufc-pay-for-strikeforce.

168   *In March of 2011, White announced the deal* Loretta Hunt, "UFC Buys Strikeforce," *Los
Angeles Times*, March 13, 2011, https://www.latimes.com/archives/blogs/sports-now
/story/2011-03-13/ufc-buys-strikeforce.

168   *The news came a week before Coker had planned* Nash, "The Secret History of
Strikeforce—Part 5: Business as Usual."

168   *Knowing Viacom wouldn't approve a new deal that was substantially bigger* Kevin Kay,
author interview.

169   *It was a losing strategy, and in August of 2011* Richard Sandomir, "UFC Lands a
Seven-Year Deal with Fox Sports," *New York Times*, August 18, 2011, https://www
.nytimes.com/2011/08/19/sports/ufc-lands-a-seven-year-deal-with-fox-sports.html.

169   *In addition to paying more than Spike, Fox had also agreed* Mike Chiappetta, "UFC and
FOX Officially Announce Details of Landmark 7-Year Broadcast Deal," *MMA Fighting*,
August 18, 2011, https://www.mmafighting.com/2011/8/18/2738071/ufc-and-fox-offi
cially-announce-details-of-landmark-7-year-broad; Kristi Dosh, "Fuel TV Scores Early
Ratings Hit with UFC," *ESPN*, April 16, 2012, https://www.espn.com/blog/sportsbusi
ness/post/_/id/607/fuel-tv-scores-early-ratings-hits-with-ufc.

169   *Zuffa announced the deal in Los Angeles, at Studio 2A* Ariel Helwani, "UFC Signs
Broadcast Deal with FOX Sports," AOL (via *MMA Fighting*), August 18, 2011, https://
www.youtube.com/watch?v=YMKElewUxFk.

169   *"We're not second class anymore"* Ibid.

169   *Asked about the split from Spike, Lorenzo claimed* Ibid.

169   *While Lorenzo was pragmatic, White was triumphant* Ariel Helwani, "Dana White
Explains Why UFC Chose to Sign with FOX Over Other Networks," *Ariel Helwani*,
August 19, 2011, https://www.youtube.com/watch?v=cbQW-81JO24.

169   *Strikeforce's legal counsel Ken Ellner looked back* Nash, "The Secret History of
Strikeforce—Part 5: Business as Usual."

169   *"I never imagined that the UFC would leave Spike"* Ibid.

170   *Instead, Strikeforce ran as a kind of zombie promotion* Matt Erickson, "Nick Diaz
Challenges Georges St-Pierre at UFC 137 in October," *MMA Fighting*, June 1, 2011,
https://www.mmafighting.com/2011/06/01/nick-diaz-challenges-georges-st-pierre
-at-ufc-137-in-october; Mike Chiappetta, "Dana White Confirms Dan Henderson vs.
Shogun Rua at UFC 139," *MMA Fighting*, September 21, 2011, https://www.mmafighting.
com/2011/09/21/dana-white-confirms-dan-henderson-vs-shogun-rua-at-ufc-139;
"Overeem Signs with the UFC; Faces Lesnar in December," UFC.com, September 6,
2011, https://www.ufc.com/news/overeem-signs-ufc-faces-lesnar-december.

170   *After three shocking losses in Strikeforce* "Fedor Emelianenko Retires Following Knockout
of Pedro Rizzo," *MMA Junkie*, June 22, 2012, https://mmajunkie.usatoday.com/2012/06
/fedor-emelianenko-retires-following-knockout-of-pedro-rizzo.

170   *White had claimed the UFC didn't want Emelianenko* Mike Chiappetta, "Dana White:
After Loss, We Have No Interest in Fedor Emelianenko," *MMA Fighting*, July 1, 2010,
https://www.mmafighting.com/2010/07/01/dana-white-after-loss-we-have-no-interest
-in-fedor-emelianenko.

Chapter 9: I Will Make You Look Like a Genius

171 *She spent her afternoons behind the bar* Ronda Rousey, with Maria Burns Ortiz, *My Fight/ Your Fight* (New York: Regan Arts, 2015), pp. 149–50.

171 *She had spent most of the previous eleven years* Athlete Biography: Ronda Rousey, US Olympic Committee website, accessed on August 31, 2022, https://olympics.com/en /athletes/ronda-rousey.

171 *When she returned to LA afterward* Rousey with Ortiz, *My Fight/Your Fight*, p. 144.

171 *Among Rousey's favorite regulars were a pair* Ibid., pp. 149–50.

171 *The short clips fascinated Rousey* Ibid., p. 150.

172 *During the first UFC in 1993, Davie had hired* Ibid., pp. 177–78.

172 *A number of early UFC champions, including Don Frye* Joseph Santoliquito, "Becky Levi: Where Is She Now?," Sherdog, December 18, 2013, https://www.sherdog.com/news /articles/2/Becky-Levi-Where-Is-She-Now-60831.

172 *In 1997, Levi became one of the first women* "IFC 4: Akwesasane Cage Combat," Tapology, https://www.tapology.com/fightcenter/events/4151-ifc-4-akwesasane-cage-combat.

172 *In the early 2000s, Jennifer Howe emerged as a regional star* "Jennifer Howe: Undefeated Female MMA Fighter," *The Fight Girls*, originally published February 23, 2002, https:// www.fightergirls.com/jennifer-howe-undefeated-female-mma-fighter/.

172 *In 2002, former UFC commentator Jeff Osborne promoted* Joe Hall, "Are You Ready for 'The Revolution'? All Women's MMA Card Becomes a Reality," *Full Contact Fighter*, April 12, 2002, https://fcfighter.com/are-you-ready-for-the-revolutionall-womens-mma -card-becomes-a-reality/.

172 *In 2007, Gina Carano became an unexpected* "Gina Carano Changed the Face of MMA," *ESPN*, July 5, 2012, https://www.espn.com/espnw/athletes-life/inthegame/story/_/id /8131825/in-game-gina-carano.

172 *After suffering her first professional loss in 2009* Mike Flemming, "Soderbergh, Carano a Knockout Pairing," *Variety*, September 6, 2009, http://weblogs.variety.com/bfdeal memo/2009/09/soderbergh-carano-in-knockout-pairing.html.

172 *Despite Carano's breakout success—her fight on CBS drew* Ken Pishna, "CBS-EliteXC, UFC, and WEC Score with Ratings," *MMA Weekly*, June 3, 2008, https://www .mmaweekly.com/cbs-elitexc-ufc-and-wec-score-with-ratings-2.

172 *In 2011, he famously told a TMZ reporter* "Dana White—Women Will Never Fight in the UFC," *TMZ*, January 19, 2011, https://www.tmz.com/2011/01/19/dana-white-ufc-women -fighters-cris-cyborg-santos-gina-carano-mma-female/.

172 *He also thought there was something that was fundamentally* Tisha Thompson, "Dana White: Bringing Ronda Rousey, Women's MMA to UFC Was 'the Best Decision I Ever Made,' " *ESPN*, available at https://www.youtube.com/watch?v=GcVnraOqL5s&t=3s.

172 *When Rousey mentioned the idea of competing* Rousey with Ortiz, *My Fight/Your Fight*, pp. 161–63.

173 *Like many gyms at the time, Hayastan had its own* Ibid., p. 162.

173 *Rousey drew up an elaborate fourteen-day* Ibid., p. 158.

173 *"This is the stupidest fucking idea I've heard"* "When Ronda Rousey Pitched MMA Career to Mom: 'Stupidest Idea I've Heard in My Life,' " *MMA Junkie*, March 25, 2015, https:// mmajunkie.usatoday.com/2015/03/when-ronda-rousey-pitched-mma-career-to-mom -stupidest-idea-ive-heard-in-my-life.

173 *She herself had been a lifelong judoka* Kelefa Saneh, "Mean Girl," *New Yorker*, July 28, 2014, https://www.newyorker.com/magazine/2014/07/28/mean-girl.

173 *When Rousey was twelve, she was worried she had broken* Rousey with Ortiz, *My Fight/ Your Fight*, p. 43.

173 *"If you want to win the way you say"* Ibid.

173 *"I am not going to be one of these parents"* Rousey with Ortiz, *My Fight/Your Fight*, pp. 163–65.

173 *It was a familiar feeling for Rousey* Jen Pereira, "UFC Fighter Ronda Rousey Delivers Message for Mom Who Helped Her Discover Childhood Speech Condition," ABC News, August 28, 2015, https://abcnews.go.com/Entertainment/ufc-fighter-ronda-rousey-delivers-message-mom-helped/story?id=33361412; Saneh, "Mean Girl."

173 *She had communicated with her parents and two older sisters* Rousey with Ortiz, *My Fight/Your Fight*, p. 24.

174 *"It wasn't just about words, it was about everything"* Ibid., p. 12.

174 *After she had begun to speak, Rousey's family relocated* Ibid., p. 16.

174 *During their first winter in North Dakota, Rousey's father* Pete Thamel, "Rousey's Journey Out of Pain, Through Judo," *New York Times*, August 11, 2008, https://www.nytimes.com/2008/08/12/sports/olympics/12judo.html.

174 *He ended up moving to the small town of Devil's Lake* Ibid.

174 *While her sisters stayed behind in Minot with her mother* Rousey with Ortiz, *My Fight/ Your Fight*, pp. 24–26.

174 *The family was eventually reunited when Rousey's mother* Ibid., p. 28.

174 *One afternoon, he called Rousey's mother at her office* Ibid., pp. 28–29.

174 *De Mars would later decide to move the family back* Ibid., p. 32.

174 *But Rousey seemed stuck in a lingering depression* Jonathan Snowden, "The Gentle Way: Strikeforce Champion Ronda Rousey and the Birth of a Judo Star," *Bleacher Report*, April 6, 2012, https://bleacherreport.com/articles/1134250-the-gentle-way-strikeforce-champion-ronda-rousey-and-the-birth-of-a-judo-star.

175 *"One hundred percent of my focus had to be in the present"* Rousey with Ortiz, *My Fight/ Your Fight*, p. 33.

175 *After two weeks of nothing but introspection and silence* Ibid., p. 166.

175 *If it didn't seem like she would be able to support herself* Saneh, "Mean Girl."

175 *A few weeks into her new training routine at Hayastan* Flinder Boyd, "How Ronda Rousey and Coach Edmond Tarverdyan Became UFC's Perfect Pair," Fox Sports, November 12, 2015, https://www.foxsports.com/stories/ufc/how-ronda-rousey-and-coach-edmond-tarverdyan-became-ufcs-perfect-pair.

175 *"I was like, A girl fighting?"* Ibid.

175 *Rather than guiding her through drills, he told her instead* Joseph Santoliquito, "Edmond Tarverdyan: The Reluctant Ronda Rousey Benefactor," Sherdog, July 29, 2015, https://www.sherdog.com/news/articles/Edmond-Tarverdyan-The-Reluctant-Ronda-Rousey-Benefactor-89745#!.

175 *"When Ronda was a kid we used to yell at her"* Snowden, "The Gentle Way."

176 *When she wasn't at the Glendale Fighting Club* Rousey with Ortiz, *My Fight/Your Fight*, pp. 188–90.

176 *Harvey booked Rousey in her first amateur fight* Ibid., pp. 194–96.

176 *The event was held at a jiu-jitsu academy* "Combat Fight League—Ground Zero," Sherdog, https://www.sherdog.com/events/CFL-Ground-Zero-18729.

176 *The lights were turned down low to give* "Ronda Rousey vs Hayden Muñoz Full Fight" (video), available at https://www.youtube.com/watch?v=9xCKnDRPWeU.

176 *As she stood in the cage for the first time* Rousey with Ortiz, *My Fight/Your Fight*, p. 196.

176 *Munoz had been so nervous about facing* Phil Murphy, "Ronda Rousey Breaks Down Tape of 3 of Her Early Fights," *ESPN*, July 4, 2018, available at https://www.youtube.com /watch?v=vKFYEnCxLiA&t=3s.

176 *"Winning feels like falling in love"* Rousey with Ortiz, *My Fight/Your Fight*, p. 11.

176 *Rousey would win each by first-round armbar* "Ronda Rousey" (Fight Finder profile), Sherdog, https://www.sherdog.com/fighter/Ronda-Rousey-73073#!.

177 *First Tarverdyan agreed to begin individually training* Santoliquito, "Edmond Tarverdyan: The Reluctant Ronda Rousey Benefactor"; "Ronda Rousey Wins in 49 Seconds, Likely Headed to Strikeforce Next," RondaMMA.com, June 18, 2011, https://rondamma.com /ronda-rousey-wins-in-49-seconds-likely-headed-to-strikeforce-next/.

177 *Rousey's opponent, Sarah D'Alelio, had originally* "Ronda Rousey vs. Sarah D'Alelio Shifted to Strikeforce Challengers 18 Main Card," *MMA Junkie*, July 4, 2011, https://mmajunkie .usatoday.com/2011/07/ronda-rousey-vs-sarah-dalelio-shifted-to-strikeforce-challeng ers-18-main-card.

177 *Rousey treated it as the most important fight of her career* Rousey with Ortiz, *My Fight/ Your Fight*, p. 208.

177 *As Rousey returned to the locker room after the victory* "Ronda Rousey: 'I Should Reconsider Being So Nice,'" Strikeforce, August 13, 2011, https://www.youtube.com /watch?v=WApfonxtiU4&t=26s.

177 *"From this day on," she told Tarverdyan* Rousey with Ortiz, *My Fight/Your Fight*, p. 208.

177 *Rousey soon developed a reputation among fans* Matthew Ryder, "Strikeforce: Is Ronda Rousey a Hero or Villain?" *Bleacher Report*, March 21, 2012, https://bleacherreport.com /articles/1113462-strikeforce-is-ronda-rousey-a-hero-or-a-villain.

177 *In her next fight with Strikeforce, against Julia Budd* UFC Holdings, Ronda Rousey vs. Julia Budd, *Strikeforce Challengers: Britt vs. Sayers*, November 18, 2011, available at https://ufcfightpass.com/video/88554/ronda-rousey-vs-julia-budd-strikeforce-challeng ers-britt-vs-sayers.

178 *Four months later, Rousey was booked against Miesha Tate* Brian Knapp, "Miesha Tate Ronda Rousey Given the Green Light for Strikeforce Women's Title Bout," Sherdog, March 2, 2012, https://www.sherdog.com/news/news/Miesha-Tate-Ronda-Rousey-Given -Green-Light-for-Strikeforce-Womens-Title-Bout-40753.

178 *In the lead-up to the fight, she described Tate* "Ronda Rousey vs. Miesha Tate: War of Words," *MMA Interviews*, February 29, 2012, available at https://www.youtube.com /watch?v=PW2KUCGkluw.

178 *More offensive still was Tate's claim* Damon Martin, "Miesha Tate Pulls No Punches About Her Disdain for Ronda Rousey," *MMA Weekly*, February 28, 2012, https://www .mmaweekly.com/miesha-tate-pulls-no-punches-about-her-disdain-for-ronda-rousey.

178 *The night before the fight, tensions escalated even further* Jeremy Botter, "Miesha Tate's Boyfriend Makes Stupid Twitter Comments Toward Ronda Rousey," *Bleacher Report*, March 3, 2012, https://bleacherreport.com/articles/1089423-miesha-tates-boyfriend -makes-stupid-twitter-comments-towards-ronda-rousey.

178 *As Rousey and Tate finally faced off in the cage* UFC Holdings, Ronda Rousey vs. Miesha Tate, *Strikeforce: Tate vs. Rousey*, March 3, 2012, https://ufcfightpass.com/video/41065 /ronda-rousey-vs-miesha-tate-strikeforce-tate-vs-rousey.

179 *Though it was just her fifth professional fight* "Jacare Sits Atop Strikeforce: Tate vs. Rousey Fighter Salaries," *MMA Weekly*, March 5, 2012, https://www.mmaweekly.com/jacare-sits -atop-strikeforce-tate-vs-rousey-fighter-salaries.

179 *In the summer of 2012, the editors of* ESPN *magazine* "Ronda Rousey Featured in ESPN the Magazine's The Body Issue," *Yahoo! Sports*, July 10, 2012, https://sports.yahoo.com /blogs/mma-cagewriter/ronda-rousey-featured-espn-magazine-body-issue-182218140 —mma.html?guccounter=1.

179 *She had never seen herself as beautiful* "All Access: Ronda Rousey, Episode 1," Showtime, August 9, 2012, available at https://www.youtube.com/watch?v=fJwdEMA-l_Y.

179 *"There were days I would look at myself"* Ibid.

179 *"I think what we really need right now is a face"* "Ronda Rousey: One-Minute Woman," Strikeforce, August 11, 2011, available at https://www.youtube.com/watch?v=FiYpWz Kt2d0.

180 *Before her next fight, against Sarah Kaufman* "All Access: Ronda Rousey, Episode 1."

180 *Lesnar's departure from the UFC a year earlier* Chad Dundas, "Brock Lesnar's Final UFC Exit Leaves UFC Fans with Unanswerable Questions," *Bleacher Report*, March 25, 2015, https://bleacherreport.com/articles/2408808-brock-lesnars-final-exit-leaves-ufc-fans -with-unanswerable-questions.

180 *After her first first Strikeforce title defense* Rousey with Ortiz, *My Fight/Your Fight*, pp. 234–36.

181 *She felt a smile break across her face* Ibid., p. 235.

181 *"In my mind, there was confetti"* Ibid.

181 *"I promise," she said, "I will make"* Ibid.

Chapter 10: Brother, I Lost Everything

182 *By 2014, the UFC offices had grown to nearly twenty thousand square feet* Alan Snel, "UFC Starts Construction on New Global Headquarters in Las Vegas," *Las Vegas Review-Journal*, December 1, 2015, https://www.reviewjournal.com/business/ufc-starts-con struction-on-new-global-headquarters-in-las-vegas/.

182 *White no longer recognized many of the faces* Bill King, "New HQ Represents Turning Point for UFC, Athletes," *Sports Business Journal*, April 24, 2017, https://www.sports businessjournal.com/Journal/Issues/2017/04/24/In-Depth/UFC-HQ.aspx.

182 *"When we started this thing, guys were at my house"* Duane Finley, "The Fighting Life of Dana White," *Bleacher Report*, February 5, 2014, https://bleacherreport.com/articles /1949634-the-fighting-life-the-fire-of-dana-white.

182 *During one representative three-month stretch* Kowal, "UFC's History and an In Depth Interview with Dana White."

182 *"I've done an entire season of* The Ultimate Fighter*"* Ibid.

182 *"It got to the point where we didn't clock time"* Stephie Haynes, "Former UFC PR Director Jen Wenk Discusses What It Was Like Working for the Organization," *Bloody Elbow*, October 11, 2012, https://www.bloodyelbow.com/2012/10/11/3487392/ufc-former-pr -director-jen-wenk-interview.

183 *With five channels to provide programming* "UFC Launches UFC Fight Pass," *UFC.com*, December 28, 2013, https://www.ufc.com/news/ufc-launches-ufc-fight-pass.

183 *"There were plenty of times when people in our offices"* Don Gold, author interview.

183 *And the international expansion continued* Mike Bohn, "UFC 2014: A Ridiculously Robust Look at Stats, Streaks, Skids, and Record-Setters," *MMA Junkie*, December 27, 2014; "UFC and BT Launch Three-Year Deal," UFC.com, May 7, 2013, https://www.ufc .com/news/ufc-and-bt-launch-three-year-deal.

183 *make up for a major decline* Nash, "What We Now Know About the UFC's Finances."

183 *The UFC partially offset the decline by raising its pay-per-view prices* Kevin Sampson, "2009 Marks Breakout Year for UFC PPV Sales," *Bleacher Report*, January 2, 2010, https://bleacherreport.com/articles/318590-2009-marks-breakout-year-for-ufc-ppv-sales; Steven Marrocco, "It's Official: UFC Pay-Per-View Prices Going Up for 2015," *MMA Junkie*, January 29, 2015, https://mmajunkie.usatoday.com/2015/01/its-official-ufc-pay -per-view-prices-going-up-for-2015.

183 *In 2013, Zuffa acquired LA Boxing* Jesse Holland, "Zuffa Buys LA Boxing and Will Re-brand as 'UFC Gym,' " *MMA Mania*, January 7, 2013, https://www.mmamania .com/2013/1/7/1816054/zuffa-buys-l-a-boxing-ufc-gym-mma.

183 *The company also released UFC Fit, a twelve-DVD* "UFC Launches UFC Fit," UFC.com, May 16, 2013, https://www.ufc.com/news/ufc-launches-ufc-fit.

184 *"This is the key to changing your life"* Ibid.

184 *In 2014, the first video game in a multiyear agreement* Damon Martin, "UFC Signs Video Game Deal with EA Sports," *MMA Weekly*, June 4, 2012, https://www.mmaweekly.com /ufc-signs-video-game-deal-with-ea-sports; "UFC Selects Future US to Oversee UFC 360 Media Brand," *PR Newswire*, February 19, 2014, https://www.prnewswire.com/news -releases/ufc-selects-future-us-to-oversee-ufc-360-media-brand-246165721.html.

184 *In December of 2014, Zuffa announced a six-year* "Reebok, UFC Announce Landmark Apparel Deal," UFC.com, December 1, 2014, https://www.ufc.com/news/reebok-ufc-an nounce-landmark-apparel-deal; Gareth A. Davies, "UFC's £45m Tie-Up with Reebok a Big Deal as Fighters Get Dressed for Financial Success," *Telegraph*, December 2, 2014, https://www.ufc.com/news/reebok-ufc-announce-landmark-apparel-deal.

184 *For Lorenzo, the deal was a milestone* Galen Moore, "Shoeless? UFC's CEO Defends Fighter Pay Under Reebok Deal," *Bostinno*, January 17, 2016, https://www.bizjournals. com/boston/inno/stories/news/2016/01/17/shoeless-ufcs-ceo-defends-fighter-pay-un der-reebok.html.

184 *Reebok had also agreed to pay every fighter* Marc Raimondi, "UFC Announces How Much Fighters Will Be Paid Through Reebok Deal," *MMA Fighting*, May 6, 2015, https://www .mmafighting.com/2015/5/6/8560867/ufc-announces-how-much-fighters-will-be-paid -through-reebok-deal.

184 *"All [the fighters] have to worry about is performing"* Moore, "Shoeless?"

184 *By 2014, just 16 percent of the UFC's revenue* Nash, "What We Now Know About the UFC's Finances."

184 *In 2014, the company spent $72 million on fighter pay:* Ibid.

185 *Zev Eigen, a labor law professor from Northwestern* Jonathan Snowden, "The Business of Fighting: A Look Inside the UFC's Top-Secret Fighter Contract," *Bleacher Report*, May 14, 2013, https://bleacherreport.com/articles/1516575-the-business-of-fighting-a -look-inside-the-ufcs-top-secret-fighter-contract#slide0.

185 *The contract's termination clause summed up the overwhelming* Ibid.

185 *"This is an unconscionable term"* Ibid.

185 *The small number of star fighters who could credibly* John S. Nash, "Lawsuit Documents Reveal Even More Details on UFC Business Structure and Fighter Pay," *Bloody Elbow*, February 3, 2020, https://www.bloodyelbow.com/2020/2/3/20922496/ufc-lawsuit-docs -reveal-more-details-ufc-business-structure-fighter-pay-class-action-business-news.

185 *Zuffa bought Ronda Rousey a BMW X6 M* Rousey with Ortiz, *My Fight/Your Fight*, pp. 252–53.

185   *"I can't have one of my champions driving"* Ibid.

185   *"I was so driven, if they said to me"* Phillipe Nover, author interview.

186   *He would go on to win all three of his bouts* Michael David Smith, "Dana White: Ultimate Fighter's Phillipe Nover Reminds Me of Georges St-Pierre," *MMA Fighting*, November 5, 2008, https://www.mmafighting.com/2008/11/05/dana-white-ultimate-fighters-phillipe -nover-reminds-me-of-geor.

186   *Though Nover went on to lose in the season finale* Phillipe Nover, author interview.

186   *It was a substantial pay cut from what the twenty-five-year-old* Ibid.

186   *Though he still had one fight left on his contract* Jesse Holland, "Phillipe Nover Released from the UFC following His Feb. 6 Loss to Rob Emerson," *MMA Mania*, February 11, 2010, https://www.mmamania.com/2010/2/11/1305835/phillipe-nover-released-from -the.

186   *In a little over a year, Nover had earned $16,000* Phillipe Nover, author interview.

186   *He had to cover the cost himself* Ibid.

186   *With 230 new fighters making their debut in 2014* "Debut UFC Fighters—UFC in 2014," Wikipedia, https://en.wikipedia.org/wiki/2014_in_UFC.

186   *The UFC had introduced a formal rankings system* Thomas Myers, "Official UFC Rankings for Fighters to Be Introduced in Feb. 2013," *MMA Mania*, January 31, 2013, https://www.mmamania.com/2013/1/31/3939412/official-ufc-rankings-fighters-intro duced-feb-2013-pound-for-pound-dana-white; "How Are Rankings Determined?," UFC .com, https://www.ufc.com/rankings.

186   *But with the average fighter's career lasting just forty-one months* Singer, *Redacted Expert Report of Hal J. Singer*, p. 16.

186   *The initial seventy-three-person panel, chosen by the UFC* "UFC Rankings—Voting Panelists," UFC.com, July 11, 2013, available at http://web.archive.org/web/2013071101 4918/http://www.ufc.com/rankings.

187   *During the Fox Sports era, the UFC's domestic television* "Payout Perspective: UFC-Fox TV Deal Q1/2012 Performance Review," *MMA Payout*, April 5, 2012, https:// mmapayout.com/2012/04/05/payout-perspective-ufcfox-tv-deal-q12012-performance -review/.

187   UFC on FOX 2 *would draw 4.7 million, and both* Ken Pishna, "UFC on Fox 3 TV Ratings Signal Significant Drop," *MMA Weekly*, May 8, 2012, https://www.mmaweekly.com /ufc-on-fox-3-tv-ratings-signal-significant-drop; "UFC on Fox 4 Up from UFC on Fox 3 While Going Head-to-Head with Olympics," *MMA Weekly*, August 7, 2012, https://www .mmaweekly.com/ufc-on-fox-4-tv-ratings-flat-opposite-olympics-record-numbers.

187   *The average audience for the first season* "Payout Perspective: UFC-Fox TV Deal Q1/2012 Performance Review."

187   *The semiweekly* Fight Night *events saw similar* Ibid.

187   *The audience for* UFC Primetime, *a documentary series* Ibid.

187   *The UFC's global television audience showed similar signs of flagging* Singer, *Redacted Expert Report of Hal J. Singer.*

187   *In 2012, ESPN produced a segment on UFC fighter pay* John Barr and Josh Gross, "UFC Fighters Say Low Pay Simply Brutal," ESPN.com, January 11, 2012, https://www.espn .com/espn/otl/story/_/page/UFCpay/ufc-fighters-say-low-pay-most-painful-hit-all.

187   *"We're basically fighting for crumbs"* Ibid.

187   *Rob Maysey, an Arizona attorney who had helped launch* Ibid.

188   *Lorenzo had agreed to be interviewed for the story* "Lorenzo Fertitta's 'Outside the

Lines' Interview Uncut and Unedited," *MMA Weekly*, January 16, 2012, https://www
.mmaweekly.com/lorenzo-fertittas-espns-outside-the-lines-interview-uncut-and-uned
ited.

188 *"Maybe it's just part of our culture"* Ibid.

188 *Yet, when asked what percentage of the UFC's annual revenue* Ibid.; John S. Nash, "Court
Filings Reveal More Info on How Much 'Top' UFC Fighters Are Paid," *Bloody Elbow*,
September 16, 2019, https://www.bloodyelbow.com/2019/9/16/20866655/court-filings
-reveal-more-info-on-how-much-top-ufc-fighters-are-paid.

188 *Eighty-three percent were contracted to earn guaranteed* John S. Nash, "Lawsuit
Documents Reveal Even More Details on UFC Business Structures and Fighter Pay."

188 *In 2014, the UFC provoked more public ire* Damon Martin, "Former WWE Champion
CM Punk Signs with UFC," Fox Sports, December 6, 2014, https://www.foxsports.com
/stories/ufc/former-wwe-champion-cm-punk-signs-with-the-ufc.

188 *One fighter described the signing as a "circus"* "Fighters React to the UFC Signing CM
Punk," *MMA Weekly*, December 7, 2014, https://www.mmaweekly.com/fighters-react
-to-the-ufc-signing-cm-punk-via-twitter; Brett Okamoto, ESPN reporter, Twitter post,
December 6, 2014, https://twitter.com/bokamotoESPN/status/541438487136710656?r41
438487136710656%7Ctwgr%5E%7Ctwcon%5Es1_.

188 *Longtime cutman Jacob "Stitch" Duran admitted Zuffa's deal* John S. Nash, "UFC Cutman:
Reebok Deal May Chase Us to Boxing," *Bloody Elbow*, July 20, 2015, https://www
.bloodyelbow.com/2015/7/20/9002195/veteran-ufc-cutman-stitch-duran-reebok-deal
-cutmen-go-to-boxing-mma-interview.

188 *"Brother, I lost everything regarding sponsors"* Jacob "Stitch" Duran, Twitter post, July 13,
2015, available at https://twitter.com/StitchDuran/status/620610258554064896?.

189 *A day later, Zuffa told Duran it would no longer be using his services* Marc Raimondi,
"Legendary Cutman 'Stitch' Duran Says UFC Fired Him for Comments About Reebok
Deal," *MMA Fighting*, July 21, 2015, https://www.mmafighting.com/2015/7/21/9012245
/legendary-cutman-stitch-duran-says-ufc-fired-him-for-comments-about.

189 *Duran was shocked by the news* Marc Raimondi, "Dana White: 'Stitch' Duran Won't Be
Back with the UFC and 'We Were Never Friends,' " *MMA Fighting*, July 26, 2015, https://
www.mmafighting.com/2015/7/26/9040767/dana-white-stitch-duran-wont-be-back
-with-the-ufc-and-we-were-never.

189 *"Dana has definitely changed"* Ibid.

189 *"We weren't friends," White said. "We're not"* Ibid.

189 *In early 2015, Burt Watson found himself in a similarly* Marc Raimondi, "Burt Watson
Explains Confrontation That Led to Him Quitting UFC: 'I Didn't Appreciate It,' " *MMA
Fighting*, March 9, 2015, https://www.mmafighting.com/2015/3/9/8177379/burt-watson
-explains-confrontation-that-led-to-him-quitting-ufc-i.

189 *One of the fighters who had been booked to compete on the prelims* Burt Watson, author
interview.

189 *Shortly after, Mike Mersch, the UFC's vice president of legal affairs* Ibid.

189 *"I went off on him," says Watson* Ibid.

189 *He would never again be asked back to work* Ibid.

189 *"I was disappointed because of the fact I had"* Ibid.

190 *After two years of negotiations with the company's debtors* Julie Triedman, "After Two
Rocky Years, Station Casinos Exits Bankruptcy," *AM Law Daily*, June 20, 2011, https://
amlawdaily.typepad.com/amlawdaily/2011/06/stationcasinosexit.html.

190 *As part of the deal, the Fertittas were allowed to reacquire* Howard Stutz, "Fertittas' Bid Seen as Highest for Station Casinos," *Las Vegas Review-Journal*, August 6, 2010, http://www.reviewjournal.com/business/fertittas-bid-seen-highest-station-casinos.

190 *The one company that could, Boyd Gaming* Ibid.

190 *In one example, they pointed to a stipulation* Ibid.

190 *While six other bids for individual properties* Ibid.

190 *The unsecured bondholders, who had collectively invested* Cy Ryan, "Fertittas Win Station Casinos Bankruptcy Auction," *Las Vegas Sun*, August 6, 2010, https://lasvegassun.com/news/2010/aug/06/fertittas-win-station-casinos-bankruptcy-auction/.

190 *Frank III and Lorenzo's losses were estimated* Liz Benston, "Why Causing Big Debt Has Not Cost Fertittas Control of Station Casinos," *Las Vegas Sun*, August 15, 2010, https://lasvegassun.com/news/2010/aug/15/why-causing-big-debt-has-not-cost-fertittas-control/.

191 *At the same time that Station was fighting with* "Culinary Union Alleges Unfair Labor Practices at Station Casinos," *Las Vegas Sun*, February 25, 2010, https://lasvegassun.com/news/2010/feb/25/culinary-union-alleges-unfair-labor-practices-stat/; Michael Mishak, "Station Casinos Workers Seek Refuge with Culinary Union," *Las Vegas Sun*, March 13, 2010, https://lasvegassun.com/news/2010/mar/13/station-workers-seek-refuge-culinary/; "Workers from Station Casinos Form Union Organizing Committee," Culinary Workers Union Local 226, February 25, 2010, https://www.culinaryunion226.org/news/press/workers-from-station-casinos-form-union-organizing-committe.

191 *The Culinary Union had successfully organized* "Vegas Union Hotel Guide," available at https://herelocal165.org/vegas-union-hotel-guide/.

191 *It held the record for the longest strike* "Nation's Longest Strike Comes to an End," *Las Vegas Sun/Associated Press*, February 1, 1998, https://lasvegassun.com/news/1998/feb/01/nations-longest-strike-comes-to-an-end/.

191 *Despite its success in organizing on the Strip* Chris Sierotyl, "Labor Board Upholds One Complaint Against Station Casinos, Dismisses Six," *Las Vegas Review-Journal*, June 29, 2012, https://www.reviewjournal.com/business/casinos-gaming/labor-board-upholds-one-complaint-against-station-casinos-dismisses-six/.

191 *In 2010, several hundred Station employees formed* Mishak, "Station Casinos Workers Seek Refuge with Culinary Union."

191 *The members cited concerns about the company's* Ibid.

191 *"Every day we come in in fear"* Ibid.

191 *Fearing that Station would try and make additional cuts* "Hourly Employees from Station Casinos Attend the Company's Bankruptcy Proceedings for the First Time," UniteHere.org, May 6, 2010, https://unitehere.org/press-releases/hourly-employees-from-station-casinos-attend-the-companys-bankruptcy-proceedings-for-the-first-time/.

191 *Also in 2010, the Culinary Union filed a complaint* "Culinary Union Alleges Unfair Labor Practices at Station Casinos."

192 *In 2012, a three-member panel from the NLRB ruled* Steve Green, "National Labor Relations Board Sides with Culinary Union Against Station Casinos," *Las Vegas Sun*, October 2, 2012, https://vegasinc.lasvegassun.com/business/2012/oct/02/national-labor-relations-board-sides-culinary-unio/.

192 *In 2011, after Zuffa announced its plan to acquire* Luke Thomas, "Culinary Union Encourages Federal Trade Commission to Investigate Zuffa," *SB Nation*, September 1, 2011, https://mma.sbnation.com/2011/9/1/2398347/culinary-union-ufc-federal-trade-commission-zuffa-mma-news.

192 *"The anticompetitive restrictions it imposes"* Ibid.

192 *In 2012, the FTC closed its formal investigation* Nate Wilcox, "UFC Strikeforce Merger: FTC Closes Probe of Zuffa," *Bloody Elbow*, January 31, 2012, https://www.bloodyelbow.com/2012/1/31/2762537/ufc-strikeforce-merger-ftc-closes-investigation-zuffa.

192 *A former FTC commissioner familiar* Paul Gift, "Former FTC Commissioner: UFC Investigations, Antitrust Lawsuit 'Ultimately About Consumers,' " *Bloody Elbow*, April 12, 2016, https://www.bloodyelbow.com/2016/4/12/11404276/former-commissioner-joshua-wright-ftc-investigation-antitrust-lawsuit-ufc-news.

192 *The websites ran stories questioning the UFC's* Investors, Unfitforchildren.org, archived at August 28, 2013, http://web.archive.org/web/20130828111350/http://www.unfitforchildren.org/p/investors.html; "The Culinary Union Has Uncovered Some Disturbing Facts About 'UFC on Fox 5,' " Unfitforchildren.org, archived on February 27, 2014, http://web.archive.org/web/20140227033156/http://www.unfitforchildren.org/2012/12/the-culinary-union-has-uncovered-some.html; "Death and Profits, UFC and Deutsche Bank," ZuffaInvestorAlerts.org, January 22, 2013, archived at http://web.archive.org/web/20130410173046/http://www.zuffainvestoralerts.org/2013/01/death-and-profits-ufc-and-deutsche-bank.html.

193 *The union also worked with its national parent organization* Ariel Helwani, "Union Memo Reveals Its Argument Against MMA in New York," *MMA Fighting*, May 11, 2011, https://www.mmafighting.com/2011/05/11/union-memo-reveals-its-arguments-against-mma-in-new-york.

193 *According to Ratner, there was overwhelming* Marc Ratner, author interview.

193 *"We'd get through every committee and we would pass"* Ibid.

193 *Silver would later step down from his role* David Klepper and Michael Virtanen, "NY Assembly Speaker Sheldon Silver Agrees to Step Down as He Loses Democratic Support," NBC 4 New York, May 21, 2015, https://www.nbcnewyork.com/news/local/ouster-new-york-assembly-speaker-sheldon-silver-bribery-charges/625820/.

193 *He was convicted on all counts* "Former New York State Assembly Speaker Sheldon Silver Sentenced to 7 Years in Prison," the United States Attorney's Office, Southern District of New York, July 27, 2018, available at https://www.justice.gov/usao-sdny/pr/former-new-york-state-assembly-speaker-sheldon-silver-sentenced-7-years-prison.

193 *In 2014, a small group of fighters went a step further* Dan Gartland, "Three MMA Fighters File Antitrust Lawsuit Against UFC," *Sports Illustrated*, December 16, 2014, https://www.si.com/mma/2014/12/16/ufc-class-action-anti-trust-lawsuit.

193 *The suit argued that the Zuffa had used a wide* Michael McCann, "Antitrust Lawsuit, If Successful, Could Unravel the UFC," *Sports Illustrated*, December 16, 2014, https://www.si.com/mma/2014/12/17/ufc-antitrust-lawsuit-cung-le; Talib Visram, "Inside the Novel Antitrust Case That Could Kick UFC in Teeth," *Fast Company*, May 3, 2021, https://www.fastcompany.com/90630571/inside-the-novel-antitrust-case-that-could-kick-ufc-in-the-teeth.

193 *As the case went through the early stages* John S. Nash, "Federal Trade Commission Re-Opens UFC Investigation, Contacting Promoters, Fighters, and Managers," *Bloody Elbow*, May 14, 2015, https://www.bloodyelbow.com/2015/5/14/8608897/federal-trade-commission-investigating-ufc-again.

194 *Ticket sales would add $67 million* Nash, "What We Now Know About the UFC's Finances."

194 *The company's remaining profit—$119 million* Ibid.

194 *Just as casinos ran on the gulf between the odds* "Odds and Return to Player," *Casino Reports*, available at https://www.casinoreports.ca/video-poker/odds-return-player/.

194   *In 2014, top fifteen UFC welterweight Robbie Lawler* "UFC on FOX 12 Salaries: Robbie Lawler ($210,000) Tops $986,000 Payroll," *MMA Junkie*, July 27, 2014, https://mmajunkie.usatoday.com/2014/07/ufc-on-fox-12-salaries-robbie-lawler-210000-tops-986000-payroll.

195   *"The reality is the UFC is the ultimate place"* Graham Bensinger, "Lorenzo Fertitta: I wanted to pay fighters $1 million," *In Depth with Graham Bensinger*, available at https://www.youtube.com/watch?v=RhiH3Mj7i6A&list=PLW5qT4HIAd1Yxu7xA-xuHND 97K-XIGhRc.

195   *After winning the UFC's welterweight championship* "UFC 189 Salaries: Conor Mcgregor and Chad Mendes Both Earn Flat $500K," *MMA Junkie*, July 13, 2015, https://mmajunkie.usatoday.com/2015/07/ufc-189-salaries-conor-mcgregor-and-chad-mendes-both-earn-flat-500k.

195   *The reality is the UFC is the ultimate place"* Graham Bensinger, "Lorenzo Fertitta: I wanted to pay fighters $1 million," *In Depth with Graham Bensinger*, available at https://www.youtube.com/watch?v=RhiH3Mj7i6A&list=PLW5qT4HIAd1Yxu7xA-xuHND97K-XIGhRc.

195   *Over the years, he had become a prolific art collector* Henri Neuendorf, "Art for High Rollers: See the Flashy Contemporary Art That Adorns Las Vegas's Most Blinged-Out New Casino," Artnet, May 24, 2018, https://news.artnet.com/art-world/palms-las-vegas-art-collection-1292057.

195   *He'd commissioned Damien Hirst to create* Graham Bensinger, "Lorenzo Fertitta and Dana White: Pranking UFC CFO," *In Depth with Graham Bensinger*, available at https://www.youtube.com/watch?v=2-vmr3JTxI8.

195   *When UFC chief financial officer John Mulkey prepared* Nash, "Court Filings Reveal More Info on How Much 'Top' UFC Fighters Are Paid."

195   *When describing the appeal of cage fighting to others* Lawrence Epstein, author interview.

195   *If American football was akin to Mark Rothko's* Ibid.

195   *In Lorenzo's office, on the wall directly behind his desk* UFC Holdings, "Three Guys and Three Letters."

196   *Taken from Hirst's* Eat the Rich *series* "Damien Hirst—Eat the Rich Series," New Art Editions, June 16, 2017, https://www.newarteditions.com/damien-hirst-eat-rich-series/.

196   *CBS had reportedly offered $1 billion* UFC Holdings, "Agents of Change."

196   *In 2014, investment firm Blackstone had expressed interest* Jeremy Botter, "Sources: Zuffa Accepts $4.2 Billion Bid for Sale of UFC," *FloCombat*, June 20, 2016, https://www.flocombat.com/articles/5052356-sources-zuffa-accepts-42-billion-bid-for-sale-of-ufc.

196   *Lorenzo had been a lifelong football fan* "Lorenzo Fertitta, Ex-UFC Owner, Gunning to Buy NFL Team," *TMZ*, June 9, 2019, https://www.tmz.com/2019/06/09/lorenzo-fertitta-ufc-nfl-ownership/; Damon Martin, "Dana White: I Would Not Be Shocked if Lorenzo Fertitta Ends Up Owning an NFL Team," *MMA Weekly*, September 13, 2012, https://www.mmaweekly.com/dana-white-i-would-not-be-shocked-if-lorenzo-fertitta-ends-up-owning-an-nfl-team.

196   *Lorenzo had paid to build a two-story* Ray Brewer, "Taking a Tour of Gorman's New Athletic Training Center," *Las Vegas Sun*, August 6, 2012, https://lasvegassun.com/news/2012/aug/06/gorman-fertitta-athletic-training-las-vegas/.

196   *During Nicco's senior year Bishop Gorman had gone* "USA Today Super 25 Expert Rankings," *USA Today*, archived at http://web.archive.org/web/20150207102507/https://usatodayhss.com/rankings/expert/boys/football/2014/19.

196   *In the fall of 2015, Nicco accepted a full scholarship* Brian Leigh, "Notre Dame Offers

Football Scholarship to Nicco Fertitta, Son of UFC CEO," *Bleacher Report*, January 22, 2014, https://bleacherreport.com/articles/1933099-notre-dame-offers-football-scholar ship-to-nicco-fertitta-son-of-ufc-ceo.

196 *At the same time, Oakland Raiders owner Mark Davis* Ken Belson, "What Happens in Vegas? The Draft and a Lot of Other NFL Events?" *New York Times*, April 28, 2022, https://www.nytimes.com/2022/04/28/sports/football/las-vegas-nfl-draft.html.

196 *Though there were competing offers* Seth Wickersham and Don Van Natta Jr., "Sin City or Bust," *ESPN*, April 13, 2017, http://www.espn.com/espn/feature/story/_/id/19143486 /the-story-how-owner-mark-davis-moved-raiders-las-vegas.

196 *With annual revenue of $10.5 billion in 2013* Chris Isidore, "NFL: Richer Than Ever, Despite Controversy," *CNN Money*, September 11, 2014, https://money.cnn.com/2014 /09/11/news/companies/nfl-revenue-profits/index.html.

197 *While nothing was certain, Lorenzo and Frank III* Nikhil Subba, "Red Rock's IPO to Value Casino Operator at Up to $2.4 Billion," Reuters, April 15, 2016, https://www.reuters.com /article/us-redrockresorts-ipo-idUSKCN0XC1G5.

197 *The IPO was targeted for the first half of 2016* Howard Stutz, "Station Casinos' Corporate Name Will Be Red Rock Resorts After IPO," *Las Vegas Review-Journal*, January 21, 2016, https://www.reviewjournal.com/business/station-casinos-corporate-name-will-be-red -rock-resorts-after-ipo/.

197 *In November, the FTC announced it was closing* Adam Hill, "Federal Trade Commission Closes Inquiry into UFC Business Practices," *Las Vegas Review-Journal*, November 24, 2015, https://www.reviewjournal.com/sports/mma-ufc/federal-trade-commission-closes -inquiry-into-ufc-business-practices/.

197 *The commission again noted that the announcement* Ibid.

197 *Around the same time, Lorenzo got a call* UFC Holdings, "Agents of Change."

197 *Ari Emanuel hadn't initially been included* Ibid.

197 *Emanuel was determined to involve himself in some way* Ibid.

Chapter 11: Maybe I Can

198 *On the morning before his first fight* John Kavanagh, "Conor UFC Fight Day," John Kavanagh video blog (YouTube), April 6, 2013, https://www.youtube.com/watch ?v=AhX_htCRSzI.

198 *In his mind, he was already a star* "UFC on Fuel TV 9 Post Press Conference," *Front Row MMA*, April 9, 2013, available at https://www.youtube.com/watch?v=xASOIYfLryw.

198 *The UFC's standard entry-level contract at the time* "UFC Fight Night 26: Fighter Salaries: Alistair Overeem Towers Over Main Event on Payroll," *MMA Weekly*, September 10, 2013, https://www.mmaweekly.com/ufc-fight-night-26-fighter-salaries-alistair-overeem -towers-over-main-event-on-payroll.

198 *It was the lowest amount of money* Katie Richcreek, "Conor McGregor Featured in New 'Call of Duty,' " ESPN.com, September 15, 2016, https://www.espn.com/mma/story /_/id/17555967/conor-mcgregor-featured-call-duty-infinite-warfare.

198 *And as far as he was concerned, one win* Ariel Helwani, "The MMA Hour 170—Conor McGregor," *MMA Fighting*, February 26, 2013, https://www.mmafighting.com/ videos/2013/2/26/4031560/the-mma-hour-episode-170-conor-mcgregor; Dean Kelly, "Conor McGregor 2008 Interview—Before Fame Interview, Predicts Future," *Irish MMA Tapes*, December 2008, available at https://www.youtube.com/watch?v=wPUVy0Kk8II.

198 *They were addressed not individually but in groups* John Kavanagh, "Conor UFC Weigh-in Day," John Kavanagh video blog (YouTube), April 5, 2013, https://www .youtube.com/watch?v=69AaezhMmFI.

199 *They had gear check and were fitted* John Kavanagh, "UFC Conor 2," John Kavanagh video blog (YouTube), April 3, 2013, https://www.youtube.com/watch?v=zcdEfWkH aI0&t=285s.

199 *Then they were sent into an even smaller, windowless conference room* Ibid.

199 *There were twenty-six fighters on the card* "UFC on Fuel TV 9," UFC.com, https://www .ufc.com/event/FUEL9.

199 *The main event, between former Strikeforce* "UFC on Fuel TV 9 Update: Alexander Gustafsson Cut Spells Demise of Main Event," *MMA Weekly*, March 31, 2013, https:// www.mmaweekly.com/ufc-on-fuel-tv-9-update-alexander-gustafsson-cut-spells-demise -of-main-event.

199 *One of his teammates who'd never fought in the UFC* Dave Doyle, "Ilir Latifi Replaces Alexander Gustafsson vs. Gegard Mousassi at UFC on Fuel 9," *MMA Fighting*, April 2, 2013, https://www.mmafighting.com/2013/4/2/4176496/ilir-latifi-replaces-alexander -gustafsson-vs-gegard-mousasi-at-ufc-on.

199 *Because of the time difference, the card would air* "UFC on Fuel TV 9."

199 *McGregor's fight in the prelims wouldn't make* ShinSplints, "UFC on Fuel TV 9 Recap: Facebook Prelims," *Bloody Elbow*, April 7, 2013, https://www.bloodyelbow.com/ufc-on -fuel-9-mousasi-vs-latifi/2013/4/7/4193714/ufc-on-fuel-tv-9-results-recap-facebook -preliminary-card-mma; and Lawrence Epstein, author interview.

199 *"It's just another contest"* Kavanagh, "UFC Conor 2."

199 *"It's always you versus you"* Ibid.

200 *He'd grown up in the gray and glamorless suburb* Conor McGregor: Notorious, directed by Gavin Fitzgerald (Universal, 2017).

200 *He was enamored with WWE and Batman movies* Ariel Helwani, "A Day in Dublin with Conor McGregor," *MMA Fighting*, November 8, 2016, https://www.youtube.com /watch?v=JcUE6Nwx3EE; "Conor McGregor Talks Reebok Shoe Launch, Sings Biggie 'Hypnotize' and Life After Fighting," *The Mac Life*, February 21, 2020, https://www .youtube.com/watch?v=Jg2K8HhVsps.

200 *His father worked as a taxi driver* Gareth A. Davies, "Meet Conor McGregor: The 'Mummy's Boy' with Fury in His Fists," *Stuff*, August 22, 2017, https://www.stuff.co.nz /sport/other-sports/96013589/meet-conor-mcgregor-the-mummys-boy-with-fury -in-his-fists; Andrea Smith, "Like Father Like Son: Meet Tony McGregor, Dad of 'The Notorious' UFC Star Conor," *Independent*, June 19, 2016, https://www.independent.ie /style/celebrity/celebrity-news/like-father-like-son-meet-tony-mcgregor-dad-of-the -notorious-ufc-star-conor-34803633.html.

200 *At his new school, McGregor befriended Tom Egan* Darren Frehill, "Conor McGregor Interview," *RTE Sport*, January 27, 2015, available at https://www.youtube.com /watch?v=-jtnF3L2cnk.

200 *"He was just a lazy prick"* Flinder Boyd, "True Stories of the Incredible, Unbelievable, Unstoppable Conor McGregor!" *Bleacher Report*, August 16, 2017, https://bleacher report.com/articles/2727681-conor-mcgregor-stories-dublin-friends-coaches.

200 *Egan's mother was a black belt in Shotokan karate* Thomas Gerbassi, "UFC's First Irish Fighter Shares His Story," UFC.com, August 14, 2016, https://www.ufc.com/news/ufcs -first-irish-fighter-shares-his-story.

200 *He and McGregor eagerly used each other* Frehill, "Conor McGregor Interview."

200 *Instead of absorbing dead bits of information* "Conor McGregor: UFC on Fuel TV 9 Pre-fight Interview" *Fighters Only*, April 3, 2013, available at https://www.youtube.com /watch?v=0JMjU4eAUnA.

201 *McGregor and Egan found a local MMA gym* John Kavanagh, *Win or Learn: MMA, Conor McGregor, & Me: A Trainer's Journey* (London: Penguin Random House UK, 2016), pp. 9–29.

201 *"I couldn't shut it off, so I just rolled"* Frehill, "Conor McGregor Interview."

201 *His family was less excited about McGregor's desire* Ibid.

201 *It was an eighteen-mile drive from the McGregor home* Ibid.

201 *"I'm looking around on the site, looking at"* "Conor McGregor—An Irish Muhammad Ali?" *Late Late Show/RTÉ One*, April 13, 2013, available at https://www.youtube.com /watch?v=2SewDhT85N0.

201 *McGregor decided to quit and instead try to* Jeremy Botter, "Outrageous Conor McGregor: His Irish Roots and Improbable American Dream," *Bleacher Report*, July 8, 2015, https:// bleacherreport.com/articles/2514254-outrageous-conor-mcgregor-his-irish-roots-and -an-improbable-american-dream.

201 *"The first thing they said was, 'Who else has done it?' "* Botter, "Outrageous Conor McGregor."

201 *The decision was especially alien to his father* Smith, "Like Father Like Son."

202 *For a short while it seemed like everything was* "In Depth MMA Roundtable—The History of MMA in Ireland," *Pundit Arena*, July 21, 2016, https://punditarena.com/mma /thepateam/on-hold-mma-roundtable-the-history-of-irish-mma/; Kavanagh, *Win or Learn*, p. 45.

202 *The events usually took place at a small venue* "In Depth MMA Roundtable—The History of MMA in Ireland."

202 *He booked his third fight just two weeks before* Kavanagh, *Win or Learn*, pp. 46–47.

202 *McGregor was humiliated, and it left his once unshakable* Ibid., p. 48.

202 *Instead of returning to training, McGregor hid from* Kavanagh Ibid., pp. 48–49.

202 *He had labeled him as a "street kid"* Paul Kimmage, "Paul Kimmage Meets John Kavanagh: My Friendship with Conor, Battling Mcgeeney and How We Blagged Our Way into J-Lo's Party," *Independent*, October 16, 2016, https://www.independent.ie/sport/columnists /paul-kimmage/paul-kimmage-meets-john-kavanagh-my-friendship-with-conor-battling -mcgeeney-and-how-we-blagged-our-way-into-j-los-party-35133838.html.

203 *But two months after the loss McGregor's mother* Kavanagh, *Win or Learn*, pp. 48–49.

203 *"I was used to this bubbly, charismatic athlete"* Kimmage, "Paul Kimmage Meets John Kavanagh."

203 *Seven years McGregor's elder, Erin had become* Jeremy Botter, "The Secret That Led Conor McGregor to Fame, Fortune, and Floyd Mayweather," *Bleacher Report*, August 25, 2017, https://bleacherreport.com/articles/2728822-the-secret-that-led-conor-mcgregor-to -fame-fortune-and-floyd-mayweather.

203 *The project began, by Byrne's account* "The History of The Secret," TheSecret.tv, https:// www.thesecret.tv/history-of-the-secret/.

204 *She assembled her own selection of insights* The Secret (Rhonda Byrne) Abstract, https:// web.iitd.ac.in/~prbijwe/Book_Abstracts/The%20Secret.pdf; Michael Shermer, "The (Other) Secret," *Scientific American*, June 1, 2007, https://www.scientificamerican.com /article/the-other-secret/.

204 *Erin had given the book version of* The Secret Botter, "The Secret That Led Conor McGregor to Fame, Fortune, and Floyd Mayweather."

204 *He let himself try it as a joke* Jack Slack, *Notorious: The Life and Fights of Conor McGregor* (London: John Black Publishing, 2017), pp. 32–33; Botter, "The Secret That Led Conor McGregor to Fame, Fortune, and Floyd Mayweather."

205 *For winning his second title in Cage Warriors* Kavanagh, *Win or Learn*, p. 79.

205 *In early 2013, Kavanagh noticed that McGregor* Ibid., p. 80.

205 *Then in February of 2013, one of UFC's matchmakers* Ibid., pp. 80–82.

205 *After the fight, in the locker room McGregor* Fitzgerald, *Conor McGregor: Notorious.*

205 *McGregor was also awarded a $60,000 bonus* "UFC on Fuel TV 9 Bonuses: Pickett, Easton, Madadi, McGregor Earn $60K," Sherdog, April 6, 2013, https://www.sherdog.com/news/news/UFC-on-Fuel-TV-9-Bonuses-Pickett-Easton-Madadi-McGregor-Earn-3660K-51511.

205 *To celebrate, he put on a shirt and bow tie* Kavanagh, "Conor UFC Fight Day."

205 *Before the fight in Sweden, McGregor fans had swarmed* Steven Marrocco, "Marcus Brimage Annoyed by Conor McGregor Fans Prior to UFC on Fuel TV 9," *MMA Junkie,* April 5, 2013, https://mmajunkie.usatoday.com/2013/04/marcus-brimage-annoyed-by-conor-mcgregor-fans-prior-to-ufc-on-fuel-tv-9.

206 *In McGregor's second fight in the UFC* UFC Holdings, "Conor McGregor vs. Max Holloway UFC Fight Night," *UFC Fight Pass,* original event date August 17, 2013, available at https://ufcfightpass.com/video/30613/conor-mcgregor-vs-max-holloway-ufc-fight-night.

206 *In his third UFC fight, McGregor was booked* Brett Okamoto, "Conor McGregor Gets Diego Brandao," *ESPN,* June 3, 2014, https://www.espn.com/mma/story/_/id/11029080/conor-mcgregor-fight-diego-brandao-cole-miller-hurts-hand.

206 *For Lorenzo, McGregor's success was the best-case* David St. Martin, "Morning Report: Lorenzo Fertitta Justifies Conor Mcgregor's Salary by Dubbing Him a PPV Needle-Mover, Reinforces Comparisons to Brock Lesnar and Georges St-Pierre," *MMA Fighting,* October 2, 2014, https://www.mmafighting.com/2014/10/2/6886407/morning-report-ufc-lorenzo-fertitta-conor-mcgregor-dana-white-cowboy-cerrone-sonnen-lesnar-mma-news.

206 *When McGregor fought Brandão, Lorenzo noted, he drew* Ibid.

206 *The event, topped by a flyweight championship fight* Dave Meltzer, "Demetrious Johnson Shows That Championship, Exposure, and Success Don't Make One a Draw," *MMA Fighting,* July 10, 2014, https://www.mmafighting.com/2014/7/10/5888421/johnson-shows-that-a-championship-exposure-and-success-doesnt-make; "The UFC 178-181 PPV Buyrate Estimates Are About As 'Meh' As You'd Expect," *Cage Potato,* January 15, 2015, available at http://web.archive.org/web/20150115104937/https://www.cagepotato.com/the-ufc-178-181-ppv-estimates-are-about-as-meh-as-youd-expect/.

206 *McGregor had signed a new contract with the UFC* Shaun Al-Shatti, "UFC 178 Salaries: Conor Mcgregor Cashes In with Quick Win over Dustin Poirier," *MMA Fighting,* September 29, 2014, https://www.mmafighting.com/2014/9/29/6865269/ufc-178-salaries-conor-mcgregor-cashes-in-with-quick-win-over-dustin.

206 *For a month prior to the event, McGregor had stayed* Kavanagh, *Win or Learn,* pp. 132–34.

206 *The week before the fight, McGregor, Kavanagh* UFC Holdings, "UFC 178 Embedded: Vlog Series—Episode 1," UFC YouTube channel, September 23, 2014, https://www.youtube.com/watch?v=PqXCBZkWWTY.

207 *A month after he knocked out Poirier* UFC Holdings, "UFC 179 Embedded: Vlog Series—

Episode 3," UFC YouTube Channel, October 23, 2014, https://www.youtube.com /watch?v=61F4iIi6sIo.

207 *"I'm not even in the fighter hotel"* "Conor McGregor Trash Talking Chad Mendes," BT Sport YouTube Channel, October 21, 2014, https://www.youtube.com/watch?v=c6HIZX 3rfpI&t=76s.

207 *ratings for the prelims, which aired* Dave Meltzer, "Ratings Report: UFC 179 Prelims Land 536,000 Viewers," *MMA Fighting*, October 29, 2014, https://www.mmafighting .com/2014/10/29/7086853/ratings-report-ufc-179-prelims-land-536000-viewers.

207 *The event generated an estimated 180,000 buys* "The UFC 178-181 PPV Buyrate Estimates Are About As 'Meh' As You'd Expect."

207 *In contrast, McGregor seemed important* UFC Holdings, "Full Blast: Conor McGregor— Aldo vs. Mendes 2," UFC YouTube Channel, July 8, 2015, https://www.youtube.com /watch?v=Ceg9qaBBBrg.

208 *In the spring, McGregor was finally scheduled* "UFC 189 World Championship Tour Dates Set," UFC.com, March 14, 2015, https://www.ufc.com/news/ufc-189-world-champion ship-tour-dates-set.

208 *In Rio, Aldo and McGregor sat on a dais* UFC Holdings, "UFC 189: World Tour Press Conference," UFC YouTube Channel, March 20, 2015, https://www.youtube.com /watch?v=B9w5C0IEzDw.

208 *"I own this town," McGregor answered* Ibid.

208 *In Ireland a week later, Aldo tried to mimic* UFC Holdings, "UFC 189: World Tour Press Conference—Dublin," UFC YouTube Channel, March 31, 2015, https://www.youtube .com/watch?v=zxoT34adJ_4&t=1605s.

209 *"I'm not here to show these people remorse"* Ariel Helwani, "UFC 178: Conor McGregor Says He's in Everyone's Head," *MMA Fighting*, September 26, 2014, https://www.youtube .com/watch?v=52Zils8TBMY.

209 *The question would be delayed when, two weeks* Brett Okamoto, "Jose Aldo Out of UFC 189 Bout Against Conor Mcgregor with Rib Injury," *ESPN*, June 30, 2015, https://www .espn.com/mma/story/_/id/13177577/jose-aldo-ufc-189-bout-conor-mcgregor-rib-in jury.

209 *Lorenzo and White both drove to the two-story stucco* Fitzgerald, *Conor McGregor: Notorious.*

209 *"This is what you call a rude awakening"* Ibid.

209 *"I didn't know that was an option"* Ibid.

209 *A day later the UFC announced McGregor would fight* Thomas Gerbassi, "Aldo Out of UFC 189; Mendes to Face McGregor," UFC.com, June 30, 2015, https://www.ufc.com /news/aldo-out-189-mendes-face-mcgregor.

210 *The event had drawn a sold-out audience* "UFC 189 Gate and Attendance: Mendes vs. McGregor Breaks US Records," *MMA Weekly*, July 12, 2015, https://www.mmaweekly .com/ufc-189-gate-and-attendance-mendes-vs-mcgregor-breaks-u-s-records.

210 *Mendes stepped onto the arena floor as country singer Aaron Lewis* UFC Holdings, "Conor McGregor vs. Chad Mendes UFC 189," *UFC Fight Pass*, July 11, 2015, https://ufcfight pass.com/video/36835/conor-mcgregor-vs-chad-mendes-ufc-189.

210 *When McGregor planted to kick or punch* Danny Segura, "Conor McGregor Reveals New Details About Extent of Knee Injury Prior to UFC 189," *MMA Fighting*, October 29, 2015, https://www.mmafighting.com/2015/10/29/9638296/conor-mcgregor-reveals -details-on-his-knee-injury-prior-to-ufc-189.

212 *In the locker room after the fight, McGregor collected* Nash, "Lawsuit Documents Reveal Even More Details on UFC Business Structure and Fighter Pay."

213 *When McGregor was rebooked to fight Aldo* Kevin Iole, "Dana White: Aldo-McGregor Set for Dec. 12 at MGM Grand in Las Vegas," *Yahoo! Sports*, August 10, 2015, https://sports .yahoo.com/blogs/mma-cagewriter/dana-white—aldo-mcgregor-set-for-dec—12-at -mgm-grand-in-las-vegas-004231499.html.

213 *When the fight finally took place, it lasted* UFC Holdings, "Conor McGregor vs. Jose Aldo UFC 194," *UFC Fight Pass*, December 12, 2015, https://ufcfightpass.com/video/37576 /conor-mcgregor-vs-jose-aldo-ufc-194.

214 *In 2008, Lorenzo had famously said the UFC's* David Samuels, "Lorenzo Fertitta (interview)," *Atlantic*, November 2008, https://www.theatlantic.com/magazine/archive /2008/11/lorenzo-fertitta/307183/.

214 *"At least one or two times in every UFC show"* Ibid.

215 *After the fight, Aldo returned to his locker room* Mookie Alexander, "UFC 194 Video: UFC Releases Aldo Locker Room Post Fight Footage," *Bloody Elbow*, December 13, 2015, https://www.bloodyelbow.com/2015/12/13/10033282/ufc-194-video-ufc-releases-aldo -locker-room-post-fight-footage; also available at https://www.youtube.com /watch?v=41XNU2uQu9g.

215 *He had grown up in the slums of Manaus* Guilherme Cruz, "The Kid from the Favela," *MMA Fighting*, December 9, 2015, https://www.mmafighting.com/2015/12/9/9834878 /the-kid-from-the-favela.

215 *Having nowhere else to go, Aldo slept at the gym* Marcelo Alonso, "17 Years Ago, I Met Jose Aldo, Who Still Slept at His Dojo," Sherdog, August 10, 2021, https://www.sherdog .com/news/articles/17-Years-Ago-I-Met-Jose-Aldo-Who-Still-Slept-at-his-Dojo-180 998#/slide/5.

215 *Aldo had been certain he would beat McGregor* Guilherme Cruz, "Jose Aldo, Cris Cyborg Reflect on What Happened After Quick Title Losses," *MMA Fighting*, April 27, 2020, https://www.mmafighting.com/2020/4/27/21236072/jose-aldo-cris-cyborg-ufc-knock out-conor-mcgregor-amanda-nunes.

215 *Meanwhile, McGregor basked in attention* Karyn Bryant, "Conor McGregor's Post-Fight Press Conference After 13-Second KO of Jose Aldo at UFC 194 (unedited)," Karyn Bryant YouTube Channel, December 13, 2015, https://www.youtube.com/watch?v=37K wXmGoD1w.

216 *"How do I look up here, by the way?"* Ibid.

216 *He seemed kind instead of cocky* "UFC 194 Draws Reported 16,516 Attendance for $10.1 Million Live Gate," *MMA Junkie*, December 13, 2015, https://mmajunkie.usatoday .com/2015/12/ufc-194-draws-reported-16516-attendance-for-10-1-million-live-gate.

216 *"I said to Dana and Lorenzo, I'm bringing"* Rachel Crane, "UFC CEO: Here's How We Made Half a Billion in Revenue Last Year," *CNN Business*, December 28, 2015, https:// www.youtube.com/watch?v=5leKNVSXsqw&t=2s.

Chapter 12: Fair Is Defined as Where We End Up

217 *In early 2016, Ari Emanuel found himself scrambling* UFC Holdings, "Agents of Change."

217 *Lorenzo had also settled on a minimum* Ibid.

217 *It was nearly twenty-two times Zuffa's* Michael Smith and John Ourand, "What Drove UFC's $4 Billion Deal," *Sports Business Journal*, July 18, 2016, available at http://web

.archive.org/web/20160804214737/https://www.sportsbusinessdaily.com/Journal
/Issues/2016/07/18/Leagues-and-Governing-Bodies/UFC.aspx; Nash, "What We Now
Know About the UFC's Finances"

217 *An internal UFC document prepared for the sale* Nash, "Court Filings Reveal More Info
on How Much 'Top' UFC Fighters Are Paid."

217 *While Zuffa had forecast that it would be able* Ibid.; Tim Burke, "Wanderlei Silva, Other
Fighters Push for Muhammad Ali Act in MMA," *Bloody Elbow*, August 3, 2015, https://
www.bloodyelbow.com/2015/8/3/9092041/wanderlei-silva-other-fighters-push-for-mu
hammad-ali-act-in-mma.

217 *Emanuel had first discussed the idea* UFC Holdings, "Agents of Change."

218 *Emanuel had befriended one of Silver Lake's managing* William D. Cohan, "The Inside
Story of Ari Emanuel's Big, Risky WME-IMG Merger," *Vanity Fair*, March 2015, available
at https://www.vanityfair.com/news/2015/02/wme-img-merger-ari-emanuel; Michael
Cieply, "A Merger of Agencies Shakes Up Hollywood," *New York Times*, April 27, 2009,
https://www.nytimes.com/2009/04/28/business/media/28talent.html.

218 *The newly combined entity, renamed WME* Nellie Andreeva, "WME at 10: Where
the Top William Morris Agents Are Now," *Deadline*, May 31, 2019, https://deadline
.com/2019/05/william-morris-agency-endeavor-merger-where-are-they-now
-1202618487/; Sharon Waxman and Lucas Shaw, "Leaked! Inside Details of $2.45 Billion
WME-IMG Financing and Why an IPO May Loom," *The Wrap*, April 13, 2014, https://
www.thewrap.com/leaked-inside-details-2-45-billion-wme-img-financing-ipo-may
-loom/.

218 *Durban was impressed with Emanuel's intensity and ambitions* "Silver Lake Looks to Turn
WME into Gold," *Financial Times*, November 20, 2014, https://www.ft.com/content/eba
1b20a-6f8d-11e4-b50f-00144feabdc0.

218 *Though the number of original television series being produced* Joe Otterson, "Number of
Streaming Shows Overtakes Basic Cable, Broadcast for First Time, FX Reports," *Variety*,
December 13, 2018, https://variety.com/2018/tv/news/number-of-streaming-shows
-basic-cable-broadcast-fx-report-1203089218/.

218 *In 2002, nearly 1.6 billion movie tickets* "Domestic Movie Theatrical Market Summary
1995 to 2022," *The Numbers*, https://www.the-numbers.com/market/.

218 *In 2012, fewer than 1.4 billion tickets* Ibid.

218 *Inspired by George Gilder's short but influential book* Richard Rushfield, "Ari Emanuel,
WME, and the Great Hollywood IPO That Wasn't," *Vanity Fair*, January 27, 2020, https://
www.vanityfair.com/hollywood/2020/01/ari-emanuel-wme-and-the-great-hollywood-ipo
-that-wasn't; Connie Bruck, "Ari Emanuel Takes on the World," *New Yorker*, April 19, 2021,
https://www.newyorker.com/magazine/2021/04/26/ari-emanuel-takes-on-the-world.

218 *"The world of 10,000 networks"* Nicole LaPorte, "What It's Like to Chase After Superagent
Ari Emanuel and WME-IMG," *Fast Company*, November 16, 2016, https://www
.fastcompany.com/3065684/what-its-like-to-chase-after-superagent-ari-emanuel-and
-wme-img.

218 *Gilder had been a favorite of libertarians and techno-futurists* "George Gilder Books,"
Regenery.com, https://www.regnery.com/george-gilder-books/.

219 *After William Morris, Emanuel's first major target had been IMG* Daniel Miller, Joe Flint,
and Dawn C. Chmielewski, "William-Morris Endeavor Targets Sports with $2.3 Billion
IMG Buy," *Los Angeles Times*, December 19, 2013, https://www.latimes.com/entertain
ment/envelope/cotown/la-et-ct-william-morris-endeavor-img-deal-20131219-story

.html; E. M. Swift, "The Most Powerful Man in Sports," *Sports Illustrated*, May 21, 1990, https://vault.si.com/vault/1990/05/21/the-most-powerful-man-in-sports-mark-mccor mack-founder-and-ceo-of-international-management-group-rules-his-empire-as-both -agent-and-impresario.

219 *IMG also represented more than ninety university* Miller, Flint, and Chmielewski, "William-Morris Endeavor Targets Sports."

219 *Originally founded in 1960 by a corporate lawyer* Ibid.

219 *Though IMG had rejected several previous acquisition attempts* Cohan, "The Inside Story of Ari Emanuel's Big, Risky WME-IMG Merger."

219 *It was over $600 million more than the next closest bid* Ibid.; "Moody's Rating System in Brief," *Moody's*, available at https://www.moodys.com/sites/products/productattachments /moody%27s%20rating%20system.pdf.

220 *"So the book department is now"* LaPorte, "What It's Like to Chase After Superagent Ari Emanuel and WME-IMG."

220 *The UFC's Fox deal was set to expire* John Ourand, "The Fight to Sell the UFC's and WME's Media Rights," *New York Business Journal*, July 11, 2018, https://www.bizjournals .com/newyork/news/2018/07/11/the-fight-to-sell-the-ufcs-and-wwes-media-rights.html.

220 *Zuffa had begun preparing bid books—containing a detailed* Darren Rovell, "Sources: UFC Owners in Advanced Talks to Sell Business," *ESPN*, May 10, 2016, https://www.espn .com/mma/story/_/id/15503004/ufc-owners-advanced-talks-sell-promotion.

221 *Both Fox and ESPN had expressed interest* Ibid.; Smith and Ourand, "What Drove UFC's $4 Billion Deal."

221 *Nick Diaz watched his younger brother, Nathan* Ariel Helwani, "UFC on FOX 17: Nick Diaz Breaks Down His Brother's Win, Potential Conor Mcgregor Fight," *MMA Fighting* (YouTube channel), December 20, 2015, https://www.youtube.com/watch?v=8uxcgrrylJc.

221 *It was the UFC's last event of 2015* UFC Holdings, "UFC Fighter Rankings," UFC.com, archived on December 18, 2015, http://web.archive.org/web/20151218064214/https:// www.ufc.com/rankings.

221 *As Nathan tried to settle into a rhythm, Johnson continually* UFC Holdings, "Nate Diaz vs Michael Johnson UFC Fight Night," *UFC Fight Pass*, December 19, 2015, https://ufcfight pass.com/video/41933/nate-diaz-vs-michael-johnson-ufc-fight-night.

221 *He had always hated watching his little brother* Helwani, "UFC on FOX 17: Nick Diaz Breaks Down His Brother's Win."

221 *Nick's own career as a cage fighter had come to an abrupt halt* Brett Okamoto, "Nick Diaz Suspended 5 Years by Nevada Commission for Marijuana," *ESPN*, September 14, 2015, https://www.espn.com/mma/story/_/id/13657932/nevada-bans-ufc-nick-diaz-5-years -marijuana.

221 *As part of his punishment, Nick had been barred* Damon Martin, "Nick Diaz Given Permission by NJ Commission to Corner Brother Nate at UFC on Fox 3," *MMA Weekly*, April 26, 2012, https://www.mmaweekly.com/nick-diaz-given-permission-by-new-jersey -commission-to-corner-brother-nate-at-ufc-on-fox-3.

222 *"It's my bad he even got into this sport"* Ariel Helwani, "UFC Brothers: Inside the Unique Bond of Nick and Nate Diaz," *ESPN*, November 11, 2019, https://www.espn.com/mma /story/_/id/28054988/unique-bond-nick-nate-diaz.

222 *They competed in triathlons in the pine-flocked mountains* "Nick and Nate Diaz Bike from Stockton to Lodi: Conditioning for Georges St-Pierre," *Fight Hub TV* (YouTube channel), March 14, 2013, https://www.youtube.com/watch?v=zxrbhy2v3Us; "UFC 143: Nate

Diaz—Brother Nick Diaz, Triathalons, and TUF 15," *MMA30tv* (YouTube channel), February 3, 2012, https://www.youtube.com/watch?v=cVQxBzto_gY; Elliot Worsell, "Nick Diaz: The UFC's Running Man," *Huffington Post*, February 1, 2012, https://www .huffpost.com/entry/carlos-condit-nick-diaz_b_1245886.

222 *They'd come home again in the evening and while away* "Rare Video: Young Nick Diaz vs Nate Diaz Sai Fight," *The Queen* (YouTube channel), October 20, 2018, https://www. youtube.com/watch?v=sJYakmLSldk; "MiddleEasy.com—Watch This Video of Nick Diaz Going into Beast-Mode with a Pair of Nunchucks," *MiddleEasy* (YouTube channel), November 27, 2010, https://www.youtube.com/watch?v=zrYanfHbqjo; "Ronda Rousey's Trip to the 209: Episode 4," *MiddleEasy* (YouTube channel), July 30, 2012, https://www .youtube.com/watch?v=dSCd16orlsw&t=459s.

222 *In June 2011, Nick had been one of the first fighters* Joe Schafer, "UFC 137 Georges St-Pierre vs Nick Diaz: A Fan's and Champion's Dream Come True," *Bleacher Report*, June 1, 2011, https://bleacherreport.com/articles/720603-ufc-137-georges-st-pierre-vs -nick-diaz-a-fans-and-champions-dream-come-true; Scott Christ, "Nick Diaz vs Jeff Lacy Off the Table: Georges St-Pierre Fight Almost Done for Diaz," *Bad Left Hook*, May 23, 2011, https://www.badlefthook.com/2011/5/23/2186055/georges-st-pierre-vs -nick-diaz-jeff-lacy-boxing-mma-strikeforce-ufc-news.

222 *He missed press conferences, and was pulled* Tim McTiernan, "UFC 137 News: Nick Diaz Pulled from Title Fight After No-Showing 2nd Conference," *Bleacher Report*, September 7, 2011, https://bleacherreport.com/articles/839628-ufc-137-news-nick-diaz -pulled-from-title-fight-after-no-showing-2nd-conference; Case Keefer, "Dana White: 'Nick Diaz Obviously Can't Handle the Pressure of a Main Event,' ".*Las Vegas Sun*, September 7, 2011, https://lasvegassun.com/news/2011/sep/07/dana-white-nick-diaz/; Ariel Helwani, "Nick Diaz Not Happy About Fighting BJ Penn," *MMA Fighting* (YouTube channel), October 27, 2011, https://www.youtube.com/watch?v=3NVywlRmnho.

222 *"They do everything they can in their power"* "UFC 158 Nick Diaz on GSP Being on Steroids, Dana White/UFC Wants Him to Lose," *ecdctech* (YouTube channel), March 14, 2013, archived at http://web.archive.org/web/20130317202853/https://www.youtube .com/watch?v=586vlvQG35I.

222 *Nick would lose a slow and largely uneventful* UFC Holdings, "Georges St-Pierre vs Nick Diaz UFC 158," *UFC Fight Pass*, March 16, 2013, https://ufcfightpass.com/video/30293 /georges-st-pierre-vs-nick-diaz-ufc-158.

223 *"You know, I think I'm gonna have to—I'm gonna"* Ibid.

223 *At the same time, Nathan began to think the UFC* Thomas Myers, "Nate Diaz: UFC 'Conned Me' with Eight-Fight Contract, 'Tried to Do Me Dirty,' " *MMA Mania*, April 8, 2014, https://www.mmamania.com/2014/4/8/5595698/nate-diaz-ufc-conned-me-with -eight-fight-contract-tried-to-do-me-dirty.

223 *"I'm over here getting chump change"* Ibid.

223 *In 2012, his one and only title fight* Jesse Holland, "UFC on Fox 5 Ratings 'Killed It' with 4.4 Million Viewers for 'Henderson vs. Diaz' in Seattle," *MMA Mania*, December 12, 2012, https://www.mmamania.com/2012/12/12/2150095/ufc-on-fox-5-ratings4-4-mil lion-average-viewers-henderson-diaz-mma.

223 *White dismissed Nathan's complaints* John Branch, "UFC Needs an Antihero: Nate Diaz Returns Just in Time," *New York Times*, August 15, 2019, https://www.nytimes .com/2019/08/15/sports/nate-diaz-fight-pettis.html.

223 *White claimed Nathan had missed a chance to make "Justin Bieber money"* Dave Doyle,

"Dana White: Nate Diaz Missed His Opportunity to 'Make Justin Bieber Money,'" *MMA Fighting*, April 9, 2014, https://www.mmafighting.com/2014/4/9/5599094/dana-white -nate-diaz-missed-his-opportunity-to-make-justin-bieber.

223 *"Guess how much money he makes sitting at home?"* Elias Cepeda, "Nate Diaz Speaks Out About UFC 'Con,' Dana White Responds," *Yahoo! Sports*, April 9, 2014, https://sports .yahoo.com/blogs/mma-cagewriter/nate-diaz-speaks-out-about-ufc—con—-dana-white -responds-162851887.html?guccounter=1.

223 *When Nathan refused to accept another fight* Brett Okamoto, "Nate Diaz Removed from Rankings," *ESPN*, May 6, 2014, https://www.espn.com/mma/story/_/id/10891979/nate -diaz-removed-rankings-ufc.

224 *After holding out for nearly a year, Nathan began* Ariel Helwani, "UFC on FOX 17: Nate Diaz Media Scrum," *MMA Fighting* (YouTube channel), December 17, 2015, https:// www.youtube.com/watch?v=LqWG7VdoSTA.

224 *By the end of the fight, Nathan had earned a unanimous decision* "UFC on FOX 17 Fighter Bonuses: Rafael dos Anjos Takes Top Honors with Fast Finish," *MMA Weekly*, December 19, 2015, https://www.mmaweekly.com/ufc-on-fox-17-fighter-bonuses-fight -of-the-night.

224 *Nick had left the locker room after the fight and watched* "Watch! Backstage Footage of Nick Diaz Reacting to Nate's Win," BJPenn.com, December 29, 2015, https://www .bjpenn.com/ufcnews/watch-backstage-footage-of-nick-diaz-reacting-to-nates-win/.

224 *As if to underscore the strange irrelevance of Nathan's* Thomas Gerbasi, "It's On! Dos Anjos/McGregor, Holm/Tate Set for UFC 197," UFC.com, January 12, 2016, https://www .ufc.com/news/its-dos-anjosmcgregor-holmtate-set-ufc-197.

225 *That plan was upended a little over a month later* Guilherme Cruz, "Coach Details Injury That Forced Rafael Dos Anjos Out of UFC 196 Clash with Conor McGregor," *MMA Fighting*, February 23, 2016, https://www.mmafighting.com/2016/2/23/11102634/coach -details-injury-that-forced-rafael-dos-anjos-out-of-ufc-196.

225 *It was the second consecutive pay-per-view main event that* Zane Simon, "UFC 196 Goes from PPV to FS1 with Hendricks vs. Thompson Headliner," *Bloody Elbow*, January 26, 2016, https://www.bloodyelbow.com/2016/1/26/10835700/ufc-196-ppv-fs1-heavyweight -title-fight-cancelled-miocic-vs-werdum-hedricks-vs-thompson-mma-news.

225 *As White scrambled to keep UFC 196 together* Pat Hanavan, "A Tour of UFC President Dana White's Bad Ass Office," *Faded Industry*, September 17, 2014, archived at http:// web.archive.org/web/20140921020340/http://www.fadedindustry.com/tour-ufc-presi dent-dana-whites-bad-ass-office/.

225 *When he got the offer, he was on a short vacation* Jason Nawara, "Nate Diaz Was Taking Shots of Tequila When He Got the Call to Fight Conor McGregor," *Uproxx*, March 7, 2016, https://uproxx.com/mma/nate-diaz-cabo-tequila-conor-mcgregor/.

225 *According to Urijah Faber, a UFC bantamweight* Luke Thomas and Brian Campbell, "Urijah Faber Talks Fighter Pay, TJ Dillashaw and Losing Conor McGregor Fight in 2016—Morning Kombat RSD," *Morning Kombat* (YouTube channel), August 4, 2022, https://www.youtube.com/watch?v=TqKV0ytYd2w&t=3829s.

225 *The UFC went back to Nathan with a new multiyear deal* Ibid.

225 *Nathan accepted the offer, and two days later* "UFC 196: McGregor/Nate Diaz (Full Press Conference)—UFC 196" *UFC on Fox* (YouTube channel), February 24, 2016, https:// www.youtube.com/watch?v=MvKU3hqH-WE.

226 *As the fight drew closer, media interest* Jane Wells, "UFC's McGregor, Diaz Trash

Talk Each Other, Then One Walks Out," CNBC, March 4, 2016, https://www.cnbc
.com/2016/03/04/ufcs-mcgregor-diaz-trash-talk-each-other-then-one-walks-out.html;
Conan O'Brien, "Conor McGregor Demos His Capoeira Kick on Conan—Conan on
TBS," *Team Coco* (YouTube channel), March 3, 2016, https://www.youtube.com
/watch?v=O6hAm0LC7dA.

226 *McGregor closed as nearly a four-to-one favorite* Alex Ballentine, "UFC 196 Fight Card:
PPV Schedule, Odds, and Predictions for McGregor vs. Diaz," *Bleacher Report*, March 5,
2016, https://bleacherreport.com/articles/2622087-ufc-196-fight-card-ppv-schedule
-odds-and-predictions-for-mcgregor-vs-diaz.

226 *Nathan closed a three-to-one underdog* Ibid.

226 *When Nathan and McGregor finally stood* UFC Holdings, "UFC 196: McGregor vs. Diaz,"
UFC Fight Pass, March 5, 2016, https://ufcfightpass.com/video/52493/ufc-196-mcgregor
-vs-diaz?playlistId=3294.

227 *In the final press conference two days before* UFC Holdings, "UFC 196 Pre-Fight Press
Conference," *UFC—Ultimate Fighting Championship* (YouTube channel), March 3, 2016,
https://www.youtube.com/watch?v=5Qq6mMVR1ng.

229 *At the post-fight press conference in the MGM Grand* UFC Holdings, "UFC 196 Post-Fight
Press Conference," *MMA Fighting* (YouTube channel), March 6, 2016, https://www
.youtube.com/watch?v=NvjVoxnBna0.

230 *"You know you have something exciting when people"* Megan Olivi, "UFC 196: Dana
White Event Recap," *UFC—Ultimate Fighting Championship* (YouTube channel),
March 6, 2016, https://www.youtube.com/watch?v=BXAY7Ltg89A.

230 *UFC 196 would go on to generate roughly* Karim Zidan, "Dana White: UFC 196 Did
1.5 Million PPV Buys," *Bloody Elbow*, March 11, 2016, https://www.bloodyelbow
.com/2016/3/11/11202190/dana-white-ufc-196-did-1-5-million-ppv-buys.

230 *It generated $8.1 million in ticket sales* "UFC 196: McGregor vs Diaz Gate and Attendance
from Las Vegas," *MMA Weekly*, March 5, 2016, https://www.mmaweekly.com/ufc-196
-mcgregor-vs-diaz-gate-and-attendance-from-las-vegas.

230 *It was the number one trending* Damon Martin, "UFC 196 Conor McGregor vs Nate
Diaz Smashes PPV Record, Says President Dana White," Fox Sports, March 12, 2016,
https://www.foxsports.com.au/ufc/ufc-196-conor-mcgregor-v-nate-diaz-smashes-ppv
-record-says-president-dana-white/news-story/c5d1b7e3e036a4c3fd7ef61a058a7870;
Jason Floyd, "Ratings Report: UFC 196 on FS1 Draws 1,843,000 Viewers," *MMA Report*,
March 9, 2016, https://themmareport.com/2016/03/ratings-report-ufc-196-prelims-on
-fs1-draws-1843000-viewers/.

230 *The morning after the fight, Lorenzo and White* Shaun Al-Shatti, "Dana White: Conor
Mcgregor Was 'Obsessed' with Nate Diaz Rematch at 170 Pounds," *MMA Fighting*,
March 30, 2016, https://www.mmafighting.com/2016/3/30/11335306/dana-white-conor
-mcgregor-was-obsessed-with-nate-diaz-rematch-at-170.

230 *He begged for a rematch, but White thought* Ibid.

231 *White and Lorenzo tried to persuade McGregor to forget* Ibid.

231 *And so three weeks later, with the UFC's bid books* Alysha Tsuji, "UFC Officially
Announces Nate Diaz?Conor McGregor Rematch Date," *USA Today*, March 30, 2016,
https://ftw.usatoday.com/2016/03/ufc-200-conor-mcgregor-nate-diaz-rematch.

231 *Lorenzo wanted the new owners to be people* UFC Holdings, "Agents of Change."

231 *"He's got huge balls"* UFC Holdings, "The Exchange: Dana White," *UFC Fight Pass*,
April 25, 2017, https://ufcfightpass.com/video/55538/the-exchange-dana-white.

231 *"I saw him scream at someone on the phone"* Adam Lashinsky, "Hi, It's Ari @#$%ing Emanuel, and I Plan to Shake Up Hollywood," *Fortune*, May 23, 2013, https://fortune.com/2013/05/23/hi-its-ari-ing-emanuel-and-i-plan-to-shake-up-hollywood/.

232 *Another employee had reportedly seen Emanuel* Rushfield, "Ari Emanuel, WME, and the Great Hollywood IPO That Wasn't."

232 *And just as White had gravitated to Tony Robbins's gospel* LaPorte, "What It's Like to Chase After Superagent Ari Emanuel and WME-IMG"; One World Academy website, archived at http://web.archive.org/web/20200805050905/https://www.oo.academy/.

232 *"It says it's OK to be mad!"* LaPorte, "What It's Like to Chase After Superagent Ari Emanuel and WME-IMG."

232 *At Zuffa's offices, White was infamous for his inability* Casey Keefer, "Lorenzo Fertitta, Dana White Built UFC into Something Big," *Las Vegas Sun*, June 29, 2014, https://lasvegassun.com/news/2014/jun/29/two-sides-octagon-white-fertitta-are-opposites-who/.

232 *Emanuel was likewise so perpetually restless* Ibid.

232 *"Most of Hollywood stays in Hollywood"* Ibid.

232 *"Fair is defined as where we end up"* Kit, "Backlot: 80 Years of The Holloywood Reporter."

232 *"It was very difficult to come up"* UFC Holdings, "Agents of Change."

232 *In March, WME-IMG raised $250 million* Julia Boorstein, "Softbank Takes $250M Stake in WME-IMG," CNBC, March 23, 2016, https://www.cnbc.com/2016/03/23/softbank-takes-250m-stake-in-wme-img-agency.html.

233 *In the spring, WME-IMG began exploring another* Mark Kleinman, "IMG Owner Eyes F1 as CVC Revs Up Options," *Sky News*, May 24, 2016, http://web.archive.org/web/20160624020554/https://news.sky.com/story/1701250/img-owner-eyes-f1-as-cvc-revs-up-options.

233 *Yet, at the end of April, Emanuel's efforts grew more* Robby Kalland, "UFC President Dana White: We pulled Conor McGregor from UFC 200," CBS Sports, April 19, 2016, https://www.cbssports.com/general/news/ufc-president-dana-white-we-pulled-conor-mcgregor-from-ufc-200/.

233 *White claimed that McGregor had refused to leave* Matt Jones, "Dana White Says Conor McGregor Responsible for UFC 200 Withdrawal," *Bleacher Report*, April 28, 2016, https://bleacherreport.com/articles/2636286-dana-white-says-conor-mcgregor-responsible-for-ufc-200-withdrawal.

233 *"Joanna Jedrzejczyk came in from Poland"* Ibid.

233 *The first public press conference livestream for UFC 200* Chris Taylor, "Report: Today's UFC 200 Press Conference Had Significantly Less Viewers Than the UFC 196 Press Conference," BJPenn.com, April 27, 2016, https://www.bjpenn.com/mma-news/ufc-200/report-todays-ufc-200-press-conference-had-significantly-less-viewers-than-the-ufc-196-press-conference/.

233 *Emanuel pushed ahead and by early May* Rebecca Sun and Georg Szlai, "WME-IMG Teams with Private Equity Firms for $4B UFC Purchase," *Hollywood Reporter*, July 10, 2016, https://www.hollywoodreporter.com/business/business-news/wme-img-group-acquire-ufc-908362/.

233 *A report from ESPN's Darren Rovell said negotiations* Darren Rovell, "Sources: UFC Owners in Advanced Talks to Sell Business," *ESPN*, May 10, 2016, https://www.espn.com/mma/story/_/id/15503004/ufc-owners-advanced-talks-sell-promotion.

233 *Providence Equity reportedly submitted a bid for $2.8 billion* Mike Ozanian, "How Ari Emanuel Danced on Debt and Grabbed the UFC," *Forbes*, July 20, 2016, https://www

.forbes.com/sites/mikeozanian/2016/07/20/how-ari-emanuel-danced-on-debt-and
-grabbed-the-ufc/?sh=5887d91f9bd8; Smith and Ourand, "What Drove UFC's $4 Billion
Deal," *Sports Business Journal,* July 18, 2016.

233 *"Yeah, we're not up for sale"* Dan Patrick, "Dana White on The Dan Patrick Show," *The
Dan Patrick Show,* May 11, 2016, https://www.youtube.com/watch?v=aIzM-nJsp6Y.

234 *"Look, if we bring on an investor or something happens"* Lance Pugmire, "Lorenzo Fertitta
Occupied This Week by Details of UFC 200, Not Sale," *Los Angeles Times,* July 5, 2016,
https://www.latimes.com/sports/sportsnow/la-sp-ufc-white-fertitta-20160705-snap
-story.html.

234 *Behind the scenes, Lorenzo and Frank III had reportedly narrowed* Dave Metlzer, "UFC
Sale Reportedly Imminent with Two Bids in $4.1 Billion Range," *MMA Fighting,* June 16,
2016, https://www.mmafighting.com/2016/6/16/11957074/ufc-sale-reportedly-immi
nent-with-two-bids-in-4-1-billion-range.

234 *While WME-IMG's involved substantially more* Jeremy Botter, "Source: Zuffa Accepts $4.2
Billion Bid for Sale of UFC," *FloCombat,* June 20, 2016, https://www.flocombat.com
/articles/5052356-sources-zuffa-accepts-4-2-billion-bid-for-sale-of-ufc; Jeremy Botter,
"Sources: UFC Sale Completed to William Morris-Endeavor-led Group," *FloCombat,*
June 22, 2016, https://www.flocombat.com/articles/5052398-sources-ufc-sale-completed
-to-william-morris-endeavor-led-group; Josh Nason, "JNPO: Flosports.com's Jeremy
Botter Reveals New Details on UFC Sale," *Wrestling Observer,* June 22, 2018, https://
www.f4wonline.com/podcasts/punch-out/jnpo-flosportscoms-jeremy-botter-reveals
-new-details-ufc-sale-215096.

234 *As Lorenzo flew with Frank III to a $28 million* Pugmire, "Lorenzo Fertitta Occupied This
Week by Details of UFC 200, Not Sale"; Jeff Collins, "Vegas Tycoon Buys Emerald Bay
Home for $28 Million," *OC Register,* June 26, 2009, https://www.ocregister.com/2009
/06/26/vegas-tycoon-buys-emerald-bay-home-for-28-million-2/.

234 *"It was nine days of hell"* UFC Holdings, "Agents of Change."

234 *In early July, three days before UFC 200* Brett Okamoto, "Jon Jones' Temporary
Suspension Extended by NSAC," *ESPN,* July 18, 2016, https://www.espn.com/mma
/story/_/id/17099953/jon-jones-tested-positive-clomiphene-letrozole-according-nevada
-state-athletic-commission.

234 *As White scrambled to find yet another replacement* UFC Holdings, "Agents of Change."

235 *Just two days before they were hoping* Ibid.

235 *Meanwhile, White persuaded Anderson Silva* Brandon Wise, "UFC 200 Card Shuffled:
Anderson Silva Replaces Jon Jones Against Daniel Cormier," CBS Sports, Juy 7, 2016,
https://www.cbssports.com/mma/news/anderson-silva-to-replace-jon-jones-against
-daniel-cormier-at-ufc-200/.

235 *White moved another fight to the main event slot* Ibid.

235 *Despite everything, the event still managed to be a hit* "UFC 200: Tate vs. Nunes Re-
cord-Setting Gate and Attendance from Las Vegas," *MMA Weekly,* July 10, 2016, https://
www.mmaweekly.com/ufc-200-tate-vs-nunes-record-setting-gate-and-attendance-from
-las-vegas; Thomas Gerbassi, "Brock Lesnar Announces Return at UFC 200," UFC.com,
June 6, 2016, https://www.ufc.com/news/brock-lesnar-announces-return-ufc-200.

235 *On Sunday evening, less than twenty-four hours* Robby Kalland and Adam Silverstein,
"UFC Sells for $4 Billion to WME-IMG Group, Dana White Remains President," CBS
Sports, July 11, 2016, https://www.cbssports.com/mma/news/reports-ufc-sells-for-4
-billion-to-wme-img-dana-white-remains-president/.

235 *worth $1.6 billion more than Red Rock* Subba, "Red Rock's IPO to Value Casino Operator at Up to $2.4B."

235 *A little after midnight on Sunday, White posted* Kalland and Silverstein, "UFC Sells for $4 Billion to WME-IMG Group."

Chapter 13: Be Happy for Me

236 *"I didn't believe it was gonna happen, at all"* UFC Holdings, "The Exchange: Dana White."

236 *The weekend before UFC 200* Ernie Clark, "Mainer Dana White Gets Rich Building UFC, But Relishes Ties to State," *Bangor Daily News*, August 4, 2016, https://www.bangordaily news.com/2016/08/04/sports/mainer-gets-rich-building-ufc-but-relishes-ties-to-state/.

236 *After UFC 200 came to an end* UFC Holdings, "The Exchange: Dana White."

236 *For fifteen years, Lorenzo and Frank III had treated* UFC Holdings, "Three Guys and Three Letters."

236 *As the reality hit, White would* UFC Holdings, "The Exchange: Dana White."

236 *In* Unlimited Power, *Tony Robbins describes his search* Robbins, *Unlimited Power*, p. 3.

236 *"How was it that this twenty-five-year-old kid"* Ibid.

237 *He rented a suite at Palace Station, pulled the blinds* UFC Holdings, "The Exchange: Dana White"; David Zinczenko, "UFC Warrior King Dana White on Creating a $4 Billion Fight Empire, Steroids in Sports, and What Fans Would Never Guess About Him," *Men's Journal*, November 2016, https://www.mensjournal.com/wp-content/uploads/mf/dana -white-newsstand-main.jpg?w=700.

237 *"I never thought I would react that way"* Ibid.

237 *White stayed in the suite for two days* Ibid.

237 *"Dude, I'm done. Be happy for me"* Ibid.

237 *Most people who worked at the UFC learned* Paul Cambria, author interview.

237 *"Nobody had any idea of what really was happening"* Ibid.

238 *On a June episode of the UFC's in-house podcast* Steven Marrocco, "Dana White Has Message for UFC Employees Stressed About Sale: 'Don't Even Worry About Stuff Like That,' " *MMA Junkie*, June 21, 2016, https://mmajunkie.usatoday.com/2016/06/dana -white-has-message-for-ufc-employees-stressed-about-sale-dont-even-worry-about -stuff-like-that.

238 *Some jokingly called it the "Zuffa two-step"* Paul Cambria, author interview.

238 *Tim O'Toole, vice president of Zuffa's event* Max Miceli, "Minding My Business with UFC VP/Event Production Tim O'Toole," *Sports Business Journal*, August 31, 2016, https:// www.sportsbusinessjournal.com/Daily/Issues/2016/08/31/People-and-Pop-Culture /MMB.aspx.

239 *It was described as a historic milestone* Darren Rovell and Brett Okamoto, "Dana White on $4 billion UFC sale: 'Sport is going to the next level,' " *ESPN*, July 11, 2016, https:// www.espn.com/mma/story/_/id/16970360/ufc-sold-unprecedented-4-billion-dana -white-confirms; Dan Reilly, "The UFC Sale: Everything You Need to Know," *Men's Journal*, https://www.mensjournal.com/sports/the-ufc-sale-everything-you-need-to -know-w212694/.

239 *The UFC was worth more than every team in the NFL* Mike Ozanian, "The NFL's Most Valuable Teams 2016," *Forbes*, September 14, 2016, https://www.forbes.com/sites /mikeozanian/2016/09/14/the-nfls-most-valuable-teams-2016/?sh=217557013068; Robert McLean and Charles Riley, "Michael Jackson's Slice of Beatlemania Goes

to Sony in $750 Million Deal," CNN Business, March 15, 2016, https://money.cnn
.com/2016/03/15/media/sony-michael-jackson-estate/index.html.

239 *Emanuel had offered a group of WME-IMG's celebrity* Gavin Evans, "These 23
Celebrities Paid At Least $250K Each to Purchase a Small Stake in the UFC," *Complex*,
September 30, 2016, https://www.complex.com/sports/2016/09/celebrities-paid-250k
-purchase-stake-ufc.

239 *When Marshall Zelaznik, the UFC's European division president* Marc Raimondi,
"Longtime Former UFC Exec Marshall Zelaznik Explains Departure from Company,
New Role as Glory CEO," *MMA Fighting*, January 310, 2018, https://www.mmafighting.
com/2018/1/31/16948700/longtime-former-ufc-exec-marshall-zelaznik-explains-depar
ture-from-company-new-role-as-glory-ceo.

239 *After relocating from London to Los Angeles in 2011* Ibid.

239 *That unease was amplified when, in October* Sridhar Natarajan and David Carey,
"Goldman Sachs Said to Receive Fed Warning on UFC Buyout Debt," *Bloomberg*,
October 6, 2016, https://www.bloomberg.com/news/articles/2016-10-06/goldman-sachs
-said-to-receive-fed-warning-over-ufc-buyout-debt.

239 *Typically, the Federal Reserve considered acquisitions unsafe* Ibid.

239 *Shortly after, WME-IMG sent a document to investors* Steven Marrocco and Ben Fowlkes,
"UFC Documents Lay Out Promotion's Plan to Grow Profits—and Increase 'Earn
Outs'—by Shrinking Expenses," *MMA Junkie*, October 27, 2016, https://mmajunkie
.usatoday.com/2016/10/ufc-documents-lay-out-promotions-plan-to-grow-profits-and
-increase-earn-outs-by-shrinking-expenses; Nash, "What We Now Know About the
UFC's Finances."

240 *In mid-October, around sixty full-time Zuffa employees were laid off* Steven Marrocco,
"WME-IMG to Lay Off 'Under 15 Percent' of UFC's Total Staff," *MMA Junkie*,
October 18, 2016, https://mmajunkie.usatoday.com/2016/10/wme-img-to-lay-off-un
der-15-percent-of-ufcs-total-staff; Ariel Helwani, "Three Months After Purchase, UFC
Laying Off Significant Number of Employees," *MMA Fighting*, October 18, 2016, https://
www.mmafighting.com/2016/10/18/13321992/three-months-after-purchase-ufc-laying
-off-significant-amount-of.

240 *If they could drive the UFC's EBITDA to $275 million* Marrocco and Fowlkes, "UFC
Documents Lay Out Promotion's Plan to Grow Profits."

240 *And if EBITDA for 2018 reached $350 million* Ibid.

240 *While regulators were alarmed by the terms* Natarajan and Carey, "Goldman Sachs Said to
Receive Fed Warning on on UFC Buyout Debt."

240 *In the preceding decade, private equity fundraising* Bain & Company, *Global Private Equity
Report 2016*, p. 2, available at https://media.bain.com/Images/Bain_and_Company
_Global_Private_Equity_Report_2016.pdf.

240 *The political environment in the US had been* Patrick Gillespie, "Finally: Fed Raises
Interest Rates for the First Time in 2016," *CNN Money*, December 15, 2016, https://
money.cnn.com/2016/12/14/news/economy/federal-reserve-rate-hike-december/index
.html.

240 *The US tax code also provided a series of loopholes* Josh Kosman, *The Buyout of America:
How Private Equity Is Destroying Jobs and Killing the American Economy* (New York:
Portfolio/Penguin, 2009) pp. 24–34.

241 *Zelaznik would be let go, along with Jamie Pollock* Dave Doyle, "Senior Execs Garry Cook,
Marshall Zelaznik Among High-Level UFC Layoffs," *MMA Fighting*, October 18, 2016,

https://www.mmafighting.com/2016/10/18/13325002/garry-cook-marshall-zelaznik
-among-high-level-ufc-layoffs; Luke Thomas, "Jaime Pollack, 'The Ultimate Fighter' and
the UFC's Push into Spanish-Speaking Latin America," *MMA Fighting*, June 1, 2014,
https://www.mmafighting.com/2014/6/1/5770420/jamie-pollack-the-ultimate-fighter
-and-ufcs-push-into-spanish.

241 *Tom Wright, who had overseen the promotion's Canadian* Daniel Austin, "UFC Cuts
Majority of Its Canadian Staff," *Toronto Sun*, October 19, 2016, https://torontosun
.com/2016/10/19/ufc-cans-a-majority-of-its-canadian-staff/wcm/650ef9bd-034b-49aa
-8d7a-4b1423b48bea.

241 *Garry Cook, who'd come to the UFC in 2012* Doyle, "Senior Execs Garry Cook, Marshall
Zelaznik Among High-Level UFC Layoffs."

241 *Even Chuck Liddell and former welterweight champion Matt Hughes* Ariel Helwani,
"Chuck Liddell, Matt Hughes Part Ways with UFC," *MMA Fighting*, December 2, 2016,
https://www.mmafighting.com/2016/12/2/13820376/chuck-liddell-matt-hughes-part
-ways-with-ufc.

241 *"It was an awful day for the company"* Raimondi, "Longtime Former UFC Exec Marshall
Zelaznik Explains Departure from Company."

241 *The layoffs had been expected, and a number of other key executives* Ben Fowlkes, "End of
an Era: Following Promotion's Sale, Matchmaker Joe Silva Leaving UFC," *MMA Junkie*,
August 31, 2016, https://mmajunkie.usatoday.com/2016/08/end-of-an-era-following
-promotions-sale-matchmaker-joe-silva-leaving-ufc; Marc Raimondi, "UFC PR Man
Dave Sholler Departing for NBA's Philadelphia 76ers," *MMA Fighting*, October 12, 2016,
https://www.mmafighting.com/2016/10/12/13265694/ufc-pr-man-dave-sholler-depart
ing-for-nba-s-philadelphia-76ers.

241 *Markwayne Mullin, a Republican member of the House* Markwayne Mullin et al., *H.R. 44
– Muhammad Ali Expansion Act*, 115th Congress, introduced January 3, 2017, available
at https://www.congress.gov/bill/115th-congress/house-bill/44/text.

241 *The Ali Act, which had been signed into law in 1999* Lance Pugmire, "John McCain's
Support for Boxing, Including Ali Act, Is Remembered Before Championship Match in
Arizona," *Los Angeles Times*, August 25, 2018, https://www.latimes.com/sports
/boxing/la-sp-mccain-boxing-20180825-story.html; *Muhammad Ali Boxing Reform Act*
(2000), available at Association of Professional Boxing Commissions website, https://
apbcboxing.com/?page_id=61.

242 *The act had rarely been invoked in the years since* Donald Tremblay, "Insider: Ali Act Not
the Greatest," *The Ring*, https://www.ringtv.com/120291-insider-ali-act-not-the-greatest/.

242 *Promoters likewise often ignored financial transparency* Thomas Hauser, "No One Is
Enforcing the Federal Boxing Laws," *ESPN*, September 25, 2007, https://www.espn.com
/sports/boxing/news/story?id=3032059.

242 *Despite the criticism, Mullin believed the Ali Act* Gene Maddaus, "Meet the Cage-Fighting
Congressman Who's Taking on the UFC," *Variety*, July 13, 2016, https://variety.com
/2016/biz/news/markwayne-mullin-cage-fighting-congressman-ufc-1201812803/.

242 *He'd fought in regional events around Oklahoma* "Markwayne Mullin—Fighter
Profile," Sherdog, https://www.sherdog.com/fighter/Markwayne-Mullin-22106#!;
Amy Dash, "Congressman: UFC Tried to Influence Witness List, Threatened to Walk
If Couture Speaks," *Bloody Elbow*, December 6, 2016, https://www.bloodyelbow
.com/2016/12/6/13847610/congressman-ufc-tried-to-influence-witness-list-threatened
-to-walk-randy-couture-ali-act-mma.

242 *"I couldn't believe what they were wanting"* Dash, "Congressman: UFC Tried to Influence Witness List."

243 *"The only way the sport is sustainable is the fighters"* Maddaus, "Meet the Cage-Fighting Congressman Who's Taking on the UFC."

243 *On December 8, 2016, Mullin scheduled* US Congressional Subcommittee on Commerce, Manufacturing, and Trade, "House Hearing on Regulating MMA Combative Sporting Events," December 8, 2016, available at https://www.youtube.com/watch?v=OVKBEkTci7Q.

243 *According to Mullin, the UFC threatened to pull out* Dash, "Congressman: UFC Tried to Influence Witness List."

243 *Following his loss to Lesnar in 2009, Couture had been* "Randy Couture—Fighter Profile," Sherdog, https://www.sherdog.com/fighter/Randy-Couture-166.

244 *"You're not gonna see me again—this was it"* UFC Holdings, "Lyoto Machida vs. Randy Couture UFC 129," *UFC Fight Pass*, April 30, 2011, available at https://ufcfightpass.com /video/29409/lyoto-machida-vs-randy-couture-ufc-129.

244 *In retirement, Couture had turned again to show business* David Whitely, "Interview: Randy Couture Talks The Expendables 2, Staying Retired, Fighting Jet Li with Frying Pans," *Complex*, August 17, 2012, https://www.complex.com/sports/2012/08/interview -randy-couture-talks-the-expendables-2-staying-retired-and-jet-li-fighting-with-frying -pans.

244 *He also resumed his former role as an occasional* Elias Cepeda, "Couture 'Enjoying the Ride' in Retirement," UFC.com, August 17, 2012, https://www.ufc.com/news/couture -enjoying-ride-retirement; "Ryan Couture—Fighter Profile."

244 *A few months before Ryan would make his UFC debut* Lesley Goldberg, "Spike Inks Randy Couture to Overall Deal, Sets Two MMA-Themed Series (Exclusive)," *Hollywood Reporter*, February 5, 2013, https://www.hollywoodreporter.com/tv/tv-news/spike-randy -couture-deal-mma-series-bellator-417508/#!.

244 *One series, called* Gym Rescue, *would see Couture* Ibid.

244 *He called Couture's lawyer and went on a tirade* "Randy Couture Can't Buy a Ticket, but the UFC Is Ryan's House—Dana White," *MMA Weekly* (YouTube channel), February 4, 2013, https://www.youtube.com/watch?v=F_1CkE9WFWc.

244 *He also barred Couture from any future events* Ibid.

244 *"The only time that Randy Couture is ever a man"* Ibid.

244 *"The issues are his, not mine, so it's up to him"* Marcos Villegas, "Randy Couture Has Not Spoken to Dana White Since Split; Talks Bellator's Fight Master," *Fight HubTV*, June 18, 2013, https://www.youtube.com/watch?v=gYCemKH4lD8.

244 Gym Rescue *was canceled after airing just three episodes* Gym Rescue (series profile), Sidereel.com, https://www.sidereel.com/tv-shows/gym-rescue/episodes; Kevin Iole, "Spike Takes It on the Chin with Shaky Ratings for Fight Master, Bellator," *Yahoo! Sports*, June 20, 2013, https://sports.yahoo.com/blogs/mma-cagewriter/spike-takes-chin-shaky -ratings-fight-master-bellator-225342981.html.

245 *Couture carried on with his acting career* Randy Couture (profile), Internet Movie Database, https://www.imdb.com/name/nm1330276/.

245 *In 2013, he began dating Mindy Robinson* "Randy Couture and Mindy Robinson Attend the World Premiere of 'Homefront' at Planet Hollywood Resort & Casino on November 20, 2013 in Las Vegas, Nevada," *Alamy*, November 20, 2013, https://www .alamy.com/randy-couture-and-mindy-robinson-attend-the-world-premiere-of-home front-image62795909.html.

245 *Robinson was also active in conservative politics* Mindy Robinson, *Red White and F U: The Unapologetically Patriotic Show*, Mindy Robinson (YouTube channel), https://www.youtube.com/channel/UC_sjTORjVqajdyUjX9CUDgQ/about.

245 *Couture became more political in his own right* "Randy Couture for MMAFA—MMA Fighters Association," *The MMAFA* (YouTube channel), August 11, 2016, https://www.youtube.com/watch?v=hbEz0U1Nq74; Shaun Al-Shatti, "Randy Couture Believes Now Is Best Shot for Fighters Association: 'Fighters Are Fed Up' with 'Taking It in the Shorts,' " *MMA Fighting*, October 30, 2016, https://www.mmafighting.com/2016/10/30/13463406/randy-couture-believes-now-is-best-shot-for-fighters-association; "MMAFA Mission Statement," *MMAFA.tv*, http://mmafa.tv/about-mmafa/.

245 *Couture had opposed the idea of a fighters union* Amy Dash, "Randy Couture Reacts to MMAAA's Invitation, Questions Bjorn Rebney's Motives," *Bloody Elbow*, November 30, 2016, https://www.bloodyelbow.com/2016/11/30/13802678/randy-couture-reacts-to-mmaaa-invitation-questions-bjorn-rebneys-motives-mma-news.

245 *In his testimony, Couture criticized* US Congressional Subcommittee on Commerce, Manufacturing, and Trade, "House Hearing on Regulating MMA Combative Sporting Events."

245 *"That conflict of interest gives the promoters a ton"* Ibid.

246 *"If a UFC fighter who is under the most stringent"* Ibid.

246 *"We just don't have any teeth to do any other kind"* Ibid.

246 *While Mullin's bill had attracted fifty sponsors* Tim Bissell, "UFC Adds an Estimated $210,000 to Ali Act Lobbying in 2017, Viacom Joins In," *Bloody Elbow*, November 15, 2017, https://www.bloodyelbow.com/2017/11/15/16655926/ufc-muhammad-ali-act-bellator-viacom-lobbying-2017-mma-politics-mullin-congress-government-news.

246 *In 2016, the Fertittas gave a combined $1.5 million* Paul Blumenthal, "Senate Races Flooded with Never-Before-Seen Sums of Super PAC Cash," *Huffington Post*, November 5, 2016, https://www.huffpost.com/entry/2016-senate-races-super-pacs_n_581cfbf5e4b0d9ce6fbc23be.

247 *The company had also paid $420,000 to several* Bissell, "UFC Adds an Estimated $210,000 to Ali Act lobbying in 2017."

247 *The company had also earmarked more than $210,000* Ibid.

247 *In New York, Zuffa had paid a company* "Case Study: Ultimate Fighting Championship," *Global Strategy Group*, archived October 22, 2012, available at http://web.archive.org/web/20121022113530/http://globalstrategygroup.com/case-studies/ultimate-fighting-championship/; Nicholas Confessore, "In Consulting Group, Hints at How Albany Works" *New York Times*, September 28, 2008, https://www.nytimes.com/2008/09/29/nyregion/29global.html.

247 *In 2001, the company had argued to state athletic commissions* Richard Sandomir, "UFC Sues State Over Ban on Mixed Martial Arts," *New York Times*, November 15, 2011, https://www.nytimes.com/2011/11/16/sports/ufc-sues-to-lift-new-york-ban-on-mixed-martial-arts-fighting.html.

247 *While the suit had eventually been dismissed* "UFC Releases Statement After Lawsuit in NY Dismissed, Judge Says MMA Law in State Is Vague," *Full Contact Fighter*, April 1, 2015, https://fcfighter.com/ufc-releases-statement-after-lawsuit-in-ny-dismissed-judge-says-mma-law-in-state-is-vague/.

247 *"Lawrence said to me it's not a championship belt"* Dash, "Congressman: UFC Tried to Influence Witness List."

247 *It was an echo of how former UFC fighter Jon Fitch* Jon Fitch, Statement Letter Submitted in Support of H.R. 44, November 9, 2017, available at https://www.scribd.com /document/364480126/Jon-Fitch-Statement.

248 *In an interview with* Fast Company, *Emanuel said WME-IMG* LaPorte, "What It's Like to Chase After Superagent Ari Emanuel and WME-IMG."

248 *"We're in conversations with Hasbro"* Ibid.

248 *"We're in the emotion transportation business"* Ibid.

248 *In three years with the promotion, her pay-per-views* "The Blue Book—Pay-Per-Views," *MMA Payout*, available at http://web.archive.org/web/20170121034505/http://mma payout.com/blue-book/pay-per-view/.

248 *She had been profiled in the* New Yorker Jesse Holland, "Ronda Rousey in the New Yorker Magazine as UFC 'Mean Girl' Who Loves to Be Hated," *MMA Mania*, July 21, 2014, https://www.mmamania.com/2014/7/21/5923177/ufc-ronda-rousey-the-new-yorker -magazine-mean-girl-who-loves-to-be-hated-mma; Sheila Marikar, "Ronda Rousey's Next Fight: Body Image in Hollywood," *New York Times*, October 9, 2015, https://www .nytimes.com/2015/10/11/fashion/ronda-rouseys-next-fight-body-image-in-holly wood.html?_r=0; Molly Knight, "Ronda Rousey Shares Why She's the Best Fighter in the World," *Self*, October 19, 2015, https://www.self.com/story/ufc-champion-ronda -rousey-best-fighter-world; Damon Martin, "Ronda Rousey Lands Sports Illustrated Cover," Fox Sports, May 12, 2015, https://www.foxsports.com/stories/ufc/ronda-rousey -lands-sports-illustrated-cover; "Ronda Rousey First Woman on Aussie Cover of Men's Fitness Magazine," *MMA Weekly*, October 5, 2015, https://www.mmaweekly.com/ronda -rousey-first-woman-on-aussie-cover-of-mens-fitness-magazine; Brent Brookhouse, "Ronda Rousey Featured on 'Ring' Cover—to Dismay of Some Boxing Fans," *MMA Junkie*, October 26, 2015, https://mmajunkie.usatoday.com/2015/10/ronda-rousey -featured-on-ring-magazine-cover-to-the-dismay-of-some-boxing-fans; *Black Belt*, November 2012, https://blackbeltmag.com/black-belt-60th-anniversary/mike-dillard -august-2011.

248 *She had appeared alongside Couture* Cory Braiterman, "Expendables 3 Cast: Ronda Rousey, UFC Female Champion, Set to Make Hollywood Acting Debut," *MMA Mania*, July 23, 2013, https://www.mmamania.com/2013/7/23/4551196/expendables-3-cast-ron da-rousey-ufc-female-champion-acting-debut-hollywood; Damon Martin, " 'Entourage' Review: Ronda Rousey Joins the Party in Her First Real Acting Role," Fox Sports, June 2, 2015, https://www.foxsports.com/stories/other/entourage-review-ronda-rousey-joins -the-party-in-her-first-real-acting-role; Meredith B. Kile, "Ronda Rousey on Filming 'Furious 7' with Paul Walker: 'He Was a Joy to Be Around,' " ET Online, March 17, 2015, https://www.etonline.com/movies/161294_ronda_rousey_on_filming_furious_7_with_ paul_walker_he_was_a_joy_to_be_around; Damon Martin, "Ronda Rousey Had Role in 'Mile 22' Reduced with More Action, Less Acting," Fox Sports, January 12, 2016, https:// www.foxsports.com/stories/ufc/ronda-rousey-had-role-in-mile-22-reduced-with-more -action-less-acting.

248 *She'd also agreed to star in* Roadhouse, *a remake* Justin Kroll, "Ronda Rousey to Star in 'Road House' Reboot (EXCLUSIVE)," *Variety*, September 9, 2015, https://variety .com/2015/film/news/ronda-rousey-road-house-reboot-1201567956/.

248 *Paramount had bought the film rights* Kayla Lombardo, "Ronda Rousey to Star in Paramount Pictures Film About Her Life," *Sports Illustrated*, August 3, 2015, https:// www.si.com/mma/2015/08/03/ronda-rousey-movie-autobiography-paramount-pictures;

Justin Kroll, "UFC Fighter Ronda Rousey Lands Two Movie Roles (EXCLUSIVE)," *Variety*, February 6, 2014, https://variety.com/2014/film/news/warners-ronda-rousey -athena-project-entourage-1201089906/#!.

248 *In 2015, she won ESPN's Fighter of the Year* Adam Guillen Jr., "ESPY's 2015: Ronda Rousey Dethrones Floyd Mayweather as 'Best Fighter,' Takes Shot at His Domestic Violence Past," *MMA Mania*, July 15, 2015, https://www.mmamania.com/2015/7/15/8974809/ufc-ronda -rousey-dethrones-floyd-mayweather-espy-awards-best-fighter-mma.

248 *And in January of 2016, she would become the first* "Ronda Rousey to Host 'SNL,' " *Hollywood Reporter*, January 5, 2016, https://www.hollywoodreporter.com/tv/tv-news /ronda-rousey-joins-snl-as-852191/#!.

248 *Rogan described her as "the best female combat sports"* UFC Holdings, "Ronda Rousey vs Bethe Correia UFC 190," *UFC Fight Pass*, August 1, 2015, https://ufcfightpass.com /video/36663/ronda-rousey-vs-bethe-correia-ufc-190.

248 *"When you watch Ronda Rousey fight, especially now"* Ibid.

249 *According to White, Rousey was "the biggest"* Saneh, "Mean Girl."

249 *"She'll do the work of twenty male fighters"* Jon Wertheim, "The Unbreakable Ronda Rousey Is the World's Most Dominant Athlete," *Sports Illustrated*, May 12, 2015, https:// www.si.com/mma/2015/05/12/ronda-rousey-ufc-mma-fighter-armbar.

249 *After six dominant wins, five of which* Dave Doyle, "UFC 193 Crowd of 56,214 Sets Company Attendance Record," *MMA Fighting*, November 15, 2015, https://www.mmafighting .com/2015/11/15/9737660/ufc-193-crowd-of-56214-sets-company-attendance-record.

249 *Holm had patiently circled around the cage in short* UFC Holdings, "Ronda Rousey vs Holly Holm UFC 193," *UFC Fight Pass*, November 14, 2013, https://ufcfightpass.com /video/38055/holly-holm-vs-ronda-rousey-ufc-193.

249 *"Champ, beautiful work," her cornerman, Edmond Tarverdyan* Ibid.

250 *Two days later, when she landed back in Los Angeles* "Ronda Rousey Covers Up at LAX Post Knock Out—TMZ Live," *TMZ* (YouTube), November 18, 2015, https://www .youtube.com/watch?v=CxHsZKkHYp4.

250 *"I really don't remember most of it"* "Ronda Rousey Discusses Her UFC Upset," *The Ellen Show* (YouTube), February 16, 2016, https://www.youtube.com/watch?v=iwCd v9iR8P8.

250 *She had adopted the nickname "Rowdy"* Georgia Slater, "Watch Ronda Rousey Recall 'Rowdy' Roddy Piper Giving 'Blessing' to Use His WWE Name in Docuseries," *Yahoo! Sports*, April 23, 2021, https://www.yahoo.com/entertainment/watch-ronda-rousey -recall-rowdy-141559667.html; Lauren Tuck, "Ronda Rousey Isn't a 'Do-Nothing- Bitch,' " *Yahoo! Life*, July 31, 2015, https://www.yahoo.com/lifestyle/ronda-rousey-isnt -a-do-nothing-bitch-warning-125521646968.html; "Ronda Rousey on Joan Jett's 'Bad Reputation,' " *Wall Street Journal*, July 16, 2015, https://www.wsj.com/articles/ronda -rousey-on-joan-jetts-bad-reputation-1434466625.

250 *At a rematch against Miesha Tate* Thomas Myers, "UFC Quick Quote: Ronda Rousey Explains Reason She Ignored Miesha Tate Handshake," *MMA Mania*, December 29, 2013, https://www.mmamania.com/2013/12/29/5253310/ufc-168-ronda-rousey-reason -ignored-miesha-tate-handshake-womens-mma.

250 *"If you're cheering and the person next to you"* Saneh, "Mean Girl."

250 *Her zest for cruelty became most acute* Michael David Smith, "Dana White: Cris Cyborg Stripped of Title, Future of Division in Question," *MMA Fighting*, January 7, 2012, https://www.mmafighting.com/2012/01/07/dana-white-cris-cyborg-stripped-of-title -future-of-division-in.

251 *Rousey had initially been scheduled to fight Cyborg* Mike Whitman, "Ronda Rousey to Defend Bantamweight Belt Against Liz Carmouche in UFC 157 Headliner," Sherdog, December 6, 2012, https://www.sherdog.com/news/news/Ronda-Rousey-to-Defend -Bantamweight-Belt-Against-Liz-Carmouche-in-UFC-157-Headliner-48001.

251 *The negotiations eventually fell apart over a dispute* Matthew Roth, "Dana White Says Tito Ortiz Advised Cyborg to Not Take Fight with Ronda Rousey," *Bleacher Report*, December 6, 2012, https://bleacherreport.com/articles/1435822-dana-white-says-tito -ortiz-advised-cyborg-to-not-take-fight-with-ronda-rousey; Mike Chiappetta, "Cris Cyborg, Ronda Rousey, and the Magic Numbers That Add Up to a Superfight," *MMA Fighting*, May 2, 2013, https://www.mmafighting.com/2013/5/2/4293762/cris-cyborg -ronda-rousey-and-the-magic-numbers-that-add-up-to-a.

251 *"In a perfect world, she wouldn't have been"* Saneh, "Mean Girl."

251 *After Rousey's comments were criticized as transphobic* Scott Harris, "Dana White Tirade: Justino Looks Like 'Wanderlei Silva in a Dress and Heels,'" *Bleacher Report*, April 24, 2014, https://bleacherreport.com/articles/2040999-dana-white-justino-looks-like-wan derlei-silva-in-a-dress-and-heels.

251 *"I think that this is the fight business"* Ibid.

251 *She seemed overcommitted to a story line that Holm* Brent Brookhouse, "Ronda Rousey on Holly Holm After UFC 193 Weigh-In Scuffle: 'Fake Humility B-Tch,'" *MMA Junkie*, November 14, 2015, https://mmajunkie.usatoday.com/2015/11/ronda-rousey-on-holly -holm-after-ufc-193-weigh-in-scuffle-fake-humility-b-tch.

251 *The loud provocations had started to feel like tells* Mike Chiari, "Ronda Rousey vs Holly Holm: Updated Odds, Predictions Before Weigh-in," *Bleacher Report*, November 13, 2015, https://bleacherreport.com/articles/2588608-ronda-rousey-vs-holly-holm-updated -odds-predictions-before-weigh-in.

252 Champions do more. Everything is easy: Rousey with Ortiz, *My Fight, Your Fight*, pp. 115, 187, 213, 221, 233.

252 *One morning in early 2015, she discovered another one* UFC Holdings, "UFC 184 Embedded: Vlog Series—Episode 2," *UFC—Ultimate Fighting Championship* (YouTube channel), February 25, 2015, https://www.youtube.com/watch?v=1bHQhBZ2FYM.

252 *Sometimes misattributed to Franz Kafka, the quote comes* "Franz Kafka: Quotes: Quotable Quotes," GoodReads, https://www.goodreads.com/quotes/475461-the-nonexistent-is -whatever-we-have-not-sufficiently-desired-only.

252 *"With everything finally ended, I suddenly felt"* Nikos Kazantzakis (translated by P. A. Bien), *Report to Greco* (New York: Simon & Schuster, 1965), p. 434.

252 *When Rousey finally returned to the octagon* Thomas Gerbasi, "Ronda Rousey Set to Return at UFC 207," UFC.com, October 12, 2016, https://www.ufc.com/news/ronda -rousey-set-return-ufc-207.

252 *She had asked that she not be required* Brett Okamoto, "Dana White: Ronda Rousey Will Fulfill Press Obligations in Future," *ESPN*, December 28, 2016, https://www.espn.com /mma/story/_/id/18366538/dana-white-says-ronda-rousey-not-addressing-media -ahead-ufc-207-one-thing.

252 *"Listen, Ronda has given more than anybody"* Ibid.

253 *The fight itself would last just forty-eight seconds* UFC Holdings, "Amanda Nunes vs Ronda Rousey UFC 207," *UFC Fight Pass*, December 30, 2016, https://ufcfightpass.com /video/47910/amanda-nunes-vs-ronda-rousey-ufc-207.

254 *After the loud weigh-ins, she'd return to her hotel room* Rousey with Ortiz, *My Fight, Your Fight*, p. 279.

254   *"We lie on my bed" Rousey wrote* Ibid.

254   *Rousey didn't appear at the post-fight press conference* Josh Peter, "Ronda Rousey Skips
       Press Conference After UFC 207 Loss," *USA Today*, December 31, 2016, https://www
       .usatoday.com/story/sports/ufc/2016/12/31/ronda-rousey-press-conference-silence-ufc
       -207-amanda-nunes/96032098/.

254   *It would be the fifth event of 2016* Dave Meltzer, "UFC 207 Does Over 1 Million Buys,"
       MMA Fighting, January 8, 2017, https://www.mmafighting.com/2017/1/8/14204530
       /ufc-207-does-over-1-million-buys; John S. Nash, "Finances: UFC's Revenues
       and Earnings Drive Endeavor IPO," *Bloody Elbow*, May 11, 2021, https://www
       .bloodyelbow.com/2021/5/11/22411542/finances-ufc-revenues-and-earnings-drive
       -endeavor-ipo.

Chapter 14: The Money Belt

255   *The day after Donald Trump was elected president* UFC Holdings, "UFC 205 Embedded
       Vlog Series—Episode 3," *UFC—Ultimate Fighting Championship* (YouTube channel),
       November 9, 2016, https://www.youtube.com/watch?v=UmK3O6BapJM&t=256s;
       "Conor McGregor Gifted Custom 'Notorious' Rolls-Royce for UFC 205," *MMA Fighting*,
       November 7, 2016, https://www.mmafighting.com/2016/11/7/13557740/conor-mcgregor
       -gifted-custom-notorious-rolls-royce-for-ufc-205.

255   *He was ebullient, splitting his days between* "Conor McGregor Shops and Trains in New
       York City: The Mac Life Series 2," *The Mac Life*, November 8, 2016, https://www.youtube
       .com/watch?v=X_3QRem-LMk.

255   *It would be the UFC's first-ever event at Madison Square Garden* Ken Boehlke, "Road to
       UFC 205: How the UFC Took 20 Years to Get to Madison Square Garden," CBS News,
       November 2, 2016, https://www.cbsnews.com/newyork/news/ufc-205-new-york-madi
       son-square-garden-history/.

255   *In Los Angeles, people had marched onto the 101* Jory Rand, "Thousands Protest Trump
       Election in LA, Block 101 Freeway Downtown," ABC 7, November 10, 2016, https://abc7
       .com/donald-trump-protests-election-2016-march/1599507/; Jim Ryan, "Anti-Trump
       Protestors March Through Portland, Close Interstates 5 and 84," *Oregonian*, November 9,
       2016, https://www.oregonlive.com/portland/2016/11/protesters_gather_at_portlands
       .html; David Matthews, "Thousands March Against Trump in Chicago: 'Hate Won't
       Make America Great,'" *DNA Info*, November 9, 2016, https://www.dnainfo.com
       /chicago/20161109/downtown/donald-trump-election-protest-tower/; Michael George,
       Ray Villeda, and R. Darren Price, "Thousands Protest Donald Trump in New York City,"
       NBC 4 New York, November 9, 2016, https://www.nbcnewyork.com/news/local/donald
       -trump-new-york-city-reaction-protests-union-square-columbus-circle-nyc/1088013/;
       UFC Holdings, "UFC 205 Embedded Vlog Series—Episode 3."

255   *McGregor was perplexed by the sudden* Zach Baron, "Conor McGregor Talks Fighting
       Floyd Mayweather, Searching for Khloé Kardashian, and Really Getting Paid by the
       UFC," *GQ Style*, February 15, 2017, https://www.gq.com/story/conor-mcgregor-gq-style
       -cover-story.

256   *"It's the wrong mindset," he'd later say* Ibid.

256   *Lorenzo and Frank had each donated $1 million to America First Action* Tarini Parti, "The
       Bros of the Ultimate Fighting Championship Are All In on Trump," *Buzzfeed*, April 23,
       2018, https://www.buzzfeednews.com/article/tariniparti/the-bros-of-the-ultimate-fight
       ing-championship-are-all-in.

256 *White had pledged his support to Trump* "UFC's Dana White Speaks at Republican National Convention," PBS, July 19, 2016, https://www.pbs.org/video/ufc-s-dana-white-speaks-at-republican-national-convention-1476232920/.

256 *In a radio interview, White described Trump admiringly* "Dana White Talks UFC at MSG, Ronda, Conor, Trump, Money, & More," *Hot 97* (YouTube channel), September 26, 2016, https://www.youtube.com/watch?v=UquD8q1jrDY.

256 *Emanuel had represented Trump as an agent until 2016* Matthew Belloni, "Ari Emanuel and Patrick Whitesell Unleashed: WME-IMG's Strategy, IPO Plans, China and the Doubters," *Hollywood Reporter*, March 30, 2016, https://www.hollywoodreporter.com/movies/movie-features/ari-emanuel-patrick-whitesell-unleashed-879003/.

256 *"I call him a lot, and we talk," Trump said* Michael Wolff, "The Donald Trump Coversation: Politics' 'Dark Heart' Is Having the Best Time Anyone's Ever Had," *Hollywood Reporter*, June 1, 2016, https://www.hollywoodreporter.com/news/politics-news/donald-trump-conversation-politics-dark-898465/.

256 *In 2015, WME-IMG purchased the Miss Universe Organization* John Koblin, "Trump Sells Miss Universe Organization to WME-IMG Talent Agency," *New York Times*, September 14, 2015, https://www.nytimes.com/2015/09/15/business/media/trump-sells-miss-universe-organization-to-wme-img-talent-agency.html; Yashar Ali, "Did Ari Emanuel Cover for Donald Trump on the Miss Universe Tapes?" *Daily Beast*, December 18, 2016, https://www.thedailybeast.com/did-ari-emanuel-cover-for-donald-trump-on-the-miss-universe-tapes; Kim Janssen, "Tom Arnold: Ari Emanuel Told Me He Lost Too Much Money on Cosby to Release Embarrassing Miss Universe Footage of Trump," *Chicago Tribune*, January 18, 2018, https://www.chicagotribune.com/news/ct-met-arnold-ari-trump-0118-chicago-inc-20180117-story.html.

256 *Emanuel was also briefly vetted for a potential position* Gene Maddaus, "Ari Emanuel Was Vetted for Trump Administration Role," *Variety*, June 24, 2019, https://variety.com/2019/biz/news/ari-emanuel-trump-administration-role-1203251204/.

256 *Though McGregor was not especially political, he had* Karim Zidan, "The Strange Politics of Conor McGregor," *Bloody Elbow*, July 8, 2021, https://www.bloodyelbow.com/2021/7/8/22566987/conor-mcgregor-politics-putin-trump-ireland-mma-news-feature.

256 *McGregor felt closer than ever to fulfilling his own vision* Jeff Cain, "Conor McGregor's Plan Was Always to Hold Two UFC Titles at the Same Time," *MMA Weekly*, January 24, 2016, https://www.mmaweekly.com/conor-mcgregors-plan-was-always-to-hold-two-ufc-titles-at-the-same-time.

257 *After he'd seen the UFC sold, he'd gone from* Lance Pugmire, "With Two Belts, Conor McGregor Doubles Down on UFC: 'I'm Aware of My Worth,'" *Los Angeles Times*, November 13, 2016, https://www.latimes.com/sports/boxing/la-sp-ufc-mcgregor-2016-1113-story.html.

257 *As much money as the UFC was paying him for his fights* "Conor McGregor Is First UFC Fighter Forbes' Highest Paid Athletes List," UFC.com, June 10, 2016, https://www.ufc.com/news/conor-mcgregor-first-ufc-fighter-forbes-highest-paid-athletes-list.

257 *"I want to put my analytics forward, man-to-man"* Baron, "Conor McGregor Talks Fighting Floyd Mayweather."

257 *"Surprise, surprise, motherfuckers"* UFC Holdings, "Conor McGregor vs Nate Diaz UFC 202," *UFC Fight Pass*, August 20, 2016, https://ufcfightpass.com/video/44070/conor-mcgregor-vs-nate-diaz-ufc-202.

257 *A little over a month later—after McGregor* Mike Dyce, "Conor McGregor Wants Eddie

Alvarez to Beg Him for Fight," *Sports Illustrated*, September 21, 2016, https://www
.si.com/mma/2016/09/21/conor-mcgregor-eddie-alvarez-beg-fight; Brett Okamoto,
"Conor McGregor to Challenge Eddie Alvarez for Lightweight Title at UFC 205," *ESPN*,
September 27, 2016, https://www.espn.com/mma/story/_/id/17648940/eddie-alvarez
-conor-mcgregor-confirmed-ufc-205.

257 *I run New York City!" McGregor shouted* UFC Holdings, "UFC 205 Embedded:
Vlog Series—Episode 5," *UFC Ultimate Fighting Championship*, November 11,
2016, https://www.youtube.com/watch?v=xzSd3XtbOSU&t=2s; Ben Coate, "Conor
McGregor Reveals Details About 'Iconic' $55,000 Gucci Fur Coat," *Fansided*, https://
fansided.com/2019/06/29/conor-mcgregor-shows-off-iconic-and-historic-gucci-fur
-coats/.

257 *When the fight finally arrived, playing out* UFC Holdings, "Conor McGregor vs Eddie
Alvarez," *UFC Fight Pass*, November 12, 2016, https://ufcfightpass.com/video/46526
/conor-mcgregor-vs-eddie-alvarez-ufc-205.

258 *Later that night, McGregor announced* "Conor McGregor's Full UFC 205 Post-fight Press
Conference—UFC 205," *UFC on Fox* (YouTube channel), November 13, 2016, https://
www.youtube.com/watch?v=PgYOODHmzco.

258 *"If you want to come at me, if you want me to stick around"* Ibid.

258 *Mysteriously, three weeks later, the California State Athletic Commission* Keith Idec,
"Conor McGregor Gets Approval for Boxing License in California," *Boxing Scene*,
November 30, 2016, https://www.boxingscene.com/conor-mcgregor-gets-approval-box
ing-license-california—111273.

258 *Conan O'Brien had asked McGregor about the matchup* "Conor McGregor: I Will Destroy
Chad Mendes & Floyd Mayweather—Conan on TBS," *Team Coco*, July 3, 2015, https://
www.youtube.com/watch?v=zOgao7UNw3E.

259 *Mayweather's uncle and trainer, Jeff Mayweather* "Conor McGregor Would Get His Ass
Whooped by an Amateur Boxer Says Floyd Mayweather's Uncle," *The Mayweather Channel*
(YouTube channel), July 9, 2015, https://www.youtube.com/watch?v=b13NcWFRZvk.

259 *"They say he talk a lot of trash and people praise him"* Ben Thompson, "Floyd Mayweather
Sounds Off on the State of Boxing: 'I Truly Believe That Racism Still Exists in the Sport,' "
Fight Hype, December 30, 2015, http://www.fighthype.com/mayweathernews/may
weather_says_boxing_still_racist.html.

259 *McGregor was quick to respond, with an Instagram post* Nick Schwartz, "Conor McGregor
Blasts Floyd Mayweather: 'Don't Ever Bring Race into My Success,' " *USA Today*,
January 9, 2016, https://ftw.usatoday.com/2016/01/conor-mcgregor-blasts-floyd-may
weather-dont-ever-bring-race-into-my-success.

259 *McGregor suggested they could settle their differences* Ibid.

259 *Later, Mayweather claimed he had contacted McGregor* David Reid, "Floyd Mayweather
Claims He Offered McGregor $15 Million for Fight," CNBC, January 12, 2017, https://
www.cnbc.com/2017/01/12/floyd-mayweather-claims-he-offered-conor-mcgregor-15
-million-for-fight.html.

260 *The following day, in January of 2017, two months* Damon Martin, " 'The Herd': Dana
White Makes Offer to Floyd Mayweather to Fight Conor McGregor," Fox Sports,
January 13, 2017, https://www.foxsports.com/stories/ufc/the-herd-dana-white-makes
-offer-to-floyd-mayweather-to-fight-conor-mcgregor.

260 *Mayweather ignored the offer, which was almost* Darren Rovell and Dan Rafael, "Payday:
Floyd Mayweather to Make at Least $220M from Pacquiao Fight," *ESPN*, July 1, 2015,

https://www.espn.com/boxing/story/_/id/13181452/floyd-mayweather-make-least-220
-million-fight-manny-pacquiao.

260 *"If Conor McGregor really wants the fight to happen"* Ben Dirs and Rob Bartlett, "Floyd
Mayweather Jr. to Conor McGregor: 'Sign the Paper,' " *ESPN*, March 7, 2017, https://
www.espn.co.uk/boxing/story/_/id/18843882/floyd-mayweather-says-conor-mcgregor
-sign-paper-potential-superfight.

261 *"Let 'em boo, it's no problem"* Top Rank Boxing, "Mayweather Jr. vs. Arroyo," *ESPN+*,
January 9, 1998, available at https://www.espn.com/espnplus/player/_/id/c81e7d0e-a205
-4923-aade-00484dc8515e.

261 *"It's my job," he said. "I go to the gym"* Kelefa Sanneh, "The Best Defense," *New Yorker*,
May 25, 2015, https://www.newyorker.com/magazine/2015/05/25/the-best-defense.

261 *Born in Grand Rapids, Michigan, Mayweather was named* Josh Peter, "Mayweather's 'White
Daddy' Also from Grand Rapids," *USA Today*, April 23, 2015, https://www.freep.com/story
/sports/2015/04/23/floyd-mayweather-manny-pacquiao/26256365/; Steven Bunce, "Floyd
Mayweather: 'I Had a Father Who Was a Hustler and a Mother Who Was on Drugs,' "
Independent, December 6, 2007, https://www.independent.co.uk/sport/general/floyd-may
weather-i-had-a-father-who-was-a-hustler-and-a-mother-who-was-on-drugs-763309.html.

261 *When Mayweather was just six months old* Sanneh, "The Best Defense."

261 *To help keep the family afloat, Mayweather Sr. sold* Ibid.

261 *As a teenager, Mayweather had thought about finding a job* Ibid.

261 *Mayweather emerged as a star amateur boxer* Bunce, "Floyd Mayweather: 'I Had a Father
Who Was a Hustler.' "

261 *When Mayweather made his professional debut a few months later* "Floyd Mayweather Jr.,"
BoxRec.com, https://boxrec.com/en/proboxer/000352.

262 *As his career progressed, Mayweather famously avoided alcohol* Lance Pugmire, "Floyd
Mayweather Jr. Is Obsessed with Perfection," *Los Angeles Times*, September 12, 2013,
https://www.latimes.com/sports/boxing/la-xpm-2013-sep-12-la-sp-floyd-mayweather
-20130913-story.html.

262 *Mayweather settled in Las Vegas and founded his* Daron Pressley, "Meet the Members of
the Money Team," *Black Enterprise*, October 5, 2015, https://www.blackenterprise.com
/meet-the-members-of-the-money-team/; George Willis, "An Inside Look at Floyd Mayweather's Controversial Money Team," *New York Post*, August 24, 2017, https://nypost
.com/2017/08/24/its-a-family-an-inside-look-at-mayweathers-money-team/.

262 *He kept a growing collection of luxury cars* "Floyd Mayweather Shows Off Insane Car
Collection of Royces, Lambos, & Maybachs!!!" *TMZ*, August 6, 2021, https://www.tmz
.com/2021/08/06/floyd-mayweather-car-collection-vegas-mansion-rolls-royce-lambo
-maybach/; Brian Jones, "The Greatest Hits in Floyd Mayweather's Car Collection,"
Autowise, October 26, 2018, https://autowise.com/floyd-mayweather-cars/; Nina Mandell,
"Floyd Mayweather Got His Son a Gold Bentley Golf Cart for His Birthday," *USA Today*,
November 17, 2014, https://ftw.usatoday.com/2014/11/floyd-mayweather-golf-cart.

262 *He also owned two mansions in Las Vegas* Julio Lara, "Floyd Mayweather Flaunts His
Prodigious Wealth in the Real Estate Market," Realtor.com, August 24, 2017, https://
www.realtor.com/news/celebrity-real-estate/floyd-mayweather-real-estate-review/.

262 *He owned a $2 million 3,100-square-foot penthouse* Ibid.

262 *"He prides himself off [money] more than the belts"* "Floyd Mayweather Jr.: Behind the
Police Report," *Yahoo! Sports*, May 1, 2013, https://sports.yahoo.com/news/boxing
—floyd-mayweather-jr—-behind-the-police-report-061849219.html.

262 *Mayweather fed his acquisitiveness with a string* Kurt Badenhausen, "Floyd Mayweather Hits Jackpot with New Showtime PPV Deal," February 20, 2013, https://www.forbes .com/sites/kurtbadenhausen/2013/02/20/floyd-mayweather-hits-jackpot-with-new -showtime-ppv-deal/?sh=7395ca3179cb.

262 *The deal helped Mayweather transform into his own enterprise* Tim Smith, "Making Money: How Floyd Mayweather Produces Boxing's Biggest Fights," *Bleacher Report*, September 10, 2014, https://bleacherreport.com/articles/2192887-making-money -how-floyd-mayweather-produces-boxings-biggest-fights.

262 *At the end of 2016, Mayweather announced another new* Jesse Granger, "Floyd Mayweather Jr.'s Las Vegas Strip Club to Open Soon," *Las Vegas Sun*, December 29, 2016, https://lasvegassun.com/news/2016/dec/29/floyd-mayweather-jr-las-vegas-strip-club-to -open/.

262 *"I feel that, as far as when it comes to females"* Daniel Roberts, "The Trouble with Floyd Mayweather," *Deadspin*, July 16, 2014, https://deadspin.com/the-trouble-with-floyd -mayweather-1605217498.

262 *Mayweather had a long and violent history with women* Ibid.; Frances McCabe and Brian Haynes, "Police Called to Another Dispute Between Floyd Mayweather Jr. and a Woman," *Las Vegas Review Journal*, September 18, 2012, http://www.reviewjournal.com /sports/boxing/police-called-another-dispute-between-floyd-mayweather-jr-and -woman.

263 *"You may be a terrific and famous fighter, but that doesn't"* Matt Pordum, "Boxer Mayweather Guilty of Battery," *Las Vegas Sun*, June 11, 2004, https://lasvegassun.com /news/2004/jun/11/boxer-mayweather-guilty-of-battery/.

263 *Perhaps the most disturbing event took place in 2010* Martin Rogers, "Life with Floyd Mayweather: 'I was a battered woman,'" *USA Today*, November 18, 2014, https://www .usatoday.com/story/sports/boxing/2014/11/18/floyd-mayweather-josie-harris-domes tic-abuse/19221605/.

263 *He returned a few hours later, at around 4:00 a.m., and knocked* Ibid.

263 *"I've just climbed to another level of this"* Baron, "Conor McGregor Talks Fighting Floyd Mayweather."

263 *Kavanagh had first caught a glimpse of this tendency in 2011* Kavanagh, *Win or Learn*, pp. 64–65.

263 *The promotion had paid for a hotel room for McGregor* Ibid.

264 *By early 2016, Kavanagh said McGregor's training habits* Ariel Helwani, "John Kavanagh: Conor Mcgregor Found His New Reason to Fight—Ariel Helwani's MMA Show," *ESPN MMA*, January 13, 2020, https://www.youtube.com/watch?v=uiJrflsbWZY.

264 *McGregor's training routines had grown more esoteric* Stephanie Hayes, "The Viral Video Star Behind the Fitness Fad That May Replace CrossFit," *Atlantic*, August 7, 2018, https:// www.theatlantic.com/health/archive/2018/08/ido-portal-the-player/566687/.

264 *Cell phone footage appeared of him poolside in a Las Vegas mansion* Brandon Wenerd, "Is This a Video of Conor McGregor Partying with His Girls Who Aren't His Girlfriend?" Brobible, March 17, 2016, https://brobible.com/sports/article/video-conor-mcgregor -partying/.

264 *A few months later, he spent three intoxicated days in Liverpool* Jonny Dillon, "Hippy Craic: UFC Star Conor McGregor's Trashed Hotel Suite in Aintree Left Strewn with Nitrous Oxide Canisters—But He 'Hired Specialists to Clean Up After,'" *The Sun*, April 18, 2017, https://www.thesun.co.uk/sport/3345024/ufc

-star-conor-mcgregors-aintree-hotel-suite-trashed-nitrous-oxide-canisters-hired
-specialists-to-clean-up/.

264 *He was filmed walking into the Aintree Racecourse* George Boulton, "High Flyer: Grand
National 2017: Conor McGregor Arrives in Style After Getting a Private Jet AND a Rolls
Royce," *The Sun*, April 8, 2017, https://www.thesun.co.uk/sport/3288204/conor-mcgregor
-arrives-grand-national-private-jet-rolls-royce/.

264 *A report in the* Sun *also described heavy damage done* Dillon, "Hippy Craic: UFC Star
Conor McGregor's Trashed Hotel Suite."

264 *In March, he was filmed at a boxing event at Madison Square Garden* Dan Rafael, "Conor
McGregor: 'I Am Boxing!' " *ESPN*, March 18, 2017, https://www.espn.com/blog/dan
-rafael/post/_/id/17470/conor-mcgregor-i-am-boxing.

265 *After months of rumor, the fight between Mayweather and McGregor* "Mayweather vs.
McGregor IT'S OFFICIAL . . . 12 Rounds, Boxing," *TMZ*, June 14, 2017, https://www
.tmz.com/2017/06/14/mayweather-mcgregor-fight-official/.

265 *Twelve minutes later, Mayweather followed up* "Conor McGregor vs. Floyd Mayweather
Happening Aug. 26 in Las Vegas," *MMA Junkie*, June 14, 2017, https://mmajunkie.
usatoday.com/2017/06/report-conor-mcgregor-vs-floyd-mayweather-happening-aug-26
-in-las-vegas.

265 *Instead of a formal title, the World Boxing Council announced* Marc Raimondi, "WBC
President Explains Origin of Over-the-Top, 'Priceless' Money Belt for Mayweather
vs. McGregor," *MMA Fighting*, August 24, 2017, https://www.mmafighting.
com/2017/8/24/16195296/wbc-president-explains-origin-of-over-the-top-priceless
-money-belt-for-mayweather-vs-mcgregor.

266 *To emphasize the magnitude of the fight, Showtime arranged* Brian Campbell, "Floyd
Mayweather, Conor McGregor Announce Press Tour with Ticket Information," CBS
Sports, July 7, 2017, https://www.cbssports.com/boxing/news/floyd-mayweather
-conor-mcgregor-announce-press-tour-with-ticket-information/.

266 *"This is what a $100 million fighter looks like"* Brett Okamoto, "Floyd Mayweather, Conor
McGregor Trade Insults as Media Tour Begins," *ESPN*, July 11, 2017, https://www.espn
.com/boxing/story/_/id/19966520/floyd-mayweather-conor-mcgregor-trade-insults
-promo-tour-begins-los-angeles.

266 *Two days later, at the Barclays Center in Brooklyn* "Mayweather, McGregor Exchanges
Profanities, Barbs in Brooklyn," CBS Sports, July 14, 2017, https://www.cbsnews.com
/dfw/news/mayweather-mcgregor-exchange-profanities-barbs-in-brooklyn/.

266 *"I run this show, this is my ho, and I threw"* "Mayweather vs McGregor: New York Press
Conference," *Showtime Sports* (YouTube channel), July 13, 2017, https://www.youtube
.com/watch?v=ktUGNEyW7To.

266 *"A lot of people have me saying I'm against"* Ibid.

267 *The tour reached its acidic conclusion in London* "Floyd Mayweather vs Conor McGregor:
London Press Conference," *Showtime Sports* (YouTube channel), July 14, 2017, https://
www.youtube.com/watch?v=XkuYRHK1WDU.

267 *He reminded White that they had known each other* "Floyd Mayweather's Early Fight
Outfits Sponsored by UFC's Dana White," *Yahoo! Sports*, April 30, 2015, https://sports.
yahoo.com/blogs/boxing/floyd-mayweather-s-early-fight-outfights-sponored-by-ufc-s
-dana-white-233757891.html.

267 *According to the betting odds, McGregor was an underdog* Brian Campbell, "Floyd
Mayweather Betting Odds Keep Falling as Conor McGregor Picks Up Steam," *CBS*

Boxing, August 25, 2017, https://www.cbssports.com/boxing/news/floyd-mayweather
-betting-odds-keep-falling-as-conor-mcgregor-picks-up-steam/.

267 *Despite that fact, the overwhelming majority* David Purdum, "Sportsbooks See High
Number of Bets for Underdog McGregor," *ESPN*, June 17, 2017, https://www.espn.com
/chalk/story/_/id/19664207/sportsbooks-sees-flurry-square-bets-conor-mcgregor-fight
-floyd-mayweather; David Purdum, "Bets on Floyd Mayweather Hit Seven Figures in
Vegas," *ESPN*, August 24, 2017, https://www.espn.com/chalk/story/_/id/20448655
/1-million-bets-come-floyd-mayweather-ahead-conor-mcgregor-showdown.

267 *He had a boxing ring and some gym equipment installed* Simon Samano, "The Story
Behind Conor McGregor Knocking Out Floyd Mayweather (in a Mural on His Gym
Wall)," *MMA Junkie*, June 20, 2017, https://mmajunkie.usatoday.com/2017/06/conor
-mcgregor-knocking-out-floyd-mayweather-huge-mural-gym.

267 *A little over three weeks before the fight* Brett Okamoto, "Paulie Malignaggi, Conor
McGregor Spar Again: 'A Lot More Intense,' " *ABC News*, August 2, 2017, https://
abcnews.go.com/Sports/paulie-malignaggi-conor-mcgregor-spar-lot-intense
/story?id=49002346; Brett Okamoto, "Paulie Malignaggi Throwing in the Towel as Conor
McGregor's Sparring Partner," *ESPN*, August 3, 2017, https://www.espn.com/boxing
/story/_/id/20240996/paulie-malignaggi-throwing-towel-conor-mcgregor-sparring
-partner.

268 *The McGregor camp refused, but shortly after* Brian Campbell, "Dana White Releases
Viral Video of Conor McGregor Sparring with Paulie Malignaggi," *CBS Boxing*,
August 12, 2017, https://www.cbssports.com/boxing/news/dana-white-releases-viral
-video-of-conor-mcgregor-sparring-with-paulie-malignaggi/.

268 *The debate only fed the fanatical optimism of those* Kevin Iole, "Conor McGregor Is Ready,
Predicts Second-Round Knockout of Floyd Mayweather," *Yahoo! Sports*, August 12,
2017, https://sports.yahoo.com/conor-mcgregor-ready-predicts-second-round-knockout
-floyd-mayweather-043049697.html.

268 *He posted videos of evening scooter rides through Miami* Elie Seckbach, "Floyd
Mayweather and Team on a 5 Hour Bike Ride in Miami," *ESPNews* (YouTube channel),
August 18, 2017, https://www.youtube.com/watch?v=hB5HhjuPU8I.

268 *He ate McDonald's and drank Coca-Cola, rode horses* "All Access: Mayweather vs
McGregor—Episode 2" and "All Access: Mayweather vs McGregor—Episode 3,"
Showtime, August 4, 2017, and August 11, 2017, https://www.sho.com/all-access
/season/22/episode/2/mayweather-vs-mcgregor—-episode-2.

269 *The night of the fight, both Mayweather and McGregor* "All Access: Floyd Mayweather
vs. Conor McGregor—Epilogue," *Showtime Sports* (YouTube channel), December 1,
2017, https://www.youtube.com/watch?v=GeOUZ_pIwB4; Fitzgerald, *Conor McGregor:
Notorious.*

269 *The final ticket sales were 13,094, and with complimentary* Scott Christ, "Mayweather vs
McGregor: Gate Big, But Well Short of All-Time Record," *Bad Left Hook*, September 7,
2017, https://www.badlefthook.com/2017/9/7/16265796/mayweather-vs-mcgregor-gate
-big-but-well-short-of-all-time-record; Marcus Vanderberg, "Mayweather-McGregor:
Why Was T-Mobile Arena So Empty?" *Yahoo! Sports*, August 27, 2017, https://sports
.yahoo.com/mayweather-mcgregor-t-mobile-arena-empty-071410953.html?guc
counter=1.

269 *Most fans were priced out by tickets that ranged* Kurt Badenhausen, "Mayweather vs.
McGregor Tickets on Sale Today Priced at Up to $10,000," *Forbes*, July 24, 2017, https://

www.forbes.com/sites/kurtbadenhausen/2017/07/24/mayweather-vs-mcgregor-tickets
-on-sale-today-priced-at-up-to-10000/?sh=39c218bf35d5; Jeremy Woo, "At $3,684,
Average Mayweather-McGregor Ticket Cheaper Than Mayweather-Pacquiao," *Sports
Illustrated*, August 8, 2017, https://www.si.com/boxing/2017/08/08/mayweather-mcgre
gor-tickets-average-price-pacquiao.

269 *Despite an arena that was nearly one-third empty* Christ, "Mayweather vs McGregor:
Gate Big, But Well Short of All-Time Record."

269 *Yet the magnitude of people looking into the event* Adam Stites, "Mayweather vs.
McGregor Finally Started After Midnight ET," *SB Nation*, August 27, 2017, https://www
.sbnation.com/2017/8/26/16209540/floyd-mayweather-conor-mcgregor-start-time
-begin-ppv.

274 *In the dressing room after the fight, White and Lorenzo* "All Access: Floyd Mayweather vs.
Conor McGregor—Epilogue."

274 *"Dude, I'm ecstatic," White said* Ibid.

274 *The event would go on to break the all-time* Jason Gay, "The Unnamed Podvideocast with
Jason Gay and Dana White," *Wall Street Journal* (YouTube channel), October 19, 2017,
https://www.youtube.com/watch?v=V2wbIUSpALY.

274 *In the US, the buy rate had been 4.3 million* Ryan Harkness, "The Official PPV Count
for Mayweather vs. McGregor Is a Staggering 4.3 Million," *MMA Mania*, December 14,
2017, https://www.mmamania.com/2017/12/14/16778920/official-ppv-count-mayweath
er-vs-mcgregor-4-3-million.

274 *White also claimed the fight was the most pirated event in history* Gay, "The Unnamed
Podvideocast with Jason Gay and Dana White"; Kevin Iole, "Mayweather-McGregor
Pirated by Upward of 100 Million Viewers," *Yahoo! Sports*, August 28, 2017, https://
sports.yahoo.com/mayweather-mcgregor-pirated-upwards-100-million-viewers
-205358627.html.

274 *The MGM claimed more than $1 billion in bets had been placed* David Purdum, "The
Betting Event of the 2010s: Mayweather vs. McGregor," *ESPN*, December 27, 2019,
https://www.espn.com/chalk/story/_/id/28366850/the-betting-event-2010s-mayweather
-vs-mcgregor.

274 *Mayweather made $100 million in disclosed pay* Dan Rafael, "Floyd Mayweather's Purse
at $100M; and Conor McGregor's $30M Biggest of Career," *ESPN*, August 25, 2017,
https://www.espn.com/boxing/story/_/id/20461204/floyd-mayweather-guaranteed
-100-million-purse-conor-mcgregor-get-30-million; Kurt Badenhausen, "How Floyd
Mayweather Made a Record $275 Million for One Night of Work," *Forbes*, June 5, 2018,
https://www.forbes.com/sites/kurtbadenhausen/2018/06/05/how-floyd-mayweather
-earned-275-million-for-one-night-of-work/?sh=3096325b6e4d.

274 *McGregor reportedly earned $85 million* Ibid.

274 *The UFC was paid an undisclosed fee as co-promoter* Mac Andrews, "UFC Secured
'Well Over' US$700m in Revenue in 2017," *Sports Pro Media*, July 5, 2018, https://www
.sportspromedia.com/news/ufc-revenue-2017-mcgregor-mayweather/.

274 *The event placed McGregor at number four on the* Forbes list Lewis Mckeever, "Conor
McGregor Comes in at No. 4 on Forbes' 2018 List of Highest Paid Athletes," *Bloody
Elbow*, June 6, 2018, https://www.bloodyelbow.com/2018/6/6/17433684/ufc-mma-news
-report-conor-mcgregor-forbes-highest-paid-athlete-fight.

275 *"It was almost like the world got a magic trick"* Joe Rogan, "JRE MMA Show #32
with Firas Zahabi," *Spotify*, June 2018, https://open.spotify.com/episode/0AZTuZ16

pZyvwQcXl5F7Ee (also available at https://www.youtube.com/watch?v=5H5sk8q
T3ZE).

275 *He was the last to speak for the night, at a podium* UFC Holdings, "Mayweather vs
McGregor: Post-fight Press Conference," *UFC—Ultimate Fighting Championship*
(YouTube channel), August 27, 2017, https://www.youtube.com/watch?v=4pWtejhHvMI.

Epilogue: A Man Must Exceed His Limits

277 *In 2017, the promotion relocated to a 180,000-square-foot* "Lorenzo Fertitta Outlines
Plans for New UFC Corporate Campus," *MMA Junkie* (YouTube channel), December 1,
2015, https://www.youtube.com/watch?v=vOP1ajkyB-M; Don Riddell, "Behind the
Scenes at the UFC's New Headquarters," CNN (YouTube channel), May 1, 2017, https://
www.youtube.com/watch?v=ilfuSGJsUDw.

277 *In addition to weight machines, heavy bags, treadmills* Jen Booton, "The New Rules of
Fight Club: You Talk About All the Tech Being Used at the UFC Performance Institute,"
Sports Business Journal/SportTechie, August 13, 2019, https://www.sporttechie.com
/ufc-performance-institute-sports-technology/.

277 *The UFC hired Forrest Griffin to help oversee the Performance Institute* "The Team—UFC
Performance Institute," UFC.com, available at https://www.ufc.com/performance-insti
tute/team.html.

278 *In 2019, the UFC opened another massive compound* Bill King, "Dana White: 'This Is the
Day I Have Been Dreaming On,'" *Sports Business Journal*, November 12, 2018, https://
www.sportsbusinessjournal.com/Journal/Issues/2018/11/12/In-Depth/UFC-HQ.aspx
?hl=dana%20white.

278 *In 2020, White announced the promotion was also* Mike Heck, "Dana White Reveals Plan
for New UFC Hotel for Fighters in Las Vegas: 'We'll Be Completely Self-Sufficient,'"
MMA Fighting, August 26, 2020, https://www.mmafighting.com/2020/8/26/21402146
/dana-white-reveals-plan-for-new-ufc-hotel-for-fighters-in-las-vegas-well-be-self-suffi
cent.

278 *Ironically, the UFC had its best year yet during* Anton Tabuena, "Dana White: UFC
'Killed It' in 2020, 'Broke Just About Every Record,' Including Revenue," *Bloody Elbow*,
December 12, 2020, https://www.bloodyelbow.com/2020/12/12/22169623/dana-white
-ufc-killed-it-in-2020-broke-just-about-every-record-including-revenue.

278 *As the new disease spread around the world* "The True Death Toll of COVID-19," World
Health Organization, https://www.who.int/data/stories/the-true-death-toll-of-covid-19-esti
mating-global-excess-mortality; "ILO: Uncertain and Uneven Recovery Expected Following
Unprecedented Labour Market Crisis," *International Labour Organization*, January 25, 2021,
https://www.ilo.org/global/about-the-ilo/newsroom/news/WCMS_766949/lang—en/index
.htm; Nash, "Finances: UFC's Revenues and Earnings Drive Endeavor IPO."

278 *According to White, the UFC's total audience* Tabuena, "Dana White: UFC 'Killed It' in
2020."

278 *the promotion's Instagram account passed twenty-five million* Ibid.

279 *The UFC also offered the same hope to Endeavor* John S. Nash, "'Biggest First Half Ever'—
Endeavor's Q2 Earnings Reveal UFC Doing Record Business," *Bloody Elbow*, August 19,
2021, https://www.bloodyelbow.com/2021/8/19/22630218/biggest-first-half-ever-en
deavors-q2-earnings-reveal-ufc-doing-record-business.

279 *The UFC became the main selling point Emanuel could offer* Joshua Franklin, "Talent

Agency Endeavor Abandons IPO Amid Weak Investor Demand," Reuters, September 26, 2019, https://www.reuters.com/article/us-endeavor-group-ipo-idUSKBN1WB2HD; Echo Wang, "UFC Owner Endeavor Raises $511 Million in IPO, Valued at $10.3 Billion," NASDAQ.com, April 28, 2021, https://www.nasdaq.com/articles/ufc-owner-endeavor-raises-%24511-million-in-ipo-valued-at-%2410.3-billion-2021-04-28.

279 *In 2017, Lorenzo started Fertitta Capital* "Fertitta Capital Launches with $500 Million," *PRNewswire*, May 1, 2017, https://www.prnewswire.com/news-releases/fertitta-capital-launches-with-500-million-300448601.html.

279 *The company's website is filled with the same kinds* Fertittacapital.com, May 9, 2017, archived at http://web.archive.org/web/20170509045945/http://www.fertittacapital.com/.

279 *The Fertittas' family business, Red Rock Resorts, has continued to thrive* Red Rock Resorts, Inc., "Red Rock Resorts Announces Fourth Quarter and Year End 2019 Results," *PRNewswire*, February 4, 2020, https://redrockresorts.investorroom.com/2020-02-04-Red-Rock-Resorts-Announces-Fourth-Quarter-and-Year-End-2019-Results.

279 *Lorenzo and Frank III each have an estimated net worth* "Forbes World's Billionaires List," *Forbes*, https://www.forbes.com/profile/frank-fertitta-iii/?sh=1ecaaac7346b and https://www.forbes.com/profile/lorenzo-fertitta/?sh=518a623863d1; "In One Map: How Many Billionaires Are in the World," HowMuch.net, April 20, 2020, https://howmuch.net/articles/world-map-of-billionaires-2020.

280 *In 2017, Frank III bought a $70 million, 9,138-square-foot* Amy Plitt, "520 Park Avenue's $70M Duplex Penthouse Sold to a Las Vegas Billionaire," *Curbed*, August 17, 2017, https://ny.curbed.com/2017/8/17/16159938/nyc-penthouse-sold-frank-fertitta-robert-am-stern.

280 *He's also continued to build his private art collection* Motoko Rich and Robin Pogrebin, "Why Spend $110 Million on a Basquiat? 'I Decided to Go for It,' Japanese Billionaire Explains," *New York Times*, May 26, 2017, https://www.nytimes.com/2017/05/26/arts/design/110-million-basquiat-painting-yusaku-maezawa.html.

280 *In 2018, Frank III spent a reported $25 million to host* Devin O'Connor, "Las Vegas Billionaire Frank Fertitta Drops $25M on Daughter's Las Vegas Red Rock Casino Wedding, Bruno Mars Headlines Reception," Casino.org, September 3, 2018, https://www.casino.org/news/las-vegas-billionaire-frank-fertitta-drops-25m-on-daughters-wedding/.

280 *In 2019, Lorenzo bought a 285-foot super-yacht* Anton Tabuena, "Former UFC Owner Lorenzo Fertitta Reportedly Buys $125 Million Superyacht," *Bloody Elbow*, February 5, 2019, https://www.bloodyelbow.com/2019/2/5/18211712/former-ufc-owner-lorenzo-fertitta-reportedly-buys-125-million-superyacht.

280 *Both Lorenzo and Frank III have also become prodigious* "Individual Contributions—Frank Fertitta III," Federal Election Commission, available at https://www.fec.gov/data/receipts/individual-contributions/?contributor_name=frank+fertitta&min_date=01%2F01%2F2009&max_date=12%2F31%2F2020; "Individual Contributions—Lorenzo Fertitta," Federal Election Commission, https://www.fec.gov/data/receipts/individual-contributions/?contributor_name=lorenzo+fertitta&min_date=01%2F01%2F2009&max_date=12%2F31%2F2020.

280 *In 2017, he bought three adjacent mansions* Eli Segall, "UFC Chief Dana White Buys 3 Homes in Exclusive Las Vegas Area," *Las Vegas Review-Journal*, June 6, 2017, https://www.reviewjournal.com/business/housing/ufc-chief-dana-white-buys-3-homes-in-exclusive-las-vegas-area/.

280 *White then had them all demolished and built* Jon Boon, "Game Boy: Inside UFC Chief Dana White's Amazing £6M Las Vegas Home with Gaming Arcade, Personalized Basketball Court and Pool," *The Sun*, May 8, 2020, https://www.the-sun.com/sport/800533/dana-white-vegas-home-ufc/; "Dana White: 5 Ways I'm Riding Out the Quarantine at Home in Las Vegas," *Haute TV* (YouTube channel), April 23, 2020, https://www.youtube.com/watch?v=PvXGa64IGro.

280 *He spent a reported $1 million to throw his youngest son* John Katsilometes, "Dana White Throws $1M Party for Son's 16th on Las Vegas Strip," *Las Vegas Review-Journal*, July 21, 2018, https://www.reviewjournal.com/entertainment/entertainment-columns/kats/dana-white-throws-1m-party-for-sons-16th-on-las-vegas-strip/.

280 *One of his most prominent pieces is Nobuyoshi Araki's* Robbie Fox, "Dana White Gives an Exclusive Tour of UFC HQ," *Barstool Sports* (YouTube channel), July 11, 2019, https://www.youtube.com/watch?v=sAGjFk9bPUI.

280 *Another favorite piece is conceptual artist Mel Bochner's* "Mel Bochner—Head Honcho," Denis Block Fine Art, https://denisbloch.com/artworks/artists/mel-bochner/head-honcho/.

281 *White also owns a full set of samurai armor from the fifteenth century* O'Brien, "UFC Tries to Prove It's Capable of a Knockout"; "Bran Symondson," House of Fine Art, https://thehouseoffineart.com/artists/41-bran-symondson/biography/.

281 *In 2019, White also donated $1 million to the Trump-tied* "Individual Contributions—Dana White," Federal Election Commission, https://www.fec.gov/data/receipts/individual-contributions/?contributor_name=dana+white+&contributor_city=las+vegas&min_date=01%2F01%2F2009&max_date=12%2F31%2F2020; "WATCH: UFC President Dana White's Full Speech at the Republican National Convention," PBS NewsHour (YouTube channel), August 27, 2020, https://www.youtube.com/watch?v=2LM98qaa1OI.

281 *The connection to conservative politics appears to have benefitted* Project Spearhead website, available at http://projectspearhead.com; Lucas Middlebrook, author interview; Leslie Smith, author interview.

281 *One, women's bantamweight Leslie Smith, filed a claim* Marc Raimondi, "Attorney: NLRB Plans to File a Complaint Against UFC in Leslie Smith Case," *MMA Fighting*, June 29, 2018, https://www.mmafighting.com/2018/6/29/17519328/attorney-nlrb-plans-to-file-complaint-against-ufc-in-leslie-smith-case.

281 *Shortly after the merit finding, a partner at the law firm* Lucas Middlebrook, author interview.

282 *Unable to win the case on the merits, Middlebrook* Marc Raimondi, "Attorney: Leslie Smith Case Against UFC Now in a 'Holding Pattern' After Change," *MMA Fighting*, June 30, 2018, https://www.mmafighting.com/2018/6/30/17520386/attorney-leslie-smith-case-against-ufc-now-in-holding-pattern-after-change.

282 *Three days after Middlebrook traveled to the main* "Colby Covington, Dana White Visit President Donald Trump at White House," *MMA Fighting*, August 2, 2018, https://www.mmafighting.com/2018/8/2/17644592/colby-covington-dana-white-visit-president-donald-trump-at-white-house; "Dana White Had a Three Hour Dinner with Donald Trump," *Jimmy Kimmel Live* (YouTube channel), October 4, 2018, https://www.youtube.com/watch?v=26MP2gCO7sM.

282 *A little over a month later, the NLRB overturned the Region 4 finding* Alexander K. Lee, "Leslie Smith to File Appeal After Dismissal of NLRB Complaint," *MMA Fighting*,

October 4, 2018, https://www.mmafighting.com/2018/10/4/17934950/leslie-smith-to
-file-appeal-after-dismissal-of-nlrb-complaint.

282 *According to Middlebrook, the UFC's treatment of Smith* Steven Marrocco, "Attorney:
'Precipitous Decline' in Union Cards Bolstered Leslie Smith's Labor Complaint vs. UFC,"
MMA Junkie, July 11, 2018, https://mmajunkie.usatoday.com/2018/07/attorney-union
-leslie-smith-labor-complaint-ufc.

282 *Renato Sobral, who fought in the UFC from 2000 to 2007* Guilherme Cruz, "Retired
Renato Sobral Believes He's Showing Signs of CTE: 'I Don't Know If I'll Be Able to See
My Grandkids,' " *MMA Fighting*, April 30, 2019, https://www.mmafighting.com/2019
/4/30/18514466/retired-fighter-renato-sobral-cte-issues-mma.

282 *"People only talk about the good things today"* Ibid.

282 *Since retiring in 2010, former UFC and Pride veteran Gary Goodridge* Ben Fowlkes,
"The Fighter Who Stayed Too Long," *MMA Fighting*, March 13, 2012, https://www
.mmafighting.com/2012/3/13/2867460/the-fighter-who-stayed-too-long.

282 *The rods later broke, and Frye developed a bacterial* Dave Meltzer, "Don Frye Rebounding
from Lengthy Medically-Induced Coma," *MMA Fighting*, December 4, 2016, https://
www.mmafighting.com/2016/12/4/13816060/don-frye-rebounding-from-lengthy-medi
cally-induced-coma.

282 *Former UFC heavyweight champion Kevin Randleman struggled* "Kevin Randleman at
a Crossroads," *MMA Weekly*, February 18, 2007, https://www.mmaweekly.com/kevin
-randleman-at-a-crossroads-2.

283 *In 2007, he suffered a life-threatening staph infection* Chris Howie, "MMANews.com
Exclusive Interview with Kevin Randleman [Pt. 1]" *MMA News*, November 2, 2007,
available at http://web.archive.org/web/20071102045204/https://www.mmanews.com
/other/MMANews.com-Exclusive-Interview-With-Kevin-Randleman-[Pt.-1].html.

283 *In 2016, he died unexpectedly from heart failure* "Kevin Randleman Dies at Age 44,"
ESPN, February 12, 2016, https://www.espn.com/mma/story/_/id/14764569/former-ufc
-heavyweight-champion-kevin-randleman-dies-age-44.

283 *Cal Worsham, who fought just three times in the UFC* Krauss and Aita, *Brawl*, pp. 119–20.

283 *"I beat Zane," he would later say of the night* Ibid.

283 *After retiring, lightweight Spencer Fisher, whom White once called* Steven Marrocco, "The
Cost of Being 'The King,' " *MMA Fighting*, January 12, 2021, https://www.mmafighting.
com/2021/1/12/21554602/the-cost-of-being-the-king-spencer-fisher-ufc.

283 *White had arranged for Fisher to remain on a $5,000* Ibid.

283 *In 2020, former heavyweight champion Tim Sylvia* Harry Davies, "Graphic: UFC Refuses
to Pay for Former Champ Tim Sylvia's Infection Caused by 2004 Frank Mir Loss," *Bloody
Elbow*, June 3, 2020, https://www.bloodyelbow.com/2020/6/3/21278836/tim-sylvia-ufc
-pay-arm-infection-frank-mir-fight-mma-news.

283 *When asked about Sylvia's request, White said he hadn't* Steven Marrocco, "Tim
Sylvia Thanks Fans, Blasts UFC Snub on Arm Surgery: 'If This Was Chuck Liddell,
There'd Be No Problem,' " *MMA Fighting*, June 6, 2020, https://www.mmafighting.
com/2020/6/6/21282134/tim-sylvia-thanks-fans-blasts-ufc-snub-on-arm-surgery-if-this
-was-chuck-liddell-thered-be-no-problem.

284 *Sylvia later raised more than $15,000 from fans* "Tim Sylvia Arm Surgery," GoFundMe
.com, https://www.gofundme.com/f/tims-arm-surgery.

284 *In 2014, the promotion announced it would join Bellator* "Cleveland Clinic Studying
Support Professional Fighter Brain Health," *Boxing Insider*, February 4, 2014, https://

www.boxinginsider.com/headlines/cleveland-clinic-studying-support-professional-fight
er-brain-health/.

284 *A 2017 study of 291 active fighters and 44 retired* "Study: Boxers, MMA Fighters May
Have Long-Term Brain Damage," CBS News, September 7, 2017, https://www.cbsnews
.com/philadelphia/news/fighters-may-have-brain-damage/.

284 *Another study, published in 2019, tracked 173 boxers* Trent Reinsmith, "Study Finds Loss
of Brain Volume in MMA Fighters and Boxers," *Bloody Elbow*, February 19, 2020, https://
www.bloodyelbow.com/2020/2/19/21142178/study-finds-loss-brain-volume-mma-fight
er-boxers-ufc-health-science-tbi-research.

284 *In 2018,* Ultimate Fighter *season one finalist Stephan Bonnar* Katherine Jarvis, "Report:
Drivers Restrained UFC Fighter Stephan Bonnar During DUI Arrest," KTNV 13 Las
Vegas, October 31, 2018, archived at http://web.archive.org/web/20190909075636
/https://www.ktnv.com/news/crime/video-shows-drivers-restraining-ufc-fighter
-stephan-bonnar-after-resisting-arrest-for-dui; "Nevada Highway Patrol Body Cam
Footage of UFC's Stephan Bonnar Arrest for DUI," *Law Enforcement Network* (YouTube
channel), November 1, 2018, https://www.youtube.com/watch?v=J9ewppSI6sk.

284 *Nick Diaz also seemed to have "gotten a little out of control"* Derek Hall, "Jake
Shields: Nick Diaz Got 'Too Out of Control,' but the Old Nick Is Back," *Middle Easy*,
September 10, 2020, https://middleeasy.com/mma-news/jake-shields-old-nick/.

284 *Nick began spending more time in Las Vegas* Chris Taylor, "Video: Nick Diaz Goes Off
on Bizarre Rant, But What Does It Mean?" BJPenn.com, December 22, 2018, https://
www.bjpenn.com/mma-news/ufc/video-nick-diaz-goes-off-on-bizarre-rant-but-what
-does-it-mean/; "Nick Diaz Is Drunk," *UberAssault* (YouTube channel—archived from
Instagram), February 11, 2019, https://www.youtube.com/watch?v=fQz_Z4k7ZsU.

285 *"Nick didn't have the childhood, the carefree life"* Steve Heath, author interview.

285 *In May of 2018, Nick was arrested in Las Vegas* Simon Samano and Steve Marrocco, "Nick
Diaz Arrested for Alleged Domestic Violence in Las Vegas (updated)," *MMA Junkie*,
May 25, 2018, https://mmajunkie.usatoday.com/2018/05/ufc-nick-diaz-arrested-domes
tic-violence-las-vegas; "Nick Diaz Accuser, He Was Coked Up and Choked Me," *TMZ*,
May 25, 2018, https://www.tmz.com/2018/05/25/nick-diaz-accuser-claims-cocaine-fu
eled-domestic-violence/.

285 *A grand jury would later decline to indict Nick* Briana Erickson, "Grand Jury Declines to
Indict UFC Fighter Nick Diaz in Domestic Battery Case," *Las Vegas Review-Journal*, July
31, 2018, https://www.reviewjournal.com/crime/courts/grand-jury-declines-to-indict
-ufc-fighter-nick-diaz-in-domestic-battery-case/.

285 *In 2019, Nick appeared in a bizarre and frequently incoherent* Ariel Helwani, "Nick Diaz
Exclusive: Opening Up on Return to the Octagon, Jorge Masvidal—Ariel Helwani's
MMA Show," *ESPN MMA* (YouTube channel), November 11, 2019, https://www
.youtube.com/watch?v=EUAlYvPjU4o&t=339s; Amy Kaplan, "Twitter Reacts to Nick
Diaz's Rambling, Incoherent First Interview in Years," *Fansided*, November 11, 2019,
https://fansided.com/2019/11/11/twitter-reacts-nick-diazs-rambling-incoherent-first
-interview-years/; Trent Reinsmith, "Opinion: Nick Diaz's Recent Video Interview
Should Not Have Aired," *Bloody Elbow*, November 27, 2019, https://www.bloodyelbow
.com/2019/11/27/20985495/nick-diaz-ariel-helwani-espn-ufc-video-interview-opinion
-editorial-mma.

285 *"It's not a good thing at the end of this tunnel"* Cesar Gracie, author interview.

285 *Nick finally returned to the UFC in 2021* UFC Holdings, "Robbie Lawler vs Nick Diaz

UFC 266," *UFC Fight Pass*, September 25, 2021, https://ufcfightpass.com/video/254915
/robbie-lawler-vs-nick-diaz-ufc-266.

285 *When they rose a few moments later* Holdings, "UFC 266: The Thrill and the Agony—
Sneak Peek," *UFC—Ultimate Fighting Championship* (YouTube channel), October 5,
2021, https://www.youtube.com/watch?v=kF0SHa-lWqc&t=248s.

286 *In April of 2018, he was arrested and charged with felony* Sarah Wallace et al.,
"Handcuffed Conor McGregor Appears in Court on Assault, Criminal Mischief Charges
in UFC Melee," NBC 4 New York, April 9, 2018, https://www.nbcnewyork.com
/news/local/conor-mcgregor-wild-rampage-barclays-center-brooklyn-nyc-arrest-war
rant/466357/.

286 *McGregor smashed one of the bus windows* Brandon Wise, "UFC 223: Michael Chiesa,
Ray Borg Forced Out of Action After Conor McGregor Incident," CBS Sports, April 5,
2018, https://www.cbssports.com/mma/news/ufc-223-michael-chiesa-ray-borg-forced
-out-of-action-after-conor-mcgregor-incident/.

286 *He would later plead guilty to one count* AP Staff, "MMA Star Conor McGregor Gets
Anger Management, Community Service in Wild Barclays Rampage," Associated Press/
NBC 4, July 26, 2018, https://www.nbcnewyork.com/news/local/conor-mcgregor-bar
clays-brooklyn-mma-ufc-rampage-court-nyc/1825384/.

286 *The UFC seized on the scandal to promote a fight* Ben Fowlkes, "How Conor McGregor's
Rampage Went from 'Disgusting' Incident to a Compelling Commercial—in Just Four
Months," *MMA Junkie*, August 6, 2018, https://mmajunkie.usatoday.com/2018/08/how
-conor-mcgregor-rampage-went-from-disgusting-to-compelling-commercial-in-just
-four-months-ufc-229.

286 *At a press conference in New York* UFC Holdings, "UFC 229 Press Conference: Khabib vs
McGregor," *UFC—Ultimate Fighting Championship* (YouTube channel), September 20,
2018, https://www.youtube.com/watch?v=s8NL-n_XgSY.

286 *"It was dark, man. It was the darkest press conference"* Andrew Pearson, "Midnight
Mania! Dana White Says McGregor-Khabib Press Conference 'Darkest I've Ever Seen,' "
MMA Mania, September 22, 2018, https://www.mmamania.com/2018/9/22/17889352
/midnight-mania-dana-white-mcgregor-khabib-press-conference-darkest-ever-muham
mad-ali.

286 *According to Kavanagh, he hardly saw McGregor* Helwani, "John Kavanagh: Conor
Mcgregor Found His New Reason to Fight."

286 *After knocking his training partners out, McGregor would* Ariel Helwani, "Conor
McGregor on UFC 246, Khabib, Mayweather—Extended Interview—Ariel Helwani's
MMA Show," *ESPN MMA* (YouTube channel), January 13, 2020, https://www.youtube
.com/watch?v=0lzbKIwLc8k.

286 *When the fight finally took place, McGregor lost* UFC Holdings, "Khabib Nurmagomedov vs Conor McGregor UFC 229," *UFC Fight Pass*, October 6, 2018, https://ufcfightpass
.com/video/64526/khabib-nurmagomedov-vs-conor-mcgregor-ufc-229.

287 *White had the octagon cleared without any post-fight interviews* Gianni Verschueren, "3
Members of Khabib Nurmagomedov's Team Arrested After UFC 229 Brawl," *Bleacher
Report*, October 7, 2018, https://bleacherreport.com/articles/2799493-3-members-of
-khabib-nurmagomedovs-team-arrested-after-ufc-229-brawl.

287 *It would go on to generate a reported 2.4 million* Ken Pishna, "Dana White Pleased, but
Admits UFC 229 Did Not Do as Many PPV Buys as Hoped," *MMA Weekly*, October 8,
2018, https://www.mmaweekly.com/dana-white-pleased-but-admits-ufc-229-did

-not-do-as-many-ppv-buys-as-hoped; Dave Meltzer, "UFC 229: Khabib vs. McGregor Destroys Previous MMA Record for Pay-Per-Views," *MMA Fighting*, October 11, 2018, https://www.mmafighting.com/2018/10/11/17962158/ufc-229-khabib-vs-mcgregor -destroys-previous-mma-record-for-pay-per-views.

287 *In January of 2019, a story in the* Irish Times *claimed* Conor Gallagher and Ronan McGreevy, "Sportsman Arrested Over Alleged Sexual Assault in Dublin," *Irish Times*, January 18, 2019, https://www.irishtimes.com/news/crime-and-law/sportsman-arrested -over-alleged-sex-assault-in-dublin-1.3762529; Tariq Panja, "Conor McGregor Under Investigation Over Sexual Assault in Ireland," *New York Times*, March 26, 2019, https:// www.nytimes.com/2019/03/26/sports/conor-mcgregor-sexual-assault.html.

287 *In 2021, the alleged victim filed a civil suit* Tariq Panja and Kevin Draper, "After Criminal Case Ends Without Charges, Conor McGregor Is Sued in Ireland," *New York Times*, January 19, 2021, https://www.nytimes.com/2021/01/19/sports/conor-mcgregor-law suit-ufc.html.

287 *In March of 2019, McGregor was arrested in Miami* Damon Martin, "Conor McGregor Arrested in Miami on Robbery, Criminal Mischief Charges," *MMA Weekly*, March 11, 2019, https://www.mmaweekly.com/conor-mcgregor-arrested-in-miami-on-robbery -criminal-mischief-charges.

287 *Charges were later dropped after the victim's attorney* Brett Okamoto, "Charges Dropped vs. McGregor in Phone Incident," *ESPN*, May 13, 2019, https://www.espn.com /mma/story/_/id/26737622/charges-dropped-vs-mcgregor-phone-incident.

287 *The following month, McGregor sucker punched* Harry Brent, " 'He's a Bully with Money'—Elderly Man Punched by Conor McGregor Speaks Out for First Time," *Irish Post*, August 22, 2019, https://www.irishpost.com/news/hes-bully-money-elderly-man -punched-conor-mcgregor-speaks-first-time-170437.

287 *McGregor would later plead guilty to charges* Sean Nevin and Marc Raimondi, "Conor McGregor Fined, Avoids Jail Time for Hitting Man at Bar," *ESPN*, November 1, 2019, https://www.espn.com/mma/story/_/id/27981990/conor-mcgregor-fined-avoids-jail -hitting-man-bar.

287 *In October, the* New York Times *reported that McGregor* Tariq Panja, "Conor McGregor Faces Second Sexual Assault Investigation in Ireland," *New York Times*, October 19, 2019, https://www.nytimes.com/2019/10/19/sports/conor-mcgregor-sexual-assault-accusation .html

287 *In a radio interview, the UFC's chief operating officer* Alan Snel, "UFC COO Lawrence Epstein Live on LVSportsBiz w/ Alan Snel on #GuerillaCrossRadio," *Guerilla Cross* (YouTube Channel), June 13, 2019, https://www.youtube.com/watch?v=gW0uuLVvsyI.

288 *Ivan Trembow, an influential blogger who began* Ivan Trembow, "Monday, September 27, 2010," *Ivan's Blog*, September 27, 2010, http://www.ivansblog.com/2010/09/.

288 *"A lot of these guys in the MMA and all other"* Skye, "High Times Interview: Nick Diaz."

288 *"In a perfect world," he said in 2015* Samuels, "One Hundred Years of Arm Bars."

288 *"Some people think I'm a classless moron"* Erik Hedegaard, "What Is UFC President Dana White Fighting For?" *Rolling Stone*, June 12, 2008, https://www.rollingstone.com/culture /culture-features/ufc-dana-white-mma-940798/.

289 *Colby Covington would describe White as a* "Colby Covington: Dana White Is a Piece of (Expletive) Person with No Morals or Values," *MMA Junkie*, January 7, 2019, https:// mmajunkie.usatoday.com/2019/01/colby-covington-says-dana-white-a-piece-of-shit -person-with-no-morals-or-values?.

289 *White's own mother publicly renounced him with a short* "Dana White's Mom Calls Him a 'Prick' and 'Tyrant,' Who Turned His Back on His Family," *Full Contact Fighter*, July 19, 2011, https://fcfighter.com/dana-white's-mom-calls-him-a-"p-"-and-"tyrant"-who -turned-his-back-on-his-family/.

289 *During his tenure as UFC president, she writes* Ibid.

289 *When asked about the book, White declined* "Dana White Responds to Reporters Questions at Australian Press Conference 2/29, on Dana's Biography, 'Dana White, King of MMA,' " *PR Web*, March 14, 2012, https://www.prweb.com/releases/2012/3/prweb 9272998.htm.

289 *"Dana never did anything to her"* Joel Stein, "Blood Sport: How Dana White Turned the UFC into a \$4 Billion Titan," *Financial Times Magazine*, September 1, 2022, https://www .ft.com/content/be73d581-c7a2-464e-be55-9dc964ea17b8.

289 *"Every time I run into problems or I have some situation"* Mike Swick, author interview.

289 *When Swick lost his entire life savings trying to launch* Ibid.

289 *In 2018, White also gave \$1 million to a support fund* Steven Rondina, "Dana White: UFC Donating \$1 Million to Las Vegas Shooting Victims," *Bleacher Report*, October 2, 2017, https://bleacherreport.com/articles/2736516-dana-white-ufc-donating-1-million-to-las -vegas-shooting-victims.

290 *The rest of the world—criticism from fighters, the press* Mike Swick, "Dana White EP 91— Real Quick with Mike Swick Podcast," *Real Quick with Mike Swick Podcast*, October 22, 2020, https://www.youtube.com/watch?v=GXen9WS4VsU.

290 *At the end of 2018, the promotion hosted an event* Greg Rosenstein, "UFC to Hold Event in Moscow in September," *ESPN*, May 16, 2018, https://www.espn.com/mma/story /_/id/23520258/ufc-hold-first-event-russia-september; "UFC Strikes Rights Deal in Russia, CIS," *Sports Business Media*, January 4, 2019, https://media.sportbusiness.com /news/ufc-strikes-rights-deal-in-russia-cis/.

290 *The company also continued broadcasting in Russia in 2022* Karim Zidan, "UFC Maintains Broadcast Relationship with State-Controlled Russian Sources," *Bloody Elbow*, March 18, 2022, https://www.bloodyelbow.com/2022/3/18/22983819/ufc-maintains -broadcast-relationship-with-state-controlled-russian-sources.

290 *Also in 2019, the UFC opened a second Performance Institute* Mathew Scott, "UFC's Shanghai Performance Institute Opens, Aiming to Give China—and Asia—a Cutting Edge," *South China Morning Post*, June 20, 2019, https://www.scmp.com/sport/martial -arts/mixed-martial-arts/article/3015416/ufcs-shanghai-performance-institute-opens.

290 *In 2020, Zhang Weili became the UFC's first Chinese champion* Alaa Elassar, "Zhang Weili Named China's First UFC Champion After Defeating Jessica Andrade in Just 42 Seconds," CNN, August 31, 2019, https://www.cnn.com/2019/08/31/china/zhang-weili -chinese-ufc-champion-trnd/index.html; John Morgan, "UFC Announces New Broadcast Partner in China, Launch of Dana White's Contender Series in Asia," *MMA Junkie*, February 24, 2021, https://mmajunkie.usatoday.com/2021/02/ufc-announces -new-broadcast-partner-in-china-launch-of-dana-whites-contender-series-asia.

290 *The following year, the UFC signed a new deal* "UFC and Migu Reach Landmark Partnership in China," UFC.com, February 23, 2021, https://www.ufc.com/news/ufc -and-migu-reach-landmark-partnership-china-read.

290 *The UFC also announced a multiyear agreement* "UFC Action Is Coming to SuperSport in 2019," UFC.com, November 22, 2018, https://www.ufc.com/news/ufc-action-coming -supersport-2019.

290 *The promotion also signed a new five-year agreement* Karim Zidan, "Arabian Fights: Inside the UFC's Long-Term Partnership with the UAE," *Guardian,* September 4, 2019, https://www.theguardian.com/sport/2019/sep/04/arabian-fights-inside-the-ufcs-long -term-partnership-with-the-uae; "Abu Dhabi to Host Historic 'UFC Fight Island,' " June 9, 2020, https://www.ufc.com/news/yas-island-abu-dhabi-host-historic-ufc-fight -island.

291 *"If you didn't believe me fifteen years ago"* Stephen Brunt, "Dana White on How He Became the Most Powerful Man in MMA—Open Invitation," *SportsNet* (YouTube channel), January 14, 2020, https://www.youtube.com/watch?v=e6sXbII2ZwU.

291 *Instead, the promotion's success simply overwhelmed its critics* Ron Suskind, "Faith, Certainty and the Presidency of George W. Bush," *New York Times*, October 17, 2004, https://www.nytimes.com/2004/10/17/magazine/faith-certainty-and-the-presidency-of -george-w-bush.html.

291 *In a lecture given to the Parnassos Literary Society in Athens in 1934* Jigoro Kano, "Principles of Judo and Their Applications to All Phases of Human Activity," *Journal of Combative Sport*, February 2001, available at https://ejmas.com/jcs/jcsart_kano_0201 .htm.

292 *The walls are covered with inspirational quotes* Fox, "Dana White Gives an Exclusive Tour of UFC HQ."

292 *White's most prized possession isn't in his gym* Ibid.

292 *He won it along with a $250,000 prize, during a fifty-two-person* Ibid.

292 *"I'm like, Yeah, fuck that shit"* Ibid.

292 *"When I tell you these people hated me"* Ibid.

292 *As he got ready to leave the Rio* Mike Swick, "Dana White EP 10—Real Quick with Mike Swick Podcast," *Real Quick with Mike Swick Podcast*, October 26, 2017, https://www .youtube.com/watch?v=2c_FF7vfP2s.

292 *"Do I need to play cards?"* "UFC Boss Fights the Clock."

INDEX

ABOUT THE AUTHOR

MICHAEL THOMSEN writes about sports, video games, technology, and political culture for the *New Yorker*, the *New York Times*, the *Atlantic*, *Vanity Fair*, *Forbes*, *Wired*, the *New Republic*, and other outlets. He lives in New York City.